# Mac OS X
# Disaster Relief

## Troubleshooting techniques
## to help fix it yourself

**Ted Landau**

with Dan Frakes

**Peachpit Press**

**Mac OS X Disaster Relief**
Troubleshooting techniques to help fix it yourself

**Ted Landau**

**Peachpit Press**
1249 Eighth Street
Berkeley, CA 94710
510/524-2178
800/283-9444
510/524-2221 (fax)

Find us on the World Wide Web at www.peachpit.com
To report errors, please send a note to errata@peachpit.com

Peachpit Press is a division of Pearson Education
Copyright © 2002 by Ted Landau

Editor: Clifford Colby
Production Coordinator: Connie Jeung-Mills
Copyeditor: Kathy Simpson
Compositor: Owen Wolfson
Indexer: Joy Dean Lee
Cover design: Nathalie Valette

ISBN 0-201-78869-1

9 8 7 6 5 4 3 2 1

Printed and bound in the United States of America

*To Brian*

# Acknowledgments

My thanks go first to Dan Frakes, who wrote the primary drafts of three chapters in this book (the ones on printing, networking, and Classic). He wrote exactly what I requested, and completed the chapters by the requested deadlines. What more could I ask? Without Dan, I'd probably still be working on getting this book finished.

Thanks also to Robert DeLaurentis, my associate at MacFixIt. The two of us produced the MacFixIt home page each day. Trying to write a book while doing a Web site such as MacFixIt can leave you with no time to breathe. With Bob's help and advice, I was able to get the breathing room I needed. Thanks also to the folks at TechTracker for their continuing support of MacFixIt.

I am also most grateful to all the MacFixIt readers who sent email on Mac OS X. Through their contributions, I was able to learn much more about Mac OS X in a shorter time than I could have ever hoped to do otherwise.

A very warm thanks to all the staff at Peachpit (a special nod to Cliff Colby, Nancy Ruenzel, Marjorie Baer, and Gary-Paul Prince). If there is a better bunch of people in the publishing industry, I have yet to find them. It has been a joy to work with them over the years. As long as they are willing to put up with me, I plan to stick with them.

Finally, I offer my thanks to my wife, Naomi. Mere thanks are not enough to compensate for the constant support she has given me through all the ups and downs of the past years. But it's a start.

Ted Landau
*ted@tlandau.com*
*www.tlandau.com*

# Contents at a Glance

# Table of Contents

## Chapter 10: Unix for Mac OS X Users . . . . . . . . . . . . . . . . . 537

# Foreword

## Why buy this book?

Mac OS X is new. Mac OS X is different. Mac OS X is popular. In the computing world, whenever something new, different, and popular comes along, you can be certain that many books will be written about it. Such is the case with Mac OS X.

So why should you buy this book—instead of or in addition to any other book on Mac OS X? The brief answer: If you want to know how to get Mac OS X working when something goes wrong, this book is the one you want. This book is not a general introduction to Mac OS X. Instead, its constant focus remains on troubleshooting—on providing how-to advice for solving problems.

I do include a good deal of basic information on Mac OS X, because you need to know these fundamentals before you can fix what may go wrong. Still, I don't start at square one. If you are a complete novice to the Mac universe, this probably is not the first book on Mac OS X that you want to read. But it might well be the second one.

Although this book may not be for novices, it does not assume you are already an expert. This book is for the average Mac user—one who understands the basics of how to use a Mac and is motivated to know more.

This book provides a wealth of specific solutions to common problems, from how to avoid installation roadblocks to how to diagnose network connection hassles. But no book can provide every imaginable bit of troubleshooting advice, especially when the latest information changes each day. That's why this book also provides the in-depth background needed for a fuller understanding of how Mac OS X works. With this knowledge, you'll be prepared to solve problems not specifically covered here.

*Mac OS X Disaster Relief* not only maintains a focus on troubleshooting but also maintains a laserlike focus on troubleshooting Mac OS X. This means that general troubleshooting issues (such as hardware failures, computer viruses, and Web pages that do not load) will not be emphasized; they will be covered only to the extent that they specifically affect Mac OS X. Without this restriction, I could not have kept this book to a manageable size.

The upside is that this focus leaves me much more room to cover those issues that *are* Mac OS X-specific. In fact, I believe there is more Mac OS X troubleshooting information here than in any other book you could purchase.

Still, this is the first edition of a book about an operating system that is barely a year old. Mac OS X continues to evolve at a rapid pace. You can expect that future editions of this book will expand and diverge in ways that I cannot yet even imagine. Welcome to the first leg of what promises to be a wild and exciting ride (at least for those who think of troubleshooting as being something potentially wild and exciting!).

For those who seek more general troubleshooting advice, together with information specific to Mac OS 9, I recommend my previous book: *Sad Macs, Bombs, and Other Disasters* (Peachpit Press, 2000).

## The sidebars

This book contains two types of sidebars:

**Take Note.** These sidebars are used to cover background material that is not directly related to solving problems or that otherwise does not easily fit into the flow of the main text but is still quite relevant to the main topic. For example, in a section where main text refers to software found on the Developer Tools CD, a Take Note sidebar provides background on exactly what this CD is and how to obtain it. Unless you already know this information, consider these sidebars to be just as essential as the main text.

**Technically Speaking.** These sidebars cover more technical or advanced topics than the Take Note sidebars. Thus, you usually can skip them without affecting your ability to understand and use the advice in the main text. They are, in essence, a bonus for more-advanced users who want to know more about the topic at hand.

## Cross-references

Often the same bit of advice or information applies to several situations. Coverage of these situations may be scattered across several chapters. To avoid covering the same advice multiple times, I make frequent reference to information already covered elsewhere. The result of this are the copious cross-references found throughout this book.

On the other hand, too many cross-references can disrupt the flow of the material, forcing you to thumb back and forth between chapters. As a result, I do sometimes repeat the same information in more than one place.

Striking a balance between these two concerns has not been easy. You, of course, will be the final judge of how successful I have been.

## Brackets

When you see text in this book that is intended for you to type on the keyboard (such as in the Terminal application), it will be in a different font. In addition, it may also be enclosed in brackets (like this: <ls>). You are not supposed to type the brackets: They are there only to indicate where to start and stop typing.

In other cases, you may see terms enclosed in curly brackets (like this: {name}). This means that what you see on the screen or what you are supposed to type is the specific example of what the general case in brackets indicates. Thus, for me, instead of {name}, I might see or type Ted. In some instances, text in italics, with or without the curly brackets, means the same thing.

## Getting more help: MacFixIt

Certain troubleshooting information, of necessity, cannot or should not be covered in this book. In particular:

- Time-sensitive problems (such as bugs that get fixed by an update that is released within weeks the bug's discovery)
- Problems that were unknown until after the book was written

For these matters, I recommend the MacFixIt Web site (**www.macfixit.com**). Created by me six years ago, the site is devoted to troubleshooting the Mac and provides extensive coverage of Mac OS X.

## Getting the software mentioned in this book

Throughout this book, I mention products (mainly shareware utilities) that can assist in troubleshooting Mac OS X. Virtually all this software can be downloaded from the Web. But you don't have to search the Web to find each program. Instead, you can get the latest versions of all the software simply by going to VersionTracker (**www.versiontracker.com**). The site has links to just about every Macintosh program in existence.

Also, I have gathered together a list of all of my personal favorite Mac OS X utilities, which includes just about everything mentioned in this book. It's accessible from MacFixIt via this URL: **http://www.macfixit.com/library/osxu.shtml**.

# 1

# Why
# Mac OS X?

Mac users who are familiar with Mac OS 9 understand that Mac OS X is not an incremental change in the Mac OS; it is more like a quantum leap. The first time a long-time Mac user launches Mac OS X, everything will seem different. Sometimes just a bit different. More often, quite a bit different.

As such, you may be wondering why Apple felt it was necessary to make this leap, abandoning what had been successful for so long and moving into uncharted territory.

This chapter provides the answers.

# In This Chapter

# Why Did Apple Need a New OS?

I still own Macintosh System Disk 1.0, which came with an original 1984 Mac. The single disk contained the first versions of MacWrite and MacPaint, as well as a System Folder. Its size? A single-sided 400 KB floppy disk!

Back in 1984, the OS did not include any support for networking or the Internet. You could open only one application at a time. There were no such things as QuickTime and PostScript. The only storage peripheral you could connect to your Mac was an external floppy drive.

Clearly, the latest version of Mac OS 9 has come a very long way from these System 1.0 roots. For starters, the System Folder alone now occupies more than 150 MB. And MacWrite and MacPaint no longer exist, having evolved into AppleWorks. We now have USB, FireWire, and Ethernet. Floppy disks have vanished. But the evidence of those 1.0 roots is still there.

More and more, it became clear that continuing to improve an OS that was tied to the priorities of two decades ago would require significant compromises. Updates of the OS too often depended on patches and add-ons that were not dependable. The original Mac OS was never intended to work in today's interconnected, multimedia-rich world. Trying to add essential new features while maintaining backward compatibility with previous OS versions was becoming close to impossible. What Apple needed was a clean start.

Mac OS X is that clean start. Yes, Mac OS 9 and Mac OS X have many similarities, but underneath the hood, they are fundamentally different. For Mac OS X, these differences are both its greatest strength and its biggest weakness.

## Mac OS 9: The up side

Apple's move to Mac OS X does not mean that Mac OS 9 has lost all its appeal. It hasn't. For starters, Mac OS 9 retains a simplicity and common-sense appeal that is the hallmark of the Mac itself. When the Mac was first advertised as the computer for the "rest of us," Apple was talking about the ease of use of the Mac OS. Even a relative novice can figure out a good deal about how the OS works, with relatively little effort. Where are control panels stored? In the Control Panels folder, of course. How do you get a new item into the Apple menu? Drag it to the Apple Menu Items folder. What's the name of the extension that enables file sharing? File Sharing. It all just makes sense. (Yes, I know that there are times it does not seem to make sense at all, but I am speaking in generalizations here.)

Mac OS 9 is also remarkably portable. The entire OS is contained in the single System Folder. With some minor exceptions, you can use the Finder to copy a Mac OS 9 System Folder from one volume to another, and the new volume instantly becomes a bootable Mac OS 9 volume. In fact, a bare-bones System Folder with a System, Finder, and very little else are still all you need to start up a Mac from Mac OS 9.

This simplicity of the Mac OS provided the impetus for my *Sad Macs, Bombs, and Other Disasters* book. The premise of *Sad Macs* was that even "the rest of us" could learn to troubleshoot their Macs.

## Mac OS 9: The down side

Unfortunately, Mac OS 9 is also burdened with the limitations that existed 20 years ago. For one thing, Mac OS 9 crashes more often than it should. Even worse, too many of its crashes require restarting the Mac—a time-consuming frustration. And diagnosing an extensions conflict can take several hours. Mac OS 9 is too often plagued by out-of memory errors, even when it seems that more than enough memory is installed. Getting on the Internet involves a tangle of extensions and control panels that sometimes confound even an experienced user.

The Mac was born in a time when the World Wide Web did not exist. Even a local network was a rarity except in large institutions. As such, the original Mac OS had no security features or multiple-user support. Although Mac OS 9 now does offer this support, it often doesn't work very well and is too easy to circumvent.

## Mac OS X: The down and up sides

Mac OS X's first up side is that clearly addresses the down sides of Mac OS 9. Mac OS X is more stable (you almost never need to restart Mac OS X) and handles memory more efficiently. Its security and multiple-user features are so ingrained and feature-rich that they drift toward becoming a down side—sometimes getting in the way of a single user who does not really need them.

Mac OS X throws in several up sides of its own. The quality of its graphics and text displays is unmatched anywhere. (Just look at the Mac OS X icons for an example.) It has more advanced networking capabilities, including simplified settings that sense how you are connected to the Internet and automatically change as needed. It also offers the potential for significantly greater application speed, including the capability to take advantage of multiple processors, should your Mac have them. Finally, you get software, such as iPhoto, that you won't find in any Mac OS except Mac OS X.

But Mac OS X also abandons some of the upsides that still exist in Mac OS 9. A standard Mac OS X installation, for example, involves thousands of files, many of which are invisible from the Finder. A peek inside the contents of the /System/Library folder reveals that Apple has abandoned the notion that the names of OS files should retain the common-sense appeal of Mac OS 9. The portability of the Mac OS 9 System Folder is completely gone in Mac OS X. Creating a bootable Mac OS X volume is now a major exercise, requiring utilities other than the Finder. Just backing up Mac OS X is significantly more difficult than in Mac OS 9.

And troubleshooting Mac OS X is inevitably a more complex task—one that the average Mac user can still master, but with more effort.

**Unix.** For most Mac users, the biggest potential hurdle in mastering Mac OS X troubleshooting will be the Unix basis for Mac OS X's core functions. Unix uses a command-line interface (CLI)—that is, it is an entirely text-based OS. You enter text via a command line and press Return. The OS then processes your command and gives you the appropriate feedback. Does this arrangement sound old-fashioned and quaint? If so, that's because it is. This style of computing was in use before a graphical user interface (GUI) and mouse input were available. Unix dates back to the mammoth, clunky mainframe computers that were in use before desktop computing was born.

Thus, you might reasonably ask, "How does moving from Mac OS 9 to Unix represent a step forward?" Here's how:

- Unix is an easily extensible operating system and, thus, has done a good job of keeping pace with the changes in the computer world. Although for better or worse, it retains its command-line interface (and some users actually find it preferable for certain tasks), it is a much faster, sleeker, and more powerful OS than it was years ago.

- Unix is an immensely popular OS for running multiple-user servers (such as those used at universities, where a central server regulates traffic among a network of client computers). Because of its speed and stability, many Web sites also favor using Unix; my own MacFixIt site runs from a Unix server. And especially via its popular cousin Linux, it has become increasingly popular for use on personal computers.

  By basing Mac OS X on Unix, Apple instantly acquires all the power and benefits of this mature OS. Mac OS X's Web Sharing feature, for example, is based on the Apache Web server included in Unix. This far exceeds the Web-sharing capabilities of Mac OS 9. If Apple had to start from scratch in building all this functionality into Mac OS X, it probably would have taken another decade before Apple reached the same level as Unix.

- Mac OS X is not merely a shell for Unix. Some people have mischaracterized Mac OS X is a graphical interface for accessing Unix. This is most certainly not the case. Mac OS X can do many things that otherwise would be impossible to do in Unix. AppleWorks could never run under Unix, for example. Mac OS X uses Unix for some of its core features, but it expands well beyond those features. It is the combination of Unix and the new unique features of Mac OS X make it the modern OS that it is.

Still, in some cases, using Unix in Mac OS X *will* feel like a step backward. Unix can be intimidating for those who expect the Mac to work the way the Mac has typically worked. This is especially true for the typical user in Apple's prime markets: home users, small-office users, and students.

For this reason, Apple designed Mac OS X so that most users should not even need to know that Unix exists in Mac OS X. The OS succeeds at this most of the time. Running applications in Mac OS X seems very little different from doing so in Mac OS 9.

Although Mac OS X succeeds in hiding its Unix underpinnings from the casual user, troubleshooters will need to become familiar with it. You need not become a Unix expert to be an expert Mac troubleshooter, but you can't be an expert troubleshooter without at least a basic knowledge of how Unix works.

Unix exists as an operating system independent of Mac OS X. Numerous very large books about Unix have been written, and there is no way I can provide a thorough background in Unix in this book. Instead, I will present specific "cookbook" examples, throughout this book, as appropriate. I will also present a primer on Unix for Mac OS X troubleshooters in chapter 10.

Bottom line: I applaud Apple's move to Mac OS X. I admit that I entered the Mac OS X swimming pool from the shallow end, taking my first steps rather tentatively—and wondering whether I would ever feel as comfortable as I did in Mac OS 9. The adjustment took some time. But now I find that when I'm forced to use Mac OS 9 for some reason, I cannot wait to revert to Mac OS X. When I am gone, I miss the elegant look of Mac OS X, its stability, its capability to do more and more things at the same time with less and less hassle, and all the rest of its advertised features. Thanks largely to the contributions of shareware software developers, I can now have my cake and eat it too. A host of utilities add back the Mac OS 9 features (such as windowshading and the Application menu) that I missed most. More specific to troubleshooting, other utilities sidestep the need to work directly in Unix by providing graphic-based Mac-like alternatives that do the Unix work for you. And upgrades of Mac OS X are expected to solve the most significant remaining issues, such as remaining difficulties in backing up a Mac OS X volume.

By the very fact that you are reading this book, I assume that you have already made the move to Mac OS X. Don't worry. You made the right decision. Mac OS X is Apple's future. It's time to get on board.

# A Brief History of Mac OS X

Now that you know why Apple decided to move to Mac OS X, it's worthwhile to take a brief look at how Apple made the move. Mac OS X has a bit of a sordid history. The road to where we are now is filled with detours, dead ends, delays, and surprises.

What we now call Mac OS X began as Mac OS 8—not the Mac OS 8 that was eventually released as Mac OS 8 but an entirely different OS that never saw the public light of day.

The original Mac OS 8 was intended to be a radical upgrade of what was then the current OS: System 7. (Back then, Apple used the word *System* to describe the OS, rather than Mac OS.) Code-named Copland, Mac OS 8 had many of the same critical features that are now part of Mac OS X, such as preemptive multitasking and protected memory (features that form the basis of Mac OS X's superior performance and stability).

Apple had been working on Mac OS 8 for several years and finally announced it publicly in 1994. Development versions soon began to ship. CDs that took you on a demo tour of the new OS were handed out at Macworld Expos. The final release version was scheduled for 1996.

Unfortunately, all this happened at the same time that Apple hit its financial nadir. During this period, Apple's sales and market share plummeted, and articles about the "death" of Apple began appearing in the media with the regularity of weather reports.

Apple took a hard look at the status of Mac OS 8 and realized that it was too far from completion and would require too much time and money to finish. The result was that Apple killed Copland in August 1996.

The Mac OS 8 that was eventually released was a much more modest update. It added some significant new features to System 7 but essentially was the same OS.

Back at the drawing board, Apple realized that it could not entirely abandon its plans for a new OS. But if not Mac OS 8, what? The company had to do something fast. Apple had promised to announce its new strategy by January 1997. Having decided that it could no longer afford to design a new OS itself, Apple decided to purchase one. The focus quickly narrowed to two choices:

**BeOS.** On the surface, BeOS seemed to be the logical choice. Be Inc. had already released versions of BeOS that ran on Mac hardware. The compact, fast code often exceeded the capabilities of the Mac OS itself, and its user interface was sufficiently similar to the Mac OS as not to be a shock to long-time Mac users. But BeOS had two strikes against it. First, many essential components (such as its printing and networking capabilities) were lacking. Second, Be Inc. demanded more money than Apple was willing to pay. The latter turned out to be the decisive strike. Be was out.

**NeXT.** NeXT was the company Steve Jobs started after he left Apple in 1986. The original NeXT product was a combination of hardware and software, much like the Mac itself. By 1996, however, all that was left was the software, which was called NEXTSTEP and which ran only on Intel processors. It eventually evolved into an open operating system called OPENSTEP, developed jointly with Sun Microsystems. OPENSTEP was a more mature OS than BeOS; it already had almost all the features that Apple was looking for. The main problem was that it lacked the familiar Mac user interface. It fact, it did not even run on Apple hardware. Nonetheless, Apple decided to tie its future to NeXT. In December 1996, the two companies announced their intention to merge.

The primary initial benefit of the merger of Apple and NeXT was that Steve Jobs returned to Apple. This eventually led to the iMac and the subsequent "supercool" hardware that allowed Apple to rise from the ashes, becoming a profitable, thriving company again.

At the same time, work proceeded on converting OPENSTEP to the next-generation Mac OS. Initial plans centered on Rhapsody, the code name for a project that largely was a direct port of OPENSTEP to the Mac. The problem was that no existing Mac software would run in Rhapsody, so all Mac applications would have to be completely rewritten. Developers let it be known that they would abandon the Mac before doing this.

So Apple returned to the drawing board one more time. Rhapsody evolved into Mac OS X (a roman numeral X that is pronounced ten). In this version of the OS, existing Mac software would be able to run with just minor modifications—a process Apple called *carbonizing* the software.

The Unix core, the Library-folder structure, and many of the development tools of Mac OS X have their origins in OPENSTEP. But the most distinctive feature of Mac OS X—the Aqua interface—came from Apple itself. Aqua was unveiled with great fanfare at a Macworld Expo in January 2000. Apple also added the capability to run Mac OS 9 within Mac OS X via a feature dubbed Classic. With these pieces in place, Mac OS X had reached its final stages.

A public beta version of Mac OS X was released in September 2000. The official release, labeled Mac OS X 10.0, came in March 2001. This first release still had some significant limitations, such as no AirPort or DVD support. But these problems were largely addressed in Mac OS X 10.1, released in September 2001. This release was the first version of Mac OS X that truly was ready for prime time.

Mac OS X 10.1 arrived seven years after the public first heard about Copland. Better late than never. It was a long road, but the hard part is over. Almost 20 years ago, the original Mac OS set the standard for elegance and ease of use. Now Mac OS X is ready to set that standard all over again.

Of course, if nothing ever went wrong with Mac OS X, there would be no need for the rest of this book. Things do go wrong. But you already knew that. That's why you're reading this book. So enough introduction. Let's get to work....

## Jaguar: Mac OS X 10.2

One more thing before we get started...

Apple's next update to Mac OS X, code-named Jaguar and expected to be called Mac OS X 10.2, will be released several months after the publication of this book.

Regarding troubleshooting matters, very little of significance will change from the current version of Mac OS X. Virtually all the tips and information included in this book will still be relevant in Jaguar. According to Apple, it may contain some notable interface changes, such as to certain System Preferences and to the Show Info window. These will result in some minor changes to the steps needed to accomplish certain tasks. But the problems you will face—and generally how to fix them—will remain the same.

That's good news for those of you (and that includes me!) concerned that the value of this book would diminish after Jaguar comes out.

Apple has said that it will make numerous under-the-hood improvements in Jaguar that should make Mac OS X run faster and with even greater stability than before (hence its code name). So while basic troubleshooting advice remains almost the same, you can expect to have trouble less often in Jaguar.

Apple has made public a few of the new features in Jaguar. To get a sneak peek, check out: "Take Note: What's new in Jaguar?" After Jaguar is released, I will post an online update to this book that will provide more details, especially as relevant to troubleshooting. You can get the update here: **www.tlandau.com/osxrelief.shtml**. MacFixIt, of course, will also cover the Mac OS X update.

**TAKE NOTE** ▶ **What's New in Jaguar?**

Here is an overview of what Apple has announced about Jaguar:

**Toolbar Fast Find.** There is search textbox in the Finder's Toolbar. Just enter text and press return, and the Finder window will change to display the results.

**Find.** Select Find from the Finder's File menu, and it brings up the new Find utility. Use this when you want to do more "complex" searches than the toolbar will allow, such as searching for items by modification date or using multiple criteria.

**Sherlock 3.** Finding information on your drives has been completely removed from Sherlock. Sherlock is now only an Internet search tool. Internet search-results features have been improved: You can now have full HTML output so that results appear as they would on a Web page, including graphics.

**QuickTime 6** features MPEG-4 video and AAC audio streaming.

**iChat.** This is an AOL Instant Messenger-compatible instant messaging application. You can use your existing Mac.com names with iChat or get a free Mac.com name if your don't already have one.

**Rendezvous.** This is Apple's proposed new standard for automatic discovery of computers, devices, and services on IP networks. With Rendezvous, you will be able to browse a network, find other Rendezvous clients, and connect to them without having to fiddle with settings. Paraphrasing Apple:"Rendezvous opens the door for a new way of networking. For example, you could keep all your music on the iMac in the den, and then listen to the iMac's playlists using iTunes on your iBook connected to the living room stereo. The only configuration panel you'd ever see is iTunes itself."

**Quartz Extreme.** This is a hardware-accelerated update to Mac OS X's Quartz graphics engine. The bad news is that it only works with the more recent graphics cards from nVidia (GeForce2MX, GeForce3, GeForce4 Ti, GeForce4 or GeForce4MX) and ATI (any AGP Radeon card).

**InkWell.** This is Mac OS X's new handwriting recognition technology. You'll need a stylus and graphics tablet to use it. Once installed, you can write directly in applications such as TextEdit or use the InkPad to write text and draw sketches before sending them to an application.

**Address Book.** This is a completely new application, not just an upgrade of the old version. It uses Apple's new system-wide database for managing contact information. It will be able to synch with Palm PDAs via Bluetooth. It also supports vcards.

**Mail.** This application has been updated to include spam filters, QuickTime playback, and more.

# 2

# Getting Started: Installing Mac OS X

Maybe your Mac came with Mac OS X preinstalled. Or maybe you already installed Mac OS X months ago. So maybe you think you can skip this chapter—because with Mac OS X already installed, you don't need to bother with how to install it. Maybe so. But maybe not.

Even in the above cases, a time will come when you will likely need to reinstall Mac OS X, because of problems with corrupted files on the currently installed OS, because a major update to the OS has been released, because you get a Mac that doesn't already have Mac OS X on it, or perhaps because you erased the drive to partition it. For all those cases, and for the benefit of those who have never installed Mac OS X before, this chapter walks you through the basics of Mac OS X installations and explains many of the things that can go wrong during an installation—and how to fix them.

I placed this chapter early in the book because, if you don't already have Mac OS X installed, installing it is the first thing you need to do. However, much of the chapter revolves around reinstalling Mac OS X and gets into topics that assume at least a basic knowledge of Mac OS X. So if you are completely new to Mac OS X, you may wish to first jump ahead to Chapter 3 and then return here.

# In This Chapter

# What Do You Need to Install and Run Mac OS X?

Well, for starters, you need a Mac OS X Install CD. But beyond that...

## Which Mac models can run Mac OS X?

Apple's official position is that only the following Macs can run Mac OS X:

- Power Macintosh G3 (beige or blue-and-white)
- Power Macintosh G4 (any model)
- PowerBook G3 (except the original PowerBook G3)
- PowerBook G4
- Any iMac or any iBook

Essentially, with the exception of the original PowerBook G3, any Mac that shipped with a PowerPC G3 or G4 processor (or anything newer that comes along) can run Mac OS X.

**Don't know what processor your Mac came with? Open Apple System Profiler, and check the Processor Info listing. If you are currently running Mac OS 9, you'll find Apple System Profiler in the Apple menu. Mac OS X users will find it in the Utilities folder inside the Applications folder.**

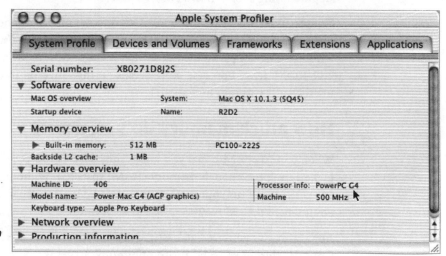

**Figure 2.1**

Apple System Profiler shows that this Mac came with a PowerPC G4. It can run Mac OS X.

Does this mean that you absolutely cannot use Mac OS X on an older Mac—even one that has been upgraded to have a G3 or G4 processor (such as a Power Mac 7500 with a processor upgrade)? Apple's position remains firm: You cannot run Mac OS X on these Macs. But there are always some users who will not take no for an answer. Users have found various ways to get Mac OS X running on at least some of these older Macs. If you want to try, a good starting point would be to get a utility called Install Unsupported X (**www.versiontracker.com/moreinfo.fcgi?id=11168&db=mac**). Be aware, however, that if you have any problems running Mac OS X on these systems, Apple will not help you solve them.

Overall, I strongly recommend that if you want to run Mac OS X, you get a Mac that is sanctioned to run Mac OS X.

Unfortunately, even some Macs that are on Apple's approved list have been known to have some problems with Mac OS X. Here are the two best-known examples:

**PowerBook G3 ("Lombard" bronze keyboard model).** There have been numerous reports that some of these PowerBooks cannot run Mac OS X if extra memory is installed in the top RAM slot. (The PowerBook typically shipped from Apple with this slot empty.) Freezes and System crashes (*kernel panics*, as they are called in Mac OS X, and as discussed in Chapter 5) are the main symptoms. The consensus view of users is that the problem is due to the processor used in some, not all, machines of this model of PowerBook. There appear to be two variations of the processor: copper-based and aluminum-based. The copper-based one appears to be the problem child. The best fix is to get the entire logic board replaced. At this writing, Apple has not officially confirmed all this information, so you may or may not have success with Apple's doing a logic-board swap for free.

**Power Macintosh G3 (beige).** This original G3 Mac generally works OK with Mac OS X—if you can get it to install. Getting it to install can be a problem if you have a partitioned drive that is larger than 8 GB or use a third-party CD-ROM drive. I provide more details on this situation In the section below titled "8 GB partition limitation."

## How much memory do you need?

When you have a Mac that you know runs Mac OS X, your next step is to make sure it has enough memory (RAM) installed. Without sufficient RAM, Mac OS X may run, but performance may be unacceptably slow—to the point where the OS may seem to freeze at times.

Apple also says you need at least 128 MB of memory to use Mac OS X. Consider this figure to be a bare minimum. To get the best performance from Mac OS X, I recommend at least 192 MB—ideally, even more.

Every Mac now shipping comes with at least 128 MB of RAM, so new Macs will not have a problem meeting the minimum.

Every Mac can accommodate more memory than the minimum that ships from Apple. Typically, you add more memory by purchasing a memory module and inserting it into the designated RAM slot or slots on your Mac. Each Mac comes with instructions on how to do this for your model. Apple makes sure that the process is relatively easy. On a Power Mac, for example, you don't need any tools. Just open the door, insert the RAM into the location described in the manual that came with the computer, and you are done.

## Other requirements

**8 GB partition limitation.** If you have an older iMac, PowerBook G3, or beige Power Mac G3 (the Read Before You Install file on the Mac OS X CD gives more precise details); you have a hard drive that is larger than 8 GB; and you partition the hard drive (more on partitioning in a moment), you must assign the first partition to be contained entirely within the first 8 GB. That is, the partition must be no larger than 8 GB, and you must install Mac OS X on that partition. Actually, some people have complained that this requirement applies even to some Macs that Apple says do not have this restriction.

If your first two partitions are both less than 8 GB total (such as 3 GB each), you should be able to install Mac OS X on either of them.

**Hard drive space.** You should have a minimum of 1.5 GB of free space on your hard drive before attempting to install Mac OS X. The amount "available" is typically listed at the top of each Finder window.

*Figure 2.2*

*The amount of disk space "available" is listed.*

**External drives.** You can potentially start up from an external FireWire or USB drive running Mac OS X. In fact, you can even install Mac OS X on the mini-drive inside Apple's iPod device, and start up from the iPod. However, some external drives will not serve as startup disks due to an incompatibility with the drive's firmware or hardware components. If no update for the drive is available, the drive may be unusable as a startup device. However, you should still be able to mount it as a nonstartup volume.

SEE: • "Take Note: Startup Failure only when starting up from a CD or External Drive," in Chapter 5, for more details.

**Firmware.** A firmware upgrade alters a special modifiable component of the hardware on the Mac's logic board. Check Apple's Web site (**www.apple.com/ support**) for the latest firmware available for your computer. If a firmware update is available that is more recent than the purchase date of your computer (or more recent than the last firmware update that you have installed), install the new firmware update. Several firmware updates are included on the Mac OS X Install CD. There is no danger in trying one if you are not sure whether it has been installed on your Mac. If you don't need it, the installer will not run.

One caution, however: You cannot undo a firmware upgrade. In some cases, a firmware upgrade can cause more problems than it solves. Thus, if you want to be extra-cautious, check a site such as MacFixIt to see whether problems have been reported for a firmware update that would make you hesitant to install it.

**Mac OS 9.** Mac OS X has the capability to run Mac OS 9 applications seamlessly within Mac OS X, which means you won't have to leave Mac OS X and restart in Mac OS 9 each time you need to run an application that does not yet run in Mac OS X. This capability depends on a Mac OS X feature called Classic Environment, which is discussed much more in Chapter 9.

To take advantage of this capability, you need Mac OS 9 installed somewhere on your drive. In fact, you need at least Mac OS 9.1 to run Mac OS X 10.0, and you need at least Mac OS 9.2 to run Mac OS X 10.1 or later.

**If you don't know what version of Mac OS 9 you have installed, just choose the About This Computer item from the top of the Apple menu. The window that opens will tell you. If you have a Mac OS 9 Install CD, the version number should be printed on the disc.**

If you don't have Mac OS 9 already installed, you should install it before installing Mac OS X. In general, to install Mac OS 9, use the Mac OS 9 Install CD that came with your computer or a newer one that you may have purchased. Actually, the Mac OS X installer will warn you about this situation and advise you to install Mac OS 9 first if it cannot find a working copy of Mac OS 9. In some cases, the Installer claims that it cannot find a copy of Mac OS 9 installed, even though you have one installed. In such cases, you typically can ignore the warning and proceed.

**Other issues.** Check the Read Before You Install file for more information that may be relevant to your particular setup or that may be more recent than I have covered here. The file is included as a text document on the Mac OS X Install CD. It also appears when you run the Install utility (as I will note again in a moment).

# How Do You Install/Reinstall Mac OS X?

## Start up from the CD

For this section, I assume that you are using a generic Mac OS X Install CD. If your Mac came with Mac OS X preinstalled, you instead may want to use the Software Restore set of CDs instead. I discuss that option in "Using Software Restore" later in this chapter.

**Install Mac OS 9 first.** If a compatible version of Mac OS 9 is already installed on your drive and you wish to add Mac OS X, you can proceed directly to the next step. Otherwise, install Mac OS 9, using the Mac OS 9 Software Install CD that came with your Mac (or a newer CD, if you have it). Or you can use the Mac OS 9 Software Restore CD that came with your Mac (the one included with Macs that did not come with Mac OS X preinstalled). Do not use the Software Restore CD to install Mac OS 9 on a volume that already has Mac OS X installed, however, unless you intend to erase the volume.

**SEE:** • "Technically Speaking: Don't Use Mac OS 9 Software Restore on a Mac OS X Volume."

The Mac OS 9 Install CD included with Mac OS X retail packages may be preferred over the CD that came with your Mac, especially if it contains a newer version of Mac OS 9. However, there is a chance the CD will not even start up on your Mac (because it does not include hardware-specific resources needed for your particular Mac model). In this case, use the CD that came with your Mac and apply any Mac OS 9 updates, as available, from Apple's Web site.

Because this book is on Mac OS X, I am not going to explore the details of a Mac OS 9 installation here. As is typical of Apple software, however, installation is fairly easy, even if you have never done it before. If you need more help using the Mac OS 9 Install and Software Restore CDs, see the documentation that came with your Mac. Or check out my previous book, *Sad Macs, Bombs, and Other Disasters.*

**TECHNICALLY SPEAKING** ▶ **Don't use Mac OS 9 Software Restore on a Mac OS X volume**

Imagine this scenario. You have a Mac that did not come with Mac OS X preinstalled. Your Software Restore CD has only Mac OS 9 and includes options that allow a restore without erasing the drive: Restore in Place and Restore Saving Original Items. At some point, you have installed Mac OS X on the same partition as Mac OS 9. Now you want to use Software Restore to restore the original Mac OS 9 software without erasing Mac OS X.

Unfortunately, you cannot do this. Using Software Restore in such a situation may render Mac OS X unusable. In particular, when you try to start up in Mac OS X, an icon of a belt around a folder will likely appear onscreen, meaning that the startup has failed. Less serious, but still annoying, symptoms may occur instead.

If you used the Restore in Place option, you generally can solve the problem completely by reinstalling Mac OS X. If you used the Restore Saving Original Items option, however, things get much more complicated. In brief, after reinstalling Mac OS X, you will also need to re-create the exact set of Users directories that existed before. Then you will need to type the following command in the Terminal utility of Mac OS X: <sudo cp –R /Original\ Items/Users/* /Users>. You are still not done. You can find details on exactly what to do next in this Apple Knowledge Base document 106294. The far simpler solution, however, is to prevent the problem in the first place:. To prevent it, never do a Mac OS 9 Software Restore on a volume with Mac OS X installed.

**Install Mac OS X next.** To install Mac OS X for the first time, you must start up from the Mac OS X Install CD. The best way to do this is to insert the CD, and launch the Install Mac OS X application. A window will appear that contains a Restart button. Click it and your Mac will restart, booting from the CD.

Alternatively, you can choose Restart from Mac OS 9's Special menu, and hold down the C key on the keyboard until the Mac starts up from the CD.

Or you can start up from the CD by selecting the Mac OS 9 Startup Disk control panel, selecting the CD as the startup volume, and finally clicking the Restart button. If a volume has more than one System, click the disclosure triangle for the volume to display the available choices, indicating what version of the System software each one represents; then select the one you want. The Mac OS X Install CD includes a copy of the Startup Disk control panel in its Utilities folder; it may be newer than the version on your hard drive. It is important that the version be at least 9.2.1; older versions will not work properly with Mac OS X.

In any case, now you will start up from the CD.

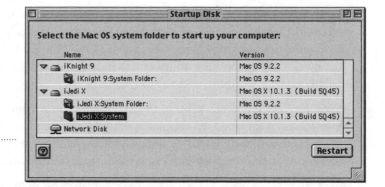

**Figure 2.3**

The Startup Disk control panel in Mac OS 9.

The Mac OS X Install CD launches the Installer application directly. The first thing you will likely see is a window labeled Mac OS X with the words *Preparing installation* visible. You cannot quit the Installer to go to the Desktop (the Finder) from here. If you try to quit this application at any point, you will simply restart the Mac.

Next, you will get to a window that starts the Install process. First, you are asked to select a main language. Presumably, most readers will be selecting English. After doing this, you click the Continue button to go on to the next screen.

## Check the Installer and File menus

But before you click the Continue button, take a moment to look at the menus available. The two of special interest are **Installer** and **File**.

**Installer.** The Installer menu contains three commands of note:

**Quit.** You use this command to quit the application if you change your mind about installing Mac OS X.

**Reset Password.** This command is of use only if you have already installed Mac OS X, so you won't be using it now. You can use it to enter a new password for any user of Mac OS X—an important back door of last resort in case you cannot recall your own password. This arrangement is also a security weakness, of course, as it means that anyone with a Mac OS X Install CD could change your password to gain access to your system. But that is the tradeoff you get for the ability to recover from a forgotten password. This command is accessible only if you start up from a CD. If you launch the Installer application from a hard drive, this option will not appear. Actually, the Installer on the CD is accessing a separate utility called Password Reset, which is also on the CD. This utility works only if you start up from the CD, however. Should you copy the utility to a Mac OS X hard drive and try to run it from there, it will not work.

**Open Disk Utility.** This command takes you to a window in which you can select either First Aid (used to repair a disk) or a variety of other options that correspond to what Drive Setup does in Mac OS 9 (for example, reformat and partition). I will cover these utilities more in later chapters of this book, especially Chapter 5. For now, note the following.

If you click the name of a drive in the left column, information about the drive (capacity, for example) appears in the Information pane. If the drive is divided into partitions, click the disclosing triangle next to the drive name to see a list of partition names. You can separately get "Information" on each one.

**First Aid.** To use First Aid, click the First Aid tab. The ability to run First Aid from the CD is important, as the First Aid component of the current version of Disk Utility cannot repair the drive currently running the OS. So if you start up from the hard drive, you cannot use First Aid to repair that drive. Don't try to use Mac OS 9 versions of Disk First Aid, as they are not designed to work with Mac OS X.

**Erase.** From the Erase pane, you can erase (also called initializing or reformatting) any writable media.

**Partition.** The Partition pane is where you can partition the drive as well as determine the type of drive formatting (for example, Mac OS Extended) you want to use. (Note: The **RAID** pane is used for setups where multiple drives are linked together; I will not be discussing this type of setup in this book.)

In general, you will not need to use Disk Utility at this point—with one exception. The default setup for a drive, as shipped from Apple, is to have one partition. Should you want to have two or more partitions, you will need to use Disk Utility now to set up the additional partitions.

SEE:  • "Take Note: Why and How to Partition" for information on how and why you would want to partition a drive when using Mac OS X.

  • "Take Note: Root Access," in Chapter 3, for more on the Reset Password command.

  • Chapter 5, for much more on startup issues, including using passwords and Disk Utility.

**TAKE NOTE ▶ Why and How to Partition**

Partitioning a drive means dividing the drive into two or more separate volumes. Each volume in turn mounts separately when you launch your Mac. In almost all respects, the partitions/volumes will behave as though you have two (assuming that you made two partitions) separate hard drives, rather than just one. The only times when it would become apparent that only one hard drive was at work would be when the hard drive failed or you needed to reformat it.

All drives ship from Apple with just one partition. Thus, if you want two or more partitions, you will need to create them yourself. Changing the number of partitions on a drive requires erasing the contents of the drive. Thus, anything on your drive that you want to save, you will need to back up first (a subject that I discuss a bit more later in this chapter, but especially again in Chapter 5).

That's why I recommend partitioning a drive the day you unpack a new Mac. You will have nothing to back up, because you haven't used it yet. This procedure simplifies the process considerably.

Why should you partition a drive? Two main reasons. First, partitioning allows you to create two separate startup volumes, if you want. If you are having trouble with volume A, for example, and need to restart from another volume to fix the problem, you have a Volume B ready to go. You don't necessarily need to seek out a CD or other external medium. This feature can be very convenient.

The second reason is that partitioning allows you to install Mac OS X and Mac OS 9 on separate volumes. Why is this ability important? The day may come when Mac OS X files get so messed up that the only solution is to erase the volume and start over. With Mac OS 9 and X on separate volumes, you can erase the X volume without losing the 9 volume. You could even use the second partition to maintain backup copies of important personal files (for documents photos, and so on) on your Mac OS X volume, simplifying the process of erasing the Mac OS X volume. The Erase Disk command in the Mac OS 9 Finder (or a similar option accessed from the Mac OS X Installer utility) erases only the selected partition, not the entire drive.

A related benefit of having separate partitions for separate OS versions occurs if you use the setup to install two copies of Mac OS 9: one on a separate partition from Mac OS X and a second on the same partition as Mac OS X. (Note: some users recommend creating three partitions—one for each OS. But I find this practice to be a bit of overkill, and it can result in each partition's being too small to fit everything you want on it, especially if your drive is not too big to begin with.) This technique allows you to use one version of Mac OS 9 (on its own partition) when you want to boot from Mac OS 9 and the other (the one on the Mac OS X partition) when you want to launch Classic. The benefit (see more in Chapter 9 ) is that some files work in Mac OS 9 directly but not in Classic. Thus, with only one Mac OS 9 installed, you might have to choose between giving up on these programs (primarily extensions and control panels) so that you can use Classic or keeping them so that you can boot from Mac OS 9 and giving up on Classic. With two Mac OS 9 Systems, you can have your cake and eat it too.

*continues on next page*

**TAKE NOTE ▶ Why and How to Partition** *continued*

Still, if you don't intend to bother with Mac OS 9 often, you can get by with a single partition without any sacrifice.

But if you do want to partition, here is my recommended procedure:

**1.** Start up from a Mac OS Install CD.

If it is a Mac OS 9 CD, launch Drive Setup, select your hard drive, and click Custom Setup.

If it is a Mac OS X CD, access Disk Utility from the Installer's Install menu and select the Partition pane.

In either case, you next choose to create two partitions (of type Mac OS Extended). For simplicity, leave both partitions the same size. Otherwise, make the intended Mac OS X volume (the one on top in the graphic display) somewhat larger than the other, as it will need to house both Mac OS X and Mac OS 9.

**2.** If your Mac came with Mac OS X and Mac OS 9 preinstalled:

a. Use the set of Restore discs to install the original software on the first partition. This step sets up the first partition to be identical to how your Mac was set up when it first arrived. All software will be there—both Mac OS 9 and Mac OS X.

b. Restart the Mac when you're done.

c. Update the OSes as needed (if newer versions are available than the ones came with your Mac).

d. Copy the Mac OS 9 System Folder (as well as the Applications (Mac OS 9) folder, if you want) to the second partition, via drag and drop, so that you have a separate copy of the System Folder there. As long as the initially installed Mac OS 9 System Folder is not the current startup System, you can delete it after you have copied it, should you want only one Mac OS 9 System on your drive.

If you prefer, you can instead use the Mac OS 9 Software Install CD to install Mac OS 9 on the second partition.

Whatever you do, don't try the reverse—that is, don't try to copy the Mac OS X System software from one partition to the other. That's a whole lot trickier to do than for Mac OS 9. Keep it simple; leave Mac OS X where it is, and move Mac OS 9.

**3.** If your Mac came with only Mac OS 9 preinstalled:

a. Use the Restore disc to reinstall the original software on the second partition.

b. Restart with the Mac OS X Install CD to install Mac OS X on the first partition.

c. Restart the Mac again when you're done.

d. Update the OSes as needed (if newer versions are available than those that are on the CDs).

e. If desired, drag the Mac OS 9 System Folder to the Mac OS X partition to make a copy of it there.

If you have any problem selecting the desired System Folder as the folder to use when launching Classic, see Chapter 9 for help.

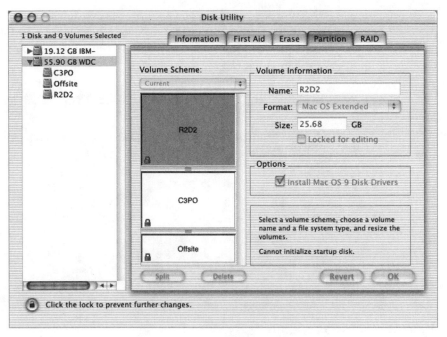

*Figure 2.4*

*The partition options of Disk Utility.*

**File.** The File menu contains two commands of note:

**Show Log.** This command gives a record of just about every action that occurs while the Installer application is running. If you make a selection in any window, it typically will be recorded in the log. The log may also list error messages, but you can most likely ignore them, as they don't imply that you won't be able to install Mac OS X. If you really trip over a show-stopper error, you will get warned about it directly, via a message alert. You won't need to check the log. The log is just a sometimes-useful detailed record.

**Show Files.** This command cannot be selected yet. In fact, it may not be selectable at all in the version of the Installer included on the CD. More typically, it works for OS updates that you run from the Installer included on the hard drive. Sometimes, it will not be selectable in the early panes of the Installer but will work later (as in the Select Destination pane, or after the installation has completed but before you restart). So experiment.

Show Files brings up a list of every file that is to be installed by the current Installer setup and the folders in which each file will be placed. This information is not so critical for the initial installation but will be of more interest when you update the OS and want to see what new files the updater installed. I will return to this topic in the "Use a Stand-alone Installer/Updater," section, later in this chapter.

OK, now you can click the Continue button. You will proceed through a Welcome screen, a Read Me screen (which is identical to the Read Before You Install file I mentioned earlier), a License screen, and finally a Select Destination screen.

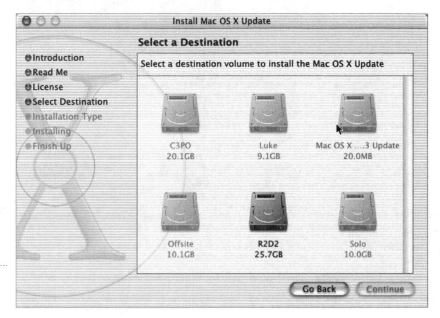

**Figure 2.5**

The Select Destination screen of the Installer.

## Select a destination

In the Select Destination screen, click the volume (partition/drive, if you have more than one) where you want to install Mac OS X. If you have enough disk space on the drive, you will be allowed to proceed.

Before proceeding, however, note the Erase Destination and Format As option at the bottom of the window. The option is unchecked by default.

Keep Erase Destination disabled if:

**Mac OS 9 is already installed on your volume, and you want it to remain there.** In this case, Mac OS X will install into remaining free space on your drive. Everything that is currently there for Mac OS 9 will remain untouched.

**Mac OS X is already installed on your drive, and you want to reinstall it without losing your customized changes.** This option typically is referred to as a *clean* reinstallation of Mac OS X, which may be required if Mac OS X files get modified or corrupted to such an extent that you cannot start up from Mac OS X anymore. In some cases, the only solution may be to reinstall Mac OS X, essentially starting from scratch. In such cases, however, you don't want to lose all the documents, added applications, and other items that you have added to the drive since Mac OS X was first installed. A clean install will accomplish this dual goal: reinstalling the essential OS files and leaving everything else untouched.

Enable Erase Destination if:

**You want everything on the selected volume to be erased before installing Mac OS X.** This option would be desirable if the volume currently contains only unwanted data or if a current install of Mac OS X is so messed up that even a clean reinstallation cannot get it to recover. In that case, if you can access the volume at all (perhaps by starting up from a Mac OS 9 second partition), back up anything you need to save before launching the Installer and erasing the volume.

If you select this option, you can choose either Mac OS Extended (HFS Plus) or Unix File System (UFS) from the pop-up menu. In almost all cases, you should choose HFS Plus. Why? For starters, this format is the same one that Mac OS 9 uses. If you select UFS, you will not be able to use that partition for Mac OS 9. About the only people who may actually need UFS formatting are those who are running Mac OS X as a server—something I will not be considering much in this book.

## Select an installation type

Finally, you will get to the Installation Type screen, which has an Install button. Click it to initiate an Easy Install of Mac OS X. After that, sit back and relax. The installation may take 20 minutes or so to complete. A variety of status messages will appear, informing you of what is happening at each stage. But unless something goes wrong and the installation fails, there is nothing that you need to do. When installation is over, you can choose to restart by quitting the Installer. If you don't, the Installer will restart automatically after a brief delay, and it should launch Mac OS X. You are done!

Before clicking Install, however, you can click the Customize button. This button will take you to a screen where you can enable and disable certain components of the installation—that is, do a Custom Install. You have at least two options. One is to choose whether to install additional print drivers; the other is to choose whether to install the BSD Subsystem. The BSD Subsystem comprises optional components of the Unix software that is at the core of Mac OS X (as discussed more in Chapter 4). Although these components technically are optional, some applications may not run correctly without them. As both options are rather small (a little more than 4 MB each), I would not even bother thinking about them; go with the Easy Install.

You may also have the option here to selectively install support for different languages. The fewer languages you select, the less disk space will be needed for the installation.

When you restart, the Mac should start up in the just-installed Mac OS X. If not, restart again, this time holding down the Option key. On virtually all Macs that support Mac OS X, this step will bring up a screen that lists all your available startup volumes. Click the desired one; then click the continue arrow.

**SEE:** • **Chapter 5 for more information on using the Option key at startup.**

# Using Software Restore

If you have a Mac that came with Mac OS X preinstalled, you can skip the preceding section, as you already have Mac OS X installed. In fact, you can skip this section as well for the same reason. As I mentioned at the start of this chapter, however, you may want or need to reinstall Mac OS X at some point. If so, read on.

## What is Software Restore?

For Macs that come preinstalled with Mac OS X, Software Restore is a set of CDs (currently, four) that install both Mac OS X and Mac OS 9, as well as all other software that originally shipped with the Mac. Thus, these CDs completely restore the contents of a drive (or partition of a drive) to the way it was the day the computer was unpacked. If you are familiar with Software Restore CD that came with Macs before Mac OS X, you will note two differences. First, the Mac OS 9-only Software Restore CD was just one CD; the new Mac OS 9 and Mac OS X combined Software Restore takes up four CDs. Second, the new Software Restore requires that the volume be erased prior to installation; the Mac OS 9-only Software Restore had additional options, such as Restore in Place, which left all non-OS software untouched. Thus, if you want to use the Mac OS 9/X combined Software Restore, you first need to back up anything you want to save that is currently in the installation volume; otherwise, it will be lost.

## Decide whether to install or restore

If you don't want to erase your drive, you don't want to use Software Restore. Instead, use the installation method covered in the preceding section.

A down side of using the Software Install CD is that it may not install all the software that came with your Mac—especially on consumer Macs (iMacs and iBooks) that come with bundled software (such as AppleWorks and FAXstf) that typically is not included in a Mac OS Install CD. Some of this software may be included in the special version of the Mac OS 9 Software Install CD that comes with each Mac, but a few programs may get installed only by the Software Restore discs. (Note: Your Mac may have come with an additional Applications CD, but even this CD may not contain all software that's missing from the Install CD.)

So if you don't mind erasing your drive, using the Software Restore CDs is the preferred choice.

**SEE:** • **"Selective installation of Software Restore files," later in this chapter, for how to separately reinstall files that are only included on the Software Restore CDs.**

## Install with Software Restore

Using Software Restore could hardly be easier. First, restart from the first Software Restore CD. Then select the volume you want to use, click the Restore button, and wait until the process is done. You will be asked to insert the second, third, and fourth CDs as needed. But otherwise, the process is automatic. Also, you can format the drive only with HFS Plus here. The Software Restore will install Mac OS 9 and Mac OS X on the same volume. You have no choice about this situation.

What if you set up your drive with two partitions, so as to have Mac OS X and Mac OS 9 on separate partitions (or to have an additional Mac OS 9 version on the second partition)? I explain how to do this in "Take Note: Why and How to Partition" earlier in this chapter.

## Back up your files via the Finder

If you decide to use Software Restore and thus erase your volume, you will likely want to save document files and other files you added to the initial installation.

Here is a relatively simple method of backing up and restoring saved Mac OS X files, using the Finder:

1. Copy everything you want to save into your Home directory/folder.

   Most of what you want to save should already be there.

2. Copy the entire folder to your backup location.

   This location will most likely be a removable medium such as a CD-RW disc, DVD-RAM disc, or ZIP disk. Or it could be an online server such as Apple's iDisk, which Mac OS X fully supports (see Chapter 8).

3. Save other users whose folders are in the Users directory, if any.

4. After reinstalling Mac OS X, set up Users directories for yourself and other users as needed, ideally using the same names as before.

Use the Users System Preferences dialog box to create directories beyond the one automatically created for yourself (see Chapters 3 and 8 for more details).

5. Copy the contents of each backed-up folder to the new folder of the same name. In some cases, such as the Desktop, you may need to copy directly from one subfolder to the other.

To replace the contents for users other than yourself, you need to be an administrator, probably with root access (as described in "Take Note: Root Access," in Chapter 3). One way to work around this and similar hassles you may encounter is to start up from Mac OS 9 and copy the Users folders' contents from there; then reboot to Mac OS X. In any case, don't just copy a folder for an individual user to the Users folder. Always create a new user directory first, while you're in Mac OS X, and then copy contents to the folder that gets created. Otherwise, the OS will not recognize the folder as a legitimate user.

6. If you moved files from other locations, such as the Applications folder, now you can now move them back.

With certain applications, you may still have problems, especially if the application installed needed files in locations other than the Applications folder—which you no longer have. That's why for applications, your best choice is simply to reinstall them.

Backing up and restoring Mac OS 9 files is a simpler process. Just copy the files to your backup volume and then copy them back to your new Mac OS 9 volume. If you saved files that go in the System Folder, you will need to drag them to the new System Folder. If you were not having any problems with your old System Folder, you can simply save the entire old System Folder and then use it to replace the one that gets installed by the Software Restore. As you cannot delete an active System Folder, this procedure is easiest when you boot from a Mac OS 9 CD.

SEE: • **"Reinstall Mac OS X," in Chapter 5, for further details on reinstalling and backing up Mac OS X, especially in regard to solving startup problems.**

## Selective installation of Software Restore files

Suppose you want to get the unique software for Mac OS 9 that is contained on the Software Restore CD, or you want to reinstall certain software (such as iDVD) that is contained on the Software Restore CDs but on no other CDs that come with your Mac. Can you do this without having to erase your drive, as is required when you do a Software Restore? Yes.

First, check again to make certain that the software is not on the Mac OS X Install CD. If it is, you probably can just copy it from there. Next, check online; you may find a newer version that you can download. Finally, if you can obtain the files only from the Software Restore CDs, you have two approaches:

If you have an empty external drive, an unused partition on your main drive, or another external medium that can hold a complete restore, do a Software Restore to this location; then copy the needed software to the desired location on your main drive.

Otherwise, copy all four of the disk-image files from each of the four Software Restore CDs to your hard drive. (The files will have names such as iBook HD Disc 1.dmg and iBook HD Disc 2.dmgpart.) Then double-click the first image. This step mounts a hard-drive image—using the Disk Copy application—that contains all the software that will be installed by Software Restore. Then you can copy applications and their needed System Folder items to your hard drive manually. Ideally, you should be running Mac OS X when you do this.

# Updating Mac OS X

After you have installed (or reinstalled) Mac OS X from a CD, you may have more installing to do in two situations:

- The Software Restore CDs will always return you to the version of the OS that came with your Mac. If a newer version exists, you may have a new Mac OS X Install CD. Your Mac may have come with Mac OS 10.0, for example, and you may already have a Mac OS 10.1 Install CD. In this case, after using Software Restore, your next option is to install the update with the newer CD.

- Software Restore and your latest software Install CD may not be the newest versions that are available. In particular, Apple may have released free updates. You need to get and install these updates.

## Use Software Update

In Mac OS X, the simplest way to check for and install updates is to select Software Update from the System Preferences window. From the pane that appears, click the Update Now button.

**SEE:**  • **Chapter 3 for more background on System Preferences.**

Or, if you prefer (and I don't), you can choose the Automatically rather than Manually option and set a time for the OS to check for potential updates (Daily, Weekly, or Monthly). You have to have an active Internet connection for this option to work.

**SEE:**  • **Chapter 8 for information on setting up an Internet connection.**

If an update is found, a separate Software Update application will launch and will list the update and offer to let you download and install it. The only updates you will find this way are OS and OS-related software (such as Internet Explorer) that ordinarily would come on a Mac OS X Install CD. The listing will often be for an update of the OS itself, such as to go from Mac OS X 10.1.2 to 10.1.3.

If you wish to install the listed software, make sure its checkbox in the Install column is enabled. Then click the Install button. The rest is automatic. The software will be downloaded to your drive and installed.

Some updates only appear in the listing if certain prior updates have been previously installed. For example, Apple at one point released an update to the Installer application itself. No newer updates would appear in Software Update until after the new Installer had been installed. Thus, after installing any update, return to the Software Update System Preference and click Update Now again. Keep doing this until no new updates appear.

Occasionally, there may be an optional update that you do not wish to install. For example, Apple released Language Support updates for Mac OS X 10.1.3. If you only use English, you could skip these updates. However, it can get to be annoying to have Software Update keep listing them each time you check for new software. The solution is to select the unwanted items and then select Make Inactive from the Update menu. At any later time, should you change your mind about installing an inactive update, you can toggle between Show Inactive Updates and Hide Inactive Updates, also in the Update menu.

(Note: In Mac OS 9, you obtain Mac OS 9 updates by using the Software Update control panel.)

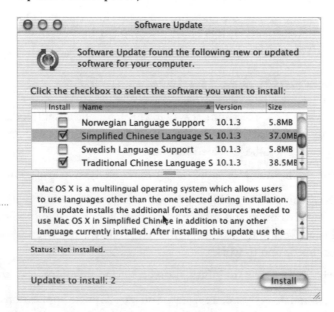

**Figure 2.6**

*Software Update shows a list of needed updates. Just check which ones you want to receive, and click Update Now.*

**TAKE NOTE ▶ Understanding Image files**

Users who are familiar with Mac OS 9 probably are familiar with the Disk Copy program and its capability to open and even create image files. These image files typically have the extension .img (for image) or .smi (for self-mounting image; such files can open without Disk Copy). Double-clicking the image file opens yet another file: the actual image. Opening an image file is similar to mounting an external read-only medium (such as a CD-ROM disc). Thus, you can use this technique to make exact copies of folders, discs, and other items, and later re-create them as image files.

Programs such as StuffIt Deluxe may also be able to open image files.

In Mac OS X, the version of Disk Copy located in the Utilities folder can open the same .img files that can be opened in Mac OS 9. It can also open another type of image file with the .dmg extension, technically referred to as a UDIF device image. If you try to open a .dmg file in Mac OS 9, you will likely get an error message unless you have Disk Copy 6.5 or later. Otherwise, for most end users, a .dmg file and a .img file will behave almost identically.

Both Apple and third-party software makers use disk images for installing updates. In many cases, there will be no separate Installer application. The software on the image can be copied directly to a hard drive and used there. Apple's official position is to prefer that third parties use this installer-free method of installing software. The installer method should be used only if the developer requires different components of the software to be copied to different folders on the drive.

## Use a stand-alone installer/updater

**Get the installer package.** In some cases, if you use Software Update, you may be able to use the new software immediately without needing to restart your Mac. In other cases, you will need to restart before the new software takes effect. In the latter case, the Installer will inform you and insist that you restart when you try to quit the installation.

As a rule, after you update software with Software Update and then restart, the OS will delete the installer file that was downloaded. This situation can be a significant disadvantage. Suppose that you have four Macs, and you want to update all four of them. Further suppose that you have a slow Internet connection, so you prefer not to use Software Update for all four Macs. Rather, you would like simply to copy the installer file that you downloaded to the first Mac for each remaining Mac. If you restart and the file gets deleted, you can't do this. What do you do? As is often the case in Mac OS X, you have more than one alternative. Here are three choices for obtaining a stand-alone installer file (also called a package file, with a .pkg at the end of its name):

**Download the stand-alone installer file from the Web.** You can
bypass using Software update altogether. Instead, go to Apple's Web site
(**www.apple.com/swupdates/**) . It typically posts the same software available
from Software Update, although it may not be available until a few days to
a few weeks after it is available from Software Update. These files are not
deleted after you use them and can be saved for multiple installations or reinstallations, as needed.

These updates may download as image (.dmg or .img) files. In this case, you
need to open the image file via Disk Copy (a utility included with Mac OS X).
•Typically, just double-click the file and it will launch automatically. An image
icon should mount. Double-click the image icon to open its window. The actual
installer .pkg file will be located here. Drag it out of its window if you wish to
save it to your hard drive. You can also run it directly from the image window.

**SEE:** • "Take Note: Understanding Image Files," for more details.

For certain OS updates, there may be two similarly named files available, such
as *Mac OS X 10.1.3 Update* and *Mac OS X 10.1.3 Combo Update*. The difference is that the Mac OS X 10.1.3 Update can only update a system currently
running Mac OS X 10.1.2. The Combo update can update any prior version
of Mac OS X 10.1 (for example, 10.1, 10.1.1, 10.1.2). As a result, the Combo
update is a significantly larger file.

**Save the installer file via Software Update's Save As command.**
After installing an update via the Software Update System Preference, the
Save As command in the Update menu should be enabled. You can use this
to save a copy, to whatever location you select, of the installer file that was
just downloaded.

**Save the installer file via the Finder.** If for some reason the Save As
method does not work, you can still preserve the installer file for later use.
To do so, you just have to locate it and copy it before you restart. Fortunately,
in Mac OS X, dialog boxes typically are not modal, as they are in Mac OS 9.
This means that even if a dialog box with a Restart button appears on your
screen, you can still click elsewhere and work with your Mac, returning to
click the Restart button when you are ready to do so. (Actually, you could quit
the Installer without restarting if you wished.) In this case, here's what you
need to do:

1. Choose Go to Folder from the Go menu.
2. In the text box that appears, type: </private/tmp>.

    This step takes you inside a folder that normally is invisible. Here, you may
    find the update installer. More likely, you will either find a folder with a
    number for a name (such as 501). Double-click this folder to open it.

    Inside this will likely be a folder called Temporary Items. Double-click
    this folder to open it.

If you don't see any such folders here, it is because these folders are currently invisible. To "see" them, get a shareware utility called TinkerTool, and enable its "Show hidden and system files" option. You can turn this option off when you are done.

3. Inside the Temporary Items folder should be the installer file. If there are multiple files here, you should be able to recognize the one you want by its name (and its name should typically end in ".pkg").

4. Drag the installer file to the Desktop or any other desired location.

5. Restart, if needed, to get the already-installed software to work.

The installer file you copied to the Desktop will remain even after the restart. The copy in the tmp folder will be gone.

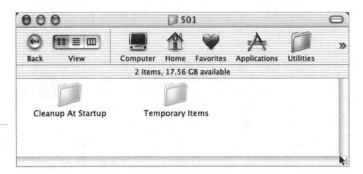

**Figure 2.7**

*The Temporary Items folder inside a 501 folder.*

SEE:  • "Invisible Files," in Chapter 6, for much more information on working with invisible files, including more on using TinkerTool.

• Chapter 10 for more information on using Terminal and Unix commands.

---

**TECHNICALLY SPEAKING ▶ Using Terminal to Save the Installer File**

If you want, you can use Terminal to navigate to the tmp file and copy the installer document to a new location. Here's how:

1. Launch Terminal.

2. Type: cd /private/tmp.

   This step takes you to the tmp directory/folder.

3. Type: ls.

   This shows the contents of the tmp directory.

4. Look for a directory with a numerical name (such as 501). Type: cd {*name of folder*}. Then again type: ls.

   If you do not find this folder, proceed directly to the next step.

5. From this output, look for a directory called Temporary Items. If you find such a folder, type: cd Temporary\ Items. Then type: ls.

   Hint: If you type cd T and then press the Tab key, Terminal will fill in the rest of the name.

   *continues on next page*

**TECHNICALLY SPEAKING** ▶ **Using Terminal to Save the Installer File** *continued*

**6.** The installer file should be here (it should have a .pkg extension at the end of its name).

**7.** Type mv *{name of file} ~/{name of file}*.

   This step moves the file to the root level of your home directory. Remember that to type a space in the name of a file, you should use the backslash character—that is, *my file* becomes *my\ file*.

**8.** You can now quit Terminal.

**9.** In a Finder window, click the Home icon in the toolbar.

   You should see the file in the window. If not, relaunch the Finder via a forced quit (Command-Option-Esc) and check again.

**Run the Installer.** Most Mac OS X updates come in the form of package (.pkg) files. As already stated, these files have a .pkg added to the end of their name (such as MacOSXUpdate10.1.3.pkg).

To install the update, simply double-click the .pkg file. This action launches the Installer application (in the Utilities folder) and opens the update document. At this point, you will be greeted with an installer screen that looks almost identical to the one that appeared when you installed Mac OS X. You will likely be required to enter an administrator password before you can continue. To do this, click the lock icon next to the words *Click the lock to make changes*. After entering your password, you will be taken to the introduction screen. Proceed through the next few screens as described earlier in this chapter until you get to the Select Destination screen.

Before you install the update, check out the File menu. The Show Files item should be enabled (unless instructions contained within the package file specifically disable this option). Choosing this command will open a window with a list of all files to be installed on your drive and where the files will be installed. With the Files window open, you can choose to print the list or save it as a text file.

Now simply click the Install button, and the installation should proceed. That's it.

Note: Some updates may not be .pkg files but may use their own self-contained installer. This is especially true for third-party applications not available from Apple. A VISE Installer is currently the most popular alternative; it makes no use of Apple's Installer utility. In this case, follow whatever instructions appear when you launch the Installer application.

**SEE:** • **"Technically Speaking: Understanding Packages," later in this chapter, for more information.**

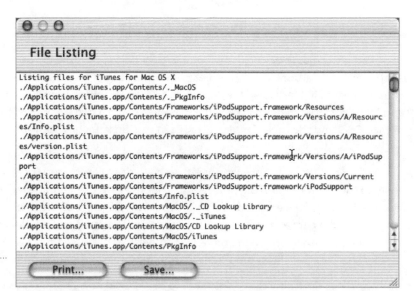

File Listing

```
Listing files for iTunes for Mac OS X
./Applications/iTunes.app/Contents/._MacOS
./Applications/iTunes.app/Contents/._PkgInfo
./Applications/iTunes.app/Contents/Frameworks/iPodSupport.framework/Resources
./Applications/iTunes.app/Contents/Frameworks/iPodSupport.framework/Versions/A/Resourc
es/Info.plist
./Applications/iTunes.app/Contents/Frameworks/iPodSupport.framework/Versions/A/Resourc
es/version.plist
./Applications/iTunes.app/Contents/Frameworks/iPodSupport.framework/Versions/A/iPodSup
port
./Applications/iTunes.app/Contents/Frameworks/iPodSupport.framework/Versions/Current
./Applications/iTunes.app/Contents/Frameworks/iPodSupport.framework/iPodSupport
./Applications/iTunes.app/Contents/Info.plist
./Applications/iTunes.app/Contents/MacOS/._CD Lookup Library
./Applications/iTunes.app/Contents/MacOS/._iTunes
./Applications/iTunes.app/Contents/MacOS/CD Lookup Library
./Applications/iTunes.app/Contents/MacOS/iTunes
./Applications/iTunes.app/Contents/PkgInfo
```

( Print... )     ( Save... )

*Figure 2.8*

A Show Files listing
in an installer.

---

**TECHNICALLY SPEAKING ▶ Understanding Packages**

**What are packages?** A package (also referred to as a bundle) is really a folder in disguise. In its disguise, it acts as though it is an single file, rather than a folder with a collection of files inside. The purpose of creating this disguise is to simplify the user's experience in working with these folders. One of the key advantages of this approach is working with installer packages. Rather than dozens of files scattered among several folders (as OS updates typically require in Mac OS 9), the end user sees what acts like a single file. Double-click this item, have it launch the installer, and you are on your way. Packages similarly help prevent users from moving needed files to incorrect locations or deleting them.

Several types of package files are included in Mac OS X, including .framework and .bundle files, as will be covered in more detail in Chapter 4 . I will focus on just two package types for now:

**Installer .pkg files.** These files, which have a .pkg file extension, essentially are the installer-package documents opened by the Installer application. Thus, a package file installs an application or an update of an existing application. Because all needed files and resources are combined in one package, the user sees that the installer is actually one file. Receipts files are also .pkg files.

**Applications.** In Mac OS X, applications can be packages. Such files have the .app file extension. The Finder hides the extension, however, so all the user sees is a single file called AppleWorks, as opposed to a file called AppleWorks.app—or more properly, a folder called AppleWorks.app. In these packages, the actual application file itself, as well as various accessory files used by the application (such as international language support) is stored within the package.

*continues on next page*

**TECHNICALLY SPEAKING** ▶ **Understanding Packages** *continued*

**Mac OS 9 and packages.** Mac OS 9 can also recognize packages (if the OS version supports and includes the needed CarbonLib extension, as current versions of Mac OS 9 do). Packages similarly appear as single files in Mac OS 9. Thus, certain application packages can run equally well in Mac OS 9 and Mac OS X. Sometimes, the package may even contain two versions of the application—one for Mac OS 9 and the other for Mac OS X. Each version launches appropriately for its OS.

In Mac OS 9, however, the traditional format for applications is single files, not packages. Mac OS X can run these single-file applications if they have been carbonized for Mac OS X. (See Chapter 4 for more information on Carbon applications.) Apple encourages developers to use the package format, however. It also prefers that developers place as much of a program's accessory files in the package as possible, so that an application remains self-contained and does not need files elsewhere on the drive. Nonetheless, as discussed more in Chapter 3, applications and their installers sometimes place needed files in other locations.

**How does the Mac OS know that a folder is to be treated as a package?** In some cases, just changing the name is enough to convert a folder to a package. For example, if you take an ordinary folder and change its name from sample to sample.pkg, you will likely get a message that says, "The folder 'sample' may no longer appear as a folder if you rename it." If you go ahead anyway, the file will turn into a package file and will launch the installer if you double-click it. You may be able to make the same package conversion with the .app extension (although it did not work when I tried it). In either case, you have not created a true installer file or application by doing this, so the file will not function as a real .pkg file or application would. To do so also requires that all the files within the package be set up correctly. Thus, I do not advise trying these tricks unless you are experimenting with files that you have backed up elsewhere or don't care if they get ruined.

What happens if you have an ordinary folder to which you (or someone) has added a .pkg extension and you now want to revert it back to its prior ordinary folder status? You might think that removing the .pkg extension would do the trick. Indeed, if you try, you may get an alert message warning you that this will happen if you proceed. I have found, however, that the procedure typically does not work out as expected. Instead, the .pkg file may be turned into a text document and still cannot be opened. In other cases, the Finder may give the item a document icon, rather than a folder icon, but it will at least still act correctly as a folder and can be opened directly.

An alternative way to convert misassigned-packages to folders is to boot from Mac OS 9 (see Chapter 5 for more information on how to do this, if you are in doubt), and use the Package First Aid utility included on the Mac OS 9 CD. As Apple states: "Package First Aid is a utility that resets folders that have been incorrectly configured as packages. If you have a package or folder that cannot be opened, drag it on this utility to reset it as a folder." Do not drag a file correctly intended to serve as a package to this utility—just use it for folders that have been incorrectly assigned as packages.

*continues on next page*

**TECHNICALLY SPEAKING ▶ Understanding Packages** *continued*

Yet another alternative is to use the BoxCutter, a contextual-menu item (again, available only in Mac OS 9 at this writing) which accomplishes the same thing. BoxCutter is included in a shareware application called Tape (which I mention later in this sidebar).

**Bundle bits.** How is the Finder really determining whether or not a folder is a package? The answer lies in something called Finder attributes (or bits). In Mac OS 9, these attributes are on/off settings that can be set for each file. They determine how the Finder treats the file. These bits determine whether a file is locked or invisible or both, for example. Although bits are mainly intended to be manipulated by developers, numerous shareware utilities allow anyone to manipulate these bits (my personal favorite is one called Snitch). One of these bits is called the bundle bit. Before the invention of packages, this bit was relevant only to applications and had no effect for folders, whether it was on or off. The bundle bit usually was enabled for applications; it told the Finder to check the application for information about the type of documents the application creates. Starting in Mac OS 9, Apple decided to use the bundle bit or folders to indicate that a folder should really be treated as a package. Turn the bundle bit on to indicate a package; turn it off to indicate a normal folder.

Mac OS X continues to use some, not all, of the Finder attributes used in Mac OS 9. You can use utilities such as x-Files to turn these attributes off and on in Mac OS X. In any case, you should not have to do this very often, if at all. In fact, in Mac OS X, simply having the needed extension (.pkg or .app) added the folder's name is all that is needed for the folder to be treated as a package, even if the bundle/package bit is not enabled.

**Creating a package.** Creating a functional package (one that operates as an installer file or an application), as opposed to one that looks like a package but does nothing requires more than just converting a folder to a package. It requires setting up the contents of the package according to quite-specific guidelines described in Apple's Mac OS X documentation for developers. Developers can get help automating this process somewhat by using Apple's PackageMaker utility (available on the Mac OS X Developer Tools CD or from Apple's developer-support Web site) or via third-party utilities such as Tape. The details exceed what you need to know for typical troubleshooting, but it does pay to examine the overall structure of a typical package at least briefly.

**Viewing the contents of a package.** If you want to view the contents of a package from the Finder, simply Control-click the package icon and choose Show Package Contents from the contextual menu. If that contextual menu choice does not appear, the file is not a package.

Although the Finder is designed to see a package as a single file, other applications can play by different rules. It is possible, for example, that the Open or Save dialog box of an application will view a package as a folder and allow you to navigate within it. As a rule, you should not attempt to add new files to packages or delete or modify files within packages via this route unless you are confident of the consequences and specifically intend to do this (as is in some hacks).

*continues on next page*

**TECHNICALLY SPEAKING ▶ Understanding Packages** *continued*

**What's inside a package?** If you use the Show Package Contents command to open a package file, the first thing you will typically see is yet another folder, called Contents. Inside most Contents folder are at least two files: PkgInfo and Info.plist. The Info.plist file is a key file; it contains all the critical information that the Finder and other System software need to understand what is inside the package and how the package files should be treated. You can look at this plist file (and similarly structured files) with any text editor (I especially recommend the freeware BBEdit Lite) or, even better, with the Apple Developers utility called Property List Editor (covered more in Chapter 3). PkgInfo contains a subset of the Info.plist data; the Finder uses it for quicker access.

If the package is an application, the top level (where the Contents folder is) will also contain an alias file to the actual executable code file, which will be more deeply nested within the package.

Depending on the type of package, inside the Contents folder may be MacOS and MacOS Classic folders (where the actual applications are stored) and a Resources folder, which contains graphics and other accessory items, as well as information for multiple-language support (in .lprog folders).

SEE:   • **"Take Note: Understanding Receipt (and Installer) Files," later in this chapter, for more information on what is inside certain package files.**

## Selective installation of individual files from an update

Suppose that you have isolated a problem to one particular Mac OS X file, which apparently is corrupted. The quick solution would be to replace this likely damaged file with a fresh copy. But further suppose that you do not have a convenient fresh copy in your backups. What can you do? You have several choices:

**Reinstall.** You could just redo the installation of the entire update. This approach is probably the simplest but carries some risk that you may overwrite some file that you do not want to modify. Also, in some cases, as discussed elsewhere in this chapter, an update may not reinstall software that has already been installed.

**Copy from the CD.** If the latest version of the file you want is on the original Install CD, as an accessible file, you can copy it directly from the CD.

**Extract the file.** Often, the latest version of the file you want is available only from an update package file. In this case, what you would most like to do is extract the suspected culprit file from the update package file. Can you do this? Yes, with some degree of hassle.

In Mac OS 9, an Apple utility called *TomeViewer* makes it easy to view and extract individual files from the Tome archive files that contain the actual updated files (see *Sad Macs* for more details). Apple has not provided a similar utility for Mac OS X. Here's what to do instead:

1. Locate the pax.gz file inside the installer package file.

**SEE:** • **"Take Note: Understanding Receipt (and Installer) Files," later in this chapter, for more details about this file and how to access it.**

2. Make a copy of the file outside the package.

   This step is not necessary but is desirable.

3. Decompress the file.

   The current version of StuffIt for Mac OS X does not decompress these files (although I suspect that this capability will be coming in an updated version). But you can expand/decompress them with other utilities, such as the shareware application OpenUp. Be prepared for all this output to take up a healthy amount of disk space, because it will contain every file in the update.

4. Locate the desired file, and use it to replace the corrupted original.

   You may need root access to do this. You can delete the remaining expanded files, if you want, or you can save them for the possibility that you may need to do this again someday.

Note: A receipt file does not contain the pax.gz file. For this reason, if you double-click a receipt file, it will launch as though it were a true installer file, but when you finally click the Install button, you will get an error message stating, "There were errors installing the software."

**Use Pacifist.** Fortunately, a shareware author has come up with a TomeViewer-like utility that simplifies this process. This utility is called Pacifist. You simply open a update package file with it, and you see a complete list of all files in the update. Then you can choose to extract the file, either to its intended destination location or to any location you select.

The only problem I have had with Pacifist was in the case of reinstalling Internet Explorer. Internet Explorer updates are available only via the Software Update application. Thus, after extracting the version of Internet Explorer on your Mac OS X Install CD, if an update is available and you have already installed it, you will want to get it again, because the reinstall wiped it out. Software Update will not list the update, however, apparently believing that it was already installed (from when you previously did install it). I have still not been able to determine what the OS is checking in deciding whether to list Explorer in Software Update, so I am not sure how to fool it. Had you planned for this possibility, however, you would still be OK. In particular, when downloading the Explorer update, you should save the update package file, as explained earlier in this section. Then you can run the updater, and it should work.

**SEE:** • **"Take Note: Understanding Receipt (and Installer) Files," later in this chapter, for more details on these files and the pax.gz file inside installer files.**

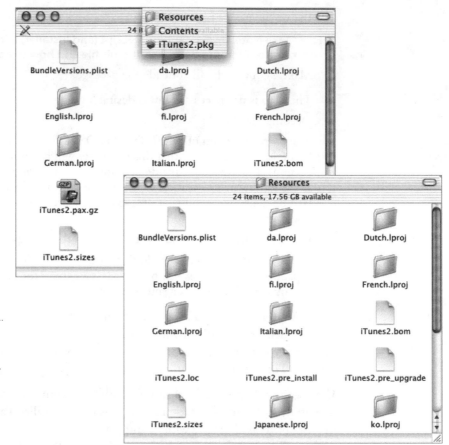

**Figure 2.9**

*Inside the package file of (top) an iTunes Updater and (bottom) the receipt file for the iTunes updater. Note that the pax.gz file is missing from the receipt file.*

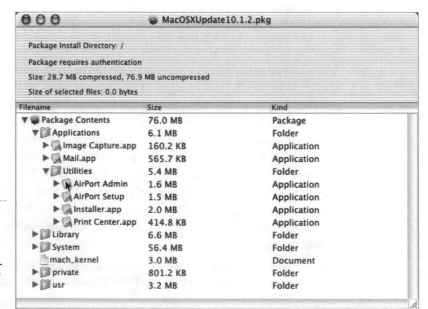

**Figure 2.10**

*Pacifist window showing the contents of an Mac OS X update file. Clicking the disclosing triangles would reveal subdirectory contents.*

**Use DesInstaller.** DesInstaller is another shareware utility. This one will not help in dealing with an installer .pkg file. However, it can help resolve dilemmas such as the one with Internet Explorer, as just described. What DesInstaller can do is use the information in the receipt file for any installed software to uninstall, create an archive, and create a reinstaller for the specified software. Thus, you could use it to create a reinstaller for the currently installed version of Internet Explorer (useful if you forgot to save its pkg file). Assuming you do this prior to any potential problems with Explorer, you can then use the reinstaller to replace a corrupted copy of Explorer at any later time.

Note: Do not use this utility to remove Mac OS X Updates, as it would likely delete critically needed files.

**TAKE NOTE ▶ Understanding Receipt (and Installer) Files**

**What are receipt files, and why have them?** Receipt files, as their name implies, are used by the OS to maintain a record of what has been installed by the Installer application. Each one is created and placed in the Receipts folder of the root-level Library folder after you install software from an installer file.

The main use of these files is by the Software Update application, which uses these files to determine what software you have already installed. That is why if a receipt file is present for an update you are trying to reinstall, Software Update may not list the update as available, even if you have deleted the application. If the receipt file is still present, Software Update will think you still have the software installed. In such cases, you may get a message from an Installer application indicating that you cannot install the update or that the update is already installed—even though it is not.

In actuality, when I tested the "rules" of how receipts are used, I found the process to be less than completely predictable. Here is what I found:

- In no case did the presence or absence of a receipt file prevent a stand-alone installer from reinstalling an update.

- A receipt file sometimes affected whether Software Update listed an update as needed or not, but it did this mainly for non-OS updates (such as for Explorer, and even then only in some cases). For updates of the OS itself, such as an update to Mac OS X 10.1.3, Software Update checks the OS version in a way that does not depend on receipts files. In at least some cases, it uses information stored in the System Version.plist file, as described in the main text later in this chapter.

Still, I would play it safe and leave these receipt files in place unless you need to move them to get an update to work. If you do need to move them, drag them to the Trash but do not delete them; then check Software Update to reinstall the software. After the software is reinstalled and a new receipt file has been created, you can empty the Trash.

*continues on next page*

**TAKE NOTE ▶ Understanding Receipt (and Installer) Files** *continued*

**How to look inside a receipt file.** As with full stand-alone installer files, receipt files are package files. Indeed, both types of files have the same icon and the same description (*Installer package*) in the Kind line of the Show Info window (accessed by clicking the file's icon and choosing Show Info from the Finder's File menu). Thus, you can open receipt files by Control-clicking the .pkg icon and choosing Show Package Contents from the contextual menu.

**What's inside installer package files (installer and receipt) files?** Typically, inside either of these types of files, you will find a Contents folder. Inside the Contents folder will be a large collection of files and folders that represents the contents of the package. Of all the different files, only two need concern you for now:

*{name of file}.bom.* The file extension .bom stands for *bill of materials*. This file contains the list of everything that the installer will install; it creates the list that appears when you choose Show Files from the installer's File menu. You may also see a matching file with the extension .bomout. This file contains essentially the same data but in a form that can be read by any text editor, such as TextEdit, included in Mac OS X.

*{name of file}.pax.gz.* The extensions .gz and .pax refer to separate compression schemes designed to reduce the size of this file, which contains all the files to be installed by the update. A crucial difference between the actual update .pkg file and the matching receipt .pkg file is that the receipt file is missing this pax.gz file. This is why the receipt file is much smaller than its .pkg file sibling and why you cannot use the receipt file to install an update.

**The Install CD vs. pkg files.** The software on a full Mac OS X Install CD is not simply a single .pkg file. Instead, it has the files needed to be a bootable CD plus the files needed for a complete installation of Mac OS X, not just the relatively fewer files needed for an update.

Some of the files on the CD are available directly; you don't need to delve into a package's contents to access them. Inside the System folder on the CD, for example, is a Library folder that contains most of the files that eventually get installed in System/Library on your hard drive. Should you ever need to replace one of these files (perhaps because you tried a hack on one of the files, it failed, and you don't have a backup), the files are readily available.

The remaining files are stored in packages. For example, inside the same System folder is another folder called Packages. Inside this folder are several .pkg files (most notably Essentials.pkg) that contain the bulk of the Mac OS X software.

In either case, if you have updated your OS to a newer version than the one on the CD, you will need to determine whether one of the updates installed a newer version of a given file—before you decide to replace the file with one from the CD. If there is a new version on your drive, you should get the update from the update .pkg file instead (for example, by using Pacifist, as described in the main text).

SEE: • "Technically Speaking: Understanding Packages," earlier in this chapter, for more details regarding packages.

**TAKE NOTE ▶ Mac OS X Update CD vs. Install CD**

A major update of Mac OS X (typically where the first digit after the decimal point changes, such as going from 10.1 to 10.2) will almost always require getting a new full installation Mac OS X CD. Expect Apple to charge for this CD.

Between major updates, however, Apple releases free minor updates. These updates typically are available via Software Update or by downloading the update file from the Web.

Mac OS X 10.1 did not quite fit either pattern, however. It was a "free" update, but you could get it only on a CD that was not quite free; you had to pay $20 in shipping and handling in most cases. Further, this Mac OS X 10.1 Update CD would install only on volumes that had Mac OS X 10.0.x already installed on it. However, at this point, the Update CD acted as though it were a full installation CD—that is, you could erase the volume and install a fresh complete copy of Mac OS X 10.1.

There was also a Mac OS X 10.1 full installation CD, which would install on any volume, even if no earlier version of Mac OS X was detected. This CD was what you would purchase if you had not already purchased an earlier version of Mac OS X.

## Software Update or stand-alone installer: Which is better?

The advantages of the Software Update method are that (1) it automatically checks what you need, so you do not have to; (2) it handles the download and installation automatically, simplifying the process; and (3) it typically lists updates as available sooner than Apple's Web site does. In some cases, it may be the only way to obtain an update.

The main advantages of using a stand-alone installer are that (1) it may offer more control of what gets installed, especially if there is a Customize option; and (2) it is saved on your drive so that you can reuse it without an Internet connection or additional download time.

# Troubleshooting Mac OS X Installation

In most cases, the installation of Mac OS X will go quite smoothly. As with any OS, however, problems can occur. The following covers most of the things that may go wrong as well as what to do to get it right again.

## Cannot start up from Mac OS X CD

Some users cannot get the Mac OS X Install CD to act as a startup disc for their Mac. They may get an error message that says, "Startup Disk was unable to select the install CD as the startup disk.(-2)." In another case, users may simply see a ripped-in-half System Folder icon at startup, with no further progression of the startup sequence.

This problem appears to affect some Macs and not others, even with the same CD. Thus, the problem usually is not a defect in the particular CD. Still, as starting up from the CD is a requirement for installing Mac OS X, you cannot ignore this symptom!

In one example of the "broken" System Folder symptom, the cause turned out to be a third-party CD-ROM drive that replaced the internal drive that came with the Mac. The drive worked in general, but not for the Mac OS X CD. In this case, if you are up to the task, you can reinstall the original CD drive and see whether that works. Otherwise, you can borrow or buy an external CD drive and try that.

**SEE:** • **Chapter 5 for more information on the broken System Folder startup problem.**

By the way, if you installed an internal CD or DVD drive, you need to be careful about its settings. In particular, the drive, which is an ATA device, should be set for the master position, not the slave position. Users have reported that drives in the slave position do not work in Mac OS X. If you don't have a clue what this discussion means, don't worry—unless you decide to install an internal CD or DVD drive and start having problems. At that point, check with *Sad Macs* or Apple's support Web site for more help.

More generally, Apple has offered this advice for dealing with an inability to startup from a Mac OS X Install CD:

1. Inspect the Mac OS X CD.

    Verify that the shiny side of the CD is relatively clean (no particles, smudges, or other abnormalities).

2. Make sure that current firmware is installed.

   Your computer may require a firmware update for best Mac OS X compatibility. The latest firmware updates are available at **http://www.apple.com/swupdates**.

3. Disconnect peripheral devices connected to your computer except for the Apple keyboard and mouse, including USB devices, SCSI devices, and PCMCIA cards.

4. Remove third-party hardware upgrades such as third-party memory (RAM) and third-party PCI cards.

After doing all of this, try starting up from the CD again.

## Volume cannot be selected

In some cases, the installer will launch and run correctly until you get to the Select Destination screen. At this point, you may find that the drive that you intended to use to install Mac OS X is not listed—especially likely for an external SCSI drive.

In some cases, the problem is with the destination drive itself. You may need to get a firmware update for the drive or abandon the drive altogether. Check with the drive vendor for exact recommendations. The drive vendor's name is available from the Apple System Profiler listing.

The problem may be that the desired destination volume is a partition that does not include the first 8 GB of the drive (as discussed earlier in this chapter). In this case, the volume will most likely be listed, but dimmed, so you still cannot select it.

Finally, if the drive is listed but its icon is dimmed so that it cannot be selected, make sure you are not using an Update CD and trying to install the OS on a volume that does not have a required version of Mac OS X already installed. Similarly, for update pkg files, make sure that the required prior version of Mac OS X is on the destination volume. You can check your current version from the About This Mac window, accessed from the Apple menu.

If you have moved, deleted or modified files in the /System/Library folder, it is possible that the Installer will not recognize the OS as the correct version, even if it is correct. In this case, you will likely need to start over with a reinstall from a full Mac OS X Install CD.

**SEE:** • " Installation refuses to run," later in this chapter.

## Installation is interrupted

If an installation of a Mac OS X update via Software Update should get interrupted for any reason, such as power failure, go to Apple's Web site and download the stand-alone version of the installer. Or save the file via Software

Update's Save as command, if it is enabled. Use the downloaded/saved installer file to try again to install the update. If you instead try to use the Software Update method again, it may report incorrectly that you no longer need the update.

If you are already using a stand-alone update file and it "unexpectedly quits" or otherwise fails to complete, simply run the installation a second time. It will likely work. If not, the file itself may be corrupted. In this case, download a new copy of the update file and run the install again.

If the update fails during the point where it says "optimizing drive," don't worry too much. You already have a completed installation. The only problem may be that you will have slower overall performance than you otherwise would get. To fix this, trying running the installer again. Otherwise, you can run an optimize/update prebinding command.

SEE:  • **"Optimize Mac OS X volumes," in Chapter 5.**
      • **"Technically Speaking: Monitoring and Improving Performance," in Chapter 6.**

---

**TECHNICALLY SPEAKING ▶ Checking logs After An Install Error**

The following comes from Apple Knowledge Base document 106692:

If an alert box appears with a message that says: "There was an error while installing," check the logs for the specific issue.

**Installer log.** When started up from an installation CD-ROM disc or installing a package file from a disk image, choose Show Log from the File menu. If the information in the log window is not helpful, select the Show More Detail option. If you are going to call Apple, save the log file or write down the last few lines.

**Software Update log.** This log is available from the Software Update pane of System Preferences. This log just lists which update had an issue. It does not give you detailed information about the issue.

**Console log.** Use the Console utility to check the logs used by Mac OS X, which are "console.log" and "system.log". Look for messages containing the word "Install" or messages that appeared during the time of the installation.

SEE:  • **Chapter 3 and Chapter 5 for more on Console and logs**

---

## Software Update does not list the update

If you believe a software update is available (perhaps you read about it on a Web site) but Software Update does not list it, there are several possibilities:

• Make sure you have a working Internet connection.

• If you get a "server busy" error, there is probably a problem at Apple's end. Try again later (ideally in a day or so).

- If you get a message that says "Your software is up to date," it may be that the desired software cannot be downloaded via Software Update. For examples: (a) QuickTime updates are handled via its own software Updater; (b) iPhoto is only available from Apple's Web site.

  Also make sure the file you want is really newer than what you already have. For example, if you are trying to obtain Mac OS X 10.1.2, make sure you do not have Mac OS X 10.1.3 already installed. To check the current installed version, select "About this Mac" from the Apple menu.

- If you just installed some other software via Software Update, try running Software Update again. The desired software may only appear after the initial software has been installed.

- The software may not be needed for your computer. For example, a DVD Player update may not appear if you do not have a DVD drive. For a PowerBook, the Update may not appear (or the Installer may not work even if you can access it) if the DVD drive is not currently inserted in the expansion bay.

## Installation refuses to run

When you choose to install Mac OS X, the installer may fail to cooperate. This might happen for any of the following reasons. Work your way through the list until you have success.

1. Make sure that you have at least the minimal installed RAM and free hard drive space for the installation to proceed.

   The Read Me file that accompanies the installer should supply these minimums (we also noted general requirements earlier in this chapter). The Read Me file should also tell you whether the software only works with certain versions of Mac OS X.

2. Restart the Mac and try again. Do not attempt to perform any other actions with the Mac while the install is proceeding.

3. Quit all open applications. Also turn off any settings, in Energy Saver or Screen Saver System Preferences, that automatically put the Mac to sleep or shift to a screen saver. Make sure Classic is disabled as well.

4. If you used Software Update to attempt the installation, see whether you can download and use a stand-alone version of the software installer instead.

5. Check to see whether disk repairs are needed.

**SEE:** • **Chapter 5 for more information on disk repairs.**

6. Disconnect all peripheral hardware devices and try the installation again.

7. Create a new user (if the drive has only one local user), and install from the new user's account.

   If the installation succeeds, you can delete the newly created user account when you are done.

**SEE:** • **Chapters 3 and 8 for more information on creating additional users.**

**Installing Mac OS X updates.** If the software to be installed is an update of existing software, the update will obviously not proceed unless you have the previous version of the software available. In some cases, you may need a specific version of the to-be-updated software available. In such cases, the solution is to go back and reinstall the needed older software and then return to the update.

In certain situations, an update may fail, claiming that you have already installed this update. Most often, this may happen after a reinstallation of the original System software from a CD and a subsequent attempt to upgrade, especially when you are upgrading via Software Update. Suppose that you reinstall an original version of Mac OS X from the CD that takes you all the way back to Mac OS X 10.0.0. Now you want to proceed with the subsequent updates. Software Update may not list a particular update, however, and tell you that you are in fact up to date.

A similar problem may occur if you try to reinstall an update (perhaps to fix potentially corrupted files) that you previously installed and that is still there.

Even if you run a stand-alone installer file, you may be greeted by an initial message that says, "You cannot install this software on this machine" or "This volume does not meet the requirements for this update," even though you believe that the update should run on your machine despite whatever restrictions are built into the update.

To attempt to solve this, first make sure that you have selected the actual update package, not a receipt file. Second, make sure that you really have installed all the needed updates. When you're trying to install Mac OS X 1.1.1, for example, the installer will refuse to install over Mac OS X 1.1, unless you first install a security update that was released after the initial 1.1 release. The security update changes the build number listed in About This Mac, but the version number remains 1.1.

Otherwise, if you still have a problem, try the following:

1.  Open the /Library folder (not System/Library, but just Library) at the root level of the drive.

2.  Open the folder called Receipts.

    In this folder, you will find a collection of .pkg receipt files that correspond to almost every .pkg file update you have installed. Look for one with the same name as the update that you cannot install (such as MacOSXUpdate10.1.3.pkg).

3.  Drag the .pkg file to the Trash, but do not delete it yet.

4.  Try to run the update installer again.

    Note: You will likely need to enable root access to have permission to move this file.

**SEE:** • **"Take Note: Root Access," in Chapter 3, for details.**

**5a.** After the update is complete, restart and then delete the receipt file that is in the Trash.

The reason to wait to delete the file until after restarting is that deleting a receipt file without reinstalling the same or related software could render the system unusable. At least, that's what Apple has warned.

**5b.** If the installation still fails to run, return the receipt file to its original location instead of trashing it, and delete the entire Software Update folder inside the Preferences folder in the Library folder of your Home directory.

**5c.** If deleting the Software Update folder fails to work, you likely have more-serious problems; you may need to start over with a complete rein-stallation of Mac OS X from a Mac OS X Install CD.

**5d.** If even a complete reinstallation fails, try deleting the entire Mac OS X System folder on your drive (you will have to boot from Mac OS 9 to do this) and then reinstall Mac OS X.

**SEE:** • **"Take Note: Understanding Receipt (and Installer) Files," earlier in this chapter, for related information.**

*Figure 2.11*

*Partial contents of the Receipts folder.*

**SystemVersion.plist .** Before you consider something as extreme as deleting the Mac OS X System folder, there is one other alternative to consider. It involves a file called SystemVersion.plist, located in /System/Library/CoreServices. This file contains the Mac OS X version and build number of the currently installed OS. If you change the information in this file, the version number and build number change in the About This Mac window. Follow these steps:

**1.** Login as a root user (or open the file via a third party utility, such as Pseudo, that can open files with root access).

2. Open the SystemVersion.plist file with Property List Editor.

3. Click the build number in the Value column of the ProductBuildVersion row, and edit it as desired.

4. Click the version number in the Value column of the ProductVersion row, and edit it as desired.

You can use this procedure to change the listing for Mac OS X 10.1.1 back to 10.1, for example, or to make any other change you want. This process does not really change any of the other software on your drive; all it does is fool an installer so that it agrees to install when it might not have before. The procedure won't work in all cases, but it is worth a try.

Warning: In some cases, circumventing these restrictions works because the Installer is being overly cautious about when the update is permitted. However, in other cases, you really *should* only attempt to install the software over the correct version. If you don't trust your own ability to make this distinction, seek out guidance from Web sites such as MacFixIt.

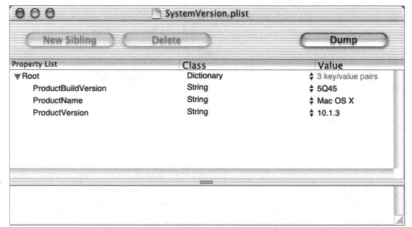

*Figure 2.12*

*SystemVersion.plist viewed in PropertyList Editor.*

**SEE:** • **Chapter 3 for more information on the root user, Pseudo, and PropertyList Editor.**

When you are done with the installation, make sure that the About This Mac window now lists the correct version. Otherwise, you should modify SystemVersion.plist again so that it is correct.

# Downgrade installation

Occasionally, you may want to reinstall an older version of Mac OS X.

For one example, suppose you started with a Mac OS X 10.1 CD and proceeded to update to Mac OS X 10.1.3 via Software Update. Now, you decide you want to completely reinstall Mac OS X. To do so, you would have to reinstall Mac OS X 10.1 (from your Mac OS X 10.1 Install CD) first and then reinstall the online updates. It would not be sufficient to just re-run the latest update (for example, 10.1.3). The online update only contains files that have been modified for that update; it does not have a complete set of Mac OS X software.

If you only have the Mac OS X 10.1 Update CD (rather than the full install CD), you will have even bigger problems. The Mac OS X 10.1 Update CD will not install over a newer version of the OS (for example, 10.1.3). In this case, you would have to revert back to your original Mac OS X full install CD, presumably a 10.0 version. You will then have to reapply all subsequent updates, possibly also needing to use the tips regarding updates described in the previous section.

You can do all of the above without erasing your existing volume. The Installer overwrites Mac OS X files, leaving the rest of your software intact.

Now for the really bad news! Even if you can get any or all of this to work successfully, Apple warns that you should not do so. Instead, Apple recommends that you select the Erase Destination option from the Installer utility, completely erasing your volume when you select to reinstall Mac OS X (after first backing up needed documents and applications that are not part of the OS). Apple does not want you to do a downgrade installation without erasing. Apple's apparent concern is that not all files will be downgraded and reupgraded correctly, leaving you with a mixture of files from different OS versions. The result could lead to unpredictable symptoms, including startup failures.

At a practical level, many users have done this sort of downgrade reinstallation without first erasing their drives and have had not problems. Still, if erasing the hard drive would not be a hardship, it is the safest way to go.

Reinstalling the current version of the OS (for example, rerunning the Mac OS X 10.1.3 update over a 10.1.3 system) is acceptable, even by Apple's standards. This can be useful for fixing OS-related problems.

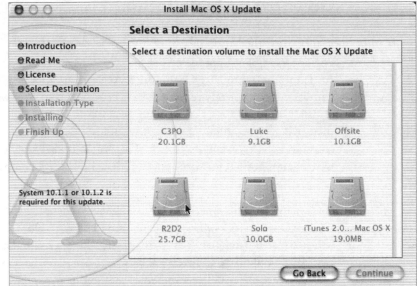

**Figure 2.13**

*Message that appears (in lower left of window) when trying to install Mac OS X 10.1.2 Update over a system currently running Mac OS X 10.1.3.*

SEE: • " Select a destination," earlier in this chapter, for more on Erase Destination.

• "Installation refuses to run," earlier in this chapter, for more on re-installing without erasing.

• "Reinstall Mac OS X," in Chapter 5, for more on reinstalling to fix problems.

## Installer utility bug

A bug in the initial version of the Installer utility is related to the use of pax as a compression format for files. As described at the stepwise.com Web site (`www.stepwise.com/Articles/Technical/Packages/InstallerOnX.html`): "If during the installation of a package pax encounters a directory that already exists, it will set its permissions and ownership to the permissions of the version in the archive. This is especially annoying in the case of the /Library or Applications directories, since many packages install into this location. However, it can have a much more serious impact, including preventing your system from booting, or applications from running." The site also describes a second problem involving symbolic links (a type of alias used by Unix).

Without going into details, I will just say that these problems appear to be more likely to occur when you are trying to install the same update a second time. So be cautious about doing this. If you do wind up with permissions problems, the likely symptom will be an inability to modify the contents of the Library and Applications folders. I discuss how to fix this problem in Chapter 6.

In any case, I expect that Apple will address this bug in a subsequent update of the utility.

## Crash on restart

An installation of Mac OS X may appear to be entirely successful. Yet when you restart the Mac, it refuses to start up running Mac OS X, typically crashing even before login. Why?

**SCSI.** The most common cause is SCSI devices attached. SCSI refers to a technology for connecting peripheral devices, such as hard drives, to a Mac. No current Mac comes with an SCSI port as part of the logic board; instead, new Macs use USB and FireWire as alternatives. The main places where you will still find SCSI included are Power Mac G4s that have a separate SCSI card installed in one of the PCI slots. In some cases, the SCSI PCI card itself is incompatible with Mac OS X and may lead to startup problems. Fixing this problem may require a firmware upgrade of the card or, at the very least, a driver-software upgrade.

In other cases, the problem may be with a device connected to the card or how multiple devices are chained together, mainly involving what is called SCSI termination. This term refers to how SCSI devices are connected in a chain when you have more than one device. Mac OS X is much more sensitive to SCSI termination, so setups that did not cause a problem in Mac OS 9, even though they may have been technically incorrect, can cause a problem in Mac OS X.

Check with the vendor of the card (or Apple, if your Mac came with a SCSI card) for specific recommendations. Apple itself has an update for its Apple Ultra Wide SCSI PCI card (http://docs.info.apple.com/article.html?artnum= 25176); you need this update if you intend to use the card with Mac OS X.

**Memory.** In some cases, a Mac will not start up in Mac OS X due to a problem with a third-party memory (RAM) module, even though the same memory module works fine in Mac OS 9. If you get a black screen immediately at startup, I would suspect this problem. To check, remove the extra installed memory and try again. If startup succeeds, contact your memory vendor about getting a replacement that works.

If problems persist even after you remove the extra RAM, try running the Apple Hardware Test CD that is included with all recent Mac models. This CD will diagnose a variety of possible hardware problems and offer advice about what to do.

**SEE:** • Chapter 5 for a more general discussion of startup problems, beyond those that immediately follow a Mac OS X installation.

# Miscellaneous other installation problems

What follows is an assortment of installation issues that do not conveniently fall into any of the previous categories.

**iTunes 2.0 and Installer's deleting more than it should.** When Apple first released iTunes 2.0 as a free upgrade on the Web, the Installer had a nasty quirk: It tried to delete any older version of iTunes that it found on your drive before installing the new version by running a Unix shell script. Unfortunately, due to an error in the script, the installation might fail and not install iTunes at all. Even worse, in some cases, installation could remove much of the data on your drive rather than just an older version of iTunes. This problem was fixed the same day via an updated install file, but not before hundreds of users lost files. The moral: Always have backups of critical files before running an installer.

**AirPort 2.0 and a problem with moving files from their default location.** The installer for AirPort 2.0 installed updated versions of the AirPort software. The installer expected to find the AirPort Admin utility in its default location inside the Utilities folder. If that utility was not in its default location (probably because you decided to move it elsewhere), the installation was not successful. In particular, the installer placed a nonfunctional version of the Admin utility in the Utilities folder (it was not even launchable). Meanwhile, the copy of the Admin utility that you relocated remained unchanged at the old version, with no warning message from the installer that a problem occurred. A similar situation occurred with the update of the Mail application in Mac OS X 10.1.1.

If you are comfortable working inside packages, you could fix this problem by dragging the new files installed in the default location to the respective folders located inside the application package of the original version. The process is a pain, but it should work. Otherwise, return the application to its default location and try reinstalling the update (using tips covered earlier in this section as needed). The moral: Save yourself some hassle. Files that are installed by Mac OS X should always remain in their default location.

The real solution is for Apple to revise its Installer application substantially so that these problems do not occur. In the meantime, you can also use a utility such as Pacifist to do a separate reinstall of an individual utility.

**Installation folder.** At least in initial versions of Mac OS X, the only folder directly inside the Mac OS X System folder was the Library folder. More recently, you may also see an Installation folder. Inside this folder will be files related to hardware devices that connect to the Mac. I first saw this situation while installing the AirPort 2.0 software (which works with the AirPort Base Station hardware). An Installation folder was created; inside it was another folder called AirPortPrePostScripts. Inside that folder was a version of the AirPort.pkg file.

An Installation folder is also located in the System folder of the Mac OS X Install CD. But this folder serves another purpose: It holds the .pkg files that contain the files to be installed by the installer.

# Uninstalling Mac OS X

Suppose that you want to uninstall Mac OS X—because you no longer want to use it (which I certainly hope is not the case!), because you no longer want it on that particular volume, or you are having such problems getting the OS to start up that an uninstallation followed by a fresh installation is the only possible solution, short of erasing the volume entirely.

Can Mac OS X be uninstalled? Yes, but the process is not as easy as it should be. As of now, Apple offers no officially supported uninstallation method. If you have Mac OS X installed on its own partition (as I recommended earlier in this chapter), and you have backed up all documents and third-party software you want to save, the process is relatively painless. Just erase the partition when installing Mac OS X; then restore your backed-up software.

If you have Mac OS 9 and Mac OS X on the same partition, however, and you want to delete Mac OS X without disturbing any Mac OS 9 files, the process is complicated by the fact that many of the Mac OS X files are invisible. The following procedure should work (although I offer no guarantees!):

1. Restart in Mac OS 9.

   See Chapter 5 for details on switching OSes at startup.

2. Locate the following visible folders/files, and move them to the Trash:

   - Applications—but not Applications (Mac OS 9)
   - System—but not System Folder
   - Library
   - Users
   - mach, mach_kernel, and mach.sym
     (if visible; otherwise, delete them in the next step)

3. Using a utility that can locate and delete invisible files (File Buddy is one such example), locate and delete the following files, aliases, and folders from the root level of the hard drive that contains Mac OS X:

   | | | |
   |---|---|---|
   | • .hidden | • dev | • usr |
   | • Network | • etc | • var |
   | • Volumes | • private | • .vol |
   | • bin | • sbin | • .DS_Store |
   | • cores | • tmp | • .Trashes |

This list may not include every last Mac OS X file, but it should be enough so that the remnants, if any, present no lingering problems.

4. Rebuild the Desktop (by holding down the Command and Option keys at startup in Mac OS 9).

People occasionally report problems even when following this advice successfully. That's why erasing the volume remains the best option.

There are indications that receipt files may someday be used to uninstall what their matching installers previously installed (similar to what DesInstaller can already do), but Apple has not implemented this as yet. There are also hints that you may someday be able to uninstall Mac OS X from a special command in the Mac OS 9 Finder. Again, this feature has not been implemented yet.

**SEE:** • **Chapter 6 for more information on Mac OS X and invisible files and folders.**
     • **Chapter 9 for more information on installing and using Classic.**
     • **Chapter 10 for more information on what Unix and invisible files and folders do.**

# 3

# Using Mac OS X: An Overview

For those who may still be largely unfamiliar with Mac OS X, this chapter comes closest to being a general introduction to the OS and will bring you up to speed. You'll be taking a basic tour of the major features in the Mac OS X Finder, Dock, and Desktop.

Even if you are familiar with Mac OS X, however, don't be too eager to skip to the next chapter. Before you're done here, you'll also be looking in considerable depth at such issues as file extensions, privileges, and preferences files.

This chapter is not a comprehensive overview but a selective survey of those topics that are especially relevant to troubleshooting. In later chapters, I will make frequent reference to the topics covered here.

# In This Chapter

**TAKE NOTE ▶ Mac OS X vs. Mac OS X Server**

Mac OS X Server is a special version of Mac OS X that includes software needed to set up Mac OS X as a central server of a large network of client computers. It is the Mac OS X equivalent of what, in Mac OS 9, was referred to as AppleShare IP. For this book, I assume that you are using the standard (client) version of Mac OS X, not the server version.

# The Dock

When you arrive at the Mac OS X Desktop, the predominant item visible will be the Dock, which is Mac OS X's primary navigational tool. No matter where else you are in Mac OS X, you can almost always return to the Dock, either by clicking it directly or clicking the Desktop background (which makes the Finder/Dock the active applications).

*Figure 3.1*

*The Dock.*

## Dock basics

The basics of the Dock are quite straightforward. Icons in the Dock represent the applications, documents, and folders on your drive. By convention, the Dock is divided into two parts. If your Dock runs across the bottom of your screen, applications appear on the left side. On the right side are folders, documents, and anything else.

The last item in the Dock is the Trash icon, which is where you place items when you want to delete them.

To launch an application or open a document, simply click it. For applications, if the application is open, a triangle appears below its icon. Clicking an already-open item makes it the frontmost window.

While an application is opening, its icon will bounce up and down. Similarly, the icon for an open application will bounce as a means of alerting you that it requires your attention. An email application's icon, for example, will bounce if it has received email in the background while you are working in another application. The bouncing will stop as soon as you make the email program the active application.

When you move the pointer over a Dock icon, its name will pop up in text. No clicking is needed.

# Add and remove items from the Dock

**Add items to the Dock.** To add an item to the Dock permanently, simply drag its icon from its Finder window to the Dock. You cannot place an application icon on the right side of the Dock; neither can you place other types of icons on the left side of the Dock. Otherwise, you can put Dock icons pretty much where you want. You can even rearrange the icon order by dragging an icon to the desired location.

When you open an application that does not have an icon in the Dock (by double-clicking its icon in a Finder window, for example), its icon appears in the Dock temporarily. When you quit the application, the icon is removed.

**Minimize windows to the Dock.** By clicking the appropriate button in a Finder window (discussed in "The Finder" section, later in this chapter), you can minimize a window to the Dock. What this means is that the window moves from its location on the Desktop to become an icon in the Dock. If you later click the window icon, the window maximizes out to the Desktop again. An animation effect typically accompanies this moving back and forth.

**Remove an icon from the Dock.** To remove a "permanent" icon from the Dock, simply drag its icon off the Dock. You will see a "poof of smoke" animation, and the Dock icon is gone. Don't worry—removing a Dock icon does not delete the item itself from your drive; it just removes its representation from the Dock. The icon serves as a pointer to the actual item. You can still locate the item in its Finder window.

All nonpermanent icons in the Dock are removed automatically when you log out, restart, or shut down.

*Figure 3.2*

*A Dock menu for (left) an open application (iTunes) and (right) a folder (Microsoft Office).*

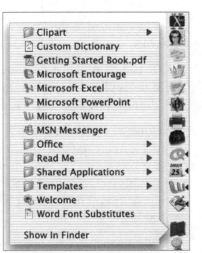

# Dock menus

If you click an item in the Dock and hold down the mouse button, a pop-up menu will appear. What is in the menu depends on the nature of the item. At the very least, you should see the item Show in Finder. If you choose this command, the Finder window that contains the selected item will open.

For open applications, the menu will likely include at least one additional item: Quit, which quits the application. Depending on the open application in question, you may see additional items, intended to provide convenient access to specific features of the program. When iTunes is open, for example, you can play songs from its Dock menu.

For folders, the Dock menu will be a list of every item contained within the folder. If the folder contains subfolders, you will get hierarchical submenus containing the contents of the subfolders. Drag the pointer to any item in the menu and you select that item, opening the folder or launching the application as appropriate.

If you drag the icon of your hard drive to the Dock, you will have access to a hierarchical menu listing every location on your drive!

Finally, the menu for the Trash icon offers the Empty Trash option. This command actually deletes the contents of the Trash. Before doing this, you can always click the Trash icon to open its window and drag an item out of the Trash before emptying it, should you decide that you placed the item there in error.

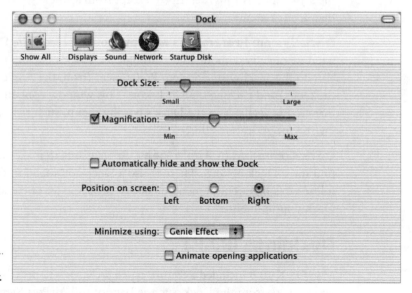

**Figure 3.3**

*The Dock System Preferences window.*

## Dock preferences: Customize the Dock

You can customize the appearance of the Dock and how several of its features work.

If you move the pointer over the Dock's white separation line, for example, the pointer changes to a bar with arrows on either side. If you click and drag the pointer in the direction of either arrow, the entire Dock will get larger or smaller.

If you press and hold the Control key while the arrow pointer is visible, it brings up a special pop-up menu. From here, you have several options:

**Turn Magnification On/Off.** With this option enabled, the Dock gets larger in the region where the pointer is. This option can be convenient if the Dock is set very small by default.

**Turn Hiding On/Off.** With this option enabled, the Dock vanishes from the screen until you move the pointer to the edge where the Dock resides. This option can be convenient if need some extra screen real estate.

**Position on Screen.** This option lets you place the Dock on the left, right, or bottom edge of the screen.

**Minimize Using.** This option lets you decide what type of animation effect will be used for windows that get minimized to the Dock.

**Dock Preferences.** Choose this option to open the System Preferences window for the Dock. (I discuss System Preferences in more detail later in this chapter.) For the Dock, this option simply is a way to access more or less the same options I just described, except from a single window layout, rather than from a menu.

**Dock System Preferences window.** You can access the Dock Preferences window directly without going through the Dock's pop-up menu, of course. You do this by choosing System Preferences (from the Apple menu or from the Dock) and clicking the Dock icon. This window contains some options that are not available in the Dock's pop-up menu, such as a slider for adjusting the magnification effect.

**Dock Command in Apple Menu.** Apple wants to make sure that you can find these Dock options. There is also a Dock command in the Apple menu; it leads to a hierarchical menu of almost the same set of choices as in the Dock pop-up menu.

## Docklings (R.I.P.)

Mac OS X 10.0 included a feature called *docklings*—items whose only function was to work from the Dock, such as Battery and AirPort Signal docklings. These docklings graphically displayed the amount of battery charge left and the AirPort signal strength via their Dock icons.

The Dock is a jack of all trades for Mac OS X. If you are familiar with Mac OS 9's features, you will recognize that the Dock serves to replace Mac OS 9's Launcher, control strip, and Application menu. Still, many longtime Mac users preferred the flexibility of the Mac OS 9 approach. That is partly why Apple dropped support of docklings in Mac OS X 10.1.

Apple chose instead to go with Menu Extras, which are items that appear at the right end of the menubar at the top of the screen (see "Take Note: Menu Extras"). Also, developers can now customize the menus that pop up from the application icon in the Dock. Thus, you will not likely find any docklings on your Mac. I mention them here only so you will know what they are in case you do find one.

**Figure 3.4**

Menu Extras items in the menubar (with the PPP menu dropped down).

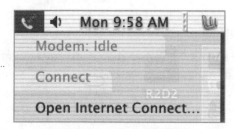

---

**TAKE NOTE ▶ Menu Extras**

You can now access docklinglike features from small icons that appear at the right end of the menubar. These features are called Menu Extras. You should have a Volume extra, for example; when you click it, it reveals a slider that allows you to adjust speaker volume. The clock is also a Menu Extra. Other extras include Battery and AirPort. A Displays extra gives you access to a menu that allows you to change screen resolution and color depth.

Mac OS X installs some of these extras by default, and only if appropriate for your Mac. The Battery extra will be installed on notebooks but not on desktop Macs. The AirPort extra is installed only if you have an AirPort card installed.

Third-party developers can create extras as well, so expect to see some that do not come from Apple. These extras will likely be used in conjunction with some application and will get installed when you install the application.

**Add and remove Menu Extras.** In some cases, you can add or remove extras by choosing it in the relevant System Preferences window. (I discuss System Preferences a bit later in this chapter.) To add the Displays extra, for example, enable the Show Displays in Menubar option in the Displays System Preferences window. To remove it, uncheck that option.

*continues on next page*

**TAKE NOTE ▶ Menu Extras** *continued*

The actual Menu Extras files are located in the /System/Library/CoreServices/Menu Extras folder. If you cannot locate a preferences option to add an extra, you can do so by going to this folder. Each item will have the .menu file extension. Thus, the Volumes extra is called Volume.menu. To add an extra to the menubar, simply drag its .menu file from this folder to the menubar location where the icons appear. In some cases, this method will work only if your Mac supports the feature referenced by the extra. You cannot add the AirPort extra to a Mac without an AirPort card installed, for example.

An alternative method to remove any extra is to hold down the Command key and drag the extra's icon off of the menubar.

You can rearrange the left-to-right order of menubar items by clicking an item with the Command key held down and dragging the item to the desired location.

**Items in the menu bar that are not extras.** Some menubar items may be installed directly when you launch an application. Most of these items will come from third-party developers, not the OS itself. QuicKeys and StuffIt Deluxe's MagicMenu do this, for example; they do not use the Menu Extras method, so there are no items from these extras in the Menu Extras folder.

Finally, several utilities, such as ASM, mimic the functions of the Application Switcher menu in Mac OS 9 (that is, they provide a list of all open applications). These utilities, too, have icons in the menubar but do not use Menu Extras to create them.

## Troubleshooting the Dock

Dock is quite reliable. Most often, it works exactly as described here. Occasionally, however, problems may occur. The following tips should get you out of most trouble:

**Question-mark icon in Dock.** A question-mark icon in the Dock means that for whatever reason, the Dock can no longer locate the item that the Dock icon represents. In some cases, the item may have been deleted. If the item is still on your drive, however, the solution is simple:

1. Place the pointer over the question-mark icon.

   The name of the missing file will appear. Make a note of it.
2. Drag the question-mark icon off the Dock.

   The icon will disappear.
3. Locate the missing file in its Finder window, and drag its icon to the Dock.

   Problem solved.

If you delete an item that has a Dock icon, the Dock icon will not turn to a question mark until the Dock is relaunched (typically after a logout or restart). Until then, the item's normal icon remains but will show no response if you click it. In this case, the solution is simply to delete the icon from the Dock.

*Figure 3.5*

*Question mark in the Dock.*

**Dock fails to function as expected.** Very rarely, the Dock may appear to stop functioning altogether. Clicking any item in the Dock will have no effect.

To fix this problem, you need to quit and relaunch the Dock. The Dock is a special application, however, so no easily accessible Quit command is available for the Dock. Even if you force quit (by pressing Command-Option-Escape, as discussed in Chapter 5), the Dock will not be listed.

The solution is to launch ProcessViewer, a program included with Mac OS X and located in the Utilities folder. This utility shows all open processes (an application is a type of process), even ones that are not accessible directly from the Finder. From the ProcessViewer window that appears, do the following:

1. Choose User Processes from the Show pop-up menu, if it is not already selected.

2. Scroll to locate the item called Dock in the list of processes, and select it.

3. Choose Quit Process from the Processes menu (Command-Shift-Q).

4. When a dialog box appears to asks whether you really want to force a quit, click Force Quit, click the Quit button (or, if that fails to work, return to the dialog box and choose Force Quit).

The Dock should quit, vanishing temporarily. Then it will relaunch, and all should be normal again.

**Poof does not evaporate.** When you drag an item off the Dock, and the poof of smoke appears, the "poof" may never go away; it just lingers on your Desktop. All else responds as normal, but the poof is not very attractive. Logging out and logging back in will fix this problem, but it forces you to close all open applications and can be a bothersome waste of time. There is a better way! Simply quit the Dock as just described, and the poof will be gone, with no other ill effects.

**Application fails to open or quit.** Occasionally, you may click a Dock icon to open an application, but the application never opens. Instead, the Dock icon continues to bounce indefinitely. Alternatively, you may quit an application, and although it appears to have quit, its Dock icon remains, even though it is not a permanent icon and should therefore be removed. These matters are more a problem with the application itself, rather than the Dock. As such, you usually can fix them by force-quitting the application.

You can force-quit directly from the Dock in some cases by holding down the Option key while accessing the application's menu. In this case, the Quit command should change to Force Quit. Choose it. If this command does not work (you see the words *item not responding* in the Dock menu), you can still force-quit via Command-Option-Escape.

---

**TAKE NOTE ▶ Dock and Finder Shortcuts**

Keyboard shortcuts provide an alternative method for accessing various commands and features. If you look at the menus of almost any application, such as the Finder, you will see shortcut equivalents for many of the commands. In the File menu, for example, you will see that Command-W is the equivalent of the Close Window command.

Some mouse-related shortcuts are less obvious, however, because they are not conveniently listed in menus. I cannot possibly list all of them here. I recommend that you experiment on your own by clicking your mouse button while holding down the Command, Option, Control, and Shift keys in various combinations and in various locations. See what happens.

To help you get started, here are some of the most common shortcuts for the Dock and Finder.

### Dock shortcuts

**Command-click.** This shortcut is equivalent to choosing Show in Finder. If you hold down the Command key and click an item in the Dock, a new Finder window opens, showing that item.

**Command-Option-click.** If you hold down Command-Option and click an item in the Dock, that application becomes the active frontmost application, and all open windows for other applications become hidden.

Clicking the Dock icon for any hidden item makes its windows visible again. To get everything back at the same time, choose Show All from the Finder menu (or a similar menu for whatever application is active).

**Command-Tab.** Click the Dock, press and hold down the Command key, and repeatedly press the Tab key. This action will rotate you through all open applications. When you let go of the keys, the highlighted application becomes the active one.

### Finder-window shortcuts

**Option.** When you double-click a folder to open it, if you also hold down the Option key, the folder opens in a new window, and the previous window closes.

**Command.** When the toolbar is visible in a window, double-clicking a folder icon typically replaces the contents of the current window with those of the folder you just chose to view— that is, a new window does not open. If you hold down the Command key when clicking a folder, the folder opens in a new window. It will also do open a new window automatically if the toolbar is not visible.

*continues on next page*

**TAKE NOTE ▶ Dock and Finder Shortcuts** *continued*

***Finder copy/move shortcuts***

**Option-drag.** When you drag an item's icon to a different folder on the same volume, it moves the item to that location, rather than copying it. That is, the item no longer exists at its original location; it exists only where you moved it. If you hold down the Option key when doing this, however, you will make a copy rather than move the file.

**Command-drag.** When you drag an item's icon to a different volume from the one in which it resides, the Finder copies the item rather than moves it. If you hold down the Command key when dragging the item, however, you will move the item rather than copy it.

Note: These last two commands may not work as described if you do not have sufficient privileges to make the desired move or copy. (See later in this chapter and Chapter 6 for more information on this topic.)

# The Finder

The Finder is the application in Mac OS X that you use to navigate to the different locations on your mounted volumes. Whenever you click the Desktop background, you make the Finder the active application. Similarly, clicking any open Finder window or the Finder icon in the Dock makes the Finder active. In this section, you take a tour of the many things you can do in the Finder.

**SEE:** • "Take Note: Folders vs. Directories," in Chapter 4, for an explanation of the use of these two important terms.

**TAKE NOTE ▶ Windows in Applications Other Than the Finder**

Most applications use windows. An open document in a word processor is a window, for example. But the options and actions in a document window are somewhat different from the ones in the Finder.

If you have an unsaved change in a document, for example, the *X* that appears in the red jewel button will turn to a dot. This dot indicates that a dialog box will appear, warning you that you have not yet saved your changes, should you try to close the window before saving it. Document windows also will not show the toolbar or other special features of Finder windows.

**Applications with no open windows.** If you close the last open window in an open application, in most cases, the applications remains open. This arrangement makes sense for most productivity applications, such as word processors.

*continues on next page*

**TAKE NOTE** ▶ **Windows in Applications Other Than the Finder** *continued*

It also works this way for most utility applications, such as Mac OS X's own System Preferences, which you can use at times to speed up your Mac. When the System Preferences window is closed, it uses very little memory or processor (CPU) time, so you incur little cost by closing it. Still, you can reopen the window faster than you can relaunch the application, had you quit it.

## Finder windows

To see a typical Finder window, click the Finder icon in the Dock. This action will likely open the window generically referred to as Computer, which lists all mounted volumes. Using this window as an example, you'll work your way through the major features of Finder windows in general.

**Figure 3.6**

*A typical Finder window, in icon view, without the toolbar and status bar visible.*

**Figure 3.7**

*The same Finder window as in Figure 3.6, with the toolbar and status bar now visible.*

**Jewel buttons.** The top row of the window is sometimes called the *title bar.* In the top-left corner of the title bar are three jewel-like buttons. If you move the pointer over these buttons, an X, minus sign (–), and plus sign (+) appear over each button in turn. If you click the left (red) button, you close the window. If you click the middle (yellow) button, the window is minimized to the Dock; clicking the window icon in the Dock maximizes it again. The name of the window appears when you place the pointer over it, allowing you to tell what's what when you have several windows in the Dock. (See "The Dock" earlier in this chapter for more information on this feature.) The right (green) button changes the size of the window, rotating among several sizes and shapes; experiment with clicking the button repeatedly to see what happens.

**Hide/Show Toolbar button.** In the top-right corner of the window is an oval button. If you click it, you toggle between displaying and hiding the toolbar.

**Window title.** In the middle of the title bar is the title of the window. If you Command-click the title, a pop-up menu appears, showing all folders that are higher up in the directory hierarchy than the window itself, back to the Computer level. Select any one, and go directly to that window.

**Toolbar.** The next row in the Finder window is the toolbar, assuming that you set it to be visible. I discuss the toolbar in more detail in the following section of this chapter.

**Status bar.** The next row is called the status bar. If it is not visible, go to the Finder's View menu and choose Show Status Bar. The text in the center of this row will list how many items are in the displayed folder, as well as how much space is left on the volume that contains the folder.

Depending on the particular window, you may also see symbols at the left end of the status bar. If you see an icon of a pencil with a line through it, for example, the current window's contents are read-only.

**Scroll bars and resize box.** If you cannot see the full contents of the window at the window's current size, scroll bars on the right and bottom allow you to bring the other items into view. In the bottom-right corner of the window is the resize box. Drag this box to resize and reshape the window as desired.

**Window contents.** You can open the files and folders in the window by double-clicking them, as is typical of the Mac OS. You can edit the name of an item by clicking the icon and then clicking the name. At this point, the name should have a box around it, indicating that you can edit it. If the name exceeds what can fit on one line, you will move to a second or even a third line as needed.

If an item's name is still deemed too long to display, an abbreviated version of the name will appear. If you hold the pointer over the shortened name for a few seconds (or hold down the Option key to get an instant response), the full name will appear in an expanded text window.

# Toolbar and Finder views

Last, in your tour of Finder windows, you return to the toolbar. The toolbar has two sections, separated by a dividing line.

**Figure 3.8**

*The same Finder window as in Figure 3.6, in List view.*

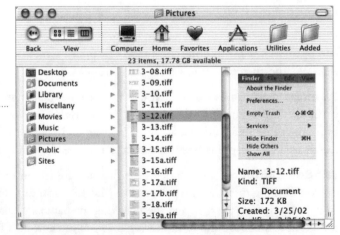

**Figure 3.9**

*(Top) The same Finder window as in Figure 3.6, in Column view; (Bottom) A similar Column view, this one showing a file "preview" in the rightmost column.*

**Left end.** At the left end of the toolbar are the following buttons:

**Back.** Click this button to go back to the folder that was visible in this window previously. The toolbar has no Forward button. To go forward, double-click any folder icon in the window being displayed.

**View.** The View button is really three separate buttons, each of which affects how the contents of the window are displayed:

**Icon View.** This view is the traditional view, in which every file is indicated by an icon with a name below it. You can move icons by dragging them.

**List View.** In this view, all items are in a text list, with each item in its own row. The contents of a row are organized by the columns listed at the top. On the far-left side is a column of icons and names for each file. This column typically is followed by columns for last modification date, file size, and kind (such as application, document, or folder). Clicking any column title sorts the window by that column. Click the triangle in the column name to go from an A–Z to Z–A sort of that column.

To the left of each folder in the list is a disclosure triangle. Click the triangle to reveal a subdirectory list of the folder's contents within the current window (as opposed to opening the folder in its own window). If, instead, you double-click a folder, you open the window, replacing the current contents displayed.

**Column View.** This view is new to Mac OS X; Mac OS 9 has no counterpart of this view. In this view, you have multiple columns. The contents of a folder appear in the leftmost column. If you click a folder in that column, its contents appear in the folder to the right. This arrangement can continue until there are no more folders to open in the rightmost window.

You can use the horizontal scroll bars to slide back and forth among the columns, if they do not all fit within the current size of the window.

If you click an item that is not a folder, the column to the right typically displays summary information about the file (such as its name, kind, size, version, and modification date). For documents, you may see a preview of the document's contents.

By clicking the small double vertical bars at the bottom of each column divider and holding down the mouse button, you can move the pointer to resize the column widths.

**Right end.** At the right end of the toolbar are buttons that mainly represent commonly accessed volumes or folders. Mostly, these buttons will be folder or volume icons, but they can be any type of Finder item. Click one of these buttons, and you open that folder.

By default, the buttons located here include:

**Computer** takes you to a window that shows all mounted volumes, including hard drives, CD-ROMs, and iDisks.

**SEE:** • "Take Note: The Computer and 'Root Level' Windows," in Chapter 4, for more details on this window and its contents.

**Home** takes you to the top level of the Home directory of the logged-in user. Your Home directory is the one with your name on it, located within the Users folder.

**SEE:** • **Chapter 4 for more information on the Home directory concept.**

**Favorites** takes you to a folder contained within the Library folder of the logged-in user. It lists whatever items you have deemed to be your personal favorites—a feature I describe more in the next section. Technically, it contains aliases to the locations of these favorites.

**SEE:** • **"Aliases and Symbolic Links," in Chapter 6, for more on aliases.**

You can add a new item to the Favorites folder simply by clicking the item and then choosing Add to Favorites from the Finder's File menu (Command-T). To delete an item from Favorites, just drag the item to the Trash.

**Applications** takes you to the Applications folder, located at the root level of the Mac OS X volume. It houses all the applications initially installed by Mac OS X, as well as any other applications that may have been installed there.

**Customize items in the toolbar.** To add an item to the toolbar, simply drag its icon to the bar. (The first item I add to my toolbar is the Utilities folder!) Drag an icon off to remove it. You can rearrange the left-to-right order of items in the bar by Command-dragging them. For more customization, choose Customize Toolbar from the Finder's View menu.

If you have more items in the toolbar than you can see in the window, an arrow will appear at the right end. Click it to access a pop-up menu of the remaining items.

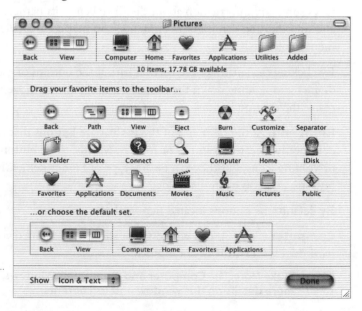

*Figure 3.10*

*Customize the toolbar.*

*Figure 3.11*

The Apple menu.

## Finder menus

Here is a tour of key items in the menus that are accessible when the Finder is the active application.

**Apple menu.** This menu is common to all applications, not just the Finder. From here, you access a variety of universally available features. When you are done with your work, you can choose Sleep, Restart, Shut Down, or Log Out (all covered in more detail in later chapters). Because of the stability of Mac OS X and the low power consumption of Sleep, most users will likely not need to restart or shut down very often.

You use the Force Quit command to quit applications that do not quit when requested to do so via the application's own Quit command (see Chapter 5).

---

**TAKE NOTE ▶ About This Mac: Version, Build, and Serial numbers**

The About This Mac command in the Apple menu opens a window that tells you the amount of installed memory and the type of processor in your Mac. It also tells you the version number (such as Mac OS X 10.1).

If you click the version number, you get something called the *build number*. A version of Mac OS X may have numerous builds, including prerelease builds and, occasionally, postrelease builds. Shortly after Mac OS X 10.1 was released, for example, a security update was released that fixed a small but important bug that could allow a user to get root access without needing a password. After you installed the update, the About This Mac window still said you were at Mac OS X 10.1, but the build number went from 5G64 to 5L14.

If you click the build number, you get the serial number for your computer.

**Finder menu.** The name of this menu is always the name of the active application. For the Finder, therefore, it is called Finder. For virtually all applications except the Finder, you will see a Quit command, which quits the application. (The Finder normally is never quit, so the option is not listed.)

This menu is also where you can choose Empty Trash. Again, anything you place in the Trash icon is not actually removed until you empty it. Also note that each user maintains his or her own separate Trash. Thus, any items left in your Trash when you log out cannot be deleted by other users who may log in later. If you double-click the Trash icon in the Dock, it opens a window showing the current contents of the Trash. You can drag an item out of the window before emptying the Trash, if you decide the item was placed there in error.

**SEE:  • Chapter 6 for help in troubleshooting problems with deleting files.**

The Finder (as well as certain other applications) also includes a command called Services in this menu. From the Services submenu, you can access specific functions in other programs, if those programs support this Services feature. You could select text in one program and have it pasted directly into another, for example.

Finally, you can choose Finder Preferences from this menu. In the window that appears, you can choose such options as the following:

- Whether to show volume items (such as hard disks) as icons on the Desktop. If this option is not selected, you access these items primarily via the window generically named Computer.

- Whether a new Finder window shows the Computer window or the Home directory by default.

- Whether to open a new folder within the same window or a new window by default.

- Whether you get a warning message when you choose Empty Trash.

- Whether to show file extensions (discussed more later in this chapter).

**File menu.** This menu contains many of the most commonly accessed features of the Finder, including the capability to create a new folder, create an alias for an item, add an item to the Favorites list, move an item directly to the Trash (bypassing the need to drag its icon there), ejecting removable media, open or close windows, or choose Find (which opens Mac OS X's Sherlock application, described later in this chapter).

*Figure 3.13*

The Finder's File
menu.

**Edit menu.** This menu where you cut, copy, paste, and undo. One note for Mac OS 9 users: The Undo command in the Mac OS X Finder supports multiple levels of undo. In Mac OS 9, you could undo only one level.

Starting in Mac OS X 10.1, this menu contains a new feature. If you click an item in a Finder window and then access the Edit menu, the Copy command now reads Copy {*name of item*}. If you choose that command, you activate a Paste {*name of item*} command in the menu. If you choose that command, you will paste a copy of the item in the new location. This setup is a way to copy and paste from one window to another without needing both windows open at the same time.

> **TAKE NOTE** ▶ **Contextual Menus**
>
> If you Control-click an item in the Finder, you will bring up a *contextual menu* for that item. What is in the menu will vary, depending upon the nature of the item (such as a file versus a folder). Common selections include Open, Show Info, Move to Trash, Duplicate, Make Alias, and Copy {*name of item*}.

**Figure 3.14**

*A contextual menu (with some third-party items, such as XRay, added).*

**View menu.** This menu has options that largely overlap with the toolbar, allowing you to switch among Icon, List, and Column views, for example. You can also choose Clean Up to affect the arrangement of icons or Arrange by Name, which is useful to push all icons to the top-left corner of the window. The Show View Options command lets you select different icon arrangements (such as Always Snap to Grid).

Mac OS X still seems to have some problems with cleanup. More than occasionally, a window that you cleaned up will have its icons return to their messy state on a subsequent visit. Ideally, this bug will have been fixed by the time you read this book.

 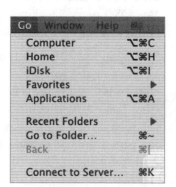

**Figure 3.15**

*The Finder's (left) View and (right) Go menus.*

**Go menu.** The Finder's Go menu lists the same Computer, Home, and Applications options that are available in the toolbar. You can access your Favorites selections from this menu. You can also choose Customize Toolbar.

Of special importance are the following three commands:

**Go to Folder.** This command lets you select a specific folder. If you know the exact pathway to a folder, you can also use it to access folders that otherwise would be invisible (as you learned in Chapter 2, when you used it to access the private/tmp folder).

**Connect to Server.** This command lets you connect to other volumes accessible on a local network or over the Internet. Typically, at least two items will be listed, even if you are not connected to the Internet: AppleTalk and Local Network. These two choices represent two different protocols (AppleTalk and TCP/IP) for accessing volumes on a network. Some volumes may be set up to work with both protocols and thus will be listed in both locations.

To mount a volume, click its name and then click Connect. For local networks (such as in a home or small office), despite the word *Server* in the name of the command, most listed volumes will simply be other locally connected computers. Most users will use this feature for file sharing.

SEE:  • Chapter 8 for more information on file sharing.

**iDisk.** This command mounts your iDisk volume, assuming that you are connected to the Internet and previously set up an iDisk account with Apple (which you do from the iTools tab of the Internet System Preferences window).

SEE:  • Chapter 8 for more information on iDisk.

**Window menu.** This menu lists all open windows and lets you choose which one you want to bring to the front. You can also enlarge (zoom) or minimize (move to the Dock) the current window.

**Help menu.** You can choose Mac Help from this menu. Given the sparse documentation that comes with your Mac, this option is an important one. To get help, click the text box in the Help window, and type the keywords for the quest you seek. Type format disks, for example, if you want to learn how to do that. Then click the Ask button, and a list of suggested items will appear. Select the ones that sound most relevant and read the help provided.

For more help, you have two main alternatives: (1) Go to the Web (especially to Apple's support site or my own MacFixIt site) or (2) purchase a book on the Mac (such as the one you are now holding).

# System Preferences

System Preferences is a central location from which you can set up or customize a variety of features of Mac OS X. In most cases, these features are not linked to any particular application and are not accessible any other way. In some cases, especially if an application is a background application or otherwise does not have its own menus, this window is also where you would likely find an application's preferences settings, so it is comparable to Control Panels in Mac OS 9.

You can access System Preferences from a variety of locations. The Dock icon probably is the most common way. Or you can choose System Preferences from the Apple menu or simply double-click the System Preferences application icon in the Applications folder. Whatever method you choose, you wind up at the same place.

*Figure 3.16*

The System
Preferences window.

## System Preferences window: An overview

The top row of the System Preferences window starts with a Show All button. You can click this button at any time to return to the default display that shows all available preferences windows.

To the right of Show All is a collection of commonly accessed preferences. Several are placed there by default when you install Mac OS X, but you can customize this collection. To add an item, drag its icon from the bottom part of the window to the Favorites row; to remove an item, drag it off.

The remaining part of the window lists all preferences in four categories: Personal, Hardware, Internet & Network, and System. There may also be a fifth category called Other. Click any icon, and the window is filled with the options for that particular preference. To go to another preference, click its icon in the Favorites list (if it is listed there), choose System Preferences from the View menu, or click the Show All button in the Preferences window and select the desired preference from the full display.

Following are brief descriptions of selected preferences that are most relevant to troubleshooting. I'll cover some in more detail in later chapters, when I explore the topic for which they are used. You can also choose System Prefs Help from the Help menu for additional information.

# Personal

**International** includes options for adjusting the characteristics of your Mac to match conventions used in different countries. You can change number, time, and date formats, as well as the language used for menus and dialog boxes. The ability to switch languages in third-party software requires that the developer build in the needed support.

**Login** is a critical system preference. For starters, the Login Items window is where you create a list of applications to be opened automatically at startup. If you have QuicKeys installed and want it to launch automatically at each startup, you would add it to this list. The Login window is where you specify whether you want to log in automatically at startup. If this option is enabled, you are logged in via the account that was first set up when you installed Mac OS X (which may be the only account that exists). No login window ever appears. Otherwise, you see a login window at startup; you must enter a name and password before you can proceed.

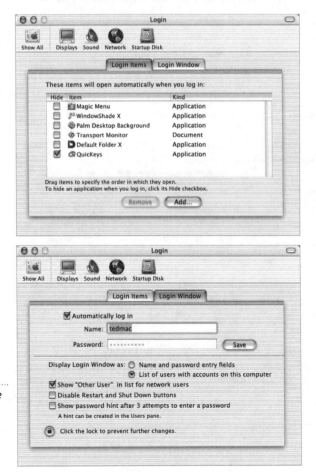

**Figure 3.17**

The two tabs of the Login System Preference: (top) Login Items and (bottom) Login Window.

This tab is also where you select options, such as whether you want the login window have just a name and password entry box or a list of users. If you choose the latter option, all users with local accounts will be listed in the login window. If you choose Show Other User, an additional Other option will be added for network users. You would use this tab to log in as the root user (which I explain more later in this chapter).

**Screen Saver** allows you to enable a screen saver that kicks in after a specified period of time, as set in the Activation window. You can also set it so that you must enter a password before you can wake the screen saver.

## Hardware

**Displays** is where you set the resolution and color depth of your monitor, as well as select a color profile to match your display.

**Energy Saver** is where you set the options that determine when the Mac goes to sleep. You can set times for display and hard-disk sleep separately.

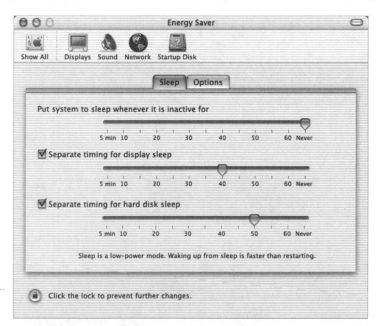

*Figure 3.18*

*The Energy Saver System Preference.*

**Keyboard** features an option called Full Keyboard Access that allows you to use Control-key combinations to access menus and Dock items without using the mouse or trackpad. This option works only with Mac OS X-native applications (and only the ones that do not also run in Mac OS 9).

**Sound** is where you select an alert sound and volume.

**TAKE NOTE ▶ Sleep failures**

System Sleep is the low-power mode in which the Mac appears to be off, except for the pulsing light on the power button (on desktop Macs) or other location (on notebooks). Be aware that problems have occurred with this "deep sleep" in Mac OS X, especially on Power Macs that have SCSI cards. It may be that the Mac will not go to sleep or will crash when waking from sleep. In some cases, this problem can be fixed by software or hardware updates for the SCSI card. (Check the vendor's Web site for details. You can find out the vendor via the Devices tab of the Apple System Profiler window; if your SCSI card shipped from Apple; check Apple's site regardless of the vendor.) Otherwise, you simply won't be able to use sleep—at least, not deep sleep.

## Internet & Network

**Internet** is where you can enter your iTools name and password (you can sign up for Apple's iTools if you do not have an account), plus basic account information and preferences for email, Web, and news. This data will be used by all email and Web-browser software that supports this system preference, eliminating the need to enter the same data multiple times.

This feature is separate from the Internet Connect application (in the Applications folder) that you use to log on to the Internet via a dial-up modem. **Internet Connect** is where you enter the telephone number, name, and password for your Internet service provider (ISP). Actually, Internet Connect gets its default settings from the Network System Preferences window, described in the following paragraph. For broadband connections, such as a cable or DSL connection, Internet Connect is not needed.

**Network** is an essential system preference if you plan on using the Internet or accessing a computer beyond your own (even for two Macs connected via an Ethernet cable). This tab is where you enter the TCP/IP settings for Ethernet, AirPort, and modems. You can create different settings for each type of connection. By choosing Active Network Ports, you can also determine which of these options is enabled and the order in which the options should be tried (should the first choice fail to work). You can set your Mac up so that it tries to connect via Ethernet automatically, and if it fails to find an Ethernet connection, it will next try to connect via AirPort. Unlike Mac OS 9, Mac OS X does not require you to make any changes manually for this setup to happen. You can also create different settings for different locations (such as home and work). I cover this topic in much more detail in Chapter 8.

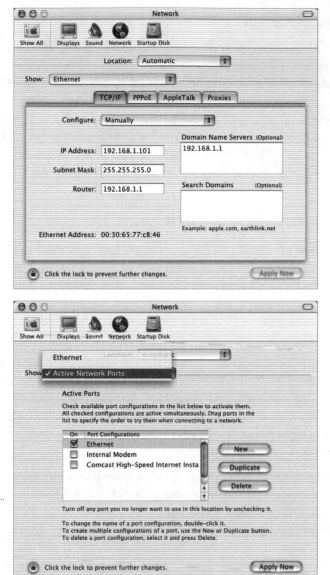

**Figure 3.19**

*Network System Preferences: (top) the Ethernet TCP/IP tab and (bottom) the Active Network Ports pane.*

**Sharing** is mainly used to turn file sharing on and off. Unless it is on, no one will have any network access to your computer. The Allow FTP Access option enables users with local accounts to connect to your Mac via any FTP client software, including a Web browser. These users just need to know the IP address and enter it (ftp://192.168.1.878, for example, followed by a user name and password when asked).

Web sharing is also enabled in this tab. This option allows users to have Web-browser access to the files (such as HTML files) in the Sites folder of your home directory.

In the Application tab, the Allow Remote Login option allows access to your computer via the Terminal application. This option can be useful in some troubleshooting situations when your Mac appears to be frozen. Despite the freeze, you may be able to access the computer via Terminal from another Mac on the network.

I discuss all these options more in Chapter 8.

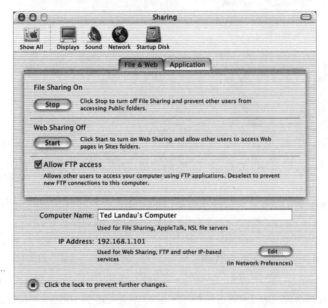

*Figure 3.20*

*The Sharing System Preferences pane.*

## System

**Classic** is where you select what Mac OS 9 System Folder you want to use for running Classic (if more than one is available). You can also start, stop, restart, or force-quit Classic from this pane if problems occur or if you no longer want it to be running.

The **Advanced** tab provides other useful troubleshooting options, including the option to start up with extensions off or to access Extensions Manager at startup. You can also rebuild the Desktop from this tab—a useful option if Mac OS 9 icons are incorrect or if double-clicking a document does not open the expected application. I cover Classic in Chapter 9.

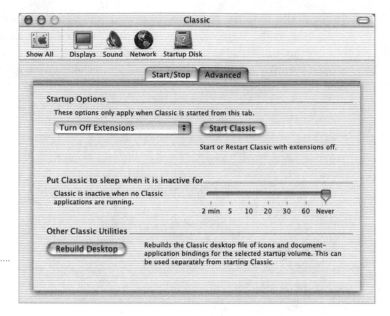

**Figure 3.21**

*The Advanced tab of Classic System Preferences.*

**Date & Time** is where you set the current date and time (of course!). You can also have the correct time maintained via a check with a network clock. Finally, you can enable or disable the clock that appears in the menubar. This feature is separate from the Clock application, which creates a clock that appears in the Dock or floats over the Desktop.

**Software Update** checks for new Mac OS X software that Apple makes available. You should check it at least once a week or set it up to do so automatically. Click Update Now to download and install the software. In Chapter 2, I cover some potential problems with using this feature to update the OS.

**Figure 3.22**

*The Software Update System Preferences window. Click the Update Now button to launch the Software Update application that actually lists the available updates.*

**Startup Disk** is where you select the startup OS and volume. If you have both Mac OS 9 and Mac OS X installed on your drive, for example, you would use this tab to tell the Mac which OS to use on the next restart. In Mac OS 9, you would use the Startup Disk control panel to reselect Mac OS X. You can accomplish this System switching in other ways, as I discuss in Chapter 5.

**Figure 3.23**

*The Startup Disk System Preferences window.*

**Users** is another important system preference. In this tab, you can create users beyond the initial account created for yourself when you installed Mac OS X. Each new user is given a name, a shortcut name, a password, and a log-in picture. You also decide whether the user is to have administrative status (something I discuss more later in this chapter). Each account has its own folder in the Users folder. For the user who is currently logged in, his or her folder becomes the Home folder/directory for that session.

You can also edit the settings of existing accounts, such as changing a password. If you are an administrator, you can even delete an account.

**SEE:** • "Technically Speaking: Delete a Deleted User's Folder," in Chapter 6.

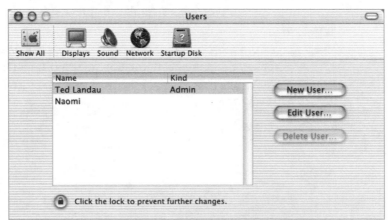

**Figure 3.24**

*The Users System Preferences window.*

## Other

Third-party software can also use system preferences. If you have installed any non-Apple system preferences, those settings will appear in the Other tab. TinkerTool and ASM are two shareware programs that do this.

**Where system preferences files are stored.** The system preferences files installed by Mac OS X are stored in /System/Library/PreferencePanes. You will see files with names such as Classic.prefPane and Displays.prefPane. In the Show Info window, these files are listed as Mac OS X Preference Pane. In most ways, however, they function as ordinary applications, with the exception that launching them also launches the system preferences shell.

Third-party system preferences files will be most likely stored in the Library/PreferencePanes folder in your User directory. As a result, installed preferences will be available only for the user in whose account the file resides. If you have created more than one user account and want all users to have access to a specific preference, you will need to install it in each user's directory.

**If user-installed preferences panes do not appear in System Preferences.** If user-installed third-party preference panes don't show up in the Other section of the System Preferences window, here is what to do:

1. Quit System Preferences.
2. Use a utility such as TinkerTool to make normally invisible files visible.
3. Go to the Library/Caches folder of your home directory and locate the file named .ApplePrefPanesCache.
4. Delete the file and undo the change you made TinkerTool.

Alternatively, you can launch Terminal and immediately type:

`<rm ~/Library/Caches/.ApplePrefPanesCache>`

In either case, a new default version of this file will be created the next time you launch System Preferences. Ideally, the previously missing panes should now appear.

**SEE:** • **"Take Note: The Location of Desktop and Trash Folders," later in this chapter, for additional information on using TinkerTool.**

• **The "Invisible Files," sections in Chapter 6, for much more information on this topic.**

# Applications and Utilities

Mac OS X installs several programs in the Applications folder. In this section, I offer a brief overview of the most troubleshooting-relevant of these programs. As always, I will return to most of them later in the book when discussing the particular troubleshooting problem for which the software is used.

Most of the applications of troubleshooting interest are in the Utilities folder, located within the Applications folder. I start by describing two programs located in the Applications folder: Preview and Sherlock. Then I move to the all-important Utilities folder.

## Preview

Preview opens graphics files of various formats. You can use it to view the GIF and JPEG files that are common on most Web pages, for example. You can also use Preview's Export command to convert a graphics file from one format to another; choices include TIFF, JPEG, PICT, QuickTime Image, and Photoshop. The default choice, if you just choose Save, is TIFF.

Perhaps the best feature of Preview, however, is its link to the Preview button in the Print dialog box of almost any application that works with documents. If you click the Preview button, the Preview application launches and opens the selected document as a PDF file. PDF, which stands for Portable Document Format, is the native format used by Acrobat Reader. The document should look virtually identical to how it looked in its creating application. At this point, you have two choices:

- You can print the document from Preview. This option may be useful for occasions when printing from the creating application does not work, for some reason.

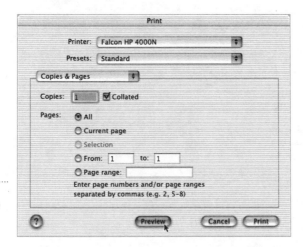

*Figure 3.25*

*The cursor is over the Preview button in the Print dialog box.*

- You can save the file as a PDF file via the Save As PDF command. Then you can open the saved document in any application that can view PDF files, including Preview itself and Acrobat Reader. This option can be useful for exporting files to other platforms (such as Windows) that could not otherwise open the original document. As a Windows version of Acrobat Reader is available, Windows users will be able to open the PDF file.

Note that Acrobat Reader has some options that Preview does not (such as a Find command), so don't throw out your copy of Acrobat Reader just because Preview is available.

**SEE:** • **Chapter 7 for more information on printing.**
- **"Take Note: Type and Creator vs. File Extensions," later in this chapter, for information on how to fix a situation when the Preview button launches Acrobat Reader instead of Preview.**

---

**TAKE NOTE ▶ Open and Save Sheets**

When you choose Save As to save a document (or when you save an untitled document), a sheet pops down below the title bar. In this sheet, you name the file and choose where to save it. The default choice will be the Documents folder in your Home directory. A pop-up menu will give you a few other basic choices: Home, iDisk, anything you may have created as a Favorite, and other recent choices.

For anything else, click the disclosure triangle next to the Where pop-up menu to open a view similar to the column view of a Finder window. From here, you can navigate to wherever you want, just as you can in the Finder itself. You could also add a particular destination to your Favorites list.

**SEE:** • **"Take Note: Type & Creator vs. File Name Extensions," later in this chapter, for more on file name extensions and saving files.**
- **"Opening and Saving Files," in Chapter 6, for a more extended discussion of opening and saving documents. Especially see: "Take Note: File Name Extensions."**

---

**Figure 3.26**

*The "collapsed" version of the Save as sheet.*

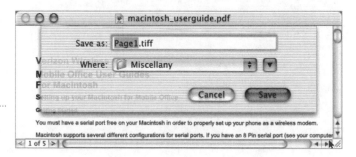

# Sherlock

Sherlock is the application that the Finder uses to locate files on your drive as well as to locate information on the Internet. If you have used Sherlock in Mac OS 9, you are already familiar with it, as the Mac OS X version is much the same. To launch Sherlock, click its Dock icon, click its listing in the Applications folder, or press Command-F in the Finder. I divide my coverage of Sherlock into two section: Search Files and Search the Internet:

**Search Files.** Sherlock's initial screen lists all mounted volumes. By checking or unchecking the box next to a volume, you can determine whether that volume is included in a search.

To perform a search, enter the search text in the text box, and click the magnifying-glass icon. The results will appear in the area where the volume listing had been.

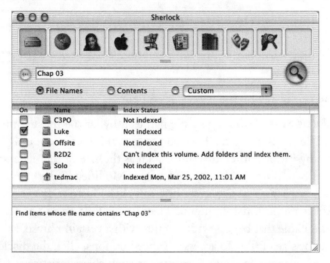

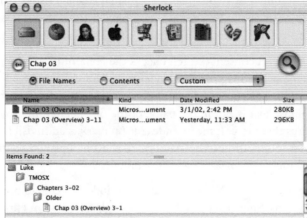

*Figure 3.27*

*Sherlock's Search Files screen (top) before and (bottom) after searching for results.*

If you click any item in the results pane, the area at the bottom of the window will show the path to that item. Double-clicking any location in the path will open that window in the Finder. Double-clicking a document or application will launch the file.

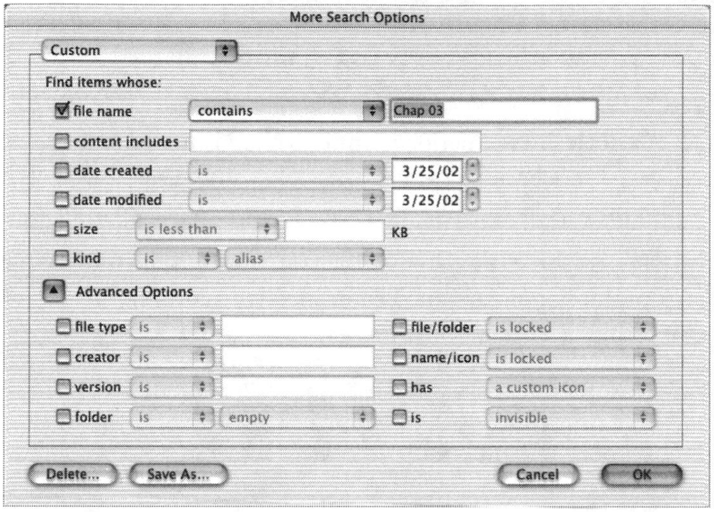

*Figure 3.28*

*Sherlock's More Search Options window; accessed by selecting Edit from the Custom pop-up menu.*

You can search by file names or contents.

**File names.** Searching by file names is by far the most common thing you will do. This method allows you to search for a file not only by its name but also by various other attributes, such as the size of the file and when it was last modified. A few such options (such as Modified Today) are accessible via the pop-up menu that appears when you click Custom. For more options, choose Edit from the Custom menu. Then you will be able to choose criteria such as a file name that begins with or ends with a certain phrase, as well as search by date or size of file. To access advanced options, click the disclosure triangle; these options allow you to search for such characteristics as files that are locked or invisible. You can also combine criteria. If you don't select any option, you will search for all items that contain the search term you enter.

**Contents.** A contents search checks the content (that is, the actual text that you type in a word processing document) for documents of selected applications. This option can be useful if you are looking for a file that contains some key phrase that is not in the name of the file. Searching by content, however, requires that the volume be indexed. An *index* is an invisible file that stores all the text information to be searched; it must be updated continually to reflect any changes you make in your documents.

Currently, Mac OS X volumes cannot be indexed. Due to privileges/permissions restrictions, Sherlock cannot create a single index of an entire volume (as Mac OS 9 does). The best Sherlock can do in Mac OS X is create an index for a given folder. As a result, your Home folder/directory is listed in Sherlock by default. Because this folder is where most (if not all) of the documents you create will be stored, a contents search restricted to this folder is still likely to be useful. You can add other folders for indexing, if you want; just choose Add Folder from the Find menu.

Indexing is done (and updated) automatically every time you launch Sherlock. Indexing can take a lot of time and slow your Mac, so you may want to turn off this feature if you do not intend to use it. You can stop and start indexing manually via the Stop Indexing and Index Now commands in the Find menu. Or you can prevent automatic indexing by disabling the Automatically Index Items When Sherlock Opens option in Sherlock's Preferences window. Unlike the Mac OS 9 version, the Mac OS X version has no command to schedule indexes at preset times (such as while you are asleep).

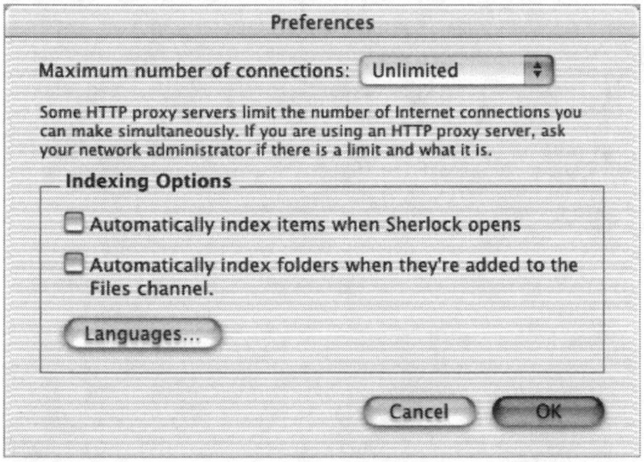

*Figure 3.29*

*Sherlock's Preferences window.*

---

**TECHNICALLY SPEAKING ▶ Index formats**

Index formats are different and stored separately in Mac OS X and Mac OS 9. The Find by Content option in Mac OS 9's version of Sherlock does not see the indexes created by the Mac OS X version. Similarly, the Mac OS X version does not see indexes created in Mac OS 9.

In particular, for storing indexing data, Mac OS X uses invisible .FBCIndex and .FBCLockFolder files within each indexed directory (plus a .FBCSemaphoreFile inside a Private folder in the same directories), whereas Mac OS 9 uses an invisible TheFindByContentFolder folder containing a TheFindByContentIndex file) at the root level of each indexed volume.

This situation explains why Sherlock cannot index an entire volume at the same time. To modify a folder, as is needed to place the invisible index file in the folder, a user must have permission to do so. Sherlock cannot create an index in a folder for which the user does not have write permission. By default, even an admin user does not have write permission for every folder on a startup disk. This setup prevents the entire disk from being indexed.

**Search the Internet.** The remaining icons—or *channels*, as they are called—across the top of the Sherlock window access various categories of Web sites. Select the Globe channel, for example, and you will see a list of basic search engines such as Excite and Lycos. Select the Apple channel, and you get a list of several locations on Apple's Web site, most notably its Knowledge Base site for technical support and troubleshooting information. I'll leave it to you to experiment with the other channels.

Similar to selecting volumes in file searching, you can select which sites in a given list to search, via the checkboxes to the left of each name. After you make your selection and enter a search term, click the magnifying-glass icon to initiate a search. In the results that appear, click any link to go that Web page. To do all this, you must be online, of course. Whenever you select a particular channel, Sherlock will check to see whether the search sites listed there need updating. If so, it will add, delete, or modify the sites as needed.

*Figure 3.30*

*Search Apple's Web sites.*

The last channel (with the Sherlock hat and magnifying glass) is My Channel. This channel is where you will most likely put channels that you add yourself. To do so, first download the Sherlock plug-in from a Web site that provides one (such as MacFixIt!). Then, with My Channel selected, install the Sherlock plug-in by choosing the Add Search Site command from the Channels menu. The site will appear in the My Channel window. You can even create new channels, if you want (via the Add Channel command).

**TECHNICALLY SPEAKING ▶ Where are the Search Site files stored?**

Sherlock search site files are stored in the Internet Search Sites folder, inside the Library folder in your Home directory. Thus, every logged-in user can have his or her own customized set of search sites. Drag search sites into and out of the subfolders to add or remove search sites, bypassing the need to use the Add Search Site command.

# Utilities-folder applications

The Utilities folder, contained within the Applications folder at the root level of your volume, holds a wealth of troubleshooting utilities. Here is an overview:

**Apple System Profiler** provides details about the software and hardware currently in use. You have five tabs to choose among. The two most useful ones are System Profile and Devices and Volumes.

System Profile provides details about your Mac model, including the processor you have installed, how much memory you have, and the Boot ROM version (which is what gets updated if you ever install an Apple firmware update for your Mac). If a particular problem is linked to a particular version of the Boot ROM, for example, you could check this tab to see which version you have.

Devices and Volumes lists details about all the ATA, USB, FireWire, and PCI-card connected devices communicating with your Mac, including hard drives, CD drives, and scanners. It does not list devices connected via an Ethernet network (such as a printer). If you are having problems with any external device, this tab would be a good place to check first. If the device is not listed, the Mac doesn't even recognize it as being connected.

To see more information about any item, click the disclosure triangle next to the name.

The remaining tabs list all extensions, frameworks, and applications on your drive. You would rarely need to check this information here.

**SEE:** • **Chapter 4 for more information on extensions and frameworks.**

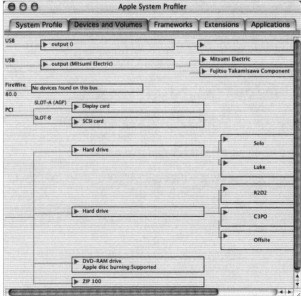

**Figure 3.31**

*Apple System Profiler's Devices and Volumes tab. (See Figure 2.1 for another view of Apple System Profiler.)*

**CPU Monitor** graphically displays the level of CPU (central processor unit) activity. If the level remains high, you may have too much processor activity. The result will likely be a decrease in the overall performance of the Mac. To reduce the processor load, you could quit some open applications, especially if they are doing processor-intensive tasks that are not needed at the moment (such as doing a transformation in Photoshop).

CPU Monitor's Processes menu (shown in Figure 6.46) contains a command to open other utility applications automatically, including ProcessViewer (a utility that provides more detail about open applications and how much processor time they are using) and Terminal (going to the Top command, which is yet another way of viewing this activity information, this time via a command-line Unix interface).

**SEE:** • **Chapter 5 and later in this chapter for more on ProcessViewer.**

       • **Chapter 10 for more information on Terminal.**

**Disk Copy** primarily opens or creates disk images. Disk images, as I first discussed in Chapter 2, are files that typically end in .img or .dmg. When you mount one of these files, it opens a virtual volume, as though you were mounting a volume such as a CD-ROM disc. Then the contents of the image file are accessible from the Finder. To do this with Disk Copy open, just drag an image file to its window. Typically, you can also double-click an image file to open it. From the Image menu, you can choose commands to create a new image or burn a CD of a given image.

**Figure 3.32**

Mounting a .dmg
file via Disk Copy.

---

**TAKE NOTE ▶ Mounting Disk Copy image files**

Occasionally, if you double-click an image file, it will not mount its image. Instead, it may open as text in a text editor or otherwise fail to open. This may happen because the file is corrupted. If the file was downloaded from the Web, the solution may be to try to download it again.

More likely, however, the problem is simply that the Finder doesn't know what application is needed to open the file. If, instead of double-clicking the file, you drag it to the Disk Copy window, it should mount just fine.

*continues on next page*

**TAKE NOTE ▶ Mounting Disk Copy image files** *continued*

If you want to fix the file so that double-clicking works, you will need to change the creator for the file. A utility called DMG Fixer can do this for you automatically. Otherwise, see "Show Info Window," later in this chapter, for information on how to use Show Info for this purpose. In both cases, you need not know anything about a file's creator code to make the desired change. But several third-party utilities, such as FileXaminer and Magic Menu (included with StuffIt Deluxe), let you modify a file's creator code directly, assuming that you know what code change you want to make.

**SEE:** • "Take Note: Type and Creator vs. File Extensions," later in this chapter, for background.

**TAKE NOTE ▶ Create a Bootable CD**

Troubleshooters often depend on startup disks other than the one that is normally used—typically, the Mac's internal drive. Alternative startup disks can be convenient when you're doing something that cannot be done to the current startup drive (such as doing disk repairs with some utilities) and become especially valuable if the data on your default drive gets corrupted in such a way that the disk cannot start up at all.

Fortunately, the Mac OS discs that come with your Mac, as well as most OS discs you might purchase later, can serve as startup discs. Still, sometimes you may want additional copies or even customized startup/bootable discs.

Creating a bootable drive in Mac OS 9 is about as simple as can be. Just drag a copy of a System Folder to the drive and (assuming that the software is recent enough to run on the Mac in question), you can start up your Mac from that drive. This method works with hard drives and most removable media such as Zip disks. CDs present a special problem. CDs need some special boot code so that the Mac will recognize the disc as a startup volume at a time in the startup process when it typically would not have loaded the code needed to recognize CDs in the first place. This problem is solved by utilities such as Toast, which create a bootable CD with the needed special code from any original that contains a System Folder. Even the most recent versions of Apple's Disk Copy can burn a bootable CD if you first create a disk image of a bootable CD for it to copy.

Creating a bootable Mac OS X volume presents considerable more difficulties. The primary reason is that the essential System files are not all in the Mac OS X System folder. Also, numerous invisible files, mostly related to the underlying Unix OS, need to be copied as well. And there is the potential issue of setting up a default user account.

Thus, you cannot simply copy a Mac OS X System folder to a Zip disk, for example, and expect it to function as a startup volume. In fact, given that Zip discs max out at 250 MB, and given that a typical Mac OS X system can require more than 600 MB, it is unlikely that you will even be able to use a Zip disk as a Mac OS X startup disc under any circumstances.

*continues on next page*

**TAKE NOTE  ▶  Create a Bootable CD**  *continued*

**Bootable hard drive.** If you divided your internal hard drive into several partitions, the simplest thing to do would be to use a Mac OS X Install CD to install Mac OS X on more than one partition. If the entire hard drive fails, however, you will be unable to start up from any partition.

A better alternative is a second, ideally external, hard drive. Especially useful, if you want to travel with an emergency startup drive, are the small portable FireWire drives (such as LaCie's PocketDrives), but they are more expensive than standard external drives.

Even more cool: Apple's iPod contains a FireWire drive. You can install Mac OS X on the drive and have it serve as a portable emergency startup drive. To do so, you enable iPod's Enable FireWire Disk Use option. See Apple Knowledge Base article 60920 (http://docs.info.apple.com/article.html?artnum=60920) for more details.

You may also be able to use a utility such as Retrospect to back up a hard drive partition to another medium (such as a tape drive) and then restore it to a second partition. This technique gives you an exact duplicate of the original drive, including all user accounts and additionally installed software.

Note: Depending on the version of Mac OS X you are using, the Mac you are using, and the specific external drive, you may have problems starting up from an external SCSI or FireWire hard drive. I cover this more in Chapter 5. Otherwise, check with Apple's support pages or MacFixIt for the latest details.

**Bootable DVD-RAM.** You should also be able to install Mac OS X onto a DVD-RAM disc, which has capability of at least 2.6 GB). You must have a DVD-RAM drive (which is different from a DVD-R drive), as well as a second CD drive; most Mac users do not. If you do have such a setup, you don't even have to restart from the Mac OS X CD to get it to work. Simply mount the Mac OS X Install CD in the CD drive while you're booted from your Mac OS X hard drive; then locate the OSInstall.mpkg file in the System/Installation/Packages folder on the CD. Double-click this file, and the Installer will launch. After entering your administrator's password, you will be able to install Mac OS X on the DVD-RAM disc. Expect the process to be quite slow, however.

**Bootable CD.** By far the most useful and most commonly used bootable disc for a trouble-shooter will be a bootable CD. If you have a CD-RW drive, can you create a bootable CD? At this writing, the answer is yes and no. You certainly can create an exact copy of a bootable CD that will also be bootable, but making a useful customized bootable CD is not a user-friendly procedure.

I'll start with the basics. Suppose that you want to make an exact bootable copy of a Mac OS X Install CD. Here is what you need to know:

Do not expect the Burn Disc feature in Mac OS 9's or Mac OS X's Finder to work. At least as of Mac OS X 10.1, you cannot create a copy of a bootable CD with this method.

*continues on next page*

**TAKE NOTE ▶ Create a Bootable CD** *continued*

Toast (both the Mac OS 9 or the Mac OS X versions) can make a bootable Mac OS X CD. According to some reports, using Toast is as simple as clicking the Copy Disc button and then copying the Install CD. Other users report that you might first have to first create a .dmg or .cdr image of the Install CD and then copy the unmounted image file for Toast to work. You could do this by creating the image file via the Disk Copy utility in Mac OS X. But if you need to go this route, you might as well skip Toast altogether and just use Disk Copy.

The Mac OS X version of Disk Copy can create a startup CD all by itself. Here is how:

1. Booting from your hard drive, insert and mount the Mac OS X Install CD.

2. Launch Disk Copy.

3. From the Image menu, choose New Image from Device.

   In the Mac OS 9 version of Disk Copy, this command brings up a friendly window listing each mounted volume/device (such as the CD-RW drive). Mac OS X is less friendly. Here, you see a series of listings: disk 0, disk 1, and so on. Some items have a disclosure triangle next to them. Click the disclosure triangles until you find one that says CD_ROM_Mode_1. This is the Install CD.

4. Select the Install CD, and click the Image button.

5. In the window that appears, give the file a name in the Save As text box.

6. Choose an image format.

   I chose DVD/CD Master. One or more of the other formats may have worked as well, but this one seemed best, given that what I wanted was a CD master. If you want to modify the contents of the image before burning the CD, and you have problems with the DVD/CD Master selection, try Read/Write as the format.

7. Leave encryption set to None.

   The resulting image file will be named {your selected name}.cdr.dmg.

8. Eject the Mac OS X Install CD.

   Do not try to mount the image.

9. Choose Burn Image from Disk Copy's Image menu.

10. When you are asked to insert a blank CD, do so.

    Note: Don't try to use the Finder's Burn Disc option instead of Disk Copy. That option will not work!

11. Click the Burn button (now enabled) to burn the CD.

    When you're finished, you should have a bootable Mac OS X Install CD.

Note: In Mac OS X, you may see two types of image files: .img and .dmg. A .dmg file is a device image, whereas an .img file is a normal image file. The two types of files have a few differences of practical significance. For one, .dmg files work primarily, or exclusively, in Mac OS X; .img files work equally well in Mac OS X and Mac OS 9. Also, .img files can be made of almost any unit: a folder, partition, or volume. By contrast, .dmg files are made of an entire device (such as a CD),

*continues on next page*

**TAKE NOTE  ▶  Create a Bootable CD**  *continued*

including all invisible files. Thus, device images (.dmg files) are necessary for making bootable CDs. See also "Take Note: Understanding Image Files" in Chapter 2.

**Modified bootable CD.** The above procedure is all well and good. But what if you want to make a customized CD with your own utilities on it? In principle, the procedure would work, because the cdr.dmg image that you create is modifiable. After you complete step 8, you can mount the image file (and remove nonessential files, such as those in the Applications folder, if you need more room) and then copy your own files to the image. The changes you made are saved to the .dmg file. Then you can unmount the image and proceed with step 9.

But the bootable CD does not load the Finder. In fact, the Finder is not even on the CD. Instead, the CD boots directly into the Installer utility, which is the only way that the CD can start. Thus, although you may have other utilities on the drive, you would have no way to access them. Could you get the CD to boot into another utility or even boot the Finder if you installed it? Booting to the Finder remains a question mark, because I am not sure how it would handle not having any accounts in the Users folder. It certainly could boot into another application, however. There are already bootable Mac OS X CDs (such as the one for Micromat's Drive 10) that serve this purpose. The Drive 10 CD, however, appeared to be set up differently from the Mac OS X Install CD; its System folder did not even have the BootX file, which normally is needed for all bootable volumes.

How would a typical end user manage this task, as opposed to a developer? The information that tells the CD what application to launch at startup is contained in the rc.cdrom file, located in the etc directory on the CD. You can read the contents of the file with a text editor such as BBEdit or TextEdit. At this point, I stopped. I confess that the procedure has become more complicated that I believe should be required for an end user to make a modified bootable CD.

I believe that this situation is one of the major weaknesses of Mac OS X compared with Mac OS 9. A shareware alternative, however, provides at least a partial solution.

**BootCD.** You can create a bootable CD with the freeware utility called BootCD, which allows you to go further than any of the options I have described so far. In particular, it lets you create a bootable CD that contains a Finder and a Dock. The Dock can be set up to contain any applications you choose. Here are the details:

1.  Launch BootCD. Type the desired Volume Name and click the "Create Bootable CD image" button.

2.  Give a name to the dmg file that BootCD will create and click to Save.

3.  Next, choose which applications you would like included on the CD and put on the CD's Dock. You do this via a file browser window that appears. Typically, you would add utilities that you might need for repair or recovery in an emergency. Click Open to add a utility. Click Cancel when done. Disk Utility and Terminal are automatically included so you do not need to select them.

*continues on next page*

**TAKE NOTE ▶ Create a Bootable CD** *continued*

**4.** Quit BootCD and launch Disk Copy and select to Burn Image of the image file you created.

**5.** Mount the newly created CD and select to Restart. Boot from the CD (by holding down the C key at startup).

When done starting up, you should be at the Finder. There will be a Dock that contains all the utilities you selected (plus Disk Utility and Terminal). Your startup drive volume/partitions will also be mounted. You have root user status at this point. BootCD has the root password set to "BootCD."

With the full contents of the hard drive now accessible, you can work with most applications on the drive, in addition to the emergency utilities on the CD. I could play chess or create a document in TextEdit, for example.

The Restart, Shut Down, and Log Out commands in the Apple menu do not work on a CD created with BootCD. So to reboot again from your hard drive, use the reboot command in Terminal. To make sure that you do not reboot from the CD, hold down the Eject button on your keyboard until the CD ejects.

See this Web page for more tips on using BootCD:
`http://www.macfixit.com/library/usingbootcd.shtml`.

**Disk Utility** is a combination of what were two separate utilities in Mac OS 9: Disk First Aid and Drive Setup. Disk First Aid is a repair utility; I cover its use in Chapter 5. The remaining tabs are used to format disks (akin to Drive Setup in Mac OS 9). I cover its use, especially for creating partitions when formatting a volume, in Chapter 2.

The Erase tab is the only place in Mac OS X where you can erase the contents of a CD-RW disc.

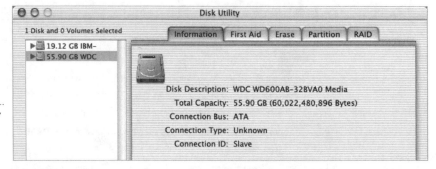

*Figure 3.33*

*The default window that appears when you launch Disk Utility.*

**Grab** creates screen captures (pictures of your Desktop), which are the sort of pictures that illustrate this book. Personally, I find Grab to be rather a kludge. It has one saving-grace feature: a time-delayed capture, useful for setting up what you want to see after choosing to take a capture. Beyond that, it is inconvenient to use and too often prevents you from getting the shot you want.

Fortunately, starting in Mac OS X 10.1, the main screen-capture shortcuts from Mac OS 9 are back. Command-Shift-3 takes a snapshot of the entire screen, and Command-Shift-4 allows you to select a portion of the screen for capture. Command-Shift-Caps Lock-4, which lets you select a window to capture automatically, works only in a Classic application. Captured files are saved to the Desktop as TIFF files, named Picture 1, Picture 2, and so on. If you are in a Classic application, however, the files are saved as PICT documents at the root level of the volume containing the Classic application.

If you want the ultimate in power and convenience for taking screen captures, get the shareware program Snapz Pro X, which even allows you to create movies of your screen actions.

**Installer** is the utility that launches when you open an installer package file. I cover this topic in Chapter 2.

**Keychain Access** simplifies having to remember multiple passwords used by other applications. If an application supports this feature (that is, if it is keychain-aware), the password used by the application can be stored as a key-chain file. Typically, when you enter your password in a supported application, you will have the option to add it to your keychain. If you choose this option, Keychain Access will enter the password for you automatically the next time you need to do so. You just need to have created a Keychain account and have it open at the time. Mac OS X typically handles this procedure for you auto-matically when you log in. It couldn't be much simpler.

**Network Utility** tests and troubleshoots network connections. If you are having trouble with an Internet connection, this utility can help you diagnose the source of the problem. I discuss this topic more in Chapter 8.

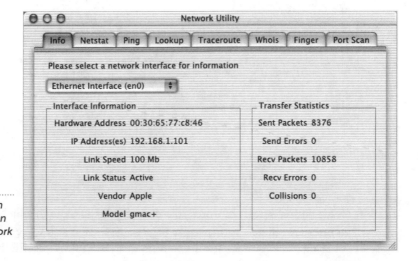

**Figure 3.34**

*The default screen that appears when you launch Network Utility.*

**Print Center** helps you select and set up printers you will use in Mac OS X. You need a printer driver for your printer before setting it up via Print Center. Mac OS X ships with many printer drivers; others may be available from the printer manufacturer. For details on this procedure, including working with AppleTalk vs. TCP/IP, see Chapter 7.

**ProcessViewer** is a nearly essential troubleshooting utility that can view every open process. An application is a process, but many processes that Mac OS X can open are not applications. The most important feature of ProcessViewer for troubleshooting purposes is that it can force-quit any application, even ones that are not listed in the Force Quit window that opens when you press Command-Option-Escape. I cover this topic in Chapter 5. I also discussed its use in "The Dock" earlier in this chapter.

ProcessViewer also shows you the percentage of CPU time and memory each process is using. This feature can be useful in diagnosing which processes are hogs that could be causing your computer to slow.

**SEE:** • **CPU Monitor, earlier in this section.**

• **Chapter 5 and Chapter 6 for more information on ProcessViewer**

**Terminal** allows you to access Mac OS X's Unix command line environment.

As a troubleshooter, you will need to use Terminal occasionally when things go wrong. Still, whenever possible, this book offers alternative solutions that do not require Terminal.

**SEE:** • **Chapter 1 and Chapter 4 for background on Unix**

• **Chapter 10 for details on how to use Terminal**

**Console** is a utility, provided by Apple rather than by a third party, that does what I just described—that is, it allows you to access a feature of Unix via an Aqua-based application instead of Terminal.

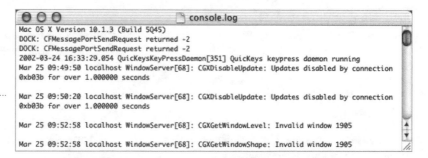

**Figure 3.35**

*A Console window showing the most recent output in console.log.*

In this case, it provides access to the log files that Unix maintains. These files track various events—primarily, errors that occur while using your Mac. Viewing these log files can be useful in diagnosing the cause of a problem such as a system crash. In truth, unless you are very familiar with Unix, the text may appear to be meaningless. But developers or tech-support people may want this information when you go to them for help.

**SEE:** • **Chapter 5 for more information on Console, Crash Reporter and related topics**

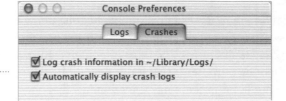

**Figure 3.36**

Console's Crashes Preferences.

---

**TECHNICALLY SPEAKING ▶ Crash Reporter**

Of special note regarding Console is an option in the Crashes tab in Console's Preferences window: Log crash information in ~/Library/Logs. When this option is enabled, a feature called Crash Reporter will log information at the time of a system crash. To developers, this information can provide important clues as to why the crash may have occurred. If you also enable Automatically display crash logs, Console will launch and show the crash log immediately after a crash.

At this point, Mac OS 9 users may be asking, "How can it show anything after a crash? Don't you have to restart the computer after a crash?" Well, no. This is one of the key advantages of Mac OS X. Crashes bring the application down but rarely bring down the OS itself. So everything but the crashed application will still be working, including Console.

If you want to see an example of the sort of output you might get, here's a way to do it without actually crashing an application. Install the applications included in the Developer Tools CD. In the Developer/Applications/Extras folder is an application called BombApp. Run it after enabling Crash Reporter, and you will see what sort of error messages a crash produces.

---

**TAKE NOTE ▶ The Developer Tools CD**

The Developer Tools CD is (at least, as I write this chapter) included with the retail purchase of Mac OS X. Most of what is on the CD, as its name implies, will be useful only to developers.

Still, a few items, such as PropertyList Editor, BombApp, and the Carbon version of SimpleText (all mentioned in other sections of this chapter), are useful even for basic troubleshooting.

If you do not have a copy of the Developer Tools CD, you probably can order it from Apple. Otherwise, you can become a ADC online member (it's free) at Apple's ADC (Apple Developer Connection; connect.apple.com) site. Online members may download the Developer Tools from the Download Software area of the ADC member site.

**TECHNICALLY SPEAKING** ▶ **Log Files and Cron Jobs**

**Where are the log files?** The log file that opens when you launch Console is console.log. It is just one of several logs that Console can open.

Some files, such as the crash logs, are in the Logs folder inside the Library folder.

The Console.log itself is in an invisible Unix directory located at /private/var/tmp. To access this log from the Open dialog box of Console, type the following in the Go To text box: /private/var/tmp. Alternatively, you can make all invisible files visible (such as via the Show Hidden and System Files option in the shareware utility TinkerTool). Now you can go to this directory from the Finder and double-click the Console.log file. This action, too, will open it in Console.

Most of the remaining log files that Console might access are stored in another invisible location: /private/var/log, accessible via the methods I just described. Here, you will find logs such as system.log and `ftp.log`.

Console.log is sort of a condensed version of all the information you see in system.log. In some cases, files have names such as system.log.1.gz. The extension .gz indicates that the file has been compressed to save space. Essentially, these compressed files contain data older than that in the current system.log file. The Unix system periodically creates these compressed log files, deleting the oldest one.

You can clear the contents of any single log file by choosing the Clean command from Console's File menu while the file is the active window.

**Doing maintenance with cron jobs.** One problem with cron jobs is that they typically are set to run at night—say, at 2 or 3 a.m. The decision to do this is a leftover from the Unix mainframe heritage of the OS, when computers were left on 24 hours a day, and maintenance tasks were carried out in the early morning, when things were less busy. Thus, if you turn your Mac off each night, these tasks may never get run. In truth, this situation probably will not matter much, although it can lead to very large log files (or very many log files) that never get cleared. One solution is to get a shareware utility called MacJanitor. This Aqua-based utility allows you to run the daily, weekly, and monthly cron jobs easily.

If you are a bit more technically inclined, you can see the system cron job listing without using Terminal. To do so, get a shareware utility called CronniX. Launch it, and choose Open System Crontab from the File menu. You will see the daily, weekly, and monthly entries. You can also create your own user-specific cron jobs here. I strongly suggest not making any changes unless you know what you are doing. Although this utility bypasses the need for Terminal, it doesn't make the task itself any easier to understand.

If you are comfortable using Unix, you can do all these things from the Terminal application. For those who would prefer to avoid the Terminal, you can still get much more flexible control of the log files on your computer by using the shareware BetterConsole instead of Mac OS X's Console.

**NetInfo Manager.** Apple states: "NetInfo is the directory system that is built into computers running Mac OS X and Mac OS X Server. NetInfo facilitates the management of administrative information used by Mac OS X computers. For example, NetInfo lets you centralize information about users, printers, servers, and other network devices so that all Mac OS X computers on your network, or only some of them, have access to it. It helps you set up and manage home directories for Mac OS X users on multiple, integrated Mac OS X Servers. And it simplifies the day-to-day management of administrative information by letting you update information that's used across the network in one central place."

Every time you log in to Mac OS X or add a new user via the Users System Preferences window, for example, the NetInfo database checks whether your password is correct or stores the new user's information.

If you are a network administrator, especially one who's running Mac OS X Server, understanding NetInfo is of critical importance. Most users of Mac OS X client will rarely, if ever, need to deal with the NetInfo database directly. When you want or need to do so, however, NetInfo Manager is to the tool to use. I use this tool occasionally for tasks such as enabling root access, checking on printer setups, and determining group ownership. I will reserve discussing details until the specific occasions appear in this book.

Users who are familiar with Unix will recognize that in a pure Unix system, much of what is handled by NetInfo Manager would be handled instead by something called lookupd. Lookupd exists in Mac OS X as well and works with NetInfo Manager. Actually, lookupd acts as a superset of NetInfo, getting information from other sources (such as a DNS server). It is beyond the scope of this book to go into much detail about this feature. But if you are interested, I suggest that you check out a shareware utility called LookUpManager (once again, an Aqua-based utility that bypasses the need for Terminal). The utility and its documentation (**http://www.bresink.com/ osx/DocsLookupManager/intro.html**) provide just about everything you might want to know about this topic.

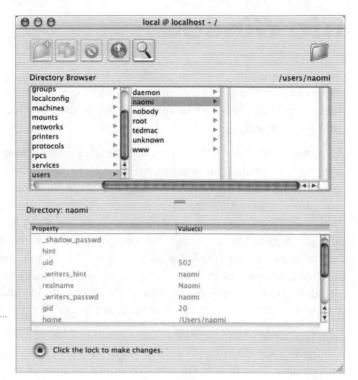

*Figure 3.37*

*NetInfo Manager, with the listing shown for the user named "Naomi."*

## Third-party utilities

As rich as the programs in the Utilities folder are, they do not come close to providing all the troubleshooting help you might want. Fortunately, third-party software developers have jumped in to fill the gaps, providing an array of useful utilities. Most of these programs are shareware or freeware. Rather than list them all here, I will describe them as I cover the topics for which the utility was intended. When I discuss modifying privileges settings, for example, I will mention utilities such as FileXaminer and XRay.

# Show Info Window

To get the Show Info window for any file, folder, or volume in Mac OS X, simply click the item's icon (or its name in List or Column view) and press Command-I (or choose Show Info from the Finder's File menu). The Show Info window will appear.

With the Show Info window open, if you click any other icon or even the Desktop background, the window will shift to display the information for your current selection. You cannot have two Show Info windows open at the same time. This method can be a convenience when you want to see information from several files in succession. (You do not need to press Command-I for each item and have several windows open.) But it can be inconvenient if you want to compare two Show Info windows side by side. Some third-party methods, such as StuffIt Deluxe's Magic Menu Command-Shift-I command, do allow you to compare Show Info windows side by side (although the content of the windows is not identical to what you get from the Finder).

The Show Info window includes a pop-up menu. Choosing different items from the menu shifts the content of the window to display different information and options. This display will vary depending on the type of item (application, document, or folder) you are selecting.

Following is an overview of what you can expect to find in Show Info windows.

## General Information

General Information is the tab that appears when you first open the Show Info window. It gives basic information such as the type of file (application, document, folder, volume, or alias), the file's size, where on the drive it is located, the version number of an application (if the application provides that information), and the creation and modification dates of the item.

If the file is an alias, General Information will tell you where on your drive the original is located.

**SEE:** • "Aliases and Symbolic Links," in Chapter 6, for more information on aliases.

At the bottom of the window may be one more checkboxes. One checkbox will be Locked. With this option enabled, you are prevented from deleting the file. Actually, you will not even be able to place it in the Trash. If you do, you will get a message stating that you do not have sufficient privileges to do so.

**SEE:** • Chapter 6 for more information on problems with locked files and with deleting files in general.

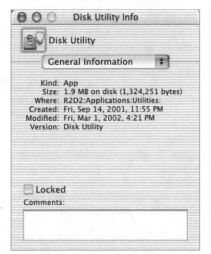

**Figure 3.38**

Show Info's General
Information pane
for an application.

For some documents, you will have a Stationery Pad option. If this checkbox is checked, opening the document opens a copy of the document, rather than the document itself. This setup allows you to make changes in the copy and still preserve the original. As its name implies, this option is useful for documents such as stationery, in which you have some element (such as a name and address) that you want to preserve for use with other future documents (such as letters you are writing).

Some applications can be opened in either Classic (Mac OS 9) or Mac OS X. These applications usually open in Mac OS X by default. But you may have some reason to want one of these applications to open in Mac OS 9. You can do so by choosing the Open in the Classic Environment option in the General Information tab of the Show Info window. If that option does not appear, the application probably is not a "switch hitter" and can open in only one environment or the other.

As described in Chapter 9, there are cases (such as AppleWorks 6) in which an application can open in Classic or Mac OS X even though the Open in the Classic Environment checkbox does not appear.

**SEE:** • **Chapter 4 for more information on Carbonized applications and applications that can open in Classic.**
• **Chapter 9 for more information on Classic.**

The Comments field is where you can type your own personal comments about the item. You can enter anything you want, such as the Web site where the file was obtained or the serial number of the product. If you reboot in Mac OS 9, you can access a similar window called Get Info; it, too, has a Comments field. Mac OS 9 stores the comments in a different invisible file from the one that Mac OS X uses, however. Thus, comments created in Mac OS X are not visible in Comments fields in Mac OS 9, and vice versa.

Finally, the icon of a file or folder is visible in this window.

**TAKE NOTE ▶ Icons with Bars**

Do you ever find that some of your icons mysteriously acquire black horizontal bars? Apple has confirmed this as a bug in the OS, identifying it as a "cosmetic" problem (which means that it causes no further harm beyond its appearance). It appears to get triggered when you have many applications open and are using most of the Mac's virtual memory. However, quitting applications will not help get rid of it. Relaunching the Finder often works to eliminate the bars. Restarting the Mac is an almost certain fix. Otherwise, you can just ignore it.

**TECHNICALLY SPEAKING ▶ Changing icons**

Changing a file or folder's icon is something you usually do more for fun than out of any need.

**Change icons via Show Info** In most cases, if a Finder item has a custom icon, you can copy it from the item's Show Info window and paste the copied icon into the Show Info window of another item. The other item will then display that icon in the Finder. To do this:

1. Select Show Info for the file that has the desired icon.

2. Click the icon in the Show Info window and select Copy (Command-C).

3. Select the Show Info window for the destination file.

4. Click its icon and select Paste (Command-V). (Note: If the file already has a custom icon, you may first have to cut it before you can paste a new one.)

Pasting a custom icon will not work for files that do not have a resource fork (such as dfont font files), but will work in most other cases.

You can also select to cut (Command-X) rather than copy a custom icon. In this case, what remains will either be a default icon (as assigned by the Finder, based on its creator or file name extension) or a blank icon.

You can also obtain graphics to be used as icons from sources other than the icons of other files. For example, you can create your own icons with the IconComposer utility included on the Developer Tools CD. Third-party utilities such as Iconographer X also work well and are more end-user-friendly. You may even be able to paste graphics other than icons, such as images in opened in the Preview application (but they won't look as good as a graphic specifically designed to be an icon). Alternatively, you can paste an icon from an icon file downloaded from the Web.

**Change icons of package files** Package files (such as .app applications) typically do not permit pasting of a new icon over their existing one, via the Show Info window of the file. However, there is a solution to this. You need to have the desired icon in the form of an icns file rather than as a graphic on the clipboard. Icns files are available for download on the Web, can be created via icon editing utilities, or can be "borrowed" from an existing package file (assuming it has the icon you want). For example, to use the icns file from one package to place in another, do the following:

*continues on next page*

**TECHNICALLY SPEAKING ▶ Changing icons** *continued*

1. Select the application that has the icon you want to copy and Control-click to access its contextual menu. If a "Show Package Contents" item appears, the application is a package. [Note: Not all applications will be packages in Mac OS X, but most will be.]

2. Select "Show Package Contents." From the window that opens, navigate to the Contents/Resources folder. There you will find at least one icns file. Look for the one named {name of application}.icns. This is the file that is used to create the Finder icon for that application.

3. Option-drag this icns file to the Desktop. This creates a copy of it on the Desktop.

4. Select the application where you want the icon to go and, using the Show Package Contents contextual menu, go to the same Resources folder inside the package.

5. Rename the icns file on the desktop to match the name of the one in the destination package's Resources folder.

6. Drag the renamed file to the Resources folder of the destination package, and say OK when asked if you wish to replace the file already there.

7. Close all folders you opened.

8. Select Command-Option-Escape to open the Force Quit window. Select to Relaunch the Finder. When the Finder reappears, the application with the replaced icns file should now display the new icon.

Or alternatively, try this:

1. After obtaining the icns file you wish to use (as described above), go to the Contents folder inside the destination package.

2. Using a text editor (such as BBEdit) or PropertyList Editor, open the info.plist (or info-macos.plist) file.

3. Change the value of the CFBundleIconFile key to the name of the new icns file. Save the change.

4. Move the new icns file into the package's Resources folder. With this method, you don't overwrite the original icns file or change the name of your newly added one.

*continues on next page*

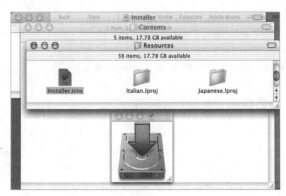

**Figure 3.39**

*The Installer.icns file in the Installer.app package.*

**TECHNICALLY SPEAKING ▶ Changing icons** *continued*

Note: I recommend working with copies of the files involved so that you don't have to worry about doing any permanent harm in case things do not work out as desired. There is an apparent bug in Mac OS X that affects this method. When you're making a copy of any package file, you may not be able to open the Contents folder inside the package of the copy. Thus, you will not be able to get to the needed .icns file. The solution seems to be simply to log out and log back in again. You should be able to open the Contents folder.

SEE: • **"Take Note: Preferences Files in Mac OS X," later in this chapter, for more on using Property List Editor.**

## Name & Extension

Name & Extension is the tab of the Show Info window that lists the name of the file and its file extension (if any). All applications have the file extension .app. Other files, especially documents, may have extensions that identify the type of file (such as .gif to identify a file as a GIF graphic). Mac OS 9 did not use file extensions, so Mac users may find it inconvenient or confusing to see these extensions listed in the Finder. That is why the .app extension is almost always hidden for applications. You can choose to hide an extension for a given file by choosing the Hide Extension option in this tab.

More generally, you can choose to hide virtually all file extensions in the Finder by deselecting Always Show File Extensions in the Finder Preferences window.

*Figure 3.40*

*The Name & Extension tab of the Show Info window.*

SEE: • **"Take Note: Open and Save Sheets" and "Take Note: Type and Creation vs. File Extensions," elsewhere in this chapter, for more information on this subject.**
• **"File Name Extensions," in Chapter 6.**

## Open with Application

Open with Application is a tab that appears only when you open the Show Info window for a document. You use this tab when double-clicking a document's icon does not open the document with the application you expected to be used (or does not open the document at all).

The tab has two parts. At the top are an icon for an application and the name of the application. This application will try to open the document if you double-click it. In the corner of the icon will be a triangle. Click the triangle and hold down the mouse button to access a list of applications in a pop-up menu. The bottom choice is Other—useful if none of the listed applications is what you seek. In general, just choose the application you want to use with this document. Now when you double-click it, the document will open in that application. In most cases, the icon of the document will also change.

One of the choices in the list will have the word *(default)* next to it. This option typically is used for documents of the type you are working with and probably is the type that was selected when you accessed the Show Info window.

You might have reason to make a change in this tab when you have .dmg files downloaded from the Web. When you double-click these files, they may launch TextEdit in error. You can change the setting to Disk Copy instead.

**SEE:** • **"Take Note: Mounting Disk Copy Image Files," earlier in this chapter.**

At the bottom of the tab is a section named Use This Application to Open All Documents Like This. This section will also display the type of document and what application the document was created with. Sometimes, the type is listed as unknown or the creating application is listed as not available. Most often, these displays will match the default application. A document that is opened by AppleWorks by default, for example, will be listed as an AppleWorks document (actually, a com.apple.appleworks document—a terminology I will explore in "Take Note: Preferences Files in Mac OS X" later in this chapter) and as created by AppleWorks.

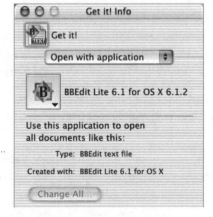

*Figure 3.41*

Show Info's Open with application pane for a BBEdit Lite document.

If you change the application in the top half of the tab, the Change All button in the bottom half will be enabled. If you click this button, all documents of the same type as the current document will open in the selected application. In essence, you are changing the default application. One reason you might want to do this is if all files in a certain graphics format (say, JPEG files) open in Application A by default, but you would rather that they open in Application B. Or perhaps all documents of a certain type are opening in a Classic version of Application C, and you have a Mac OS X version that you prefer to use. The Change All button can make such changes.

---

**TAKE NOTE ▶ Type and Creator vs. File Extensions**

The controversy regarding type and creator vs. file extensions is a heated one. Here, I try to explain what the controversy is about and what you need to know to navigate these troubled waters.

**Type and creator.** In Mac OS 9, every file is identified by a type and a creator. The type identifies the type of file (application, system extension, AppleWorks document, and so on), and the creator is mainly used to identify what application the Finder views as being as the creator of a document. What is listed in the Kind line in a file's Show Info window is typically determined by the type and creator code for the file.

Type and creator information are essentially two separate four-letter codes stored in a special area of a file called its *resource fork*. This situation is especially significant for document files, as they have little use for a resource fork except to store this information (sometimes referred to more generally as *metadata*). The rest of the file's contents are stored in the data fork.

Although Apple provides no utility for changing creator and type codes in a standard installation of either Mac OS 9 or Mac OS X, many third-party utilities that do so. In Mac OS X, for example, you can use xFiles or FileXaminer.

The creator is especially important for documents that can be opened by several applications. When you double-click a plain-text document in the Finder, it opens in SimpleText if SimpleText is listed as the creator. The same file opens in AppleWorks if AppleWorks is listed as the creator.

The type can also affect how documents are treated. Read-only SimpleText documents (the ones with the newspaper icon) have a type of ttro, whereas read-write SimpleText documents have a file type of TEXT (case matters!). You can change a read-only file to an editable one simply by changing this type. In both cases, the creator for SimpleText should be ttxt.

By the way, in TextEdit (Mac OS X's equivalent of SimpleText), you can change an editable document to a read-only one via the Make Editable and Make Read Only toggle commands in the Format menu.

A consequence of this system is that no matter what name you gave a file, the Finder can figure out what type of file it was and (for documents) what application it should open in, simply from the type and creator information.

**Problems with type/creator.** Mac OS X can use the same type and creator information but does not require it. In fact, Apple prefers that developers no longer depend on it. Documents saved in Mac OS X's TextEdit, for example, include no type or creator code.

*continues on next page*

**TAKE NOTE** ▶ **Type and Creator vs. File Extensions** *continued*

Why has Apple gone this route? First and foremost, no platform except Apple uses this system. Thus, when you send a file from the Mac to the Windows platform, the resource fork in a document—and, thus, its type and creator data—typically is lost. Conversely, files created on Windows machines and sent to a Mac do not have this data. Also, type and creator data are not supported in Unix, so a Mac OS X drive formatted with UFS (se Chapter 2) could not use this data to identify files. In these other platforms, the files consist only of a data fork. Mac OS X is going in this direction.

**Extensions.** What does Apple prefer to use to identify a file in Mac OS X? It prefers file extensions. File extensions are abbreviations stuck on the end of a file's name, such as .jpg in picture.jpg, in which .jpg is used to indicate that the file is a JPEG document. This system is essentially what other platforms use.

**Problems with file extensions.** The system has numerous problems, however. For starters, it is much easier to change the name of a file inadvertently than it is to change a file's type or creator. You could give a file an extension that does not make sense, such as .jpg for a word processing document. Although the Finder might think you now have a .jpg file, the file really is not a JPEG and will not open in applications designed to work with .jpg files.

A second problem occurs if you eliminate the extension, which could make it difficult to figure out what type of document it is and what application to use with it.

Finally, by relying on just one bit of information (file extension) instead of two (type and creator), you lose some significant flexibility. With type and creator, you can have two JPEG files with different creators. One may open in Preview; the other may open in AppleWorks. You can't do this with file extensions. All JPEG files open in the same application by default unless you override the setting in the file's Show Info window.

Thus, there has been a considerable backlash against Apple's use of file extensions in preference to type and creator. The feeling is that Apple took something that worked well and substituted something more likely to have problems. For now, regardless of your opinion, Mac OS X users are stuck with Apple's decision. So you might as well get used to it.

**How it all works.** Here is what you need to know about how Mac OS X decides what application to use when trying to open a document:

**Priorities.** Mac OS X uses a technology called Launch Services to do what its name implies (service the launching of files). It is responsible for launching applications and their associated documents. Launch Services uses the following rules to decide how to open a document:

1.  Open the document via the application specified by the user in the Show Info window, if the user has made a nondefault selection.

2.  If the document has a creator assigned to it, open the file with the application indicated by the creator.

*continues on next page*

**TAKE NOTE ▶ Type and Creator vs. File Extensions** *continued*

3. If no creator is present and a file extension is included, find the applications that can open this document.

4. If neither a creator nor a file extension is present, check for a file type.

   If a file type is present, look for the applications that can open that type of file.

5. If more than one matching application is found in step 3 or 4, give preference to Mac OS X applications first, then to Classic ones; also, give preference to newer versions of the same application, if more than one exists.

Finally, if one application is designated as the default application for a particular file extension, that application is preferred.

In brief, Mac OS X will use creator information over extensions if the creator information is present. This is why Mac OS X may appear to ignore extensions in some cases; it is trusting the creator type instead. If you want Mac OS X to use the extension, you can use a utility to eliminate the file's creator.

You could use utilities such as xFiles to remove a document's type and creator codes, if you want. After that, the Finder would have to rely on file extension to determine how to treat the file.

**File-extension hiding.** Apple recognized that many Mac users might be confused by or even hostile to the presence of file extensions and keep all these file names hidden in the Finder. To see them, you need to go to the Finder Preferences window and enable the Always Show File Extensions option.

Even when the Always Show File Extensions option is disabled, you can have the file extension for an individual file displayed in the Finder by unchecking the Hide Extension option in the Show Info window's Name & Extension tab. This option is not always available, however. Applications, for example, have the extension .app, which is always hidden and typically is never shown in the Finder. Still, you can at least see the .app extension listed in the Name & Extension tab of the Show Info window for the application.

**Editing file extensions.** You can edit a file name in Name & Extension tab, including removing its extension. Be careful, however. If you remove .app from the application name, for example, you will get a dialog box that asks whether you are sure that you want to do this; doing so may change the application into a folder. If you say yes, you will no longer be able to launch the application until you undo the change.

**Problems with editing file extensions.** Behind this file-extension setup is much inconsistency. Even if you choose to have extensions hidden, this setting will be overridden for files downloaded from the Internet. If a downloaded file was named fileone.rtf, it will remain that way. If you later change the name to myfile, however, the Finder will change the name and hide the .rtf extension (because you did not type it). Thus, the .rtf extension will still be in the Name & Extension tab of the Show Info window; you just don't see it in the Finder. Similarly, you can wind up with a situation in which an .rtf file downloaded from the Web has its extension visible but another that one you created with TextEdit does not.

*continues on next page*

**TAKE NOTE ▶ Type and Creator vs. File Extensions** *continued*

You can change a file's extension, either in the Finder directly (if the extension is visible) or in the Show Info window. If the edit just changes what application the Finder uses to open the file, and the application can open the file, the change should work well. But if changing an extension forces the Finder to think that you have changed the format of the file (when you really have not), problems are likely.

Remember that simply changing a file's extension from .jpg to .gif (different graphics formats) does not really change the graphics format of the file; it just changes what the Finder thinks the file is; the Finder will now be in error. Similarly, changing a file extension from .rtf to .rtfd does not really make the file an .rtfd/package file.

In any case, the Finder will warn you about the potential danger of changing a file extension whenever you try to do so, offering you the chance to change your mind.

More complications can occur when you save files. Mac OS X-compliant applications typically add the appropriate extension for their document type when you save a new document, even if you do not type the extension. Thus, when you save an AppleWorks word processing document, AppleWorks will add .cwk to the name of the file. Although AppleWorks shows that it is adding this extension, other applications may do so without indicating it. Even if you delete the extension from the name in the Save As dialog box, the extension still gets added.

The application should also warn you against trying to assign an invalid extension (such as .jpg to an AppleWorks .cwk file). If you try to do this, you will have the option to end the name in both extensions (such as name.jpg.cwk), but the Finder will looks at only the .cwk extension in deciding how treat the file.

Ideally, applications should respect whether you specified for extensions to be hidden in the Finder, but sometimes, they do not. Extensions may be visible in a saved file's name even if you chose to keep extensions hidden, and vice versa.

Adding still more complication is the interaction with the Open with Application tab of the Show Info window. In particular, changing the application used to open a document and then choosing Change All will change the default application associated with that extension. Files with the extension .txt and .rtf, for example, are opened by TextEdit by default. If you choose Change All for a .txt file, the Finder will open all .txt files in the new application you selected. This system also respects type and creator. Thus, if the .txt file is specifically listed as having been created by AppleWorks, Mac OS X will change all .txt files created by AppleWorks. If no creator is listed, Mac OS X will change all .txt files that have no creator listed.

*continues on next page*

**TAKE NOTE ▶ Type and Creator vs. File Extensions** *continued*

**Info.plist.** In Mac OS X, creator and type information for a particular application is stored in the information property list file (Info.plist) file, located inside the application package. This file is where the Finder goes to determine what codes to assign to documents created by that application. You can use PropertyList Editor to open the .plist file. Look for CFBundlePackageType and CFBundleSignature as the file type and creator. This information will be listed in the Value column of the row of that name. If the column says ????, no type or creator has been assigned. As I stated earlier, this information can also be viewed (and edited) via third-party utilities such as xFiles.

**The LS preferences files.** Beyond the information stored in each application's info.plist file, all information about default applications associated with given extensions and overrides of settings such as hiding extensions are stored in the LS (for Launch Services) preferences files in the Library/Preferences folder of your Home directory. These files are LSApplications, LSClaimedTypes, and LSSchemes. To delete these files, drag them to the Trash, log out, and log back in; then empty the Trash. The OS should re-create default versions of these files. If this method does not work, try the ">console" method, described in Chapter 5.

By doing this, you may lose customized changes that you made (in the Show Info window, for example), but you may also fix various problems that you may be having, such as documents that do not open as expected, applications that look like folders, and icon errors. The process is sort of like rebuilding the Desktop in Mac OS 9.

### Putting it together: Print Preview opens Acrobat in error

When you click the Preview button in the Print dialog box of most applications, Mac OS X should create a PDF version of the file and open the file in the Preview application (described earlier in this chapter). I have seen cases, however, in which the file opens in Adobe Acrobat Reader instead (typically, the Classic version of Acrobat, if you have that on your drive). To fix this problem:

1. In Preview, allow Acrobat to open the document.

2. Save the document, using Acrobat's Save command.

3. Locate the saved file, and open it with a utility, such as FileXaminer, that can modify type and creator data. For this example, I dragged the document icon to the FileXaminer icon.

4. Select "Type/Creator" (Command-3) from the pop-up menu.

5. Select "Generic PDF Document" from the Favorites pop-up menu.

6. Quit FileXaminer.

7. In the Finder, open the Show Info window for the same file, and choose Open with Application tab.

8. Click the icon with the disclosure triangle to access the pop-up menu.

9. Choose Preview from the menu.

10. Click the Change All button.

*continues on next page*

**TAKE NOTE ▶ Type and Creator vs. File Extensions**  *continued*

Now when you click Preview in the Print dialog box, it Preview should open the document instead of Acrobat. Ideally, the icon for the file should shift from Acrobat to Preview. If not, try switching back and forth between the two applications in the Show Info window.

In general, any application without a creator will open in the default application for that type of document. So you can use any utility (such as XRay or FileXaminer) that allows you to strip out the creator. If the document, when double-clicked, was opening in the wrong application, it should now shift to the default choice, which ideally will be more to your liking.

Alternatively, for the Acrobat problem, a few users have reported that deleting the LS preferences files (LSApplications, LSClaimedTypes, and LSSchemes) from the Library/Preferences folder in the Home directory may also fix this problem. After you log out and log back in, the problem should be gone.

### *Putting it together: System Preferences window does not open*

Suppose that you choose Dock > Dock Preferences from the Apple menu, and the Dock System Preferences window does not open. Or Mac OS X may attempt to launch iDVD, as though system preferences were iDVD documents. (This situation has been known to happen after iDVD is installed.) The likely reason is that the link between the Dock Preferences window and the System Preferences application has been broken. Some file corruption during the installation of a Mac OS X update or other software might cause this problem. To fix it:

1. Go to the /System/Library/PreferencePanes folder.

2. Click Dock.prefPane, and choose Show Info.

3. Go to the Open with Application tab of the Show Info window.

4. If the icon pop-up menu reads anything other than System Preferences, and especially if it reads Not Applicable, choose the Other item from the menu.

5. In the window that appears, select the System Preferences application.

6. If it is dimmed, change Recommended Applications to All Applications.

7. Click Add.

   A dialog box will appear, stating, "You don't have privileges to change the application for this document only. Do you want to change all similar documents to open with application System Preferences?"

8. Click Continue.

   At this point, the Dock and any other Preferences windows with this symptom should open correctly.

# Privileges

Privileges is a tab of the Show Info window that looks deceptively simple but opens a Pandora's box of problems. I will look at these problems in some detail here and return to the matter more in subsequent chapters when dealing with such issues as problems in copying and deleting files.

**Figure 3.42**

The Privileges pane of the Show Info window.

**Owner & Group.** The top of the Privileges tab lists the owner and group name of the item in question. You cannot edit items in any way. The owner of a file typically is the person who created the file. Thus, when you create and save a new document in AppleWorks, you are the owner of the file. You also own files that you first copy to a drive. Thus, you will be the owner of files you download from the Web.

Finally, although there are exceptions, you are the owner of the files in your Home directory. One notable exception: If you move a file into your Home directory (such as from the Applications folder), it retains its original ownership. If you instead copy the same file, so that the original remains in its original location, the copy will inherit the properties of the folder where it now exists—that is, you will be the owner of the copy in your Home directory. Thus, copying a file can change the ownership of a file.

The function of the group name is a bit more complex. I will explain it in the following paragraphs.

**Read & Write.** The bottom of the tab contains the actual privileges settings. Three separate settings are listed: Owner, Group, and Everyone. Next to each name is a pop-up menu. For applications and documents, the choices will be Read & Write, Read Only, and None. If the item is a folder, the menu will also have an option called Write Only (Drop Box). The meaning of each option is pretty much what the name implies. A Read Only file can be opened but not modified; Read & Write allows modification; None prohibits any access. Write Only for a folder means that you can add something to the folder but cannot otherwise access its contents.

Typically, the owner of a file has Read & Write access to the file, which makes sense. If you own the file, you should be able to modify it, including deleting it, if you want. In fact, only the owner of the item can change the settings in these pop-up menus. The most common setting is Read Only, which means that anyone can read the file, but no more. This option makes sense for files in the Applications folder, for example. Anyone can run these files, but not anyone can change them. So if you set up your daughter with a nonadministrative account, for example, she will be able to run the applications in the Applications folder, but you need not worry that she may delete a file from that folder accidentally or deliberately.

Actually, if you do not have write privileges to a file, you cannot drag that file to the Trash, even if it is unlocked. This issue is entirely separate from a file's being locked or unlocked.

**TECHNICALLY SPEAKING ▶ Mac OS X Privileges vs. Mac OS 9 Multiple Users**

Users who are familiar with Mac OS 9 will instantly recognize Mac OS X's privileges as being similar to the file-sharing settings used in Mac OS 9. There are three major differences, however.

First, the Mac OS X settings are always enforced. In Mac OS 9, they mattered only if you enabled file sharing or multiple users. In Mac OS X, the equivalent of multiple users is enabled by default, so these settings always matter.

Second, in Mac OS 9, if you were the only user of your computer (or were the administrator for multiple users), you had read/write access to every file on the drive. No owner was higher than you. The situation is different in Mac OS X. The user called System is higher than you. If the System owns a file, you cannot modify its privileges even if you are an administrator. Similarly, if you have set up users besides yourself, you do not have access to the files in their Users directories. Well, you can get this access, but you need to get root access to do so (see "Take Note: Privileges vs. Permissions" later in this chapter).

Similarly, you cannot change the owner or group name for an item, even if you are the owner of the file. Thus, even though you may own all the documents in the Documents folder of your Home directory, you cannot reassign the ownership of those files to someone else. You certainly cannot change the owner of a file owned by System to something else. You can often do the next-best thing, however. You can place a copy of the file in the directory of another user (such as in his public Drop Box). When you do so, the ownership of the copy of the file will change to that of the person who owns the directory.

Third, the privileges settings in the Show Info window of Mac OS X are actually determined by—and are a subset of—the much more complex permissions settings of the underlying Unix base of Mac OS X. Mac OS 9 has no underlying base.

**Group settings.** Back up a minute. If you look at the files in the Applications folder, you will see that they are owned by System. Even so, you can work with these files almost as though you were the owner (you can delete them, for example). Why? The reason is that the group setting is Read & Write, and the group name is admin. If you are an administrative user (which you are if you were the person who set up Mac OS X initially), you are part of the admin group—and thus have read/write access to the files in the Applications folder. All administrators have admin-group privileges to any file that is assigned to the group admin.

Administrators are also members of the group wheel (or primary group). Members of this group are the only ones with permission to enable root access. (I'll discuss this more later in this chapter.) Typically, files are assigned as read-only for group wheel. The files in the /System/Library directory are like that. Thus, as an administrator, you can look at and use these files, but you cannot modify them in any way. If you want to make any changes in the files in System/Library, you will need to enable root access. This setup is designed to protect these files from being moved or modified. As these files are essential to the operation of the OS, this safety precaution is obvious. Remember that the heritage of this setup dates back to when Unix was used primarily as a mainframe OS in large multiple-user systems. The last thing you wanted was some individual user playing with system files and bringing the entire system down.

Most items that are owned by individual users are also assigned to the group staff by default. For most purposes, this privilege is largely irrelevant. But if you were to change the staff group privilege for a file you own from None to Read Only, all other users (who are all also members of staff) would have access to that file.

Sometimes, you may find that the group is listed as unknown. This listing is not necessarily an error; it simply means that the OS cannot determine what the group should be, which is typically the case for all folders and files on a Mac OS 9 partition or on many forms of removable media. But if you see Mac OS X files on your Mac OS X drive listed as unknown, especially if they are in the /System/Library folder, it could spell trouble. As these files should have admin or wheel as their group, so that you have access to them, you could be unable to access files you need to get the OS to work as expected. This situation usually happens if you made some change you should not have made, perhaps when you booted in Mac OS 9 (because you can make changes that would be prohibited in Mac OS X). I discuss more specific examples, and explain how to fix them, in Chapter 6.

**Who is in a group?** How would you know whether you are a member of wheel, admin, or any other group? You can check NetInfo Manager. Simply launch it and select the groups item in the first column in the window that appears. In the next column on the right will be a list of all groups (many more than you might think; most are used by the Unix operating system and need not concern you). Scroll to find the group wheel, for example. Click it. In the section at the bottom of the window will be a line called users. The names associated with this item are the users who are part of the wheel group.

As an administrator, you could make changes here, including creating new groups. If you were a network administrator, such as at a university, you would likely need to do this. (You would also likely be running Mac OS X Server rather than the client.) Most Mac OS X users need not worry about setting up or modifying groups. Reassigning a file or folder to a new group is easy enough with the right shareware utility, such as XRay.

Actually creating a new group, or reassigning the names that are members of a group, requires more work. You will need to use NetInfo Manager. In particular, you will need to navigate to the groups directory, where you will be able to edit existing groups or create new ones. Alternatively, you could use a utility such as SharePoints, as I cover in "Take Note: Using SharePoints," in Chapter 8. However, you probably will never need to do this in typical troubleshooting.

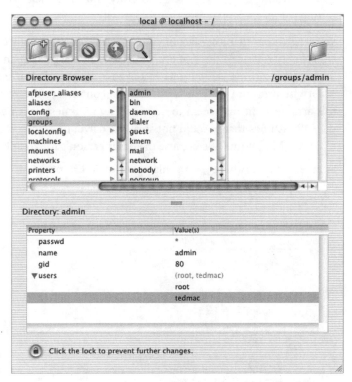

*Figure 3.43*

*NetInfo Manager shows the members of the admin group.*

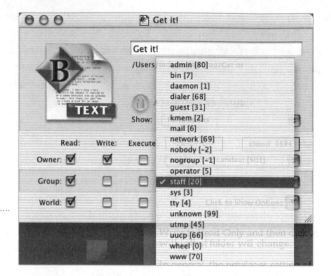

**Figure 3.44**

XRay lets you change the group assignment for a file.

**Special settings for folders and volumes.** The Privileges tab contains an additional item for folders and volumes and a second item just for volumes.

Folders have the additional option to *Apply to all enclosed folders* any change in settings to the enclosing folder. Thus, if you change the Everyone privilege for a folder from Read & Write to Read Only and then click Apply, the Everyone setting for all folders within that folder will change.

Volumes (other than the startup volume) have an option called *Ignore privileges on this volume*. You need this option primarily when accessing an external storage device from a third party. It lets you bypass the permission security that might otherwise prevent you from accessing the contents of the volume. Although this arrangement may seem to be a security weakness, it is necessary. Basically, the OS assumes that you did not steal the drive; therefore, if you can connect it to your Mac, it must be because the other person gave you permission.

**SEE:** • " Ignore privileges on this volume," in Chapter 6.

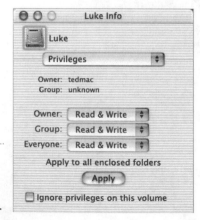

**Figure 3.45**

Show Info's "Apply to all enclosed folders" and "Ignore Privileges" options for the Luke volume.

**Bottom line.** Taken together, these permissions settings help explain several apparent mysteries. If you try to move something from the System/Library, for example, you make a copy rather than move it, because you cannot make changes in the System directory except as a root user, so you cannot move a file from there. Conversely, if you try to move something into the /System directory or drag something from the /System directory to the Trash, you will be prevented from doing so. You will get an error message that says you cannot do this because the item is owned by root, or you will get a more general error message stating that you do not have sufficient privileges to do what you just attempted. When you understand the implications of privileges settings, this arrangement begins to make sense.

---

**TAKE NOTE ▶ Root Access**

Mac OS X often gives the impression that you are only a guest on your own computer. In a sense, this is true. But as an administrator, you have the option to give yourself what is called root access and become the "real" owner of the machine. Root access means that you are the equivalent of the user System and can do pretty much anything you want. Root is sometimes referred to as the superuser. You have several ways to get root access, each with its advantages and disadvantages. I'll cover three methods here.

- **Mac OS X utilities.** The easiest and most user-friendly method is to use a third-party utility that offers temporary root access. Essentially, you log in as you normally would and launch the utility. Typically, whenever you try to make a change that would require root access, the utility will ask again for your password. If you give it, and if you are an administrator, you will have temporary root access and will be able to make the change. As soon as you quit the application, your root access is stopped. Several utilities use this method to allow you to make changes in the privileges settings that you otherwise could not make. Most significantly, you can use them to change the owner and group of a file—something you can never do in the Show Info window. Two of my favorites are the shareware programs FileXaminer and XRay.

  The main disadvantage of this utilities approach is that it allows you to do only what the application is designed to do. Want an option that's not included? You either need to find another utility that provides that option or give up on this approach. Still, for the Unix-phobic user or anyone who values ease of use in a familiar GUI interface, this method is the way to go.

  A shareware utility called Pseudo works a bit differently. It allows you to open almost any application with root access, even if the application itself does not support doing this directly. Drag an application to the Pseudo icon, and the application launches with root access. (You will still be prompted to enter your password.) Pseudo allows you to open and modify documents that you could not modify otherwise. You can use it to modify the contents of files in the System folder, for example (not something that I recommend doing in most cases, but I thought you should know this). BBEdit Lite (a freeware text editor) is a good application to try; it includes an Open Hidden method of accessing even the invisible files in Mac OS X. PropertyList Editor (included on the Developer Tools CD) is another utility that works well for this purpose, as it is designed to work with the preferences (.plist) files used by Mac OS X.

*continues on next page*

**TAKE NOTE ▶ Root Access** *continued*

- **Terminal.** Anything that you can do with Unix in Mac OS X, you can do via the Terminal application—the command-line interface utility that accesses the Unix OS.

  You can enable root access from Terminal in two ways. The first way is to use the su (for superuser) command. Type su, and press Return. You will be asked for your administrator password. Give it, and you have root access. As confirmation, you will see the word *root#* at the end of the string that precedes each line you type. Anything you do for the rest of the Terminal session (or until you type the command exit), you will do as a root user.

  Second, you can type sudo plus a command in the same line. This action gives you root access just for that one command, returning you to your normal access when you are done. Again, you will be asked for your password. One practical use of this method is to mimic the action of the Pseudo utility, described earlier in this section. Type sudo open {path of application}, for example, and you will launch the named application in the Finder with root access. You can't just type the name of the application; you must type its full path, starting at the root level of the drive, through all the directories needed to reach it. Due to some convenience tricks in Terminal, this procedure is easier than you might expect. In this case, just drag the icon of the application from its Finder window to the Terminal window; Terminal instantly enters the path for that file. Specifically, type sudo open, and press the spacebar. Now drag the icon; the path will be added to the command line. Press Return, and you are done.

  The rationale for using sudo instead of su is to keep root access as limited as possible. Even with the best of intentions, root access can allow you to make a change that can have devastating consequences for your Mac, such as wiping out the files the OS needs to work. Thus, Unix tries to keep your risk to a minimum by restricting root access to the task at hand.

  By the way, chmod (CHange MODe) is the Terminal command used to change an item's read and write privileges.

  I discuss su, sudo, chmod and numerous other Unix commands in Chapter 10.

- **Log in as root.** If you want (or need) to ignore the preceding advice about keeping your root access as limited as possible, you can log in as the root user. You remain in the familiar Aqua environment, except that you now have the power accorded to a root user. You can now add files to or delete files from the System folder, for example. You can access the Home directory folders of all users on the drive.

  Before you can log in as a root user, you need to set up a root user account. There are two main ways to do this.

**Use Reset Password.** This option is available when you start from the Mac OS X Install CD. Follow these steps:

1. Start up from the Mac OS X Install CD.

   To do so, hold down the C key at startup with the disc installed, or (if booted from Mac OS 9) launch the Install Mac OS X application and restart.

2. Choose Reset Password from the Installer menu.

3. In the window that appears, select your Mac OS X startup drive's icon.

*continues on next page*

**TAKE NOTE ▶ Root Access**  *continued*

4. From the pop-up menu, choose System Administrator (root).

5. Enter the desired password in the text boxes.

6. Click Save.

**Use NetInfo Manager.** Follow these steps:

1. From the Domain menu, choose Security and then choose Authenticate from the hierarchical menu that appears.

2. Enter your administrator password at the prompt.

3. Go back to the same menu and choose Enable Root User.

   If you are using this method for the first time, you will get a message that the password field for root user is blank. You will be asked to set a password. Do so.

4. From this same menu, you will later be able to change the root password, if you want, as well as disable root access, so you cannot log in using it.

   Note: After you have do all this, when you go to the Users System Preferences window, System Administrator will be listed as a user. This user is the root user.

Although this practice has a slight security risk, I use the same password for root as I do for my own admin accounts. It keeps things simple and is all the protection most people need in most home and small-office environments. If you expect more than one person to have root access, however, you will want to use a unique password.

After you have enabled the root account, you can log in as root. To do so, follow these steps:

1. In the Login pane of the Login System Preferences window, if you have chosen Display Login Window As List of Users, also choose Show "Other User" in List.

2. Disable the Automatically Log In option, and restart.

   You don't want to log in automatically if you are going to log in as root.

   Alternatively, if you choose to Log Out, you will get the needed Login screen, even if you normally log in automatically .

3. When the login window appears, if you have chose Display As List, choose Other.

4. For User Name, enter root.

5. For Passwords, enter the password you selected.

6. Click the Log In button.

Now you will be logged in as the root user. Note that any customizations you have made, such as items on the Desktop or additions to the Dock, will not be visible, because the Mac now considers you to be a different user from your normal login.

*continues on next page*

**TAKE NOTE ▶ Root Access** *continued*

Even when you are logged in as the root user, some options will not be available instantly. The Finder's Show Info window, for example, still will not include an option to change the owner of a file (although you can do this via the alternative methods described elsewhere in this chapter). In general, however, you now have the keys to the kingdom. Use them wisely. Remember: Log in as root only as a last resort. When possible, use the more temporary methods of gaining root access, so as to minimize the chance of making a change that you will regret. In any case, log out as the root user as soon as you have completed whatever task you intended to do.

Bottom line: Different levels of users have different levels of access. An ordinary user can modify the files in the Library folder of his Home directory but not any other Library folders. An admin user can modify the files in the Library folder at the root level of the drive, but not the System/Library folder. An admin user with root access can modify anything.

SEE: • **Chapter 4 for more information on access to the different Library folders.**
    • **Chapter 10 for much more information on Unix and using Terminal.**

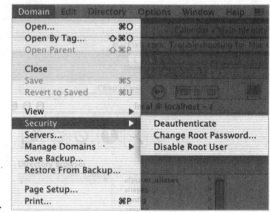

*Figure 3.46*

*NetInfo Manager's menu commands for root user options.*

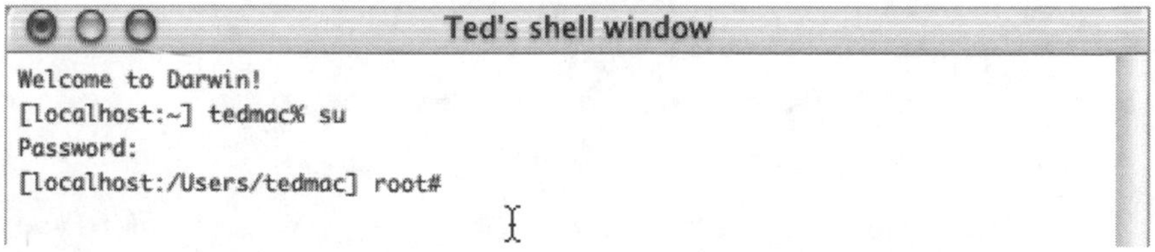

*Figure 3.47*

*Using the* su *command in Terminal to get root access.*

**TECHNICALLY SPEAKING ▶ Privileges vs. Permissions**

The Mac OS X Show Info window is called Privileges. But Unix refers to the same concept as permissions. The difference is more than just the name.

Mac OS X's privileges limit you to the choices in the pop-up menu—typically, Read/Write, Read, and None.

In Unix, there are three somewhat different attributes: Read, Write, and Execute. Further, unlike Mac OS 9, they are not mutually exclusive. To get read and write access, for example, you enable the first two of the permissions settings. To eliminate all access (the equivalent of None in Mac OS X), you turn off all permissions. Thus, there are six possible combinations of settings, from all off to all on. In addition, some special options—such as setuid, setgid, and sticky bit— have no corresponding option in the Show Info window. Also, the Execute (sometimes referred to as the search) permission does not apply directly to Aqua-based applications—that is, you can run an Aqua application even with this setting off. It does apply to commands that run directly within Unix. It also has a special meaning when applied to folders.

When you make a change in the Show Info window, you are actually making the corresponding change in the Unix permissions settings. To make changes that do not fit into the subset of possibilities included in Show Info, you need to use a utility such as FileXaminer or XRay. They both have options for editing owner and group names, privileges settings, and type/creator settings. They even include options for editing more obscure permissions settings (such as setuid and setguid).

**SEE:** • Chapters 6 and 10 for more background on privileges and permissions.

**Figure 3.48**

*Unix permissions settings as viewed from XRay; Compare to Figure 3.42. Also see Figure 10.11 for how permissions are listed in Terminal.*

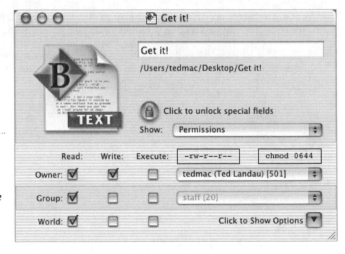

## Preview

Preview shows you a preview of the contents of the document. If the document does not support this feature, you will see just an enlarged icon of the document file.

## Languages (Mac OS X applications only)

Languages allows you to enable/disable or add/remove the language-support files needed for having an application display its menus and dialog boxes in different languages.

**SEE:** • "International Language Support," in Chapter 4, for more details.

## Memory (Mac OS 9 applications only)

Memory allows you to set the amount of memory (RAM) used by Mac OS 9 applications. This option appears only for applications that run only in Mac OS 9. It lists a suggested size and allows you to set a preferred size and a minimum size. The application will not open unless the amount of memory in the Minimum Size setting is available. You should almost never change this setting to be lower than the default. The Preferred Size setting is how much memory the application typically uses (assuming that the amount is available). This setting usually is the same as the suggested size, although you can make it larger if you feel that the program is not working well (running slowly, for example) due to the preferred size's being insufficient.

Mac OS X programs are not assigned any preset level of memory, as the OS itself allocates the appropriate amount of memory dynamically as needed. That's why this option does not appear for Mac OS X applications. The Mac OS X approach is a much more flexible, because it permits on-the-fly adjustments that the Mac OS 9 system does not allow.

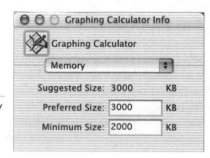

*Figure 3.49*

*Show Info's Memory pane (available for applications that run only in Classic).*

# Applications and Their Accessory Files

As I discussed in Chapter 2, most applications as viewed in Mac OS X are actually packages—that is, they are really folders in disguise. In fact, removing the .app extension from their names (which you can do via Show Info's Name & Extension tab) changes the application to an actual folder. The true application file is contained within the package/folder.

One advantage of this package concept is that it permits the developer to store virtually all the files needed for the application in this single location. In Mac OS 9, an application might also have installed files in the System Folder's Extensions folder, Fonts folder, Preferences folder, Application Support folder, and other places. In Mac OS X, all these files can be stored in one package file. Among other things, this arrangement makes installing and moving the application to a new location a breeze; just copy the package file to the new location, and you are done!

Even with these Mac OS X applications, however, files still occasionally need to be stored in locations outside the package. Also, some applications that run in Mac OS X may not be packages. (Some applications still use the format designed primarily for Mac OS 9, as I discuss in the Chapter 4.) These applications often have accessory files in other locations. In some cases, the files are self-regenerating. If the accessory file is deleted, the application will create a new default version the next time the application is launched. Others can be reinstated only by reinstalling the application from its Installer utility.

Following is a brief overview of where you can expect to find application accessory files.

**System/Library/Startup Items.** Some applications need to run at least a component of their software at startup to work. I am referring to something beyond getting an application to launch at the end of a log in by adding its name to the Login Items tab of the Login System Preferences. . In this case, I am referring to applications that add an item to the Startup Items folder in the System/Library directory. Timbuktu Pro is an example of a program that does this. In general, this task should be handled by the application's installer; if something goes wrong, try reinstalling again rather than dragging files to or from this folder yourself.

**SEE:** • **Chapters 4 and 5 for additional coverage of Startup Items.**

**Root-level Library folder.** The Library folder is accessible to all local users. Thus, when you install an application, and it wants to have its accessory files (those that are not in its package) available to all local users, the installer typically installs the accessory files here. In the Application Support folder, you may find StuffIt Engine.cfm, a file needed by the StuffIt software (Expander, DropStuff, and Deluxe). Internet plug-ins, fonts, and preferences may also be stored in the folders of the same names.

**Home-directory Library folder.** Almost all other accessory files for an application you install will be located in the Library folder of your Home directory. Again, check especially in the Application Support and Preferences folders, which are especially likely locations for such files. Files in this Library folder will be available only to the user who owns that Home directory. Thus, separate files of this type will need to be created for each new user.

In some cases, these files will be created automatically when the application is launched. (Most preferences files work this way.). Inside the Preferences folder, for example, is an Explorer folder, inside which you will find several important files used by Internet Explorer, including the Favorites.html file that Explorer uses to create the list of items in its Favorites menu. Explorer will create a separate file for each user who logs in.

In other cases, the application will need to be reinstalled for each new user. The latter situation is especially likely if you installed the application directly in a user's Home directory, as opposed to the root-level Applications folder.

Note: If you enabled Crash Reporter in Console (discussed earlier in this chapter), the Logs folder in your Home directory's Library folder will contain the log files for any crashes of specific applications.

**Home-directory Documents folder.** Finally, the Documents folder in the Home directory may contain application-related support. iTunes keeps its Music Library file in this folder, for example. Also, the Microsoft User Data folder is located here, and Microsoft Office's Entourage application keeps its email database (among other things) in this folder. Again, if these files are deleted or are not present, the application typically creates a new default version when the application is launched.

**TECHNICALLY SPEAKING ▶ Troubleshooting StuffIt Engine.cfm**

The StuffIt Engine.cfm file in the Library/Application Support folder is installed there by the Mac OS. When you are upgrading to a newer version of StuffIt Deluxe, the StuffIt installer may not update this file. One symptom is that StuffIt may keep telling you that a newer version of StuffIt is available, when in fact you have the latest version installed. This problem occurs when the version.plist file in the StuffIt Engine.cfm package (which StuffIt Expander uses to decompress and decode files) causes StuffIt to think that an older version is still present. Following is the easiest way to solve the issue permanently :

1. Drag the StuffIt Engine.cfm file to your Desktop.
2. Drag the StuffIt Deluxe folder (probably located in the main Applications folder) to the Trash, and delete it.
3. Reinstall StuffIt Deluxe.

The correct version of the StuffIt Engine.cfm file should be placed in your Application Support folder. To be certain, confirm that the new StuffIt Engine.cfm is actually located in that folder. Then you can delete the copy placed on your Desktop. If the OS refuses to delete the file due to insufficient permissions, use a utility such as XRay or BatCHmod to change the permissions accordingly (I discuss this topic more in Chapter 6).

**TAKE NOTE ▶ Preferences Files in Mac OS X**

Preferences files primarily refer to those files that store the customized changes you can make to an application, most commonly through its Preferences command. These files are entirely separate from the System Preferences panes. I have occasionally mentioned these preferences files throughout this chapter. In this sidebar, I provide a more detailed overview of where these files are stored and how they work (see also Chapter 4 for some additional information).

### *Locations of preferences files*

If you are looking for where preferences files are stored, here's where to find them:

**Preferences files in Home/Library/Preferences.** Most preferences files are located in the Library/Preferences directory in each user's Home directory. These files are the ones that are specific to each user. This is why when different users log in, they can have different preferences settings.

Most files in this folder are the standard type of Mac OS X preferences files, ending in .plist. The loginwindow.plist file, for example, contains the list of items that you selected in the Login Items tab of the Login System Preference window. You may also find Mac OS 9-type preferences files in this folder, however. And a few files, such as the LS (Launch Services) files (mentioned earlier in this chapter), do not fit into either category.

*continues on next page*

**TAKE NOTE ▶ Preferences Files in Mac OS X** *continued*

**Preferences files in Library/Preferences.** A few preferences files will be stored in the Preferences folder of the /Library directory. These files will be the same for all users. Therefore, they typically are ones that, if they can be changed at all, can be restricted so that only administrators can change them, such as via the Click Lock to Prevent Changes option in System Preferences windows. com.apple.PowerManagement.plist, for example, contains Energy Saver's settings.

**Preferences files in Unix directories.** Occasionally, you will find preferences files in the invisible Unix directories on your drive. The /var/db/SystemConfiguration/preferences.xml file, for example, contains various settings related to networking. Assorted other files are in these folders, such as config files that essentially act like preferences files. This topic quickly gets beyond what you need to know for now. However, we do mention a few more examples in "Modifying Unix files," in Chapter 6.

### Format of preferences files

As I stated earlier, the most common preferences file in Mac OS X are files that end in .plist (such as com.apple.finder.plist). plist is an abbreviation for Property List. Thus, it should not come as a surprise that plist files can be opened in the PropertyList Editor application (included with the Developer Tools CD). As the .plist files are simply text files, they can also be opened in any text editor. PropertyList Editor, however, provides a graphical interface for the file's contents that makes it easier to read and modify the file. I will use PropertyList Editor in all my discussions of viewing and manipulating .plist files.

.plist files actually are written in XML (Extensible Markup Language), which is essentially a superset of the HTML markup language used for most Web pages. For those who are familiar with XML, the document type declaration (.dtd) file for property lists is propertylisr.dtd and is located in System/Library/DTDs.

Note: The <defaults> command, used in Terminal, can access and modify the same data as does PropertyList Editor. Users comfortable with Unix may prefer this alternative.

### Content of preferences files

Preferences files contain nonessential information. The application should still launch even if its preferences file is deleted; it will simply create a new default .plist file in such a case. But applications sometimes include "hidden" preferences settings in the .plist file that are not accessible from the application. These settings can be changed only by modifying the .plist file directly, such as via PropertyList Editor or a third-party utility.

Each .plist file is mainly a list of items called keys, which can have different values. By changing the value of a key, you modify a given preference.

*continues on next page*

**TAKE NOTE ▶ Preferences Files in Mac OS X** *continued*

**Internet preferences change not saved.** Several Microsoft applications all store their inter-net-related preferences in the same file: com.apple.internetconfig.plist. This can result in a glitch where changes you make do not get saved. For example, suppose you have Internet Explorer and Entourage open at the same time. Next, suppose you make a change to Explorer's preferences, such as its "auto-fill" settings. Now quit Explorer and then Entourage. Finally, relaunch Explorer. You will see that the changes you made have vanished! What appears to have happened is that, when you quit Entourage, it "updated" the preferences data and over-wrote the change you made in Explorer. The work-around is, if you're going to be changing set-tings that would get written to com.apple.internetconfig.plist, make sure you first quit all applications except the one where you are making the change.

### Modifying a .plist file with PropertyList Editor

Following is an example of how to modify a .plist file. In this case, you will change the Finder preferences so that normally invisible files are visible in the Finder.

1. Double-click the com.apple.finder.plist file in your Home directory's Library/Preferences folder.
2. If you are asked what application you want to open this document with, choose PropertyList Editor.

More likely, the document will open directly.

3. Click the disclosure triangle next to the word *root* to reveal the list of keys.

Some keys will seem quite familiar. Click the disclosure triangle next to the key for DesktopViewOptions, for example, and you will see some of the same choices you get when you choose Show View Options from the Finder's View menu. Similarly, the WarnOnEmptyTrash key is the option you change via the Preferences window that you open from the Finder menu.

4. To change a setting, simply change the entry in the Value column.

Typically, you need to know what the alternative choices are, because only the current choice will be listed. Occasionally, however, the value will be in the form of a pop-up menu, which facilitates making changes. In such a case, just choose a different value from the menu, and you have made the change. The AppleShow AllFiles key, for example, should have a value of No. Choose Yes from the pop-up menu instead.

5. Save and close the file.
6. If invisible files are not yet visible, choose Force Quit from the Apple menu, and relaunch the Finder.

See "Take Note: The Location of Desktop and Trash Folders," later in this chapter, for more infor-mation on seeing invisible files. Also see the section on Invisible Files in Chapter 6.

You can also use PropertyList Editor to create new preferences keys or delete existing ones. But, as a troubleshooter, it is rare if ever that you will need to do this.

*continues on next page*

**TAKE NOTE ▶ Preferences Files in Mac OS X** *continued*

Note: In some cases, you may be able to open a .plist file in PropertyList Editor but will not be able to save changes due to insufficient permissions. This situation is most likely for .plist files that are not in your Home directory. In general, avoid making changes in such cases, especially if the file is in the System folder. Changing files in this folder is always a risk. You may do more harm than good and may even render your system unbootable. In any case, changes you make will likely get wiped out the next time you update the OS (sometimes, the next time you restart). Still, if you want to make such changes, all you need to do is open PropertyList Editor with root access. I explain a variety of ways to do this in "Take Note: Root Access" earlier in this chapter.

**Why the com notation?** You will notice that most .plist files begin with the abbreviation com. This is Apple's way of making sure that each application has its own unique preferences file. Suppose that two developers created an application with the name SuperText, and you had both of these apps on your drive. If both .plist files were named supertext.plist, how would the applications tell them apart? To deal with this problem, Apple has requested that developers prefix their files with their Web sites' domain-name information. Because no two domain names are identical, this setup ensures that each file will have a different name. Thus, Apple's Web site is **www.apple.com**, which converts for .plist purposes to com.apple. A .plist file for Apple's Finder is com.apple.finder.plist.

**Property Lists beyond preferences files.** .plist files show up in various locations besides Preferences folders. Application packages, for example, all contain at least one essential .plist file: info.plist. This file contains the following information:

- Name of application (displayed by the Finder)
- Type and creator codes (type APPL for applications, for example)
- Icon file name
- Version string
- Descriptive information (displayed by the Finder)
- Documents handled by this application, including document name, icon, role, types, and extensions
- URLs handled by this application, including URL name, icon, and schemes

The Finder uses the information from these files to determine how to work with the application, such as what documents go with what applications.

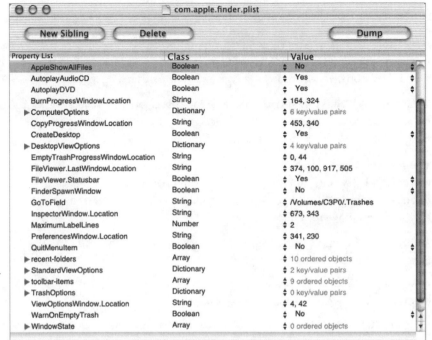

*Figure 3.50*

*Viewing the Finder's preferences from the com.apple. finder.plist file in PropertyList Editor.*

---

**TAKE NOTE ▶ The Location of Desktop and Trash Folders**

**Desktop folders in Mac OS X.** Anything that you place on your Desktop in Mac OS X is actually stored in a folder in your Home directory called, appropriately enough, Desktop. To confirm this fact, simply open a Finder window, click the Home button in the toolbar, and open the Desktop folder that will be in the resulting window. Inside will be a duplicate of every file and folder on your Desktop. Any changes you make in this folder will be reflected on the Desktop as well.

A consequence of this situation is that when a different user logs in to your computer, he will neither see nor have access to the files on your Desktop. Instead, he will see what is in the Desktop folder in his own Home directory. There is no systemwide Desktop folder whose contents are visible to everyone. Thus, things that you want to make accessible to everyone need to be placed in shared locations, such as the Applications folder or the Shared folder in the Users directory.

**Mac OS 9 Desktop folders and Mac OS X.** Each Mac OS X volume (if formatted via HFS Plus) typically has a folder called Desktop Folder. This folder contains the items that are visible on the Desktop when you boot from Mac OS 9. For all volumes except the current startup volume, these Desktop Folders (which normally are invisible when you boot from Mac OS 9) are quite visible and accessible in Mac OS X. The only exception is the Desktop Folder on the Mac OS X startup volume (which is present if you also have Mac OS 9 installed on this volume, as is the case with all Macs shipped from Apple); this one remains invisible. In this case, you have no direct way to access the items stored on the Mac OS 9 Desktop of your startup volume.

*continues on next page*

**TAKE NOTE ▶ The Location of Desktop and Trash Folders** *continued*

Apple solves this problem by creating, when Mac OS X is installed or a new user is created, a special alias called Desktop (Mac OS 9) in the Mac OS X Desktop folder in your Home directory. This alias, when opened, shows the contents of the otherwise-invisible Mac OS 9 Desktop Folder.

**The root-user Desktop.** If you log in as a root user, you also have a Desktop. Because there is no root user folder in the Users folder, however, a question arises: Where is the Desktop folder for the root user?

This folder is located in an "invisible" location at /private/var/root/Desktop. You can view the folder icon by typing `/private/var/root` as the pathway in the window that opens when you choose the Finder's Go to Folder command. You will not be able to open the folder, however, as you do not have root access.

To see the contents of the folder, you can log in as root. Then you can also move or delete the files located in the folder.

Or you can use Terminal, even when you're not logged in as root, if you are an administrative user. To do so, type the following commands:

- `<su>` (then enter the administrator password when requested to do so)
- `<cd /private/var/root/Desktop >` (to move to that directory location)
- `<ls>` (to list the contents of the Desktop directory)

A third method is to boot from Mac OS 9 and go to the /private/var/root/Desktop folder. As this folder is invisible in Mac OS 9, however, you will need to use a utility that can access invisible files and folders (such as File Buddy).

Overall, logging in as a root user in Mac OS X is the simplest approach in this case.

**Trash folders.** As is the case with the Desktop folder, each user in Mac OS X maintains his or her own Trash folder. Thus, any item you place in the Trash but do not empty will not be visible or accessible if you log out and some other user logs in. These other users will not be able to delete any folders you left in the Trash. Mac OS X has no universal emptying of the Trash, as Mac OS 9 does.

The files that you place in the Trash in Mac OS X are actually stored in an invisible folder in your home directory called .Trash. You can see this easily enough via the Terminal utility. Simply launch Terminal, and type `ls –a`, which lists all files, including invisible ones. The capability to access this invisible folder via Terminal plays a role in deleting files that refuse to be delete from the Finder, as discussed in Chapter 6. For now, I simply want to point out the existence of the folder. Each user's directory has its own.

Items placed in the Trash when you boot from Mac OS 9 are stored in the invisible Trash folder used by Mac OS 9. There is one such folder at the root level of every Mac OS 9 partition.

*continues on next page*

**TAKE NOTE ▶ The Location of Desktop and Trash Folders** *continued*

Note: If you start up in Mac OS 9, any files that you left in the Trash while in Mac OS X will not appear in the Mac OS 9 Trash. To access their contents and try to delete them from Mac OS 9, you will need a utility that allows you to view and modify the contents of invisible folders (File Buddy, for example). Then you will need to navigate to the directory in the Users folder containing the .Trash file that you want to empty. Again, I cover this topic in more detail in Chapter 6.

Back in Mac OS X, if you have any additional mounted partitions or volumes beyond the Mac OS X startup partition, anything that you drag to the Trash from those volumes will appear in the Trash window that you access by double-clicking the Trash icon in the Dock. If you empty the Trash, those files will be deleted. The files are not stored in the .Trash folder in your Home directory, however; they remain stored in invisible .Trashes folders on each volume. These .Trashes folders have write-only privileges set by default; so you would need to change the privileges (as described earlier in the chapter) to view its contents, such as via a list (ls) command in Terminal. You also will find a Network Trash Folder for dealing with trashing files when you're connected to another Mac over a network. But I think this is enough Trash talk for now.

**Seeing invisible files: an alternative method.** You can bypass some of the inconveniences in the procedures mentioned earlier (such as using Terminal) by using TinkerTool or a similar utility that allows you to see normally invisible files in the Finder. Simply enable the Show Hidden and System Files option in the Desktop window of TinkerTool. If invisible files do not appear immediately, relaunch the Finder from the Force Quit menu or from TinkerTool's own Relaunch Finder button. Now the normally invisible Mac OS 9 Desktop folder and .Trash or .Trashes folders will be visible and can be accessed directly. You can undo the change in TinkerTool to make the invisible items invisible again.

You can always access these files via Terminal, where they can be listed even if they are invisible in the Finder.

SEE: • "Take Note: Screen Captures," in Chapter 5, for more on the root-user Desktop.

　　• "Deleting Files" and "Invisible Files," in Chapter 6, for more information on these subjects.

　　• Chapter 10, for more on using Terminal.

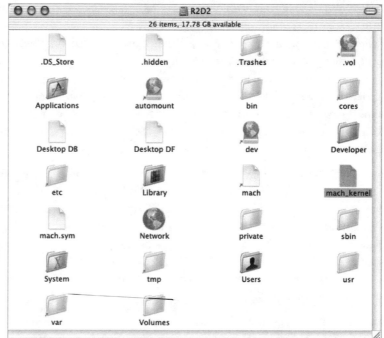

**Figure 3.51**

*The root level of a Mac OS X volume (top) before and (bottom) after making normally invisible files visible.*

# 4

# Understanding Mac OS X: In Depth

There is more than one way to think about dividing up a pizza. First, there is the familiar method of dividing it into slices. Alternatively, you could divide it into layers: topping, cheese, sauce, crust. Theoretically, you could also divide it into its basic ingredients: flour, water, tomatoes, garlic, milk. Each method makes a different contribution to your enjoyment of the pizza. The first method (slices) is best when you're getting ready to eat the pizza; the second is best when you are deciding what to order (such as pepperoni with extra cheese); the third is best if you are concerned about nutrition (needing to know the exact ingredients to calculate calories).

The same is true for Mac OS X. There are multiple ways to look at it and take it apart. Each way makes its own contribution to your understanding of the OS. In this chapter, I look at the major ways to "take apart" Mac OS X. Having at least a minimal knowledge of Mac OS 9 will help, as I occasionally make comparisons between the two OS versions. But even if you've never used Mac OS 9, you'll be able to follow along.

# In This Chapter

# The Layers of Mac OS X: Aqua

Aqua is the name given to what most users think of when they think of Mac OS X: the user interface, the Finder, the Dock, the windows, the translucent buttons, the high-resolution icons, the menus, and all the rest. Many users may never explore Mac OS X beyond its Aqua layer.

From this perspective, a user upgrading from Mac OS 9 will feel quite at home, at least initially. Much still works the same way. You still double-click icons in the Finder to launch them; you still choose the Save command from an application's File menu to save a document; you still open a folder icon to see its contents.

But you will soon notice some significant differences: a new column view, a very different Apple menu, the Dock. I discussed the basics in Chapter 3, when I presented an overview of Mac OS X.

# The Layers of Mac OS X: Application Environments

The main thing you do when you are in Aqua is use applications. On the surface, almost all applications in Mac OS X appear to function in a similar way: You launch them; you use commands from their menus; you quit them. Mac OS X has some fundamentally different types of applications, however. As a troubleshooter, you need to understand these categories.

## Cocoa

The Cocoa environment is unique to Mac OS X—that is, software developed via Cocoa uses Mac OS X-only programming tools, and the finished application runs only in Mac OS X. The advantage of Cocoa-based software is that it potentially can take advantage of every feature built in to Mac OS X. The TextEdit application that comes with Mac OS X is an excellent example of such an application. Its Font Panel window, its spelling checker, and its capability to access Services from the Services command in the TextEdit menu are all, at least in part, due to the fact that TextEdit is a Cocoa-based application. Other types of applications will not be have such features or will be much less likely to include them. In non-Cocoa applications, items in the Services menu are likely to be dimmed and unselectable; they will have a Fonts menu instead of a Font panel, and so on.

Apple probably hopes that down the road, almost all Mac OS X applications will be Cocoa-based. But for now, they are relatively uncommon, because writing a Cocoa-based application means pretty much starting from scratch. If you already have written a Mac OS 9 application that you now want to get to work in Mac OS X, Cocoa would not be the fastest way to go.

# Carbon

Applications written for the Carbon environment also run in Mac OS X. In most cases, a user would be hard-pressed to tell whether a particular application is Cocoa-based or Carbon-based. Carbon-based (or Carbonized) applications can offer all the basic Aqua features that you expect to find in Mac OS X, such as the look and feel of its windows. You cannot look at an application in the Finder and see quickly whether it is a Cocoa or a Carbon application.

To some extent, however, when a developer Carbonizes an application, he can decide how much of the Aqua interface features to support. As a result, some Carbon applications may look and feel more like Mac OS X applications than others do.

Carbon exists for two main reasons. First, it reduces the development time needed for rewriting existing Mac OS 9 applications to work in Mac OS X. That's why major Mac OS 9 applications, such as AppleWorks and Microsoft Office, are Carbonized applications rather than Cocoa ones. Second, some developers find it preferable even when they're starting from scratch. REALbasic, for example, is a programming language that creates Carbonized applications for Mac OS X.

Making matters a bit more complicated, Carbon applications have two distinct subcategories. Their difference depends on an OS feature called a library manager. Library managers are special programs that prepare other, more "ordinary" programs to be run. Library managers exist in both Mac OS 9 and Mac OS X. Carbon applications in Mac OS X can use two different types of library managers. Bear with me as I introduce some esoteric jargon:

- **CFM (code fragment manager)** is essentially the same as the CFM used in Mac OS 9. It works with an application's executable binary code, which is in a format called **PEF** (for Preferred Executable Format). Unfortunately, this format is not preferred in Mac OS X.

- **Dyld (dynamic link editor)** is the manager that only Mac OS X uses. It works with an executable binary-code format called Mach-O. Mach-O format is what Mac OS X's kernel uses; it is derived from Unix.

Exactly what all these managers and formats do, and how they differ, need not concern you. What does matter is the following:

- **CFM is not optimized for Mac OS X.** Mac OS X is a native dyld platform. This means that for CFM-based programs to work, they must bridge to the dyld platform via Carbon routines. This bridging step takes time, resulting in a performance penalty that dyld-based software does not have—that is, CFM-based software will not run as fast in Mac OS X as the same program would if it had been written to use dyld instead.

The most visible sign of this bridging is the LaunchCFMApp application. The file itself is located in /System/Library/Frameworks/Carbon.framework/ Versions/A/Support/LaunchCFMApp. More important, this file (which is an updated version of the Mac OS 9 Code Fragment Manager) is used every time you launch a CFM-based application. In fact, if you launch ProcessViewer and look at the list of open applications in User Processes, you won't see any of the CFM-based applications by name. Instead, you will see multiple instances of LaunchCFMApp . This intermediary causes the performance hit for CFM-based applications. LaunchCFMApp is itself a Mach-O program.

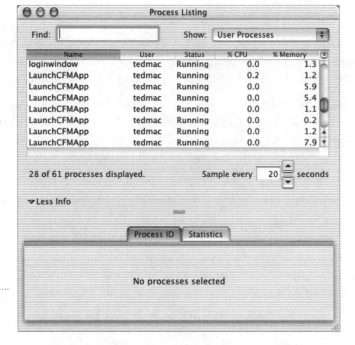

**Figure 4.1**

LaunchCFM App items in Process Viewer.

Also, CFM applications, although they can be packages, may still use the single file format common in Mac OS 9. Thus, if you open the contextual menu for an application and no Show Package Contents command is listed, the application is almost certainly a CFM application. Dyld software will always use the preferred package format.

**SEE:**  • "Technically Speaking: Understanding Packages," in Chapter 2.

• **Dyld (Mach-O) software cannot run in Mac OS 9.** So why bother with CFM at all? Two reasons. First, it may be easier to convert an existing Mac OS 9 application to its CFM-based cousin than to a dyld one. Second, CFM-based programs can run equally well in Mac OS 9 and Mac OS X. Thus, you need only one application for both environments. Dyld-based software runs only in Mac OS X. By the way, Cocoa-based software also uses Mach-O.

For those who want a dyld-based Carbon program to run in Mac OS 9 and Mac OS X, a solution is to create two versions of the application, a CFM version and a dyld version. These versions can be combined into an application package that appears as a single file in the Finder. When the application is launched in Mac OS 9, however, the CFM version will be used; in Mac OS X, the dyld version will run. This situation allows the optimized version for each OS to be used with its respective OS. Actually, this type of division is more common with Classic and Carbon software versions in the same package, as described a bit later in this chapter.

When a program is said to be a native Mac OS X program, this generally means that it is either a Cocoa program or a dyld Carbon one (although some people consider any Carbon application to be native).

---

**TAKE NOTE** ▶ **Faceless Applications; Hidden Applications**

Some applications run without an icon in the Dock or without being listed in the Force Quit window. Such applications are often called faceless applications, as they run without any user interface. The log-in window application, discussed in Chapter 5, is an example.

You can also simulate the effect of a true faceless application by setting it to launch at log in (via choosing it in the Login Items list in the Login System Preferences window, and checking the Hide checkbox). Installers for some applications automatically set up software this way. iTunes does this with the iTunes Helper application (which is actually located within the iTunes package).

Be careful when you hide an item in the list. You might lose its functionality. When I chose to hide items that created menus in the menu bar, for example, the menus no longer appeared.

This Login Items type of hiding is separate from hiding the windows of open applications, as you can do by holding down the Command and Option keys when clicking an application icon in the Dock. This technique hides the windows of all open applications except the one you clicked. Shareware utilities such as ASM, which mimics the Mac OS 9 Application menu, offer similar window-hiding options.

**SEE:**   • "Take Note: Dock and Finder Shortcuts," in Chapter 3, for more details.

---

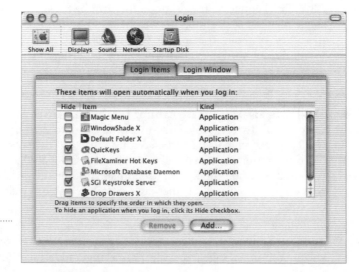

*Figure 4.2*

*Note the Hide checkboxes in the Login Items list.*

**TAKE NOTE** ▶ **Identifying Application Formats**

Suppose that you needed to know whether a given application is Cocoa, Carbon-cfm, Carbon-dlyd, or Classic. What's the fastest way to find out? A utility called Get Info for App works great—if it works (in the most recent versions of Mac OS X it kept crashing on me). Just drag the application in question to the Get Info for App icon, and a window will open that shows you what you want to know.

For TextEdit, for example, you will see that the Framework is Cocoa and the Binary Kind is Mach-O.

On the other hand, if you select Internet Explorer, the window will say Carbon for the Framework and CFM for the Binary Kind.

As an alternative, you can use the ever-handy XRay. It does not distinguish between CFM vs. Mach-O, but it does distinguish between Cocoa, Carbon, and Classic applications.

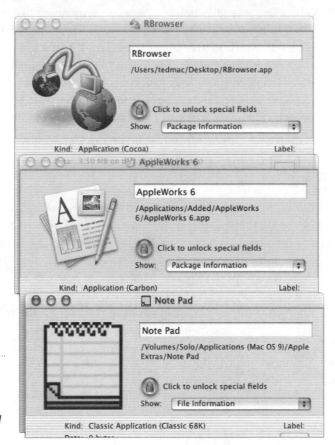

*Figure 4.3*

*Three applications as listed in XRay. Note the Kind line distinction of Cocoa, Carbon, and Classic 68K.*

## Classic

Mac OS 9 programs that have not been Carbonized can still run in Mac OS X, but this capability requires a special trick. Mac OS X needs to launch what is called the Classic environment. I discuss this topic in detail in Chapter 9. For now, here's a brief summary of what happens. When you launch Classic, a working version of Mac OS 9 (including extensions and control panels) is loaded. The Mac OS 9 application then runs in this environment. In many ways, going back and forth between the two environments is almost seamless. You can cut and paste from a Classic program to a Mac OS X one, for example. Classic can even borrow your Mac OS X Internet and printer settings, so Classic applications can maintain access to the Web and to your connected printers.

Still, running a program in Classic has a huge disadvantage: You are not really using Mac OS X and thus get almost none of the advantages of running Mac OS X. Running an application in Classic is pretty much like running it in Mac OS 9, and maybe even a bit worse; it will likely run slower and have more potential conflicts than if you booted from Mac OS 9. The sole advantage of Classic is that it allows you to run Mac OS 9 programs that otherwise would not run in Mac OS X. As time goes by, however, you will want to find Mac OS X alternatives to these applications (or hope that Mac OS X versions of them get released) so that you can reduce your use of Classic to zero.

**SEE:**  • **Chapter 9 for more information on the Classic environment.**

## Java

Mac OS X can run programs written in Java. Most users, if they are familiar with Java at all, think of it as being something used by certain Web sites and accessed from your Web browser. But Java software can be created to run independently of a browser. and Mac OS X is set to do this. Apple has even provided a means for developers to incorporate Mac OS X's Aqua interface into Java code so that a Java application can have the look and feel of a typical Mac OS X application. The main advantage to Java, for the programmer, is that Java is platform-independent. The same Java software (with some minor modifications to accommodate the platform's user interface) can run on any computer that supports the use of Java, including a Windows PC. At present, few Java applications are available for Mac OS X. The jury is still out as to whether Java will someday play a significant role in Mac OS X.

## Putting it together

All these application environments are unified within the Aqua interface. There are signs—some subtle, some obvious—that occur when you shift from Classic to Carbon to Cocoa to Java applications. Still, one of the great successes of Mac OS X is that you can accomplish these switches almost effortlessly. And at least most of the time, it all works as Apple intended.

One other type of application that can run in Mac OS X: Unix software. I discuss it in "Darwin" later in this chapter.

# The Layers of Mac OS X: Graphics Services

Running underneath the application layer is a set of core technologies that create the elements you see on the screen: fonts, graphics, movies, and so on. As a troubleshooter, you need not be concerned with the inner workings of this layer. Still, you should be familiar with the terminology.

## Quartz

Quartz is the name of the technology used to create all two-dimensional images, including text. It is quite different from the technology used in Mac OS 9, which is called QuickDraw. Some of the most spectacular differences show up when you work with text. First, Quartz uses PDF (Portable Document Format) as a native format for documents. This format is the one employed by Acrobat Reader. Almost anything you create—in any application—can easily be saved as a PDF document. This capability in turn makes it easy for anyone to view these documents, even on Windows PCs, with all fonts, formatting, and graphics preserved intact. As PDF is a PostScript-aware format, it also makes it easy to render any PDF document to a PostScript printer. Quartz also allows virtually all text in Mac OS X to have a smoothed (antialiased) look.

Also of relevance is **Apple Type Solution** (or ATS). This technology unifies the display of fonts, no matter what format they may have (TrueType, PostScript, and so on), as well as provides the basis for multiple-language support.

---

**TECHNICALLY SPEAKING ▶ ATSUI and Unicode**

Some more Apple jargon:

**ATS** Apple Type Solution (ATS) manages fonts in Mac OS X. It checks for all fonts in Mac OS X's Library/Fonts folders, as well as in the Classic System Folder, and prepares them for use in Mac OS X applications.

**ATSUI** (Apple Type Services for Unicode Imaging) is the technology used for printing and displaying Unicode text in Mac OS X.

*continues on next page*

> **TECHNICALLY SPEAKING** ▶ **ATSUI and Unicode**   *continued*
>
> **Unicode** is Apple's name for the font technology Mac OS X uses for multiple-language support. Unicode, for example, allows you to use multiple languages in applications such as Mail, TextEdit, and the Finder. Unicode-enabled programs allow text characters to be displayed consistently regardless of the language and language software selected for display, due to a single worldwide character set that works with most of the world's languages. See "Fonts in Mac OS X" later in this chapter for more information on fonts.
>
> Note: The display of Unicode text in the Finder has a bug; certain characters in file names appear correctly in Mac OS 9 but appear as garbled text in Mac OS X.

## Multimedia: OpenGL and QuickTime

Three-dimensional graphics use Mac OS X's OpenGL software, which comes into play mainly with 3-D game software.

Mac OS X also supports QuickTime for multimedia. This software is used for playing QuickTime movies, such as the popular movie trailers available on Apple's QuickTime Web site.

On a related note, Mac OS X also handles a variety of sound formats and has DVD movie support.

# The Layers of Mac OS X: Darwin

Now you delve into the deepest layers of Mac OS X. The umbrella name for this layer is Darwin. Darwin is open-source code, which means that Apple makes the code publicly available (http://www.publicsource.apple.com/). This availability allows developers to better understand the code as well as modify and improve it. Darwin is sometimes referred to more generically as the Mac OS X kernel environment.

In discussing the layers of Mac OS X, what determines whether something is considered to be at a higher or lower level? The answer is that as a general rule, a component at a lower level is used by all higher-level layers. But the converse is not necessarily true. Thus, an application, whether it is Carbon and Cocoa, uses the core Darwin technology, but Darwin can function without a need for any additional application layer.

Darwin is the core of Mac OS X. The Darwin kernel consists mainly of the FreeBSD and Mach 3.0 technologies. Darwin includes various core services, such as those involved in networking and device drivers. I discuss this topic in more detail in Chapter 5, as I walk through the startup sequence of events. Beyond that, as an end-user troubleshooter, you need be aware only of the two key kernel components.

## Mach

As a troubleshooter, you will rarely, if ever, be working directly with Mach code. Nonetheless, it is important to understand its basic concepts. Mach refers to the code that handles the most fundamental aspects of Mac OS X. It is also responsible for several of Mac OS X's most touted benefits:

**Preemptive multitasking.** This term refers to how Mac OS X can schedule its processor activity among different open applications or processes. (All applications are processes, but not all processes are user-accessible applications.) Mac OS 9 used *cooperative multitasking*, which was not very intelligent. In Mac OS 9, unimportant but CPU-intensive background events might take up so much of a processor's time that more important activities in the foreground would become sluggish and unresponsive. Neither you nor the OS could do much about this situation. Mac OS X's Mach has much more flexibility in how it handles these matters. In essence, it can preempt any running process, giving something else more attention. It can note intelligently what activities are in the foreground and make sure that they get the lion's share of attention. Developers can also write hooks in their software to increase (or decrease) the priority that their software should get. As a result, operations that need the most processor activity at any moment should get the most, enhancing overall performance. This is a good thing.

A related benefit of Mac OS X's multitasking capability is that fewer modal functions prevent you from doing other tasks. That is, Mac OS X offers *multithreading*. In Mac OS 9, when you launched an application, you typically had to wait for it to finish launching before you could do anything else. This process could take a minute or two. Mac OS X doesn't have these waiting games. Instead, once a program starts to launch, you can begin another activity right away. You could check your email while waiting for Classic to launch and Photoshop to open, for example.

**Protected memory.** Metaphorically, protected memory means that the memory assigned to each open process is entirely separate (protected) from that of every other open process. The result is that systemwide crashes should almost vanish from the landscape. If and when an application crashes, it should cause only the application itself to go belly up; the rest of the operating system should remain functional. In the event that a program freezes (such as when you get an endlessly spinning beach-ball pointer), you will still be able to switch to a different program (such as the Finder) and continue to work as normal, even while the problem application remains frozen. This would be impossible to do in Mac OS 9. Protected memory also means that you should almost never need to restart the Mac to recover from a crash.

**Virtual memory.** Virtual memory allows you to simulate memory (RAM) via a special file on your hard drive. The main advantage of virtual memory is that if you do not have sufficient physical (built-in) RAM for what you want to do, you may get the RAM boost you need via virtual memory.

In Mac OS 9, you could choose to turn virtual memory on or off. As virtual memory tended to slow performance, it typically was wise to turn it off if your physical RAM was more than adequate for your needs. In Mac OS X, virtual memory must always remain on. Until you really start pushing its limits (by having way too many applications open at the same time, for example), you should not notice a performance hit.

Still, you can't have too much physical RAM. And given the current low prices of memory, I would recommend buying as much RAM as you think you will ever need—or more.

**Dynamic memory.** In Mac OS 9, the amount of memory assigned to an application is fixed (or *static*) when the program is launched. You assign this fixed amount via the Memory settings in the application's Get Info window. After an application was launched, if it needed more or less memory than was assigned to it when it launched, the OS could not do about the situation. You had some limited ability to add RAM assigned to an application, via an OS feature called temporary memory, but not all programs could use this feature, and it did not solve the problem completely.

One result is that you would still wind up getting "out of memory" error messages in Mac OS 9, even when you technically had enough memory available for what you wanted to do. The OS could not shuttle the memory around to where it was needed at the moment.

In Mac OS X, memory assignment is dynamic, which means that the amount of memory assigned to an application can be increased or decreased as needed. Thus, if an application is idling in the background and hogging unused memory, the OS can grab some of this memory for another application that needs it more. The combination of dynamic memory assignment and Mac OS X's virtual memory means that you should almost never see "out of memory" error and should have fewer memory-related system freezes and crashes.

Similarly, the total amount of memory available as virtual memory can be adjusted on the fly in Mac OS X. You could not do this in Mac OS 9. Making a change in the total size of virtual memory required restarting the Mac.

Mac OS X manages all these tasks and also allocates memory intelligently from physical and virtual memory so as to maximize the performance of each application.

Still, as I implied earlier, memory availability in Mac OS X is not infinite. If you push your Mac to its memory limits, you will start noticing an overall decline in the performance of everything. Applications may succeed in opening without an error message, but you will still see the effects of too-little memory. That's why getting more physical RAM still makes sense.

Note: Mac OS X's Show Info window still includes a Memory tab for Classic applications, because Classic applications do not take advantage of Mac OS X's dynamic-memory feature.

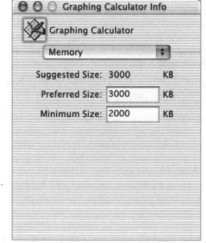

*Figure 4.4*

*The Memory tab of the Show Info window for a Classic application.*

## BSD (Unix)

BSD stands for Berkeley Software Distribution. It used to be called the Berkeley version of Unix but is now referred to as BSD, so referring to it as Unix is a bit incorrect. For all practical purposes, however, the term is synonymous with "a version of Unix." A portion of the Mac OS X kernel is based on FreeBSD, a version of BSD.

Note: Part of the BSD installation is optional when you install Mac OS X. The optional component is installed by default, however, unless you do a custom installation and choose not to install it. Overall, there is little cost (other than some disk space) in installing the optional files, and there are some Mac OS X features and some third-party software will not work without the files present. So I advise going with the default installation.

**SEE:** • **"Mac OS X: The down and up sides," in Chapter 1, for background on why Unix is included as part of Mac OS X.**

• **Chapter 2 for more information on installing Mac OS X.**

The integration of Unix in Mac OS X represents a significant change from Mac OS 9. In Mac OS 9, the System Folder was the OS. Except for a few invisible files (such as the Desktop files), all OS files were in the System Folder where they were easily accessible. In Mac OS X, the entire Unix layer remains largely invisible from the Aqua Finder. Thus, Mac OS X has a sort of secondary OS underneath the visible OS.

Occasionally, troubleshooting will require that you access or modify these hidden Unix files. One place where this requirement will likely crop up is file privileges. The Show Info window's Privileges settings are only a subset of the underlying Unix permissions that are really in use. The settings that you can't see can cause a variety of unexpected problems with opening, moving, or deleting files.

SEE: • "Technically Speaking: Privileges vs. Permissions," in Chapter 3, for more background on this subject.

• Chapter 6 for solving troubleshooting problems that require modifying privileges/permissions settings.

• Chapter 8 for more coverage of file sharing.

You access Unix commands and files in Mac OS X in three main ways:

**Terminal.** The Terminal application (included with Mac OS X) essentially provides a command-line environment where most Unix commands will work, just as though you were in a true Unix environment. Still, Terminal let's you know right away that you are not exactly in standard Unix, via its "Welcome to Darwin!" greeting. Any changes that you make in Terminal, such as renaming or deleting files, will modify the Aqua environment as well, so you need to be careful.

**Finder and text editors.** Tasks such as moving or deleting Unix files can usually be directly done from the Finder. You can also modify some Unix files via text editors such as TextEdit and BBEdit. In many cases, this will require you to log in as a root user or use a utility that makes invisible files visible.

**Aqua utilities.** Via an Aqua-based interface, many third-party utilities allow you to more easily do what otherwise would require you to use Terminal.

SEE: • "Take Note: Root Access," in Chapter 3, for more information on logging in as a root user.

• "Technically Speaking: Log Files and Cron Jobs," in Chapter 3, for an example of accessing Unix invisible files from the Finder and via GUI utilities.

• Chapters 3 and 6 for several examples of how to access the invisible Unix files from the Finder.

• Chapter 10 for more information on understanding Unix and using Terminal.

**TAKE NOTE ▶ What and Where Are the Unix Files?**

The "system" software for Unix is located at the root level of the Mac OS X volume. You can see these invisible directories and files from the Finder by using a utility, such as TinkerTool, to make invisible files visible (as described more in Chapter 6).

Or you can use Terminal. To do so from Terminal, type: <cd  />. Now type <ls>. This will list the contents of the root level.

Here is a sampler of the Unix directories and files found at the root level:

**bin** is the directory where most of the main Unix commands (or executables) are stored. These are the equivalent of what in Mac OS X would be called applications.

**dev** is where device drivers are stored. This are the files needed for your computer to interact with other hardware, such as external drives.

**etc** contains a mish-mash of administrative files.

**tmp** as its name implies, contains files created by programs that are only needed temporarily. Unfortunately, some programs may forget to delete these tmp files, so you may find some files here "permanently."

**usr** is another place where critical Unix OS commands are found, especially in /usr/bin. For example, the ditto and open commands are stored here.

**mach** is Unix's kernel, or core code, of the operating system. This is a file, not a directory. It is the software equivalent of the Mac's CPU, the central processing location for all Unix commands. Without the mach, nothing else would work.

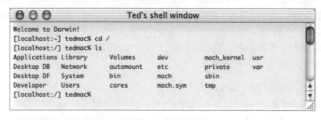

*Figure 4.5*

*Unix directories and files (for example, usr and bin) in the root directory, as viewed from (top) Terminal and (bottom) the Finder. The Unix items are normally invisible in the Finder; non-Unix visible items are also intermixed.*

**TECHNICALLY SPEAKING** ▶ **gdb: The Mac OS X Debugger**

In Mac OS 9, developers and some end users employed a program called MacsBug, mainly used by developers to debug software. In the event of a system crash, it could occasionally be used to recover from the crash without restarting. For this reason, and for a few other uses, it was a valuable troubleshooting tool.

MacsBug does not work in Mac OS X. The debugger in Mac OS X is gdb, a Unix tool accessed via Terminal. I will not be discussing its use further in this book.

**TAKE NOTE** ▶ **Folders vs. Directories**

In Finder windows, you will see many icons that look like folders. Indeed, that is the Desktop metaphor for what they are: containers that hold other items (documents, applications, or other folders).

**Folders vs. directories.** In Unix jargon, a folder is referred to as a directory. And as Mac OS X has a Unix basis, I sometimes find it convenient to refer to these folders as directories, especially so when I am in a Unix environment, such as the Terminal application. Even in the Finder, I occasionally refer to folders as directories. I typically refer to the user's Home *directory* rather than Home *folder*, for example, because of the special significance that the Home directory has in Unix. (The directory is a default location where you log in via Terminal, for example.)

Thus, an Aqua folder is best viewed as being a graphical representation of a Unix directory. Moving an item in to or out of a folder in the Finder changes the underlying directory in Unix. The terms *folder* and *directory* are sometimes used interchangeably when the distinction is not relevant.

Note that not all Unix directories are displayed in the Finder. Most of them remain invisible to the Finder, because a typical Mac OS X end user will rarely, if ever, need to manipulate these files—and modifying them accidentally could lead to serious problems, including taking down the whole system. Still, as I said in the main text, I will cover throughout this book the essentials of how to access these files for troubleshooting.

**Pathnames .** A *pathname* is what Unix uses to define the location of a file or directory. An *absolute pathname* starts at the top or root level of the hierarchy and works its way down. /System/Library/Fonts/Geneva.dfont, for example, is an absolute pathname. Slashes separate the directory names. An initial forward slash indicates that you are starting at the root level. This setup is important, for example, in distinguishing otherwise-identical fonts in multiple Fonts folders (such as (/Library/Fonts vs. /System/Library/Fonts).

A *relative pathname* is the path starting from your current location. Thus, if you were already in the System/Library directory, the relative path to the same font file would simply be Fonts/Geneva.dfont.

The ~ symbol means to start at the top of the current Home directory. Thus, ~/Library/Fonts mean to look in the Fonts folder inside the Library folder inside your Home directory.

Because the forward slash is used in all these designations, you should not use the forward slash in the actual name of a file or folder in Mac OS X (much as the colon was not permitted in file/folder names in Mac OS 9).

# Domains: An Overview

Having dissected the layers of Mac OS X, it's time to take Mac OS X apart again, but from a different perspective. In this section, you will examine why Mac OS X has multiple Library folders/directories. You will learn the different functions of each folder and directory and get an overview of the files and folders contained within them.

First, a bit of background. Mac OS X was born when Apple acquired the NeXT OS, often referred to as OpenStep, back in 1997. This was when Steve Jobs, the founder of Apple and NeXT, returned to Apple. The result is that much of the higher-level OS software is based on NeXT code. In fact, it is not unusual to peek inside some System software file and see a reference to NeXT or OpenStep.

At a practical level, this means that the System Folder of Mac OS 9 is gone from Mac OS X. Gone also are the control panels and extensions that populated the System Folder. Instead, you have the Library folder—or, more precisely, a multitude of Library folders. The reason relates to the fact that Mac OS X is inherently a multiple-user system. Different Library folders correspond to different domains or levels of the OS. At the top level (System), for example, changes affect all users of the Mac in question. At the bottom level (User), changes affect only the individual user who is logged in.

The Classic Mac OS was designed with the idea that only one person (or perhaps one family) would be using a Mac. The ability to set up security so that Person A could not access the files created by Person B was irrelevant to the original Mac OS. Such security was added to the Mac OS eventually, but it was never completely successful. Mac OS X, in contrast, enforces a multiple-user setup. This setup can be annoying if you are the only person who intends to use your Mac, as you will have to deal with an overhead and complexity that you will never need. The up side is that if you ever do need a multiple-user setup, Mac OS X is far better equipped to handle it than Mac OS 9 ever was.

**SEE:** • **"Take Note: Mac OS X and Multiple Users," in this chapter, for more detailed information.**

      • **"Mac OS X: The down and up sides," in Chapter 1, for more background on why Unix is included as part of Mac OS X.**

      • **Chapter 8 for more information on file sharing.**

**TAKE NOTE ▶ Mac OS X and Multiple Users**

To fully understand the why and where of all the Library folders in Mac OS X, you need to understand the multiple-user nature of Mac OS X. I cover this important topic from different perspectives at several points in this book.

**Mac OS 9.** Mac OS 9 is an inherently single-user system. All users share the same resources in the single System Folder on the drive. In fact, the basic OS makes no attempt to distinguish whether a different user is accessing the Mac. When you sit down to play a game on a Mac running Mac OS 9, you could be John Doe or Elton John; the Mac would not know or care about the difference. This is the way most Mac users use their Macs.

There are two main exceptions to this rule:

- **The Users & Groups tab of the File Sharing control panel** allows you to set up restrictions on who can access your Mac—either over a local network or a remote connection— and what sort of access such users can have. In particular, you can make some folders accessible and mark others as off-limits.

- **The Multiple Users control panel** allows you to set up your Mac so that different users have their own separate log-in passwords and—to some extent—maintain their own separate preferences settings (stored outside the System Folder). This arrangement allows separate users to access the same Mac, each with their own customized settings and their files secure from access by other users. Unfortunately, the Multiple Users feature has never been a complete success. Too often, you wind up tripping over problems that stem from the fact that the OS was never designed to cope with such matters. A given application may not be aware of Multiple Users'"rules" and may refuse to store its preferences settings anywhere other than the System Folder. This situation would block each user from maintaining his or her own customized preferences.

**Mac OS X.** Mac OS X is an inherently multiple-user system. You cannot turn this feature off.

Bear in mind that Unix was created as an OS for large networked systems. As such, it needed to allow hundreds of people to log in to the same system. At the same time, it needed to maintain a level of security such that no user could access the private data of another user. Just as important, no user (other than the few people who needed such access) could access the main system software needed to keep everything running. This restriction prevented any user from deliberately or inadvertently bringing down the entire system.

Mac OS X adopts the same Unix-based security features. In general, there are three levels of users:

- **Ordinary.** These users have access only to files that are in their own Home directories, unless an administrator specifically grants them access to other files.

- **Administrative.** These users have access to those sections of the OS designed to be shared among all users, such as the Applications folder. An ordinary user cannot add anything to or remove anything from the Applications folder. By default, even an administrative user cannot access certain areas used by the System that are considered essential to running the OS. Administrators can access these files via root access, however, if they have the root password.

*continues on next page*

**TAKE NOTE ▶ Mac OS X and Multiple Users**  *continued*

- **Root.** These users are the only ones who can modify and access the essential System software needed to keep the OS running, as well as anything else on the volume.

Thus, even as an administrative user, you don't own the OS in the way you do as a Mac OS 9 user. In particular, the OS may tell you that you don't have permission to move or delete certain files or to add files to certain folders. The truth is that you don't own Mac OS X; Mac OS X owns Mac OS X. You are just a privileged visitor.

The software needed to sort everything out is set up by default when you install Mac OS X. You don't do anything to start it working, and you can't turn it off.

When you install Mac OS X, you set up an initial account for yourself. You are given administrator status automatically. The OS also, by default, turns off the requirement to log in at startup. (You can change this setting via the Login System Preferences window). Thus, when the OS starts up, you are not required to enter a password, so it may appear that no security is being enforced. But don't be fooled. The security features are indeed in effect.

SEE:  • "Privileges," in Chapter 3 (especially "Take Note: Root Access"), for more information on privileges settings and logging in as a root user.
- Chapter 6 for solving troubleshooting problems that require modifying privileges/permissions settings.
- Chapter 8 for more coverage of permissions and file sharing.

## System domain

The first Library folder on your tour is at the root level of the Mac OS X volume. To get there, open any Finder window. In the toolbar of the window that appears, click the Computer button. If no toolbar is present, click the oval icon in the top-right corner of the window to reveal it. Alternatively, you can Command-click the name of the window in the title bar and, from the pop-up menu that appears, choose the bottom item (the name of your computer). You almost always have multiple ways to do the same thing in Mac OS X!

SEE:  • Chapter 3, especially "Toolbar and Finder views," for more background on navigating Finder windows and using the toolbar.

Within the Computer window, double-click the volume icon that is the current Mac OS X startup volume. You are now at the root level of Mac OS X. Locate the folder called System; it should have an X on it. Double-click the icon. Inside will be a folder called Library. You have now arrived at the first stop on your tour.

**TAKE NOTE ▶ The Computer and "Root Level" Windows**

**The Computer window.** If you click the Computer icon in the toolbar of a Finder window, the Computer level window opens. This window lists all mounted volumes, including hard drives, CD-ROMs, and iDisks. It also includes the Network item/icon, as described elsewhere in this chapter.

A hard drive can be divided into multiple *partitions*. In this case, each partition functions almost as though it were a separate drive and will have a separate listing in this window. The term *volume* refers to a drive, a partition of a drive, or anything else that can be mounted in Mac OS X.

The name of the Computer window will not be Computer but the name you assigned to your computer when you first set up Mac OS X. This name is accessible (and editable) from the Network Identity tab of the Sharing System Preferences window.

The icons at the Computer level are also represented by identically named icons on the right border of the Desktop (assuming you enabled the feature to show these icons on the Desktop via the Finder's Preferences command).

**The root level of the startup volume.** If you double-click any of the icons in the Computer window, you are taken to the root level of that volume. If you go to the root level of the volume that is the current Mac OS X startup volume, the window that appears will contain at least four folders:

- **System.** This is the folder that holds "core" Mac OS X software, as described in the main text.
- **Library.** This is the folder that contains "local domain" Mac OS X software, as described in the main text.
- **Applications.** This folder houses all the applications initially installed by Mac OS X, as well as any other applications that may have been installed there by you or by third-party installers. The Utilities folder is also within this folder.
- **Users.** This folder contains the "home" directories for each user with an account on the volume. The Shared directory is also here.

If Mac OS 9 is installed on this volume, there will also be a folder called **System Folder**; it may have a 9 icon on it. This folder is *not* the Mac OS X System folder/directory referred to in the main text! In addition, there will be a folder called **Applications (Mac OS 9)**. This contains application software installed by Mac OS 9, such as SimpleText and QuickTime Player.

If you installed the software from the Developer Tools CD, a folder named **Developer** is located at the root level.

Finally, the Unix directories (normally invisible in the Finder) are located here.

**The root level of other volumes.** If you click any of the other volume icons in the Computer window, you will similarly go to the root level of those volumes. What is located in each one depends, of course, on the nature of the volume. It could be another Mac OS X volume, a Mac OS 9 volume, or simply a volume that stores files (with no OS software at all).

*continues on next page*

In the structure of Mac OS X, the root level volume of the startup volume has a special status. For example, the "root level" in Terminal (as covered in Chapter 10) refers only to the Mac OS X startup volume's root level. Other volumes are structured differently. For example, select the Finder's Go to Folder command and type: </Volumes>. This will take you to the Unix Volumes directory, located at the startup volume's root level. Here you will see a listing for every mounted volume except the startup volume.

SEE:  • "Take Note: What and Where are the Unix Files?" earlier in this chapter.

• Chapter 2 for more information on partitioning a drive.

• Chapters 3 and 8 for more on the Sharing System Preferences and Users folders.

*Figure 4.6*

*The Computer and root Mac OS X volume (R2D2 in this case) windows (normal views; with invisible items invisible). Note: Mac OS 9 is not installed on R2D2.*

If the Mac OS X System folder strikes you as being the Mac OS X equivalent of the Mac OS 9 System Folder, you are more or less correct. The Library folder here contains the files that are essential to the operation of the OS. Every file in this folder is installed by the Mac OS X Installer itself (or another Apple-supplied updater). The contents of this folder rarely get modified, other than by an update to the OS. In fact, Apple warns against modifying the contents, as doing so could result in failure to start up the computer. If you even try to make a change in this folder, you will be blocked from doing so, getting a message such as "The item could not be moved because Library cannot be modified." Only users with root access can make changes.

**SEE:** • "Take Note: Mac OS X and Multiple Users," earlier in this chapter, for background.

Occasionally, you will want to modify files in this folder; I mention examples elsewhere in this book. But by and large, I concur with Apple's assessment: Troubleshooting will rarely require modifying the contents of this folder.

**SEE:** • "Miscellaneous other installation problems," in Chapter 2, for a mention of folders, other than Library, that you may find at the root level of the Mac OS X System folder.

## Local domain

Return again to the root level of the drive. You will see a folder called Library. Inside it is an assortment of folders—some with the same names as the ones in the /System/Library folder.

The contents of this Library folder are populated when you install Mac OS X. But unlike the System/Library folder, it can be modified directly by any administrative user—as well as by installer applications for third-party software.

The function of this Library folder is to contain all the resources to be shared by all the local users of the computer. Note: A local user is anyone who has physical access to the computer and can log into it directly.

## User domain

Next, click the button in the toolbar that says Home. This button will take you to the top level of the directory for the person who is logged in (presumably, you!).

*Figure 4.7*

*Inside my Users folder.*

Another way you could get Home is to open the Users folder at the root level of Mac OS X. Inside, you will see at least two folders:

- **Shared.** The Shared folder houses files that any user can access and modify.

**SEE:** • Chapters 6 and 8  for more information on the Shared folder and file sharing.

- **Home.** This folder will have the name you assigned when you first set up the OS (such as landau). If you have created more than one user, you will find additional folders with those user names. Your folder (if you are the logged-in user) will have a house icon; the others will have a generic folder icon. If you open your own folder, you will be at the same place as if you clicked the Home button.

Inside your Home folder will be a third Library folder. Every user will have a comparable Library folder. These user-level Library folders contain the resources specific to each user. Any personal preferences you set for an application will be stored here. That way, when you log in, those preferences will be in effect. When another user logs in, the preferences set by that user will be in effect instead.

## Network domain

Your drive has a fourth-level Library folder. To find it, return to the Computer window, and double-click the globe icon called Network. In the window that appears will be yet another Library folder.

If you open this Library folder, it is likely to be empty. The folder comes into play only if you are on a network that is connected to a central server (such as a computer running Mac OS X Server software). In such a case, this Library folder would contain the shared resources (usually stored on the server itself) that can be used by all those on the server's network.

At this level, you will also find an alias icon called Servers. If you double-click this icon, you will see a list of networks to which you can connect. Typically, if you are not on any network, the only thing that will appear is an icon called localhost. If you double-click this icon, you will be back at the root level of your Mac OS X volume.

I will not be discussing troubleshooting server networks in this book, as that is best left to server administrators, not end users. Thus, I will rarely mention the Network domain again.

**TAKE NOTE ▶ Multiple Folders of the Same Name in Multiple Library Folders**

As noted in the main text, several folders (such as Fonts and Sounds) appear in more than one Library folder. The reason for these multiple folders, including the multiple Library folders themselves, is for the different levels of access that each folder provides. To make this arrangement as clear as possible, here is an overview, using the different Fonts folders as a specific example.

- **User [~/Library/Fonts/].** The fonts here are accessible only to that user. The user can add fonts to or remove fonts from this folder, as desired. This method is how a nonadministrative user can access new fonts.

- **Local [/Library/Fonts/].** Any local user of the computer can use fonts installed in this folder. A set of these fonts is installed by the OS. The OS does not require these additional fonts for system operation, however. An admin user can modify the contents of this folder, which is the recommended location for fonts that are shared among applications and users.

- **System [/System/Library/Fonts/].** This folder contains the essential fonts required for the OS to run (such as the ones needed for creating menus and dialog-box text). These fonts should not be altered or removed.

- **Network [/Network/Library/Fonts/].** The Network folder is for fonts shared among all users of a local area network. This feature normally is used on network file servers under the control of a network administrator.

- **Classic [/System Folder/Fonts/].** This folder contains fonts used by the Classic environment. If more than one Mac OS 9.x System Folder is present, only fonts in the System Folder selected in the Classic pane of the System Preferences window are used. Mac OS X applications can use these fonts even when the Classic environment is not active. These fonts can be accessed even if they are in locations other than the Fonts folder.

  Classic applications can access only fonts in the Classic System Folder, however, not those stored in Mac OS X Fonts folders. An exception: The third-party software Suitcase includes an extension called Suitcase Bridge. When installed in the Classic System Folder, this extension allows fonts activated in Mac OS X to be available to Classic applications.

Fonts may also be stored in association with specific applications. Inside the Office folder of the Microsoft Office X folder, for example, is a folder called Fonts. This folder contains an assortment of fonts that get installed when you install Microsoft Office. The fonts are copied to the Fonts folder of your Home directory the first time you launch Office.

SEE: • "Take Note: Problems with Duplicate Fonts in Fonts folders," later in this chapter, for related information.

# The Libraries of Mac OS X: /System/Library

I now take a more detailed look at the contents of each of the main Library folders in Mac OS X, starting with /System/Library. The number and variety of files and folders in any of these Library folders are far too great for me to cite even a bare majority of them. so I will limit the list to the ones that are most relevant for any troubleshooting you may have to do. Feel free to open these folders and browse around yourself, however. There is no fee for just looking.

**Figure 4.8**

*The /System/Library folder (partial view; items A through I seen).*

The /System/Library folder contains the essential OS software. Inside this folder, you will find the following folders.

## Core Services

Core Services is the most critical folder in the /System/Library folder. Like the System folder itself, it has an X on it to denote its special status. It contains the BootX file, required for starting up from Mac OS X (as described in Chapter 5).

The folder also contains the Dock, Finder Classic Startup, Help Viewer, and Software Update applications, as well as the loginwindow process (also covered in Chapter 5) and the Menu Extras (covered in Chapter 3). There are also fake Mac OS 9 Finder and System files, created so that Carbon applications that expect to see these Mac OS 9-type files will "find" them. Yes, you will see the word Fake used in the Version description in the files' Show Info windows.

The SystemVersion.plist file determines what Mac OS X version is listed in the About This Mac window.

**SEE:** • " Installation refuses to run," in Chapter 2, for more on this plist file.

*Figure 4.9*

*Some of the files and directories in the Core Services folder.*

# CFMSupport

CFMSupport contains software used for running Carbon applications. The CarbonLib file is in this folder, for example.

# Extensions

This folder contains the kext (for kernel extension) files that load at startup, primarily acting as driver software for hardware peripherals (covered in Chapter 5). As their name implies, kext files are extensions of the basic kernel software that loads at startup.

# Fonts

This folder is one of several Fonts folders in Mac OS X. This one contains the fonts that are considered to be essential for Mac OS X.

**SEE:** • "Take Note: Multiple Folders of the Same Name in Multiple Library Folders," earlier in this chapter.

## Frameworks

Frameworks are an important component of Mac OS X, but you will have little reason to work with them directly in troubleshooting.

Briefly, frameworks are the Mac OS X equivalents of Mac OS 9's dynamic shared libraries, which means that they contain code that can be used by more than one application simultaneously. The basic idea is to eliminate the need to repeat code that will be used by multiple applications.

Frameworks have the structure of package files, although they appear to be ordinary folders and can be opened without the Show Package Contents contextual menu. A framework package can contain multiple versions of the shared software; applications that require the newer version can access it, and those that are incompatible with the newer version will be able to access the older version.

Frameworks can occur in other locations besides this folder. The ones in this folder are simply the ones that are most essential for the OS.

SEE:  • Technically Speaking: "Understanding Packages," in Chapter 2, for more details on packages.

## PreferencePanes

This folder contains the panes that you access via the System Preferences application.

SEE:  • "System Preferences," in Chapter 3.

## Printers

This folder contains files needed for printers to work with Mac OS X. Among other things, it contains the PPD and PDE files required for LaserWriter printers in Mac OS X.

SEE:  • Chapter 7 for more information on printing, including details on PPD and PDE files.

## QuickTime

This folder contains some QuickTime-related software, such as the QuickTime Updater application.

## ScreenSavers

This folder contains the basic screen-saver options (Beach, Forest, and so on), which you accessed from the Screen Saver System Preferences window.

## Services

This folder contains software needed for some of Mac OS X's Services feature, which allows you to access certain features of one application while you are in another application. You typically access this feature via the Services command in the menu that has the name of the active application (such as Finder, if Finder is the active application). If this feature is working, it allows you to open TextEdit with the selected text of your open application already pasted into an untitled TextEdit document, for example. This feature works only if the given applications support Services technology. Most do not, so most often, these options will be dimmed.

In the current context, Services also refers to some options that can be incorporated into any Cocoa application. As of Mac OS X 10.1, just two such Services are stored here: AppleSpell and Summary. AppleSpell, for example, allows a developer to include a spelling-checking feature in his application without having to write his own code.

## Sounds

This folder contains the sound files (in AIFF format) that are listed in the Alerts tab of the Sound System Preferences window.

Note: AIFF is one of several sound formats supported by Mac OS X. Another is the well-known MP3 format, commonly used for music files stored on your drive and used by iTunes and iPod.

## StartupItems

This important folder contains the various protocols that load at startup while you wait for the log-in window and Desktop to appear. These items include the Apache Web server, AppleShare, AppleTalk, Networking, and Network Time.

**SEE:** • **Chapter 5 for more information on the startup sequence.**

# The Libraries of Mac OS X: /Library

As I explained earlier in this chapter, this folder stores files that are available to all local users and that can be modified by an administrative user. Inside this folder, you will find the following folders.

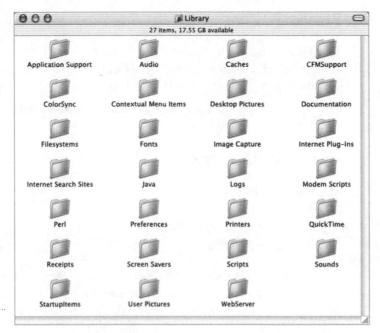

●●●                    Library
27 items, 17.55 GB available

Application Support    Audio    Caches    CFMSupport

ColorSync    Contextual Menu Items    Desktop Pictures    Documentation

Filesystems    Fonts    Image Capture    Internet Plug-Ins

Internet Search Sites    Java    Logs    Modem Scripts

Perl    Preferences    Printers    QuickTime

Receipts    Screen Savers    Scripts    Sounds

StartupItems    User Pictures    WebServer

*Figure 4.10*

*The /Library folder.*

# Application Support

This folder contains accessory software for various applications, such as the StuffIt Engine.cfm file, used by StuffIt compression software.

# ColorSync

The profiles you create via the ColorSync System Preferences window are stored here.

# Contextual Menu Items

Third-party software that adds items to Mac OS X's contextual-menu feature (accessed when you Control-click an item) is stored here.

# Desktop Pictures

The background pictures that you can select via the Desktop System Preferences window are stored here.

# Documentation

Some programs that provide Read Me files and other documentation, accessed via commands within the application (such as Help), store their documentation files here.

## Fonts

This folder is similar in function to the Fonts folder in /System/Library, except that these fonts are not considered to be essential. As an administrator, you can add fonts to or remove fonts from this folder.

SEE:   • **"Take Note: Multiple Folders of the Same Name in Multiple Library Folders," earlier in this chapter.**

## Internet Plug-Ins

Plug-ins used with your browser, such as the QuickTime and Shockwave plug-ins, are stored here.

## Modem Scripts

This folder is the location of the modem scripts that you can choose from the Modem pop-up menu. You specify these scripts in the Modem tab for the Internal Modem protocol in the Network System Preferences window. (Whew—that was a mouthful of terminology!)

SEE:   • **"Take Note: Modem Scripts," in Chapter 8, for related information.**

## Preferences

A few systemwide preferences (.plist) files are stored here, such as those for loginwindow. In general, you will have little reason to modify preferences files in this folder.

SEE:   • **"Take Note: Preferences Files in Mac OS X," in Chapter 3, for more information on .plist files.**
        • **Chapter 5 for more information on loginwindow.**

## Printers

This folder is where you will find support software for printers, in addition to the LaserWriter support files located in System/Library/Printers. In particular, drivers for Epson, Hewlett-Packard, and Lexmark printers are stored here.

SEE:   • **Chapter 7 for more information on printing, including details on PPD and PDE files.**

## Receipts

Every time you install a Mac OS X update, a receipt .pkg file for the update is stored in this folder. In certain situations, as discussed in Chapter 2, the OS (especially Software Update) uses these files as a means of knowing that a given update has been installed.

### StartupItems

This folder is the equivalent of the StartupItems folder in /System/Library. The main difference is that this folder is used for third-party software, as opposed to the preinstalled Mac OS X items stored in the /System/Library folder. If you install Timbuktu Pro, it will install a Startup Item in this folder. This item is needed for the Timbuktu software to be active at startup, no matter which user logs in. The actual Timbuktu application is located elsewhere, most likely in your Applications folder. Similarly, the Retrospect backup software also installs an folder, called RetroRunHelper, in the Startup Items folder.

# The Libraries of Mac OS X: /Users/"Home"/Library

This folder is the Library folder for files that are accessible to you only if you are the logged-in user. I have also referred to this via the < ~/Library> notation. Each user account has a separate folder of this kind. Where the expression "Home" appears, you actually substitute your user short name. The following list is selective, emphasizing folders that do not have duplicates in the Library folders that I have already discussed.

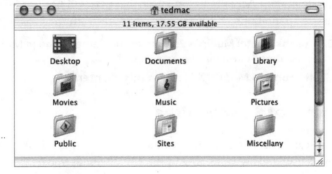

*Figure 4.11*

*My /Users/"Home"/ Library folder.*

### Application Support

This folder serves the same purpose as the Application Support folder in /Library, except that items in it are available only when the owner of the directory logs in and the directory becomes the current Home directory.

### Caches

Cache files, such as the cache files created by Internet Explorer (selected in the Advanced tab of Internet Explorer's Preferences window), are located here.

## Favorites

This folder is the location of the aliases that form the Favorites list, which you access by choosing from the Favorites command from the Finder's Go menu.

## Font Collections

Open a Cocoa application, such as TextEdit, and choose Font Panel from the Font submenu of the Format menu. The names in the Collections column on the far-left side of the Font Panel are stored in this folder. You can edit Collections items via the Edit Collections command in the Extras pop-up menu that appears at the bottom of the Font Panel.

**SEE:** • "Font Panel window," later in this chapter, for more information on the Font Panel.

## Fonts

This folder is the third of the main trio of Fonts folders. This one is used for fonts that will be accessible only when you are the user who is logged in.

Note: I copy third-party fonts from my Classic System Folder and place them here if I intend to use them in Mac OS X. This method seems to result in fewer problems than if I access the font from the Classic Fonts folder. (Mac OS X uses a font in a Mac OS X folder before it uses the same font in the Classic folder.) Actually, if you know that you will not need these fonts for Classic applications, it is best to delete them from the Classic System Folder.

**SEE:** • "Take Note: Multiple Folders of the Same Name in Multiple Library Folders," earlier in this chapter.

• "Fonts in Mac OS X," later in this chapter.

## Internet Search Sites

The search sites listed in Sherlock are stored in this folder. Sites that you add yourself will likely be located in the My Channel folder.

**SEE:** • "Sherlock," in Chapter 3, for more information on Internet search sites.

## Keychains

If you create a keychain file (which you access from the Keychain Access application in the Utilities folder), the data you create are stored here. A key-chain file is a convenience feature that stores passwords for any number of applications and services. The relevant software must support Apple's Keychain technology for this feature to work. If it does, when entering or creating a password, there may be a checkbox that says something such as "Add password to Keychain." Enable it, and the password is added to the Keychain data.

**SEE:** • **"Keychain Access," in Chapter 3.**

## Preference Panes

System Preferences panes that appear in the Other section of the System Preferences window are installed here. Typically, if you download a preferences pane, you install it simply by dragging it to this folder. The next time you launch System Preferences, this pane will be listed.

## Preferences

This folder is the single most important folder in this Library folder and the one you will likely access most often. It contains the preferences files created by most applications you use, so it stores any customized changes you make via the Preferences command of these applications. Some OS-level preferences files are also stored here (such as the ones used by the Finder, for example).

Whenever anything goes wrong with an application, a common early step in troubleshooting is deleting its preferences file, because preferences files may get corrupted when they get modified. Deleting the corrupted preferences file fixes the problem. The application automatically creates a new default version of the file the next time it launches.

Note: Don't get overly eager to delete preferences files. A few of these files contain important information that you cannot re-create easily after Mac OS X creates a new default version. The Favorites.html file (inside the Explorer folder in the Preferences folder), for example, contains all the URLs listed in Explorer's Favorites menu. You would not want to lose this list. To be safe, make a backup copy of any file you intend to delete so that you can restore the deleted file if it turns out not to be the source of your problem.

Most of the preferences files you will work with have the .plist extension.

**SEE:** • **"Take Note: Type and Creator vs. File Extensions" and "Take Note: Preferences Files in Mac OS X," in Chapter 3, for more background on preferences files.**
   • **"Delete preferences," in Chapter 5, for more information on trouble-shooting preferences-related problems.**

## Application-specific folders

Various applications, such as QuicKeys, may install their own folders in this Library folder.

**TAKE NOTE ▶ Other Folders in the Home Directory**

The Home folder/directory for each user contains other standard folders (installed by Mac OS X). These include:

**Public.** This folder is used for anything that you want to make publicly available. Any user who can access your computer, via a local network or even the Internet, will be able to access what is in the Public folder. Those users won't be able to modify anything, but they will be able to copy the files to their own drives.

**Documents.** Here is where you will save most documents that you create in applications. Most applications select this folder as the default location for saving documents. Some applications also install important data for using the application in this folder. AppleWorks installs an AppleWorks User Data folder here, for example. This folder contains information about the list of starting points that appears when you launch the program.

**Desktop.** This folder contains all the files and folders that are scattered about the Desktop. Because each user has his or her own Desktop folder, what appears on the Desktop will change depending on who is logged in. The Desktop folder also typically contains an alias called "Desktop (Mac OS 9)" if you have Mac OS 9 and Mac OS X installed on the same volume; the folder contains all the files and folders that are in the Mac OS 9 Desktop.

# Fonts in Mac OS X: Font Formats

Given the complexities involved, Apple did a great job of implementing fonts in Mac OS X. For the casual user of Mac OS X, working with fonts included in Mac OS X is as simple as selecting a font and using it. The user will also be able to switch to different languages with greater ease than in Mac OS 9. But for users who want to add and delete their own fonts, who have problems getting certain fonts to work, or who have troubleshooting symptoms that may be font-related, this section provides essential background.

More than one type of font can be used on a Macintosh. As font formats are not a Mac OS X-specific issue, I will not go into great detail on font formats for this Mac OS X book. But especially for those who are new to the subject, following is a brief overview.

## TrueType fonts

TrueType fonts are Apple's preferred type of font for Mac OS X. Most or all of the fonts that ship with Mac OS X are TrueType fonts. With TrueType, the font displays and prints smoothly (with no irregular jagged edges), no matter what size (such as 10 point vs. 13 point) or style (such as plain text vs. bold) you select.

For this feature to work, you need only a single font file for a given TrueType font. However, there will often be separate style variations within a font file (such as Times Italic and Times Bold). Without these variations present, you will not be able to select different styles for a given font in most Mac OS X applications.

Windows PCs can also use TrueType fonts, but a Windows TrueType font file has a somewhat different format from a Mac TrueType font. Fortunately, Mac OS X recognizes the following Windows versions of TrueType fonts: TrueType fonts (with the extension .ttf) and TrueType collections (with the extension .ttc). Note: Mac OS X believes that any font with a .ttf extension is a Windows TrueType font, so don't use this extension for Mac TrueType fonts.

## PostScript fonts

These font files contain the PostScript instructions needed to print to PostScript-supported printers. If you don't have a printer that includes PostScript support, you are better off avoiding PostScript fonts and sticking with TrueType ones, if possible. No PostScript fonts ship with Mac OS X, but you may have some in your Mac OS 9 System Folder or may have added PostScript fonts to your Mac OS X System folder.

In Mac OS 9, you could not display PostScript fonts on the screen. PostScript fonts are printer font files that contain instructions only for printing the text to a PostScript printer. A matching screen font version (either a bitmap or TrueType version) was needed for display. This screen/printer font pairing did not always work well. Often, what you saw on the screen was different from what was printed. This situation improved significantly with the release of Adobe Type Manager (ATM). This utility uses the PostScript printer's font instructions to display the fonts on the screen.

ATM does not work in Mac OS X, but it is not really needed. Whereas Mac OS 9 used a technology called QuickDraw to display fonts, Mac OS X uses Quartz. Quartz can display PostScript printer font information with no additional software (such as ATM) required. Note: ATM still works in Classic for displaying text in Classic applications.

You may still need at least one matching TrueType or bitmap font to get some PostScript fonts (with a type of LWFN, as displayed by a utility such as XRay) to be listed in Fonts menus. PostScript fonts of the SFNT type should work without any separate matching version needed.

PostScript Multiple Master fonts (font files that end with MM) are not yet supported in Mac OS X.

## OpenType fonts

This font format is relatively new, designed jointly by Microsoft and Adobe. A touted advantage of OpenType is that the same font file works on both the Mac and Windows platforms. At this writing, most Mac users still use TrueType instead of OpenType. OpenType fonts typically have the extension .otf. Microsoft started OpenType as an attempt to free itself from its dependence on Apple's TrueType. In a sense, the two formats are competitors.

## Bitmap fonts

These fonts are the oldest type of fonts and are rarely used anymore. These fonts require a separate file for each size of the font (Times 10, Times 12, Times 14, and so on). If you select a size that does not have a separate file, the font will be jagged.

Although you may get these fonts to work in Mac OS X, especially when you're working in Classic, they are not supported, so you should avoid them. Especially avoid older bitmapped versions of Chinese/Japanese/Korean/ Vietnamese language fonts; these fonts will not work in Mac OS X. Also, older bitmapped fonts of the type FONT are not supported. Fonts of the type NFNT are supported for Classic/QuickDraw applications but ignored by applications based on Cocoa (such as TextEdit).

---

**TAKE NOTE ▶ True Type fonts, Data-Forks, and the .dfont File Extension**

**Mac OS X TrueType and .dfont.** In Mac OS 9, a font file (like almost all Mac OS 9 files) has both a resource fork and a data fork. In brief, this fork distinction means that a file's main data (such as the text of a text document) is in the data fork, and the rest of its metadata (type and creator information, icon, and so on) would be stored as separate resources in its resource fork. Mac OS X's preference is to avoid resource forks and keep everything in the data fork. For fonts, Apple claims that this arrangement facilitates the capability of fonts to work in other OS systems, such as Windows, that do not recognize resource forks.

Data-fork-only font files must have the file extension .dfont. They may also have the file type dfon.

Essentially, a .dfont file is a TrueType font with all the resource-fork info moved to the data fork so that only the data fork remains. Mac OS X can read both old-style TrueType fonts and the new .dfont type. Apple clearly prefers the. dfont type, however, so that type is mainly what gets installed by Mac OS X. Old-style TrueType fonts may still be installed by third parties.

*continues on next page*

**TAKE NOTE** ▶ **True Type fonts, Data-Forks, and the .dfont File Extension** *continued*

**OpenType and Windows TrueType.** OpenType fonts and Windows TrueType fonts also have all their data in the data fork and do not have the additional resources of Macintosh fonts. The data fork for Mac OS X TrueType format, however, is different from the data fork for TrueType font format used by Microsoft Windows. The difference is that data-fork Mac OS X files contain all the resources associated with a Macintosh font, including FOND and NFNT resources, which are used with QuickDraw Text. OpenType and Windows TrueType fonts do not have this information.

**Want more info?** By the way, if you are unfamiliar with terms such as FOND and NFNT resources, you can check out my other book, *Sad Macs*, for more details. You can also experiment with Apple's ResEdit utility to see these resources in Mac OS 9. Or you can pick up any number of books that delve into the details of Mac typography, such as the chapter on fonts in the latest edition of *The Macintosh Bible* (Peachpit Press).

## Identifying font formats

You open a Fonts folder and see an assortment of fonts there. How can you tell which fonts are TrueType, PostScript, and Open Type? You can tell in several ways.

**File extension.** As I discussed earlier in this section, if a font file has an extension in its name, this extension can indicate the font type. The extension .otf, for example, is used for OpenType fonts.

**Icon.** You can identify PostScript printer font files via the file icons. Most PostScript printer font files have a distinctive icon such as the one shown in Figure 4.12.

*Figure 4.12*

*TrueType font vs. PostScript printer font file icons.*

**Show Info.** Unfortunately, the Show Info window rarely is helpful in identifying fonts. You may get lucky; the Kind line in the General Information tab may say something like Data-Fork TrueType Font. Just as often, however, it will simply say Document.

**Type/creator utility.** As I discuss in chapters 3 and 6, numerous Mac OS X utilities can list a file's type and creator information. In Mac OS 9, every file needs to have these codes assigned. In Mac OS X, this information is optional. Most files (including most fonts), however, still include this information. I have already noted the use of such types as FONT, NFONT, SFNT, and LWFN. Additionally, most TrueType fonts will have a type of FFIL and a creator of DMOV.

Utilities that can display type and creator data include XRay and FileXaminer.

**X Font Info.** The useful freeware utility X Font Info will identify whether a font is TrueType, bitmap, or a screen font for a PostScript font. It cannot open PostScript printer font files directly, however.

SEE:  • "Take Note: Type and Creator vs. File Extensions," in Chapter 3, for more information on type and creator codes.

*Figure 4.13*

*The FileXaminer utility, showing the type, creator, and extension data for two TrueType fonts: (left) a dfont file in the System folder Library and (right) a OS9-type file in the User's Home directory Library.*

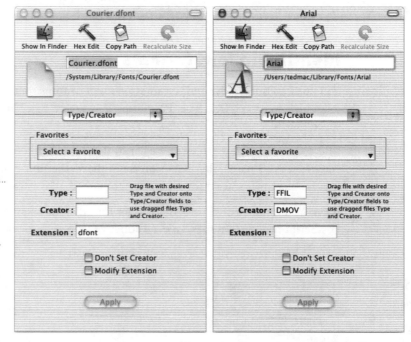

**TAKE NOTE ▶ Font Suitcases**

In Mac OS 9, a font could exist as an individual file or as one of several font files in a font suitcase. Mac OS X does not make this distinction as clearly. In particular, a font suitcase file in Mac OS X typically appears in the Finder exactly as a single font file does. In describing fonts in Mac OS X, Apple often uses the term *suitcase* to refer to virtually all font files.

Similarly, in Mac OS 9, if you wanted to remove a font file from a font suitcase, you could double-click the suitcase icon to open a window displaying its contents. Then you could drag a font file from the suitcase to remove it. You cannot do this in Mac OS X.

Thus, to remove a font from a suitcase file, the simplest approach is to reboot in Mac OS 9 and modify the font suitcase as desired via the Finder. Otherwise, you may find utilities that let you do this from Mac OS X (either in Mac OS X itself or via Classic), but I have not found any good ones so far.

A suitcase can contain unrelated fonts (such as Times and Helvetica). As a result, I prefer not to include mixed suitcases in Mac OS X, as the name of the font will likely give no clue about the variety of fonts within. In general, restrict suitcase files to the Mac OS 9 Classic System Folder, assuming that you need to use them at all.

More generally, it's wise to avoid as many Mac OS 9 Fonts as possible. These older fonts remain a too-common source of problems.

SEE: • "Check fonts," in Chapter 5, for more on troubleshooting font problems.

*Figure 4.14*

.................

*An Error message that may appear when you try to open a font in Mac OS X.*

*Figure 4.15*

.................

*(Left) TrueType font file icon and font suitcase icon as viewed when booted in Mac OS 9; (right) the icons for the same files after rebooting in Mac OS X.*

**TAKE NOTE ▶ Opening Font Files in the Finder**

In the Mac OS 9 Finder, if you double-clicked an individual font file, a window displayed what the characters in that font looked like. If you double-clicked a font suitcase, it opened to list all the fonts in that suitcase.

In Mac OS X, this method no longer works. Typically, double-clicking most types of font files in Mac OS X leads to an error message, stating, "There is no application available to open document {*name of font*}." If you happen to have the ancient Font/DA Mover utility on your drive, fonts may launch that utility in Classic; but don't expect it to work very well.

If you want to duplicate the Mac OS 9 Finder feature for fonts, the best solution I have found is a freeware utility called X Font Info. If you drag any font file or font suitcase to this application's icon, a window shows the name and kind (such as TrueType) of the font, as well as the alphabet in the characters of the font itself. In addition, two pop-up menus allow you to see this display in different styles (bold or italic, for example) and sizes. If the file you opened is a font suitcase that contains multiple fonts, the Font pop-up menu allows you to choose among the fonts in the suitcase.

You can go one better, however. When you double-click a font file, it can launch X Font Info, coming close to duplicating the Mac OS 9 Finder effect. To do this, follow these steps:

1. Select almost any TrueType font in the Mac OS X /Library or /System/Library folder.

2. Press Command-I to open the Show Info window for the font.

3. Choose Open with Application from the pop-up menu in the Show Info window.

   The default application listed will likely be Finder, nothing, or (amazingly!) the old pre-Mac OS 9 Font/DA Mover 4.1.

4. Click the box next to the application name and choose Other from the pop-up menu.

5. From the pop-up menu list, choose X Font Info as the new application. If X Font Info is not in the list, select the "Other…" item to locate it.

6. Click the Change All button so that all font files of the same type also open with this application.

Now, any similar font files that you double-click should launch X Font Info and display the font. If you selected an Mac OS 9-style TrueType font initially, this technique probably will not affect TrueType .dfont files. If so, simply repeat the procedure after selecting a .dfont file.

Overall, this method has worked well for me. There is a chance, however, that some font files may not display their Finder icon after you do this. And I have heard one report that this conversion prevented some fonts from being displayed in Microsoft Word and perhaps other applications. But this problem has never happened for me.

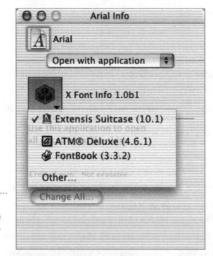

**Figure 4.16**

*The "Open with application" option in a font file's Show Info window.*

**Figure 4.17**

*The X Font Info window.*

# Fonts in Mac OS X: Working with Fonts

The following sections cover issues regarding using fonts in applications.

## Font Panel window

The Font Panel is a new way to display your Font choices in Mac OS X applications.

Most Carbonized applications running in Mac OS X, including AppleWorks and Microsoft Office, continue to provide user access to font choices in the same way that they did in Mac OS 9. That is, they use the same Font menus that they used in the Mac OS 9 versions of the application. There is no Font Panel here.

Mac OS X-only Cocoa-based applications, however, typically use the Font Panel. TextEdit is an example of an application that does so. To access the Font panel, choose Font Panel from the Font submenu of the Format menu (Command-T).

**The columns in Font Panel.** The Font Panel window contains four main columns:

- **Font Collections.** Use this column if you want to restrict your accessible fonts to a subset of the total fonts installed. This method may be advisable when you're working on a project that will use only certain fonts and you do not want to be bothered seeing the rest. Mac OS X comes with a couple of sets preconfigured (Fun, Web, and so on)

- **Family.** The fonts included in a selected collection appear in the Family column to the right of the Font Collections column.

- **Typefaces.** If you select a specific font in the Family column, its available typefaces appear in the next column over. What typefaces appear (italic, bold, and so on) will vary with the font.

- **Sizes.** Finally, you can choose sizes for a font via the Sizes column. If you choose the Edit Sizes command from the Extras menu, you can modify which sizes appear in this column or switch to using a slider.

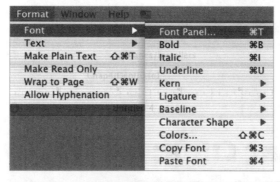

*Figure 4.18*

*(Top) Selecting Font Panel from the Format menu and (bottom) the Font Panel main window.*

**Figure 4.19**

*(Top) Selecting Edit Collections from Font Panel's Extras menu and (bottom) the window that appears.*

**Modify Collections.** You can edit the fonts in a collection, create a new collection, or delete an existing one by choosing Edit Collections from the Extras pop-up menu at the bottom of the window. This command opens a new window. To edit a collection, follow these steps:

1. Click a collection name.

   The fonts in that collection appear in the Family column.

2. Using the arrow keys, you can move fonts to and from the Family and All Families columns, as desired.

   The plus-sign (+) button adds a new collection; the minus-sign (–) and Rename buttons do what you would expect.

3. When you finish, click Done.

**Other Font-menu commands.** The Font menu in TextEdit includes other choices, such as Kern, Ligature, and Colors. If you know what these options mean and how to use them, great. Otherwise, the topic gets beyond the level of font troubleshooting that's appropriate for this Mac OS X book.

**TAKE NOTE ▶ Font Styles and Copy/Paste**

In most Mac OS 9 text applications, as well as Carbonized Mac OS X text applications, a Style menu allows you to change the style of text from plain to italics to bold, and so on. Although the situation gets a bit more complicated with PostScript fonts, these menu options generally allow you to change a font's style even if the font file itself has only the regular (plain) variant. In essence, the application uses built-in OS routines to create a good estimate of the style variant. Mac OS X Cocoa applications such as TextEdit, however, support only styles that exist in the font file itself. Thus, if you used the X Font Info utility to examine a font file and found that it contained only regular and bold styles, only those styles would appear in TextEdit; you could not display that font in italics. As a result, even if you were to paste text of that font that had been italicized in another application, the italics would be lost when you pasted the text into TextEdit.

Yet another oddity: When you paste text into TextEdit from another application, the Font Panel window will not highlight the font name. Thus, you cannot determine the font of the pasted text easily.

Finally, if you add a version of a font to the Fonts folder in your Home directory, it will generally take precedence over versions of the same font in other Fonts folders (as covered more in the next "Take Note" on duplicate fonts). For applications such as TextEdit, adding a duplicate font could thus result in a shift in what Style options are available.

**TAKE NOTE ▶ Problems with Duplicate Fonts in Fonts Folders**

While it is usually OK to have two versions of the same font in different Fonts folders, do not(!) place two versions of the same font in the same Mac OS X Fonts folder. This will almost certainly cause problems, especially within Carbon applications. The most likely symptom is a crash of the application when attempting to display the font or sometimes immediately when the application is launched. This has been known to affect Suitcase (a font management utility), Microsoft Office applications, several Adobe applications, and more.

The consensus opinion is that a bug in Mac OS X is the primary cause. Thus, it will likely require an update to the OS to fix it.

How or why would you wind up with two versions of the same font in a Fonts folder? It could happen by "accident," such as if a Mac OS 9 font suitcase containing several fonts is copied to a Mac OS X Fonts folder (most likely the Fonts folder in your Home directory, at ~/Library/Fonts). If one of the fonts in the suitcase has the identical name to one of the fonts already in the Fonts folder, you may trigger the symptoms.

*continues on next page*

**TAKE NOTE ▶ Problems with Duplicate Fonts in Fonts Folders** *continued*

Less often, problems can occur if the same font is in two *different* fonts folders. This has been most commonly seen when there is a duplicate between a TrueType dfont in the /System/Library/Fonts folder and a PostScript version of the same font that the user installs in either /Library/Fonts or ~/Library/Fonts. It has been reported, for example, after installing an Adobe Helvetica PostScript font. In this case, in addition to potential crashes, there may be additional oddities when displaying the font.

Problems occur here because an application must, of necessity, chose one or the other versions when deciding how to display the font. If different versions of the same font appear in multiple Library/Fonts folders, the more "local" version generally takes priority. Thus, if you place a font in your Home directory's Fonts folder that is a different version from the same-named font in the System/Library/Fonts folder, the version in your Home directory should be used in applications' Font menus. However, there is at least one situation where this does not occur.

In particular, several Adobe applications will choose the version of the font with the most glyphs (for example, visual displays of font characters) if there are multiple font versions available. This could be the system TrueType version in the System directory rather than the PostScript version in the Home directory. The result is that you may have less style variations available than you had expected via installing the PostScript font. That is, if the TrueType version does not include an italics font, you may not have italics available (as Mac OS X does not create an italics display "on the fly" from the plain text version, as Mac OS 9 can do).

A solution to this problem, assuming you wanted access to the PostScript version of the font, would be to delete the corresponding TrueType font from the System/Library/Fonts folder. However, modifying the fonts in this folder is generally considered a bad idea, as these are fonts reserved for system use by the OS and may trigger other problems if modified or deleted.

If you use the third-party utility Suitcase, it includes an option to "Override System Fonts," but even this does not prevent these crashes and display problems from occurring.

Bottom line: Until Apple (and Microsoft and Adobe, as needed) fix the cause of these symptoms, there is no ideal solution.

**TAKE NOTE ▶ TextEdit: Plain Text vs. Rich Text Format; Other Format Options**

**Rich Text vs. Plain Text.** The default format for files saved in TextEdit is Rich Text Format (RTF). Such files will have the extension .rtf. Rich Text Format allows you to include the specialized font, justification, stylized text, and other options that TextEdit is capable of producing. You can also open RTF files in applications such as Microsoft Word.

Some applications (some email applications, for example) may not be able to understand Rich Text Format. In such cases, you may need to save the file in plain-text format (which has the file extension .txt). To do so, choose Make Plain Text from the Format menu and save the file. Now virtually any application should be able to read this file.

You can reconvert the text to Rich Text Format via the Make Rich Text command, which you will find in the Format menu when you view plain-text files. Any of the RTF formatting you did previously will not return, however.

**.rtfd.** You can paste graphics into an .rtf document. When you try to save this document, you will likely get an alert box that says: "You cannot save this document with the extension 'rtf' at the end of the name. The required extension is 'rtfd.'"

An .rtfd file is actually a package that combines the text and graphics (as TIFF images) data as separate elements within the package. Should you ever decide to remove the .rtfd extension from the file's name in the Finder (such as via the Name & Extension tab of the Show Info window), the file will revert to a folder. Adding back the .rtfd extension should get it to appear as a document file again.

**Read-only.** The Format menu also includes the option to save a file as read-only, via the "Make Read Only" command. You may want to do that when creating the Read Me files that accompany applications. Conversely, if you open a read-only file, the command in the Format menu will say "Make Editable."

**Saving SimpleText documents.** You can use TextEdit to open and edit documents created in Mac OS 9's SimpleText application. However, as also covered in Chapter 6 (see: "Saving Files"), when you select to Save a modified SimpleText document, you will get an error message that states: "Please supply a new name. TextEdit does not save SimpleText format; document will be saved as rich text (RTF) instead, with a new name." If you click OK, you will be given the chance to Save the document with a new name.

**Wrap.** Finally, the Format menu has a command that toggles between Wrap to Window and Wrap to Page. If text continues beyond the right border of a window (so that you cannot read it), choosing Wrap to Window will readjust the text so that you can read it all.

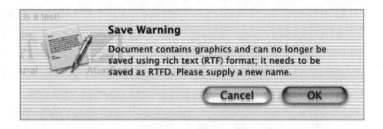

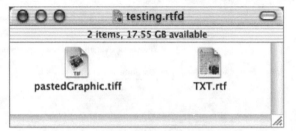

*Figure 4.20*

*(Top) The warning message when attempting to save an rtf file after pasting a graphic into it and (bottom) inside the resulting .rtfd package file.*

## Font smoothing and Mac OS X

Even without any special font-smoothing effect, the display of PostScript and TrueType fonts would be quite smooth in Mac OS X. At the very least, text will likely appear as smooth as it does when displayed in Mac OS 9.

**Antialiased text.** Mac OS X, via its Quartz layer, adds a font-smoothing option that was not built into Mac OS 9 (although special utilities could provide it): *antialiasing*. This feature modifies the edges of the fonts to eliminate the inevitable "jagginess" of the display (which is due to the fact that an edge—especially an oblique edge—is a string of square pixels, rather than a true line). Antialiasing fills in the gaps left by the pixels with various shades of gray pixels. The human eye, in almost an optical-illusion effect, views this display as a smooth line (unless the magnification level gets so high that you start seeing the gray shades).

Although antialiased text generally looks superior to nonantialiased text (which is why the technology exists in the first place!), it may not look especially good for smaller fonts. Smaller fonts may wind up looking more blurry than smooth, which makes them even harder to read.

For this reason, Mac OS X gives you the option to turn off the antialiasing effect for small font sizes. To do so, follow these steps:

1. Open the General pane of the System Preferences window.

   The last command reads: "Turn off text smoothing for fonts sizes {#} and smaller."

2.  Choose the font size from the pop-up menu that appears in the # location.

    Your choices are point sizes 8, 9, 10, and 12. Thus, if small fonts are too blurry, choose a higher number to turn off smoothing for more font sizes. Conversely, if large fonts are too jagged, choose a lower number.

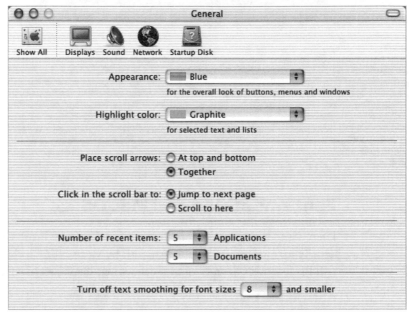

**Figure 4.21**

*The General pane of the System Preferences window.*

The General pane does not allow you to disable font smoothing for sizes larger than 12. Some users would like to turn off font smoothing for larger sizes or turn the option off altogether. You can do this easily enough with the shareware utility TinkerTool, a user-installed system preference. Here's what to do:

1.  Choose TinkerTool in the Others section of the System Preferences window.

2.  Select the Font Smoothing tab.

3.  To disable font smoothing, choose "Disable Font Smoothing in Core Graphics."

    You can also manipulate font smoothing selectively for Cocoa vs. QuickDraw (Carbonized) applications. In each case, you can choose virtually any size as the threshold font size for when smoothing should occur.

Note: Due to a bug in earlier versions of Mac OS X, some fonts were not smoothed as expected in certain applications (especially Microsoft Word). This problem appears to be fixed in the latest OS versions (Mac OS X 10.1.2 and later). If you still have a problem modifying the font-smoothing size range, TinkerTool should be able to get the display to look at least reasonably smooth.

**Modify default fonts.** TinkerTool includes a Fonts tab, where you can change the default font settings (such as font name and size) that Mac OS X uses for its system font and applications. You cannot access these modifications from any Mac OS X-supplied System Preference. Not all applications will use these changes, however, and the changes will not affect the menu-bar font.

Note: You may be surprised to learn that TinkerTool doesn't implement any features of its own; it instead unlocks features that Apple built into the Mac OS X software but did not make easily accessible (so-called hidden features).

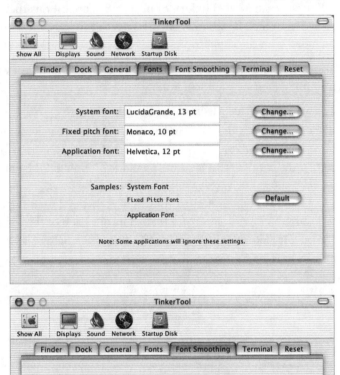

**Figure 4.22**

*TinkerTool's (top) Fonts and (bottom) Font Smoothing tabs.*

# International language support: basics

Mac OS X allows you to change the language used in its menus and dialog boxes. You can also use these international language characters in text that you create in applications. For this book, I am sticking mainly with troubleshooting in English (for which there's already more than enough to know!). But it still pays to be aware of some basics regarding multiple-language support.

**Multiple-language support files.** Support for multiple languages in the OS itself (such as the Finder), or in specific applications that run in Mac OS X, is determined by whether the files needed for any additional language are included with the application.

To see how this situation works, use iTunes (an application with excellent multiple-language support). Follow these steps:

1. Select the iTunes icon in the Finder.

2. Control-click the icon, and choose Show Package Contents from the contextual menu.

3. In the window that appears, open the Contents folder and then the Resources folder within the Contents folder.

   Here, you will find numerous folders that end with the extension .lproj (such as English.lproj and French.lproj). Each of these folders represents the needed support for iTunes to run in the named language.

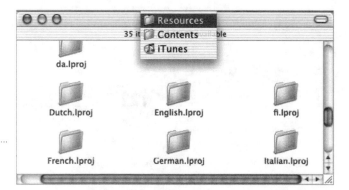

*Figure 4.23*

*Some of the lproj folders in iTunes' Resources folder.*

**Disabling or removing language support files.** The language support files in iTunes take up most of the iTunes application (around 20 MB). Eliminating these files (assuming that you have no need for additional languages in iTunes) could save a considerable amount of space.

To do this, you could remove the undesired .lproj folders from the iTunes package and drag them to the Trash (or somewhere else, should you want to save them). Or, if you want to save the files within iTunes but not have them accessible for display, drag them to the Resources Disabled folder that is also in the Contents folder.

Alternatively, if you do not want to bother with delving into package contents, you can do the same thing via iTunes' Show Info window. Follow these steps:

1. Select the iTunes icon in the Finder.

2. Press Command-I to bring up its Show Info window.

3. Choose Languages from the pop-up menu.

4. To disable a language, simply uncheck the appropriate checkbox. This action moves the language into the Resources Disabled folder.

   *or*

   To delete the language resource (which is what you need to do to reduce the size of the iTunes application), select an enabled language and click the Remove button.

You cannot remove a language that has been disabled. To remove a disabled language, first reenable it. If the Remove button is still dimmed when you select an enabled language, Force Quit the Finder and try again.

Choosing to remove a language places its .lprog folder in the Trash. Until you actually empty the Trash, you could drag the language folder from the Trash and save it elsewhere. In this way, you could use the Add button to return it to the list later, should you want. Note: You will have to close the Show Info window and reopen it before it will show that you have added a language.

iTunes will display its menus and other text in the first language listed in the International System Preferences window, if that language is available and enabled for iTunes. If the preferred language has been disabled or removed, iTunes will use the next enabled language listed in the International System Preferences window.

Note: The Show Info window for iTunes also has a Plugins tab that allows you to enable/disable or add/remove the files (located in the Plug-Ins folder inside the Contents folder) that provide support for various MP3 players (such as the Rio).

**Figure 4.24**

*Languages tab of the Show Info window for iTunes.*

## International language support: troubleshooting

Following are some potential problems—and solutions—with using multiple languages in Mac OS X.

**Additional software needed.** Some languages may require additional software, such as a Mac OS 9 language kit or font. Apple writes: "For example, Mac OS X 10.1 includes script bundles for Cyrillic and Central European languages. However, such a script bundle does not activate unless at least one font for that script is present. Installing a font that is compatible with the script bundle will activate it. Keyboard layouts associated with the activated bundle then appear in the International Preferences panel."

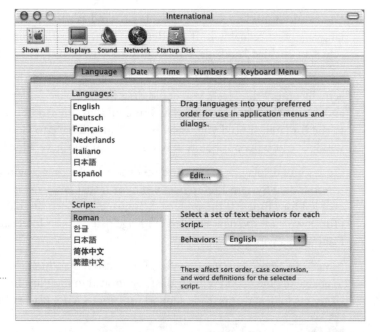

**Figure 4.25**

*The International System Preferences Language tab.*

**Localized OS needed.** Some languages work only if you have a region-specific, or localized, version of the Mac OS installed. Thus, you may not be able to use these languages with a typical North American-English Mac OS X system. You may need to install the version of Mac OS X specific to the language in question. Apple now releases each version of Mac OS X in a variety of localized versions.

**Selected keyboard needed.** To type text in a given language, you may also need to select a keyboard or input method for it via the Keyboard Menu tab of the International System Preferences window. After you select additional keyboards or input methods, a new Keyboard menu with a flag icon appears in the menu bar of all applications. This menu allows you to choose among keyboards or input methods. Some input methods may create an additional menu next to the keyboard menu when they are active. Keyboards listed as Unicode in the International System Preferences window are available only in Unicode-compatible applications such as Mail, TextEdit, and the Finder. When you're typing in an application, the availability of these keyboards in the Keyboard menu indicates whether that application works with Unicode.

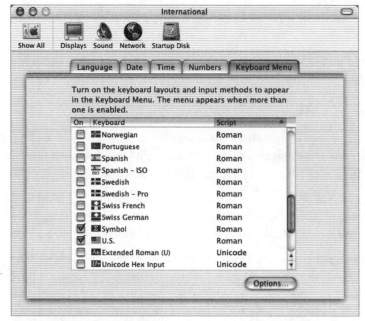

**Figure 4.26**

*The International System Preferences Keyboard Menu tab.*

**Figure 4.27**

*A keyboard menu in the menu bar.*

---

**TAKE NOTE** ▶ **Getting "Graphic" Fonts to Display in TextEdit**

In a few cases, you may need to select a keyboard in the International System Preferences window even if you are using only the English language. You will need to do this to use graphic fonts–such as Symbol and Zapf Dingbat–in Cocoa applications such as TextEdit.

Specifically, if you select some text in TextEdit and then try to change it to the Symbol or Zapf Dingbats font via the Font Panel window, the text will most likely revert to the Lucida Grande font instead. If you want to use these fonts, here is what to do:

1. Open the International System Preferences window, and select the Keyboard Menu tab.

2. Enable the Symbol and Zapf Dingbats keyboards by checking their On checkboxes.

*continues on next page*

**TAKE NOTE** ▶ **Getting "Graphic" Fonts to Display in TextEdit** *continued*

3. Close the International System Preferences window.

   You will see a menu to the right of the Help menu, indicated by a flag icon. If you are a U.S. user, you should see a U.S. flag icon. In this menu will be the names of the keyboards you just enabled.

4. Pull down the menu, and choose the menu option you want to use (such as Symbol).

   *or*

   Press Command-Option-spacebar to rotate among all the menu options until the one you want is selected.

   Now when you type text, it should be in the font you selected (such as Symbol). If it is not, choose the desired font in the Font Panel window.

This system is awkward at best, and it still does not always work the way it should. Selecting some Zapf Dingbats text and changing it to a different fonts appears to be almost impossible, for example. The system works only for text that you add after making the change.

Also, shifting to these keyboards apparently is not a prerequisite for using these fonts in Carbon applications, such as Word and AppleWorks. If you do change the keyboard, however, you can get odd effects in these applications, such as characters mapped to incorrect keys. So watch out!

**Keyboard Menu options.** In the Keyboard Menu tab of the International System Preferences window, click the Options button. You will find an option called Font and Keyboard Synchronization. This option sounds like it is designed to select the appropriate keyboard layout automatically when you select a font (such as switch to the Symbol layout when you switch to the Symbol font). The option does not seem to work as expected, however. In Cocoa applications such as TextEdit, before I could select the Symbol font, I had to select the Symbol keyboard menu manually. In Carbon applications such as Word, I could select and display the Symbol font just fine, even though the keyboard layout remained as U.S. and did not switch to Symbol.

In any case, whether this option was on or off had no effect on my inability to change existing Zapf Dingbats or Symbol text to a different font. Changing the menu affected only text typed after the change.

At this point, you may be asking why is it so much more difficult to use fonts such as Symbol in Mac OS X than it was in Mac OS 9. The key to the answer is Mac OS X's use of Unicode (see "Technically Speaking: ATSUI and Unicode" earlier in this chapter). More specifically, this is what Apple had to say on the matter: "In Mac OS 9, the Symbol and Zapf Dingbats fonts acted like other fonts, as if they worked with the usual alphabetic and numeric characters, when in fact they contained symbol characters. In a Unicode system, the special characters in the Symbol and Zapf Dingbats fonts have their own unique Unicode character codes. Typing a character like 'A' does not work when these fonts are used with Unicode, as the fonts don't contain an 'A' character. Thus, you need to use special keyboard layouts provided for those fonts."

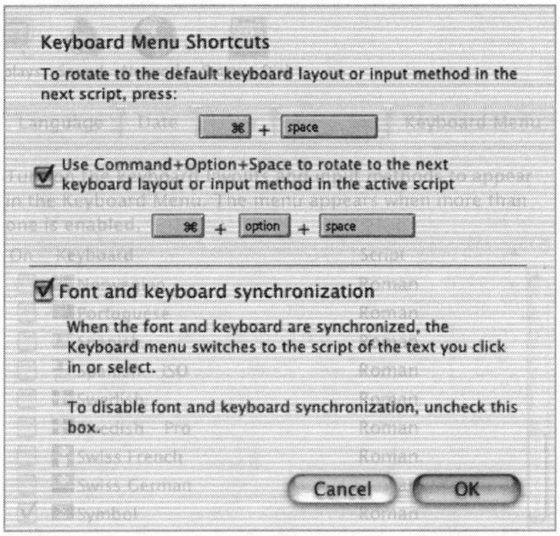

*Figure 4.28*

*International System Preferences: Keyboard Menu tab's Options window.*

## Font utilities

In addition to the X Font Info and TinkerTool utilities, mentioned earlier in this section, you should consider several useful font-related utilities.

**FontDoctor** finds and repairs an assortment of font problems. This Mac OS 9 utility has been updated to work in Mac OS X. Here's a partial list of the things it can do:

- Repair damaged and corrupt fonts
- Locate missing fonts
- Find and eliminate duplicate fonts
- Fix font ID conflicts

**FontExampler** shows all your installed fonts in WYSIWYG mode in a single window. You can also see how any selected font looks at different sizes.

**ForkSwitcher** is an Apple utility that can convert a traditional Mac OS 9 font suitcase file (with a data and resource fork, and with the file type FFIL) to one that uses the Mac OS X (.dfont) data-fork-only format. Note: ForkSwitcher cannot change individual font files in Mac OS 9 that are not inside a font suitcase.

**Suitcase** allows you to view all fonts (including Mac OS X .dfonts) in all Mac OS X Fonts folders. It can activate or deactivate individual fonts separately for Cocoa, Carbon, and Classic applications. This utility can be especially useful when two fonts conflict or when a font causes a problem with a specific application. In such cases, you can use Suitcase to deactivate the problem font. Note: Suitcase was briefly mentioned earlier in this chapter in "Take Note: Problems with Duplicate Fonts in Fonts folders" and "Take Note: Multiple Folders Of The Same Name In Multiple Library Folders."

**Font Reserve** is another excellent utility in the same genre as Suitcase.

# 5

# Crash Prevention & Recovery

Of all the things that can go wrong with a computer, the one users typically most want to avoid is a crash. Actually, the word *crash* and its first cousin, *freeze,* are generic terms that cover a wide range of symptoms and causes, some far more serious than others.

At the relative low end of the seriousness scale is an application crash or freeze. In the simplest case, the application quits itself (often referred to as an unexpected quit). You may have trouble relaunching the application at this point, but otherwise, your computer will likely be running just fine. A bit more frustrating is the hang or freeze. In this case, the application remains open and visible but nothing works. In some cases, until you thaw things out, other programs may also be inaccessible.

More serious is a crash or freeze that is not limited to a single program but brings almost everything to a complete halt, forcing you to restart your Mac. For obvious reasons, the most serious of these situations is a crash that occurs during startup, so that you cannot even get to the Desktop in the first place.

In this chapter, I'll cover all these variations of crashes and freezes. I'll tell you how best to recover from these problems as well as offer some tips on how to prevent crashes in the first place.

One bit of good news: The more serious crashes, the ones that bring down your entire system, occur much less often in Mac OS X than in Classic (Mac OS 9 and earlier) OS versions. The reason is explained in Chapter 4, in the section on "Protected Memory."

# In This Chapter

# Uh-Oh!

This initial section offers an overview of why crashes/freezes occur and what to do about them.

## What causes crashes and freezes?

The ultimate causes of crashes and freezes can be distilled down to three main reasons:

**A software bug.** Some error in the programming code of some software is causing the crash. Sometimes, it can be a "pure" bug—that is, one that occurs independently of any other software or hardware in use. If an error in the code for a word processing application, for example, causes the program to crash every time you try to save a file that includes italic text—no matter what other software you are running—that's a pure bug. At other times, a bug is the result of an interaction between two or more programs. An application may crash on launch, but only if a particular other program is already open. The question then becomes which program has the bug and which is innocent. As the saying goes, however, "Fix the problem, not the blame." Ideally, no matter who may be at fault, at least one of the developers will agree to fix the code so that the conflict is resolved.

**A corrupt file.** Sometimes, a file on your drive gets modified so that it contains data that is not supposed to be part of the file or that it is missing data it needs. Perhaps you started to save a word processing document just as a power failure occurred, resulting in a partial save of the file. When you try to open the file later, you get a crash. Or some critical OS file (such as a file in the System folder) gets updated periodically, but an error occurred when the file was last written to disk, so that the file no longer works. Again, this situation can lead to a crash—in this case, including an inability to start up your Mac. Corrupt preferences files are also common sources of system crashes. These files are usually updated quite often, increasing the odds of a copy error.

**A hardware conflict.** A problem with a hardware component, either external or internal, may lead to a crash. A circuit may burn out on the logic board, or memory may have been defective from the day it shipped from the factory. Or you may have hardware that is not compatible with your particular Mac. RAM comes in many speeds and sizes, but most Mac models work only with very specific types of RAM. Although two RAM modules may look identical, and both may fit in your Mac, one may be the wrong type. The wrong type can lead to a startup crash.

Finally, hardware components that should work with your Mac may not work due to software problems. In particular, devices (such as hard drives, printers, and scanners) require that *driver* software be present on your startup drive for the hardware to work. Bugs in the driver software can result in crashes, just as any other software bugs can. Hardware devices may also have a feature called firmware. *Firmware* is a middle ground between software and hardware; it is software code that resides in a component of the hardware itself. Typically, you can upgrade firmware by running a special firmware-update program. Often, as new Macs and OS updates come out, hardware devices will require these firmware updates to remain compatible.

## General strategies for fixing crashes

Most crashes will be limited to specific applications. You will still be able to continue using your Mac despite the crash. At this point, if the crash does not occur the next time you duplicate the same procedure (you may need to restart your Mac to get the crash to stop recurring), you may well decide to ignore the crash—and hope that it never happens again or happens so infrequently as to not be a problem. Otherwise, your goal will be to locate the cause of the crash and fix it. In general, the exact fix will depend on the type of crash.

For crashes caused by corrupt files, the solution may be as simple as deleting the file. If the problem is a preferences files, for example, deleting the file causes a new default version to be created the next time the relevant application is launched. The default file should be free of whatever corruption was causing the crash. You will need to re-create whatever custom changes you made that were stored in the preferences file, but at least the crash is gone.

Similarly, for a corrupt document, especially if you have a backup of the file, delete the corrupt version and start again with your backup. For corrupt OS files, deleting and replacing may also work, assuming that you know where and how to get the replacement (a subject I cover in more detail in Chapter 2). In some cases, you need a disk-repair utility, such as Apple's Disk Utility or Norton Utilities. A general reinstallation of the OS software is also a potential cure. (In the worst case, you may need to erase your drive before doing a reinstallation.)

For buggy software, you simply have to hope that the software gets updated with a bug fix. In the meantime, you can try to find a workaround that prevents the crash. As the old joke goes: "I told the doctor it hurts when I do this. He told me, 'Don't do that.'"

OK—that's the bare-bones outline of dealing with system crashes. What follows are all the details. Actually, I start with a prelude. Because so many problems are a function of what happens during startup (including, of course, crashes that occur during startup), I begin with a tour of the startup sequence of events. After that, I'll take a closer look at the various types of crashes and tell you what to do about them.

# The Startup Sequence of Events

When you first turn on your Mac, you typically have to wait a few minutes before you can start using it—as the Mac goes through its "startup sequence." For you, this time may simply be an opportunity to go and make yourself a cup of coffee. For the Mac, it is a critical period where a multitude of events occur that will determine the success or failure of everything that follows. Here's what you need to know about this sequence, starting from the earliest events and continuing to the final ones:

## BootROM and Open Firmware

BootROM is software code that is stored within the circuitry of the Mac's logic board. Because the data does not reside on any hard drive, it can be run even before a startup hard drive has been selected. Thus, this code is just about the first thing that gets checked when you turn on your Mac. This software is also independent of what OS version you are using. Thus, it gets checked whether you are booting Mac OS 9 or Mac OS X.

The BootROM performs two main checks:

**Power-on self-test (POST).** This test is a check of the Mac's hardware and RAM (memory). The power-on self-test resides in the ROM (read-only memory) of the computer. This test runs at startup, but only a startup that occurs from a Mac that is currently shut down (that is, it does not occur when you select the Restart command from a running Mac). If a problem is detected, the startup sequence will likely halt almost instantly. In addition, you will hear a sound other than the normal startup chime. In particular:

- One beep: no RAM installed/detected
- Two beeps: incompatible RAM type installed
- Three beeps: no RAM banks passed memory testing
- Four beeps: bad checksum for the remainder of the boot ROM
  [Note: checksum refers to a method for determining if data is corrupted.]
- Five beeps: bad checksum for the ROM boot block

The first three beeps indicate a problem with the Mac's RAM. Especially if you installed RAM beyond what came with your Mac, it's time to check whether it may be defective or otherwise incompatible with your Mac. The simplest way to check is to remove the RAM and see whether the POST warning goes away. If so, contact your RAM vendor about getting a replacement.

Otherwise, for recent Macs that shipped with a Hardware Test CD, it's time to get it and use it. This disc can help diagnose whether your startup failure is due to a hardware problem. If you cannot start up even from the Hardware

Test CD, you almost certainly have a hardware problem. It's probably time to take your Mac in for repair.

Other symptoms that indicate a likely hardware failure include:

- If you don't hear the hard drive spinning, but everything else appears to be normal, your hard drive may be damaged. In this case, you should still be able to start from a CD, but you will likely need to replace the hard drive.

- If you don't hear any noise, not even the fan, and the Mac is plugged in and has power, the power supply has probably failed. It will need to be replaced.

As none of this information is specific to Mac OS X, I will not delve into this matter further here. For more detailed help, you can try my other book, *Sad Macs,* or go online to MacFixIt (**www.macfixit.com**).

---

**TECHNICALLY SPEAKING ▶ The Apple Hardware Test CD**

The Hardware Test CD is specific to each type of Mac (iBook, iMac, PowerBook, and so on), so don't try to use a disc that came with a Mac other than the Mac model for which it was intended.

To start up from the CD, turn on your Mac, insert the CD, and hold down the C key. Then follow the instructions for the Quick and Extended tests.

If the test detects an error, it will display an error code (such as ata1/6/3 HD:2,1). You can go to Apple's Knowledge Base (`http://kbase.info.apple.com/`) and search for a document that mentions that error. The document may tell you what the error code means and what you need to fix things. If your search comes up empty, contact Apple directly.

---

**Open Firmware.** Open Firmware is essentially responsible for selecting the operating system that you will use. It also makes first contact with (or initializes) hardware beyond the Mac itself, such as external drives. You can access Open Firmware directly by pressing Command-Option-O-F at startup. This access consists of a simple command-line interface from which you can type commands. These commands carry out actions beyond what Open Firmware does by default. Normally, you would have little need to do any of this. Due to some bug, however, your Mac may display the Open Firmware screen at startup before continuing with a normal startup sequence. Even more rarely, it may halt at the Open Firmware screen. Finally, at times you may need to run a specific Open Firmware command to solve a troubleshooting matter. In all these cases, pressing Command-Option-O-F and knowing a few of the Open Firmware commands will come in handy.

**SEE:** • "Take Note: Open Firmware Updates" and "Technically Speaking: Open Firmware Commands," later in this chapter.

**TAKE NOTE ▶ Open Firmware Updates**

Apple periodically releases software called firmware updates. When you run these update utilities (which currently run only in Mac OS 9), they update the Open Firmware software. Instructions on how to install these firmware updates vary from computer model to model but are included with each update. Essentially, on most models, the procedure consists of running the update, shutting down as instructed by the update, and restarting while holding down the Interrupt button until you hear a long tone. The Mac should do the rest.

Note: The Interrupt button is on the Mac itself, usually as part of a pair of buttons; the other button in the pair is the Reset button (it has a triangle symbol on it) and is the one you press when nothing else is able to restart your Mac.

Normally, I would recommend installing firmware updates as Apple released them, because they fix bugs in the preceding version and may add new features. Occasionally, however, problems occur. A recent firmware update, for example, placed new restrictions on the type of memory that the Mac found to be acceptable. As a result, some previously installed RAM was no longer recognized (primarily, RAM purchased from vendors other than Apple). In some cases, the problem RAM needed to be replaced. But an enterprising developer wrote DIMMFirstAid (**www.mactcp.org.nz/DIMMFirstAid.sit**), which can patch the DIMM so that it is accessible again. Read the complete details on this MacFixIt page: **www.macfixit.com/reports/firmware.shtml**.

Be especially cautious not to interrupt the installation of a firmware update while it's in progress. Doing so could leave the firmware in a nonfunctional state, and you may not be able to start up again. There is no easy way to reinstall the firmware at that point. A trip to an Apple Service Provider will likely be needed. Even if you complete the update successfully, there is also no way to downgrade to an older version of the firmware. So if you don't like something about what the update does, you are out of luck.

Finally, all this information refers to updating Apple's Open Firmware. Other peripheral devices, from Apple's AirPort Base Station to SCSI cards, may have their own firmware, which can be updated. This firmware is separate from Open Firmware on the Mac itself.

**TECHNICALLY SPEAKING  ▶  Open Firmware Commands**

Press Command-Option-O-F at startup, and you get dumped into the Open Firmware environment, where you can run Open Firmware commands. To get a command to run, type the command and press Return. Open Firmware has dozens of commands. An Apple Knowledge Base document (`http://karchive.info.apple.com/article.html?orig=til&artnum=60285`) provides a useful summary. For most troubleshooting, however, you need to know only a few of these commands. The ones I have found most useful are:

**Eject CD/DVD.** Typically, to start up from a CD, you need to hold down the C key at startup with the CD inserted into the drive. Occasionally, the Mac may attempt to start up from the CD, even if you do not hold down the C key (if you selected the CD as the startup disk in System Preferences, for example). Usually, holding down the mouse/trackpad button or the Eject key at startup will force the CD to eject before it is selected as the startup device. But if even this method fails, you can boot into Open Firmware and type `eject cd`. That command will get the CD tray to open. Then you can remove the CD.

Alternatively, you may want to start up from a CD that is not in the CD drive. If due to a system crash, you cannot access the drive before restarting, you will need get the CD tray to open (unless it is a slot-loading drive, as in iMacs), insert the CD, close the tray, and hold down the C key, all before the Mac selects the hard drive as the startup device. If this is too much to do in so short a time, use Open Firmware. Open the tray via the `eject cd` command, insert the CD, and close the tray. Then type `shut-down`. This command does what its name implies. Now you can restart as normal, holding down the C key, to use the CD as the startup disc.

**reset-all.** There has been some confusion among Mac users as to what the reset-all command does. Some people believed that it resets the Open Firmware code to some default state, possibly all the way back to what it was when your Mac first shipped, thus erasing any subsequent firmware updates. This is not the case. The command makes no changes in Open Firmware itself. Instead, it appears to initiate the same sort of changes that would occur if you pressed the Mac's Reset button or even simply restarted as normal. It rechecks what peripheral devices are attached to your Mac, for example. So if you Mac appears not to recognize a device such as a FireWire drive, using reset-all could help.

**printenv reset-nvram and set-default.** I have never found a need to use these commands, but you may find them to be of interest. Type `printenv`, and you will get a list of all the settings in the Mac's nonvolatile RAM (NVRAM). These settings are stored in a special type of RAM on the Mac's logic board. You can modify the contents, as you can with ordinary RAM, but the contents are preserved even after you shut down the Mac. Among other things, NVRAM maintains the name of the default startup device.

*continues on next page*

**TECHNICALLY SPEAKING** ▶ **Open Firmware Commands** *continued*

Then you can use the reset-nvram and set-default commands to reset the NVRAM settings back to their defaults, assuming that you wanted to do so. One potential use for this technique is if your Mac will not attempt to start up from your internal hard drive, no matter what you do. The combination of reset-nvram and set-default is similar to a well-known Macintosh trouble-shooting technique called zapping the PRAM (parameter RAM).

**mac-boot.** Whenever you want to exit Open Firmware and start up from the default startup device (typically, your internal hard drive), simply type bye or mac-boot. Or type shut down or reset-all to shut down or restart immediately.

**Open Firmware password.** The latest versions of the Open Firmware software allow you to add a password requirement. If this option is enabled, on each restart, the Mac automatically defaults to Open Firmware and requires you to enter the correct password. Without the password, startup would not proceed. This option could be useful in public and semipublic environments if you are concerned about users' bypassing the OS's less-secure password protection. A user could bypass the Mac OS X security by starting up with a bootable CD, for example. A CD would not bypass the Open Firmware protection.

To create a password, simply type password. You will not be asked to use it at startup, however, until you enable the password-checking feature. To do this, type setenv security-mode {*mode*}. The {mode} is none, command, or full. The none mode means no password protection is enforced. The command mode allows you to startup without a password, but you can make no Open Firmware changes without entering the password. The full mode prohibits you from starting up without entering the password. Type reset-all after making any change. That's it.

The risk is that when full mode is enabled, if you forget your password or the Mac does not accept it for any reason, you are locked out of your Mac. In this case, I have read (but have not confirmed) that the following procedure will remove the password protection:

1. Add or remove a DIMM module (assuming that you have more than one).
2. Reset (zap) the PRAM three times by holding down Command-Option-P-R at startup until the Mac chimes three times.

Finally, Apple has made it a bit easier to work with Open Firmware passwords. On the Mac OS X Install CD, tucked away in the Applications folder located at the root level of the CD, is a utility called Open Firmware Password. If you run it and enter your administrative password, you will be able to create a password and enable its use so that a password is required to change Open Firmware settings. This option is equivalent to the command mode, which apparently prevents starting up from a bootable CD without the password, thereby making the Mac more secure.

*continues on next page*

**TECHNICALLY SPEAKING** ▶ **Open Firmware Commands** *continued*

You can run this utility directly from the CD. You can also run it from your hard drive, if you can copy it there successfully. I have discovered, however, that a setUID Unix permissions setting prevents copying the file to your drive. The workaround is to change the setting (as I explain in Chapter 6) or copy the utility to your hard drive while you're booted in Mac OS 9.

When the password is required, you will not be able to do certain startup operations, such as resetting the PRAM, starting up in single-user mode, starting up in verbose mode, or starting from a CD-ROM. To do these things, temporarily disable the password requirement from the Open Firmware Password utility. If you do not have access to the utility, start up in Open Firmware and then do the following:

1. Type: reset-nvram.

2. When you are prompted for your password, enter it and then press Return.

3. Type: set-defaults.

4. Type: reset-all.

The computer will restart, and you will be able to reset the PRAM and start up in single-user mode, in verbose mode, or from a CD.

*Figure 5.1*

*The Open Firmware Password utility.*

**TAKE NOTE ▶ Zapping PRAM and Resetting Power Manager**

The following information is not specific to Mac OS X, but it can still be helpful if you are having problems starting up.

**Zap/reset the PRAM.** Zapping the PRAM resets your Mac's parameter RAM and NVRAM settings to their default values. To do this, shut down your Mac and then turn it on again while holding down the Command, Option, P, and R keys. Wait until the Mac chimes three times. Then let go of the keys and let startup proceed. See this Apple Knowledge Base document for more details: `http://docs.info.apple.com/article.html?artnum=2238`. Or check out the section on this topic in Sad Macs. You may also be able to zap the PRAM via Open Firmware, as noted in "Technically Speaking: Open Firmware Commands" earlier in this chapter.

Apple warns: "If you have a RAID set up, your computer may not start up if you reset parameter RAM (PRAM) when you restart. To fix this, restart your computer while holding down the Option key to select your startup system. If this doesn't work, restart your computer while holding down the Command, Option, Shift, and Delete keys."

**Reset the Power Manager.** On laptops, resetting the Power Manager does the same thing as a PRAM zap, with one addition: It also resets the circuitry on the laptop that is responsible for power management, especially as regards sleep and battery use. Exactly how to do this reset varies with each Mac laptop model. This Apple Knowledge Base document provides the details: `http://docs.info.apple.com/article.html?artnum=14449`.

More recently, even desktop Macs have a Power Management Unit (PMU). Resetting this unit can eliminate certain system-crash problems. Again, exactly how to do this varies from model to model. This Apple Knowledge Base article explains the technique for flat-panel iMacs: `http://docs.info.apple.com/article.html?artnum=95165`.

## Startup Manager: Option key at startup

If you hold down the Option key at startup, you will invoke the Startup Manager. You can use this feature to select a startup volume different from the one that is the normal default (as selected in the Startup Disk System Preferences window).

The result of holding down the Option key is a screen that contains icons for the various volumes (drives, discs, and partitions) from which you can boot your Mac. Here are some guidelines for what you should expect to see in this screen and how to proceed once it appears:

- If you have Mac OS 9 and Mac OS X installed on different partitions, you should see two icons—one for each OS. If a bootable CD is in the CD drive, you should see an icon for it as well.

- If you have Mac OS X and Mac OS 9 on the same partition, only one of them can be *blessed* at a time, which means that only one of them will ordinarily be recognized as a potential bootable OS. So when you hold down the Option key at startup, you will see either the Mac OS X icon or the Mac OS 9 icon, but not both. Which one you will see will depend on which one was most recently selected as the bootable OS.

- If you do not see a volume that you expect to see, click the curved-arrow button (located below the icons), and the Mac will check again for potential startup volumes.

- Otherwise, click the icon of the volume that you want to use as the startup volume. Then click the straight-arrow button, and startup will proceed.

- If you hold down Command-period in this screen, the Mac's CD drive tray should eject, giving you the opportunity to mount a CD and use it as the startup disc. This screen also allows you to eject a CD at this point, should you want to do so. This method is an alternative to the other methods for accessing the CD tray, as described in "Technically Speaking: Open Firmware Commands" earlier in this chapter.

---

**TAKE NOTE ▶ Startup Manager vs. Startup Disk vs. Command Keys**

**Startup Disk System Preferences and Control Panel.** Using the Startup Manager screen to change a startup disk selection does not change the default choice of startup drive. That is, if you normally boot into Mac OS X and select Mac OS 9 in the Startup Manager screen, you will boot back into Mac OS X the next time you restart as normal. In most cases, the way to change the default setting is to make a different selection in the Startup Disk System Preferences window (Mac OS X) or Control Panel (Mac OS 9), as discussed in Chapter 3. Simply select the volume (and the OS within the volume, if more than one exists), and restart. That's it.

Unlike Startup Manager, the Startup Disk control panel in Mac OS 9 and Startup Disk System Preferences window in Mac OS X list both Mac OS 9 and Mac OS X as startup choices, even if both System folders are on the same partition.

In general, use Startup Disk to change your startup-disk selection. Use the Startup Manager only if the standard methods do not work or if they are inaccessible (perhaps because you cannot start up successfully).

**C key at startup.** You can hold down the C key at startup to start up from a bootable CD that is already in the drive.

**X key at startup.** Holding down the X key at startup shifts a Mac that normally boots into Mac OS 9 to boot into Mac OS X instead. This method, however, works only if the Mac OS 9 and Mac OS X systems are both on the same partition—and you last started from the Mac OS 9 System Folder on that partition. This technique allows you to work around the problem when the Option-key method does not list Mac OS 9 and Mac OS X at the same time, if they are on the same partition. Also, unlike the Option-key method, a change you make is saved. That is, the next time you start up normally, you will again start up in Mac OS X.

*continues on next page*

**TAKE NOTE ▶ Startup Manager vs. Startup Disk vs. Command Keys** *continued*

**Command-key startup selection shortcuts.** I have read reports about certain Command-key shortcuts that affect the startup-volume selection, but none of them has ever worked for me. Just in case they might work for you, I'll mention them:

• Pressing Command-Option at startup may shift from Mac OS X to Mac OS 9. Results appear to vary, depending upon your Mac model and which version of Mac OS X you are using.

• Pressing Command-X at startup may result in Mac OS X's booting without any kernel extensions loading.

**SEE:** • "BootROM and Open Firmware," "Single-user mode," and "Verbose mode," elsewhere in this chapter, for other startup options.

## BootX

If you elected to start up in Mac OS X and have passed through the BootROM stage successfully, and if you are not starting up from a CD, the next thing that the Mac looks for is called the BootX booter, a file located in /System/Library/CoreServices. Its primary job is to load what is called the kernel environment. At this point, you should see the happy-Mac icon if all is going well.

Without a BootX file in your Mac OS X System folder, your Mac will not start up. This file is essential, in the same way that the System file is essential in Mac OS 9. More precisely, the file has to be on the volume somewhere. The volume will boot even if the file is not in the System folder, although I can think of no reason to move it from there! In fact, I found that if you simply copy this BootX file onto any volume—even one that has no other Mac OS X software—the Startup Disk System Preferences window will be fooled into thinking that you can start up in Mac OS X from that volume. (This attempt will fail, of course, should you try to do so.)

**Kernel extensions.** Also during this phase, the kernel extensions (kext files) will be loaded. *Kernel extensions* are mainly device drivers for attached hardware, such as PCI cards, an AirPort Base Station, graphics cards, and an iPod.

*Figure 5.2*

*The CoreServices folder with BootX highlighted.*

**TECHNICALLY SPEAKING** ▶ **Understanding Kernel Extensions**

BootX first attempts to load a previously cached set of device drivers, called an mkext.cache. If this file is missing or corrupted, BootX will create a new one by rechecking the set of extensions in /System/Library/Extensions for drivers and other kernel extensions that are set to be loaded at startup. This mkextcache file itself is called Extensions.mkext and is located at the root level of the System/Library folder. Deleting it will force a rebuild of the cache when you restart.

When you install a new kernel extension, the Installer should force an update to the cache so that the Mac recognizes the presence of the new extension. If the Installer should fail to do so, deleting the mkext file on your own will accomplish the task. You will need to log in as a root user to do this (as explained in Chapter 3).

Otherwise, simply restarting (or even better, shutting down and then restarting) your Mac should force it to reload its existing list of extensions. If you are having any problem with a hardware peripheral, this method would be a good thing to try.

If this method alone does not work, you can also force an update by changing the modification date of the Extensions folder. To do so, launch Terminal and type <touch /System/Library/ Extensions>.

Another approach is to type <sudo kextload /System/Library/Extensions/{*name of* .*kext file*>. This command should load the newly installed kext file without a restart. Still, given that installing new kext files does not happen often, I advise playing it safe and restarting.

**SCSI extensions and deep sleep.** Although ordinarily, I would not recommend altering the contents of this folder (as is the case with almost everything in the Mac OS X System folder), there are exceptions. For example, certain SCSI cards, including the most common one that Apple supplies for Power Mac G4s (based on the Adaptec 2930 card), did not support the low-power deep sleep in Mac OS X until updated drivers were released. With the original drivers, if you selected sleep, at best, you would find that the system fan remained on. Sometimes, the Mac would not even go to sleep at all.

A work-around for this sleep problem was to log in as a root user and disable all kext files with the word Adaptec in their names, either by moving them to a folder you create called Extensions (disabled) or simply by removing the files from the System folder altogether. Then, after a restart, you could use deep sleep. The down side was that you could no longer access any devices attached to the SCSI card. But if you needed to do access SCSI devices only rarely, you could boot from Mac OS 9 on those occasions. The card would still function from that OS.

# System (and kernel) initialization

During the next phase of startup, an assortment of activities of a rather technical nature takes place. For purposes of this chapter, I summarize them briefly:

- The core software (kernel) of the Unix/BSD basis for Mac OS X loads.

- A check is made if the user is booting from a CD-ROM or via single-user mode. If so, special loading procedures take over. (I discuss single-user mode and starting from a CD later in this chapter.)

- Special scripts (rc.boot and rc) in the normally invisible /etc folder are run. These scripts handle various initialization tasks, including running the SystemStarter program in /System/Library/CoreServices. This program in turn handles the launching of startup items (as described in the following section).

Note: If you are starting up from a bootable CD, the critical information needed for booting to work is in a similar file on the CD called rc.cdrom, also located in the /etc folder.

# StartupItems

During the next phase of startup, the items in /System/Library/StartupItems are launched. During this phase, text in the startup window refers to the items being run (Starting {*name of item*}). Items located in this folder include:

- **SystemTuning.** Handles virtual memory.

- **Cleanup.** Deletes temporary files left over from the preceding session.

- **Network.** Configures the local network interfaces based on the data in the /etc/iftab file (setting IP info, and so on).

- **Apache.** Starts the Web server, if enabled.

- **Network Time.** Sets up the software to check for time and date.

- **AppleTalk.** Sets up AppleTalk as defined in the /etc/host.config file.

- **DirectoryServices.** Starts the NetInfo server (nibindd) and the lookupd program.

- **Cron.** Runs cron files (for example, updates and cleans up system logs).

Technically, each item in the StartupItems folder is itself a folder that contains two items: the startup program and a .plist file (which among other things, lists whether the startup item depends on the running of yet another startup item).

Additionally, third-party startup items (ones not installed by Mac OS X itself) may be stored in and launched from the /Library/StartupItems folder. Timbuktu Pro, for example, runs at each startup via this method. The Timbuktu Installer places the item there; this procedure is not something you typically do manually.

Shareware utilities such as Boot Config and MOX Optimize allow you to enable or disable startup items. These utilities work similarly to Extensions Manager in Mac OS 9. In most cases, you should not disable any of these Mac OS X startup items, especially the core items installed by Apple. Occasionally, however, you can solve troubleshooting problems by disabling a specific item. If the Apache Web server software appears to be contributing to crashes while you're running Mac OS X, for example, the first diagnostic thing you should try is turning Web sharing off via the Sharing Startup System Preferences window. If that method does not work, you could use Boot Config to disable the item.

**Startup-item stall.** If the network setting that was in use when you shut down is no longer active the next time you restart, the Mac may stall for a long time at the Network or Network Time items. Essentially, it is trying to access a network that doesn't exist. You may speed things up by, for example, disconnecting your Ethernet cable if it is trying to connect over a Ethernet network that is down. Otherwise, if you wait long enough, the Mac will eventually continue to start up anyway.

**SEE:** • "Network Services stall," later in this chapter.

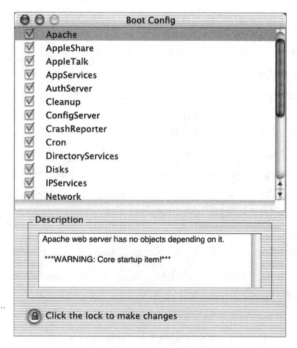

*Figure 5.3*

*Boot Config's list of startup items.*

# Log in

The last stage of the startup process begins with the appearance of the log in window. However, if you have enabled the "automatically log in" option in the Login System Preference (as described in Chapter 3), you will bypass this screen.

The log in window is, appropriately enough, handled by the loginwindow application, located in System/Library/CoreServices. When loginwindow is launched during startup, the following things happen:

- Your password is checked (against the data stored in the NetInfo database).
- Your customized environment, based on the preferences settings in your Home directory, is set up (including launching items in the Login Items pane of the Login System Preferences window).
- Your permissions/privileges are assigned to files.
- Various other typical log in tasks (such as displaying alerts) are completed.

When you enter your correct user name and password, Mac OS X completes its startup sequence, launching the Finder, the Dock, and the applications in the Login Items list.

Note: The password-checking code here looks at only the first eight characters. Anything beyond that length is ignored.

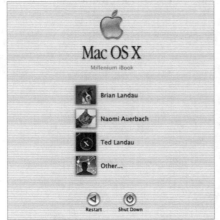

**Figure 5.4**

*Two views of the Login window: (left) "List of users" view and (right) "Name and password" view.*

**Always have your name as the login name.** If, in the Login Window tab of Login System Preferences, you chose the option titled "Display Login Window As...Name and password entry fields," the name that will appear is the name of the last person who logged in.

This situation can be annoying if you are the most common user of the computer and would thus prefer that the setting always default to your name. The simplest way to do this is to run the HideOrShowPreviousLogin application from Apple; get it at **http://docs.info.apple.com/article.html?artnum=106691**.

If you instead chose the option titled "List of users with accounts on this computer," especially if you also enabled Show "Other" User, the preceding information is moot, as all names are equally accessible in all cases.

Note: The loginwindow program continues to run while you are logged in. This program relaunches the Dock and the Finder automatically, should they quit.

---

**TECHNICALLY SPEAKING ▶ System Daemons**

If you launch Process Viewer, you inevitably will see many processes running that are not end-user applications and are not listed in any other typical place you list running applications (such as the Force Quit window, described in Chapter 3 and later in this chapter). In general, these processes are handling background processes—that is, processes that have no user interface and thus are not visible in the Finder. Typically, you will have little need to interact with them. To give you a feel for what these processes are and what they do, however, here is a list of several of the more noteworthy items:

- **kextd.** Loads and unloads device drives as needed.
- **kyslogd.** Logs system error messages.
- **lookupd.** A name resolver that expedites requests to NetInfo and DNS.
- **autodiskmount.** Automatically mounts removable media.
- **update.** Periodically flushes the system cache to help prevent data loss in the event of a crash. (I discuss this topic more later in this chapter in "Technically Speaking: Telnet to a Frozen Mac: Kill Processes, Run Sync.")
- **pbs.** Handles the Clipboard and clippings files.
- **DesktopDB.** The server for the database used by the Finder and the Dock to identify applications and documents.

---

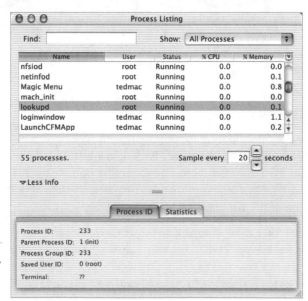

*Figure 5.5*

*ProcessViewer with "Show All Processes" selected. "lookupd" is highlighted.*

**TAKE NOTE** ▶ **Screen Captures**

You can press Command-Shift-3 (whole screen) and Command-Shift-4 (user-defined selection of screen) to take snapshots of the screen in Mac OS X, just as you can in Mac OS 9. By default, in Mac OS X, screen shots are saved to the user's Desktop as tiff files (Picture 1.tiff, for example).

**Screen captures that go the to root user.** Somewhat surprisingly, you can take a screen capture of the log in window (that is, even before your log in). The problem is that because you have not yet selected a user, it is not clear which user's Desktop should contain the saved image. The OS solves this problem by storing the image file on the Desktop of the root user.

The same thing happens when taking screen captures of applications that run as root (that is, run as if launched by the root user). For example, portions of Disk Utility is run as root. Thus, when I took screenshots of Disk Utility windows at certain points (for example, of unmount errors, as seen in **Figure 5.15**), they were saved to the Desktop of the root user.

You can access these root-level images in a couple of ways. The simplest is to log in as a root user (as described in Chapter 3). The pictures will be on the Desktop when you arrive.

Otherwise, you can view the contents of the Root's Desktop in the /private/var/root/Desktop directory. See "Take Note: The Location of Desktop and Trash Folders," in Chapter 3, for details on how to do this.

Once the Desktop contents are listed, you can move files to your own home directory via the <mv> or <cp> commands, as described more in Chapter 10. For example, I would type: <mv "Picture 1.tiff" /Users/tedmac> to move Picture 1 to my home directory. From here, I can open the picture. If the file is still owned by root, you may have to use a utility such as XRay to change its ownership to yourself. Otherwise, you will be unable to modify or delete the file.

**Changing screen capture format.** Screen-shot files are saved as TIFF images. TIFF, however, is simply the default choice among four possible choices: TIFF, JPEG, PNG, and PICT. To switch to one of the other choices, follow these steps:

1. Launch Terminal.

2. Type <defaults write NSGlobalDomain AppleScreenShotFormat ImageFormat>.

   ImageFormat is one of the four graphic formats (presumably, something other than TIFF).

3. Log out, and log back in.

   The next time you take a screen shot, your Mac should use the new format.

Alternatively, you can use a third-party System Preferences pane such as TinkerTool or OrangePref.

Note: Screen captures taken when a Classic application is active are saved to the Mac OS 9 Desktop Folder, rather than the Mac OS X one. The files are saved as PICT files, not TIFF files.

If you need even more screen-shot features, get the shareware Snapz Pro X. Forget the Grab utility that comes with Mac OS X; it is one of the weakest links in the Mac OS X software.

# Alternative Mac OS X Startup Paths

I've already covered a couple of detours from the normal startup procedure, such as starting up from a CD or booting into Open Firmware. These methods function whether you're starting up in Mac OS X or Mac OS 9. A few additional detours are specific to Mac OS X only.

## Single-user mode

If you press Command-S at startup, you will start up in what is called *single-user mode*. In essence, this mode drops you directly into Mac OS X's command-line interface. The screen will turn black and begin to fill with a series of text lines in white (perhaps with some text in yellow). You can ignore all this text. Eventually, the screen will stop at a command-line prompt, where you can enter text commands. If you have experience using Mac OS X's Terminal application, you will feel right at home.

For troubleshooting, the main use for single-user mode is to attempt disk repairs, especially when your Mac will not start up otherwise. From the single-user-mode screen, you run a Unix utility called fsck (for File System Consistency checK), which is essentially the same thing as running the First Aid component of Disk Utility. Thus, this utility may repair the cause of the startup (or other) problems.

**SEE:** • **"Run fsck," later in this chapter, for more details.**

If you get the idea that starting up in single-user mode bypasses the password-security protections that Mac OS X has in place, you would be correct. A user in single-user mode has the same authority as a root user. If you want to block unauthorized users from single-user access, you would need to enable full Open Firmware password protection.

## Verbose mode

If you press Command-V at startup, you start up in verbose mode, which looks very similar to starting up in single-user mode. The main difference is that in verbose mode, the Mac never stops for you to enter commands. After you see all the white and yellow text, a normal Mac OS X log in begins.

Thus, verbose mode is used mainly to check for error messages contained in the initial text. This information usually is of interest only to software developers. The white text, for example, gives you information about the progress of the initialization process; the yellow text is usually an alert about a possible problem with a kext file. You could view most of this information from console logs. Verbose mode would be of value, however, if the error in question is preventing a normal startup and, thus, preventing access to the Console application.

**SEE:** • Chapter 3 for coverage of the Console application.

---

**TECHNICALLY SPEAKING ▶ Kext-file Errors That Aren't**

Speaking of Console, if you check the system log in Console, you may notice an odd pair of error messages citing msdosfs.kext and webdav_fs.kext as "not a valid kernel extension bundle." If you check for these files in /System/Library/Extensions, you will indeed find that they are a bit unusual. In particular, they are ordinary folders rather than the package-file format used by the other kext files.

Apple explains that this happens because they were built in an "old format." Nevertheless, they work fine, and you can safely ignore the warnings.

---

If you are familiar with Unix jargon, verbose mode may give you a clue as to the source of a problem. One user, for example, was able to confirm that a problem with his Date & Time setting was due to a failure of the Network Time software loading at startup, as determined by a getGMTTimeOfDay error message in verbose mode. Shifting to a different server solved the problem.

For everyday troubleshooting, however, you will almost never need verbose mode. I could find only one example in which Apple recommended using it, and it involved Mac OS X Server, not the more common client software installed by almost all Mac OS X users. The problem involved a startup failure, and the solution required accessing the problem computer from another computer on the network. This problem gets beyond the level of troubleshooting covered in this book, so I will not pursue it further.

## Log in as console

When you get to the log in window, you typically log in with your user name. Occasionally (as covered in Chapter 3), you may choose to log in as the root user instead, using root as the username.

As it turns out, you can use another "name" here: >*console*. (Note: This name is unrelated to the Console application in the Utilities folder.) No password is needed yet. You will go to a screen that is much like Terminal, except that the text is white on black, as it is in single-user mode. You will need to log in at this screen, giving your name and password before you proceed.

When you are logged in via the >*console* option, it is as though you are in Terminal. The primary reason for doing this if you would like to use Terminal to solve a problem, but the problem is one that prevents you from successfully logging in via normal methods (thus prohibiting normal access to Terminal).

One example where logging in as console could help is with a symptom in which icons in the Dock, as well as application icons, appear as folders. Typically, double-clicking these icons will fail to open the files. Most often, you can fix this problem by deleting the LS files in the Library/Preferences folder of your Home directory. Ideally, drag the files to the Trash, log out, log back in, and then empty the Trash. Occasionally, however, you may be unable to delete these files from the Finder. Or this method may not appear to result in new default versions of these files; rather, the original problem versions are re-created. You could solve this problem by deleting the files from Terminal, but now Terminal is one of the applications that will not launch. The solution is to delete thee files via console access. The exact steps are as follows:

1. Type >console in the user-name field at the log in prompt (no password needed).

   If you are set to log in automatically at startup, you will have to log out and choose the Other User option to get this prompt.

2. At the next prompt that appears, log in with your normal name and password.

3. Type <cd /~/Library/Preferences>.

   This command takes you to the Preferences folder inside the Library folder of your Home directory.

4. Delete all the LaunchServices files located in this folder by typing the following, pressing Return after each line:

   rm LS*
   rm .LS*

   The rm command deletes (removes) files. By typing both command lines, you delete not only the visible LS files (such as LSSchemes) but also the invisible backup versions (such as .LSSchemes_Backup).

5. Type <logout> or <exit> to return to the normal log in window.

6. Log in as yourself, and all should be well.

**SEE:** • **"Type and Creator vs. File Extensions," in Chapter 3, for more information on LS files.**

   • **"Working with Invisible Files," in Chapter 6, for more information on invisible files.**

   • **Chapter 10 for more information on Unix commands.**

**TAKE NOTE ▶ Other Log In User-Name Options**

In addition to the >console command mentioned in the main text, a few other special commands work when you type them in the log in window's user-name text box. These commands are:

- **>restart.** Restarts the Mac.
- **>power.** Shuts down the Mac.
- **>exit.** Quits and relaunches the log in window.

**TAKE NOTE ▶ Forgot Your Password?**

What if you forget your log in password? How do you find it so that you can log in again? Here's how:

- If you are not an admin user, have an admin user log in. This user can reset your password in the Users System Preferences window.
- If you are an admin user, and there is more than one admin account, have the other admin user log in. This user can reset a new password in the Users System Preferences window.
- If you are the only admin user, use the Reset Password utility included on the Mac OS X Install CD (described in Chapter 2).

**TAKE NOTE ▶ Switching Between Mac OS 9 and Mac OS X**

A quick review:

- If you are currently in Mac OS X and want to restart in Mac OS 9, go to the Startup Disk System Preferences window, select the desired Mac OS 9 volume, and click the Restart button. Click Save and Restart in the confirmation window that appears. Note: A gold 9 badge appears on the icon of a Mac OS 9 System Folder if it is located on the same volume as Mac OS X.
- If you are currently in Mac OS 9 and want to restart in Mac OS X, go to the Startup Disk control panel and select the desired Mac OS X volume. If a volume has more than one potential startup OS, a disclosure triangle will appear to the left of its name. In this case, click the disclosure triangle to reveal all OS options. Click the Mac OS X option to select it. Then click Restart.

You can also switch startup volumes by holding down the Option key at startup, as explained in the main text. For volumes that contain both Mac OS X and Mac OS 9, however, only the most recently booted OS will be listed.

Finally, you can switch from Mac OS 9 to Mac OS X, by holding down the X key at startup, but only if both OS versions are on the same volume.

# Startup Crashes

One of the hallmarks of Mac OS X is its stability. When you get it up and running, you rarely will have a system crash that requires you to restart the computer. This fact is small comfort, however, if you get a crash or freeze during startup, preventing the system from running at all. This section explores the various causes of such startup crashes and explains what to do about them.

## Blank gray screen

When you start up a Mac, the initial screen is gray. If things are going well, a Happy Mac icon should appear soon, followed by the blue screen that indicates that Mac OS X is starting up.

Sometimes, however, the Mac never gets to the blue screen, stalling out at the gray screen. In one such case, all you see is the initial blank gray screen. In this case, a hardware incompatibility or failure looms as the most likely cause. Some of these problems may be specific to Mac OS X, in which case your Mac may still work if you try to start up in Mac OS 9. Mac OS X tends to be less forgiving of hardware anomalies than Mac OS 9 is. More likely, is the problem is a general one that will cause a failure regardless of the OS you select.

If your Mac came with a Hardware Test CD (see "Technically Speaking: The Apple Hardware Test CD" earlier in this chapter), now would be the time to use it. It may identify the problem.

Following are a few specific examples of what can precipitate a gray-screen crash:

**SCSI cards.** Mac OS X will not start up if certain SCSI cards are installed in a desktop Mac's PCI card slots. Clearly, this problem would not include any of the ones that ship from Apple, but other cards may precipitate a problem. Similarly, if you have several SCSI devices attached to a SCSI card, a startup crash may occur in Mac OS X even though Mac OS 9 boots just fine. This problem generally is the result of improper termination of devices on the SCSI chain. See the Apple Knowledge Base article on "Connecting SCSI Devices" (**http://docs.info.apple.com/article.html?artnum=9387**) or *Sad Macs* for more details on SCSI termination.

If the problem is due to the SCSI card itself, updating the firmware of the card may fix the problem. Otherwise, you may need an entirely new card. Check MacFixIt or the card vendor's Web site to see whether a firmware update is available or some other solution is suggested.

**Memory.** If you added memory (RAM) to your Mac, the RAM may not be compatible with your Mac model. There are subtle variations in the types of RAM available for Macs. You could have a module that appears to be the correct type but in fact is not. Or you may have a defective module, even if it is the correct type. All these situations could lead to a crash.

In some cases, updating the Mac's firmware, although generally recommended, may precipitate a startup failure due to a RAM incompatibility, even though the Mac worked before the upgrade.

**SEE:** • "Take Note: Open Firmware Updates," earlier in this chapter.

Sources such as Apple's own AppleSpec document (**www.info.apple.com/applespec/applespec.taf**) offer details about the precise memory specifications for each Mac. In most cases, however, if you buy from a reputable RAM vendor, you should get the correct memory simply by telling the vendor what Mac you have. You shouldn't have to investigate. If problems occur, the vendor should replace the memory free or for a nominal charge.

If the memory is defective, even though it may be the correct type, it should be replaced.

**External devices.** Finally, any device added to the Mac's other ports (USB, FireWire, or PCMCIA), may precipitate a startup crash. Most such devices should work fine. But some devices—especially those that may not have been updated to work with Mac OS X—may remain a problem. To test this possibility, disconnect all peripheral devices from your Mac and restart. If the Mac starts up successfully, one device may have been the cause. If so, start adding devices back one at a time, restarting each time. When the crash recurs, the most recently added device is the likely source of the problem. At this point, contact the vendor of the device, or check sites such as MacFixIt, to determine whether a fix is available (such as a firmware upgrade or driver update for the device) or whether you need to abandon using the device in Mac OS X.

If the problem is due to a USB or FireWire device, not plugging in the device until startup is over may be a workaround for the problem. In other cases, switching from connecting the device through a USB or FireWire hub and using the port directly on the Mac may help (or vice versa).

If none of these fixes work, you may have a disk problem. If so, try to repair it.

**SEE:** • "Solving Mac OS X Crashes," later in this chapter.

**TAKE NOTE ▶ Startup Failure Only When Starting Up from a CD or External Drive**

**CD drives.** In some cases, a hardware conflict may prevent you from starting up from a CD, even though you can start up normally from your hard drive. In this case, the solution may be simple, if a bit inconvenient. If a USB device is the cause, remove the device, boot from the CD, and do what you need to do (such as install the software from the CD). Then shut down, reattach the device, and restart from your hard drive.

If the symptom is not a crash but the Mac refuses to start up from the CD, shifting instead to the hard drive, the CD may not be a bootable CD. If you burned the CD yourself, this situation is especially likely, as burning a bootable CD requires more than simply copying the files from one CD to another, as you might do via the Finder's disc-burning feature. In this case, the solution is to reburn the CD correctly.

**External drives.** Some external hard drives, such as FireWire drives, may work just fine when they are not the startup device. If you install Mac OS X on the device and try to use it as a startup drive, however, it will fail. Fixing this problem will usually require a firmware update, either for the Mac itself or for the hard drive. Make sure that you have installed the latest firmware update for your Mac. Check with the drive vendor for possible firmware updates. In some cases, the fix may require that a hardware component of the drive be replaced. When you purchase a FireWire drive, make sure that it uses the Oxford 911 chipset, which generally is needed for Mac OS X compatibility.

For FireWire or USB startup drives, if selecting it in the Startup Disk System Preferences window does not result in starting up from the drive, restart and hold down the Option key at startup; then select the drive from the choices that appear in the Startup Manager screen. Otherwise, start up in Mac OS 9, and select the drive in the Startup Disk control panel. (Make sure that you are using version 9.2.1 or later of the control panel.)

Note: I had one case where, I could not startup from an external FireWire drive and attempting to do so prevented any startup at all. A gray screen crash occurred. Further, no startup volumes were listed if I held down the Option key at startup. The only solution was to disconnect the FireWire device from the Mac and restart.

**SEE:**   • "Take Note: Create a Bootable CD," in Chapter 3.
         • **Chapter 2 for information on problems with installing and booting from Mac OS X, especially the restriction that Mac OS X be installed.**

# Flashing question-mark icon

A variation on gray-screen startup problems is a folder icon with a flashing question mark appearing instead of the smiling-Mac icon. In most cases, this problem should occur only when you're trying to start up in Mac OS 9, if the Mac cannot find a valid Mac OS 9 System Folder for some reason. But I have also seen it when trying to startup in Mac OS X.

**Benign variation.** In the benign variation of this problem, the question mark is soon replaced by the smiling Mac, and all proceeds normally thereafter. This typically means that no default startup device is selected or that the default device is not connected to the Mac. In such cases, the Mac will search through the available startup devices and select one. This search causes the delay.

If this problem occurs at each startup, you usually can fix it by opening the Startup Disk System Preferences window and selecting a startup volume. Then close the System Preferences window to save the change. The next time you restart, the question-mark icon should no longer appear.

**Malignant variation.** If the question-mark icon persists, you obviously have a more serious problem. In this case, you will likely need to restart in Mac OS 9, typically by holding down the Option key at startup and selecting an available Mac OS 9 volume. If no Mac OS 9 volume is listed or you cannot start up in Mac OS 9, either, you will need to try to start up from a bootable Mac OS 9 CD. In either case, when you reach the Desktop, select the desired Mac OS X volume in the Startup Disk control panel, making sure that the control panel version is version 9.2.1 or later. Then restart. The Mac OS X volume should boot.

If Startup Disk does not allow you to select a System folder as the startup OS, the OS software may be damaged and will need to be reinstalled. For Mac OS 9, make sure that the minimum required software (System and Finder) is in the folder.

If you cannot start up from a hard drive under any circumstances, and if (after starting up from a CD) your hard drive volumes do not mount, your hard drive is need of repair or replacement.

**SEE:** • "Solving Mac OS X Crashes," later in this chapter, for specific advice on reinstalling Mac OS X and repairing disks.

**TAKE NOTE** ▶ **Blessed Systems and Starting Up**

A Mac OS 9 or Mac OS X System folder that the Mac recognizes as one that can be used to start up the Mac is called a blessed folder.

**The BootX file.** Located in System/Library/CoreServices is a file called BootX. As I discussed earlier in this chapter, this file is an essential piece of software for booting from Mac OS X. In fact, if it is missing, you will be unable to start up Mac OS X from this volume at all, getting the blinking question-mark icon instead. Somewhat surprisingly, I found that the file need not be in the CoreServices folder to work. If I moved it to the root level of the drive, I could still start up. Only when I deleted it did startup fail.

In some cases, the Mac OS X System folder may become unblessed. You can tell this has happened if the X icon that appears on the CoreServices folder as well as on the Mac OS X System folder no longer appears. (You see this X icon only when you boot in Mac OS X.) If this situation occurs, dragging the BootX file out of the System folder and then returning it to is location in CoreServices may help. Being able to do this means that you somehow got to the Desktop despite the fact that the Mac OS X System is not booting. Typically, you would boot either from Mac OS 9 or from another drive (an external FireWire drive, for example) that contains Mac OS X. I am not convinced that this attempt to rebless will work, but it is worth a try.

A BootX file by itself is not sufficient to start up in Mac OS X. The rest of the Mac OS X software must also be present and in working order.

**Blessed folder in Mac OS 9.** Just for the record, a similar situation exists in Mac OS 9. For the Mac to start up from Mac OS 9, it typically must locate a blessed System Folder. A blessed System Folder is one whose folder icon has a mini Mac face icon in it, as you see when you boot in Mac OS 9. If Mac OS 9 and Mac OS X are on the same volume, however, and Mac OS X was the startup OS the last time you started up from that volume, there may be no icon on the folder, because the Mac OS 9 System Folder gets unblessed when Mac OS X is selected as the startup OS from that volume. You typically can rebless the System Folder, if you want, by selecting it as the startup OS in the Startup Disk control panel. Otherwise, dragging the System file out of the System Folder and dragging it back in again should rebless the System Folder.

I mention all this to emphasize the point I alluded to in the main text: If the Mac cannot find any blessed Mac OS 9 or BootX Mac OS X System folder, you will get the persistent blinking question mark at startup.

Complicating matters a bit, the Mac OS 9 System Folder that is currently selected to launch when you launch Classic will have a 9 icon in it when viewed in Mac OS X. This icon is separate from the blessed-folder icon described earlier in this chapter.

*Figure 5.6*

*Icons on blessed System folders.*

System

System Folder

# Broken-folder icon

Yet another variation on the gray-screen startup problem occurs when before the happy-Mac icon appears, you get a folder icon that appears to be ripped in two. This icon is typically called the broken-folder icon. Startup halts at this point.

I still have some uncertainty about exactly what triggers this icon symptom. It apparently occurs more often when Mac OS X and Mac OS 9 are on the same volume. Beyond that, here is what else appears to be true:

**Old version of Startup Disk control panel used.** Selecting Mac OS X as the startup OS, when you're booted in Mac OS 9, and using a pre-9.2.1 version of the Mac OS 9 Startup Disk control panel may cause this symptom (as opposed to the related question-mark-icon symptom).

---

**TAKE NOTE** ▶ **Startup Disk Control Panel and "No Valid System Folder" error**

Using a pre-Mac OS 9.2.1 version of Startup Disk may also result in the following error message's appearing at startup: "The startup disk no longer has a valid System Folder. 'System' and 'Finder' must be in the System Folder. If you continue, you may not be able to restart the computer. Do you want to continue?" This message, which appears to be referring to Mac OS 9, may appear even if you have selected Mac OS X as the startup volume. If this situation happens, follow these steps:

1. Click the Cancel button.

2. Obtain a copy of Startup Disk 9.2.1 or later, and install it on your drive.

   If you do not have this program on a Mac OS Install CD, you can get it from Apple's Software Downloads site (http://www.info.apple.com/support/downloads.html)

3. Use the updated control panel to select Mac OS X.

---

**mach_kernel deleted.** Deleting the Mac OS X mach_kernel file (which may be visible on the Desktop when you're booted in Mac OS 9) will result in this broken folder symptom. This file likely be deleted only by someone who is using Mac OS 9 and erroneously concludes that this file is not important and can be trashed.

**Disk formatting and Mac OS X installation problems.** Formatting a drive with software other than Apple's Disk Utility could cause this symptom if the formatting software is incompatible with Mac OS X. Some versions of FWB's Hard Disk ToolKit, for example, have been known to cause this problem. Check with the vendor of the software for Mac OS X compatibility information. The fix is to reformat the disk by booting from the Mac OS X Install CD and selecting the Disk Utility option (as described in Chapter 2). Then reinstall Mac OS X.

If you tried to install Mac OS X, and the installation failed for any reason, further attempts to install Mac OS X may continue to fail. When you try to start up in Mac OS X under this failed System, the broken-folder icon will likely appear.

In this case, your best bet is to try to reinstall Mac OS X, this time with the option to reinitialize the drive selected. This technique should bypass any problems with corrupted files that were the likely cause of the installation failure. Using the Restore CDs that came with your Mac (instead of the Install CD) is also a possibility (see Chapter 2).

As reinitializing/reformatting a disk also erases the disk, reboot in Mac OS 9 and save any files you haven't backed up before proceeding.

**External devices (again!).** Having Mac OS X-incompatible PCI cards, SCSI devices, or external FireWire drives connected to the Mac can cause this symptom. The incompatibility could be in the firmware on the device or in the kext file's device driver software.

In such cases, the temporary solution is to disconnect those devices. Sometimes, they will work if they are reconnected after startup is over; sometimes, they will not.

Long-term solutions include updating the device's firmware or driver. Check the vendor's Web site for information on the availability of such updates, as well as other advice. Updating to the latest version of Mac OS X is also a good idea, as Apple generally improves support for peripheral devices with each new release. If the OS was starting successfully with the device attached but no longer does so, the existing software may have become corrupt. In this case, simply reinstalling the current version of Mac OS X (or of the device driver software) may be sufficient. As a last resort, replace the hardware device with a Mac OS X-compatible one from a different vendor.

Finally, starting up from the Mac OS X Install CD in a third-party CD drive may result in the broken-folder symptom. In this case, you will need to use the Mac's internal CD drive instead.

SEE: • "Blank gray screen," earlier in this chapter, for related information on problems with external devices, including how to determine the problem device.

---

**TECHNICALLY SPEAKING ▶ Mach Files Visible When You Boot from Mac OS 9**

When you are booted in Mac OS 9, you will see three mach files on the Desktop: mach, mach.sym, and mach_kernel. These files are needed for Mac OS X, not Mac OS 9. The first two are re-created when you start up in Mac OS X, so even if you delete them accidentally, you will be OK. The mach_kernel file, however, is critical and will not be re-created. When I deleted it as an experiment, I got the broken-folder icon at startup. Ideally, Apple should make this kernel file invisible when you're booting in Mac OS 9.

# Belted-folder icon

This final variation on the gray-screen startup problem is another rare one that most users will never see. In this case, startup stalls, and instead of the happy-Mac icon, you get a folder icon with a belt around it (as if to imply that the inside of the folder is inaccessible).

Again, there is some uncertainty about all the situations that may trigger this error. (Apple has not been all that helpful in providing details.) One example occurs if the Software Restore discs that came with your computer contain only Mac OS 9 (newer versions contain Mac OS 9 and Mac OS X), and you attempt to use these discs to restore Mac OS 9 software to a volume that now has Mac OS X on the same volume.

If you want to reinstall Mac OS 9 in this sort of setup, use the Software Install CD, not the Software Restore ones. If you have used the Software Restore CD in error, the belted-folder icon may appear the next time you try to start up in Mac OS X. Fixing this problem is sufficiently complex that I will not provide details here. You may have to use Terminal to duplicate and move your Home directory to a new location, for example. You can find the details in Apple Knowledge Base article 106294, "How to Reinstall Mac OS 9 or Recover From a Software Restore" (`http://docs.info.apple.com/article.html?artnum=106294`).

**SEE:** • Chapter 2 for more information on installing Mac OS X.

# Dumped into Unix

A rare startup problem can occur when you go from the gray screen directly to the command-line black screen that you normally see if you boot via single-user mode.

In this case, you typically see a line of text that says, "file system dirty, run fsck." You can run fsck directly at this point. You do not need to restart and hold down Command-S to restart in single-user mode.

**SEE:** • "Run fsck," later in this chapter, for more details.

If running fsck does not fix the problem, the likely cause is that critical Unix files are missing or corrupted. Unix users might be able to figure out exactly what went wrong and fix the problem from the command line. For most Mac users, however, the solution at this point will be to reinstall Mac OS X.

# Blue-screen crash

If Mac OS X successfully navigates past the gray screen at startup, the screen will turn blue, followed shortly by the appearance of the Mac OS X logo.

Within the box that contains the logo, a series of messages appears, stating that various services (such as AppleTalk) have been initialized, configured, or started. When this process is over, the Mac will either halt at the log in window or (if you have elected automatic log in) proceed directly to launching the Finder and the Dock.

During this blue-screen stage, a freeze or crash may occur. Most likely, the problem will be related to a service that failed to load. The most likely symptom will be a blank blue screen with the log in window never appearing. In this case, try the following:

**Network Services stall.** One of the most common causes of a blue-screen freeze is a problem with network services. If your network connections have changed from what you set in the Network System Preferences window, you may get a long stall. This could happen, for example, if the OS winds up looking for an Ethernet network that no longer exists. Usually, the OS will start up on its own if you simply have the patience to outwait this stall (which can take several minutes). If not, you may have success by modifying your network-connection hardware. In particular, if you have an Ethernet cable attached to your Mac, disconnect it. Conversely, if you normally have an Ethernet cable connected to your Mac but the cable is disconnected, reconnect it. If you use a cable modem and you have disconnected it or turned it off, make sure that the cable modem is active and connected. And so on.

If this technique works, the stall may end, and log in will proceed immediately. In any case, when you finish starting up, and if you intend to maintain whatever arrangement led to the stall, you may need to reestablish your settings in the Network System Preferences window to prevent the stall from happening again. You can prevent a stall by changing your active port before shutdown to one that the OS can locate on restart. (Do not leave AirPort as active if you will not be able to connect to AirPort at log in, for example.) If none of these measures has been successful, and you are still stalled at the blue screen, proceed to the next step.

**Auto-dial problem.** The PPP tab of the Internal Modem pane of Network System Preferences includes a button called "PPP Options." In the window that appears if you click that option is a checkbox for "Connect automatically when starting TCP/IP applications." Under certain conditions, if this auto-dial option is enabled, it may cause a blue-screen crash at log in. As you cannot startup in Mac OS X to disable the option at this point, the solution is to do so from single user mode. From here you can delete the preferences file where the setting is stored. This will result in a new default preferences file created at startup, with all your customized changes lost (and the relevant option disabled). You will need to reenter your customized settings when you finally log in. But at least you can startup. To do this fix:

1. Hold down the Command-S keys at startup to enter single user mode.

2. Type: <mount -uw /> and press Return.

3. Type: <mv /var/db/SystemConfiguration/preferences.xml preferences.old> and press Return.

4. Type: <reboot> and press Return.

**Restart in Mac OS 9 and remove potentially problem-causing files.**
Use the Option key at startup method to restart in Mac OS 9. These files could also be removed after booting in Mac OS X (assuming you could work-around potential permissions problems, as covered previously in this chapter and in Chapter 6). However, in the current situation, I am assuming a crash at startup of Mac OS X, which thus makes booting in Mac OS 9 a necessity.

**SEE:** • "Logout/restart," later in this chapter.

After restarting, try the following as needed:

**Remove Mac OS 9 Fonts.** When you are in Mac OS 9, remove the Fonts folder from the Mac OS 9 System Folder used by Classic and drag it to the Desktop. Also consider removing any fonts in the Fonts folders of Mac OS X (see Chapter 4 for details on Fonts folders) that you may have added since installing Mac OS X—especially older fonts originally used in Mac OS 9. Do all this to check for the possibility that an incompatible or corrupt font is causing the crash. Restart in Mac OS X by selecting the Mac OS X partition in the Startup Disk control panel. If the crash no longer occurs, one of the fonts you removed is the likely cause. You can start replacing fonts and restarting to isolate the file. If removing fonts did not eliminate the crash, you can return all fonts to their respective locations and proceed to the next step.

**SEE:** • "Check fonts," later in this chapter.

**Remove third-party startup items.** Remove items from the /Library/StartupItems folder. Certain third-party software adds items to this folder, as described earlier in this chapter. These items launch during this phase of startup. In general, do not remove items from the /System/Library/StartupItems folder, as these are the items installed directly by the Mac OS. However, if you know that a file in this folder is a third-party file, you can remove it. Restart in Mac OS X by selecting the Mac OS X partition in the Startup Disk control panel. If the crash no longer occurs, one of the files you removed is the likely cause. You can start replacing files and restarting to isolate the file. If removing files did not eliminate the crash, you can return all files to this folder and proceed to the next step.

**Remove kext files.** It is possible, although unlikely, that a kext file is at fault. If you know that third-party software has installed additional files in /System/Library/Extensions, you may experiment with removing them. Or as explained in "Technically Speaking: Understanding Kernel Extensions" earlier in this chapter, you may delete the Extensions.mkext file. In general, do not modify or remove the kext files installed by Mac OS X itself. Restart again in Mac OS X to see whether this technique eliminates the blue-screen crash.

**In general...** You can follow the same basic principles for any file that you suspect is causing the startup problem.

**Software repairs.** If none of the above methods is successful, your hard drive may need repair. To do so, run a disk repair utility from a bootable CD or run fsck from single user mode. Otherwise, you may need to reinstall Mac OS X.

SEE: • "Solving Mac OS X Crashes," later in this chapter, for specific advice on reinstalling Mac OS X and repairing disks.

**Hardware issues.** If all else fails, the problem may be hardware-related. Refer to the preceding sections on gray-screen crashes for more advice.

## Kernel panic at startup

The most serious type of system crash you can get with Mac OS X is a kernel panic. Kernel panics can occur at startup, so I discuss them here. These problems occur more often, however, while you're using Mac OS X—most often when you launch an application or choose a command from one of its menus. The logic is the same in either case.

According to Apple: "A kernel panic is a type of error that occurs when the core (kernel) of an operating system receives an instruction in an unexpected format or that it fails to handle properly. A kernel panic may also follow when the operating system is not able to recover from a different type of error. A kernel panic can be caused by damaged or incompatible software or, more rarely, damaged or incompatible hardware."

When this happens, the typical symptom is strings of text, with error messages, appearing on the screen over the current Aqua display. At this point, everything stops working. The good news is that you don't have to take the blame for the crash. The bad news is that you can't do anything to fix the problem except avoid what caused it and wait for the bug fix from Apple (or the third party that makes the offending software).

With each Mac OS X update, Apple may fix bugs that caused kernel panics in the previous OS version. Thus, a discussion of the causes of kernel panics tends to be Mac OS X-version-specific. With that in mind, here are some things that resulted in kernel panics in Mac OS 10.0.x and/or 10.1.x:

- You eject a CD while the iTunes application is opening.
- You try to make a PPP connection, especially on a dual-processor G4 Macs.

- Third-party RAM is not within the specs for your Mac, even if the same RAM works fine in Mac OS 9.

- You have a blank CD in an SCSI-connected CD-RW at startup.

More generally, there are two main causes for a kernel panic at startup:

**Hardware.** By far the most common cause is a peripheral hardware device. In general, if a peripheral device is the cause, the only way you can prevent the problem immediately is to disconnect the offending device. The long-term solution is for the hardware vendor to fix the problem by updating the hardware firmware or revising the hardware. I am refraining from listing known devices that cause this problem, as whatever I state will likely be fixed before this book goes to press. In general, be especially suspicious of third-party PCI cards if you get a persistent kernel panic at startup. The obvious way to test this possibility is to remove the card and see whether the problem disappears.

**System Software modifications.** The second major source of a kernel panic occurs if you deliberately or inadvertently modify the Mac OS System software. Making these changes from Mac OS X is hard, because unless you log in as a root user, the OS denies you permission to do so. But if you log in to Mac OS 9 or circumvent the restriction, problems can occur. In particular, be aware of the following:

- The main things to avoid are removing, deleting, or editing any files in the System/Library folders. You can make changes in these folders without harm, as you sometimes need to do to fix certain problems (as I discuss more in other sections of this book), but this technique requires knowing what is OK to do and what is not OK. Any sort of speculative troubleshooting, in which you try something just to see what it does, is could easily lead to disaster.

- Modifying (especially deleting) the contents of the normally invisible Unix folders (bin, var, and so on) is another potential path to system crashes, kernel panics, and just about anything else that can go wrong. Again, there are files here you can modify or delete without harm (as I described in various places throughout this book). But unless you know what is OK and not OK, avoid experimenting.

- Moving Applications, System, Library, or any other OS-installed folder outside its default location is very much not recommended.

- Modifying the permissions and ownership of critical Mac OS X files can cause similar problems. In essence, changing the access to a file so that the OS cannot use it when needed is functionally equivalent to deleting it. So don't even think about modifying the permissions settings for files in the Mac OS X System/Library folder. If you want to limit or expand access to these files, you have other ways of doing so, as I discuss in Chapter 6.

- If you have made any of these changes and can undo them (possibly via starting from another Mac OS X volume), do so. Then try to restart in Mac OS X from the problem volume. Ideally, the startup will work. Otherwise, you are looking at reinstalling the entire OS.

**SEE:** • **"Solving Mac OS X Crashes," later in this chapter, for specific advice on reinstalling Mac OS X.**

Finally, as kernel panics are both serious and rare, Apple is always interested in getting feedback from users about how and when a kernel panic occurred and what the text said. This information will assist Apple in figuring out why the problem occurred and what it can do to fix the bug that caused the problem. You can't take a screen shot of a Mac with a panic, because the screen-shot software will no longer work, so write down the text or take a photo of it with a digital camera. Especially note any lines that follow the word *Backtrace*. Also note any text that follows DSISR=, DAR=, or PC=. Then post the details at Apple's Discussion Boards (http://www.apple.com/support/).

# Application Crashes

Most application crashes in Mac OS X will not bring your entire system down; neither will they require you to restart your Mac. Thus, in many cases, the cure for an application crash is to ignore it, relaunch the crashed application, and hope that the crash does not occur again (or at least happens only rarely). If that is not sufficient to solve a particular crash problem, consider the following.

**SEE:** • **"Technically Speaking: Crash Reporter" and "Take Note: The Developers Tools CD," in Chapter 3, for related information, including using the BombApp program to simulate a crash.**

## Endlessly spinning cursors : freeze/hang

An application running in Mac OS X may sometimes mimic a Mac OS 9 hang; the beach-ball cursor will continue to spin endlessly, and all attempts to access the application fail. Mac OS 9's Cancel command (Command-period) often does not work in Mac OS X; I found it especially useless when trying to cancel a Sherlock search. Sometimes, nothing is wrong. The application is just taking an unusually long time to complete its task. If you come back a few minutes later, all will be well.

The silver lining is that unlike those in Mac OS 9, freezes in Mac OS X are almost always limited to the affected application. That is, if you simply click the window of another application, the spinning cursor vanishes, and your Mac is working normally again. Return to the problem application, and the symptom returns. Still, on the assumption that you would like to use the frozen application again, you'll want to fix the problem. To do so:

- Force Quit the application.

**SEE:** • "Force Quit," later in this chapter.

- If Force Quitting doesn't work, but you can still access the Apple menu, choose Log Out from that menu. When you log back in, things should be working normally again.

- If the Log Out command doesn't work, try choosing Restart. The logic is the same.

- In the worst case, the freeze will appear to affect everything. No command works in any application. In this case, you will need to do a hard restart.

**SEE:** • "Log Out/Restart/Reset," later in this chapter.

---

**TAKE NOTE ▶ Problems With Items Auto-Launching at Startup**

**Login items.** Items in your Login Items list (in the Login System Preferences window) load automatically at startup. If you have several items in the Login Items list, not all may load successfully. The workaround is to eliminate one or more of the items from the list and launch them manually as needed.

In some cases, if you have too many items in the list, you may find that if you try to open an application from the Dock—especially if the log in items are still loading—the application will fail to open. In this case, however, the application may stall permanently, with an endlessly bouncing Dock icon. At this point, even a force-quit may not get the application to quit. Your only resort will be to restart.

It is also possible that the order of log in items can cause a conflict. The Read Me file that comes with the current version of QuicKeys, for example, says that its Login List item should be last in the list.

Some items, if they are added to the Login Items list, may cause problems no matter where they are in the list or how many other items are in the list. The most notorious example is iTunesHelper, which is added automatically when you install iTunes 2. The current version seems to be stable. But in earlier versions, having this item in the list could cause a collection of symptoms unrelated to iTunes, including conflicts with third-party applications (such as Suitcase and DragThing) and even a kernel panic.

*continues on next page*

**TAKE NOTE ▶ Problems With Items Auto-Launching at Startup** *continued*

**Disable auto-launching of log in items at startup.** The worst case would be if a conflict with an auto-launched item prevented startup from completing. In this case, you could not disable the log in item, because you cannot get to the System Preferences window to do so. Apple addressed this issue in Mac OS X 10.1.3. Starting with this version, you can disable auto-launched items by holding down the Shift key at startup. (Shades of starting up with Extensions Off in Mac OS 9!) Follow these steps:

1. At startup, as soon as you see the blue background appear with a progress bar and the words Mac OS X, hold down the Shift key.

2. If the log in window appears, release the Shift key to log in; then immediately press and hold down the Shift key again.

   If you are set to log in automatically, you will not need to worry about this step.

3. Release the Shift key after the Desktop appears.

Note: The complete list of all items that are in the Login Items window is stored in ~/Library/Preferences/loginwindow.plist. Editing this file in a text editor (when booted from Mac OS 9, if necessary) is an alternative way to delete an item from the list before startup. With PropertyList Editor, you could do this more simply by deleting the entire contents of the number corresponding to the item you want to delete (0, 1, and so on) under the AutoLaunchedApplicationDictionary heading.

**Classic.** On a related note, you can choose to have Classic automatically launch automatically at startup, via the Classic System Preferences window. I have seen cases in which doing this led to a problem that could be prevented by launching Classic manually after Mac OS X finished loading. In one example, text copied from Classic applications would not paste into Mac OS X ones if Classic was auto-launched at startup. An update to Mac OS X may eventually fix this bug.

SEE: • "Log Out/Restart/Reset," later in this chapter, for more information.

• "Take Note: Preferences Files in Mac OS X," in Chapter 3, for more information on .plist files.

• Chapter 9 for more information on Classic.

**TECHNICALLY SPEAKING ▶ Telnet to a Frozen Mac: Kill Processes, Run Sync**

**Telnet access.** Even when nothing appears to be working, your Mac may be running normally under the surface. What I mean is that the Aqua interface may have temporarily gone belly up, but the Unix underbelly may still be working—if only you can get to it.

In fact, you may be able to access it via another Mac on your network if you enabled the "Allow Remote Login" option in the Sharing tab of the System Preferences window of the Mac that is now frozen. In this case you may be able to connect to the frozen Mac via a Telnet application with SSH (secure shell) support. If the connecting computer is also running Mac OS X, you can use Terminal or MacSSH as the Telnet application. You'll also need to know the IP address of your Mac (as listed in the Sharing System Preferences window) to locate the Mac from the Telnet application. Ideally, this is something you need to know before the Mac is frozen.

Once you are connected, here is what you can do:

**Kill a process.** If a particular process is causing a freeze, killing the process could be the cure. Elsewhere in this chapter, we cover using ProcessViewer to do kill processes. But you cannot use ProcessViewer if your Mac is frozen. The solution, in this case, is to issue a <kill> command remotely, via the Telnet connection. After doing so, you may be able to use your Mac again without having to restart. This technique could be valuable if you have unsaved files in other running applications that you would have lost via a restart.

**Run sync.** Another command you could run is <sync>. This command essentially takes all data in the RAM cache and makes sure that it is written to disk. This technique is also called flushing the cache. Normally, the Mac does this on its own when restarting or shutting down—as well as periodically when the Mac is idle. But when you perform a hard restart (such as by pressing the reset button on the Mac), the Mac does not get a final chance to flush the cache. In such a case, data in the cache may not get written to disk, which could result in corrupted files that will cause new (and potentially more-serious) problems when you try to restart. Although this scenario is not very likely, it is more likely in Mac OS X than in Mac OS 9, because Mac OS X flushes the cache on its own less often than Mac OS 9 does. Issuing a sync command remotely to a frozen Mac eliminates the potential danger.

If remote log in is not possible, and you are worried about sync problems, let the Mac sit idle for a minute or two before restarting. Assuming that the Unix subsystem is still running, it may sync on its own during that time. Or if you still have sufficient access to your Mac that you can run Terminal locally, try typing sync in the command line.

**SEE:** • "Kill from Terminal," later in this chapter, for more on using the "kill" command
        • **Chapter 8 for more on Telnet and other networking issues.**

## Application quits

The most common type of crash in Mac OS X occurs when an application "unexpectedly quits." When this occurs, you may or may not get a message in the Finder informing you of the "quit." Even if you do get a message, it tells you nothing about why the crash occurred.

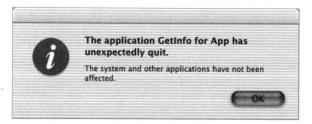

*Figure 5.7*

*The "unexpectedly quit" error message.*

**Crash Reporter.** You can get some more detailed information about the cause of the crash/quit from Crash Reporter, which you enable from the Console application.

**SEE:** • "Technically Speaking: Crash Reporter," in Chapter 3.

When Crash Reporter is enabled and set to display automatically, Console will launch immediately after a crash. It will open to at least one log file, and perhaps two. The first will be the crash.log file for the application that just quit; the second may be the default System log file. The crash file will usually begin with text such as this:

```
Command: Microsoft Word
PID: 551
Exception: EXC_BAD_ACCESS (0x0001)
Codes: KERN_INVALID_ADDRESS (0x0001) at 0x25000000
```

This text will be followed by many lines of technical text, detailing the state of the Mac at the time of the crash. In most cases, unless you are a software developer, the text will be of little use in terms of figuring out exactly what went wrong, and you can do little to fix the cause.

Noting at least the initial lines of text may sometimes be of value, however. This text may provide clues as to what went wrong and suggest a potential fix. In a case of a launch crash of Microsoft Word, for example, the first lines of Console text (after the initial ones) referred to fonts, which suggested that a corrupt font might be the cause. I removed all the fonts from the Library/Fonts folder in my Home directory. Sure enough, that action fixed the crash! Eventually, I was able to isolate the offending font.

```
     ○ ○ ○                    console.log                ┌─────────┐
     report: /Users/tedmac/Library/Logs/GetInfo for App.crash.log

     Apr 16 15:53:30 localhost /usr/libexec/CrashReporter: Succeeded writing crash
     report: /Users/tedmac/Library/Logs/GetInfo for App.crash.log

     Apr 16 16:00:16 localhost /usr/libexec/CrashReporter: Succeeded writing crash
     report: /Users/tedmac/Library/Logs/GetInfo for App.crash.log
     ●  ●  ●          📄 GetInfo for App.crash.log

     Date/Time:   2002-04-16 16:00:15 -0400
     OS Version:  10.1.3 (Build 5Q45)
     Host:        localhost

     Command:     GetInfo for App
     PID:         15567               I

     Exception:   EXC_BAD_ACCESS (0x0001)
     Codes:       KERN_INVALID_ADDRESS (0x0001) at 0x69000000

     Thread 0 Crashed:
     #0    0x706bab68 in objc_msgSend
     #1    0x70162d00 in CFRetain
     #2    0x701660e4 in CFArrayCreate
     #3    0x70831734 in -[NSPlaceholderArray initWithObjects:count:]
     #4    0x7083e688 in +[NSArray arrayWithObjects:count:]
     #5    0x70842908 in +[NSArray arrayWithObjects:]
     #6    0x00003c70 in -[AppInspector guess:]
     #7    0x0000381c in -[AppInspector inspectApp:]
     #8    0x00003620 in -[AppInspector chooseApp:]
     #9    0x70833b28 in -[NSObject performSelector:withObject:]
     #10   0x70c94698 in -[NSApplication sendAction:to:from:]
     #11   0x70c8bbb4 in -[NSControl sendAction:to:]
     #12   0x70c94778 in -[NSCell _sendActionFrom:]
     #13   0x70cdf34c in -[NSCell trackMouse:inRect:ofView:untilMouseUp:]
```

**Figure 5.8**

*Console's console.log and crash log windows following a crash for GetInfo for App.*

**Workarounds and fixes.** After a crash has occurred, and you have looked at any messages and log files, here's what to do next:

- Launch the application again. Often, it will work just fine.

- If the crash keeps recurring, log out and log back in—or restart. Again, the crash may not occur again after you do this.

- If the crash continues after a restart, you can try to diagnose the cause and search for a workaround solution.

Pay particular attention to recent changes you have made in your system. To cite one example, some users experienced an increase in system crashes (even kernel panics) after installing iTunes 2. The cause was the iTunesHelper file that was added to the Login Items list when iTunes was installed. Removing this item from the list eliminated the crash. In such cases, it remains for the developer (Apple, in this case) to fix the software so that you do not need to do the workaround.

Similarly, check the state of the Mac at the time of the crash for possible clues. A program may crash only if Classic is active, for example. In that case, quitting Classic before running the application could be a workaround.

In some cases, the names of applications (aside from the one that crashed) listed in the Crash Reporter log may provide clues as to what other software may be involved. Also check sites such as MacFixIt for possible solutions for specific instances.

- Upgrade or downgrade the software. If the crash occurred after you upgraded to a new version of the software, a bug may have been introduced in the update. Reverting to the older version may eliminate it. Otherwise, check to see whether a newer version fixes the problem.

- Consider a hardware-related cause and workaround. A crash may occur only when the Mac is waking from sleep, which in turn may happen only when peripheral devices are attached to the Mac. If so, the workaround is to disconnect the devices before putting the Mac to sleep.

- Occasionally, an application crash will result in a kernel panic. If this happens, it is almost certain that you will no longer have any access to the Mac and will need to restart. At this point, troubleshooting advice is virtually identical to what you do for a kernel panic at startup.

**SEE:** • "Kernel panic at startup," earlier in this chapter.

- Occasionally, an application will fail to launch, with its Dock icon endlessly bouncing. At this point, even a force-quit may not work. You will likely need to reset the Mac.

**SEE:** • Log out/restart/reset," later in this chapter.

- Otherwise, go to "Solving Mac OS X Crashes" later in this chapter for advice. This section lists such standard troubleshooting techniques as deleting preferences, running repair utilities, and reinstalling software. If nothing works, you may have to give up on using the crashing software until the developer addresses the cause in an update.

**TAKE NOTE ▶ Wake-From-Sleep Crashes**

Occasionally, when trying to wake your Mac from sleep (especially an iBook or PowerBook), the Mac may fail to awaken. Happily, these wake-from-sleep crashes are much less common in Mac OS X than they were in Mac OS 9.

If you do get one in Mac OS X, disconnecting peripheral cables (such as USB and Ethernet) may get the PowerBook out of its coma. If you have a PowerBook G3, Apple suggests pressing the brightness key on the keyboard.

Users report that enabling the "Wake for network administrative access" option, in Energy Saver's Options tab, can prevent some of these crashes.

**TAKE NOTE ▶ Classic Crashes**

Programs running in Classic may crash, just as they would if you were running Mac OS 9 from startup. When they do, what happens is similar to what happens if you were booting from Mac OS 9—that is, you may get a freeze, a Type 2 crash, or whatever. There is one exception, however. In general, the worst that can happen is that the crash brings down the entire Classic environment. You should not need to restart Mac OS X as a result.

If you are trying to work with a Classic application and it freezes or you otherwise appear to have little or no ability to use applications in Classic, you can try a force-quit of the application itself. If you do so, you will get a message from the OS warning you that force-quitting a Classic application is likely to quit the entire Classic environment. Indeed, this will almost always be the case.

If Classic does not quit but continues not to work, you will need to quit it manually. To do so, choose Quit or Force Quit in the Classic System Preferences window. After Classic quits, you can restart it and hope that the problem does not recur.

I have found that problems with Classic are more likely to occur after I wake the OS up from sleep or when I wake Classic up from its inactive mode (set in the Classic System Preferences window). If you intend to be working with Classic for an extended time, it probably is best to keep these options set to Never.

If you have problems with a crash or freeze when Classic first launches, you probably have an old-fashioned extensions conflict with the extensions and control panels in the Mac OS 9 System Folder. Some files that work fine when you boot from OS do not work from Classic.

There is also a known issue where, if the Startup Items folder in the Mac OS 9 System Folder contains aliases to servers that are not currently available, a hang can occur when launching Classic.

**SEE:** • Chapter 9, for information on troubleshooting Classic-related problems.

# Log Out, Restart, or Shut Down Stalls/Crashes

When you Shut Down, the loginwindow background process (mentioned earlier in this chapter) attempts to quit all open processes—first foreground ones and then background ones. If the process succeeds, logout, restart, or shutdown occurs.

If an open application or other process refuses this request to quit, the logout/restart is stalled. The stall may just slow down the exit or it may bring it to a halt. In such a case, here is what to do:

- A stall may occur if an application is waiting for you to save a modified document. In this case, simply save the document; logout should proceed automatically.

- Otherwise, you can usually get around a stall by quitting the application manually and then—if necessary—choosing the Log Out, Restart, or Shut Down command again. For background processes, loginwindow should kill the process itself if the process refuses to quit on its own; you should not need to do anything.

- If the application or background process remains stuck, Force Quit, either via the Force Quit window or ProcessViewer.

**SEE:** • "Force Quit," later in this chapter.

After logging out, the system returns to the log in window. All the initial events that occurred before the log in window appeared do not recur, however. (Kernel extensions are not reloaded, for example.) If you need everything to start over, you will need to do a restart or a shutdown/restart instead of a log out.

**Log Out failure bug.** Apple notes a log out bug in current versions of Mac OS X: "After choosing Log Out, Shut Down, or Restart from the Apple menu, you may see a plain blue screen without the spinning disc cursor. The computer may not subsequently shut down or restart as expected. If you press the Power button on the keyboard (if it has one) a dialog box appears that says: 'Are you sure you want to shut down?' If you click Yes, the computer returns to the Login Window or logs in automatically, depending on your preferences. Apple is investigating this issue. In the meantime, you can force the computer to restart by pressing Control-Command-Power, or by pressing the reset button on the computer."

**SEE:** • "Log Out/Restart/Reset," later in this chapter.

**Software Installer bug and killing loginwindow.** A problem with loginwindow may occur when you are running a third-party installer utility that insists on quitting all open applications before installing the software. In such a case, you may get a message that says, ""Warning! Quitting 'loginwindow' will log you out." Then the OS prevents loginwindow from quitting, and you are not logged out. In effect, this situation prevents the software from installing. This situation is a bug in the installer that will need to be fixed before you can get the installer to work. I have heard that logging in as a root user and running the installer is a workaround for this problem, but I have not had a chance to confirm that this is so.

I have seen various other potential workarounds. One suggestion is to try to kill the loginwindow process, overriding the OS's refusal. You cannot do this from ProcessViewer, as you will get the error message. If you look at the bottom of the ProcessViewer window when loginwindow is selected, however, the first line will say Process ID:, followed by a number, referred to as its PID number. If you launch Terminal and type <kill *PID #*>, you will kill loginwindow and log out. Still, this method is not likely to allow the installer to proceed.

Overall, I recommend not wasting too much time with these workarounds, which may not work anyway; the real solution is for the installer's developer to fix the bug.

# Solving Mac OS X Crashes

Earlier in this chapter, I covered the major startup, freeze, and crash problems you might confront when using your Mac. I also covered some specific solutions for each problem. But many of the same potential solutions are recommended for some of these problems. Rather than go over the same territory repeatedly, I summarize all of these methods in this section, listed more or less in the order I recommend trying them, barring any more-specific advice.

## Force Quit

A force-quit does what its name implies; it gets an application to quit when the normal Quit command fails to work. You can use this technique to unfreeze applications in which the menu commands are inaccessible or do not respond.

You can force-quit an application in various ways:

**Access the Force Quit window.** To do this, press Command-Option-Escape. You can do the same thing in Mac OS 9, but there's a twist: In Mac OS X, the window lists all currently running applications (not just one, as in Mac OS 9). Thus, you get to choose which one you want to quit; the OS doesn't pick it for you. You can also access the Force Quit window by choosing the Force Quit command from the Apple menu.

**TAKE NOTE ▶ Why Force Quit the Finder?**

You can press Command-Option-Escape to force-quit the Finder. Actually, if you do, the button in the window changes from Force Quit to Relaunch (as the Finder must be running for the OS to function normally). This technique can be useful in three situations:

• Fixing certain symptoms with the Finder itself (such as icons that do not display correctly).

• Forcing updating that otherwise would require logging out. If you use TinkerTool (a shareware utility) to make normally invisible files visible, for example, the now-visible files will likely not appear until you log out and log back in again. A shortcut is to quit/relaunch the Finder. The invisible files will appear. Note: The latest versions of TinkerTool now include an option to relaunch the Finder, bypassing the need to use Force Quit.

• Occasionally, the Finder may crash and not relaunch automatically. At this point, your desktop will vanish. The Finder will not be listed in the Force Quit window. However, if you quit all other applications listed in the Force Quit window, the Finder will reappear in the list. You can then relaunch it.

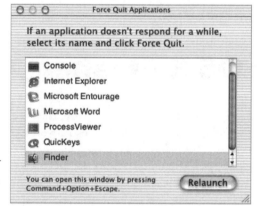

*Figure 5.9*

*The Force Quit window, with the Finder highlighted.*

**Force Quit from the Dock.** Click the icon of an application in the Dock and hold down the mouse button to get the contextual menu. Then press the Option key. The Quit command becomes Force Quit.

**Launch Process Viewer.** This application lists all running processes. An application is a process, but so are many other things that you normally do not see in Aqua. DocklingServer, for example, is the process that keeps the Dock open. Force-quit it, and the Dock disappears briefly and then relaunches. This technique can be useful if you are having some odd symptom that's confined to the Dock.

In most cases, however, you should not attempt to quit processes that are not listed in the Force Quit window, especially administrator processes (ones run by the System, as opposed to you, the user). These processes are often carrying out essential tasks that, should you quit them, could easily make a bad situation worse.

**SEE : • Chapter 3 for more information on Process Viewer.**

**Kill from Terminal.** Launch Terminal, and type <top>. You will get a list of running processes that pretty much duplicates what Process Viewer displays. The first column gives the Process ID (PID) of the process listed in the second column. Type <q> to quit top. Now you can type <kill *PID*> to kill the process with the PID you indicated. This technique is equivalent to doing a force-quit from ProcessViewer and may be useful when ProcessViewer is not working.

If kill refuses to work in it simplest form, you can try <kill –9 *PID*>. This is defined as a "non-ignorable kill." If even this is ignored, you may need root access. Try: <sudo kill –9 *PID*>.

If you are connected to the Internet (probably via a broadband connection) and applications are hanging, there's another <kill> command that may help. This is especially so if (assuming you can check) your Console log is filling up with error messages that refer to "localhost lookupd." In this case, type this in Terminal: <sudo kill -HUP *PID*> (where PID is lookupd's Process ID). This is a "hangup" kill. It may prevent you from accessing the Internet until you restart, but it should otherwise return your Mac to normal.

```
● ○ ○                Ted's shell window
Processes: 58 total, 2 running, 56 sleeping... 160 threads      14:43:54
Load Avg: 1.46, 1.61, 1.49    CPU usage: 64.1% user, 18.8% sys, 17.2% idl
SharedLibs: num = 108, resident = 24.8M code, 1.52M data, 7.21M LinkEdit
MemRegions: num = 5460, resident = 188M + 12.6M private, 113M shared
PhysMem: 43.0M wired, 136M active, 321M inactive, 500M used, 12.2M free
VM: 2.11G + 48.6M   7963(0) pageins, 472(0) pageouts

 PID COMMAND      %CPU   TIME    #TH #PRTS #MREGS RPRVT  RSHRD  RSIZE  VSIZE
13042 top        10.1%  0:04.06   1   14    15   292K   328K   532K   1.45M
13032 tcsh        0.0%  0:00.13   1   24    15   476K   656K   944K   5.72M
13031 Terminal    0.7%  0:01.99   4   90   122  1.98M  8.30M  4.98M  64.8M
13007 Snapz Pro   0.0%  0:04.75   3  104    93  5.17M  12.9M  11.7M  71.5M
12861 Console     0.0%  0:08.59   3   94   125  3.40M  8.80M  7.54M  66.2M
10133 Microsoft  71.9% 39:35.09   6  131   904  72.9M  58.5M  97.7M   194M
 9377 BBEdit Lit  0.0%  0:03.49   2   82   101  2.67M  9.95M 13.5M+ 62.9M
 5313 Internet E  1.5%  3:23.32   8  106   194  12.5M  14.3M  26.7M  98.6M
 4436 Microsoft   0.7% 16:42.40  11  154   343  21.4M  28.4M  45.5M   133M
 3103 httpd       0.0%  0:00.00   1    9    66   60K   1.08M   272K  2.38M
  368 QuicKeysKe  0.0%  0:00.27   1   58    36   376K  1.28M  1.28M  34.1M
  367 QuicKeysBa  0.0%  0:00.41   1   63    59   716K  7.04M  2.01M  61.2M
  362 MagicMenu   0.0%  0:13.59   1   47    39   476K  3.18M  1.09M  38.6M
  350 SGI Keystr  0.0%  0:00.72   1   47    44   316K  3.32M   960K  30.7M
  349 Microsoft   0.0%  0:50.30   2   74   107  3.83M  11.2M  5.44M  65.2M
```

*Figure 5.10*

*The top display in Terminal.*

# Log Out/Restart/Reset

Often, the most direct way to solve a problem is to exit your Mac OS X session and start over. Here's how to do so:

**Log Out/Restart.** Any time a problem appears while you're running Mac OS X and you cannot solve it immediately, log out and log back in. If the problem fails to go away, restart. Many problems occur only infrequently or under rare conditions. Logging out or restarting may clear those conditions, thereby eliminating the problem.

If you can't choose these commands from the Finder menu for some reason, you can try a keyboard shortcut to access these options:

- **Command-Control-Eject** should initiate a restart instantly (although it may first give you a chance to save changes in open documents). The Eject key is the one that has a triangle with a line underneath it.

- **Command-Control-Option-Eject** works the same way, except that it shuts down the Mac instead of restarting it.

- **Control-Eject** brings up a window that says, "Are you sure you want to shut down your computer now?" The window has four buttons you can click for a reply: Cancel, Sleep, Restart, and Shut Down.

- **Control-Option-Eject** puts the Mac to sleep instantly. Although this is not useful for solving a crash problem, I included it here to make the list complete.

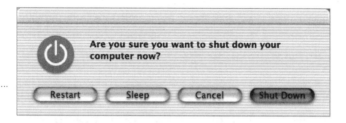

*Figure 5.11*

*The Shut Down dialog box.*

- **Hard restart/reset.** If you cannot get any of the above commands to work, you will need to do what is called a hard restart or a reset. How to do this varies a bit on different machines. In general, here is what you can try:

  **Press the Command-Control-power buttons simultaneously.** On laptops, and on older Macs that do not use a USB keyboard, this method should restart your Mac instantly. It will not work on current desktop Macs.

  **Press and hold down the power button for several seconds.** On some Mac models—notably, iMacs and iBooks—this technique should shut down the Mac. Then you can press the power button again to restart.

  **Press the reset button.** The reset button is a small button with a triangle on it. (Sometimes, it is next to another small button, the Interrupt button, which you can ignore in this situation.) On desktop Power Macs, the button typically is on the front of the machine below the power button. On iMacs, it is on the side of the machine. On recent iBooks, it is simply a small hole above the audio/video port; you'll need an unbent paper clip to access it. After you press this button, the Mac should restart instantly.

Before doing any of these resets, let the Mac sit idle for a few minutes, on the chance that it may still be able to sync.

**SEE:** • "Technically Speaking: Telnet to a Frozen Mac: Kill Processes, Run Sync," earlier in this chapter.

  • "Log Out failure bug," earlier in this chapter.

**TAKE NOTE ▶ Restart Without Restarting**

If you suspect that a restart will solve a problem you are having (typically, one that is short of a system crash but does not prevent access to the Mac), you may be able to initiate most of the functions that occur at startup without actually restarting. To do this:

1. Launch Terminal.

2. Type <sudo sh /etc/rc>.

3. Enter your password when you are asked for it.

This technique runs the rc program, which (as noted earlier in this chapter) runs the Startup Items. The Mac OS X startup logo actually appears on the screen. However, all open applications and processes remain open and functional. This method is worth a try, although some users report persisting problems after using it. You can always revert to a restart if problems persist. If not, you saved yourself a hassle.

## Check fonts

The selection of fonts accessible while you're running Mac OS X depends on the various fonts in the Fonts folders of the main Library folders on your drive (/Library; /System/Library; and ~/Library). In addition, Mac OS X accesses the fonts in the Mac OS 9 System Folder used for Classic.

Although the fonts in the /System/Library/Fonts folder should generally remain untouched, the ones in the /Library/Fonts folder—and especially those in the Library/Fonts folder of your Home directory—may contain fonts added by applications installers or by you. In some cases, these fonts can cause a crash at startup or when you're using certain applications. Even though a font may work in Mac OS 9, it may be incompatible with Mac OS X, for various reasons that need not concern you here.

Bitmap fonts are especially likely to be a problem. These fonts should be needed only to display PostScript printer fonts, which are generally imported from Mac OS 9 systems. Mac OS X does not come with any bitmap or PostScript fonts, relying almost entirely on TrueType fonts.

More specifically, Mac OS X prefers to use fonts in a new format called dfont. These fonts have a .dfont file extension and will be identified, in the Show Info window, as having a kind of Data-Fork TrueType Font. The main difference between these fonts and the older TrueType format fonts used in Mac OS 9 is that the older font format used both a resource fork and a data fork, whereas the new format uses only a data fork.

**SEE: • "Take Note: Type and Creator vs. File Extensions," in Chapter 3, for more information on resource and data forks.**

Mac OS X can still read and use the older TrueType font formats, but they are more likely to be a source of trouble than the newer .dfont format, especially if the fonts are several years old. Fonts in Mac OS 9 font suitcases, especially when there is more than one font type in the suitcase, are also a likely source of problems when imported to Mac OS X Fonts folders.

To check for problems, you can remove all these types of fonts from their folders and see whether the symptoms vanish. If so, one of the removed fonts is most likely at fault. You can return the fonts gradually to see which one is the culprit, assuming that you really need all the fonts.

Finally, as Mac OS X also reads the fonts in the Fonts folder of the Mac OS 9 Classic System Folder, corrupted or outdated fonts in this Fonts folder can cause a crash—even a startup crash—when the OS attempts to load them. To test for this problem, reboot in Mac OS 9, drag the Fonts folder to the Desktop, and restart in Mac OS X.

**SEE:** • **"Fonts in Mac OS X," in Chapter 4, for more background information.**

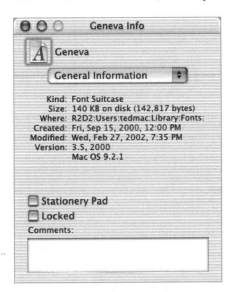

*Figure 5.12*

*The Show Info window for a font.*

# Delete preferences

As described in Chapter 3, most applications maintain preferences files in the Preferences folder inside the Library folder in your Home directory.

If preferences files associated with an application become corrupted, they can cause problems with the application, including a freeze or crash on launch. Other, less-serious symptoms, specific to accessing certain features of the application, are even more likely.

Preferences problems usually are easy to fix; you simply locate and delete the preferences file. Many of these files have names like com.apple.(*name of application*).plist. Just drag the file with the name of the problem application to the Trash. A new one will be created when you restart. This file will contain the default settings, so you may need to make some changes to get back to how you customized the application, but at least the crash will be gone.

You are best off restricting yourself to the preferences that are in the Preferences folder inside the Library folder of your Home directory. In particular, leave the preferences file in /Library/Preferences alone unless you are specifically instructed to modify or delete it by some troubleshooting document (such as from Apple's Web site or from MacFixIt). You'll need administrator access to modify it, in any case.

In extreme cases, you can solve a problem by removing all the .plist files from the Home directory's Preferences folder. If possible, however, be more selective.

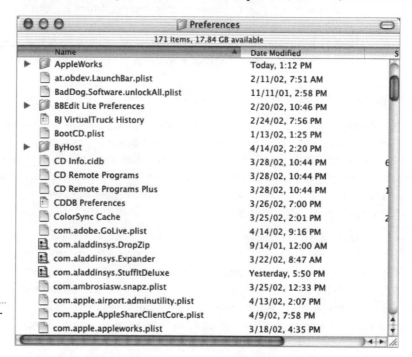

*Figure 5.13*

*A peek into the contents of a Preferences folder.*

**Locked preferences.** Occasionally, some preferences settings get reset to their default values when you log in, even if you did not delete the preferences file. You may be able to prevent this problem by locking the relevant .plist file after making the change. To do this, open the Show Info window for the file and check the Locked checkbox.

You will be unable to make any changes that would modify the preferences file unless you unlock it again. Other unusual symptoms may result from a locked preferences file; if so, you will need to unlock it.

In some cases, a preferences file may become locked even though you did not lock it. This situation can cause various symptoms, including an inability to install an update to the software. Sometimes, simply unlocking the file will cure the problem. Otherwise, unlock and delete the file.

**Finder preferences.** You can fix certain oddities in the Finder (such as applications whose icons turn to folder icons) by deleting the LSApplications, LSClaimedTypes, and LSSchemes preferences files. Note: LS stands for Launch Services.

There is also a Finder preferences file called com.apple.finder.plist. Deleting this file reportedly solves some Finder-related problems.

In some cases, users report greater success if they log out and log in again as the root user before deleting these files. The implication is that Mac OS X may re-create the corrupted file's data, via a copy in RAM, rather than create a new copy if you are logged in to the account that has the problem at the time.

---

**TAKE NOTE ▶ Editing Preferences Files**

In Mac OS X, you can do more than just delete a preferences file; you can also edit it. The best way to edit a preferences file is to use the PropertyList Editor application, which is included on the Developer Tools CD. Some of what you can do in PropertyList Editor will be self-evident when you open a file. Look at the options for the Terminal application plist in **Figure 5.14.** You can turn on or off options such as Autowrap and BlinkCursor. Make the change, save the file, and you have changed the preference.

Typically, you set these preferences in the Preferences window of the application, making PropertyList Editor unnecessary. But .plist files sometimes have settings that are not included in the application's Preferences window. In this case, PropertyList Editor gives you access to them. Terminal's .plist file, for example, has a TerminalOpaqueness option that controls the transparency of the Terminal window; this option is not listed in the Terminal Preferences window. Changing the setting to a number less than 1.00 gives the window increasing transparency. Some shareware applications also give you access to this option.

Note: If you decide to work with .plist files in /System/Library, you will need root access to do so.

**SEE:** • **Chapter 3 for more information on preferences files and root access.**

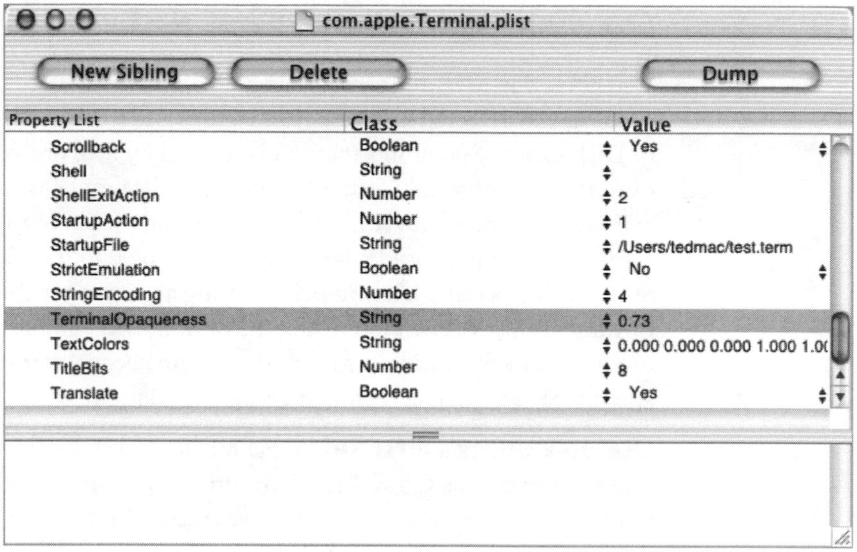

*Figure 5.14*

*Viewing the Terminal preferences file in PropertyList Editor.*

## Check for other corrupted files

Sometimes, a program may crash when it launches on your computer, even though the same program appears to work on an almost-identical machine. Why would this crash happen? Corrupted preferences files may be one reason. Otherwise, consider the following:

- **The application itself has been damaged or corrupted in some way.** Files within the application package may have been deleted or modified, accidentally or deliberately. The typical solution is to trash and reinstall the application. In the case of files installed by the Mac OS X itself, however, this procedure can be a bit tricky, as you likely do not have easy access to individual files installed by the OS update.

SEE: • **"Selective installation of individual files from an update,"** in Chapter 2, for details.

- **Accessory-file problems.** Sometimes, problems can occur with accessory files for an application that get stored in locations separate from the application itself, such as plug-in files in the Internet Plug-Ins folder inside the Library folder. The accessory files may not get updated properly when an update installer is run, for example. This situation is a form of corruption. If you know that this has happened, you usually can correct the problem by deleting the out-of-date software—in all its locations— and reinstalling the latest version.

- **Permissions and ownership of the file have been changed.** As I discussed in Chapter 3, each file has a set of privileges/permissions, as well as an owner and a group name. If these settings change, a file may not open, or you may not be able to save documents in the file. I discuss solutions to this problem in Chapter 6.

## Do disk repairs with First Aid

Whenever you have otherwise-inexplicable problems, a standard bit of trouble-shooting advice is to run a disk repair utility, such as the First Aid component of Disk Utility. Symptoms that can be caused by disk problems include applications that consistently refuse to launch, applications that repeatedly crash, and odd error messages regarding files that cannot be found or opened. Disk errors may be introduced whenever data is copied to the disk improperly; this problem is especially likely to occur during an improper shutdown (such as turning off the Mac without using the Shut Down command), a forced restart, or any power interruption. If problems occur after such events, an attempt to repair the disk should be the first thing to try.

**Use Disk Utility's First Aid.** Apple includes Disk Utility in the Utilities folder on your Mac OS X drive. This utility is a combination of what in Mac OS 9 was two separate utilities: Drive Setup and Disk First Aid.

To access the First Aid component of Disk Utility, follow these steps:

1.  Click the First Aid tab.
2.  In the column on the right, select the volume/partition you want to check.
3.  Click the Verify or Repair button.

    Verify checks for and reports problems but makes no repairs. Repair makes the needed repairs automatically.

The only problem is that with the version of Disk Utility included with Mac OS X 10.1 you can neither verify nor repair the startup volume. You will also be unable to check any other partition that is in use, including the partition that contains Mac OS 9 (if Classic is active) or any partition that contains an open application or document.

Regarding a previous version of First Aid, Apple has stated that even if you could verify the startup drive, the results may report errors that do not exist and should not be trusted.

As the most common volume you will want to check will be the startup volume (which for many Mac users will be the only volume), these restrictions present a significant dilemma.

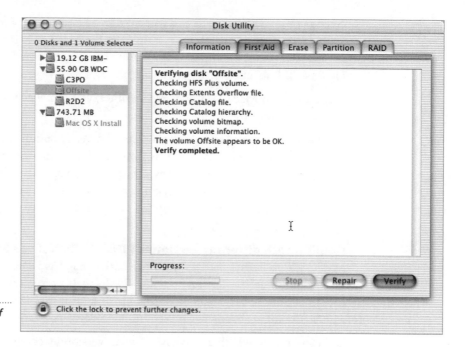

**Figure 5.15**

The First Aid tab of
Disk Utility.

**Figure 5.16**

Error messages that
may appear in First
Aid if you try to
check a volume that
cannot be
unmounted.

**Access Disk Utility from the Install CD.** The typical way to use First Aid to check the startup drive is to start up from the Mac OS X Install CD. When the Installer opens, choose the Disk Utility command from the File menu. In the First Aid tab, click Verify or Repair.

If you have two Mac OS X bootable volumes, you can check one when booted from the other.

**Why verify?** If you have a disk problem, the Verify option tells you that something is wrong but does not fix it. Why would you ever want to do this? Perhaps you are concerned that any repair might make a bad situation even worse. Thus, after the problem is confirmed, you can back up any files that you need to back up before attempting to repair. Otherwise, ignore the Verify option and choose Repair.

**Dealing with different versions of Disk Utility.** If you have updated Mac OS X via online updates, your hard drive may have a newer version of Disk Utility than the version on your CD. In such a case, it would be preferable to use the newer version to check the disk (as it may include bug fixes and checks for problems not present in the older version).

You can find out whether you have a newer version by comparing the versions numbers listed in the About Disk Utility window for each copy. The version number will be something such as 10.1 (v61). The higher the numbers, the newer the version.

On your hard drive, Disk Utility is in the Utilities folder. On the Install CD, you locate it by double-clicking the CD icon after it is mounted. In the window that opens, open the Applications folder and the Utilities folder inside that. Inside will be at least three applications: Disk Utility, Installer, and Reset Password. You probably will see Open Firmware Password, too. Launch Disk Utility, and check its About box.

What can you do if the version on the hard drive is newer than the version on the CD? Your choices are fairly limited:

- As just previously mentioned, if you have another bootable device with Mac OS X on it, such as an external hard drive or an iPod, you can start up from that device and repair the now-previous startup drive.

- If you have two Macs, you can connect them via Target Disk Mode. This procedure makes the target computer mount as though it were an external drive. Now you can run First Aid on the target computer.

**SEE:** • "Take Note: Sharing via Target Disk Mode," in Chapter 8, for more information.

- Your final choice is to create a customized bootable CD with the newer version of Disk Utility on it. To do this, make an editable disk image of the Mac OS X Install CD, replace the old copy of Disk Utility with the new copy, and burn the new CD.

**SEE:** • "Take Note: Create a Bootable CD," in Chapter 3, for more information.

**What to do after running First Aid.** What to do after running First Aid depends on the results you get, as follows:

- If First Aid reports problems and fixes them, run First Aid again. Keep doing this until First Aid no longer reports any problems. Sometimes, a repair may uncover another problem that the next repair cycle will detect.

- If First Aid reports no problems, or reports problems and fixes them, but your symptom does not go away, you could try another repair utility, just in case it can detect problems that First Aid cannot. Otherwise, disk repairs are not likely to be related to the cause of the problem.

- If First Aid reports problems but cannot fix them, definitely try another repair utility before giving up. Otherwise, erasing/reformatting your drive is the only likely way to get the damage fixed.

Finally, you may wonder what First Aid's sometimes-cryptic error messages mean. In general, they have to do with problems with an invisible area of the drive called the Directory, which is the main component that First Aid checks and repairs. The Directory has nothing to do with Unix directories or folders; it mainly keeps track of where every file is located on the drive. Also, as a file may be stored in several segments in different locations on the drive, the Directory contains the information needed to tie these segments together so that the application can run. Obviously, if this information gets corrupted, it could prevent an application from working. And if the corrupted software is critical for startup, it can prevent the OS from starting up. If this sort of error cannot be repaired, your only choice is to reformat the drive.

**Disk First Aid in Mac OS 9.** Mac OS 9 has a Disk First Aid utility. You cannot run this application from Classic within Mac OS X, but you can run it when you're booted from Mac OS 9. Can you use this utility to attempt to repair a Mac OS X volume or a volume with both Mac OS 9 and Mac OS X on it? The answer is yes. Just make sure that you are using a version that came with Mac OS 9.1 or later. Ideally, use the newest version you have available. At this writing, Disk First Aid 8.6.1 is included on the Mac OS X Install CD. Although I have no official word from Apple, I suspect that the Mac OS X Disk Utility can repair problems specific to Mac OS X that the Mac OS 9 Disk First Aid may not. So for Mac OS X problems, the Mac OS X version is preferred.

## Run fsck

The fsck utility (File-System Consistency checK and interactive repair) is a Unix program that checks for problems with Unix files and attempts to correct them. Apple has modified it so that it also includes the Mac-specific directory checks done by First Aid. Thus, in most cases, running fsck is a viable alternative to running First Aid. What makes this alternative especially attractive is the fact that you can use fsck to check your default startup drive without needing a separate startup volume to do so (as described in the preceding section). Here's what to do:

1. To run fsck, start up in single-user mode by pressing Command-S at startup.

**SEE:** • **"Single-user mode," earlier in this chapter.**

2. When the initial text scrolling has stopped and you can enter text, type: `</sbin/fsck –y>` (or simply `<fsck –y>`), and press Return.

   The fsck utility will run. The -y flag tells fsck that you want to answer yes to all questions, ensuring that the process continues without further halts.

   As fsck is running, you will see text feedback that mimics what you would get from running First Aid from the Disk Utility application, such as "Checking HFS Plus volume," "Checking Catalog file," and "Checking Volume bitmap."

3. If fsck makes any repairs, you will get a message that says FILE SYSTEM WAS MODIFIED.

   If you get this message, run fsck again, because the first run may uncover additional errors that will require a further run to fix.

4. Repeat step 3 until the MODIFIED message no longer appears and you just get the one that says, "The volume {volume-name} appears to be OK."

5. Type `<reboot>`, and press Return.

Ideally, whatever symptoms you were having that led you to run fsck will be fixed. Actually, it is a good idea to run fsck occasionally, even if you have no noticeable symptoms. The utility will often detect and fix errors that may have led to more serious problems down the road if they were left unfixed.

If fsck cannot repair the problems that it finds, or if it finds no problems but the symptoms persist on restart, your best bet is to try other repair utilities, as described in the following section.

If you have a startup problem, it is possible that incorrect or corrupted permissions settings are the cause. This situation can happen if a software installer mistakenly changes privileges during an installation or because (perhaps when you were logged in as a root user) you made such a change yourself. In either case, getting the privileges back to their correct state can be quite difficult; it can be hard to determine exactly which files have been modified and what their former settings were.

If an installer made the permissions changes, check with the vendor to see whether it has a specific fix to offer. Otherwise, a sure—albeit not very convenient—solution is to reinstall Mac OS X, erasing the drive as well if a simple reinstallation is not sufficient. If you cannot start up in Mac OS X (especially if you have a blue-screen crash) and want to do so (perhaps to back up files) before attempting a reinstallation, try the following:

1. Start up in single-user mode, and run fsck as described earlier in this section.

2. Type <mount -uw />, and press Return.

3. Type <chmod 1775 />, and press Return.

4. Type <reboot>, and press Return to restart.

If an insufficient-privileges error was preventing startup, this technique changes the permissions settings on all files in such a way that startup should be successful. This technique does not necessarily restore permissions settings to what they were when Mac OS X was first installed, however, so a reinstallation may still be needed.

**SEE:** • **Chapters 4 and 9 for more background on privileges and permissions.**

---

**TECHNICALLY SPEAKING ▶ fsck at Normal Startups and from Terminal**

When you're logging in normally, you should at some point see a line in the Mac OS X screen that says, "Checking disks..." This line is an automatic run of fsck at each startup (initiated by the rc.boot program, as noted earlier in this chapter). This run does not appear to be doing the same thing that occurs when you run fsck in single-user mode, however. The check concludes much faster during startup than fsck takes when it runs in single-user mode.

I recommend that you don't depend on this normal startup check as a substitute for fsck. The fsck program should be run in single-user mode. You cannot run fsck from Terminal while you're booted in Mac OS X.

---

## Use other disk repair utilities

When Mac OS X's built-in repair functions fail to do the job, it's time to consider third party solutions.

**Norton, TechTool, DiskWarrior.** The makers of third-party disk repair software are working on Mac OS X versions of their programs, including Symantec's Norton Utilities (also included in SystemWorks), Micromat's TechTool Pro, and Alsoft's DiskWarrior. Symantec has released their first Mac OS X version of Norton Utilities; a Mac OS X update for DiskWarrior is expected soon.

However, the latest Mac OS 9 versions of these utilities can also repair Mac OS X volumes when you run the utility while you're booted from Mac OS 9 (for example, from a bootable CD). This assumes that you used HFS Plus to format your Mac OS X volume—not the rarely used UFS.

**SEE:** • **"Select a destination," in Chapter 2, for a bit more information on UFS.**

Make sure that you are using the latest versions of these utilities. Older versions that have not been updated to work with Mac OS X can damage your directory software rather than fix it. Do not use any version of Norton Utilities before 6.0, for example. Also, when checking a drive with Norton Disk Doctor, make sure the option to "check filenames beginning with a period" is disabled. Otherwise, you may inadvertently remove the period from Unix files that need it to work correctly.

The latest versions of DiskWarrior have been cited in several cases as fixing Mac OS X problems that no other utility was able to fix. One caveat: DiskWarrior will not repair Mac OS X problems on a volume that has both Mac OS 9 and Mac OS X installed; it must be a Mac OS X-only volume.

**Drive 10.** The only completely new repair utility currently available that runs in Mac OS X is Micromat's Drive 10. This utility primarily checks for physical damage to a hard drive. These problems have nothing specifically to do with Mac OS X and, if present, will likely mean that your hard drive needs to be replaced. Drive 10's final test, however, is Volume Structure, which tests for software Directory problems, similar to what First Aid does. In its Services menu, Drive 10 also has the Rebuild Volume Structures option. Rather than repairing the directory, this option deletes the directory and creates a new one, optimized for faster performance (similar to what DiskWarrior does).

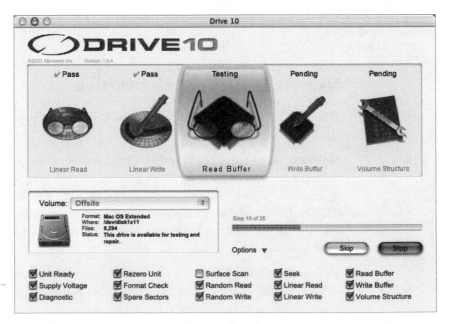

*Figure 5.17*

*Drive 10 checks a drive.*

The initial versions of Drive 10 could not repair the startup drive. Thus, unless you had two volumes running Mac OS X, you needed to run the utility from a bootable CD. Drive 10 ships on such a CD. However when an updated version of Drive 10 comes out, the update is typically free, available for download from the Web. This presents a problem if you want to have the utility on a bootable CD. The solution is to order a new CD from Micromat or to create your own customized bootable CD. As of Drive 10 1.0.4, however, you can rebuild and repair volumes without needing to restart the Mac. Still, having the utility on a bootable CD is worthwhile for those times when a problem prevents Mac OS X from starting up.

**SEE:** • **"Take Note: Create a Bootable CD," in Chapter 2.**

• **A Micromat Web page (http://www.micromat.com/product_faqs/main_product_faqs.html) for instructions on how to create a bootable CD specific to Drive 10.**

None of these utilities presently includes Mac OS X-specific fixes for such things as permissions-settings problems.

## Optimize Mac OS X volumes

Optimization is designed more to improve performance than to fix crash-related problems. But occasionally, it may solve or prevent crash problems as well.

**Optimizing with Speed Disk.** The component of Norton Utilities that makes disk repairs is called Norton Disk Doctor. Another component of Norton Utilities is called Speed Disk, which defragments/optimizes a drive. Briefly, Speed Disk combines the separately stored segments of an application into a single location, so that the number of segments for each application is reduced to a minimum (ideally, one), and then relocates the segments so that all unused space is confined to a single large block. This process may improve Mac OS X's speed noticeably.

**Optimize/update_prebinding.** When you install a Mac OS X update, as well as certain other software that uses an installer utility, there is a point at which the installer claims to be optimizing the software. This optimization is somewhat different from the optimizing that Speed Disk does. This "optimizing" in the Installer refers to a Unix-based process that can help speed up performance. Actually, you can perform optimizing at any time you choose. To do so, launch Terminal and run the Unix command <update_prebinding>. An Aqua-based shareware utility called Xoptimize does the same thing.

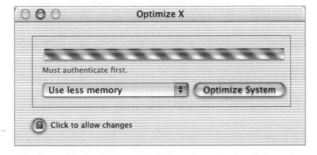

*Figure 5.18*

*Xoptimize window.*

SEE: • **"Technically Speaking: Monitoring and Improving Performance," in Chapter 6, for more on Xoptimize.**

• **The following sidebars, all earlier in this chapter, for related troubleshooting techniques:**

**"Take Note: Open Firmware Commands."**

**"Take Note: "Zapping PRAM and Resetting Power Manager."**

**"Technically Speaking: Understanding Kernel Extensions."**

**"Technically Speaking: Telnet to a 'Frozen' Mac: Kill Processes; Run Sync."**

## Log in as another user

If nothing else has fixed your problem, log out and log in again via a second account that you also own. If you have never created a secondary user account, do so now, and log into it. As I explain briefly in Chapter 3 and in more detail in Chapter 8, you use the Users System Preferences window to create a new user.

When you are logged in as the new user, see whether the problem still exists. This technique will not solve the problem for you immediately, but it is a good diagnostic.

If the problem is gone, the source of the problem is contained in your original Home directory—probably in the Library folder. In a worst-case scenario, you can transfer all your critical files to the new user account that you created and delete the former user account. As long as you are an administrator and owner of both accounts, you should have no problems in doing this. Otherwise, you can try to isolate what file in the old Home directory is the cause of the problem (presumably, based on advice earlier in this chapter, you have already considered fonts and preferences files).

If the problem remains when you are logging in as a new user, the problem is at a more systemwide level, either in the Applications folder (if the problem is specific to a given application) or in one of the main Library folders (/System/Library or /Library). If you have some idea about what the problematic file may be, you can try replacing it (assuming that you have a backup). Otherwise, you are probably looking at reinstalling the entire OS.

The problem may also be with one of the invisible Unix files. In this case, unless you are familiar with Unix, your only hope is to check a Web site (such as MacFixIt) or a book to see whether you can find specific advice about modifying one of these files to fix your problem. Otherwise, you will have to reinstall Mac OS X.

## Add memory

No matter what is wrong with your Mac, if you don't have an overabundance of physical memory (RAM), try purchasing and installing more. This procedure alone could solve the problem. At today's prices, there is almost no excuse for not having at least 512 MB. Anything less than 256 MB is asking for trouble.

## Reinstall Mac OS X

If everything else you have tried has failed to work, it's time to reinstall Mac OS X. As the absolute last resort, reinstall Mac OS X after erasing the contents of the drive.

A reinstallation replaces most of the Mac OS X files—including the files in /System/Library and /Library, as well as the invisible Unix files that work behind the scenes—with fresh default copies. Thus, if you were having a problem due to corruption of any of these files, a reinstallation would fix it. If only one file is corrupted, of course, this process can be like using a tank to shoot a fly. If you don't know which of hundreds of potential corrupt files is the culprit, however, you may have little other choice. The good news is that unless you also erase the drive, a reinstallation leaves most of your own files (such as almost all the files in your Home directory) intact and untouched. Thus, you get to keep most or all of your customizations and added software while getting to reinstall the software that is the most likely cause of the problem.

**Figure 5.19**

*The windows that appear after launching the "Install Mac OS X" application from a Mac OS X Install CD, while running Mac OS X.*

**Reinstall without erasing.** To do a reinstallation without erasing, follow these steps:

1. Insert the Mac OS X Install CD, and launch the Install Mac OS X application.

2. Type your admin password when you are asked to do so.

3. Click the Restart button.

   The Mac will restart from the CD, and the Installer will launch.

4. When you get to the Destination window, select the volume on which to reinstall Mac OS X, but do not enable the checkbox to erase/initialize the volume.

**SEE:** • **Chapter 2 for more details on installing Mac OS X.**

Although this procedure sounds simple enough, beware of a few obstacles:

- Start with the latest version for which you have a full-installation option, followed by any more recent updates that you may have installed. The latest Mac OS X Install CD you have may be older than the current version you have installed. Apple recommends that you erase the drive rather than do a downgrade reinstallation, as the downgrade (and subsequent reupgrade) may not update all OS files properly. Many users have reported success with this method, however. In any case, after downgrading via the reinstallation, run the subsequent updates to return to where you were.

**SEE:** • **"Downgrade Installation," in Chapter 2.**

- If you have updated the OS via Software Update, you probably don't have the needed update .pkg files to do the latest updates (such as to go from Mac OS X 10.1 to 10.1.1) unless you saved the .pkg file as explained in Chapter 2. Further, Software Update may not list the more-recent updates, erroneously believing that they are already installed. Not to worry. The update files are also posted on Apple's Web site; you can download the files from there and run them without using Software Update.

- In some cases, you may want to downgrade to an earlier version or reinstall the same version and not start with a full Install CD. After installing Mac OS X 10.1.4 from an update .pkg file, for example, you may want to downgrade to Mac OS X 10.1.3, or you may simply want to reinstall Mac OS X 10.1.3. Unfortunately, the update may refuse to run in such cases, claiming that the installed OS does not meet the requirements needed for the update. You can work around this problem by fooling the updater into thinking that you have the required version. One way is to modify the SystemVersion.plist file, as described in Chapter 2.

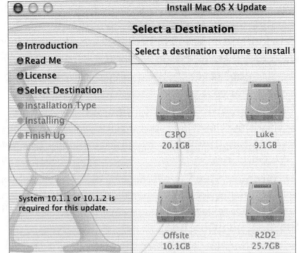

*Figure 5.20*

*Installer refuses to install. The error message on the left appeared when trying to install Mac OS X 10.1.2 on a system that was already running Mac OS X 10.1.3.*

**Reinstall with erasing.** If reinstalling without erasing does not solve your problem, your last resort is to erase your volume and reinstall. As this practice sets you back to square one, it is almost certain to fix any problem—other than ones that you may have had from square one. To erase and reinstall, run the Mac OS X Install CD as indicated in the preceding section but enable the Erase checkbox. After reinstalling, update as needed.

The main problem with erasing and reinstalling is that you lose all the additions and changes you made to the contents of your drive. Thus, before erasing and reinstalling, you should make backups of the files you want to save.

If you have installed applications in the Applications folder or added fonts to the /Library/Fonts folder, for example, you could back them up. But you likely have most of these files stored elsewhere, such as on the CDs that you get when you purchase software. Instead of choosing to back up these files, you could reinstall them from their CDs after reinstalling the OS. In fact, reinstalling the files may be the preferred way to go, as the installer utility may install accessory files (including invisible files) that you would not necessarily save simply by backing up the application file itself.

More critical are the files that you created and modified yourself. For the most part, these files will be located in your Home directory. If your drive has more than one local user, each user will have a Home directory. In this case, you will want to have backups of these Home directories. Ideally, you should back them up regularly, so that when disaster strikes and you may not be able to start up your Mac, you won't need to figure out how to back up the files (assuming it is even possible at that point).

If you do not have a current backup but have access to the problem volume, you can simply use the Finder to copy the Home directories to another medium before you erase and reinstall the OS. If you cannot access your drive from Mac OS X (perhaps because you get a startup crash), you may still be able to do so from Mac OS 9. If so, you can copy the Home directories from there. The directories are in the Users folder on the Mac OS X volume.

More specifically, here is what to do:

1.  Select a backup medium on which to store your Home directory (or directories).

    What medium you select will depend on what choices you have available and how much space the backup requires. A small directory could fit entirely on a Zip disk. Larger ones will require CD-R discs, DVD-RAM discs, or an additional hard drive.

    If you are using CD-R discs or similar media of limited size, and you cannot fit the entire contents of a directory onto one disc, you can split the contents across as many discs as needed. The only problem may be if you have a single file that is too large to fit on one disc. In that case, you may want to use a utility such as StuffIt Deluxe, which can create a segmented archive of the file; each segment can be stored on separate media. You can also create disk image files, as explained in "Take Note: Backing Up Mac OS X: Utilities to Use," later in this chapter.

2.  Erase the drive, and reinstall Mac OS X.

    As part of reinstalling Mac OS X, a fresh Home directory will be created for you, as the default administrative user. Ideally, give it the same name and password that you used previously.

3.  Drag virtually all the contents of your backed-up Home directory to your new one.

    Do not simply drag the previous directory back to the Users folder on your startup drive: Mac OS X will not recognize it as being a valid Home directory.

4.  If you are concerned that some preferences files, fonts, or other files in the Library folder of your old directory may be corrupt, you can bypass copying any or all files from the old Library folder.

    You can always copy these files later if you find that you need them and cannot re-create them. Otherwise, you should be safe in copying everything else back.

5.  Create additional users via the Users System Preferences window (as described in Chapter 3), and repeat steps 3 and 4 as needed for any other Users folders that you backed up before erasing the drive.

SEE:   • "Take Note: Backing Up Mac OS X: Utilities to Use" and "Take Note:
          Backing up Mac OS X: Hardware and Strategies," later in this chapter,
          for related information.

       • "Back up your files via the Finder," in Chapter 2.

       • "Technically Speaking: Move Your Home Directory to a Separate
          Partition," in Chapter 6, for an alternative approach to saving your
          Home directory.

---

**TAKE NOTE ▶ Backing Up Mac OS X: Utilities to Use**

For a variety of reasons, backing up an entire Mac OS X volume is more difficult in Mac OS X
than in Mac OS 9. In particular, just making a copy of a volume via the Finder in Mac OS X will
not work because:

•    File permissions are not preserved.

•    Invisible Unix files are not copied.

•    Unix symbolic and hard links are broken.

This is especially a problem if you want to make a backup that preserves what is needed so
that you can still boot from a drive after it has been restored. Fortunately, several utilities let
you back up an entire Mac OS X volume as well as allow you to restore the contents as a
bootable volume. Your main choices are:

**Retrospect for Mac OS X** is the Mac OS X version of the gold standard of backup utilities for
Mac OS 9. It allows you to restore files while you're booted from the Mac OS X volume that is
the intended destination.

**Tri-Back-Up** (or FWB's Hard Disk Backup, which is based on the same software) allows you to
create and restore a bootable Mac OS X volume.

**Carbon Copy Cloner** is a shareware utility that uses Unix's ditto command to make backups.
The author has a Web page (**www.bombich.com/mactips/image.html**) that provides many more
details about backing up Mac OS X volumes via Unix.

**Synchronize utilities.** You can use a variety of utilities, such as Synchronize Pro! X and Synk X,
to "synchronize" two folders. That is, the utility updates the folders so that they always contain
the same data. Backing up this way also saves time, as the utility will copy only what is new and
different, rather than the entire contents. Some of these utilities can also function as full
backup utilities. Synchronizing is especially useful for maintaining a backup of a folder whose
contents changes often, such as the contents of a Web site you maintain.

*continues on next page*

**TAKE NOTE ▶ Backing Up Mac OS X: Utilities to Use** *continued*

**Use Disk Copy.** If you are determined to make a full backup of your drive, and you only have Mac OS X utility software, there is a way to do it (although not very convenient). Use Disk Copy. Disk Copy can segment a large disk image into 630 MB segments, allowing you to back up to multiple CDs. (Note: If backing up to a hard drive or a DVD, you can pick a size as large as 2 GB.) To back up to CDs:

1.  Launch Disk Copy and select its Preferences command.

2.  In the Imaging Tab, select 630MB as the Segment Size.

3.  Choose "New Image from Device" from the Image menu

4.  Click the desired device (disk0 most likely), and click the Image button.

5.  Select name and destination location for the disk images.

    I use DVD/CD Master for Image Format, but the other choices should also work.

6.  Click the Image button and wait until all the images have been created.

    This requires having enough free space on a drive to hold the disk images of the contents of the drive you want to back up.

7.  Copy each image to a CD-R or CD-RW disc.

This process is tedious and time consuming, especially if you have a lot to back up, but it works.

To restore the contents of the backup later, you will need to mount the image files. To do so, copy the images back to a drive and double-click the first image.

*Figure 5.21*

*Disk Copy's "New Image from Device" (Device Selector) window.*

**TAKE NOTE ▶ Backing Up Mac OS X: Hardware and Strategies**

The preferred method for backing up data has changed over time, as the common backup media has changed (for example, from floppy disks to DVD discs) and the capacity of hard drives has increased (from, say, 20 MB to 100 GB). It also varies as a function of the type of data you are backing up (a few files vs. an entire disk). And as I discussed in the previous "Take Note," Mac OS X presents special challenges for backing up data that were not of concern in Mac OS 9. Here are my current preferred backup choices (you may find that using a combination of these methods is better than deciding on just one of them):

**CD-R or DVD-R discs.** Use a CD-RW or DVD-RW drive to back up data to CD-R or DVD-R discs. Do this mainly for a limited subset of your data, especially data that does not change often and that could not otherwise be replaced. For example, this method is perfect for backing up your MP3 music library, your collection of family digital photos, and the manuscript of that novel you are working on. This type of backup is the most reliable way to store these files without risk that the backup itself becomes damaged or inaccessible. You could use this method (especially DVD-R) to back up an entire drive, but you would not want to do this often, given how slow it is likely to be. You could also use CD-RW discs, so you can do later updates with the same media, but I recommend against this, as writing to these discs are significantly slower than the write-once media and also more prone to becoming unreadable at some later point. In general, you could use the Finder to do make these type of backups.

If you should have a complete failure of your hard drive, and you want to be able to completely recover, this method will not work. For such cases, the following alternatives are better:

**Tape backup.** I have a FireWire Ecrix tape drive (`www.ecrix.com`) and highly recommend it. With a tape drive, you are forced to backup using a utility such as Retrospect (tape drives don't mount on the Desktop, so the Finder does not "see" them). However, tape drives with Retrospect (`www.dantz.com`) have some distinct advantages: They are a cost-efficient way to backup multiple drives and computers. For example, if you have a small network of four Macs plus some external drives, and you want to keep them all backed up, you can do it all with one tape drive and multiple tapes. The cost/GB of tape is probably cheaper here than any other alternative. With this combination, you can even back up over a network (that is, you don't need to physically attached the drive to the computer you are backing up). Ecrix tape drives are also fast enough that you can back up even a large hard drive in a reasonable time. The only problem is that you cannot do an unattended backup (for example, while you are sleeping at night) if the backup will span more than one tape. The maximum capacity of an Ecrix tape is 33 GB.

With tape and Retrospect, you can also easily do incremental backups. That is, you can instruct Retrospect to only back up files that are different from the last time you backed up (saving time over a complete backup) and you can have it so Retrospect does not overwrite the old version of a file when adding a new one. This latter option is especially useful with frequently changing files. This way, if you discover that an old "deleted" version of a document contains a passage that you want to retrieve, you may still be able to do so.

*continues on next page*

**TAKE NOTE ▶ Backing Up Mac OS X: Hardware and Strategies** *continued*

**Hard drive.** Finally, you can do a full "mirrored" backup of a volume to another hard drive. This is especially useful if all you want to do is back up the internal drive in a single Mac. You can use Retrospect to do this, in exactly the same way as I described for tape drives. But Retrospect has another option, called Duplicate, that I recommend instead. Here's what to do: Get an external FireWire drive that is equal to or larger than your internal drive; format it with the same number and size of partitions as your internal drive. Now use Retrospect's Duplicate option to create a duplicate of the drive (you will have to separately do this for each partition). With this method, instead of storing your data in a Retrospect archival file format, Retrospect creates a duplicate of each file, much as the Finder would do. Except, unlike the Finder, Retrospect copies all files (including invisible files) and maintains all permissions and links correctly. The result is that you have an exact duplicate of your hard drive. You can even boot from it.

Alternatively, you can use some of the software options noted in the previous sidebar ("Take Note: Backing Up Mac OS X: Utilities to Use") to backup to another drive or to synchronize to another drive (for example, just updating those files that have changed since the last update).

**Troubleshooting tip.** I found that, before I could successfully back up my startup drive to my external FireWire drive with Retrospect, I needed to uncheck the "Ignore privileges on this volume" option in the Show Info window for the volume. Otherwise, I kept getting a –43 error. Keeping this option unchecked appears to be good advice for other backup utilities as well.

**Back up just your home directory.** Regardless of what backup method you choose, if having a complete backup of a Mac OS volume is not critical for you, or is financially impractical because of the size of your hard drive, I would recommend that you at least back up your Home directory. If disaster strikes, you can presumably re-create most or all the remaining files from your various Install CDs.

To do this, you can simply copy the files from the Finder (as described in "Reinstall with erasing," in the main text). This will not create a functional home directory but will at least have the files backed up.

Alternatively, you can use SmartTools. This shareware utility lets you copy the content of any folder, including the Home directory, into another folder including all hidden and invisible files.

A synchronizing utility may be useful if you have an especially large Home directory, as you will not need to back up the entire directory each time.

**SEE:** • **"Technically Speaking: Move Your Home Directory to a Separate Partition," in Chapter 6.**

**TAKE NOTE ▶ Having Mac OS 9 and Mac OS X on Separate Partitions**

Although you can install Mac OS 9 and Mac OS X on the same partition (which is the way they are installed by default on all new Macs), I much prefer to install the two OS versions on separate partitions . As I explained in Chapter 2, you should create the separate partitions when you first set up Mac OS X, because creating partitions requires erasing the drive.

Why should you use this arrangement in regards to backing up?

For starters, if you ever need to erase and reinstall Mac OS X, as discussed in the main text, you won't also have to erase all your Mac OS 9 files in the process.

Second, if you hold down the Option key at startup, as I discussed in "Startup Manager: Option key at startup," earlier in this chapter, you get the option to select a startup OS and volume. If you have Mac OS X and Mac OS 9 on the same partition, however, only the most recently booted OS will appear. If you cannot start up from Mac OS X, for example, you will not be able to use this method to switch to starting up from Mac OS 9, because the Mac OS 9 System Folder will not be listed as an option. Your only option is to start up from a CD. With Mac OS 9 and Mac OS X on separate partitions, the Mac OS 9 choice would be available, and you could bypass the need for the CD. This can be helpful if you need to boot in Mac OS 9 to access files for backing up before erasing a Mac OS X volume.

**SEE:**   • "Take Note: Why and How to Partition," in Chapter 2.

# 6

# Problems with Files: Open, Copy, Delete, and Beyond

This chapter covers what are likely to be the most common problems confronting a Mac OS X user: opening and saving files, copying and moving files, and deleting files. When these operations work the way they should, they are quite easy to accomplish. Due to the nature of Mac OS X, however, sooner or later (more likely sooner), you will have a problem with at least one of these operations. When you do, this chapter is the place to turn.

# In This Chapter

# Opening and Saving: Opening Files

If you are familiar with opening files in Mac OS 9, the basics of doing so in Mac OS X are very similar. Here's how the process works.

## From the Finder

To open any file, be it an application or a document, locate its icon (or name, if you are in List view) in a Finder window. Double-click the icon/name, and the file will open.

**Applications.** If you choose to open an application, it simply launches. Its icon appears in the Dock (if it is not already there as a permanent member of the Dock) and starts to bounce until the application is done opening. Thanks to Mac OS X's preemptive multitasking, if an application is taking a long time to launch, you needn't wait for it before doing something else; you can still work with other applications.

Open the application needed to work with the document (assuming that the application is not already open). Thus, if you double-click an AppleWorks document, this action will force AppleWorks to launch and the document to open within AppleWorks. If the Finder is uncertain what application goes with your document, you may have some trouble. One way to resolve this problem is to drag the document icon to the application icon.

## From the Recent Items menu

You can choose applications or documents from the Apple menu's Recent Items submenu and launch them from there.

## From the Dock

You can single-click any application icon in the Dock, or any application or document in a Dock menu, and the application will launch.

If an application has an icon in the Dock—either a permanent icon or one that appeared when you launched the application—you should be able to open a document with that application by dragging the document icon to the application icon in the Dock.

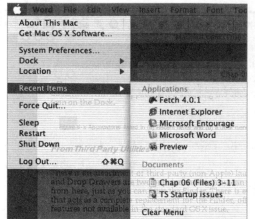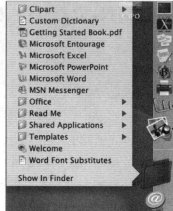

**Figure 6.1**

*Applications listed in (left) Recent Items and (right) a Dock menu.*

## From the Contextual Menu

Control-click an item in the Finder, and its contextual menu will appear. One of the items in the contextual menu will be Open. Select it, and the item will launch.

## From third-party utilities

An assortment of third-party (non-Apple) launcher utilities is available. DragThing and Drop Drawers are two popular choices. You can access and open any file from these utilities, just as you can from the Finder. A utility called SNAX even acts as a complete replacement for the Finder, offering some enhanced features that are not available in the standard Mac OS X issue.

If you have several applications open, you can also use third-party utilities to navigate among them, rather than the Dock. My favorite is ASM, a utility that brings back the Mac OS 9 Application menu, which lists each open application in a menu at the right end of the menu bar.

## From within an application: the Open command

For documents, a final option is to open a document via the Open command in the File menu of an application. This command can be used only to open documents that the application believes it is able to open. Otherwise, the documents will not be listed or will be dimmed and unselectable.

The exact style of, and options available for, the Open dialog box will vary a bit among applications, but all versions of the dialog box have basic elements in common. I'll use the Open dialog box in Microsoft Word as an example.

**File list.** The middle of the dialog box contains a list of files in the column-view format of the Finder. You can use the horizontal slider along the bottom to navigate to any place on the drive. Click a folder, and its contents appear in the column to the right. Click a file that the application can open, and the Open button is enabled. Click the Open button (or simply double-click the file name), and the file opens.

A shortcut tip: Type Command-D when the Open dialog box is frontmost and the column listing instantly shifts to highlight the Mac OS X Desktop.

*Figure 6.2*

*The Open dialog box in Microsoft Word, with the From pop-up menu visible.*

**From pop-up menu.** You can also navigate to a particular location by choosing a folder from the From pop-up menu above the file listing. This menu contains some basic locations (such as Home and Desktop) as well as recently visited folders and folders you have added to your Favorites list (such as via the Add to Favorites button in the bottom-left corner of the Open dialog box).

**Go To text box.** You can also use the Go To text box to navigate to a particular location. To do so, enter the file's Unix path name. Typing ~/Documents, for example, will take you to the Documents folder in your Home directory.

**SEE:** • **Chapter 10 for more information on Unix path names.**

**Drag and drop.** Another option is to drag the icon of a file from its Finder location to the Open window. As a result of this action, the listing will shift to the location of the file, with the Open button enabled. Just click Open, and the document opens. Why do this instead of simply double-clicking the file in the Finder? Some documents can be opened in several applications. If you want the file to open in an application other than the one in which it normally opens when you double-click it in the Finder, this method is one way to do so.

**Show pop-up menu.** Finally, if the document you want to open is not visible in the window, or is dimmed and cannot be selected, you may be able to open it by changing the selection in the Show pop-up menu. For Word, you could shift from the default choice of All Word Documents to a more-inclusive choice, such as All Documents. Just be aware that trying to open a document that is not intended for an application can have unpredictable results. The document window may be blank, for example, even though the file contains data. Or the file may be an almost-nonsensical string of characters (as might happen if you try to open some graphics files as text in a word processor).

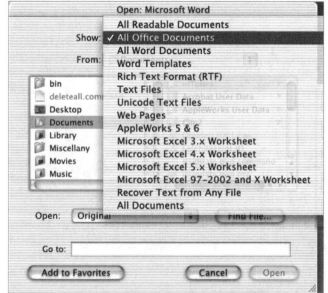

*Figure 6.3*

*The Open dialog box in Microsoft Word, with the Show pop-up menu visible.*

# Opening and Saving: Saving Files

When you are done working with a document, you will want to save it. To do so, simply choose Save from the File menu. If you want to save an already-saved document as a new file with a different name, choose Save As.

If you are choosing Save for an untitled, not-yet-saved document (or whenever you choose Save As), a sheet will drop down from the document's window; this sheet will be similar in format to the Open dialog box. In this sheet, you will have a chance to name the document and the location where you want to save it.

For the location, you will have a pop-up menu of common destinations. If none of those destinations matches where you want to save the document, click the disclosure triangle to the right of the menu. You will be presented with a full list of locations; just as you did when opening a document, you navigate to wherever you want to go.

If the application permits saving documents in more than one format, you will also have the option to select a format. Microsoft Word, for example, can save a document as a Word document, as text only, in Rich Text Format, and so on.

When everything is the way you want it to be, simply click the Save button.

The Save sheet is attached to the document to be saved. In Mac OS 9, Save was a separate dialog box. This arrangement in Mac OS X makes it easier to track what document you are saving, if multiple documents are open within the application. A few applications that are Carbonized from Mac OS 9 versions may still use the old Mac OS 9-style Save dialog box.

A document with unsaved changes will have a black dot in its close button. If you try to close the document without saving it, you will be prompted to save the document first.

## Losing track of saved files

When you're choosing Save (for a new file) or Save As, and you let the application select the location in which to save the file, be sure to note the name of the destination folder. The location will often be the Documents folder but may be something else. If the file was not saved in the expected location, and you are having trouble locating it, use Sherlock to track it down.

Occasionally, due to a bug in the OS, a newly saved file does not appear in the Finder immediately, because its Finder window is not updated to show it. Locating the file with Sherlock and double-clicking the file name in the Sherlock Results window usually forces the Finder to update and show the file.

Also note: If you have multiple partitions/volumes mounted, be careful when you save a file to the Desktop. If the application is located on a non-startup volume, the document may be saved to the Desktop folder of that partition, rather than to the Desktop folder in your Home directory. In this case, the file will not appear on your Desktop. The solution is to open the non-startup volume's root window, locate the folder called Desktop Folder, and open it. The file will be in there.

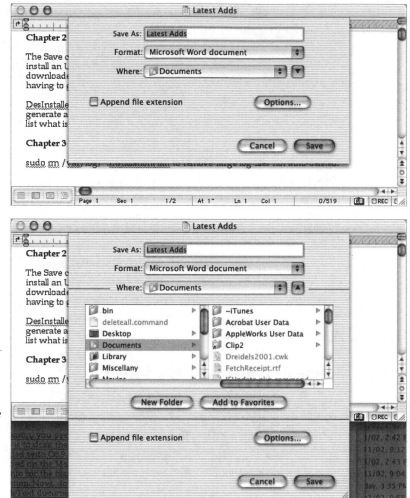

**Figure 6.4**

*A document with a Save sheet dropped down (top) before and (bottom) after the disclosure triangle is clicked. The dot in the close button indicates that the document's latest changes have not yet been saved.*

## Export instead of Save

If you want to save a document in a format other than the application's native format, but the format you want is not listed in the application's Save dialog box, check if the application has an Export command in its File menu. For example, Preview's Save dialog box has no options to convert formats. But if you select Preview's Export command, you'll be able to save a file in a variety of graphic formats, including TIFF, JPEG, PICT, and Photoshop.

In one case, I opened a PICT file in Preview and selected just to Save it to a new location. Preview created a new file that, according to the file's icon, was now a TIFF file. But when I tried to open the newly saved file, the contents were gone. All I had was a blank screen. If I instead chose to Export the file and selected the TIFF option, all went well.

# TextEdit can't save files in SimpleText format

Some operations that you do in Mac OS X may save text as a SimpleText document. If you select text in Internet Explorer and drag the selection to the Desktop, for example, the selected text is saved as a SimpleText document. If you double-click this document, however, it opens in Mac OS X's TextEdit by default. If you make any changes in the document, the following message will appear when you try to save the modified document: "Please supply a new name. TextEdit does not save SimpleText format; document will be saved as rich text (RTF) instead, with a new name."

If you prefer to keep the document in SimpleText format, one workaround is to drag the file to a copy of the SimpleText application (either the version included with Mac OS 9, which opens only in Classic, or the Carbonized version included on the Mac OS X Developer Tools CD). Alternatively, you can open the Show Info window for the file, choose Open with Application, and select SimpleText as the application. Now double-clicking the file will launch SimpleText. If you want all SimpleText documents to open in SimpleText by default, click the Change All button.

Note: If the document has been saved in RTF format, it will still open in SimpleText, but it will display all the RTF code in addition to the text.

**Figure 6.5**

*The message that appears when you're trying to save a SimpleText document in Text Edit.*

**Please supply a new name.**

TextEdit does not save SimpleText format; document will be saved as rich text (RTF) instead, with a new name.

Cancel    OK

**SEE:** • "Open with Application," in Chapter 3, for more information on using this feature.

• "Take Note: TextEdit: Plain Text vs. Rich Text format; Other Format Options," in Chapter 4, for related information.

---

**TAKE NOTE ▶ File Name Extensions**

I discussed the significance of file extensions in Chapter 3 (see "Take Note: Type and Creator vs. File Extensions"). Here, I review and extend the preceding information as it pertains to opening and saving files.

**Showing vs. hiding extensions.** In the Save dialog box of most applications, you typically see an option called Hide Extension or its opposite, Append File Extension. (The exact wording will vary from application to application.) This option most often duplicates the effect of toggling the Hide Extension setting in the Name & Extension tab of the Show Info window for that file.

*continues on next page*

**TAKE NOTE ▶ File Name Extensions** *continued*

Briefly, here is how the Show Info window's Hide Extension option works:

- If Hide Extension is enabled, a file's extension will not be shown in the Finder unless you enable Always Show File Extensions in the Finder Preferences window. That preferences setting overrides the Show Info setting.

- If Hide Extension is disabled, a file's extension is always shown, regardless of the setting in the Finder Preferences window.

- In general, if you keep Always Show File Extensions disabled, the option you choose in the Show Info window or the Save sheet will determine whether the file's extension is visible in the Finder.

- In some cases (Microsoft Word works this way), if you do not choose the Append File Extension option in the Save sheet, the Mac does not merely hide the extension; it does not add one at all. Thus, you create a file with no extension. In this case, the Hide Extension option in the Show Info window is checked, and the option is dimmed so that you cannot uncheck it (because there is no extension to show). Even in this case, you can choose to add your own extension in the Finder after the document has been saved. For the Word document, you could add .doc to the end of the document name. Now the Hide Extension option in the Show Info window will be unchecked, and you can enable it again if you want.

**What do file name extensions do?** A file name extension is one method that Mac OS X uses to determine the type of a file. For documents, this type can determine what application opens the document, should you double-click its icon in the Finder. The type also can determine what icon the document displays.

If an application can save files in more than one format, it may assign a different extension to each format. Thus, when Word saves a document in its own Word format, it uses the extension .doc; if it saves in plain text, the extension will be .txt; if it saves in Rich Text Format, the file will have the extension .rtf.

Here's a file name extension tip: Any sound file in the aiff format that you place in your ~/Library/Sounds folder can be selected to be an alert sound from the Sound System Preferences pane. However, this will only work if the .aiff extension is included in the name of the file. It has to be exact. Even .aif will not work.

**File name extension confusion.** File name extensions were largely irrelevant in Mac OS 9, and many longtime Mac users find them confusing to use. For this reason, Mac OS X gives you the option to hide them. As you have seen, however, even when they're hidden, extensions are still there.

The fact that an extension can exist even if it is not visible can be a further source of confusion. Suppose that a file has its extension hidden, and you try to add one on your own, such as changing a file named sample to sample.txt. If the .txt extension was already there but hidden, you could actually be changing the file's name to sample.txt.txt and not realize it.

*continues on next page*

**TAKE NOTE ▶ File Name Extensions** *continued*

In one case, I had an HTML file with the name reports.html, but the .html extension was hidden in the Finder, so all I saw was reports. I added the .shtml extension to the name. It looked correct in the Finder, listed as reports.shtml (as I had the Always Show Extensions option disabled), but its full name was reports.shtml.html, which was not what I wanted. I received no warning message when I made this name change. After I realized what had happened, however, the solution was simple enough: I went to the Name & Extension tab of the file's Show Info window and deleted the .html extension. I got a warning about possible problems that could occur from changing the extension, but I permitted the change anyway, and all was well.

In other cases, if you try to change an extension in the Finder (such as from .doc to .txt), you may get a message warning that this action may change the application that opens the document. Changing the extension does not really change the format of the document (changing a document from .doc to .txt, for example, does not really change the document to a plain-text document) but it can confuse the Finder into thinking that a format change has been made.

On a related note, Sherlock searches for file extensions even if they are not visible in the Finder. Take a screen shot by pressing Command-Shift-3; a file called Picture1.tiff will appear on your Desktop. If Always Show File Extensions is disabled in the Finder's Preferences window, the file name will appear as Picture1. Now, if you do a Sherlock search for the expression *tiff,* Sherlock will report Picture1 as a match (listing it as Picture1.tiff), even with file extensions disabled. This arrangement makes sense overall (Sherlock is searching for the true name of the file), but it can be confusing, especially to casual users of the Mac. Suppose that you decided to do a search for all files that end with 1, figuring that Picture1 would be among the matches. You would be wrong.

It is hopeless to try to offer every possible permutation of how all this can work. Extensions are not among Mac OS X's most logical features. To make matters worse, the file name extension is not necessarily the only method that Mac OS X uses to determine what document goes with what application. The OS can also use the type and creator information used by Mac OS 9, if that data is present in the file. In fact, if a creator is present, the Mac will use the creator setting in preference to the extension.

**SEE:** • **"Technically Speaking: How the OS Selects a Document/Application Match: Using XRay,"** later in this chapter.

• **"Take Note: Type and Creator vs. File Extensions,"** in Chapter 3, for still more details.

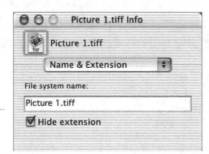

*Figure 6.6*

*Show Info window's Name & Extension tab.*

# Opening and Saving: Problems Opening Files

The two most common problems you may have opening a file are (1) when you're trying to open a document from the Finder, it opens in an application other than the one you wanted or expected; and (2) a file fails to open, yielding some error message instead. If either of these problems happens to you, here is what you need to know.

### "Item {*name of item*} is used by Mac OS X and cannot be opened"

Many files, particularly ones in the /System/Library and /Library folders, are not intended to be opened, at least not by typical end users.

In general, when you're trying to open a file from the Finder, if you get a message that says, "Item {name of item} is used by Mac OS X and cannot be opened," leave the file be. To see an example of this message, go to /System/Library/CFMSupport, and try to open CarbonLib.

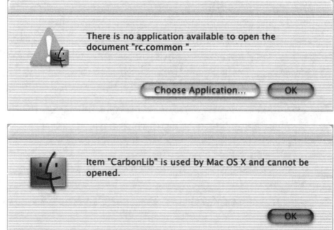

*Figure 6.7*

*Error messages that may occur when you're trying to open a file from the Finder.*

### "There is no application to open the document"

If, when you're trying to open a file from the Finder, you get a message stating, "There is no application to open the document {*name of document*}," this typically means one of two things:

**File probably should be left alone.** Go into the /System/Library/Extensions folder, for example, and double-click any kext file there. Or go into almost any other folder in /System/Library, and try to open any file with a blank icon. You will likely get this message. In most cases, unless you really need to see the contents of a selected file, simply click OK and go about your other business.

If you really need to see the contents of the file, however (perhaps advice elsewhere in this book told you to open the file and modify its contents), click the Choose Application button that appears in the error-message window, and select the desired application—if you know what application is needed to view the application. If you're in doubt, you can always start with a text editor, such as TextEdit or BBEdit.

*Figure 6.8*

*What appears if you click the Choose Application button in the error message shown in the preceding figure.*

**The Finder cannot find the needed application.** It may be that the file is intended to be opened by some application, but you do not own the application. This situation could happen if you download a document from the Internet—say, a PowerPoint slide show—but you do not own the creating application (PowerPoint). The most common solutions are:

- Acquire (purchase, if necessary) the needed application.
- Determine whether a free reader application (such as PowerPoint Viewer, in the PowerPoint example) can open the document. If so, obtain the reader application (from the Web, for example).

The remaining possibility is to open the file with some application you already own. This method may succeed because certain types of files can be opened by multiple applications. A TIFF document that appears as a Photoshop document, for example, usually can be opened in Mac OS X's

Preview application. In fact, Preview can open most graphics applications. More generally, your options are:

- Drag the file icon to the icon of the application you want to open it with (such as Preview). Or open the application and then try to open its document from the Open dialog box. If the application includes an Import command, it might succeed if Open does not.

- Choose the Open with Application tab of the Show Info window for the file, and check the pop-up menu attached to the icon. If the Finder knows that other applications on your drive can open the document, those applications will be listed. Choose any one that is listed, as desired.

- Use a utility such as Zingg!, as described in "Document opens in the wrong application," later in this chapter.

- Click the Choose Application button in the error-message window that appears when you double-click the document icon. Select the desired application from the browser list. You also can access this browser list by choosing Other from the pop-up menu in the Open with Application tab of the Show Info window, mentioned earlier in this section.

- If the application you want is not included in the list of recommended applications, you can choose All Applications from the Show pop-up menu. Be a bit cautious, however. If you try to open a document in an incompatible application, results can vary from the document's opening and displaying gibberish instead of what you expected to see to the document's not appearing at all or the application's crashing.

If none of the preceding tips help, and you have no idea what remaining applications on your drive might open a given document, how can you start narrowing down your choices? Here are some guidelines:

- For preferences files (files that end in .plist), it typically is best to open them with PropertyList Editor. This application is installed when you install the contents of the Developer Tools CD that comes with Mac OS X. (Updated versions of this CD typically are available at Apple's Developer Connect Web site.) If this application is on your drive, double-clicking a .plist file should launch PropertyList Editor automatically.

- For log files (files that end in .log), try Console. If double-clicking the file does not open Console automatically, drag the file's icon to the Console application.

- For font files (in the Fonts folder), try the freeware program X Font Info (discussed in Chapter 4) or another font-viewing utility.

- For text files, including many of the files in the Library folders and in the invisible Unix directories, try a text editor such as BBEdit.

**It's a Unix application.** Some "applications" on your hard drive are really Unix programs and run only in the Unix environment, as accessed via Terminal. Most of them normally are invisible, so there is little chance that you will try to open them accidentally. Occasionally, however, you may download a Unix program from the Web, thinking that it is in fact a normal Aqua-based Mac

OS X application. Also, the Developer Tools CD contains a folder called Tools that holds Unix programs. Double-clicking these programs in the Finder will lead to the "There is no application…" message. In this case, there is no way to open this application directly in Mac OS X, but it will run from Terminal.

**SEE:** • "Technically Speaking: Copying from Terminal," later in this chapter, for an example of using CpMac, a Terminal "application."

• Chapter 10, for much more information on running Unix software.

## Document opens in the wrong application

In some cases, if you double-click a document in the Finder, it will launch and open an application, but the application may not be the one you want to use. A PDF document may launch in Preview rather than Acrobat Reader, for example. This section covers what to do in such situations. Some of the solutions are the same as those in the preceding section for documents that do not open.

**Drag and drop.** If you are unconcerned about any general issue of why the wrong application opens and simply want to get the document opened in the desired application, drag and drop the document icon over the icon of the desired application—either in its Finder window or in the Dock.

This method usually solves the problem. Occasionally, a document may still refuse to open, even if you are certain that the application can access that document. I have seen GoLive refuse to open HTML files downloaded from the Internet when I tried to open them by dragging the document icon to GoLive's Dock icon. In such a case, continue with the following options until you find one that works.

**Use a utility such as Zingg!** The Zingg! shareware utility adds an Open With… command to the contextual menu for a file. The utility displays a submenu that lists every application that Zingg! believes can open the file safely and successfully. Choose the one you want, and the document will open in that application.

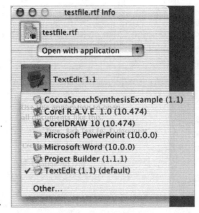
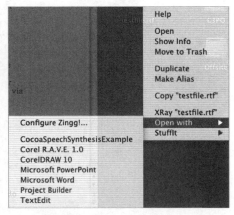

*Figure 6.9*

*The (left) Show Info and (right) Zingg! menus, listing recommended applications for opening a document.*

**Open from within the application.** Launch the application, and locate the desired document from the application's Open dialog box. This method almost always works. If the Open dialog box has a pop-up menu of the types of documents it lists as available for opening, choose the one that matches what you are trying to open. If all else fails, and you see an All Documents option, choose it.

**Bypass Classic.** Occasionally, if you have both a Classic-only and a Mac OS X version of an application, when you try to open a document created by that application, it may launch the Classic version erroneously, rather than the Mac OS X version. In general, you can prevent this problem by using the preceding techniques.

SEE: • "Launching Applications" and especially "Take Note: Applications Packages with Two Application Versions Inside," in Chapter 9, for related information.

**Delete Launch Services database files.** If you have two Mac OS X versions of the same application on your drive, you may find that double-clicking documents created by the newer application incorrectly launches the older version. If the icons are different in the two versions, the documents may also display the older version's icons. You may even be unable to get a document to open by dragging the document icon to the application's Dock icon.

To solve this problem, follow these steps:

1. Delete the older version of the application from your drive.
2. Delete the LS (LSApplications, LSClaimedTypes, and LSSchemes) preferences files from the Library folder in your Home directory.

   This procedure deletes the Launch Services database files and re-creates new default copies, and it should fix the problem.

It is important that you delete these files in such a way that a default copy is created, rather than the original version restored. You can accomplish this task in various ways. The simplest is to drag the files to the Trash, log out, log back in, and then empty the Trash.

If this method does not work, an alternative is to delete the files as a root user. Log in as a root user, navigate the relevant Library/Preferences folder, and delete the files. Yet another alternative is to log in via the >console command, described in Chapter 5. After the files are deleted, log back in as normal, and launch the application from its Finder icon. All should work as expected.

It may also help to delete the related com.apple.LaunchServices.plist file in the ~/Library/Preferences folder.

SEE: • "Take Note: Type and Creator vs. File Extensions," in Chapter 3, and "Log in as console," in Chapter 5, for more details.

**Change the file's extension.** Sometimes, changing a file extension for a document can change which application opens the file. Typically, I would avoid using this approach. More likely, the document will open in the same application, but the application will consider it to be a different type of document.

SEE: • "Technically Speaking: How the OS Selects a Document/Application Match: Using XRay," later in this chapter, for more details.

**Change the file's settings.** If you want to open the document (and others like it) in the desired application simply by double-clicking the document, you will need to change the file's settings in the Show Info window. Open the Show Info window for the file, and choose Open with Application. Then you have two choices:

• Change the application for this specific document.

• Click Change All so that this document and all documents like it open in the newly selected application.

SEE: • "Open with Application," in Chapter 3, for more details.

For even greater flexibility in assigning documents to open with specific applications, use a utility such as XRay. This utility not only allows you to make the same sort of changes you can make in the Show Info window (including changing the file extension) but also allows you to change type and creator settings.

SEE: • "Technically Speaking: How the OS Selects a Document/Application Match: Using XRay" and "Take Note: Can't Lock Folders from Show Info," later in this chapter.

• "Take Note: Type and Creator vs. File Extensions," in Chapter 3, for much more background information.

**TECHNICALLY SPEAKING ▶ How the OS Selects a Document/Application Match: Using XRay**

XRay is one of several utilities (FileXamimer is another) that allow you to change a file's settings in ways that exceed what you can do with Show Info. I use these utilities for two main functions:

• Extending the options accessible via the Show Info window's Open with Application tab

• Extending the options available via the Show Info window's Privileges tab.

Here, I focus on the first of these two functions. The second one is covered in "Permissions/privileges problems with opening files" and "Permissions/privileges problems with copying/moving files" later in this chapter.

**XRay basics.** To use XRay, follow these steps:

1. Drag the icon for the document you want to modify to the XRay icon (or if XRay is open, drag the icon to the XRay window).

2. Choose Type Creator & Extension from the Show pop-up menu.

*continues on next page*

**TECHNICALLY SPEAKING** ▶ **How the OS Selects a Document/Application Match: Using XRay** *continued*

3. Make whatever changes you want (as described in the following paragraphs).

4. Close the window.

5. Save the changes you made when you are prompted to do so.

**Modifying Type, Creator & Extension settings.** The Type, Creator & Extension window includes four categories that you can modify, listed in the order of priority in which Mac OS X checks them. That is, when deciding which application matches which document, the Finder first checks the top item in the list. If it does not find a match there, the Finder moves to the second item in the list, and so on. If it finds no match anywhere, the Finder will likely tell you that it cannot identify an application to open the document. Following are the details on the four categories:

- **Bind This Item To.** This category is equivalent to the Show Info window's Open with Application option. the XRay presents pop-up menus listing every native and Classic application on your drive and lets you pick the one you want. It is much more efficient than using the Show Info window.

  If you make a selection, the Bind All Similar Items button at the bottom of the window is enabled. This button works similarly to the Show Info window's Change All button. Any other documents that match the creator, extension, and type settings of this document will be "bound" to open with the selected application.

- **Creator.** The creator refers to the Mac OS 9 four-letter code that typically tells the Finder what application goes with what document. If you don't know what code to use, don't worry; XRay will help you out. Simply choose the desired application from the pop-up menu, and XRay will fill in the correct code for you. If you have not selected a specific application for the Bind This Item To option, the Finder will use the creator code to decide what application goes with the document.

- **Extension.** This category refers to the file extension—usually, three or four letters that appear after a dot in the file's name (as discussed in "Take Note: File Name Extensions" earlier in this chapter). Changing the extension here changes the extension in the file's name, as you can also do in the Name and Extension tab of the Show Info window or in the Finder directly. In XRay, a pop-up menu lets you choose an extension that works with the application specified by the creator or binding option.

  Note: By removing a file's creator (such as choosing No Specific Creator from the Creator pop-up menu), you force the Finder to rely on the extension to determine a matching application (assuming that you did not bind a specific application). This method can be useful if you do not want a given file to open with the application designated by the creator. I give an example of when this technique might be useful in "Take Note: Type and Creator vs. File Extensions" in Chapter 3.

  XRay also includes the same Hide Extension option that is available in the Show Info window's Name & Extension tab.

*continues on next page*

**TECHNICALLY SPEAKING ▶ How the OS Selects a Document/Application
Match: Using XRay** *continued*

- **Type.** Type is another code initially used in Mac OS 9. Type identifies the format of the file; it does not necessarily specify an application to work with that format. Microsoft Word, for example, can open many formats/types of files: Word documents, plain-text documents, Rich Text Format documents, and so on. Thus, type overlaps with file extension, which ideally should match. A document with an extension that specifies plain-text format should also have a plain-text type code. If a disparity occurs, the order of priority comes in: The extension takes precedence over the type. Again, XRay gives you a pop-up menu listing all the types associated with the creator or extension you selected.

If you don't select a binding or creator option, the OS will search for any applications that claim the extension (if one is listed) or type (if one is listed and there is no match for the extension). If a match is found, that application will be listed at the bottom of the window. If more than one matching application is found, the OS will select native applications over Classic ones and newer versions over older ones.

To understand what claimed types and claimed extensions are, click the XRay Application button at the bottom of the window. This button will open the application listed to the left of the button. Go again to the Type, Creator & Extension window, which will be quite different from what you see when you select it for a document. You will not be able to change much of anything; the window is mainly for viewing. But the two pop-up menus (Claimed Extensions and Claimed Types) will show you what the application will accept as a document that it can/will open.

There is more to XRay that I can explore in this book. Just play around with it and experiment with what changes do. As long as you work with a copy of the file you are modifying or do not save changes, you can do no harm.

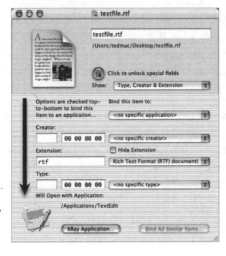 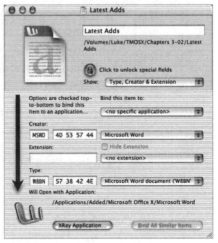

*Figure 6.10*

*XRay's Type, Creator & Extension window for documents: two examples.*

**An application takeover.** Sometimes, after you install an application, you may find that the application takes over opening certain documents that previously opened with something else (or with nothing at all).

I found that after installing the shareware program Font Checker, for example, almost all files in /System/Library that had a type of BNDL were assigned to be opened by Font Checker. (You can determine type by using a utility such as XRay.) Previously, these files had not been assigned to any application, and trying to open them would have led to the "There is no application…" message. Getting things back to the initial "no application" state can be tricky, because the Show Info window offers no option for this purpose. If getting this situation fixed is important, you can delete the application from your drive and restart. Otherwise, you may be able to use XRay to bind to no specific application.

Or you can choose to ignore the problem, which affects only what happens if you double-click a document. And in the Font Checker case, you would likely never double-click those documents anyway. If you ever need to open an affected document in a different application, follow the general advice given earlier in this section for documents that open in the "wrong" application.

In another, more-serious example of a takeover, after I installed iDVD, attempting to open a System Preferences window, which should have launched the System Preferences application, launched iDVD instead.

**SEE:** • "Take Note: Type and Creator vs. File Extensions," in Chapter 3, for the solution to the iDVD/System Preferences problem.

## File is corrupted

Occasionally, an application will not open because it is corrupted. Usually, this problem occurs with a file that you have downloaded from the Internet. Either the file only partially downloaded or an error was made during the copy process. In either case, the file cannot open because of the missing or corrupt data.

For downloaded files, the usual solution is to try to download the file again. In some cases, you may have greater success by holding down the Option key when you choose to download the file. Otherwise, try shifting to a different browser. If the URL begins with ftp, rather than http, you may also have better luck by using an FTP client, such as Fetch, rather than a Web browser. And when you use an FTP client, if it fails to work at first, use *passive FTP transfer* (typically, an option in the FTP preferences settings) and try again.

**SEE:** • "Take Note: Troubleshooting Downloading Files," in Chapter 8, for more on this issue.

If the problem persists, there may be a problem with the server that contains the file. If so, you might check on MacFixIt for possible confirmation and a solution. Otherwise, check with the site's Webmaster for advice.

If the problem occurs when you're copying files from one volume to another, the drive itself may have a corrupted directory or a hardware problem. In this case, it is time to attempt disk repairs.

**SEE:** • **Chapter 5 for more information on repairing disks.**

• **Chapter 8 for more information on Internet-related problems.**

## File is compressed or encoded

A file, especially one you download from the Internet, may download in a compressed or encoded format. If you do not have the proper application to decompress or decode the file, you will not be able to open it.

Many compressed-file formats (files with .sit, .hqx, and .bin extensions, for example) can be expanded with the StuffIt Expander utility, which is included with Mac OS X. If the file does not expand automatically on download, drag the file to Expander or launch Expander and select the file.

A few compressed-file formats do not open in Expander. In such cases, try the shareware utility OpenUp. With Expander, Disk Copy, and OpenUp, I have never failed to get a compressed file to open.

iPhoto.dmg

iPhoto

Files with .dmg or .img extensions are disk images, which you typically mount by using Disk Copy. This method opens a virtual volume that behaves as if though were a physical disk. The application or document you seek is actually on the image. So you have to open the image window, locate the file, and either launch it directly from the image or copy the file to your hard drive and then launch the copy.

*Figure 6.11*

*A .dmg file and an alias of the image that opens when you open the file in Disk Copy; you can open the image to access its contents, just as though it were an external drive.*

Occasionally, a compressed/encoded file may download erroneously as a text file. If you double-click it, it may open in a text editor, such as TextEdit or BBEdit. You can work around this problem by dragging the file to the required application (such as Disk Copy or Expander). If this problem happens with many files, you may want to make a change, via the Show Info window or a utility such as XRay, so that similar files open correctly in the desired application.

Finally, your browser may give you a message that it does not recognize the file type of the file you are trying to download. It may offer to search for a needed plug-in or other helper file. If you just want the file to download, the best advice is to choose whatever option allows you to ignore the warning and download the file; then drag the downloaded file's icon to the desired decompression utility. The cause of these problems is either at the server end (someone mislabeled the file, for example, in which case you can do nothing to fix the problem) or possibly with your browser settings (especially the Helper settings). The latter problems can be fixed, but this topic gets beyond the Mac OS X-specific scope of this book.

SEE: • **"Take Note: Mounting Disk Copy Image Files," in Chapter 3, for one example.**

• **Chapter 8 for more information on Internet problems.**

## Problems with .app files

Launching an application generally creates fewer problems than launching documents. In a few instances, however, things may go wrong.

Most Mac OS X applications are actually package files (also referred to as bundles). A package (covered in Chapter 2) is actually a folder. You can view the contents of the folder by choosing Show Package Contents from the contextual menu that appears when you Control-click the icon of the application. If Show Package Contents does not appear, the application is not a package.

Note: Most Open dialog boxes, as well as the Finder itself, will not allow you to navigate inside packages. This situation is part of maintaining the illusion that a package is really a single application file. The Show Package Contents option is the main way to access these files. An exception is the excellent BBEdit utility, which includes an Open Hidden command that allows you to navigate to almost every location on your drive, including inside a package.

**The .app extension.** Package applications have an .app extension. The Finder keeps this extension invisible, however, even if you enable the Finder preference to show file extensions. The main way to confirm that the extension exists is via the Name & Extension tab of the Show Info window. If you do this for the Mail application, for example, you will see that its real name is Mail.app.

If you were to eliminate the .app extension via the Show Info window, the Finder would change the application to a folder, which also means that the "application" would no longer launch. Clearly, you would ordinarily not want to do this. Fortunately, if you add the extension back, the folder reverts to an application; its icon returns, and it will launch properly when you double-click it.

*Figure 6.12*

*The Show Info window for the Mail application, showing that its true name is Mail.app.*

Note: Turning a folder into a functioning .app package by adding the .app extension works only if the folder already contains the elements it needs to function as an application: the Contents folder, with the .plist files inside it, and so on. Thus, simply adding a .app extension to a folder with several Word documents in it will not turn the folder into a functioning application.

**Applications as folders.** Occasionally, applications may appear as folders rather than applications, even though you made no apparent change to cause this. If this problem occurs, you usually can fix it by deleting the LS preferences files in the Preferences folder of your Home directory.

SEE: • "Delete Launch Services database files," earlier in this chapter.

> • "Take Note: Type and Creator vs. File Extensions," in Chapter 3, and "Log in as console," in Chapter 5, for related details.

**The application is in the "application."** The fact that the .app file is really a folder implies that the actual application that launches when you double-click a .app file is contained within the folder/package. This is true. In fact, sometimes more than one application is contained in the folder.

You may have two versions of the same application (such as a Classic and Mac OS X version, as is the case for AppleWorks). In such cases, you may want to launch an application directly from within the package, rather than from the package file itself.

SEE: • "Take Note: Applications Packages with Two Application Versions Inside," in Chapter 9, for an example of this situation.

In other cases, a helper application for the main application may be included in the package. iTunesHelper, for example, is included in the iTunes application package, because iTunesHelper is designed to launch only at startup via the Login Items setting. As there is no need for the typical end user to see it in the Finder and double-click it, iTunes keeps the helper hidden. But should you want to launch it directly (perhaps the iTunesHelper process quit, and you want to relaunch it), you can do so by entering the package.

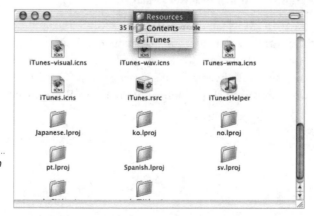

**Figure 6.13**

The hidden location of iTunes Helper inside the iTunes package.

**.app files and installing Mac OS X updates.** Apple's Mac OS X Installer leaves much to be desired. (I've probably said this before, but it bears repeating.) Suppose that you install a Mac OS X update, and the update includes a new version of an application (such as Mail). The application will likely not get updated properly if you moved it to a location other than the location where it was installed (typically, the Applications folder). If only some of the files in the application package are being updated, and only those files are included in the Mac OS X update, those files—and only those files—will be placed in the Applications folder, where the Installer expected to find the old version of the application. The old version of the application, located wherever you moved it, remains untouched. Thus, you wind up with a nonupdated version of the application and a partial updated version that will not work. What can you do in this situation? You have these choices:

- You can move the original Mail.app application back into the Applications folder, delete the partial update, and attempt to reinstall the Mac OS X update. In some cases, this method may not work; the updater may refuse to run, believing that the update is already installed. If this situation occurs, you can try to work around it by fooling the Installer into running. Or you can downgrade to or reinstall a version of Mac OS X that you can install, and reupdate again from there. Or you can erase your hard drive and start over. But before you reach that extreme, consider the next alternative.

- You can open the packages of both the updated/partial and old/complete Mail.apps. Copy the new files from the updated application to the old one. Now you should have a complete application that will work.

In some cases, the updater may contain a complete copy of the application, but the installation messed up something anyway. In this case, you can simply extract the Mail.app application from the update package file. The easiest way to do this is via the shareware utility Pacifist, which lists all files contained in an update package file and lets you extract the ones you want.

**SEE:** • Chapter 2 for more information on fooling the Installer, selective reinstallations, and using Pacifist.

**Application must be in required folder.** Some applications will not launch unless they remain in the folder where they were first installed. In rarer cases, the application will only work if installed in a specific folder, most often the /Applications folder. In such cases, the Read Me file for the software, or its Installer utility, should inform you of this. But it may not.

**Can't open a copy of an application.** If you Option-drag an application package to another folder on the same volume or drag it to a new volume, the Finder creates a copy of the application. Similarly, pressing Command-D makes a duplicate of the file. Ideally, in all these cases, the resulting application should launch and run identically to the original. Problems occur occasionally, however.

SEE: • "SetUID and 'Items could not be copied' error," later in this chapter, for details on these problems.

• Chapter 5 for more information on what to do if a file crashes on launch.

**TAKE NOTE ▶ Opening .app files from Within Terminal**

If you search the Contents/MacOS folder of some package applications, you will find a typical launchable application. Acrobat Reader 5.0 is one example; the actual Acrobat application is in that folder.

In other cases, however, the MacOS folder will contain a *document* with the name of the application, rather than an application. If you double-click this document, it will produce the error message, "There is no application available to open the document."

But you can usually launch the application from this document if you use Terminal.

Normally, you can open an .app application from Terminal by using the Open command for the overall package. To launch Print Center, for example, type: <open "/Applications/Utilities/ Print Center.app">.

Should this command fail, however, you can execute/run the aforementioned Print Center document. To do this, launch Terminal and type: <cd /Applications/Utilities/"Print Center.app"/ Contents/MacOS> to navigate to the relevant directory. Then type <./"Print Center">. That's it.

If Terminal says you do not have permission to do this, try it again with root access, typing <sudo ./"Print Center">. Actually, this is a practical use of the technique. In the latest versions of Mac OS X, you cannot use Terminal's open command to launch an .app file with root access. That is, <sudo open *name of application.app*> will not work. In such cases, using sudo with the file within the .app package will still succeed. It is thus an alternative to using a utility such as Pseudo.

SEE: • "Take Note: Root Access," in Chapter 3, for more background.

# Permissions/privileges problems with opening files

Occasionally, you won't be able to launch a file because you do not have sufficient permission/privileges to do so, and you get an error message to that effect. Similar problems can occur (and occur more often) when you're attempting to copy or move an application. I cover this topic in great detail in the sections on copying and moving files later in this chapter. For now, here are some specifics as they apply to opening files.

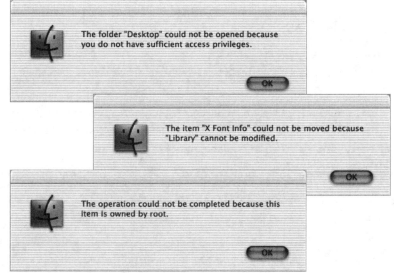

**Figure 6.14**

The insufficient-privileges error message and two related messages, all of which appeared during an attempt to modify a file or folder in the /System folder or in another user's Home folder.

**Can't access secondary folder/file.** If launching the application requires accessing files or folders beyond the application itself, such as a preferences file or a file in your Documents folder, you may not be able to launch the application if you do not have permission to access the required folder or file.

I saw one odd instance in which a user could not launch iTunes. Whenever he tried, he got the insufficient-privileges error. There seemed to be no problem with the privileges settings for iTunes itself, so I looked elsewhere. I found the answer in the iTunes folder located in the Documents folder of the user's Home directory. Somehow, the owner of that folder was listed as his son (who also had an account on the system).

You cannot fix this problem from the Show Info window, as only the owner of a file/folder can change settings there. This dilemma has various solutions (as I have covered at various points in this book). The one I recommend, however, is a utility such as XRay or FileXaminer. Follow these steps:

1.  Drag the iTunes folder to the XRay icon.

2. In the window that appears, choose Permissions from the Show pop-up menu.

3. Click the lock icon to unlock all fields.

4. Enter your password (assuming that you are an administrator).

5. From the Owner pop-up menu, choose your own name.

6. Save the change.

   The iTunes application will launch.

A similar situation may occur when you're trying to install an update to an application on your drive. I know of a case in which the owner of the Adobe folder located in /Library/Application Support was somehow changed to "unknown." This change prevented the successful update of an Adobe application that needed to access this folder but did not have permission to do so. The solution is to change the owner of the Adobe folder to system or to your administrator name.

**Access set to None.** Virtually all applications should have at least Read Only access assigned to Everyone (as set in the Privileges tab of the file's Show Info window). This access is the minimal access needed to launch the application. If the privileges setting for Everyone is None, and especially if you are not an administrator, you may not be able to launch the application. If you find this None access, here's the solution:

1. Drag the application icon to the XRay icon.

2. In the window that appears, choose Permissions from the Show pop-up menu.

3. Click the lock icon to unlock all fields.

4. Enter your password (assuming that you are an administrator).

5. In the World section, make sure that the Read and Execute checkboxes are checked.

6. Save the change.

SEE: • **"Permissions/privileges problems with copying/moving files," later in this chapter, for related information.**

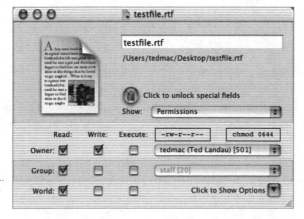

**Figure 6.15**

*The Permissions tab of XRay.*

> **TAKE NOTE ▶ Default Settings of Applications**
>
> For applications installed by Mac OS X in the Applications folder (such as Mail and Preview), the default settings, as displayed in XRay, should be the following:
>
> - Owner and Group: Read, Write, and Execute all enabled
> - World: Read and Execute enabled
> - Group should be "admin"
> - Owner should be "root (System Administrator)"
>
> Files that you install in the Applications folder by using other installers or by dragging them to the Applications folder may list your user name, rather than root, as the owner. Otherwise, the settings will likely be the same as for Mac OS X-installed applications.
>
> If Mac OS X-installed applications in your Applications folder have their permissions settings changed for any reason, you can return them to their default state by using a utility such as XRay or FileXaminer. Also note: Apple has created an application called FixApplicationsFolderPermissions that fixes these settings. It is available from Knowledge Base document 106609 (`http://docs.info.apple.com/article.html?artnum=106609`).

# Copying and Moving: Copying vs. Moving vs. Duplicating Files

In Mac OS X, users probably have more trouble copying, moving, and (especially) deleting files than with any other type of problem. In this section, I explore what you need to know to have success when copying and moving. In a later section, I cover deleting files.

## The basics

The primary ways to transfer a file from one location on your Mac to another are:

**Copy**, as its name implies, places a copy of the original file in the new location while leaving the original file intact in its original location. The simplest way to copy a file is simply to drag its icon to the new location, assuming that it is on a different volume or partition from the original file. If the file is on the same volume, Option-dragging the icon copies it to the new location.

**Duplicate** is almost the same as Copy, except that the copy is created in the same location as the original and assigned a new name. To do this, choose the Duplicate command (Command-D) from the Finder's File menu. The copy will have the word *copy* appended to its name. If you otherwise drag an icon of a file to a different location within the same folder, you neither move nor copy the file; you just reposition the icon.

**Move** literally moves the file to the new location without retaining a copy in its original location. To do this, drag the file to its intended location on the same volume.

To move a file to a different volume, you can Command-drag the item (a feature that does not exist in Mac OS 9!). A word of caution, however: If the move to a new volume fails for any reason, the OS may delete the original without creating the copy, leaving you with no file at all. So if you get an error message when using Command-drag, choose Stop rather than Continue. Or to be even safer, avoid this feature and just copy the file. Then delete the original after you know that the copy was made successfully.

## Beyond the basics

Beyond the basics, you should know several additional variations.

**Copy Item.** Copying a file from one folder to another, via dragging its icon, can be inconvenient, as you need to be able to open and position the originating and destination folders on the Desktop so that both are visible and you are able to drag the icon from one to the other. That's why Mac OS X offers an alternative: the Copy Item command. Here's how it works:

1. Select an item in the Finder.

   The Copy command in the Edit menu changes to Copy {*name of selected item*}.

2. Choose the new Copy command.

3. Click inside the window of the destination location.

   The Paste command in the Edit menu now reads Paste Item.

4. Choose Paste Item.

   The item is pasted to the new location, as though you had done a drag-copy.

The Copy Item and Paste Item options are also available via contextual menus. Thus, if you Control-click an item, a Copy {*name of file*} command will appear. Then you can Control-click the destination location and choose Paste Item from the contextual menu.

*Figure 6.16*

The Copy Item command.

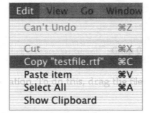

**Copy/Replace.** When you attempt to move or copy a file to a location where a file of the same name already exists, you typically get an alert message warning you that the action will replace the existing file, essentially deleting it. Be careful about clicking OK. If the two files have different content, you could erase something you wanted to save.

In some cases, such as when you're downloading files from the Internet, rather than offering to replace a file with the same name, the Internet software may instead append an extension to the duplicate file so that both files are saved. Thus, if you download the file CoolApp twice to the same location, the second download will likely have the name CoolApp.1.

**Move results in a copy.** If you attempt to move a file from a folder where you do not have sufficient permission to modify the folder contents, dragging the file typically results in a copy's being placed at the new location rather than the file's being moved. The original file remains intact, even if that was not your intention. No error message will appear. In some situations, the copy may fail completely, with an error message appearing.

In the next section ("Problems copying and moving files"), I explain how permissions settings affect the ability to copy and move files.

**Copy results in an alias.** When you drag the icon of one partition over to another or drag a disk image file to a folder on a hard drive, an alias of the original volume is created, rather than a copy's being made. This situation is not an error. Mac OS X assumes that when you drag a disk image or a volume to a new location, you want to create an alias of it. You rarely would copy these typically large volumes except for backup purposes.

If you truly want to copy the actual volume contents, select the volume and choose the Copy Item command, followed by the Paste command, as explained earlier in this chapter. Or open the window for the originating volume, choose All, and drag the selected files to the new location.

SEE: • "Aliases and symbolic links," later in this chapter, for more information.

**Move to Trash.** The only other common variation of moving of a file is moving the file to the Trash. This special case deserves a section of its own, which is coming up later in this chapter.

# Copying and Moving: Problems Copying and Moving Files

If you attempt to copy, move, or duplicate a file and are unsuccessful, consider the following causes and solutions.

## Insufficient space

If you try to copy a large file to a volume that has less free space than the size of the file, you will be unable to do so. Not a surprise.

The solution is to delete unneeded files from the destination volume, so as to free more space. Or you can attempt to copy the file elsewhere, on a volume that has more free space.

Occasionally, a volume may seem to have less space than you expected, based on the files you installed. This situation usually happens because some OS-related file—sometimes, an invisible file—is taking up more than the usual amount of space. Examples include the Console log files. If these files are not updated periodically, or if a recurring error is filling them rapidly, they can become very large. Explorer cache files can also become quite large. The solution is to locate these files and delete them. You can use Sherlock to search for files by size. This technique will help you spot unexpectedly large files.

**SEE:** • **Chapter 3 for more information on Console.**

## File is corrupted

Sometimes, you will be unable to copy a file because the file is corrupted, and the Finder is unable to read the file's contents. In general, your best bet is to delete the file and start over with a fresh download, backup copy, or new document. If you absolutely need to try to recover the information in the file, you can try opening it in its creating application (such as Word for a Word document), copying what you can to a new document and saving the new document. In other cases, an text editor such as BBEdit will allow you to at least view the text within a document, allowing you to save it even if nothing else can be saved. Otherwise, attempting disk repairs (such as with Disk Utility) may recover the item. Barring that, give up on the file and delete it.

**SEE:** • **"Problems opening files," earlier in this chapter, for related advice.**

## File does not appear after being moved

Occasionally, when you're copying a file, especially to the Desktop, the file may not appear on the Desktop when the copy is complete. This situation most often happens when you're decompressing a file from an archive or downloading a file from the Internet, or when the file is being moved or created from an application other than the Finder itself.

In almost all cases, the file is really there; the Finder has not been updated to reveal it. You need to give the Finder a bit of a push. For files that do not appear after being downloaded from Explorer, open Explorer's Download Manager; double-click the name of the missing file; and in the window that appears, click the Reveal in Finder button. The item should become visible. As a last resort, choose Force Quit and reload the Finder. This procedure should get the file to appear.

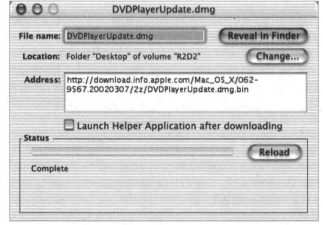

*Figure 6.17*

*The Reveal in Finder button in Explorer's Download Manager.*

One other possibility, for files on the Desktop, is that the file was copied to a Desktop other than your Mac OS X Desktop. The file may have been copied to a Mac OS 9 Desktop that resides on the same volume as Mac OS X, for example. In this case, double-click the Desktop (Mac OS 9) icon that should be on your Mac OS X Desktop if Mac OS 9 and Mac OS X are on the same volume. When Mac OS 9 is on a separate volume, simply open the Desktop Folder on the Mac OS 9 volume. You will find the missing file there.

## Permissions/privileges problems with copying/moving files

If you try to copy or move a file, and you get an error message that says, "The operation cannot be completed because you do not have sufficient privileges for {*item or folder name*}," you have a privileges-related problem.

For a copy, the problem is always at the destination end—where the copy is to go.

For a move, the problem could be at either end. When you move a file, you may not have sufficient privileges for it to be removed from its original location, or you may not have sufficient privileges for it to be copied to its new location.

SEE:  • "Permissions/privileges problems with opening files," earlier in this chapter.

Why do these permissions errors occur, and what can you do about them?

**Files that should not be moved.** In general, you should not touch files in the /System folder. Unless you are confident that you know what you are doing or are specifically instructed to modify this folder by someone else who knows what he or she is doing, avoid removing or modifying any files in this folder. Generally, Mac OS X will prevent you from making changes anyway. But just in case…you've been warned.

Similarly, you cannot add a file to the System folder for the same basic reason. If you try, you will likely get an error message that says, "The item {*name of file you are trying to move*} could not be moved because {*name of System-folder directory*} cannot be modified." Generally you want to follow this advice.

If you absolutely need to move a file to or from these forbidden locations, you will need root access to do so. You may also need to change permission settings, as described in the following paragraphs.

SEE:  • Chapter 3 for more information on root access.

There are similar limits on access to other Mac OS X folders. Administrators can add files to or remove files from the Applications folder, for example, but other users cannot. This limit can cause some odd situations. A file can be copied from the Applications folder by a nonadministrative user, but that user cannot copy the file back to the folder (due to insufficient privileges). The best solution is to have someone with administrative access handle these tasks.

**Files with incorrect permissions/privileges settings.** Almost every file in Mac OS X has an owner and a group assigned to it. In addition, the owner and group (together with a third category that includes everyone who is not the owner or in the group) each has certain permissions to read or manipulate the file. You can see the basic permissions settings (called privileges in Mac OS X) by opening the Show Info window for a file and choosing Privileges from the pop-up menu.

SEE:  • "Privileges," in Chapter 3, for many more details.

If you are neither the owner of a file nor a member of its group, and especially if read or write access is not given to Everyone, you may be unable to copy, move, or otherwise modify the file due to insufficient privileges. You cannot move a file out of a folder, for example, if you are not the owner of the folder or a member of its group. (An exception can be if you are the owner of the file.) This is the reason that nonadministrator users cannot move files into or out of the Applications folder, which is owned by system with a group assignment of admin. Only the system (which essentially means Mac OS X itself or the root user) or a member of the admin group (which includes all administrators) can modify the contents of this folder.

The /System folder lists its owner as system and its group as wheel. In this special case, you cannot move files into or out of this folder, even if you are a member of the wheel group (which you are, as an administrator), without first getting root access. This is because the wheel group only has Read access for the /System folder.

When you're copying or moving a file, the file's ownership may get modified. In particular, here's what may happen and why:

**Moving and permissions.** If you move a file from one location to another, the file generally retains its permissions settings. Thus, if you move an application from the Applications folder to your Home directory, it will retain system and admin as its owner and group.

Conversely, if you move a file from your Home directory to the Applications folder, it will retain the permissions settings it had in your Home directory. Depending on what those settings were, nonadministrative users may not be able to launch the file due to insufficient access. In such a case, the solution is to modify the file so that it acquires the system and admin attributes of most other files in the Applications folder.

**Copying and permissions.** If you copy a file from one location to another, the copy generally acquires the attributes of its enclosing folder. Thus, if you copy a file from Applications to your Home directory, it will acquire your user name as the owner and staff as the group.

Conversely, if you copy a file from your home directory to the Applications folder, its permissions change to that of system and admin. Thus, you are no longer the owner of the file you just copied. In this slightly odd situation, you may be able to modify the privileges settings (via Mac OS X's Show Info window) of the original file but not those of the copy.

Note: When creating a new file (such as via an application's Save command) or a new folder (such as via the Finder's Command-Shift-N command), you are assigned as the owner of the item. The group assignment for the item is typically the same as that of the folder containing the item. Thus, items created in the Applications folder would belong to the admin group.

Occasionally, usually due to some bug in an installer utility, the ownership of a file may get modified so that even as an administrator, you do not have immediate access to move or replace the file. Usually, the utility assigned system/wheel as the owner/group of the file.

In one example, the Applications folder may be locked or have incorrect permissions after you install a Mac OS X update. This situation may also happen after you use an installer utility for third-party software. Later, when you drag a file or folder to the Applications folder, the following error message will appear: "The item *'filename'* could not be moved because 'Applications' cannot be modified." To fix this problem, you can use the techniques described later in this section.

As an administrator, you can change whatever you want; you just need the right tools and a bit of know-how. In particular, you can accomplish your goal by using one or more of the following techniques:

- Rebooting in Mac OS 9 (where Mac OS X privileges settings are not enforced) and then copying or moving the file as desired.
- Making changes in Terminal (as covered briefly in Chapter 10).
- Logging in as a root user (as covered in Chapter 3).
- Using a utility such as XRay to change the owner, group, or read/write settings—or some combination of the three.

Of all the choices, I prefer staying in Mac OS X's Aqua interface and being logged in as usual. Thus, I prefer using a utility such as XRay. In particular, here is how to use XRay to change permissions:

**Change permissions of an individual item.** To change the settings for one file or folder, follow these steps:

1. Launch XRay, and drag the icon of the file you want to modify to its window.

2. Choose Permissions from the Show pop-up menu.

3. Change the owner and group name to whatever you want (such as system and admin for files in the Applications folder or select your own name as the owner).

   Pop-up Owner and Group menus make it easy to see what your choices are and to make your selection.

4. Make sure that owner and group have Read, Write, and Search/Execute status enabled.

5. Save your changes.

   Note: If you are the owner of the file, you will be able to change read/write settings from the Finder's Show Info window for the file. If you are not the owner, the Privileges options will be dimmed. Even if you are the owner, the Show Info window will not let you change the owner or group name. That is why you need to use XRay.

**Change the permissions of all items in a folder.** Suppose that you want to reset all applications in the Applications folder so that they have the same settings as they did when you installed Mac OS X. It might seem that you could do this by opening the Show Info window for the Applications folder, going to the Privileges tab, and clicking the Apply button. This method would convert all the contents of the Applications folder to match the attributes of the Applications folder itself. Unfortunately, you cannot do this directly, because you need to be the owner of the folder, and system is listed as the owner.

XRay allows you to work around this problem. Follow these steps:

1. Launch XRay, and drag the icon of the folder you want to modify to its window.

2. Choose Permissions from the Show pop-up menu.

3. Click the padlock icon to unlock special fields, and enter your administrator's password.

4. Click the disclosure triangle next to Show Options.

5. Click the *Change Enclosed* button.

6. Make the Owner, Group, and World options match the settings for the folder itself.

7. Click the *Save & Change Enclosed* button. You are done.

Follow the same general principles for making these permissions changes for any file or folder.

**SEE:** • "Sticky bit and the root volume," later in this chapter, for a special case of changing settings to enable moving a file.

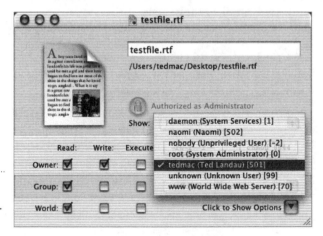

*Figure 6.18*

*XRay's Permissions tab (with the pop-up menu for changing owners visible).*

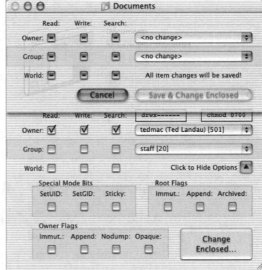

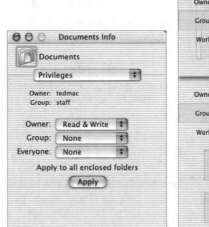

*Figure 6.19*

*(Left) The Show Info window's Privileges tab and (right) XRay's Permissions tab (with its Changed Enclosed window open) for a folder.*

**Folders with incorrect privileges settings.** The same logic that applies to files applies to folders. In one case, however, Apple has noted that the Mac OS X Applications folder may wind up with incorrect permissions after you update the OS. The result will be that you cannot modify the contents of the folder. As a quick fix for this problem, Apple released a FixApplicationsFolderPermissions application.

**SEE:** • "Take Note: Default Settings of Applications," earlier in this chapter.

**Ignore privileges on this volume.** On all mounted volumes except the Mac OS X startup volume, if you go to the Privileges tab of the Show Info window of the volume, you will see an option called *Ignore privileges on this volume*. If you enable this option, it should do what its name implies; you will be able to access files on this volume, even if you otherwise would not have the privileges to do so.

*Figure 6.20*

*The Ignore Privileges option enabled for a volume.*

This option is intended primarily to deal with mounting external volumes that you get from other users. The permissions settings for such a volume may be set so that unless you are the person who loaned you the volume, you cannot access the files. More than likely, if the person lent you the volume, this was not his or her intention. Clicking Ignore Volumes works around this dilemma.

A word of advice: I have found that enabling this option when it is not needed can precipitate problems. Without going into details here, I'll just say leave this option off unless you need to enable it to access a file on a volume. Turn it off when you no longer need to use it.

## Accessing other users' folders

Assuming that you are the person who installed Mac OS X on your Mac, you are an administrative user. Further assume that you set up a few additional nonadministrative users via the Users System Preferences window (covered in Chapters 3 and 8)—say, for other family members or colleagues. Each user gets his own Home directory, as stored in the Users folder. Finally, assume that as the administrator, you would like to be able to check on the contents of the Home directories of these other users. Can you do this? Of course. But you will have some obstacles to overcome.

**No entry.** For starters, if you open the Home directory folder for another user, you will find that your access to most of the folders within it is blocked (the Desktop, Documents, Library, and most of the other folders created by Mac OS X when the directory was set up) because the folders have a privileges setting of None for Group and Everyone, as can be seen in the Privileges tab of the Show Info window for the folders. Thus, only the owner of the directory can access these folders, and the folders have a red "no entry" icon on them. Some files and folders may have different privileges settings, providing you with some access, but they will likely be the exceptions.

**Figure 6.21**

Inside another user's Home directory. Note the "no-entry" icons on most of the folders.

**Public and Sites folders.** The only sure exceptions will be the Sites folder (where you would store a Web site enabled by Web sharing, which needs to be available publicly) and the Public folder (which is where you store files that you want anyone to be able to access, such as other local users on your Mac or people who accesses your Mac with guest access via file sharing). These two folders have the Group and Everyone privileges set to Read Only (as opposed to None, so you can open and view the contents of the folder. What you can do with the viewable contents will depend on the privileges setting of each file and folder:

- If a document has *Read & Write* privileges enabled for Everyone, you will be able to open and modify the file.

- If privileges are set to None, you won't be able to open the file, even though you can see its icon in the Finder.

- If privileges are set *to Read Only*, you will be able to read but not modify the file. If you open the file, make a change, and try to save the file, you will get an error message. You will be able to copy the file to your drive, however, and modify the copy there.

**Drop Box.** Within each user's Public folder is an additional folder named Drop Box. This folder is designed so that you can add to its contents but not see them. This folder is almost the opposite of the rest of the Public folder, which is designed to allow you to see the contents but not necessarily modify them.

The Drop Box allows you to leave files for the user who owns the Drop Box without being able to see or access what other people may have left. To accomplish this goal, the Show Info privileges for a Drop Box have been set to Write Only for Group and Everyone.

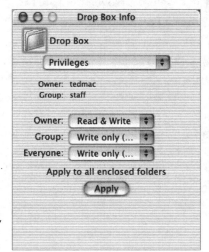 

*Figure 6.22*

*The Privileges settings of your (left) Drop Box and (right) Public folders, as viewed in their Show Info windows.*

**Administrative access.** In the preceding examples, being an administrator has not given you access beyond what any other user would have. But as an administrator, you have additional options. To peek inside restricted folders and possibly modify the files within, use these methods:

- **Use Terminal.** Type <sudo ls>, followed by a space. Then drag the folder you want to inspect to the command line. You will see the absolute path name for the folder. Press Return. You may be asked to enter your password. Do so. The contents of the folder will appear. You also can use the Terminal's open command to open a file within the folder (although you may not be able to modify the file).

- **Log in as root.** You will have complete access to all no-entry folders. You can not only view the contents but also modify them.

- **Connect to Server.** If you have two Macs connected via a local network (as discussed in Chapter 8), use the Connect to Server option to mount the Mac you want to access from the other Mac. When you're asked to log in, use the name and password of an admin user (presumably, you). You will have access to the contents of all users, even though you do not when you are working directly from the Mac in question.

  Note: If you log in as a guest, you will be able to access only the Public folder in Users directories. If you log in as an administrator instead, you will be able to access the entire contents of the drive.

---

**TAKE NOTE ▶ The Shared Folder**

In addition to all the personal Home directory folders in the Users folder is a folder called Shared. The privileges of this folder are set so that Everyone has Read & Write access. Thus, this folder is like a community folder; any local user can view, modify, copy, or move anything there. This setup is not very secure, but it can be convenient for low-security items.

As it turns out, some applications also install items in this folder. Applications use it to store accessory files that need to be accessed by multiple users but that are not stored with the application itself. Font Reserve uses this folder for its Font Reserve database, for example, and America Online Instant Messenger (AIM) uses it for its icon and sound files. This situation can present a problem should you want to move the application. For starters, to copy the application to another volume, you would also need to remember to copy the files in the Shared folder. In some cases, however, simply moving the application from one location to another on the same volume can break the application's link to the files in the Shared folder, leading to problems with using the application. That's why it often makes more sense to use the application's installer to place the application in another folder rather than copy it.

Note: The contents of the Shared folder are not available to nonadministrative users when logged in remotely (a topic I cover more in Chapter 8).

**TECHNICALLY SPEAKING ▶ Move Your Home Directory to a Separate Partition**

You can copy your Home directory to a separate partition via the Finder simply enough. This method can serve as a useful backup for your personal files, should you ever need to erase your Mac OS X volume and reinstall the OS from scratch. You cannot simply drag the backup copy of your Home directory to the new Users folder and expect it work, however. Instead, you will need to create a new Home directory and drag the individual files and folders from the backup copy to the folder locations of the new one.

If that process sounds like more hassle than you would like, there is an alternative: You can move your Home directory to a separate partition, where you can access it when running Mac OS X (instead of accessing it from the Users directory). In this case, if you need to reformat your Mac OS X partition, you will still have your Users directory preserved and can reconnect to it. Borrowing from the Mac FAQs & Tips site (**www.bombich.com/mactips/homedir.html**), here is what you need to do (for clarity, I have added an underscore wherever a space occurs; when you enter the commands, enter a space in lieu of the underscore):

1.  Launch Terminal, and type <sudo_ditto_–rsrc_/Users_/Volumes/*OtherPartition*/Users>. *OtherPartition* is the name of the partition where the new Home directory is to go.

2.  Type <sudo_niutil_-createprop_/_/users/username_home_\_/Volumes/OtherPartition/Users/*username*>. *username* is your user name.

3.  Check that the newly created directory is working by logging out and logging back in. Repeat the previous step for any additional Home directories you want to save.

4.  If all seems well, type <sudo_rm_-dr_/Users>. This command removes the old directory.

5.  Type <sudo_ln_-s_/Volumes/OtherPartition/Users_/Users>.

If you erase and reinstall your Mac OS X volume, you presumably can reconnect to the backup directory via step 2. Personally, I have never bothered to do any of this, so I cannot vouch for its success, although others have done so. Use this method at your own risk.

## Sticky bits and the Drop Box

In this section, I take a closer look at the privileges/permissions settings of a Drop Box. Along the way, I will also explain some generally relevant tidbits about something called the sticky bit.

**The permissions of the Drop Box.** As I have already noted, the Show Info window's privileges for a Drop Box folder are set to Write Only for Group and Everyone. You might think that this setting means what it says: No one except the owner (or someone with root access) can read or modify the files in that folder. But you would be wrong.

Leaving the Show Info window, take a closer look at the actual Unix-style permissions settings of the Drop Box, using either Terminal or a utility such as XRay. When you do this, you discover that the permissions for Everyone are <-wx>, which means that Everyone has write (w) and execute (x) permission for the folder. For applications, execute permission means that you can run/execute the file. For folders, however, all that the execute permission does is allow the other permissions (r and w) to have any effect at all. In fact, when used with folders/directories, the x bit is often referred to as the search bit rather than the execute bit.

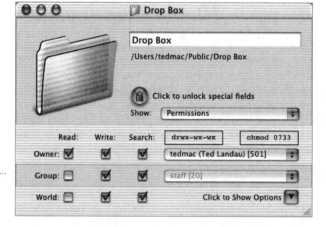

**Figure 6.23**

The permissions of the Drop Box, shown in XRay.

Thus, with <-wx> permission for Everyone for a folder, a user can add files to the folder and also remove files from the folder. In fact, omitting read access means only that you are unable to view/read the contents of the directory. That is why when you drag a file to the Drop Box, you get a message that says, "You do not have permission to see the results of this operation." Similarly, if you double-click the Drop Box, you will get the "You do not have sufficient privileges" error.

This situation does not mean that you cannot read individual files within the directory, however. You *can* read the files—if their individual permissions settings allow. Even though the folder does not have read permission set for the Drop Box, you potentially can still read and modify a file within the folder (including deleting the file). Thus, files in such a folder are less secure than they may seem.

Typically, this situation is not much of a concern. As you can't view what is in the Drop Box folder, it would be hard to open anything inside it. But if you knew the name of a file in someone else's Drop Box, you could read it and (depending on the file's permission settings) modify it. Even if you did not know the name of the file, you might be able to use a utility that lists what is in these off-limits folders and thereby gain access to it. You could take a guess at part of the file's name, for example, and enter the partial name in Sherlock. If your guess matches anything contained in the Drop Box, the file will appear in Sherlock's results. If you have read or write permission for the file, you will be able to double-click the file in Sherlock's window and open it—despite its Drop Box location.

**The sticky bit.** So is there a way to improve on the security of the Drop Box? Yes. To restrict access further to the contents of this (or any other) folder, you can set the *sticky bit* for the folder. The sticky bit is a special Unix attribute setting beyond the standard read, write, and search/execute ones I have described so far.

If the sticky bit is set for a folder, anyone can add files to the folder, but only the owner of the folder can remove anything from it. Actually, the owner of a file should also be able to remove that particular file. This situation does not prevent someone from opening and reading a file in a Drop Box (assuming that the person knew the name of the file and had read access to it), but it does prevent that person from renaming or removing the file. In some cases, the setting will also prevent modifications to the file. However, to guarantee that any non-owner read access or modification for a file is prohibited, you need to modify the permissions of the file itself (setting Group and Everyone access to None), not the folder that contains the file.

Bottom line: The Mac OS X Show Info window's Write Only privileges setting suggests a different meaning to non-Unix savvy users than it actually means. Despite the name, you have more than Write access to files in the folder. This setting is also different from what it means in Mac OS 9, in which all access to files in a Drop Box are blocked with Write Only access.

---

**TECHNICALLY SPEAKING ▶ Conceptualizing Directories in Unix**

Conceptually, the sticky-bit discussion may make more sense if you realize that in Unix, a directory is not really a folder in the way that a folder appears in the Finder—that is, it is not a container but simply another file that lists the contents of what is considered to be in that directory. Thus, the permissions settings for a directory determine only the extent to which you can modify the listing. But this setting is separate from your ability to modify the files themselves. The latter capability is determined by the permissions set for each file. In other words, a lack of read access for a directory means that you cannot read the directory listing. It does not mean you cannot read the files within the directory. Nor does it mean that you cannot change the contents of the listing.

**Set the sticky bit.** Having decided that you want the extra security of setting the sticky bit for your Drop Box, how do you set it? Two ways: Use Terminal or a utility such as XRay. I'll explain both alternatives briefly.

To use Terminal to add the sticky bit to the Drop Box folder, follow these steps:

1.  Launch Terminal, and type <cd Public>.

2.  Type <ls -l>.

    The permissions for the Drop Box should read drwx-wx-wx, which means that you have a directory (d), that the owner has rwx (read, write, execute) permission, and that Group and Everyone have just -wx permission.

3.  Type <chmod 1733 "Drop Box">.

    The permissions should now read drwx-wx-wt. The last t indicates that the sticky bit is set.

    *or*

    Type <chmod go=wxt>.

    This command has the same net effect as <chmod 1733 "Drop Box">. Briefly, it sets the access for Group (g) and Other (o) to be equal to (=) write, execute, and sticky bit but provides no read access (-wxt).

**SEE:** • **Chapter 10 for more information on using the chmod command.**

To use XRay to add the sticky bit to the Drop Box folder, follow these steps:

1.  Open the folder you want to modify in XRay (Drop Box, in this example).

2.  Go to the Permissions tab via the Show pop-up menu.

3.  Click the disclosure triangle next to Show Options.

4.  In the Special Mode Bits section, click the Sticky checkbox.

5.  Save the changes.

Note: Examine the boxes just below the Show pop-up menu. You will see the same sort of attribute listing for the folder that you can see in Terminal when you list files by using <ls –l>. When you enable the Sticky checkbox, the last letter in the listing will change from *x* to *t*. For Drop Box, it will change from <drwx-wx-wx> to <drwx-wx-wt>. Again, this change indicates that the sticky bit has been set.

The adjacent text box in XRay will change from <chmod 0733> to <chmod 1733>. This setting refers to the chmod (change mode) commands needed to turn the sticky bit on and off. A 0 as the first digit means that the sticky bit is off; a 1 means that it is on.

**Figure 6.24**

*Figure 6.24*

*The Drop Box folder with sticky bit enabled, shown in XRay.*

**Sticky bit and the root volume.** The sticky bit is enabled automatically for the root-level directory when you install Mac OS X. The root level is the level that has the name of the volume as its window name in the Finder (where you see System, Library, Users, Applications, and other folders). Thus, anything that is copied to that window cannot later be moved via a simple Finder drag by anyone other than the owner of the item or by someone who has root access. Thus, if another user on your Mac adds a file to that window when he or she is logged in, you will not be able to drag the item to the Trash, for example, even though you are an administrator.

The simplest way to get rid of the file is to use XRay to make yourself the owner of the file or folder (as described in "Permissions/privileges problems with copying/moving files" earlier in this chapter). Then you can move it or trash it as desired.

More generally, for almost any problem with moving a file from a folder with the sticky bit enabled, you can turn off the sticky bit temporarily, complete your move, and then turn the sticky bit back on. To do this via XRay for the root directory, drag the Mac OS X startup-volume icon to XRay, and uncheck the Sticky checkbox. Or use the following command in Terminal: <sudo chmod 775 />. After returning to the Finder and completing whatever you wanted to do, recheck the Sticky checkbox in XRay or type <sudo chmod 1775 /> in Terminal.

## SetUID and "Items could not be copied" error

Occasionally, when you try to copy an application, you may get an error message that says: "One or more of items can't be copied. Do you want to skip them and copy the remaining items?" If you click Continue, you will get what appears to be a copy of the application, but if you try to launch it, it will not work. Typically, you will not get an error message. Instead, the application will simply start to launch and then quit.

This happened to me, for example, when I tried to copy the Open Firmware Password utility (discussed in Chapter 5) from the Mac OS X Install CD to my hard drive. It also happened on one occasion when I was making a copy of the Mail application.

The following paragraphs explain what causes the problem and how to work around it.

**Boot and copy from Mac OS 9.** You can work around the problem by booting from Mac OS 9 and copying the utility from there. When you return to Mac OS X, the utility will run. Yet again, the problem is related to permissions settings and is enforced only in Mac OS X.

---

**TAKE NOTE ▶ Package Contents Won't Open**

After making a copy of an .app application, if you try to access the contents of the package (by choosing the Show Package Contents command from the contextual menu), you may meet with resistance. The Show Package Contents command opens the package normally enough, but the Contents folder inside is dimmed and cannot be opened.

Solution? Just log out and log back in. All should be well.

---

**Get copy to work in Mac OS X.** What is it about permissions settings in Mac OS X that causes this odd behavior? To find out, start by comparing the package contents of the original application and the failed copy to see what is different, if anything.

In the case of the Open Firmware Password utility, you will see that the essential Open Firmware Password file, located in Open Firmware Password/ Contents/MacOS, was present in the utility on the CD but not in the failed copy. Similarly, for Mail.app, the critical Mail file itself (in the Mail.app/ Contents/MacOS folder) is missing from the copy. As these files essentially contain the program code of the applications, it is no wonder that the copies did not work.

**SetUID setting.** Why didn't the files within the package copy successfully? The file has its SetUID bit enabled! You can determine whether this bit is enabled by using Terminal or XRay.

To use Terminal, mount the Mac OS X Install CD and type:

```
<ls -l /Volumes/Mac\ OS\ X\ Install\ CD/Applications/Utilities/Open\
Firmware\ Password.app//Contents/MacOS/>
```

Or, more simply, type <ls –l>, followed by a space; drag the icon of the file (for example, Open Firmware Password) to the Terminal window, automatically add the preceding path; and press Return. The Open Firmware Password document will have its attributes listed as <-rwsrwxr-x>.

Note the *s*, instead of the more common *x*, at the end of the first trio of letters (rws instead of rwx). This setting means that *setUID* (set user ID) bit has been enabled for the owner.

To use XRay to confirm that the setUID bit has been enabled, follow these steps:

1.  Drag the Open Password document from the MacOS folder within the utility's package to XRay.

2.  Go to the Permissions tab.

    You will see rws as the first trio of letters. In addition, if you click the disclosure triangle to Show Options, you will see that the SetUID checkbox has been enabled.

---

**TECHNICALLY SPEAKING ▶ SetUID and SetGID**

Occasionally, Unix users need access to a function that they would be prohibited from accessing otherwise. To change your password, for example, you need access to the function that changes passwords. But this access is restricted to the root user; otherwise, any user might be able to change anyone's password. Unix works around this dilemma by providing an option that allows a user to access the password function just to change his or her own password. This task is accomplished by having the SetUID bit enabled for the function. This bit has a similar effect for any other command for which it is set. With SetUID enabled for a command, the command is run as though the person running it has the permissions of the owner of the file (root, in the password example) for the action attempted. As long as you have permissions to access the other files needed to complete your request, the command should work. So any user can change his or her own password.

The SetGID bit works similarly, except that the normal group permissions are shifted temporarily to those of the group that owns the command in question. This bit has a somewhat different effect when applied to a directory rather than a file. In any case, you will have no need for this command, and I mention it only for the sake of completeness.

As covered in the main text, setting the SetUID bit for a file also has some effects in Mac OS X that are a bit different from those described here for standard Unix.

Apparently, if a file has its SetUID bit enabled, it cannot be copied in the Finder. In Unix, the result of the copy attempt would be for the file to copy with the SetUID bit stripped off. In Mac OS X, the file apparently refuses to copy at all.

Thus, the solution to the problem with copying programs such as Open Firmware Password is simple enough: Disable the SetUID bit for the file. Then the file will copy successfully. The copy should also run successfully with SetUID still off. If you have any problems, you can always reenable the SetUID bit.

To disable (or reenable) the SetUID, the simplest method is to use XRay or some similar Mac OS X utility. To do so with XRay, follow these steps:

1. Select Show Package Contents from the contextual menu of the application that contains the setUID-enabled file.

2. Open the setUID-enabled file with XRay (see XRay instructions earlier in this chapter for more details, if needed).

3. Click the padlock icon, and enter your administrator's password when requested.

4. Select Permissions from the Show pop-up menu and click the *Click to Show Options* disclosing triangle.

5. Uncheck the SetUID checkbox.

6. Save the change.

   You can reverse the change later, if necessary.

To use Terminal, follow these steps:

1. Type <sudo chmod u-s>.

2. Press the spacebar, and drag the Finder icon of the setUID-enabled file (in the package of the application) to the Terminal window.

   This action will enter the full (absolute) path name for the file.

3. Press Return.

4. Give your administrator password when you are asked for it.

   The change should be made. If you navigate to the directory that contains the file and type <ls -l>, permissions for the file should read <-rwxrwxr-x>.

After using either method, if you attempt to copy the original package utility, it should copy successfully. If you are familiar with Unix and the Mac OS X Developer Tools software, you may be able to use commands such as <ditto> or <CpMac> to copy a file in Terminal, even without disabling the file's SetUID bit. I recommend that most users stick with the more basic methods described in this section, however.

Whatever the rationale Apple had for enabling the SetUID bit on certain files, one thing becomes clear: It can be an effective form of copy protection. If you enable the SetUID bit on a volume for which the user does not have administrative access, there is virtually no way for the user to copy the file.

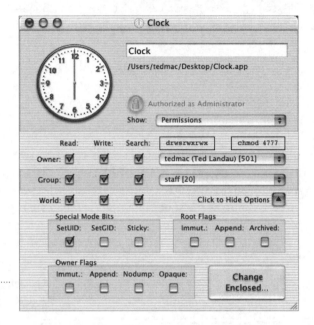

**Figure 6.25**

*The SetUID option enabled in XRay.*

---

**TECHNICALLY SPEAKING ▶ Copying from Terminal**

If you are having trouble getting a file to copy from the Finder, you may be able to succeed by copying the file via Terminal. In one case, an application (called GetInfo.app) that I had backed up to a CD would not copy back to my hard drive. I kept getting an "unexpected error (Error code –50)" message.

This error usually is the result of a bug in the OS. In this case, I found that some files in the Frameworks folder inside the application package had an alias icon, even though they were not alias files. Somehow, these files were triggering the error.

**cp.** To solve this problem, I launched Terminal, navigated to the location of the file on the disc (by using the <cd> command) and typed:

<cp –r GetInfo.app ~/GetInfo.app>

This command instructed the OS to copy the entire application to my Home directory. Use the –r option if what you want to copy is a directory rather than a single file, because the application—being a package—is really a directory.

This method successfully copied the file for me. End of story.

*continues on next page*

**TECHNICALLY SPEAKING ▶ Copying from Terminal** *continued*

This command works as long as there are no resource forks in the files being copied. The <cp> command does not copy resource-fork code. If you are unsure whether a file contains a resource fork, don't worry. If <cp> fails to work, you can delete the resulting partial copy and try again with another alternative. Or you can skip <cp> and go directly to the potential alternatives.

**ditto.** One alternative is the <ditto> command (a built-in Unix command created by Apple). Its format is the same as that of <cp> except that you will likely need to log in as a root user to use it. To do so, type:

<sudo ditto GetInfo.app ~/GetInfo.app>

No -r option is needed , as <ditto> is designed to copy directories. In fact, you cannot use it to copy just a file. The <ditto> command overwrites existing files, symbolic links, and devices in the destination when they are copied from a source. The resulting files, links, and devices will have the same mode, owner, and group as the source items from which they are copied. This command was not created specifically to deal with the problem of resource forks, but users report that it does copy them successfully. Some users have even employed this command as a way of backing up their drives.

**CpMac.** Finally, if you have installed the Developer Tools software (available on a CD included with a purchase of Mac OS X or otherwise available for download from Apple's developers' Web site), you can use the <CpMac> command. This command is a special version of <cp> that does copy resource forks. You can execute the <CpMac> command by typing its directory entry in Terminal, followed by the paths of the file you want to copy and its destination location. For example, for GetInfo.app, it might look like this:

</Developer/Tools/CpMac −r -mac GetInfo.app ~/GetInfo.app>

Note: There is no manual (man) entry for CpMac. But if you type the command with no items to be copied, you will get a brief explanation of its use.

SEE:　• **"Take Note: Type and Creator vs. File Extensions," in Chapter 3, for more information on resource forks.**

　　　• **Chapter 10 for more information on Terminal and copying files.**

*Figure 6.26*

*Error message that may appear when you're attempting to copy a file.*

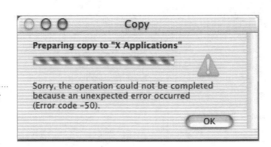

### Copying to back up

If you are wise, you will want to back up the contents of your drive periodically. Backing up is a protection against software or hardware damage that could mean the loss of the contents of your drive. Backing up a drive in Mac OS X—especially if you want to make a backup that can restore a volume, including making it bootable—presents some challenges that do not exist in Mac OS 9.

**SEE:** • "Take Note: Backing Up Mac OS X: Utilities to Use" and "Take Note: Backing Up Mac OS X: Hardware and Strategies," in Chapter 5.

# Aliases and Symbolic Links

An *alias* is a file that is pointer to a real (original) file located somewhere else. Thus, when you double-click an alias, the other (original) file opens. By using aliases, you can list the same file in many locations without having to have real copies of the file in each location, which provides convenient flexibility in organizing files on your drive.

For example, suppose that you have a collection of applications at various locations on your drive, and you want to bring them together in the same folder for a specific task. Yet you also want to retain them in their original locations. You can do both things by creating aliases of the files and placing the aliases in the new location. Now whenever you click an alias, it launches the original file, as though the file were in two locations at the same time. As the alias takes up next to no disk space, this arrangement is often more advantageous than having two copies of the full application.

You can use aliases in other ways, such as the following:

- Sometimes, a program may look for a preferences file in the startup System Folder (in Classic). If you have different startup System Folders, the preferences may be different in each case. You could prevent this problem by placing an alias of the original preferences file in each of the other System Folders. Now all the folder will use the same preferences file, no matter what changes you make at what time.

- If you place an alias of a folder in a new location, when you open the alias folder, the original folder actually opens. By placing such an alias in a convenient location, you get instant access to the folder contents, even though the folder may be nested several folders deep in some other location.

- Making an invisible folder temporarily visible and making an alias of it is a useful trick for maintaining easy access to folders that normally are invisible. You can use this technique to maintain access to the invisible tmp folder, for example.

**SEE:** • "Saving movie trailers that have the Save option disabled," later in this chapter, for an example of using this tmp folder.

## How to recognize an alias

The icon for an alias looks identical to that of the original file, except that that a small arrow appears in the bottom-left corner of the icon.

An alias also behaves differently when you open the Show Info window for the file. The differences are:

- A button called Select New Original will be in the main Show Info window. Clicking this button allows you to change the file attached to the alias. You will not need to do this often unless the original file has been deleted.

- The Kind setting for the file may be alias, and the Size setting of the file will be only 4 KB. I say "may" because in what appears to be a bug, an alias file may instead list the original file's kind as its own and be listed with a larger size. In this case, the Select New Original button will be the main clue that you are dealing with an alias.

Get it! alias

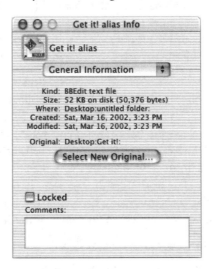

*Figure 6.27*

*An alias file and its Show Info window.*

# How to locate an original via its alias

What if you want to locate the original file from its alias? First, right above the Select New Original button will be the path to the original file. You can navigate there on your own.

More simply, you can choose Show Original from the Finder's File menu (or use the keyboard shortcut Command-R). The Finder will go directly to the folder where the original is located and display it with the file selected.

## How to create an alias

To create an alias, click the original file and choose Make Alias from the Finder's File menu (or use keyboard shortcut Command-L). Alternatively, you can choose Make Alias from the contextual menu for the file.

Which ever method you select, an alias will be created in the same location as the original file—with the word alias added to its name. (The word will precede the file's extension, if it has one.) Then you can rename or move the alias, as you want. The alias's relation to the original file will be preserved no matter where you move either file, at least as long as you stay in the same volume.

Often more conveniently, you can hold down the Command and Option keys and drag the file's icon to a new folder. This technique creates an alias at the new location with the same name as the original. (The word alias is not added.)

When you use the Add Favorites command to add an item to your Favorites folder, you are creating an alias of the item.

## Fixing a broken alias link

If you delete the file to which an alias is linked or move or modify the file so that the alias can no longer locate it, you will get an error message when you double-click the alias file. This message will state, "The alias {name of file} could not be opened because the original item could not be found." This situation is called a broken alias.

At this point, you can click OK (thereby ignoring the issue for the moment), Delete Alias (with the obvious result), or Fix Alias. This last option opens a window similar to what appears when you click Select New Original in the Show Info window. From here, you can navigate via a directory window to the desired destination file and select it as the destination for the alias.

*Figure 6.28*

*The broken-alias error message.*

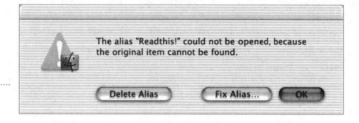

## Aliases vs. symbolic links: What's the difference?

If you are familiar with Mac OS 9, much of this alias discussion probably has a familiar ring, as aliases work in a similar way in Mac OS 9. But Mac OS X introduces a new wrinkle, compliments of Unix. Unix includes something similar to aliases: symbolic links. When you're in the Mac OS X Finder, a symbolic-link file looks and acts almost identically to an alias file, with these exceptions:

**Aliases** are linked to the file or folder to which they point. If you move the original file to a new location, the alias is able to keep track of this situation and maintain the link. When you double-click the alias, the original file still opens.

**Symbolic links** refer to a specific pathway. Thus, for example, a symbolic link to a file called Testing in your Documents folder will work only if Testing remains in the Documents folder. Move it anywhere else, and the link is broken. Just as important, if you move or delete the original file and create a new file with the same name in the original location, the symbolic link will point to that new file (because it has the same pathway). An alias would not do this; it would not link to the new file despite its identical name.

When you install Mac OS X, the OS places symbolic-link files in various locations, including inside the Library folders, inside application packages, and in the invisible Unix directories. As these locations are off the radar of most users, the typical Mac user rarely needs to work with symbolic links. Symbolic links may also appear in more commonly visited locations, where they will seem to be just ordinary aliases. As I'll describe a bit later in this chapter, there may be one such symbolic link on your Desktop.

If you want to create a new alias, my general recommendation is to stick with the traditional Mac variety. Aliases are easier to create than symbolic links are, and they generally work more the way you would expect. But if you want an alias always to refer to a file with a specific name in a given location, whether or not the file has been replaced, a symbolic link will do the trick. To link to a file that gets overwritten by a new file with the same name periodically, you would want a symbolic link.

Still, an alias link may break in a situation in which a symbolic link would be maintained, and vice versa. For this reason alone, at least understanding the distinction is useful.

Finally, if you format a drive by using UFS (which I do not recommend) rather than HFS Plus, the Mac will *not* recognize aliases; it will recognize only symbolic links.

**SEE:** • "Select a destination," in Chapter 2, for more information on UFS vs. HFS.

## Determine whether a file is a symbolic link or an alias

You cannot tell from Finder icons whether the file is an alias or a symbolic link. Both types of files have the same icon with the curved arrow.

Even the Show Info window for the two types of files does not offer an obvious answer, as both types may be identified with a Kind setting of alias. In my experience, however, the Select New Original button will be dimmed, and thus not selectable, for symbolic links. For traditional aliases, the button is selectable, meaning you can use this difference to distinguish between an alias and a symbolic link.

Another way to determine whether a file is an alias or a symbolic link is to move the original file and then double-click the alias. If the original file still launches, you have a traditional alias. If you get a message that says the original could not be found, without the usual Delete Alias and Fix Alias options, you have a symbolic link.

Yet another, more-tedious way to figure this out is to reboot in Mac OS 9. In that OS, traditional aliases are identified in the Finder's Get Info window as having a Kind setting of alias, whereas symbolic-link files will be identified as Mac OS X alias. In Mac OS X, both types of files are identified simply as alias.

As I describe in the next section of this chapter, symbolic links also differ from aliases in terms of how they are listed in Terminal.

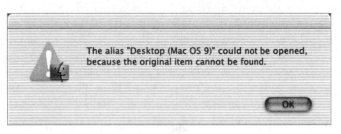

*Figure 6.29*

*The message that appears when a symbolic link cannot find its original file.*

## Create a symbolic link

Any alias that you create via the Finder's Make Alias command is a traditional alias. What if you want to create a symbolic link instead? You have two choices: take the Terminal or the Mac OS X utility (such as XRay) approach.

**Terminal.** To create a symbolic link in Terminal, follow these steps:

1. Launch Terminal.

2. Type <ln -s {*pathway of original file*} {*pathway of symbolic link*}>.

    Note: Use an absolute pathway for the original file, not a relative one. A shortcut for adding the absolute pathway is to type ln -s, a space and then drag the Finder icon of the original file to the Terminal window.

    **SEE:** • "Take Note: Folders vs. Directories," in Chapter 4, for background on absolute vs. relative pathway names.

    • Chapter 10 for more information on pathways and shortcuts in Unix.

You can now navigate to the directory where you created the link (via Unix's cd command), and type <ls –al>. This will result in the display of a list of all items in the directory, including symbolic links. Notice two things in the list:

• In the file-attributes column (where permissions are indicated), the first letter listed for a symbolic link file is *l* (rather than *d* for directory or a hyphen for files).

• For symbolic-link files, the path to the original file will be listed to the right of the file name. Traditional aliases have neither of these attributes.

Now if you go to the Finder, the symbolic-link file should appear in the same directory as seen in Terminal. If it does not, search for it via Sherlock and then double-click its name in the Search Results output. This method will force it to show up. As a last resort, log out and log in again.

**XRay.** To create a symbolic link with XRay, follow these steps:

1. Open the original file with XRay and then choose Make Alias from its File menu.

2. In the window that appears, from the Alias Format menu, choose Normal Alias, Absolute Symbolic Link, or Relative Symbolic Link.

   Ignore the rarely needed Relative Alias and Minimal Alias options.

   With an absolute symbolic link, any movement of the original file to a new location will break the link. With a relative symbolic link (most commonly used in Mac OS X packages), the link will be maintained if both the link file and the original file are always in the same relative locations within a folder, even if that folder is moved. This arrangement allows you to move an .app package file (which is actually a folder)—that contains symbolic-link files to other files within the package—without breaking the links.

Again, the link file should appear in the Finder at this point.

Note: The current version of XRay cannot show the permissions for a symbolic link correctly; instead, it lists the permissions of the original file. Thus, you cannot use XRay easily to check whether an alias is a symbolic link.

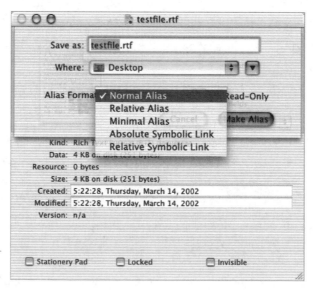

**Figure 6.30**

*XRay's option to create symbolic links.*

# "Desktop (Mac OS 9)" file is a symbolic link

An alias file called *Desktop (Mac OS 9)* is placed on the Desktop on Macs that ship with Mac OS X and Mac OS 9 installed on the same volume. This alias is of value because the Mac OS 9 and Mac OS X Desktops are entirely independent. That is, what you place on the Mac OS 9 Desktop (when you're booted in Mac OS 9, for example) and what you place on the Mac OS X Desktop are stored in different locations. Thus, the items from one Desktop are not visible when you're viewing the other. Furthermore, accessing the contents of the Mac OS 9 Desktop, when you're booted in Mac OS X, is complicated by the fact that the Mac OS 9 Desktop folder is invisible in Mac OS X ( located at the root level of the volume). The Desktop (Mac OS 9) alias allows you to work around this situation. When you open it, a window opens, showing the contents of the invisible Mac OS 9 Desktop. The contents are visible even though the folder itself is not.

If you have partitioned your drive into multiple volumes, you will not need a separate similar alias for the Desktop folders of the other volumes, because the Desktop folders for these volumes remain visible on these volumes. These folders contain the files from these volumes that appear on the Desktop when you're booted in Mac OS 9. Thus, the Desktop (Mac OS 9) folder shows only the Desktop items that are stored on the Mac OS X boot volume.

Why am I mentioning all this in this section of the book? Because the Desktop (Mac OS 9) alias is actually a symbolic link. I am not sure what Apple's rationale was in making this item a symbolic link. Perhaps Apple did not want it to continue to work if you moved the Desktop folder elsewhere. In any case, if you delete this alias/symbolic link accidentally, you will have double trouble trying to re-create it. First, the original folder is invisible (although, as I discuss later in this chapter, you can access invisible items in several ways). Second, using the Finder's Make Alias command would create a traditional alias, not a symbolic link. So duplicating the original alias takes a bit more work. The simplest way probably is to use Terminal. Follow these steps:

1.  If the symbolic-link file is present but broken, delete it; if it is deleted, proceed to the next step.

2.  Launch Terminal, and type:

    ```
    <ln -s /"Desktop Folder" ~/Desktop/"Desktop (Mac OS 9)">
    ```

3.  Press Return.

4.  Click the Desktop.

    The new symbolic-link icon should appear.

**SEE:** • **"Take Note: The Location of Desktop and Trash Folders," in Chapter 3.**

# Symbolic links and hierarchical menus in the Dock

If you drag a folder icon, or even a volume icon, to the Dock, you create a Dock item for that folder/volume. The main benefit is that if you click the Dock icon of the volume and hold down the mouse button, you will get a hierarchical pop-up menu of all the folders and files in the folder/volume. You can choose any item to open it.

If the volume contains an alias file pointing to a folder, the alias will work in the Dock icon's pop-up menu as though it were the original folder itself. Its submenu will show the contents of the original folder.

This technique appears to work only for traditional aliases, however. If the alias is actually a symbolic link, you will see only the name of the folder listed. You will not be able to view its contents hierarchically.

To see an example, drag the Favorites folder to the Dock. (The folder is located in the Library folder of your Home directory.) A Documents folder alias is placed in Favorites automatically when you install Mac OS X. This alias is actually a symbolic link. Thus, the pop-up menu will not list the contents of the Documents folder.

Note: In the first versions of Mac OS X, the situation was reversed. Symbolic links were the ones that showed submenus; traditional aliases did not.

*Figure 6.31*

*The pop-up menu from the Favorites folder in the Dock. Note that the Documents icon does not show a hierarchical menu.*

# Fixing a broken symbolic link

What if you click a symbolic-link icon and find that it is broken (you get the error message that the original file cannot be found)? In most cases, to fix the link, you create a new symbolic link file, using the ln command in Terminal, as described earlier in this chapter.

A potentially more serious problem involves the multitude of symbolic links that exist in package files, Library folders, and invisible Unix directories. If these links get broken, you may have problems that range from the failure of an application to work to inability to start up Mac OS X. You want these problems to be fixed. Fixing them, however, is not a trivial task, as you may have trouble locating the problem files and reestablishing the links correctly, especially if the problem is preventing you from starting up your Mac.

To fix these problems, try these methods:

**Disk repair utilities.** You may get some help from disk repair utilities such as Norton Utilities. If you have broken symbolic or hard links in the Unix directories, for example, run Norton Utilities (booting from its CD or from a Mac OS 9 volume, if you are not using the Mac OS X version). The utility attempts to fix the problem.

**Reinstall Mac OS X.** Otherwise, you will likely need to reinstall the problem applications or Mac OS X itself.

**SEE:** • **Chapters 2 and 5 for advice on reinstalling Mac OS X.**

How, you may ask, do these links get broken in the first place, assuming that you made no obvious change that should have caused any breakage? There are several possibilities, including the following:

- If you back up and restore files via a backup utility, symbolic links may get broken unless the backup utility specifically knows how to restore these links. (The best-known Mac backup utility, Retrospect, does handle this restoration correctly.)

- Archiving a folder/directory and later expanding it can cause problems unless the archiving utility knows how to handle the process. (At this writing, StuffIt Deluxe still has some problems.)

- An installer for an application, if not designed correctly, could move files during the installation in such a way that symbolic links get broken.

  There is a relatively rare but significant problem with the .pax files that are contained in installer packages (see Chapter 2). If an installer .pkg file (likely one from a third party, not Apple) writes to the invisible Unix files on your drive (such as the etc directory), it may do so in such a way that it breaks existing symbolic links to these directories. In extreme cases, this situation can result in the failure of your drive to start up, ultimately requiring a reinstallation of Mac OS X unless you are skilled enough to recognize and fix the broken symbolic links or have a third-party utility that can do it.

There is no sure way to prevent these problems other than not using the software in question or checking online (such as MacFixIt or the software vendor's Web site) before using a backup/archiving/installation utility to determine whether it has any known problems with symbolic links.

> **TECHNICALLY SPEAKING ▶ Unix Hard Links**
>
> A hard link in Unix is a duplicate directory entry for a file. Even if you delete the original file, the hard link will still access the file's contents, because the original file and all its hard links point to the same data. Think of the data as being stored somewhere on your drive and the original file as being just a pointer to the data. Then a hard link is another pointer to the same data. I am not aware of any case in which a hard link is used in the Finder. so hard links are relevant mainly for the workings of the invisible Unix files. About the only time they may become relevant for troubleshooting is when you're attempting to copy a Mac OS X volume to another drive. As is the case with symbolic links, the copy procedure will need to be able to maintain the hard links correctly.

# Deleting: Using the Trash

Deleting an item is a two-step process. First, you put the item in the Trash; then you empty the Trash. I discussed the basics of this process in Chapter 3. Here is a brief overview of Trash essentials.

## Place items in Trash

To place an item in the Trash, you can (a) drag the file's icon to the Trash icon in the Dock or (b) click the item and then choose *Move to Trash* from the Finder's File menu (or press Command-Delete).

Until you empty the Trash, files placed there are not really deleted. You can view the contents of the Trash by double-clicking the Trash icon to open its window. Any item in the window can be dragged out again. You can also place an item in the Trash by dragging it to this open window.

Each user maintains his or her own Trash. Thus, anything in some other user's Trash, but not emptied, will not be present when you log in. The contents will return for that user the next time he or she logs in.

Mac OS X does not include a feature that allows you to create a Trash icon on the Desktop, separate from the Dock. A shareware utility called Trash X provides this feature, however.

## Empty the Trash

To empty the Trash, do one of the following:

- Choose Empty Trash from the Finder's Finder menu.

- Press Command-Shift-Delete. This technique is especially convenient (combined with Command-Delete to get the file to the Trash) as a quick way to delete a file. Just click the file's icon and press Command-Delete, followed by Command-Shift-Delete. The file is gone.
- Choose Empty Trash from the Trash's Dock menu.

After you delete an item, there is no easy way to recover it. Norton Utilities 7.x for Mac OS X includes an Unerase feature. Beyond that, I know of no utilities that let you recover deleted files. So be careful before you delete anything.

Mac OS X will not let you delete files that are critical to the running of the OS. Later in this chapter, I explain how you can get around this prohibition, but don't be in a hurry to do so. If you are not careful, you could delete the entire contents of your drive accidentally or wreak similar havoc.

## Show warning

If you have the Show warning before emptying the Trash option enabled in the Finder's Preferences window, every time you try to empty the Trash, you will get a warning message: "Are you sure you want to remove the items in the Trash permanently?" This is useful because Empty Trash is one of the very few Finder commands that cannot be undone via the Finder's Undo command (Command-Z).

If you choose Empty Trash from the Trash's Dock menu, the Mac will empty the Trash without warning, even if the Finder warning option is enabled.

## Eject/Disconnect and Burn icons

If you click-drag a volume or server icon, the Trash icon will change to indicate that placing the volume in the Trash will unmount, disconnect, or eject the volume—rather than delete its contents.

If you drag the icon of a CD-R—that has been set up for burning—to the Trash, the Trash icon will change to the burn icon to indicate that placing the CD-R icon in the Trash will initiate the burn.

**Figure 6.32**

*Talking Trash: The Trash's Empty Trash option; the Empty Trash warning; the Trash icon changes to an Eject icon.*

**TAKE NOTE ▶ File Names in Mac OS X**

Here's an assortment of items regarding the limits of what you can and cannot do with file names in Mac OS X:

**Can't rename a file.** Normally, if you click the name of a file in the Finder (or simply click the file's icon and press Return), the name is shifted to an editable text box that allows you to change the file's name. If this text box does not appear, you either do not have the privileges/permissions to make such a change or the file is locked. See "Permissions/privileges problems with copying/moving files" earlier in this chapter and "Problems deleting files" later in this chapter for details and solutions.

**Long file names.** Mac OS 9 had a limit of 31 characters for a file name. In Mac OS X, the name of a file can be as long as 256 characters. Try renaming a file in the Finder, and you'll see what I mean. The file name can span several lines to accommodate your long name.

Still, a couple of glitches are possible:

- In many applications (especially non-Cocoa ones), the Open and Save dialog boxes show only the first 31 characters of a file name. If you simply open and save a document that already has a longer name, the full name is preserved even though you don't see it in the Open and Save dialog boxes. If you use the Save As command to save a file under a new name, however, you will be limited to 31 characters (although you can add extra characters in the Finder later).

- At this writing, StuffIt Deluxe (and perhaps other compression utilities) will truncate a long name to 31 characters when compressing the file/folder.

**Do not use / in file names.** The forward slash (/) is used in Unix as the separator for directories. Thus, Library/Fonts means the Fonts folder inside the Library folder. Adding the / character to the name of a file can confuse Unix into thinking that a reference is being made to a subdirectory, rather than a file name. The solution is to avoid using this character in file names.

**Do not use . at the start of a file name.** As discussed in "Invisible files" later in this chapter, a dot (.) at the start of a file name indicates that the file should be invisible, so the OS typically blocks you from adding a dot to the start of a file name. Unless you are deliberately attempting to create an invisible file, do not attempt to work around this block.

**SEE:**  • **"Take Note: File Name Extensions," earlier in this chapter, for related information.**

# Deleting: Problems Deleting Files

This section covers the most common reasons (and a few uncommon ones) why you may have trouble deleting a file and explains what you need to do to get things fixed so that the file can be deleted.

## Locked files

The most basic reason why a file refuses to delete is that the file is locked, via the Locked checkbox in the file's Show Info window.

If a file is locked, a small padlock symbol is visible in the bottom-left corner of the file's icon.

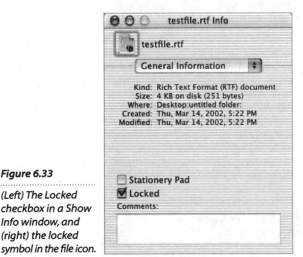

**Figure 6.33**

*(Left) The Locked checkbox in a Show Info window, and (right) the locked symbol in the file icon.*

Additionally, if you attempt to move a locked file to the Trash (or even to another folder on your drive), you typically get an error message that says, "The operation could not be completed because you do not have sufficient privileges." In Mac OS X, holding down the Option key (a technique that works in Mac OS 9) has no effect on your capability to drag the item into the Trash or empty it from the Trash.

**Figure 6.34**

*The "do not have sufficient privileges" error message that appears when you're trying to move or delete a locked file.*

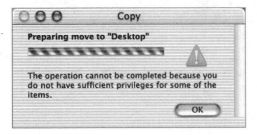

Thus, to delete a file that is locked, open the Show Info window for the file, and uncheck its Locked checkbox. Then you can drag the item to the Trash and empty it.

If a file is already in the Trash, you can still enable its Locked option, but doing so will have no effect. If you empty the Trash, the file will be deleted.

Occasionally, you may find that a locked item made it into the Trash and now refuses to be deleted. In such a case, you may not even be able to drag the item out of the Trash. Apple claims that pressing and holding down the Shift-Option keys while selecting to Empty Trash should work here. However, I have been unable to confirm this.

---

**TAKE NOTE ▶ Batch-Deleting Locked Files**

If you put a locked file in an unlocked folder, you can drag the folder to the Trash and (usually) delete the folder and its contents, including the locked file, even though you could not delete the locked file by dragging it to the Trash directly. This method is a trick way to delete a group of locked files without unlocking each one individually.

Alternatively, if you select several files and then choose the Show Info command (Command-I), you will get one Show Info window for all the selected items. The top of the window will say "# of items are selected." Any change you make (such as unlocking) will affect all selected files simultaneously. When they are unlocked, the files can be deleted.

A shareware utility, unlockAll, can batch-lock or unlock files.

---

**TAKE NOTE ▶ Can't Lock Folders from Show Info**

Mac OS X currently does not permit locking or unlocking folders via the Show Info window. Although the Locked checkbox appears, it is dimmed and cannot be selected. So you cannot lock Mac OS X applications that are packages, because a package is actually a special type of folder (as I explain in Chapter 2). Neither can you lock certain types of documents, including .pkg and .rtfd documents, as both are also packages.

You can still lock folders without needing to resort to Terminal, however. The shareware utility XRay allows you to enable the Locked option (as well as the invisible and package attributes, also not available in the Show Info window).

Note: An .rtfd document is a text document that contains graphics. The graphics and text are combined into a single document that is really a package. TextEdit saves files in this format automatically if you have a document that combines text and graphics.

SEE:  • "Take Note, TextEdit: Plain Text vs. Rich Text format; Other Format Options," in Chapter 4, for more on TextEdit formats.

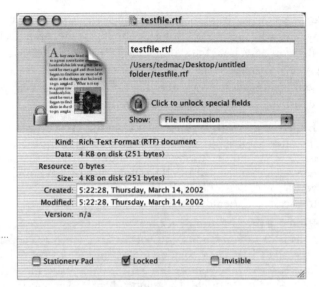

**Figure 6.35**

*XRay window with the Locked option enabled.*

## Too many aliases

If you have too many alias files in the Trash at one time, you may be unable to delete them. The solution is to drag the alias files from the Trash and return them in smaller groups (one at a time, if necessary). Then delete each group separately.

## Unlocked item cannot be placed in Trash or Trash cannot be emptied

You may get an insufficient-privileges or similar error message when you try to place an unlocked item in the Trash. Or you may succeed in placing the item in the Trash, but an error message appears when you try to empty the Trash.

**The causes.** The cause almost always has something to do with the file's permissions/privileges settings. Some of the specific causes are similar to the ones that can prevent a file from being moved. (After all, placing an item in the Trash is just a special case of moving the item.) These causes can include not having write access for the file, as follows:

- Having read-only access for a folder that contains the file you want to delete. This setting prevents you from moving the file from the folder. (Note: Having read-only access for the file itself will not prevent you from deleting it. The settings for the containing folder matter more.)

- Similarly, if the sticky bit is set for a folder, and you are not the folder's owner, you will likely not be able to move items within it to the Trash.

**SEE:** • **"Problems copying and moving files,"** earlier in this chapter, for more details and examples.

Regardless of what the permissions settings are, how the settings came to be that way, or why they cause trouble, your goal is the same: Delete the file. Usually, you can ignore the settings and focus on the delete task. The following procedures assist in this task. At least one of them will surely delete a problem file. (Again, be wary of trying to delete system files that refuse to delete; usually, you want to leave them alone.)

- **Empty the Trash.** If you try to drag a file to the Trash when a file with the same name is already in the Trash, the Finder usually renames the file that's already in the Trash (such as adding a 1 to the name) so that the new file can be added. But the Finder may balk at doing this and block you from adding a file with the same name. If so, the solution is to empty the Trash and then drag the file to the Trash.

- **Rename the volume or folder.** If a file to be deleted contains a slash (/) in its name—or any other unusual character (such as a copyright symbol), it may fail to delete. The solution is to change the name to remove the characters. Further, if the volume that a file is on contains these characters, the file may also refuse to delete. The solution here is to change the name of the volume. If needed, you can change the name back after deleting the file.

- **Create a new folder.** Create a new folder, place the uncooperative item in it, move the folder to the Trash, and empty the Trash.

- **Boot from Mac OS 9.** Boot from Mac OS 9, and delete the file there. Before switching to Mac OS 9, remove the problem file from the Trash and place it in a location that you can view easily when you're booted in Mac OS 9, such as the root level of your Home directory. The reason is that the contents of the Mac OS X Trash are invisible in Mac OS 9. The files will *not* appear in the Mac OS 9 Trash folder; Mac OS X and Mac OS 9 Trash are not stored in the same location. Thus, if you do not remove the file from the Trash in Mac OS X, you will need to locate and move the file with a utility (such as File Buddy) that allows you to view and manipulate invisible files. The Trash folder is called .Trash and is located at the root level of your Home directory.

  In the unlikely case that Mac OS X does not permit you to remove the item from the Trash, deleting the file in Mac OS 9 will again require accessing the invisible Trash location.

  SEE: • "Invisible files," later in this chapter, for more information on working with invisible files.

- **Use XRay or a similar utility.** If you cannot delete a file because you do not have the needed permissions, open the file with XRay and change the permissions. Make yourself the owner of the file, for example, and make sure that the owner has both read and write access. Now you should be able to delete the file.

  BatChmod includes a Force Empty Trash command that automates this process and appears to work well in most situations.

- **Use a delete utility.** Several utilities may be able to empty the Trash when the Finder refuses to do so. DropNuke is the name of one such utility. These utilities do not always work, but they are worth a try.

- **Repair the disk.** Start from the Mac OS X Install CD, and run the First Aid component of Disk Utility. First Aid may repair a problem that is preventing the files from being deleted. If First Aid does not work, try other repair utilities, such as Drive 10, Norton Utilities, or DiskWarrior.

- **Delete a user's account.** Here's a special case: If the files to be deleted are in a user's account, and that user no longer works on your Mac, you can delete the user's account via the Users System Preferences window. Select the name, and click Delete User. When you do this, you will be prompted to reassign ownership of the files to an administrative user— typically, you. Now you can delete or move the files as you see fit.

    **SEE:** • "Technically Speaking: Delete a Deleted User's Folder," later in this chapter, for more details.

- **Use Unix.** When all else fails, turn to Unix, which will always be able to delete your file. I explain exactly what to do in the following section.

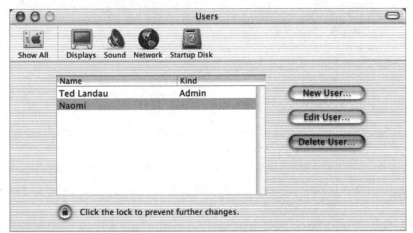

*Figure 6.36*

*Deleting a user in the Users System Preferences window.*

---

**TECHNICALLY SPEAKING ▶ Delete a Deleted User's Folder**

After you delete a User's account (via the Users System Preferences window), neither the user's folder nor its contents is deleted. Instead, the word *Deleted* is added to the name of the former user's Home directory. At this point, the deleted user can no longer access the folder. The Home directory of the deleted user reverts to the ownership of the admin user who deleted the account.

As an administrator, you can save any files you want by copying them elsewhere and then drag the rest of the folder's contents to the Trash. You cannot simply delete the folder itself, however. If you try to drag this folder to the Trash, an alert message appears: "The item '*user name* Deleted' cannot be moved to the Trash because it cannot be deleted."

*continues on next page*

**TECHNICALLY SPEAKING** ▶ **Delete a Deleted User's Folder** *continued*

To remove the user's folder from the drive, follow these steps:

1. Delete the user's account in the Users System Preferences window.

2. Launch Terminal.

3. Type: <sudo rm -rf /Users/*shortname*\ deleted>.

   *shortname* refers to the deleted user's short name, which is the name (preceding Deleted) of the Home directory you want to delete.

4. Enter your password when you are requested to do so.

The former user's Home directory is deleted. The Finder may not display this change immediately. You may have to relaunch the Finder or log out and log in again to see the effect.

Note: In general, do not attempt to move or delete the folders in the Users directory (or the Users directory itself). Doing so is an almost-certain recipe for disaster.

**SEE:** • "Technically Speaking: Move Your Home Directory to a Separate Partition," earlier in this chapter, for advice on how to safely move the Home directory.

## Use Unix to delete files

Although I prefer Aqua-based methods whenever possible, at times, the only path to success is through Terminal. Problems deleting files are examples. There are two main methods to try. If one fails to work, move to the other. I have never failed to have success with them.

**Use chflags.** The chflags (change flags) command can turn off a Unix lock attribute that prevents a file from being deleted. With the flag off, you should be able to return to the Finder and delete the file. Follow these steps:

1. Drag the files you want to delete to the Trash.

   Usually, this action will be permitted.

2. Launch Terminal.

3. Type: <chflags -R nouchg>.

4. Press the spacebar one time.

5. Open the Trash window in the Finder, and drag all the files you want to delete to the Terminal window.

   The files' pathway names should be appended to the line following the space.

6. Press Return.

Now you can return to the Finder and empty the Trash.

**Use rm.** The rm (remove) command deletes files in Unix. In most cases, if the basic rm command would work, choosing the Empty Trash command in the Finder would have worked just as well, so there would be no point in bothering with rm. The need for it arises when you want to delete an item of which you are not the owner (and changing the owner name had no effect) or in any odd situation for which the preceding suggestions did not work. In this case, using the remove command with root access (via the sudo command) should do the trick. To do this, follow these steps:

1.  Launch Terminal.
2.  Type: <sudo rm –R>.
3.  Press the spacebar one time.
4.  Open the Trash window in the Finder, and drag all the files you want to delete to the Terminal window.

    The files' pathway names should be appended to the line following the space.
5.   Press Return.
6.   If you are prompted to enter your password, do so and then press Return.

    The files and folders should be deleted. You will not need to empty the Trash from the Finder.

**Files in Trash window may come from multiple locations.** In most cases, the files listed in the Trash window (opened when you double-click the Trash icon in the Dock, for example) are stored in the invisible .Trash folder in your Home directory. Files in the Trash window may also originate in two other locations:

*   If you have multiple partitions/volumes, files dragged to the Trash from a nonstartup volume are stored in a .Trashes folder on that volume.
*   Some files deleted by the system may be stored in the .Trashes folder at the root level of the startup volume.

To make sure that you deleted all files from all these locations, launch Terminal and then follow these steps:

1.  Type <sudo rm -R ~/.Trash/>, and press Return.

    This step deletes the contents of your personal Trash folder.
2.  Type <sudo rm -R /.Trashes/>, and press Return.

    This step deletes the root Trash folder.
3.  Type <sudo rm -R /Volumes/*volumename*/.Trashes/>, and press Return.

    This step deletes the Trash from the nonstartup volume with the name *volumename*.

Repeat step 3 as needed for as many volumes as you have.

**SEE:** • **"The Location of Desktop and Trash Folders," in Chapter 3, for related information.**

**TAKE NOTE** ▶ **Using rm: Risk Management**

You can delete a file via the rm command even if the file is not in the Trash. This fact makes rm a potentially dangerous command, as it can delete a file anywhere on your drive instantly.

The –R option for the rm command is even more dangerous. Normally, rm will not delete a folder that has files or folders within it. The –R option instructs the OS to override this restriction. It deletes all listed files and folders—as well as all the files and folders contained within the listed folders.

This option is essential when you're attempting to delete a package application. Although such applications may appear in the Finder as a single file, they are actually viewed as a folder/directory in Terminal, which means that you need the –R option to delete them with rm.

That said, be very careful when using the –R option, as it will irrevocably delete everything contained in the directory you select. If you make a typing error, the error could have devastating consequences. If you type <sudo rm –R /Applications/Clock.app>, for example, you will delete the Clock application. If you mistakenly type <sudo rm –R / Applications/Clock.app>, the extra space between / and Applications means that Unix interprets the item as two separate items. The first item, /, is shorthand for the root level. Thus, you essentially are instructing rm to delete the entire contents of your drive! As I said, be *very* careful.

Note: As I mentioned in Chapter 2, Apple made a mistake like this in a script that was part of an iTunes updater. Before Apple fixed this mistake, hundreds of users wound up deleting entire volumes.

To minimize risks, you can do several things:

**Put file names in quotes.** In Terminal, if a file name is in quotes, Unix treats any spaces within the quotes as part of the file name. If the space is typed intentionally, this is what you want. If the space is typed unintentionally, the file will not be deleted, but at least no other files will be deleted either.

The other way to instruct Unix to treat a space as part of a file name is to precede the space with a backward slash. Thus, <"file name"> is equal to <file\ name>.

If you have any spaces in a name and do not use either quotes or a backward slash, the space is misinterpreted as being a separator between two items, which is where the trouble can occur.

**Drag the file from the Finder.** Dragging the file from the Finder to the Terminal window adds the correct file name automatically, saving you the trouble of figuring out how to use backward slashes or quotes.

**Use the Tab key.** Launch Terminal and then follow these steps:

**1.** Type <cd .Trash>.

This step moves you to your own Trash directory.

*continues on next page*

**TAKE NOTE** ▶ **Using rm: Risk Management** *continued*

2. Type <1s>.

   This step lists all the files that are in the Trash. You need this list only if you want to see the files in Terminal; you can always look at them in the Finder's Trash window instead.

3. Type <sudo rm –R {*initial part of file name*}>.

   You can type just the first two or three letters of the file's name.

4. Press the Tab key.

   Terminal will fill in the rest of the name (as long as you don't have two or more files that start with the letters you typed; in that case, you need to type more letters until you get a unique sequence).

**Use –i.** If you type <rm –Ri *filename(s)*>, the OS will request confirmation from you before anything gets deleted, asking "Remove *filename*?" after you press Return. Type y for yes or n for no. This situation gives you a second chance to check that what is about to be deleted is really what you want to delete.

The –f option is the opposite of –i. When you use it, this option instructs the OS to remove the files without prompting for confirmation, regardless of the file's permissions. Use this option with care, if at all.

**SEE:** • **Chapter 10 for more information on using Terminal.**

## Can't eject/unmount disks

To eject removable media or unmount a server volume or disk image, do one of the following:

- Drag the volume's icon to the Trash.

- You cannot use Command-Delete as an alternative to dragging a volume's icon to the Trash. Instead, try the Eject command (Command-E) in the Finder's File menu.

- If your keyboard has an Eject key (or uses F12 as an Eject key), pressing the key should cause a mounted removable volume to eject/unmount. For a drive such as a CD drive, if there is no disc in the drive, the tray will simply open.

   **SEE:** • **"Technically Speaking: Open Firmware Commands," in Chapter 5, for more information on ejecting a CD or DVD at startup.**

   If you have multiple removable devices mounted, select the one you want to eject before pressing the Eject key. Otherwise, you may eject/unmount multiple devices.

- Press the Eject button on the drive itself, if one exists.

If the preceding methods do not work, try the following:

- If you get the message that says the volume could not be ejected (or put away) because the volume is in use, some document or application on the volume is open. Thus, the fix is to close the open file. For a document, you may have to quit its application entirely, not just close the file.

- If you get this message when all files on the volume are closed, just try to unmount the volume again. It will usually succeed.

*Figure 6.37*

*The "in use" error message that appears when you're attempting to unmount a volume with an active process on it.*

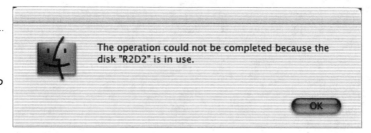

The operation could not be completed because the disk "R2D2" is in use.

OK

- For volumes that still will not unmount, log out and log back in. This technique almost always fixes the problem.

- If a disc is stuck in a drive, you may be able to eject it manually, typically by inserting an unbent paper clip into a hole located near the drive opening. Check with Apple or the vendor of the drive for specifics.

**Problems with copy-protected audio CDs.** In recent months, audio CD manufacturers have begun to release copy-protected CDs. These CDs typically have a sticker on them that reads: "Will not play on PC/Mac." Indeed, they will not. Even worse, the CD may get stuck in your drive, refusing to eject when you press the Eject button. If this happens, try the procedures described in this section. Especially try (a) holding down the mouse button at startup; (b) using the manual eject hole (if one exists on your Mac); or (3) typing `eject cd` in Open Firmware at startup. If none of these fixes work, you should probably bring the Mac to a service representative to get the CD removed. However, Mac users have found ways to get a CD tray to open manually despite the lack of any obvious manual eject hole on some Macs, especially the flat-panel iMac. Check sites such as MacFixIt (**www.macfixit.com**) for the latest suggestions.

**How to remount a volume.** Occasionally, the opposite issue may arise; you may unmount a volume that you did not intend to unmount. For removable media or remote volumes, the solution is simple: Reinsert the media or reconnect to the server. But what if you have a hard drive (especially a multiple-partition one), and you unmount a partition by mistake? (Typically, if you unmount one partition, you unmount all of them, unless one is the startup partition.) To get the volume back on the Desktop, follow these steps:

1. Launch Disk Utility.

2. Click the disclosure triangle to the left of the hard-drive icon to display the names of your hard-disk volumes and partitions.

3. Select a partition from the volume you want to remount.

4. Choose Mount from the Options menu.

# Invisible Files: What Files Are Invisible?

Numerous files on a Mac OS X volume are deliberately set to be invisible. In this section, I explore what these files are and why they are set to be invisible. I also explain why and how to access them.

## Files that begin with a dot (.)

If the first character of a file name is a period/dot (.), Mac OS X interprets that to mean that the file should be invisible. Some invisible files of interest that begin with a period include:

**.Trash.** This directory contains items you place in the Trash and is located at the root level of your Home directory.

**.DS_Store.** This file, which is likely to pop up in virtually every folder you access, stores the data needed to remember the location of icons in icon view for that folder.

Unfortunately, its memory is not always good. I still have problems when icons rearrange themselves spontaneously, especially on the Desktop and after waking from sleep.

**.FBC files** (such as .FBCIndex). These files are used in the Find by Content (FBC) Sherlock index searches. The .FBCIndex file is located at the root level of your Home directory.

**.hidden.** This special file contains a list of files (whose names do not begin with a dot) that are to be kept invisible. I discuss this file in the following section.

## Files in the .hidden list

The .hidden file is stored at the root level of the Mac OS X volume. The easiest way to open and view its contents is to use the freeware program BBEdit Lite for Mac OS X. Follow these steps:

1. Launch BBEdit, and choose Open Hidden from the File menu.

2. In the window that appears, slide the browser's scrollbar all the way to the left.

3. Select the name of your Mac OS X startup volume in the leftmost column.

   The .hidden file should be listed in the column immediately to the right.

4. Double-click .hidden to open it.

   You will see that its list contains root-level items, including the Mac OS 9 Desktop database files (Desktop DB and Desktop DF), the Mac OS 9 Desktop folder, the mach files (the mach_kernel file in particular is critical to the running of Mac OS X), and Unix folders (such as etc and bin).

The rationale, as in virtually all cases of invisible files, is that keeping these files invisible minimizes the chance that users will meddle with them. Typical users will rarely, if ever, need to modify these files, but the files could cause trouble if they are moved or deleted.

Although you could modify this .hidden file (you would need root access to do so) and thus change the invisibility of the listed files, I generally recommend not doing so. You can modify invisibility in other ways, if necessary.

**SEE:** • **"Modifying Unix Files," later in this chapter, for one example of using BBEdit to modify an invisible file.**

Note: Some of the files that are invisible in Mac OS X may be visible in Mac OS 9. Also, some files that are invisible on the Mac OS X startup volume may be visible on other volumes, even when you're booted in Mac OS X. The Desktop and Temporary Items folders, for example, are visible in all partitions other than the Mac OS X partition.

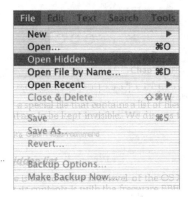

*Figure 6.38*

BBEdit's Open Hidden command.

# Files with the Invisible (Hidden) bit set

The Invisible bit is a leftover from Mac OS 9. Turning on this bit was the main way of making a file invisible in Mac OS 9, and it still works in Mac OS X. Some files may have the Invisible bit set and also have their names begin with a dot. Perhaps this setup makes them doubly invisible.

Accessing and modifying the Invisible bit requires special utilities, described in the following section.

# Invisible Files: Making Invisible Files Visible (and Vice Versa)

Should you ever need to locate, view, modify, or delete an invisible file, this is the section that explains how to do it.

## Toggle a file's Invisible bit

If a file is invisible because its invisible bit is enabled, just disable the bit to get the file to appear. Conversely, enable the bit get a file to disappear.

**XRay and Locator.** Mac OS X's Show Info window does not allow you to modify the Invisible bit directly, but you can do it in utilities such as XRay. Just open the file in XRay, and check the checkbox for the Invisible bit. When you click back to the Finder, the file should vanish.

**Figure 6.39**

XRay's Invisible-bit option.

When a file is invisible, its invisibility prevents standard methods of opening the file in XRay so as to turn the invisible bit off again. In this case, if you had just finished working with the file, it should be listed via XRay's Open Recent command in the File menu. Otherwise, you can use XRay's Open Quickly command and type the Unix pathway for the file. This method will open even invisible files. Type <~/.Trash> to load the invisible .Trash folder in XRay, for example.

If you don't know the pathway to type, you can use a utility called Locator. Type the name of the file (or even a partial name), and Locator will find all matching files, including invisible files. (Note: Locator is case-sensitive in deciding on matches.) In addition, Locator lists the pathname for each file.

You can select the file you want, choose Copy Path to Clipboard, and paste the pathway in XRay's Open Quickly window. The item will load, and you can deselect its Invisible bit.

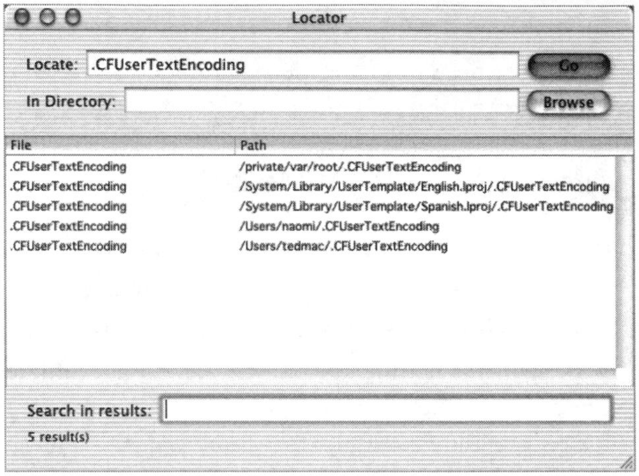

**Figure 6.40**

Locator finds all copies of an invisible file and their paths.

**Sherlock.** With Sherlock, you can do a custom search for invisible files. But Sherlock gives you no capability to modify or even open such files, which limits its value.

**File Buddy and beyond.** Several third-party utilities, such as File Buddy X, allow you to view invisible files and modify the Invisible bit. File Buddy even includes options that allow you not to list the .DS (Directory Store) files in search results, thereby reducing the amount of clutter you would have to sift through otherwise.

## Add or remove a dot at the start of a file name

Recently, I downloaded a file from a remote Web server, via FTP, to my local desktop. The file name began with a dot. The result was that the file was invisible after the download was complete. To locate and work with the file, I wanted to eliminate the dot (at least temporarily) so that I could see the file. Following are some options for doing this.

**XRay or File Buddy.** If you try to add a dot to the start of the file name in the Finder, you will be told that you cannot do so because "these names are reserved for the system."

Third-party utilities will allow you to do this, however. You could add a dot to a file name in XRay, for example. The dot at the start of the file name makes the file invisible, of course, which can make it more tricky to do the reverse (remove a dot from a file's name). In this case, a utility such as File Buddy will be more convenient.

You can similarly use File Buddy to remove a dot from the start of a file name.

**SEE:** • "Toggle a file's Invisible bit," earlier in this chapter, for related details.

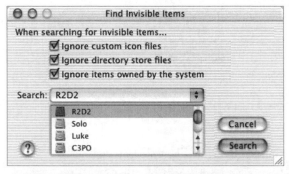

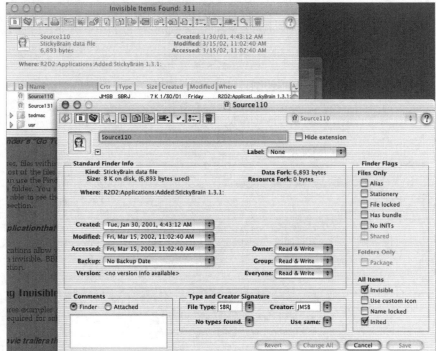

*Figure 6.41*

*(Top) File Buddy's option to search for invisible files. (Bottom) File Buddy's list of results and the Info window for one of the found files.*

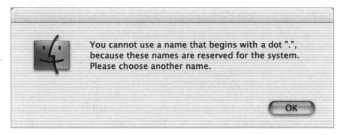

*Figure 6.42*

*The error message that appears if you try to add a dot to the start of a file name.*

You cannot use a name that begins with a dot ".", because these names are reserved for the system. Please choose another name.

OK

**Terminal.** You can also use Terminal to add a dot to or remove a dot from a file's name quickly. To do so, launch Terminal, and type:

<mv {name of file} {.name of file}>

As I have commented before, the easiest way to enter the name of a file is to drag the file icon from the Finder to the Terminal window. This technique gives you the full absolute-pathway name of the file. Then type a space and a dot, followed by the same text that you just pasted. This move (mv) command will create a new file (with a dot as the first character of the file name) to replace the original file in the same location. If you go to the Finder, the file icon will vanish.

You can make an invisible file visible by typing the opposite:

<mv {.name of file} {name of file}>

Note: Typing <ls> in Terminal does not list invisible files. For a listing that contains invisible files, type <ls –a>. You can use this command to see the names of invisible files, which is helpful, as they are not visible in the Finder.

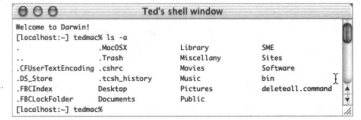

**Figure 6.43**

*Getting Terminal to list invisible files.*

**TinkerTool.** You could also use TinkerTool to make all invisible files visible, as described in the following section—and then delete the dot in the name if desired.

## Use TinkerTool or PropertyList Editor to make invisible files visible

Yet another alternative to working with invisible files is making the files visible in the Finder. Whether you can see invisible files in the Finder is determined by a setting in a .plist (property list or preferences) file, stored in the Preferences folder of the Library folder in your Home directory. Although you can edit this file's setting with any text editor, I recommend using either TinkerTool or the PropertyList Editor application (included as part of the Mac OS X Developer Tools software). Here's what to do.

**TinkerTool.** Use the shareware System Preferences utility TinkerTool, and enable its Show Hidden and System Files option. This modifies the plist file's preferences setting for you.

**PropertyList Editor.** Locate the com.apple.finder.plist file in the Preferences folder of your Home directory/folder. If PropertyList Editor is on your drive, and you double-click this file, it should open in PropertyList Editor automatically. Then follow these steps:

1. Click the disclosure triangle to the left of the word *Root* to reveal the list of properties.

2. Locate the property called AppleShowAllFiles.

3. In the Value column, click the word *No* and hold down the mouse button.

4. When the pop-up menu appears, choose Yes.

5. Save and close the document.

In either case, you may need to relaunch the Finder (via the Force Quit window or via the Relaunch Finder button included in the Preferences pane of the latest versions of TinkerTool)—or log out and log back in—before the change takes effect. All hidden files should appear in the Finder. You can navigate directly to the folder or file you want.

After you have done what you want with the invisible files, reverse what you did to return everything to the invisible state.

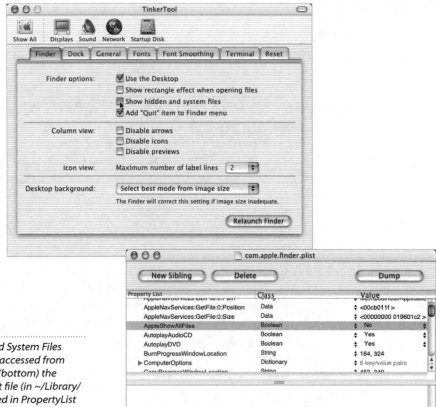

**Figure 6.44**

*The Show Hidden and System Files Finder preference, as accessed from (top) TinkerTool and (bottom) the com.apple.finder.plist file (in ~/Library/ Preferences), as viewed in PropertyList Editor. The option is off (No) by default.*

## Use the Finder's Go to Folder command

In some cases, files within a folder are set to be visible, but the folder itself is invisible. Most of the files in Mac OS X's invisible Unix folders work this way. In this case, you can use the Finder's Go to Folder command to open a window for the invisible folder. You simply need to enter the folder's full Unix pathway. Then you will be able to see the files in the invisible folder. I give an example in the following section.

## Use an application that lists invisible files in its Open dialog box

Some applications allow you to access and work with invisible files, even while they remain invisible. BBEdit is a good example, as I describe in the following sections.

# Invisible Files: Working with Invisible Files

Here are three examples of situations in which the ability to work with invisible files was required for solving a problem.

## Saving movie trailers that have the Save option disabled

When you're viewing QuickTime movies on the Web, such as movie trailers, you usually can choose to save the movie to your hard drive (although you need to have upgraded to QuickTime Pro). Still, the Web site can choose to have this option disabled, even for QuickTime Pro users. Nonetheless, you usually can save the file. Assuming that you are using Internet Explorer, follow these steps:

1. Enable the Save Movies in Disk Cache option in the Plug-In tab of the QuickTime System Preferences window.

2. Immediately after viewing the movie, go to
   `<~/Library/Preferences/Explorer/Temporary Items/>`.

   The QuickTime movie file may be stored there (although it will likely have a different name than the name of the movie itself).

3. If you find the file, drag it out of that folder.

   You are done.

If the preceding method does not work, access to invisible files comes into play. Follow these steps:

1. Enable TinkerTool's Show Hidden and System Files option.

2. Choose Go to Folder from the Finder's Go menu, and enter /tmp/ in the text box of the window that appears.

   The tmp folder window should now open in the Finder. You should find a folder in the window with a number as its name (probably, 501). This number is the same as the User ID number for the logged-in user.

   Note: In case you were curious, you can identify your user ID number by launching NetInfo Manager, choosing Users, and then selecting your user name. At the bottom of the window, search for the property that says <uid>. The number in the adjacent Value column is your user ID. Alternatively, when you're in Terminal, type <id>.

3. Open the 501 (or whatever number it is) folder.

   Inside, there should be a file with a name that starts with QuickTimePlugIn.

4. Drag the file to the Desktop.

5. Turn off TinkerTool's Show Hidden and System Files option.

6. Use a utility such as FileXaminer or XRay to change the type and creator of the file from whatever they are to MooV and TVOD, respectively.

7. Open the Show Info window for the file, and make QuickTime Player the Open with Application selection.

   This change should also change the file's icon.

8. Rename the file however you want.

9. Double-click the file, and enjoy.

**Saving package files downloaded from Software Update.** I use essentially the same method to save files downloaded from Software Update.

**SEE:** • **"Use a stand-alone installer/updater," in Chapter 2.**

## Saving the Stickies database file

The Stickies application included with Mac OS X allows you to save notes in colored windows that resemble Post-it notes. Unfortunately, due to an apparent bug in Mac OS X, the data file that contains all your saved notes may get deleted after certain actions. I have seen this situation happen after some users installed the Mac OS X 10.1.2 upgrade . The result is that Stickies reverts to the default notes that appear the first time you launch it; your saved notes are lost.

Although you may not be able to prevent this file from being deleted, you can protect yourself against the loss of the data by maintaining a backup of the Stickies data file. Doing so, however, is complicated because the data file is invisible. The following paragraphs explain how to solve this problem.

**Use TinkerTool.** Follow these steps:

1.  Enable TinkerTool's Show Hidden and System Files option.

2.  Go to ~/Library (such as the Library folder in your Home directory).

3.  Locate a file called .StickiesDatabase, make a copy of this file, and drag the copy to another location.

4.  Eliminate the period at the start of the file name.

    This step allows the file to remain visible even after you reverse the TinkerTool option.

5.  Turn off the TinkerTool option so that invisible files are invisible again.

    Now you have a backup of your Stickies database file. Back up the file again as often as needed, especially before performing an action (such as an OS upgrade) that is known to be a potential cause of the file deletion.

If your Stickies file gets deleted, reverse the preceding procedure and follow these steps:

1.  Use TinkerTool to make invisible files visible.

2.  Make a copy of your backup database, and give it the same name as the original except for the dot added as the first character.

3.  Drag the file to the ~Library folder (replacing the file that is already there, if necessary).

4.  Undo the TinkerTool change so that invisible files are invisible again.

    Your Stickies notes should be restored.

**Use Terminal.** You can also use Terminal to back up and restore the Stickies database.

To back up the database file, launch Terminal, and type <cp Library/ .StickiesDatabase Documents/StickiesDatabase>.

To restore the database file, launch Terminal, and type <cp Documents/ StickiesDatabase Library/.StickiesDatabase>.

To facilitate using these commands, save a copy of each command line as a text clipping. Then simply drag the text clipping to the Terminal window to paste it in. Press Return, if necessary, and the command will execute. (Note: In Chapter 10, I describe an alternative to text clippings for commands such as these: shell scripts.)

These commands create a file called StickiesDatabase in your Documents folder. You can select a different destination, if you want.

## Modifying Unix files

Mac OS X keeps its essential Unix directories invisible in the Finder. These directories include bin, etc, sbin, tmp, var, usr, and Volumes. In both Chapter 4 ("Take Note: What and Where are the Unix Files") and Chapter 10, I provide more detail about what is in these directories and how to use Terminal to access their contents. For now, I want to focus on how and why to edit some of these Unix files from the Finder.

Note: In Unix (as accessed from Terminal), only files that begin with a dot are considered to be invisible. Other files are listed as visible, even if they are invisible in the Finder.

Unix uses several configuration files to determine the settings and preferences of a variety of features (such as network settings). Actually, in some cases, when you change a System Preferences setting in the Finder, you are modifying the contents of one of these Unix files. These files are mostly stored as text files in Unix's etc directory. Occasionally, you may want to change a setting in one of these files that cannot be changed via System Preferences or any other Mac OS X feature. The solution is to edit the configuration file directly.

Assuming you are familiar with Unix, you can always use Terminal to access and edit these files, such as by typing <sudo pico {*path of file*}> to open a file in Unix's pico text editor via root access. I prefer to work in Aqua whenever possible, however. Fortunately, BBEdit Lite makes this especially easy to do. You do not even have to make the invisible folders or files visible in the Finder. Follow these steps:

1.  Launch the shareware utility Pseudo (needed to open BBEdit with root access).
2.  Drag the BBEdit Lite icon to the Pseudo window, and enter your password when you are requested to do so.

    Now BBEdit Lite is open with root access.
3.  Choose Open Hidden from BBEdit's File menu.
4.  Navigate to the desired folder, and open the desired file.
5.  Edit and save the file.

BBEdit includes a feature that allows owners of a read-only file to change the file's permissions so that it is writable. You cannot use this feature to modify a file owned by root, however. That is why you need to follow the above steps instead.

Note: You used to be able to type <sudo open {*path of application*}> in Terminal to mimic the effect of the Pseudo utility. But starting with an update to Mac OS X 10.1, Apple disabled this feature.

**SEE:** • See "Take Note: Opening .app Files from Within Terminal," earlier in this chapter, for an exception to this exception.

**Unix files that may need editing.** Following are three examples of Unix files you might need to modify at some point.

**Inetd.conf.** Mac OS X uses TelnetSSH for making Telnet connections over a network. The SSH protocol provides greater security than the older plain Telnet. If you want or need to use the older, less secure Telnet, you will need to change the /etc/inetd.conf file. To do so, open the file in BBEdit and then follow these steps:

1.   Locate the lines that read #telnet; #shell; and #login.

2.   Remove the # character from the start of each line.

3.   Save the file.

4.   Restart the Mac.

**SEE:**   • "Technically Speaking: Secure Connections," in Chapter 8, for more
             on SSH.

**Hostconfig.** If, when you're trying to mount a removable medium (such as a CD), you get an error message that states, "You have inserted a disk containing volumes that Mac OS X can't read," you may need to modify the /etc/hostconfig file. See Apple Knowledge Base article #106345 **<http://docs.info.apple.com/article.html?artnum=106345>** for complete details.

**Httpd.conf.** If Web Sharing refuses to start up, you may need to modify the /etc/httpd/httpd.conf file. See Apple Knowledge Base article #106505 **<http://docs.info.apple.com/article.html?artnum=106505>** for complete details.

Note: Updates to Mac OS X eventually fix identified problems, such as the latter two described in this section, so that these file changes are no longer needed. Still, new reasons to edit these files keep cropping up.

**SEE:**   • "Technically Speaking: The Root User Desktop," in Chapter 9.

# Maximizing Performance

Most computer users are never completely satisfied with how fast their computers run. They could always be faster. Although the hardware and software place certain limits on how fast a computer can go, a computer often runs slower than it is capable of doing. In this section, I describe some ways to make sure that you are getting the best performance from your Mac.

As a starting point: A native Mac OS X program running in Mac OS X should run about as fast as a Mac OS 9 version of the same program would run in Mac OS 9. A Mac OS 9 program running in Classic, while booted from Mac OS X, will generally be slower than the same program running in Mac OS 9.

Otherwise, if your Mac appears to be running significantly slower than it typically runs, or just runs too slowly in general, consider the following techniques.

**SEE:** • "Technically Speaking: Monitoring and Improving Performance," later in this chapter, for other ways to enhance the speed of your Mac and for how to monitor memory use.

## Not enough memory

Due to Mac OS X's dynamic memory, you will rarely, if ever, see "out of memory" messages, no matter how many applications you have open. Thus, it may sometimes appear that your Mac has unlimited memory. This is not so. At some point, as you open more and more applications, the overall performance of every aspect of your Mac will slow. Keep pushing the memory envelope, and you will likely precipitate a crash. Following are two solutions:

**Add more memory.** The best solution to memory problems is to purchase more memory. How much? As much as you can afford or your Mac can hold. You can't have too much. Mac OS X devours whatever RAM you give it. And the less RAM you have, the more performance slowdowns you will have.

**Quit unneeded applications.** If you are not adding more RAM, the more immediate alternative is to quit any open applications that you do not need. Quitting Classic, if you don't need to use it, is always good advice. In some cases, if a problem has become severe, you may need to log out and log back in before performance improves.

Different programs use different amounts of memory. Thus, quitting application A may have little effect, whereas quitting application B may have a tremendous effect.

**About This Mac.** How do you know how much memory you have and how much you are using? The About This Mac window, which you open from the Apple menu, tells you how much physical memory (RAM) you have installed.

**SEE:** • Chapter 4 for more background on dynamic memory and related Darwin issues.

## Too slow a processor

If your Mac is more than two years old, getting a new Mac will likely give you significantly better performance. Upgrading the processor or graphics card on your existing Mac may be a more cost-effective solution.

A Mac with a PowerPC G4 processor, for example, will be noticeably snappier than one that uses a PowerPC G3. Presumably, PowerPC G5 processors will be faster still. The difference in processor speed usually is more noticeable when you're running Mac OS X than it is in Mac OS 9, as Mac OS X places more demands on the processor. Mac OS X also includes dual-processor support for OS functions; Mac OS 9 did not. So if you have a dual-processor Mac, it should seem faster in Mac OS X than it does in Mac OS 9.

A faster graphics card (ATI and nVidia are always coming out with new and improved models) can also enhance speed, especially when you're using multimedia or playing games.

## Not enough free space on the drive (especially for the swap file)

If your hard drive is nearing capacity (generally, for most current hard drives of 10 GB or larger, if you have less than 1 GB of unused space), you may start to see a performance decline.

Too little free hard drive space is a concern especially when the size has become so small as to present problems for maintaining the virtual-memory swap file. Mac OS X's virtual-memory system works by storing information on your hard drive in a file called a swap file, located in the invisible /private/var/vm directory. This file can be quite large—80 MB at minimum. With too little free hard-drive space to accommodate the growth of the swap file as needed, you will start to see a performance decrease. Actually, even with a minimally sufficient amount of space available, fragmentation of the swap file can lead to a performance decrease.

The common solutions are:

- Reduce the need to access virtual memory by decreasing the number of processes/applications you have running at one time.
- Add more physical memory.
- Delete unneeded files from your hard drive and defragment your hard drive to make more contiguous free space. (See "Insufficient space," earlier in this chapter, for some specific advice.)
- Purchase a larger hard drive to replace your existing one or as an additional drive to offload rarely used files. Newer hard drives also tend to be faster than their older predecessors.

**TECHNICALLY SPEAKING** ▶ **Moving the Swap File to a Separate Partition**

A hard drive becomes fragmented when a file is stored in several segments in different locations on the drive, typically because no single free section of the drive is large enough to hold the entire file as one segment. As more files become fragmented, the overall level of disk fragmentation increases. If the fragmentation level gets sufficiently high, drive performance can start to decline. Disk optimizers such as Norton Utilities' Speed Disk are designed to reduce this fragmentation.

Larger files are more subject to fragmentation than smaller ones. As the swap file is a large file, it is especially vulnerable to fragmentation. Moving the swap file to a separate volume (presumably, one with lots of free space) from the one that contains Mac OS X can help reduce fragmentation. This change may in turn improve virtual-memory performance as well as disk performance.

I am still not convinced that the benefit is worth the effort. But if you want to give it a try, a utility called Swap Cop automates the procedure for you. Otherwise, the procedure, which requires considerable work in Terminal and with Unix files, is beyond the scope of this book. If you want the details, see ResExcellence (`www.ResExcellence.com/hack_html_01/06-01-01.shtml`) or Mac FAQs and Tips (`www.bombich.com/mactips/swap.html`).

**SEE:** • "Technically Speaking: Monitoring and Improving Performance," later in this chapter, for more information on memory and the swap file.

## Too slow an Internet connection

If your speed problems are primarily restricted to online problems (such as slow loading of Web pages), and you have a dial-up modem connection, it's time to think about moving up to a broadband connection (cable or DSL). Your speeds be much faster, and you will have a 24/7 connection with no need to log on and no dropped connections.

If you already have a broadband connection, you can still do some things that may improve performance. The utility MOX Optimize, for example, includes an option to speed Ethernet networking by optimizing buffers. This option essentially simplifies doing what you could otherwise do in Terminal.

**SEE:** • Chapter 8 for more information on Internet issues.

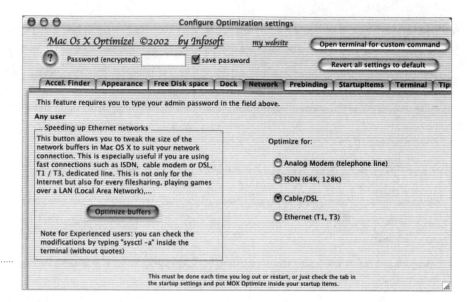

**Figure 6.45**

MOX Optimize's
Network tab.

## Miscellaneous other tips

Finally, you can do a host of other minor that have a small incremental effect on performance. These techniques mostly involve turning off certain Finder and Dock features, thereby reducing the CPU usage. It's up to you to decide whether the tradeoff is worth it. You could turn off the following features:

- Dock magnification
- Zoom rectangles
- Text antialiasing
- Window shadows
- Bouncing icons in the Dock (which can slow your Mac considerably)

You can do all these things via one or more of the following: Finder and Dock Preferences settings, TinkerTool, ShadowKiller, MOX Optimize, Dock Detox, and a host of other shareware utilities. MOX Optimize has an especially rich selection of options, including the capability to increase the Finder's Unix nice priority (see "Technically Speaking: Monitoring and Improving Performance" later in this chapter).

**Quit Sherlock.** Don't leave Sherlock running if you are not using it, especially if you have enabled its option to index volumes and folders. On one occasion, my Mac slowed down to the point that I could barely use it. When I ran the top command in Terminal, I discovered a process called ContentInd (presumably from Sherlock) was monopolizing almost all of the CPU usage. Quitting Sherlock, if you can, might put an end to this. I chose instead to use the kill command in Terminal (see "Kill from Terminal" in Chapter 5) to kill the process. This immediately eliminated the slowdown.

**Check the Web.** Various Mac Web sites have posted additional tips for enhancing Mac OS X performance. One good example (beyond my own MacFixIt) is Mac OS X FAQ (**www.index-site.com/Macosxspeed.html**).

**TECHNICALLY SPEAKING ▶ Monitoring and Improving Performance**

Insufficient memory, too slow a processor (CPU), a nonoptimized drive—all these things (and more) can decrease the performance of Mac OS X. But if you suspect that your Mac is not up to par, how would you determine which, if any, of these factors is the major cause? And beyond adding hardware (such as more memory or a faster processor), what, if anything, can you do to improve performance? The answers to both of these questions reside in a host of utility software. Some solutions require using Terminal; others are Aqua-based. Following is an overview.

**CPU Monitor.** CPU Monitor, which is included when you install Mac OS X, is located in the Utilities folder. When you launch it, the program displays a small thermometer-type gauge, with a current level that keeps rising and falling. The level indicates the ever-changing extent of CPU use. Don't be alarmed if the level occasionally gets to 100 percent; that's OK as long as it doesn't stay there for a sustained period. If the gauge remains at its peak, you are likely trying to do too many processor-intensive activities at the same time. Quitting some applications or reducing how many tasks you have going simultaneously will likely help. I have rarely found this gauge to be diagnostically useful. But the CPU Monitor Processes menu also serves as a convenient launch pad for two more-useful functions: Process Viewer and top.

**ProcessViewer.** ProcessViewer is also part of the basic Mac OS X installation. I have discussed this utility before, primarily in Chapter 5, as a means to force-quit processes. Now I want to focus on two additional features of the utility: its %CPU and %Memory column listings. Each process listed in ProcessViewer's display has a value in each of these two columns. These values indicate how much CPU attention and memory availability the process is using. You can sort either column by clicking the column name. If you do so, the processes that move to the top are the ones that are the most likely culprits in any CPU- or memory-related performance problems. In general, regardless of what the results may be, do not quit any processes that you do not recognize, especially administrative processes. If a process name is for an application you do know, its CPU or memory percentage remains high, and you don't need it open at the moment, quitting that application would be a good idea.

One difficulty is that all Carbon applications will have the name LaunchCFMApp, making it difficult to tell which one represents a particular Carbon application. Similarly, Classic applications are not listed separately but are included under the TruBlueEnvironme process. You may need to do trial-and-error guesswork to figure out the culprit.

Also note: Some applications may claim to be using 0 percent of memory. This can happen; it does not mean that something is wrong.

*continues on next page*

**TECHNICALLY SPEAKING** ▶ **Monitoring and Improving Performance** *continued*

**Terminal commands.** You can view (and, in some cases, modify) a variety of important performance measures via Unix commands you enter in Terminal. Following are some examples:

- **top.** If you choose the top command in CPU Monitor, it will launch Terminal and execute. You can also get there simply by launching Terminal and typing <top>. The top display is Unix's version of ProcessViewer. The PID column, for example, gives the Process ID number for a process, the Command column gives the name of each process, and the %CPU gives current CPU use. The numbers continue to update as you watch. To exit this display, type <q> (for *quit*).

  Note: Unlike ProcessViewer, Terminal does not list the names of all Carbon applications as LaunchCFMApp.

  At the top of the top display are some other important numbers. *Load Avg* is one indication of CPU use. The three numbers represent the most recent average and two averages from minutes before. Generally, the load should stay below 2.0. If it gets higher and stays there, and if performance slows, you may be trying to do something beyond what the processor can handle. If what you are trying to do is essential to your work, an upgrade to a faster processor may be required. Otherwise, you need to try to do less at the same time.

  The *CPU Usage* numbers give a different perspective on how the CPU is being used. These numbers indicate how much of the CPU is allocated to the system (kernel) vs. the user vs. how much is not currently being used at all (idle). Be especially on guard as the idle percentage approaches 0, which is likely to correlate with performance slowdowns.

  Finally, the VM (virtual memory) line gives an indication of memory use. The VM line looks something like this:

  VM: 3.19G + 50.7M 25092(0) pageins, 24969(0) pageouts

  If the initial number (3.19 GB in the preceding example) is getting close to the size of your remaining free hard-drive space, you are likely to see performance slowdowns. This number indicates that your swap file does not have sufficient space. (Note: The amount of free space on your volume is listed in the status bar of any Finder window for that volume, assuming that Show Status Bar was chosen from the Finder's View menu.) For further details on memory use, read on.

- **vmstat.** Unix's vmstat command provides a more focused look at Mac OS X's memory use than top provides. Of particular interest is the number of pageouts (also listed in the top display). The pageout value is an indication that physical memory is being paged (swapped) to the swap file on your drive. The higher the number of pageouts, the greater the disk access and the worse your performance is likely to be. A performance problem is especially indicated if you see pageouts continuing to increase over time.

  If pageouts equal 0, you are not using the swap file at all. This situation is the ideal, as any use of the swap file will likely result in slower performance. As long as the pageout number is near 0 and relatively stable, you need not be too concerned about memory use, even if other statistics indicate that your memory use is at or near 100 percent.

*continues on next page*

**TECHNICALLY SPEAKING** ▶ **Monitoring and Improving Performance**  *continued*

- **renice.** As I discussed earlier in this book (see "Darwin" in Chapter 4), Mac OS X's preemptive multitasking attempts to allocate the processor's attention such that the most important tasks get the most attention (generally giving greater attention to a foreground application over a background one, for example). Tasks that get the greatest attention complete the fastest. One way the OS makes these decisions is by assigning each process a priority ranking. When two processes are competing for the CPU's attention, the one with the greater priority will receive the greater attention.

  On occasion, however, you may want to override the OS's default priorities. Some users have found they can give Virtual PC a needed speed boost by assigning a higher priority to it. To do this, you use Terminal's renice command. The default nice level for most applications is 0. The potential range is between –20 and +20. To increase an application's priority, you lower its nice level from 0 to a lower number. (The lower the number, the more attention a process gets.) There are limits, of course. If you give everything a score of -20, for example, you won't be increasing the performance of anything. The benefits are always relative to the priorities assigned to other processes.

  To change a nice value, type <sudo renice {*nice #*} {*pid*}>, in which where {*nice #*} is the integer from –20 to +20 and {*pid*} is the process ID number of the process you want to change. (You can determine a process pid from the top command or from ProcessViewer.) Unfortunately, these changes may not be saved after you quit the application or restart the Mac. So you may need to reenter a change each time you use the application.

  By the way, users have noticed that Virtual PC runs slower in Mac OS X than it does in Mac OS 9. Connectix claims that this slowdown is due to a rare case in which preemptive multitasking (used in Mac OS X but not Mac OS 9) turns out to be a disadvantage. In Mac OS 9, Connectix can make sure that Virtual PC gets as much processor priority as possible. In Mac OS X, preemptive multitasking prevents this situation, resulting in slower performance. An upgrade to Mac OS X is supposed to provide a workaround for this situation.

- **Optimize (update_prebinding).** When you run a Mac OS X update via the Installer utility, at some point, the Installer typically says that it is optimizing the software. This process often turns out to be the longest part of the entire update.

  What the Installer is doing at this point is running the Unix update_prebinding command. To explain the process in the most nontechnical language possible, the command updates the linking among applications and the shared library files that may be required to run an application. Whenever a new application is installed, this information map needs to be updated. If the information is not updated, the resolving of these links is calculated when you launch the application, which takes added time and thus slows performance. Installers perform this task because, following the installation of new software, updating this map is desirable.

  If you add applications to your drive by any method that does not do this updating (which would be the case for most applications that do not use Apple's Installer utility), running the update_prebinding command yourself could increase the speed of Mac OS X.

*continues on next page*

**TECHNICALLY SPEAKING** ▶ **Monitoring and Improving Performance**  *continued*

The simplest way to do this is to bypass Terminal and use Xoptimize, an Aqua-based utility that accesses the same update_prebinding command. Xoptimize also includes options (such as using less memory when running the optimization) that can prevent problems that might occur if you simply ran update_prebinding from Terminal.

Note: Mac OS 9 users may be familiar with the term *optimizing,* as it refers to defragment-ing the files on a disk and optimizing their locations as done via a utility such as Norton Utilities' Speed Disk. This process is different from the Unix-based optimization referred to in this sidebar. You may still get benefit from using Speed Disk on a Mac OS X volume, but I confess that I no longer bother to do this. The process is not likely to be of much value if you have a large hard dive with a good deal of unused space. The issue did come up, how-ever, when I decided whether to move the swap file to a separate partition (see: "Technically Speaking: Moving the Swap File to a Separate Partition" earlier in this chapter).

- **netstat.** Terminal's netstat command gives you a quick indication of whether your network connection is performing up to par. In Terminal, type <netstat −i>. In the display that appears, if the incoming packet count is 0, you probably don't have a connection at all. If your error count is greater than 1 to 2 percent, there is likely to be some problem with your connection (perhaps a network difficulty at your cable company's end). Type <netstat −i 10>, and the display is updated every 10 seconds. This technique allows you to test hypotheses. You could start your browser to see whether the error counts change as the browser attempts a connection, for example.

**Aqua-based utilities.** Many Aqua-based utilities that measure performance are actually graphical user interfaces (or GUIs) for a Unix function otherwise accessed via Terminal. I have already mentioned some of the utilities, including ProcessViewer, CPU Monitor, and Xoptimize. Following are some others.

*Perfboard* is an Aqua-based shareware utility that provides a quick view of most of the data covered in this sidebar. In its default view, you get a constantly updated look at CPU percentage, system load, memory use (including pageouts), network ins and outs, and disk reads and writes.

Other Aqua-based utilities provide similar feedback—usually, a subset of what Perfboard pro-vides, but in the form of a menu-bar item or a Dock icon. One example is *GMem!,* which shows memory use.

The *Renicer* and *Nicer* utilities allow you to modify the nice level of a process without using Terminal.

The Netstat tab of *Network Utility* (included in the Utilities folder of Mac OS X) offers similar functionality to Unix's netstat command.

SEE:  • **"Optimize Mac OS X volumes," in Chapter 5.**
       • **Chapter 8 for more information on networking issues.**

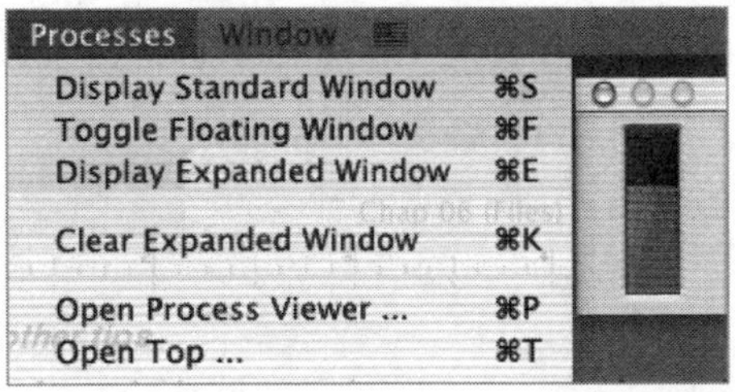

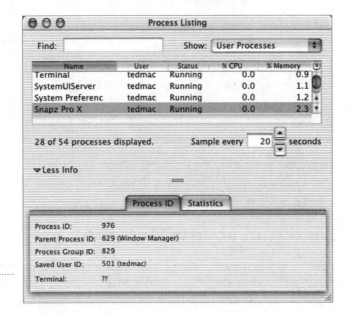

**Figure 6.46**

CPU Monitor's Processes menu and CPU gauge.

**Figure 6.47**

Process Viewer's display.

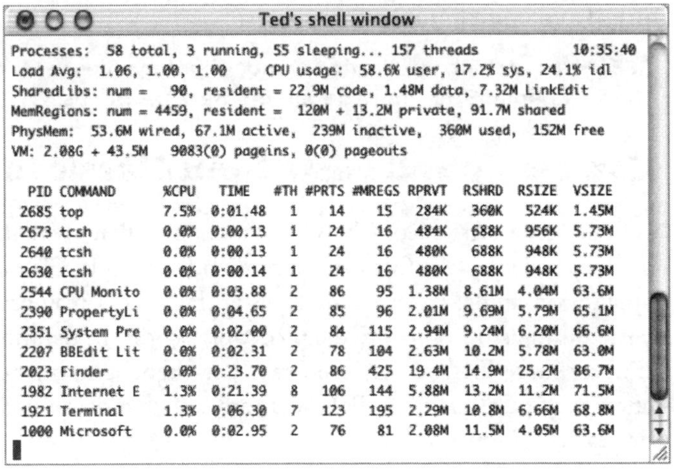

**Figure 6.48**

The top command output viewed in Terminal.

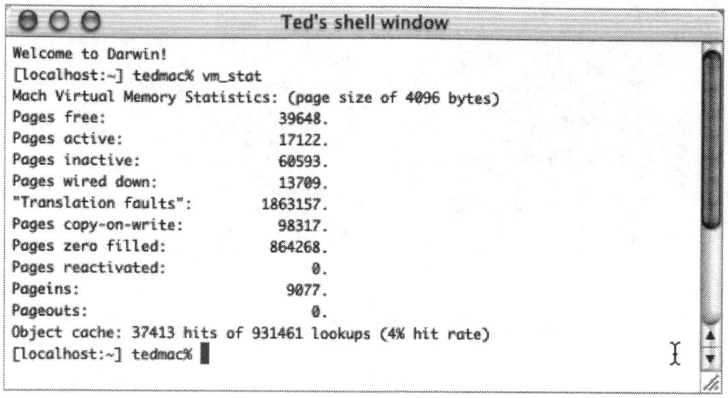

```
 ○ ○ ○              Ted's shell window
Welcome to Darwin!
[localhost:~] tedmac% vm_stat
Mach Virtual Memory Statistics: (page size of 4096 bytes)
Pages free:                39648.
Pages active:              17122.
Pages inactive:            60593.
Pages wired down:          13709.
"Translation faults":    1863157.
Pages copy-on-write:       98317.
Pages zero filled:        864268.
Pages reactivated:             0.
Pageins:                    9077.
Pageouts:                      0.
Object cache: 37413 hits of 931461 lookups (4% hit rate)
[localhost:~] tedmac%
```

*Figure 6.49*

*The vm_stat command output viewed in Terminal.*

# Quick Fixes

This final section includes a variety of troubleshooting tips and fixes that fit within the scope of this chapter but did not conveniently fit in any of the preceding sections.

## Files do not open in Mac OS 9

Occasionally, when you're booted in Mac OS 9, if you try to open a document for an application that exists in separate Mac OS 9 and Mac OS X versions, you will get an error message that says you need to be running Mac OS X to open the document. Or you may get a more general error message that indicates that the file could not be opened.

**SEE:** • "Launching applications" and "Clippings files in Mac OS 9 vs. X," in Chapter 9, for more details on these problems.

## Can't copy and paste from Classic to Mac OS X

At least some versions of Mac OS X have a bug that prevents you from pasting a Clipboard selection from an application running in Classic to a Mac OS X application. In the lesser form of this problem, you may have to copy and paste multiple times before the procedure works; in the more annoying form, it never succeeds. You may even get a persistent spinning pointer when you attempt to paste the item. Following are some workarounds for this symptom. Try each fix in turn until one work.

• Update to the latest version of Mac OS X. It may fix this bug.

• Quit and relaunch Classic via the Classic System Preferences window.

• Deselect the option titled Start up Classic on Login to This Computer, if it is selected. This change should prevent the problem in the future.

- Quit Classic, and delete the following two files from the Classic System Folder: Classic (located at the root level of the System Folder) and Classic RAVE (located in the Extensions folder of the System Folder). When you relaunch Classic, Mac OS X will ask you whether it can add files to the System Folder to replace the two you just removed; allow it to do so.

- Log in as root, and delete Finder preferences (such as /Users/username/Library/Preferences/com.apple.finder.plist). Then log out and log in again in your normal account.

## Date & Time settings

The Date & Time System Preferences window allows you to set the date and time. If you want to change the format of the date and time (such as a 12-hour vs. a 24-hour clock), you need to access the Date and Time tabs of the International System Preferences window.

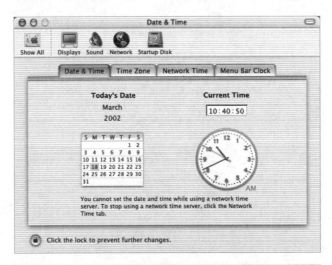

*Figure 6.50*

*Time settings in (top) Date & Time and (bottom) the International System Preferences window.*

## Can't select window

If you click a window in the background and it does not become the foreground active window, try clicking the header portion of the window. This method typically does the trick.

---

**TAKE NOTE ▶ CD Burning**

**Burning basics**

Mac OS X makes burning a CD especially easy. You have several options:

**Burn a CD via the Finder.** When you insert a CD-R or CD-RW into a CD-RW drive, a message should appear: "This disk needs to be prepared for burning. Do you want to prepare this disc?" The message window contains several options. To burn the CD, follow these steps:

1. Select a format: *Standard* (for data), *MP3 CD*, or *iTunes (Audio)*, which is the format you use if you want to play the CD in a standard audio CD player.

   Most often, you will be doing data copies from the Finder, whereas MP3 and audio CD burning will be done from iTunes.

2. Click the Prepare button.

   If you do not want to burn the CD at this point, click Eject to eject the disc. Or to leave the disc in the drive, for possible use in another application, click Ignore. (You may have to click Continue in yet another message window that appears.)

3. After clicking Prepare, an icon for the CD will appear.

4. Drag the files you want to burn to the CD icon.

5. Drag the icon of the CD to the Trash.

   The Trash icon will turn to the icon used to indicate burning a CD. Completing the drag will initiate the burning of the CD.

**Burn a CD via iTunes.** To burn a CD via iTunes, follow these steps:

1. Choose New Playlist from the File menu.

2. Add the desired songs to the playlist—either by dragging MP3 files already in the iTunes Library to the playlist or by adding new files from audio CDs via iTunes' Import option.

3. Click the playlist name in the left column.

4. Click the Burn CD button in the top-right corner.

5. Insert a blank CD.

   You will create a music CD that can be played in a standard audio CD player.

**Burn a CD via Disk Copy.** To burn a CD via Disk Copy, follow these steps:

1. Choose the Burn Image command from the Image menu.

2. Select an image (.img or .dmg) file in the window that appears.

3. Insert a disc.

*continues on next page*

**TAKE NOTE ▶ CD Burning** *continued*

**4.** Click the Burn button.

Note: Disk Copy is the only method you can use to create a bootable copy of a bootable CD (such as the Mac OS X Install CD). See "Take Note: Create a Bootable CD" in Chapter 3 for more information.

**Third-party software.** You can also burn CDs with third-party software, such as Toast Titanium.

## Troubleshooting CD burning

In most cases, burning a CD will work without hassles—especially if you have an internal CD-RW drive that shipped with your Mac. If problems do occur, consider the following:

**CD drive not compatible.** This is probably the most common CD-burning problem. After you insert a blank CD, the Finder (or other software) does not appear to recognize that a CD has been inserted. You may have an external CD-RW drive that is not compatible with Mac OS X.

To check for this situation, first go to the list of compatible drives that Apple maintains on its Web site (**www.apple.com/itunes/notes.html**). If your drive is listed, make sure that you are using the latest version of Mac OS X . Also make sure that you have the latest firmware update for the drive. (Check with the drive vendor for help.)

**External drive not connected properly.** If drive compatibility does not appear to be an issue, but you are still having problems getting the CD-RW drive to work, launch Apple System Profiler and select the Devices and Volumes tab. See whether the drive is listed in the relevant section (USB or FireWire).

If the drive is not listed, make sure that all cables to the drive are connected properly (including power cables). Make sure that the drive is on. If you are using a USB or FireWire hub, try bypassing the hub and connecting the drive directly to the Mac.

If the drive is listed in Apple System Profiler, restart the Mac with the drive already on.

**Burn fails.** You may get to the point where you can click a Burn button and the burn is initiated, but the resulting CD-R disc does not mount or play as expected. In this case, try again with a new CD-R, making sure to keep other CPU activity to a minimum. (Do not try to play a QuickTime movie while burning a CD, for example.) If you are using software that allows you to adjust the burn speed, make sure that you use a speed that does not exceed the maximum needed to make a successful copy. (Toast Titanium has a feature that allows you to test the maximum speed.) Also, set Energy Saver to disable any sleep that might occur during a burn.

**Recover space after an interrupted burn.** If a burn was interrupted, such as due to a power failure, run Disk Utility (from the Mac OS X Install CD), and repair the Mac OS X volume. This technique will reclaim disk space that was reserved for temporary files needed to burn the CD.

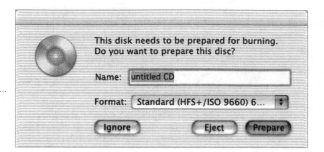

**Figure 6.51**

*Message that appears in the Finder when you insert a blank CD.*

**Figure 6.52**

*Burn CD features of iTunes and Disk Copy.*

# 7

# Troubleshooting Printing

Given the historically strong position of the Mac OS in the graphics and publishing industries, you might assume that Mac OS X would include advanced printing features...and you would be right. Mac OS X provides Mac users with a brand-new, high-tech printing engine, includes built-in support for many printers, and gives you tools to manage your print jobs. It also does some things differently from previous versions of the Mac OS, however, and requires different solutions when things go wrong. In this chapter, I'll show you how printing works in Mac OS X and what to do when it doesn't.

# In This Chapter

# Printer Support in Mac OS X

Before I talk about how to set up printing in Mac OS X, it will help to understand what types of printers and connections are supported as well as the differences among types of printers.

One of the initial problems when Mac OS X was first released was that it didn't support many of the most common printers—especially inkjet printers. It also had little, if any, support for connecting to printers over an AppleTalk network. These limitations have largely been addressed via the latest versions of Mac OS X and the various printer updates that have been released, by Apple and printer vendors. Thus, if you are having any printer problems, the first thing you should do is make sure that you are using the latest software available for your printer.

## What types of printers does Mac OS X support?

Mac OS X supports both PostScript (specifically, PostScript Level 2 and Level 3) and non-PostScript printers. The nature of Mac OS X's support differs between the two classes of printers, however.

**PostScript printers.** PostScript is a programming language, developed by Adobe, that allows the operating system to precisely describe the appearance of a printed page to the printer. PostScript has long been the standard for professional publishing and printing, but as technology has advanced, PostScript support has become fairly common among home and small-office printers. As PostScript is a standard language, all PostScript-compatible printers receive the same basic instructions from the operating system on how to print the same document, so a single PostScript driver can provide basic printing support for *any* PostScript printer. Mac OS X has a built-in PostScript driver, so it can talk with any PostScript 2 or 3 printer on a supported connection right out of the box.

**SEE:** • "What types of printer connections does Mac OS X support?" later in this chapter.

If a particular PostScript printer provides added features or functionality (multiple paper trays, various resolutions, different paper sizes, and so on), the printer manufacturer provides a *PostScript Printer Description* (PPD) file. A PPD tells the PostScript driver what is different about (or what additional features are provided by) that printer. Mac OS X includes PPD files for many PostScript printers from Apple, Hewlett-Packard, Lexmark, Tektronix, and Xerox. Even better, Mac OS X's Software Update may provide updates for these PPDs automatically, as well as PPD files for additional printers as support is added.

**TAKE NOTE ▶ Printing: a Behind-the-Scenes Intro**

As with Fonts folders (described in Chapter 4), there are multiple Printers folders in the various Library folders on your drive. Each folder serves a different function.

**/System/Library/Printers/.** This folder is where Mac OS X directly installs printer software. This folder contains a collection of other folders. In general, you should not modify any of the files here. The folders of most interest are:

- **PPDs.** This folder contains (buried in PPDs/Contents/Resources) the lproj (language-specific) folders that contain the PostScript Printer Description files for all of Apple's LaserWriter printers. The en.lproj (English language) folder must be there for the system to work; the rest are optional.

- **PDEs.** This folder contains the Printing Dialog Extensions files, which determine the options available in the Page Setup and Print dialog boxes. The names of these files hint at their functions: CopiesPages.pde, Duplex.pde, OutputOptions.pde, and so on. (See "Take Note: PDE Files," later in this chapter.)

- **PBMs.** This folder contains Printer Browser Modules files, which determine the basic options available in the Printer List pop-up menu. The names of the files mirror the options they provide: PB_AppleTalk.plugin, PB_LPR.plugin, PB_USB.plugin, PB_NetInfo.plugin, and so on.

**/Library/Printers.** This folder is primarily for third-party printer software (HP, Epson, Canon, and so on.) installed by the user. It includes PPDs for PostScript laser printers, as well as separate vendor-specific folders for inkjet printers.

**~/Library/Printers.** This folder, located in each user's Home directory, can contain the same sorts of folders and files as /Library/Printers. The only difference is that files in this folder are accessible only when the user of that name is logged in, whereas files in /Library/Printers are accessible to all local users. In general, you want printing software to be accessible to all users, so it would be common to find the ~/Library/Printers folder empty or not present at all.

If files that correspond to the same printer appear in more than one of these folders, Mac OS X will use the most local one first—that is, it will use the one in your Home directory in preference to the one in the /Library directory, which in turn overrides the one in the /System/Library folder. You should avoid having multiple files for the same printer in the same folder; in such cases, you cannot predict which one will be used.

Mac OS X will also look in the Printer Descriptions folder (inside the Extensions folder) of your Classic Mac OS 9 System Folder for additional PPD files, but only if it has not already found a match in the Mac OS X Library folders.

When you're printing from Classic (or booted from Mac OS 9), however, none of the Mac OS X folders or printing architecture is used. When you print in Classic, the OS checks for PPDs only in the Mac OS 9 System Folder and uses the Chooser (rather than Print Center) to select a printer.

The remainder of this chapter provides more details on the items covered in this sidebar.

**SEE:** • **Chapter 9 for more information on printing in Classic.**

**Non-PostScript printers.** Other recent printers (such as most inkjet printers) commonly use Printer Control Language (or PCL) rather than PostScript. Because such printers don't support a universal printing system, each printer requires its own model-specific driver. Because these drivers are printer-specific, PPD files aren't necessary; the print driver itself usually includes all the information the OS needs for full feature support. Mac OS X comes with drivers installed for many inkjet printers, such as Apple, Canon, Epson, and Hewlett-Packard models. Again, Software Update may update these drivers or install new ones from these and other manufacturers.

**QuickDraw printers.** In what may be disappointing news for some users, Mac OS X does *not* support older QuickDraw printers. Some older Apple printers (such as the ImageWriter series, StyleWriter series, and a few LaserWriter models) use Apple's own QuickDraw printing technology to communicate between the OS and the printer. Unfortunately, these printers are currently unsupported, and there is no indication that Apple will be supporting them in future versions of Mac OS X.

If your printer is advertised as being Mac OS X-compatible, but Mac OS X does not come with a driver or PPD for it, you'll probably need to install the appropriate support files manually.

**SEE:** • **"Installing Printer Drivers," later in this chapter.**

## What types of printer connections does Mac OS X support?

Mac OS X supports several connection types for printing. You can connect a non-AppleTalk printer directly to your Mac, using USB, Ethernet, FireWire, or (on older Macs) serial/printer/modem ports. You can also connect non-AppleTalk serial-port printers to newer Macs by using third-party serial-port adapters.

If you have an AppleTalk printer, your options for direct connections are a bit more limited. Because Mac OS X does not support LocalTalk (AppleTalk via serial/printer/modem ports), and because AppleTalk is generally not supported over USB or FireWire, your only real option is Ethernet. If you have a LocalTalk printer, you would need to purchase a third-party LocalTalk-to-Ethernet adapter. Unfortunately, these adapters cost approximately $100, so unless your LocalTalk printer is worth a lot of money, your best bet may simply be to get a newer printer that has a supported connection type.

In addition to the direct connections described in the preceding paragraphs, Mac OS X fully supports network printing to both AppleTalk and non-AppleTalk printers. If your Mac can "see" a printer, it can print to it. You can use any printer on a local or AirPort (wireless) network, as well as any printer anywhere on the Internet that has its own IP address (by using LPR, described later in this chapter).

The type of connection you use is largely determined by the printer itself. If it requires a USB connection (as most current inkjet printers do), that connection is how you connect the printer to the Mac. Some printers have multiple connection options. An inkjet printer, for example, may include a USB port and—via a network card—an Ethernet network connection. This card may come with the printer, or you can purchase it as an add-on.

Unfortunately, Mac OS X does not handle IrDA printing to printers with InfraRed ports. Apple claims to have no plans to support IrDA printing in Mac OS X.

# Installing Printer Drivers

As mentioned earlier in this chapter, Mac OS X comes with drivers or PPD files installed for many Apple and third-party printers. If you have a recent printer model, you should be able to configure Mac OS X to use your printer right out of the box. If support is not included, you'll need to install the appropriate software first.

If your printer is Mac OS X-compatible but a driver is not already installed, you'll need to install it. You generally have two ways to do this: Software Update or a third-party installer.

## Is my printer already supported?

You have several ways to determine whether Mac OS X already supports your printer. For newer USB printers, whether or not they are PostScript, the easiest way is to connect the printer to the Mac via the USB ports on both devices. Mac OS X can recognize a supported USB printer automatically, select the appropriate PPD file (for PostScript printers) or driver (for non-PostScript printers), and set up a print queue for it in Mac OS X's Print Center utility, which is where all printer and print-queue management is coordinated (as described in detail later in this chapter).

For other printers, you can see whether support is included by checking the printer support files on your hard drive.

For non-PostScript printers, check /Library/Printers/{*name of printer vendor*}. Within these directories, you'll find support files listed by model number. Drivers for Canon printers, for example, are in /Library/Printers/Canon/ BJPrinter/PMs. Drivers for Epson inkjet printers are in /Library/Printers/ EPSON.

You may also find manufacturer-specific printer utilities in these directories. Inside /Library/Printers/EPSON/Utilities is the EPSON printer utility, for example. Launch this application to access the ink-level, nozzle-check, head-cleaning, and head-alignment features of the printer software.

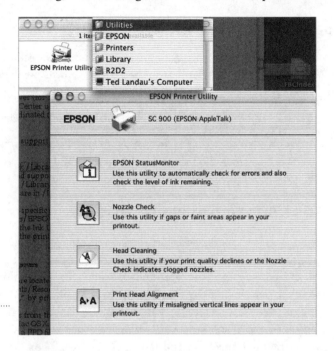

**Figure 7.1**

EPSON printer utility.

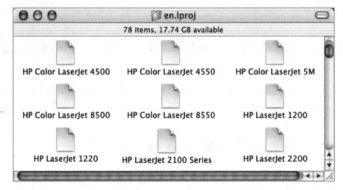

**Figure 7.2**

Partial contents of the en.lproj folder, showing PPD files for HP LaserJet printers.

PPD files for PostScript printers are located in the /Library/Printers/PPDs/ Contents/Resources/*name*.lproj folders. English-language PPD files, for example, are in the directory en.lproj—listed by printer manufacturer and model number.

Note: You can also copy PPD files from the Mac OS 9 System Folder to the appropriate language folder in Mac OS X. The files will work in Mac OS X. In addition, if Mac OS X cannot find a PPD file for your printer in the pre-ceding directories, it will search for PPD files in the Mac OS 9 System Folder.

Finally, Apple maintains a list of printer drivers and PPDs provided with Mac OS X on its Web site.

**SEE:** • "Take Note: Printer Models with Drivers Built into Mac OS X," later in this chapter.

---

**TAKE NOTE ▶ Printer Models with Drivers Built in to Mac OS X**

Mac OS X includes printer drivers and PPD files for many popular printers. Although the list of printers supported out of the box by Mac OS X is too long to list here, Apple maintains such a list on its Web site at `www.apple.com/macosx/whatyoucando/applications/printcenter.html`.

Support for additional printers not listed there may be available via Software Update.

In addition, a third-party Web site (`www.index-site.com/printersx.html`) has compiled a list of printers supported by Mac OS X, including drivers not provided by Apple.

---

## Updating via Software Update

The first place to look for additional printer drivers is Mac OS X's Software Update feature. Open the System Preferences utility (from the Apple menu or Dock), and click the Software Update button. In the resulting window, simply click the Update Now button. Software Update will check with Apple's software servers and see whether any updates are available for the printing software. If so, they usually will be listed by printer manufacturer. If your printer manufacturer is listed, click the Install box next to it and then click the Install button at the bottom of the window. (You usually need to enter your administrator/user password to install printer software.) After the software has been installed, you can check to see whether it included support for your printer by using the procedures described earlier in this chapter.

Note: Apple has now removed some of its printer updates, referring users instead to the Web site of the vendor for the "same or newer" versions.

## Installing third-party drivers

If Mac OS X doesn't include the appropriate support files for your printer, and you aren't able to get them via Software Update, you'll have to install them manually, using an installer application provided by the printer manufacturer. Some printers include a CD with the driver installer; others will tell you to go to the manufacturer's Web site to download the installer. (Going to the Web site is probably a good idea either way, because the drivers available from the Web site are often newer than those that come with the printer.) After you have the appropriate installer, installation usually is simply a matter of double-clicking the installer application and following the instructions.

# Deleting unused printer drivers

If you use only a single printer and don't plan on getting a newer one for a while, it's possible to regain quite a bit of hard-drive space (well more than 100 MB) by deleting unused printer drivers and PPDs in the /Library/Printers folder. The easiest (and safest) way is simply to delete the folders belonging to other manufacturers' support files. (If you have an Epson printer, for example, you can delete the Canon and HP folders.) If you are using only the U.S. English version of the Mac OS, you can also delete all the folders except en.lproj within the /PPDs/Contents/Resources folder, as the other folders provide support for non-English languages. As a side note, even if you *don't* use the U.S. English version, the en.lproj folder must be present; if it's not, Mac OS X won't be able to find the non-English versions of your printing software automatically. You will still be able to use non-English versions, but you will have to select it manually in Print Center.

To do this deleting, you'll need to be an administrative user. The down side to removing these is that if you ever need support for other printers or other languages, you'll need to reinstall all the support files.

SEE:  • "Take Note: How to Reinstall the Mac OS X Printer Drivers," later in this chapter.

---

**TAKE NOTE ▶ How to Reinstall the Mac OS X Printer Drivers**

If you have deleted any of the printer drivers or printing support files that come installed in Mac OS X (perhaps to save hard-drive space) and later need one or more of them, you'll find that the Mac OS X installer does not seem to allow you to install just printer drivers; you must reinstall the entire OS. To make matters worse, many of the drivers that come with Mac OS X are not available as separate downloads either from Apple or from the printer manufacturer.

The solution to this problem is to boot into Mac OS X and then insert the Mac OS X Install CD so that it mounts in the Finder. On the CD, find the application package /System/Installation/Packages/AdditionalPrinterDrivers.pkg. Double-clicking this package will allow you to install just the printer drivers.

This method will not reinstall updates to the CD software that you may have installed via Software Update, however. In most cases, you can get the same printer updates as stand-alone files from Apple's Web site. With these files, you should be able to reinstall the software. If you have any problems, see Chapter 2 for more information on installing Mac OS X updates.

# Setting up Printing with Print Center

Print Center is an application installed by Mac OS X (located in the /Applications/ Utilities folder) that you use to set up the communication between a printer and the OS . It also manages the queue of documents selected for printing on each printer. The following discussion assumes that the needed printer drivers and PPD files for your printer are already installed.

## USB

As described earlier in this chapter, after you plug a newer USB printer into a USB port on your Mac, Mac OS X should recognize the manufacturer and model automatically, select the appropriate PPD file (for PostScript printers) or driver (for non-PostScript printers), and set up a print queue for it in Print Center. If you open the Print Center application, your printer should be listed by name/model.

If you have an older USB printer, or if your printer was not recognized automatically, you will need to add your printer manually. To do this, follow these steps:

1. Launch Print Center.
2. Click the Add button in the dialog box that may appear; otherwise, click the Add Printer button.
3. In the Add window that appears next, choose USB from the pull-down menu.

   Your printer should appear in the list.
4. If the appropriate driver or PPD file is not auto-selected, choose it from the Printer Model pop-up menu.
5. If your printer model isn't listed, choose Other from the Printer Model pop-up menu, and navigate to the appropriate driver/PPD for your printer (in the /Library/Printers folder).
6. Select the printer name, and click the Add button.

   You will return to the Printer List window, where the printer should be listed.

Note that some USB printers do not work properly when they're attached to a USB hub (including the hub built into Apple USB keyboards). If your supported USB printer does not show up in the Add dialog box, make sure that it is attached directly to one of the USB ports on your Mac. Also make sure that the printer is attached and powered on before you start up the Mac.

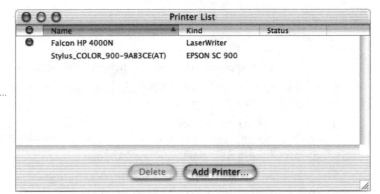

**Figure 7.3**

*The initial window that appears when you launch Print Center. (Printers listed here were created during a previous launch.)*

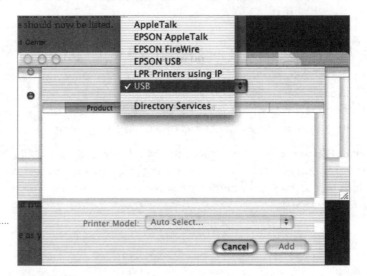

**Figure 7.4**

*Selecting the USB option in Print Center.*

## AppleTalk

If you have an AppleTalk-networkable printer, here is what you need to do to get it to work with Mac OS X.

**Enable AppleTalk.** The first thing you need to do is make sure that AppleTalk is enabled for the appropriate network type. To do this, go to the Network System Preferences window, and from the Show pull-down menu, choose the network type by which your printer is connected (Ethernet or AirPort). Select the AppleTalk tab, and make sure that the Make AppleTalk Active checkbox is checked.

**Use Print Center.** Next, follow these steps:

1.  Launch Print Center.

2.  Click the Add button in the dialog box that may appear; otherwise, click the Add Printer button.

3. In the Add window that appears next, choose AppleTalk from the pull-down menu.

   (If you're on a large multiple-zone AppleTalk network, you'll also need to select the appropriate zone.) Your printer should appear in the list.

4. If the appropriate driver or PPD file is not auto-selected, choose it from the Printer Model pop-up menu.

5. If your printer model isn't listed, choose Other from the Printer Model pop-up menu, and navigate to the appropriate driver/PPD for your printer (in the /Library/Printers folder).

6. Select the printer name, and click the Add button.

   You will return to the Printer List window, where the printer should be listed.

---

**TAKE NOTE ▶ Using the Print Command to get Summary Information**

For USB and AppleTalk printers, Print Center will select a PPD or printer driver for many printers automatically. It won't necessarily tell you what PPD or driver file it selected, however, and may select a PPD that differs in name from the name of the printer itself. Print Center will not show you this information. Instead, the Printer Model pop-up menu will simply say Auto-Select.

To find out what PPD file was selected, choose the Print command in any Mac OS X application, choose the appropriate printer from the Printer pop-up menu, and choose Summary from the main Options menu. The PPD or printer driver selected by the OS will be displayed in the summary info for the printer.

---

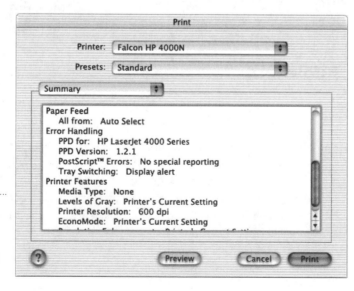

**Figure 7.5**

*Summary information in the Print dialog box shows the HP LaserJet 4000 Series as the PPD.*

## LPR printers using IP

Mac OS X also supports Line Printer (LPR) connections. LPR is a way to print to a networked or Internet-accessible printer via a TCP/IP connection rather than AppleTalk. If you have a printer (or print server) that supports LPR, here is how to set it up:

1.  Launch Print Center.
2.  Click the Add button in the dialog box that may appear; otherwise, click the Add Printer button.
3.  In the Add window that appears next, choose LPR Printers Using IP from the pop-up menu.
4.  In the LPR Printer's Address text box, enter the IP address or domain name of the printer or printer queue (see: "Take Note: What is the Printer's IP Address?" later in this chapter).

*Figure 7.6*

*Setting up an LPR printer in Print Center.*

5.  If you want to give the LPR printer a name, uncheck the Use Default Queue on Server checkbox and enter the name.

    Do not use spaces; if you need a space, use an underscore character instead. One benefit of giving the LPR printer a name is that you create a separate print queue just for the LPR printer.

6. To select a PPD for the printer other than the default Generic setting, choose the appropriate PPD file (typically, one with the same name as your printer) from the Printer Model pop-up menu.

   This setting will allow you to access specialized features of your printer that are not available via the generic PPD.

7. Finally, click the Add button.

   You will return to the Printer List window, where the printer should be listed.

In many cases, a printer connected to an Ethernet network may work via either AppleTalk or LPR. In this case, you can set the printer up for both methods and select the one you want to use.

*Figure 7.7*

*An LPR host printer (192.168.1.121) has been added to the Printer List window. It's actually the same HP 4000 printer listed in the preceding line; the Falcon listing is for connecting via an AppleTalk connection.*

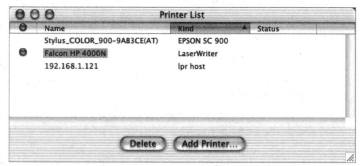

*Figure 7.8*

*Selecting AppleTalk in the Add Printer screen confirms that the HP 4000 is listed.*

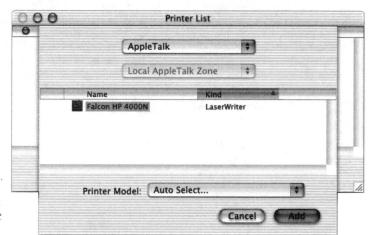

**TAKE NOTE ▶ What Is the Printer's IP Address?**

If your printer supports LPR printing, you will need to enter its IP address in Print Center's LPR Printer's Address text box. How do you know what the IP address is? The procedure varies, depending on your specific printer and network setup. I'll describe my own situation to provide one example. Follow these steps:

1. With a HP LaserJet 4000N printer, use the HP LaserJet utility (which currently runs only in Classic).

2. Choose the Settings tab, and choose Edit the TCP/IP Settings.

3. In the window that appears, choose the option to specify a TCP/IP address manually.

4. Enter the information necessary to set up the printer as a device connected to your router, just as you would do in the Network System Preferences window for the Mac itself.

5. Enter that IP address in Print Center's LPR Printer's Address text box.

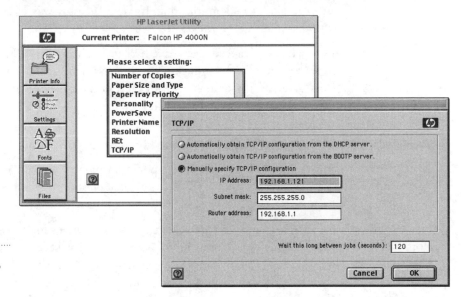

*Figure 7.9*

*Setting up an IP address via the HP LaserJet utility.*

## Directory Services

Mac OS X works with several types of network services, such as NetInfo (which is part of Mac OS X) and LDAP. Used mostly in large networked environments, Directory Services provide a way for users to print to shared network printers. To add a printer by using Directory Services, follow these steps:

1. Launch Print Center.

2. Click the Add button in the dialog box that may appear; otherwise, click the Add Printer button.

3. In the Add window that appears next, choose Directory Services from the pop-up menu.

4. Select a printer in the resulting list.

   Note that with Directory Services, you do not have the option to select a PPD or printer model, because the printing queue has already been set up by a network administrator somewhere else on the network.

## Using unsupported printers

Some printers that are not supported officially will still work in Mac OS X if you choose a similar printer driver from the Printer Model pop-down menu or (for PostScript printers) if you choose the generic PPD file. Some Epson inkjet printers that do not have drivers for use in Mac OS X work fairly well with the drivers for similar Epson printers. Keep in mind that if you try this method, you may not get the full functionality of all your printer's features or may experience problems printing. If this is the only way you can use your unsupported printer, however, it's worth a try.

In some cases, advanced users have hacked a driver designed to work with one printer so that it works with similar printers. Such hacks are available on the Web. Again, use these methods with caution, as they may cause problems due to the unintended way in which they are used.

---

**TECHNICALLY SPEAKING ▶ Creating a PostScript File for Printing**

Although most people choose to print directly to a printer, at times, it is useful to save a file in PostScript format. Such a file is saved in the language of PostScript printers, and you can send it to a printer without needing to open any application.

You can save a Microsoft Word file as PostScript, for example, and later send the file to an LPR printer via Terminal without needing to open Word. Similarly, you can save a document in a Mac OS X application and then boot in Mac OS 9 (or, in some cases, use Classic) to print the document on a printer that does not have Mac OS X support. In the latter case, however, it will likely be simpler to save the file as a PDF document, as described in "Take Note: Why and How to Create PDF Files," later in this chapter.

To create a PostScript file, open the document you want to convert. Then follow these steps:

1. Choose Print from the File menu of a Mac OS X application.

2. In the Print dialog box, choose your desired PostScript printer from the Printer menu.

3. Choose Output Options from the Options menu. The dialog box changes to display the options available.

*continues on next page*

**TECHNICALLY SPEAKING** ▶ **Creating a PostScript File for Printing** *continued*

4. Check the Save As File checkbox that now appears in the dialog box.

5. Choose PostScript from the Format menu.

 The Print button will change to Save.

6. Save the file, in PostScript format, in your desired location.

When you're saving to PostScript, you are really "printing" to a PostScript printing queue on your own computer. If you do not have a PostScript printer set up in Print Center, and no such printer is connected to your Mac, you will need to create a virtual local printing queue. To do this, follow these steps:

1. Launch Print Center, and click the Add Printer button.

2. Choose LPR Printers using IP from the pop-up menu in the dialog box that appears.

3. In the LPR Printer's Address text box, type: <localhost>.

4. Choose Generic PPD or (if you know what printer you'll eventually be printing to) a particular PPD file.

5. Click the Add button.

Your PostScript "printer" is ready.

### *Printing PostScript Files from Terminal*

You can send a PostScript file directly to an LPR or AppleTalk printer for printing.

If you have an LPR printer set up, launch Terminal and type: <lpr -P printername filepath andname.ps>

If you are using an AppleTalk printer, first you need to designate it as your default printer. To do so, follow these steps:

1. Open Terminal.

2. Type: <sudo at cho prn>, and enter your password.

 This step will give you a list of all available AppleTalk printers, with a number (1, 2, 3, and so on) at the start of each line. An "ITEM number" prompt will then appear.

3. At the prompt, type the number of the printer you want to use as your default printer for printing PostScript files.

To print a PostScript file to this printer, type the following command in Terminal: <cat filepathandname.ps | atprint printername>

### Setting/changing the default printer

When you first add a printer in Print Center, you'll notice a small "jewel" circle to the left of its name in the main Print Center window. This circle indicates that this printer is the default printer. If you have multiple printers set up in Print Center, the default printer is the one that will be used unless you switch to another printer by choosing it from the Print menu (as described in "Printing" later in this chapter).

You specify which printer will be the default by clicking its name in Print Center and then choosing Make Default from the Printers menu (or pressing Command-D).

### Deleting printers from Print Center

In addition to adding printers, you can delete printers in Print Center. When you select a printer and click the Delete button, the printer will be removed from Print Center and will no longer be available for printing. (Don't worry: If you delete a printer that you wanted to keep, you can always add it again.)

If a printer has queued print jobs, you will be asked whether you would like to wait for them to finish before deleting the printer or whether you want to cancel them and delete the printer immediately.

---

**TAKE NOTE ▶ Updating PPD Files**

Printer manufacturers often provide updated/improved printer drivers and PPD files (often via a software download). If you have already installed, and are using, a PostScript printer in Mac OS X and later install an updated PPD file, you won't be able simply to select the new PPD file. You need to delete the printer in Print Center and then set it up again, using the updated PPD file.

SEE:  • "Clear corrupt printer queues," later in this chapter, for details on deleting a printer from Print Center.

---

# Printing

After you've set up your printer or printers in Print Center, you're ready to print. In most cases (assuming that you do not want to modify any default settings and no problems occur), printing is as simple as choosing Print from the File menu of an application. In the standard Print dialog box that appears, select the number of copies you want and the desired page range. Then click the Print button. That's it.

Print Center launches at this point; you'll see its icon appear in the Dock. Then your document will be printed on your default printer. When it is no longer needed for the selected jobs, Print Center will close automatically.

Aside from selecting the Print command, you may need to make two other choices: (1) Choose Page Setup from the File menu to modify page-layout options, and (2) Open Print Center to manage print queues and resolve printing errors, should any occur. You can also modify additional options in the Print dialog box; I discuss them in the following sections.

## Page Setup

Usually, you need the Page Setup dialog box only if you want to modify the default layout settings.

The first item in this dialog box is the Settings pop-up menu. Two of its options are available in all applications: Page Attributes and Summary.

In the Page Attributes tab (which is what you see when the Page Setup dialog box first opens), you choose a printer from the Format For pop-up menu; you also choose a paper size, an orientation (portrait, landscape, or reverse landscape), and a scale (to reduce or enlarge the copy by a given percentage). Documents that are open in the application, as well as any new documents that you create in the application, will take on these attributes.

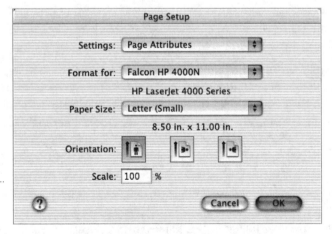

*Figure 7.10*

*The Page Attributes tab of the Page Setup dialog box.*

The Summary tab simply provides a table that summarizes the settings you have chosen, along with a bit more detail on what these settings mean (such as the current margin settings in the application).

Applications may provide additional options. For example, Microsoft Word adds its own settings screen, which provides options for custom page sizes and paper-feed method, and allows you to apply the Page Setup settings to only part of the document, if desired. Additionally, the Summary tab includes summary information on these options.

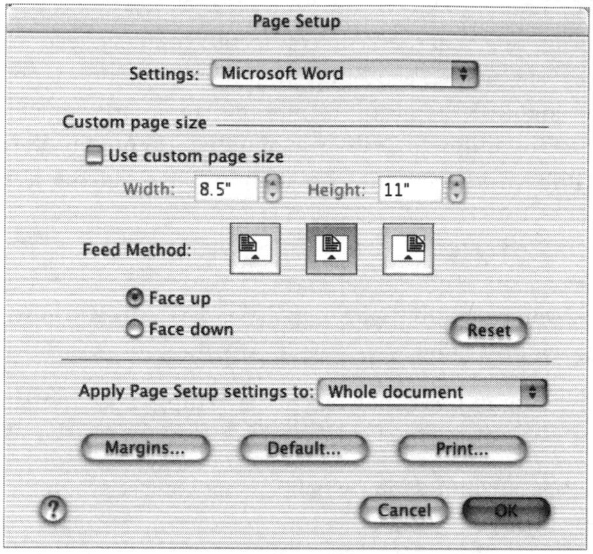

*Figure 7.11*

*Microsoft Word's additional Page Setup options.*

---

**TAKE NOTE ▶ Changing the Default Paper Size in Page Setup Dialog Boxes**

You can choose your preferred paper size in the Page Setup dialog box of each application. If you use a different paper size from the default, however, you have to change to your preferred size in every application, one by one. Many Mac users who live outside the United States, for example, use U.S. English as their language of choice in Mac OS X but use the A4 paper size.

**The default paper size.** Systemwide printer defaults are based on the language chosen in the Localization System Preferences window. Thus, if you set your preferences so that the first language is English, your default paper size is U.S. letter. This situation applies to any printer that uses Apple's system defaults (Epson printers do not, as discussed later in this sidebar).

**Changing the default.** You have two ways to change the default paper size (such as from U.S. Letter to A4) without changing your preferred language from English.

The first method is to edit the default-paper-size section of the English printing preferences. To do this, follow these steps:

1. Open a text editor (such as BBEdit or TextEdit) as the root user, using a utility such as Pseudo.

2. In the text editor, such as BBEdit, open the file /System/Library/Frameworks/ApplicationServices.framework/Versions/A/Frameworks/PrintCore.framework/Versions/A/Resources/English.lproj/Localizable.strings.

3. In the line that says DefaultPaperSize = na-letter, change na-letter to iso-a4.

*continues on next page*

**TAKE NOTE ▶ Changing the Default Paper Size in Page Setup Dialog Boxes**
*continued*

4. Save the file.

5. Log out and then log back in.

The second method is to replace the entire English printing preferences file with the British version. If you use this method, all your printing preferences will default to the British settings. To do this, follow these steps:

1. Open Terminal.

2. Type the following command (on one line, inserting a space wherever you see [space]):

   ```
   <sudo cp [space]
   /System/Library/Frameworks/ApplicationServices.framework/Versions/A/
   Frameworks/PrintCore.framework/Versions/A/Resources/en GB.lproj/Localizable.strings
   [space]/System/Library/Frameworks/ApplicationServices.framework/Versions/A/Framewo
   rks/PrintCore.framework/Versions/A/Resources/English.lproj/Localizable.strings>
   ```

3. When you are asked for your password, enter it and press Return.

4. Log out and then log back in.

   From this point on, the default paper size in all applications will be A4.

Note that Epson printers do not use Apple's systemwide printing defaults. Instead, each model has its own default settings. To change the default paper size for an Epson printer, follow these steps:

1. Open the /Library/Printers/EPSON/ folder.

2. Find the plug-in for your Epson printer.

3. Control-click the plug-in's icon, and choose Show Package Contents from the contextual menu.

4. In the package contents, find the file /Contents/Resources/English.lproj/Localizable.strings.

5. Open the file in TextEdit by dragging its icon to the TextEdit icon.

6. In the line that says DefaultPaperSize = na-letter, change na-letter to iso-a4.

7. Save the file.

8. Log out and then log back in.

You can use a similar procedure for other paper sizes.

# Print

As I have already said, when you are ready to print a document, choose Print from the application's File menu. In the Print dialog box, you can select a variety of options before printing the document. Note that unlike settings in the Page Setup dialog box, changes in the Print dialog box apply only to the document about to be printed. The following paragraphs describe the options.

**Printer.** If you have more than one printer connected to your Mac, you can use the Printer pop-up menu to choose a printer other than the default printer. Any printer you have set up in Print Center will be available in this menu. If you want to use a printer that is not listed, you can choose Edit Printer List to open the Print Center utility and then add or delete printers.

**Presets.** The Presets pop-up menu lists the standard settings by default. If you have a particular group of settings (which you created by using the following options) you use frequently, you can save it as a custom preset and choose it from this menu.

**Printing Options.** Just below the Presets pop-up menu is an unnamed pop-up menu, commonly called Printing Options. The options in this menu may vary from application to application. Virtually all applications provide the following options, however.

- **Copies & Pages.** These options allow you to select the number of copies to print (and whether they should be collated or printed by page) as well as whether to print the entire document or a subset of pages.

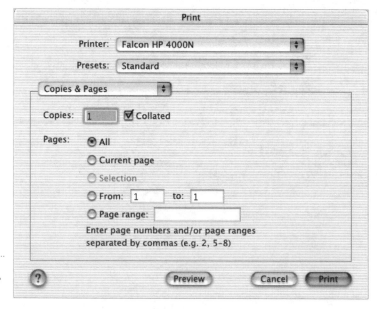

*Figure 7.12a*

*The Copies & Pages option screen in the Print dialog box.*

- **Layout.** These options allow you to print multiple document pages on each piece of printer paper as well as how to arrange the pages. You can also choose to include a thin border around each page. On the left is a sample printer sheet that shows you how document pages will be printed.

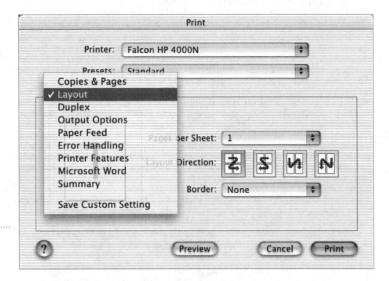

*Figure 7.12b*

The Layout option screen in the Print dialog box.

- **Output Options.** These options allow you to save the current document as a PostScript file or a PDF file. To do so, check the Save As File checkbox, and choose PDF or PostScript as the format. If you choose this option, the Print button at the bottom of the window will change to Save; click it to save the file. Next, give the document a name, specify where to save it, and click Save.

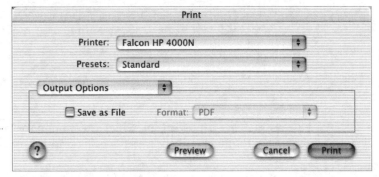

*Figure 7.12c*

The Output Options option screen in the Print dialog box.

**SEE:** • "Technically Speaking: Creating a PostScript File for Printing," earlier in this chapter, and "Take Note: Why and How to Create PDF Files," later in this chapter.

Other common options in this pop-up menu, depending on the selected printer, include the following.

- **Duplex.** If your printer supports double-sided printing, choose this option to enable it.

- **Paper Feed.** If your printer has multiple paper trays or feeds (an envelope feed, a manual feed slot, or so on), you can specify which tray you want to use. You can even have the first page come from one source, with the rest of the document being printed on paper from another source. (This option is frequently used for letterhead for the first page of multiple-page correspondence.) The specific options here may vary as they are typically provided by the printer driver or PPD for the printer chosen in the Printer pop-up menu.

- **Error Handling.** For PostScript printers, you can choose to ignore reporting of PostScript errors or have your printer create a detailed report. This screen also provides printer-specific options such as Tray Switching, which specifies what to do when a tray runs out of paper on a multiple-tray printer.

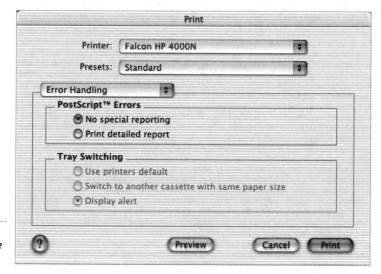

*Figure 7.12d*

The Error Handling option screen in the Print dialog box.

- **Printer Features.** This screen, which is common for laser printers, allows you to modify other printer-specific features, such as printing resolution.

- **Print Settings** (may also be called Mode or Quality). Common for inkjet printers, this screen allows you to specify the type of paper, type of ink (black or color), and print quality you want to use.

- **Color Management.** These options may be available for color printers. They include printer-specific options for adjusting how screen colors are translated to printed colors.

Applications may also provide a menu choice, usually named after the application, that provides extra options specific to the application. Most of these application- and printer-specific options are determined by the PPD and PDE files that are installed.

**SEE:** • "Take Note: PDE Files," later in this chapter, for details on PDE files.

• "What types of printers does Mac OS X support?" and "Is my printer already supported?," earlier in this chapter, for more information on PPD files.

Finally, all Print dialog boxes have the following two choices.

**Summary.** Similar to the companion tab in the Page Setup dialog box, this tab presents a table that summarizes all your settings in the different tabs.

**Save Custom Setting.** If you have a certain group of settings that you use frequently, you can choose this option. Your current settings will be saved as a custom preset, which you can access from the Presets pop-up menu. Unfortunately, you can have only a single custom preset.

---

### TAKE NOTE ▶ PDE Files

PDE (Printer Dialog Extension) files allow an application or printer (PostScript or non-PostScript) to add application- or printer-specific options in the Print dialog box. (Note: These files differ from the PPD files described earlier in this chapter. PPD files allow Mac OS X's built-in PostScript driver to support features specific to a particular PostScript printer.)

PDE files can add options to the Printing Options pop-up menu, such as the Print Settings and Color Management options noted in the main text. You can also use them to modify the options available in the default choices.

Mac OS X's built-in PDEs are located in /System/Library/Printers/PDEs. They have names such as Duplex.pde and Layout.pde. As is the case with most files in the /System directory, you should leave these files alone.

Printer-specific PDE files are located in the /Library/Printers directory. Hewlett-Packard DeskJet printers, for example, use a custom PDE file named hpdjPDE.plugin, located in the /Library/ Printers/hp/deskjet/directory. This file adds features to the Print dialog box that are specific to HP printers.

Application-specific PDEs are typically located inside the application package. Microsoft Word v. X is one exception; its WordPDE.plugin file is located in the Office folder.

**The bottom buttons.** The bottom of the Print dialog box contains three buttons: Preview, Cancel, and Print.

- **Preview.** This option creates a temporary PDF file of the current document and opens it in Mac OS X's Preview application. This feature is especially useful for applications that do not provide their own Preview command. It allows you to see exactly how the document will look when it's printed. If you like what you see, you can close the preview and return to the Print dialog box to print the document. Alternatively, you can print directly from the Preview application, but your document will be printed with the preferences you set in Preview rather than those you set in the Print dialog box of the original application. You can also save the previewed document as a PDF file, which is an alternative to using the Output Options feature to save a document as a PDF file.

- **Cancel.** Click this button to exit the Print dialog box without printing.

- **Print.** As noted earlier in this chapter, click this button to print the document. If you've chosen to save the document as a PDF or PostScript file, the button will change to Save.

---

**TAKE NOTE ▶ Why and How to Create PDF Files**

Saving a document as a PDF file can be useful for two main reasons:

- PDF files are cross-platform documents that can be viewed on almost any platform via the free Acrobat Reader utility; no conversion is necessary.

- As all files, graphics, and formatting are embedded within the document, you don't have to worry whether the recipient has the appropriate fonts or styles to view the document properly.

The main drawback is that PDF files are formatted for the specific printer you choose when you "print" them, so if the recipient prints a PDF file on a printer that is drastically different from yours, he or she may experience minor margin or spacing issues.

In Mac OS 9 and earlier, creating PDF files required separate applications, such as Adobe Acrobat or Print2PDF. Because PDF support is built in to Mac OS X, however, you can create a PDF file of any document you can print.

As covered in the main text, you have two ways to create PDF files in Mac OS X:

- Choose Output Options in the Print dialog box, and save the document as a PDF file.

- Click the Preview button at the bottom of the Print dialog box, and choose Save As PDF from the File menu.

In either case, next you give the document a name, specify where to save it, and click Save. Now you have a cross-platform PDF file of your document. One advantage of using the Output Options method is that you can save that setting. This method may be helpful if you save to PDF often or if you use the PDF option within AppleScript solutions.

# Print Center as a print manager

Each printer you have set up in Print Center has a corresponding print queue. After you click the Print button in an application, your document (now known as a print job) is sent to the print queue for the appropriate printer, where it is spooled to the printer or, if other documents are already waiting to be printed, waits in line for its turn. Just as Print Center lets you see all your printers, it lets you view and manage the print queue for each of them.

**The Printer List window.** When you open Print Center, it displays the Printer List window, where you see the list of printers you have set up. In the Status column, you will see an indication of the current status of each printer: blank (if idle), Printing (if a print job is being printed), or Stopped (if the queue for the printer is stopped).

**The Print Queue window.** Printer Queues give you a more complete picture of the status of all your print jobs. To access the queue for a given printer, double-click its name in the list. Alternatively, you can click the name and then choose Show Queue from the Printers pop-up menu (or press Command-O).

The window that appears will show a list of all documents currently printing and waiting to be printed. If there are no such documents, it simply states, "No job printing." By default, documents are listed in the order in which they will be printed. The document that is being printed will be listed at the top of the window by name, and its entry in the Status column will be Printing.

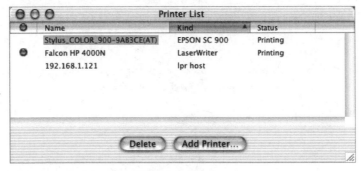

*Figure 7.13*

*Print Center's Printer List window, with documents being printed on two printers.*

**Stop Queue/Start Queue.** You can halt an entire print queue by choosing Stop Queue from Print Center's Queue menu. When you want to restart the queue, choose the toggled Start Queue command from the same menu.

This method could be useful if you notice that your printer is about to run out of paper, for example. You can stop the queue until you get the chance to add more paper. It can also be helpful if you are not connected to your printer continually. When you're using a laptop, for example, you could stop the print queue while you're on the go; any documents that you "print" will be sent to the queue and held there. When you connect to your printer later, you can start the queue, and the documents will print.

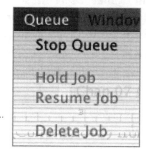

**Figure 7.14**

Print Center's
Queue menu.

**Hold Job/Resume Job.** If there is more than one job in the print queue, you can stop a particular job from printing, allowing remaining items to continue. To do this, select the item to be stopped and then choose Hold Job from the Queue menu or click the Hold button in the Print Queue window. When you want to let printing proceed, choose Resume Job from the Queue menu or click the Resume button.

Unfortunately, although the Print Queue window has a Priority column, Mac OS X does not yet allow you to change the priority of print jobs. Using the Hold button to delay the printing of less-important documents is the closest approximation you will get until a future version of Mac OS X is released.

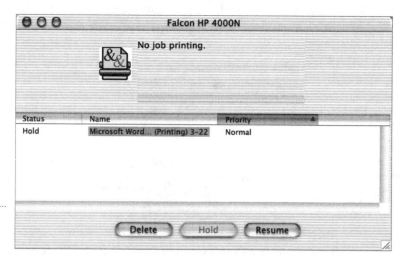

**Figure 7.15**

A Print Queue
window showing a
document on hold.

**Delete.** If you decide that you do not want to print a job at all (perhaps after clicking Print, you discovered that you selected more pages than you intended or used the wrong formatting options), you can select the job in the queue and then choose Delete Job from the Queue menu or click the Delete button in the Print Queue window.

An important use of these options is after a printing error. A printing error may prevent a job from being printed, triggering an automatic hold or stop of the queue. If the problem is something that you can fix, you can make the necessary adjustment and then click Resume or Start. Otherwise, you can delete the problem job and at least allow other documents to print.

**SEE:** • **"When Documents Fail to Print," later in this chapter.**

# Printing from Classic

As long as you have a printer supported by Classic, you can print directly from Classic applications. To do so, however, you need to set up your printers within Classic, even if you have already set them up in Mac OS X.

Selecting USB and AppleTalk network printers in Classic is pretty much identical to the method you use in Mac OS 9. Essentially, you use the Mac OS 9 Chooser as you would do if booted from Mac OS 9.

If you use an LPR printer in Mac OS X and want to do so in the Classic Environment as well, use Desktop Printer Utility (installed by Mac OS 9). To do so, follow these steps:

1. Launch Desktop Printer Utility. This will launch Classic if it is not already running.

2. A New Desktop Printer window should appear by default. If not, choose New from the File menu.

3. Choose Printer (LPR) from the list in the window, and click OK. A new window, named Untitled 1, will open.

4. From the new window, click the upper Change button to select the appropriate PPD file for your LPR printer.

5. Click the lower Change button to enter the IP address or domain name of the printer and the queue name.

6. Click the Create button.

   With the newly created Desktop printer set as the default in Classic, you will be able to print to the LPR printer from Classic applications.

Finally, some printers are supported in the Classic environment but will not print in Mac OS X. If you have one of these printers, you can save a document as a PDF file in Mac OS X and then print it in Classic.

**SEE:** • **"Printing in Classic vs. Mac OS X" and "Printing problems," in Chapter 9, for more information on how to set up printers in and print from Classic.**

# When Documents Fail to Print

When you attempt to print a document and Mac OS X encounters a problem, a Printer Error dialog box usually appears, providing a brief description of the problem. The dialog box includes two buttons: Show Queue and OK. If you click OK, you can resume your work but nothing will print. If you click Show Queue, it will go directly to the Printer Queue in Print Center. Here another dialog box will typically be present. It may include a more specific description of the nature of the error. It will also offer three options, similar to the ones described previously in "Print Center as a print manager."

**Delete Job.** This deletes the print job from the queue. The document itself remains intact.

**Stop Queue.** This stops any attempt to print the current job as well as any other items in the queue. If and when you later fix the problem, you can start the queue again via Print Center's Start Queue command. Note: In some cases, the printer error may trigger an automatic stop of the queue.

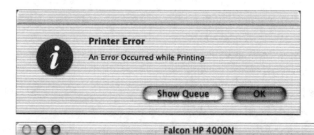

**Figure 7.16**

*Two examples of print error messages: (top) Printer error (appeared in the Finder), and (bottom) Unable to open printer connection (appeared when Print Center was launched after a document failed to print).*

**Stop Job.** This stops just the problem job. Any other items in the queue will continue to print. If and when you later fix the problem, you can try to print the job again via Print Center's Resume Job command.

Other variations of the basic format are possible, including error dialog boxes that include Continue or Retry buttons, to allow you to try to print again immediately (although, unless you addressed the cause of the problem, it will likely fail again!).

Although these messages are often clear in telling you what the problem is (your printer is out of paper, for example), at other times, they leave you with little information about what went wrong or what to do about it. To make matters worse, sometimes you don't even get an error message; your documents simply don't print.

*Figure 7.17*

*Message that appears in Print Center if you try to print when there are no printers in the Printer List window.*

There are lots of hardware reasons why things may go wrong with printing: bad connections, bad cables, the use of certain hubs for USB printers, faulty printers, and so on.

There are also numerous user errors that can lead to a print failure. The power button on the printer is off, for example, or the printer is out of paper. Or you may be trying to print to a non-networkable printer via a network connection.

As this book focuses on Mac OS X, however, I'm going to focus on what might be wrong in terms of Mac OS X software. Thus, I assume that you've already double-checked your printer and cables, successfully printed a test page, and thus determined that the cause is likely to be software-related. In this case, try each of the following methods in turn until one works.

# Check the drivers and connection ports

For starters, if you are having a printing problem that you cannot diagnose, make sure that (1) your printer is connected to the proper port (USB, Ethernet, or FireWire), (2) you have Mac OS X-compatible print drivers and PPD files installed for your printer, and (3) the printer is listed in Print Center.

If you are printing over an Ethernet network, make sure the settings in Network System Preferences are correct. If you are using AppleTalk, make sure AppleTalk is enabled.

If your printer has worked previously but has suddenly stopped working, these situations are not likely to be the cause. If you recently upgraded or modified your hardware or software, however, it pays to start by checking these possibilities.

**SEE:** • "Printer Support in Mac OS X," earlier in this chapter.

# Check that Print Center is in /Applications/Utilities

To print in Mac OS X, the Print Center application *must* be located in the /Applications/Utilities folder. If you moved your Utilities folder out of the Applications folder, or if you renamed either folder, printing will not work, and you will not even get an error message.

# Check for Print Center memory problems

Sometimes, Print Center claims to be printing a particular document, yet the document isn't printing. Other documents may print. If you can print simple documents but not larger or more-complex documents, the problem may be memory-related. Despite Mac OS X's superior memory-management skills, Print Center may have insufficient memory to print. Unfortunately, no error message appears to indicate that this is the case.

If you suspect this problem, cancel the print job, quit all open applications that you do not need at the moment, and try to print again.

# Check the printer queue

If a printer appears to be set up correctly but is not printing and especially if you are not getting any error messages, go to Print Center and check the Status column for the printer. Often, the problem is simply that the printer's queue has stopped. Typically, some previous print error (perhaps from a now deleted print job) stopped the queue, and you did not realize it.

In many such cases, choosing Start Queue from Print Center's Queue pop-up menu will get printing to resume again. Even if the queue appears to be running normally, stopping it and starting it sometimes gets a printer printing again.

## Clear the queue of corrupt print jobs

If restarting the queue fails to get a document to print, the problem document (or another one ahead of it in the queue) may have become corrupt. In this case, the only solution is to delete the print job. If you have more than one item in the queue, it generally is a good idea to delete all other queued jobs. After all jobs have been deleted, make sure that the queue is started, and try to print the document or documents again.

Remember that deleting a print job does not delete the document itself; it deletes the temporary spool file created to print the document.

## Delete printing preferences

If the preceding methods have not helped, your printing preferences may have become corrupted. To get rid of the offending preferences file, follow these steps:

1. From Print Center's Queue menu, select Stop Queue for the problem printer.
2. Open the printer's Queue and select Delete for all print jobs.
3. Go to Library/Preferences/folder in your Home directory and delete the file named com.apple.print.PrintCenter.plist.
4. Log Out and then log back in.

Before you can print again, you'll have to set up your printer queues manually by clicking the Add Printer button in Print Center, as described earlier in this chapter. Then select to Start Queue, if it is still stopped.

If this method does not work, a second set of printing preferences in Mac OS X contains the compiled printer information for all the printing queues you have set up. To delete this file, follow these steps:

1. From Print Center's Queue menu, select Stop Queue for the problem printer.
2. Open the printer's Queue ,and select Delete for all print jobs.
3. Launch Terminal and type: <cd /private/var/spool/printing>.
4. Type: <sudo rm com.apple.printing.plist>.
5. Enter your password when requested.
6. Log out and then log back in.

You will again have to set up your printer queues. See the following section for yet another variation on this theme.

# Clear corrupt printer queues

If printing problems persist, you can move from deleting the preferences for a queue, to deleting the queue entirely.

**Delete all printers and their queues.** On rare occasions, it's not a particular print job that becomes corrupt but the entire print queue. To fix this problem, you need to clear both the printer queue and the printer spool files. To do this, follow these steps:

1. Launch Print Center.

2. While holding down the Option key, choose Quit Print Center (or press Command-Q) from the Print Center menu.

   A dialog will appear, asking, "Are you sure you want to delete your list of printers and any current print jobs?"

3. Click OK.

   Print Center will quit.

To print again, you'll need to manually set up your printer queues again. Ideally, deleting the printer queues and spool files will eliminate whatever problems existed and allow you to print.

*Figure 7.18*

*Message that appears if you hold down the Option key when quitting Print Center.*

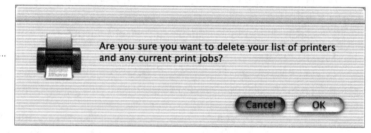

Are you sure you want to delete your list of printers and any current print jobs?

Cancel    OK

**Delete a single printer.** A less drastic approach, which can be successful if problems are specific to a single printer (but do not appear to be specific to documents in the queue), is to delete the printer from the Printer List window by selecting the printer name and clicking the Delete button in Print Center. Then return the printer to the list by clicking the Add Printer button.

In earlier versions of Mac OS X, this method might not have worked, because the OS stores a compiled version of the information for each printer driver (especially PPD info for PostScript printers) in the invisible directory /private/var/spool/printing. Deleting the printer and then adding it again would not change these files, so if the problem was within these files, the problem would remain. In more recent versions of Mac OS X (10.1.3 and later), however, deleting a printer deletes these files as well—a good thing, because the other way to delete these files requires getting root access in Terminal. To use that method (should you ever need to do so), launch Terminal and follow these steps:

1. Type <`cd /private/var/spool/printing`> to move to the directory that contains the preferences file.

2. Type <`sudo rm com.apple.printing.plist`> to delete this preferences file.

3. Type <`sudo rm –R *.Q`> (entering your password when requested) to delete all directories that end in .Q within this directory. This also deletes all the files within these directories. These files contain the compiled information.

Deleting these files may occasionally be required to fix less serious printing problems, such as to get a change you make in a PPD file to take effect (for example, modifying the default paper size).

**SEE:** • "Setting up Printing with Print Center" and "Take Note: Changing the Default Paper Size in Page Setup Dialog Boxes," earlier in this chapter.

## Remove corrupt or incompatible printer support files

The software for one printer may prevent printing on another brand of printer. This situation may be due to corrupt printer software, software that was not installed properly, or software that otherwise causes a conflict with the printer in use. In some cases, printing to an Epson printer did not work if Canon printer software was installed, and vice versa.

Especially if the problematic software is for a printer that you do not own (it probably was installed by Mac OS X, in this case), the obvious solution is to delete the unneeded software. To do so, go to /Library/Printers/, and delete the folders for printers that you do not have.

If you are still unable to print to your printer, but it previously worked fine, the driver or PPD file for the printer that you do use may have become corrupt. If so, the solution is to remove the software and then reinstall it. You need to be an administrative user to do this; in some cases, you may need root access as well.

**SEE:** • "Is my printer already supported?" and "Take Note: How to Reinstall the Mac OS X Printer Drivers," earlier in this chapter, for more details.

## Use Console

You may be able to track down the cause of a printing failure by using the Console application. Launch Console before printing. The error text that is generated when the print job fails may provide a clue to the source of the problem. If the error message makes references to fonts, for example, a font selection in the document may be the cause of the problem.

**SEE:** • Chapters 3 and 5 for coverage of the Console application, especially the Crash Reporter feature.

## Check for application or document problems

If problems persist, try printing another document from within the application you were using. Ideally, create a new test document and just type a few characters; select to print it.

If that fails, try printing a document from a different application, one that currently has no documents in the print queue.

If either of these attempts succeed, it suggests that the problem is more likely due to the application or document that would not print, rather than a more-general problem with the printer software or the OS.

What do you do in this case?

- If testing indicates that the application is at fault, try deleting and reinstalling the application. Make sure that the application and its accessory files have the correct permissions and are installed in their required locations (if such requirements exist). In general, the Read Me file for the software should inform you of any requirements. Otherwise, follow the same guidelines you would use if the application would not launch, as covered in Chapter 6.

- If the preceding methods do not work, see if you can print the document from another application. This is especially useful for documents that can be opened in several different applications, such as plain text files, graphics files, or PDF files.

- If testing indicates that the document is at fault and thus possibly corrupted, try to copy and paste the text from the document to a new blank document. If you were using any unusual page layouts, fonts, or graphic inserts, avoid them in the new document, if possible. This work-around hopefully avoids the need to start from scratch and retype the text.

- If the document is being printed in the Classic environment, try instead printing it from an application that runs native in Mac OS X. This works around the possibility that the problem is specific to the Classic environment.

## Check for font problems

Occasionally, a printing problem may have nothing to do with the document itself, the application being used, or the printer software. Instead, it may be a font selected for use in the document. The font file may be corrupt or otherwise incompatible with Mac OS X—with the result that printing fails when you select the problem font in your document.

The workaround is to select a different font. Be especially suspicious of older fonts located in the Classic System Folder or transferred from a Mac OS 9 System Folder to a Mac OS X Library/Fonts folder (most likely, the one in your Home directory). To prevent a repeat of the problem, delete the font after you have identified it as the cause. If you need that font, check the font vendor to see whether a newer version of the font may prevent the problem.

**Older versions of Times New Roman and Arial cause problems.**
These two fonts ship with Mac OS X but are provided by Microsoft. Some versions have been reported to cause printing problems in several applications, usually manifested in PostScript or general printing errors (in both Mac OS X and Mac OS 9). Microsoft has updated the fonts, but some people have found that the updated versions were not installed by Mac OS X or by any Microsoft products (Office or Internet Explorer, for example). The solution is to download the current version of these fonts from **www.microsoft.com/mac/download/ office2001/fontsupdate.asp**.

**SEE:** • "Fonts in Mac OS X," in Chapter 4, for much more information on fonts.

# Printing Quick Fixes

Following are an assortment of specific printing-related problems and their solutions/fixes.

## Errors printing PDF files in Preview

Some PDF files fail to print in Mac OS X's Preview application, resulting in the error message "ERROR NAME: limitcheck ... COMMAND: Type42BuildGlyph ... OPERAND STACK." This error is due to a bug in the Preview application that affects certain files, rather than a problem with the file itself or your printer. The solution is to open and print the offending PDF files in Acrobat Reader. If you get this error often, you may want to make Acrobat Reader the default application for opening PDF files.

## Previewing files launches Classic Acrobat Reader

If you click the Preview button in a Mac OS X Print dialog box, and the Classic version of Acrobat Reader launches instead of Mac OS X's Preview application, the problem is that Mac OS X is set to open PDF files with Classic Acrobat Reader. The solution is to save a file as a PDF (using the procedure described earlier in this chapter) and then open the Show Info window for the resulting PDF file. Choose Open with Application, select Preview as the application, and then click the Change All button.

**SEE:** • "Take Note: Type and Creator vs. File Extensions," in Chapter 3, for more details on this fix, including changing the type and creator codes.

## Error -108 when you attempt to select a printer in Print Center

If you attempt to select your printer in Print Center and get an *unknown error -108*, the problem could be that the Print Center application has had its privileges altered. For some reason, some third-party printer driver installers change these privileges during the installation process. To fix this problem, type the following sequence of commands in Terminal:

```
<cd "/Applications/Utilities/Print Center.app/Contents/MacOS">
<sudo chown root:daemon "Print Center">
<sudo chmod u=rwx,g=rsx,o=rx "Print Center">
<sudo chown root:daemon "PrintingReset">
<sudo chmod u=rsx,g=rx,o=r "PrintingReset">
```

## "No AppleTalk printers are available because AppleTalk is currently disabled" message

If you are using an AppleTalk printer and get this error when you're attempting to add your printer in Print Center, there are two possible reasons.

The first is that you did not enable AppleTalk for the appropriate network (the one on which your printer is located). The solution is to select the appropriate network (Ethernet or AirPort) in the Network System Preferences window and then check the Make AppleTalk Active checkbox in the AppleTalk tab.

The other possible cause is that you have AppleTalk enabled on multiple networks. Mac OS X may be unable to print to an AppleTalk printer unless only a single AppleTalk network is active. The solution is to disable AppleTalk (by unchecking the Make AppleTalk Active check box) for all network types except for the one on which your printer is located. If you use both Ethernet and AirPort network connections, the best solution is to use two different locations settings: one with AppleTalk enabled via Ethernet and the other via AirPort.

## AppleTalk does not work even when it is enabled

Sometimes, you may not be able to add an AppleTalk printer in Print Center, even if you have correctly enabled AppleTalk in the Network System Preferences pane. In this case, open Network System Preferences and choose New Location from the Location pop-up menu. Type a name for the location, and click OK. Then change the location back to your original location (Automatic, if you are using the default choice). This method often fixes the glitch, and you should be able to add the AppleTalk printer.

**SEE:** • **Chapter 8 for more on Network System Preferences and changing locations.**

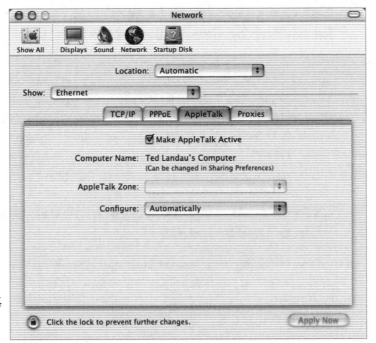

**Figure 7.19**

The AppleTalk tab of
the Network System
Preferences pane.

**No printer connection.** In one case, I could not print to my networked
laser printer via the AppleTalk connection I had set up. When I tried, I got a
No printer connection error message. The message included a Retry button,
but it, too, failed to produce results. I could print via the LPR connection I had
set up for the same printer, however. It turned out that I modified my settings
in the Network System Preferences window so that Ethernet was no longer
the top choice in the Active Network Ports list. This appeared to trigger the
error. When I put Ethernet back on top, AppleTalk printing succeeded.

## Office v. X applications refuse to print

If you are unable to print from Microsoft Office v. X applications, choose
Page Setup from the File menu, and check the Scale value in the Page Setup
dialog box. If the value is a very large number (such as 1,500 percent), change
it back to 100 percent. Printing should succeed. The incorrect value reportedly is due to an installation bug in Office; it will likely be fixed in a future
version of the software.

## Cannot print from LaserWriter NT or LaserWriter Pro 400 or 405

These printers are PostScript Level 1 printers. Unfortunately, Mac OS X supports only PostScript Levels 2 and 3. The only solution is to boot into Mac OS 9 and print. This method can work for applications that have both Mac OS 9 and Mac OS X versions, such as Microsoft Office (assuming that you have both versions). Otherwise, you can try the PDF-file trick noted earlier in this chapter.

**SEE:** • "Take Note: Why and How to Create PDF Files," earlier in this chapter.

## LaserWriter 16/600 PS cannot use the PhotoGrade option

In Mac OS X, the PhotoGrade feature of the Apple LaserWriter 16/600 PS printer cannot be enabled; the On button will be dimmed in the Printer Features dialog box. The only way to print with PhotoGrade enabled is to boot into Mac OS 9.

## HP All-in-One printer fails after USB disconnect

With Hewlett-Packard multifunction printers, such as the HP G85, avoid disconnecting the printer from the USB port while the Mac is running. If you do, the printer may no longer respond if and when you reconnect the USB cable, unless you also restart the Mac. Even letting the Mac go to sleep can trigger this symptom.

The problem is due to a bug in the current version of the HP All-in-One Communications file, located in the /Library/Startup Items folder. You may be able to avoid the need to restart the Mac by killing this process (via ProcessViewer), turning the printer off and then back on, and relaunching the file.

## Cannot print in Mac OS X when Classic is active

Some printers will not print in Mac OS X when Classic is running. In this case, the usual solution is to quit Classic before attempting to print.

In some cases, however, this printing failure occurs only the first time you try to print the document. If you launch Print Center and go to the Print Queue window for the printer (select the printer and press Command-O), you will see a Retry button. If you click it, printing may succeed, and you won't have to quit Classic.

## Cannot print in Classic

See Chapter 9 for help in solving problems with printing in the Classic environment.

---

**TAKE NOTE ▶ Scanners and Mac OS X**

During the first year after Mac OS X was released, there was very little Mac OS X support for scanners. The primary reason for this drought was that, until Mac OS X versions of photo-editing software such as Photoshop were released, there was too little incentive to write scanner software for Mac OS X.

Now that Photoshop for Mac OS X is out, scanner software for Mac OS X is finally taking off. For example, Epson and Canon have released Mac OS X drivers for at least some of their scanners. Agfa had previously released a Mac OS X scanner driver. Also, shareware drivers, such as VueScan, work with a variety of scanner models.

Even if there is no Mac OS X driver for your scanner yet, you can probably still use it in Mac OS X. You just have to use it via Mac OS 9 software, which you access from the Classic environment.

# 8

# Troubleshooting Networking: File Sharing and Internet

You can merrily run Mac OS X independently of the rest of the computing universe, creating documents in your word processor, listening to music with iTunes, and much more. In fact, flying solo was the norm for Mac users until about 10 years ago. Now it is the rare exception. These days, almost all Mac users are on some type of network.

You have two common reasons to network your Mac. The first is to access the Internet, which is what you need to use email, browse the Web, or connect to remote servers. In networking terms, this situation is often called connecting to a wide area network (WAN). The second reason is to interconnect devices (mainly, computers and printers) that are in the same home or office to permit easy file sharing from one computer to another, as well as printing from any connected computer. In networking terms, this situation is called connecting to a local area network (LAN).

Closely related is the capability to share information among the multiple users who may have accounts on the same Mac.

Although these topics are a diverse set, there is a good deal of overlap in what you need to know about and use for the different tasks. That is why I have tied all these issues together in this chapter.

# In This Chapter

Apple has done a good job of making Mac OS X's network capabilities fairly straightforward. In this chapter, I'll show you how to get your Mac on the Internet, how to share files with and access files on other computers, and what to do if either function doesn't work the way it should.

The Network System Preference is a key element for everything from file sharing to Web browsing. It and related Preferences panes are a main focus of this chapter.

Many of Mac OS X's networking features depend on its Unix underpinnings. For example, the Web Sharing feature, enabled in the Sharing System Preferences pane, really is taking advantage of the Apache Web server software included in most Unix installations. Actually, Mac OS X's Web Sharing taps into only a small fraction of what Apache can do. If you want, you can access these untapped features via Terminal. In this chapter, I will occasionally explore these options as well.

# Network and Connection/ Port Types

When computer types talk about *networks,* they are generally referring to a type of system in which multiple computers exchange data. A network may be two computers and a printer in an office, or it may be 200 computers around the world. A connection to the Internet is simply a connection to a global network. Regardless of what arrangement exists, the purpose of a network is to allow computers to communicate.

Network *connection* types (called *ports* in Mac OS X), on the other hand, are the ways in which a computer connects to other computers on a network. Mac OS X supports various types of ports: Ethernet, modem, and AirPort (wireless). Mac OS X also supports FireWire network connections, but few FireWire networking devices are available, so I won't spend much time talking about this type.

I make this distinction because it is important to understand that the type of connection and the type of network are not intimately linked. Each *connection* type can be used for any *network* type. You can use each of them to communicate both locally and over the Internet.

Although this situation can be a bit confusing, it means that Mac OS X is incredibly flexible in its networking capabilities. You can use Ethernet to communicate with other computers in your home or office and at the same time use a modem to connect to the Internet. Or you can use an AirPort Base

Station for both local networking and Internet access. In addition, if your connection and network types change frequently (if you use a PowerBook or access multiple AirPort networks, for example), Mac OS X allows you to set up locations that store sets of network settings; you can switch among your locations when necessary.

In the sections that follow, I'll explain each type of network connection and how to set it up for local and Internet connectivity.

Note: The first time you launch Mac OS X, the setup software offers to walk you through setting up your Internet connection. In answering the questions that it asks, you are actually entering data in Network System Preferences and related software. This arrangement simplifies the setup process—an especially welcome accomplishment for novice users. If you ever want to make changes in these settings, however, or if you opted out of entering the data via setup in the first place, you will need to know how to interact with Mac OS X's networking software.

# Setting up System Preferences: Network

The Network System Preferences pane is where all network settings are managed. It can seem a bit overwhelming at first because of the myriad combinations of settings that you can use. To make the preferences pane easier to understand, consider that there are basically three types of network settings:

**Active Network Ports.** These settings show which connection types are active (enabled by you for use) and the order (priority) in which Mac OS X tries to use them.

**Connection-specific settings.** These settings are your network settings for each type of connection. They can be different for each connection type.

**Locations.** You can create different combinations of active network ports and connection-specific settings for different network environments. Especially if you use a laptop, you may have one set for home, a second set for work, and a third set for when you travel. You can create different locations settings to facilitate these switches.

In all the following sections, after you change a setting, click the Apply Now button at the bottom of the dialog box to modify the files where the settings are stored, so that the change actually takes place.

# Active network ports and port priority

I have an iBook that is wirelessly connected to my cable modem via an AirPort Base Station. At times, however, I would prefer to connect the iBook via an Ethernet cable as part of my wired local network. Finally, in case my cable modem goes down, I am also set up to access the Internet via the iBook's internal dial-up modem. With Mac OS X, I can set up all three of these connection types and have them active simultaneously, via the Active Network Ports settings. Technically, this process is called *multihoming*. Mac OS X users just call it great.

You could make similar setups in Mac OS 9. But Mac OS X offers a unique advantage that's not present in Mac OS 9: You can set priorities in Mac OS X, and the OS will try each port automatically, in the order you specify, until it obtains a working connection. If the AirPort software is disabled, for example, the iBook automatically skips the attempt to connect via AirPort and tries Ethernet instead. Unlike Mac OS 9, Mac OS X requires no modification of settings for this switching to work. You can have multiple ports active at the same time, even for the same network type. In truth, the switching does not always work as well as it is supposed to do. I cover what to do in such cases in "Troubleshooting File Sharing and Internet," later in this chapter.

*Figure 8.1*

*The Active Network Ports tab of the Network System Preferences pane.*

To set your Active Network Ports, follow these steps:

1.  Launch System Preferences, select the Network pane, and choose Active Network Ports from the Show pop-up menu.

    The window will change to show a list of all available ports, with a checkbox next to each.

2.  Turn on each port you will be using by checking the checkbox next to it.

    If you know for sure that you won't be using a port, uncheck it. If you will be using your modem and AirPort card but will never use your Ethernet port, you can uncheck the Built-in Ethernet checkbox.

    Only checked items are listed in the Show menu.

3.  If a port type that you know you have available isn't listed, add it by clicking the New button.

    If you have an internal modem, for example, but a port configuration for Internal Modem is not listed, click New and then choose Internal Modem from the Port pop-up menu. You can name the connection type anything you want, but for clarity, I recommend something obvious (such as Internal Modem).

4.  If necessary, create additional ports for the same type of connection.

    Suppose that you have more than one dial-up Internet service provider (ISP). You can create a separate Internal Modem setup for each ISP. To distinguish among them, you can give each one a different name. To do so, again click the New button. Alternatively, if you want to create a setup that uses existing settings as a starting point, you can click a particular setup (such as Internal Modem) and then click the Duplicate button.

5.  Drag the ports to rearrange their order in the list, as desired.

The order in which ports are listed in this dialog box is important. If you try to initiate a network connection (local or Internet), Mac OS X first tries to connect via the port listed first. If it connects, it stops there. If Mac OS X is unsuccessful, it tries the next port. This process continues down the list until a successful connection is made or all ports have been tried to no avail (at which point, you generally get an error message). What this means for you is that if you have both DSL and dial-up Internet access and want your computer to try to use the DSL connection first, using the modem only if DSL is not available, you should click Built-in Ethernet and drag it above Internal Modem. Likewise, if you want your laptop to attempt to dial up your ISP only if it cannot find your AirPort network, make sure that AirPort is listed above Internal Modem.

You can also delete port configurations. If you have added a configuration that you no longer use, simply select the configuration and click the Delete button. (You will be asked to confirm the deletion.) You can also delete the built-in configurations, but if you find that you don't use one of them, I recommend simply making it inactive rather than deleting it, because there's no harm in having an inactive configuration.

# Ethernet (including cable/DSL Internet)

In the Network System Preferences pane, choose Built-in Ethernet from the Show pop-up menu to access the Ethernet settings. You will be able to configure the various types of connections that you'll be using over your Ethernet port.

This port is the one that you use if you are connected to any type of network (including the Internet) via an Ethernet link. The most basic Internet connection is one that goes from the Ethernet port on the back of your Mac to a cable or DSL modem. More-complex setups involve using an Ethernet hub or router to join multiple devices on the same local network.

Note: If you have added extra Ethernet ports via third-part Ethernet PCI cards, the configuration for them will be the same, and you will be able to choose each port's configuration panel from the same Show pop-up menu.

---

**TAKE NOTE ▶ Ethernet Hubs, Switches, Routers, and Cables**

Even before you take the first step to setting up your Ethernet network, you should be familiar with some basic terminology.

Hubs, switches, and routers. If you have only two Ethernet devices, your network is simple: a single cable connecting the two devices. If you have more than two devices with Ethernet ports (multiple computers, printers, and so on), you need a way to connect them. Hubs, switches, and routers provide such functionality in different ways. Here is a brief description of each device.

- **Hub.** A hub takes incoming data from an Ethernet port and broadcasts it to every other Ethernet port on the hub. This setup is fine for small networks, but when it's used in larger networks with many devices, performance can degrade, because every device attached to the hub has to filter through the data being sent by every other device.

- **Switch.** Switches are similar to hubs, but instead of sending incoming data back out to every connected device, a switch checks the destination address (usually, the MAC address of the appropriate Ethernet port) contained in the data and forwards the data to the appropriate machine. In addition, if the destination address is not valid (doesn't exist on any devices connected to the switch), the data basically dies at the switch. Switches learn the MAC address of connected devices by examining the data that passes through the switch.

- **Router.** Routers are similar to switches, but instead of directing traffic based on hardware (MAC) addresses, routers rely on network addresses (IP addresses). In addition, because routers can isolate parts of your network on different subnets, they allow you to share a single IP address among several network devices. An Internet router, used for sharing a broadband or modem connection to the Internet (discussed elsewhere in this chapter), is a specific type of router. In addition, although a switch generally configures itself, routers need to be configured by the user.

*continues on next page*

**TAKE NOTE ▶ Ethernet Hubs, Switches, Routers, and Cables** *continued*

**Ethernet cables.** The various devices on an Ethernet network are connected by Ethernet cables. Two kinds of Ethernet cables are available: standard and crossover. The difference between the two has to do with how the strands of wire in the cable are arranged.

- **Standard.** This type of cable has the strands of cable used for sending and receiving data in the same location on both ends. You generally use this type of cable to hook devices to a hub/switch/router in a multiple-device network: computers to hubs, printers to hubs, hubs to routers, and so on. The data is transferred from the send wires of the incoming cable to the receive wires of the outgoing cable as data passes through the hub, switch, or router. Most printers also use a standard cable to connect to a computer.

- **Crossover.** This type of cable has its send and receive wires switched (so that the signal crosses over), so you should use it when you are networking two computers directly, without any kind of hub, switch, or router. Note that many hubs, switches, and routers have an Ethernet port marked Uplink. This port is designed to accept a crossover cable rather than a standard cable. The port for an Internet connection also may use a crossover cable.

Because there is no easy way to visually tell the two types of cables apart, the cables are a frequent source of trouble. Using a crossover cable where a standard cable is needed (or vice versa) will result in a failed connection. One positive note: The latest Macs use an Ethernet port that can sense the type of cable and work with either type.

**SEE:** • "Take Note: Internet Routers," later in this chapter, for more information on routers.

   • "Take Note: What Are the TCP/IP Settings?" later in this chapter, for more details about MAC addresses.

**TAKE NOTE ▶ Internet Routers**

What if you have a single Internet connection, but you have multiple computers? Many companies manufacture what are commonly known as Internet routers. These devices typically provide a variety of special features for Internet connections: (a) firewall protection, preventing unauthorized access to your computer from outside the network and (b) access to the Internet for multiple computers. When you use a router, all the computers on your network can share the same cable modem or DSL connection and gain some degree of protection from unauthorized Internet intruders.

Most Internet routers are broadband-based devices, meaning that they are designed to work with cable or DSL Internet connections. Instead of hooking your DSL or cable modem up to your computer, you hook it up to a special WAN port on the router. Then you connect multiple computers to the router via additional Ethernet ports on the router. In the case of wireless routers (including Apple's AirPort Base Station), additional devices may be connected via a wireless connection (see "Take Note: Setting up an AirPort Base Station and Network" later in this chapter). Then the Internet router directs Internet traffic between your ISP and each computer on the network, using Network Address Translation (NAT). All your computers get Internet access, but it appears to the outside world that a single computer is accessing the Internet.

*continues on next page*

**TAKE NOTE** ▶ **Internet Routers**  *continued*

Some Internet routers include modems; Apple's AirPort Base Station is one. These routers are useful to people who have only modem-based dial-up Internet access. Internet routers work the same way that broadband devices do, except that when someone on the network tries to access the Internet, the router dials up the ISP just as you would when you use a modem on your own computer. When the router dials up, everyone on the network can access the Internet (although at much slower speeds, because multiple users are sharing a single modem line).

In addition to hardware Internet routers, several software Internet routers are available, such as IPNetRouter. This type of software is installed on the computer that is connected directly to the Internet, and you connect other computers to the base computer via an Ethernet hub or switch. Then the base computer routes Internet traffic to and from the client computers so that all the computers on the network have Internet access.

Apple includes a software Internet router in its AirPort software: a software Base Station. This router allows multiple devices with AirPort cards to connect to the Internet via the base computer without the need for a hardware Base Station. Unfortunately, Apple does not yet support this feature for Mac OS X, but a third-party application is available (see "Take Note: Setting up an AirPort Base Station and Network" later in this chapter).

**Configuration.** Here is a brief overview of what to expect when you set up a router. See the instructions that came with your router for more details.

The settings for connecting to the Internet (via DHCP or static IP) are made in the router itself, either via a special utility designed to work with the router or via a Web-based interface provided by the router.

For example, to access my LinkSys router, I type http://192.168.1.1 in a Web browser. This brings up a dialog box where it asks for my password (if this is the first time you were doing this, there is a default password that you would enter). After entering a successful password, I get a screen that provides access to all the router's settings. By clicking the appropriate link, I can set up the router with the needed TCP/IP information for my ISP, as well as make the appropriate choices for other features.

One such "other feature" is to specify whether and how you want addresses to be distributed to other computers on the network (that is, Network Address Translation). Typically, you have the router assign IP addresses to computers dynamically, via DHCP. To do this with a LinkSys router, you would click the DHCP tab in the router's browser display. Otherwise, you can have each computer use its own manually assigned local IP address (such as 192.168.1.101, 192. 168.1.102, and so on).

If you connect to the Internet via a dynamic IP address (such as via a cable modem using DHCP), the router screen is also where you go to locate your current IP address. For example, with a LinkSys router, click the Status tab to view your WAN IP address. With an AirPort Base Station, access the information via the Internet tab of the AirPort Admin Utility.

*continues on next page*

**TAKE NOTE ▶ Internet Routers** *continued*

**Network Address Translation.** The ability to share one Internet address among multiple computers requires enabling a router feature called Network Address Translation (NAT). When you have a dial-up or broadband connection, you generally have only a single IP address assigned to your household/connection. If you were connecting a single computer to the Internet, that IP address would be assigned to your single computer. An Internet router, however, works by *masquerading* as that single IP address and then managing all traffic among the various computers on your network and the Internet. It does this by assigning each computer on the network an internal address (such as the 192.168.1.*x* address noted above) and then *translating* that address to the single IP address that is supposed to represent your Internet connection. The router uses this Network Address Translation to keep track of which Web site you just requested, which email account your coworker or family member is checking, and which file the computer down the hall has asked to download. Conversely, when the Web page, the email, and the file are sent back to your IP address, the router knows where on your network to send them.

**Network System Preferences settings.** With these tasks done, you enter the settings in Network System Preferences on each computer. Your settings will differ from what they would be for a direct connection to the Internet, especially if you are using a manually assigned IP address. In particular, note the following:

- **Ethernet router.** For a manually entered IP address, in the TCP/IP tab of the Built-in Ethernet tab, enter a local IP address (usually, 192.168.1.*x* or 10.0.0.*x*, where *x* varies for each computer on the network). The IP address entered in the Router field typically will be 192.168.1.1 or 10.0.0.1. The subnet mask typically is something like 255.255.255.0. Again, the router instructions will provide specifics. For a DHCP address, just choose Using DHCP.

- **Wireless router.** The logic is the same, except that you enter the information after choosing AirPort from the Show pop-up menu. You will be accessing the Internet via an AirPort card through the router.

SEE:  • "Technically Speaking: Internet Routers and Port Mapping" and "Take Note: Firewalls and Antivirus Software," later in this chapter.

**TCP/IP.** If you get Internet access through a DSL or cable modem or via a company network, you typically enter the required settings in the TCP/IP tab. There are too many possibilities to cover in this chapter. In general, you either know what you are doing (and do not need this book to advise you), or you don't know what you are doing (in which case you will simply enter whatever your network provider tells you to enter). Still, it is worthwhile to provide a broad overview of what these settings do.

**Configure.** This setting basically determines whether you will be entering IP addresses and related information manually or whether the server will provide the information.

- **Manually.** If you have a static IP address, you will enter the IP address and other ISP information (subnet, router, and domain servers) here.

- **Using DCHP.** If you are assigned an IP address via your ISP or office network's DHCP server, you choose this option. You may be asked to provide a DHCP Client ID or domain name server, but, in most cases, you need supply nothing. After choosing Using DHCP, you are done.

- **Manually Using DHCP Router.** This option is a less common variation of DHCP, and you do need to enter an IP address.

- **Using BootP.** If you are assigned an IP address via a BootP server (a protocol used mostly by large office networks), and your network administrator asks you to enter DNS information, you enter it here.

If your ISP requires you to use certain domain name servers, you will also need to enter those servers' addresses, regardless of the option you choose.

Note that if you have cable/DSL Internet access but are using an AirPort card with an AirPort Base Station or third-party wireless router/access point, you should set up TCP/IP in the AirPort settings, rather than in the Ethernet ones.

**SEE:** • "AirPort" and "Take Note: Internet Routers," elsewhere in this chapter.

---

**TAKE NOTE ▶ What Are the TCP/IP Settings?**

The entries in the TCP/IP tab of the Network System Preferences pane are vital to a successful Internet connection, but most users have no idea what they really mean. If you're curious, here's a quick primer.

**IP Address.** If you want a friend to be able to write you a letter, you give him or her your street address. Likewise, if you write a letter to a company, you generally include a return address so that the company can reply to you. The Internet works in much the same way. For someone to contact you, that person needs to know your address, and if you contact someone else, you must give your address so that person can send data back to you.

Your IP (Internet Protocol) address is that address. An IP address is a unique string of numbers (in the format xxx.xxx.xxx.xxx, in which each xxx is a number from 0 to 255) that specifically identifies your computer to the rest of the Internet. If you request a Web page, your Web browser provides your IP address to the Web server; then the Web server sends the content of that Web page back to your IP address.

If you have a static IP address (entered manually), your IP address is always the same. If you have a PPP, PPPoE, or DHCP Internet account, your ISP or network hardware (such as a router) provides you a temporary IP address when you connect; it lasts until you disconnect or for a certain amount of time set by the ISP or your network administrator. This type of address is generally called a *dynamic* IP address.

*continues on next page*

**Subnet Mask.** As I just mentioned, an IP address is a string of numbers in the format xxx.xxx.xxx.xxx. The address actually has two parts. The first part identifies the specific local network on which the IP address resides; the second is the particular node (location) on that network of the computer in question. A subnet mask delineates which part of your complete IP address refers to the local network and which refers to the node. For a hypothetical IP address of 148.152.168.02, a subnet mask of 255.255.255.0 indicates that the 148.152.168 part of the address refers to the local network, and the .02 refers to the node. A subnet mask of 255.255.0.0 means that the local network is described by 148.152, and .168.02 refers to the node. These delineations are also referred to as subnet classes.

**Router.** An Internet router generally provides a gateway between your computer and the Internet. You send data to the router, which then forwards it on the appropriate path to its destination; data sent to your computer hits your router and then is directed to you. If you connect via PPPoE, PPP, or DHCP, your ISP or DHCP server will provide you the appropriate router. If you have a manual IP address, your ISP or network administrator will provide you the correct address.

If you are using an Internet router, you generally enter a specific local-only "private" address, as described in "Take Note: Internet Routers" earlier in this chapter. An address of this type is used for LAN connections because it has been arbitrarily assigned for this purpose. These addresses will never be assigned to any device on a WAN, so there is no chance for confusion between a LAN and a WAN IP address.

**Domain Name Servers.** When you enter a Web address, such as www.apple.com, you are entering a substitute for the true numeric IP address of the site. Special software on the Internet, called domain name system (DNS) servers, converts this domain name to the appropriate IP number. More specifically, domain name servers host databases that translate the readable text domain name to the specific IP address to which it corresponds. Thus, when you enter www.apple.com, your computer contacts the DNS servers listed in this field and retrieves the actual IP address of that domain name; then it contacts the IP address directly.

This setup allows you to use an easy-to-remember URL without having to know the actual IP address. It similarly means that a Web site can change its IP address without your needing to learn a new URL. If the DNS server is not working correctly, however, you may find that you cannot access a Web page via its domain name, although you can still access it via its IP address.

What if you don't know the IP address of a Web site? You can find it in several ways. One method is to use the ping function of the Network utility included with Mac OS X. (although you need to do this before a DNS problem appears for the function to work). Enter www.apple.com as the address to ping, and the results window will show you the IP address (17.254.0.91). You can test it yourself by entering http://17.254.0.91 in your Web browser. This action should take you to the Apple site (unless Apple's IP address has changed since I wrote this chapter, which is always a possibility).

*continues on next page*

**TAKE NOTE ▶ What Are the TCP/IP Settings?** *continued*

The Domain Name Servers section of the Network System Preferences pane is where you enter the address where the DNS server resides. This address is usually optional, as with most types of connections, the ISP connection will find it on its own. Some setups, however, may require an address to be entered. More problematic, entering the wrong address can prevent you from having a successful Internet connection. When I was switched from @home to Comcast for my cable connection, the DNS address that I had been using no longer worked. Until I realized this fact and deleted the address, I was unable to connect to the Internet. Finally, if you are using an Internet router, entering the router address in the DNS field (as opposed to leaving it blank) may help circumvent connection problems.

**Search Domains.** If you frequently access servers or Web sites that reside *within* a single larger domain (*sales*.domain.com, *finance*.domain.com, and so on), you can place the local network name (domain.com) in this field. The contents of this field will be added to the end of any incomplete domain names (*sales, finance*). Personally, I have never used this feature.

**Ethernet Address** (for Ethernet configurations). An IP address is assigned in software and can be changed at any time. By contrast, an Ethernet address (also called a MAC or Media Access Control address; it has nothing to do with the Macintosh) is a hardware address that identifies your computer uniquely and is hard-coded into your computer before it ships. ISPs and network administrators often use your Ethernet address for verification purposes (to make sure that it really is you trying to connect via your DSL connection, for example).

**AirPort ID** (for AirPort configurations). Just like an Ethernet address, this sequence of letters and numbers uniquely identifies your AirPort card or Base Station.

**PPPoE.** Some ISPs that provide DSL or cable Internet access use a protocol called PPPoE (short for Point-to-Point Protocol over Ethernet). This protocol is a variation of the older modem-style Point-to-Point Protocol (PPP) that has been adapted for use for broadband connections. If your ISP uses this protocol, PPPoE verifies your user name and password when you connect to its servers.

Enabling *Connect using PPPoE* in the PPPoE tab allows you to connect via PPPoE. This will also change your settings in the TCP/IP tab; the only options will be Manually or a new option, PPP. You can also choose to show the status of your PPPoE connection via an icon in the menu bar. Note that another application, Internet Connect, lets you initiate PPPoE connections as long as you have selected PPPoE and enabled Ethernet as an active network port.

**SEE:** • **"The Internet Connect Application," later in this chapter.**

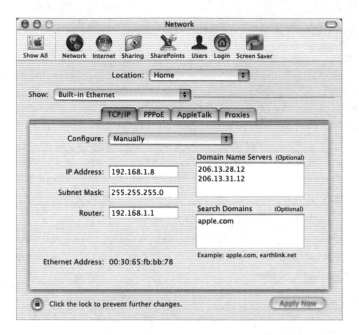

***Figure 8.2***

*The Built-in
Ethernet settings
in the Network
System Preferences
pane: (top) TCP/IP
tab and (bottom)
AppleTalk tab.*

**AppleTalk.** AppleTalk is a protocol used primarily to connect multiple local devices, such as a few Macs and a printer. A TCP/IP connection can accomplish the same task. In general, Mac OS X prefers that you use TCP/IP whenever possible. In fact, AppleTalk may not even be supported in future versions of Mac OS X. Still, if you prefer to use it, or if you have devices that can connect only via AppleTalk (such as a Mac running an old version of the Mac OS that does not support TCP/IP sharing or an Ethernet printer that is AppleTalk-only), you will need to enable AppleTalk over the Ethernet port.

To enable AppleTalk, check the Make AppleTalk Active checkbox in the AppleTalk tab.

You will need the remaining AppleTalk settings only if you are on a large network, such as at a university. If your network has multiple AppleTalk zones, you can select the zone in which you want your computer to appear. In addition, if you need to change your AppleTalk node or network IDs (do this only if you've been told to do so by a network administrator), you make the change by choosing Manually from the Configure pop-up menu.

The Computer Name option in this panel is set in the Sharing tab of the System Preferences application window.

**SEE:** • "Setting up System Preferences: Sharing," later in this chapter.

**Proxies.** Most users do not use proxies; if your ISP or network requires them, you usually will be given the information you need to use them. You enter such information in this tab.

## AirPort

If your Mac connects to a network via an AirPort wireless network card, you will need to set up the Network System Preferences pane for AirPort. Before you do, however, you should set up an AirPort Base Station or compatible wireless router.

Note: After you have everything set up, you can connect or disconnect to an AirPort network via the Internet Connect application.

**SEE:** • "Take Note: Activating Multiple AirPort Configurations," "Take Note: Setting up an AirPort Base Station and Network," and "The Internet Connect Application," later in this chapter, for related information.

The initial step in setting up your AirPort connection is choosing AirPort from the Show pop-up menu. Setting up the TCP/IP, AppleTalk, and Proxies data is very similar to what I described for Ethernet, but I offer a few specific tips in the following paragraphs. The one tab that is new is AirPort.

**AirPort.** Although it is the last tab on the screen, the AirPort tab is the first one you should configure, as it connects your Mac to a wireless network. From the Preferred Network pop-up menu, choose the AirPort network to which you want to connect. If you're a home user, this menu generally will show only the network you have already set up via a Base Station or wireless router. If you're a user in a large wireless environment (or even a home user in the vicinity of other AirPort networks), you may see multiple networks.

If the network you have chosen does not require a password, you should be connected. If the network requires a password, enter it in the Network Password field, and press the Return key. This action will authenticate you and connect you to the network. (Note: If you are setting up your own AirPort network, you can create passwords via the AirPort Setup Assistant application.)

A useful tip is to enable the Show AirPort Status in Menu Bar checkbox. This option will place a small icon in the menu bar, giving you a graphical representation of whether you are connected to an AirPort network and how strong the signal is. If you click the icon, you access a menu that includes options to turn AirPort on or off, join an existing AirPort network, or open Internet Connect.

Note: Both the AirPort icon menu and the Internet Connect application include a choice called Create Network. This is used to create a Computer-to-Computer network. These networks are a temporary setup directly between two computers. You can create such a network even if there is no Base Station in the vicinity. Cool.

**SEE:** • "The Internet Connect Application," later in this chapter, for more details on these matters.

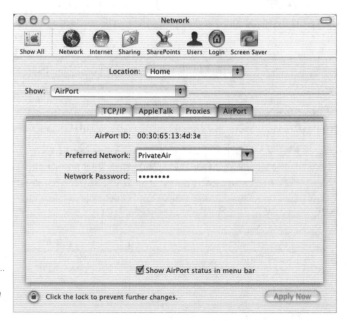

*Figure 8.3*

*The AirPort tab of the Network System Preferences pane.*

**TCP/IP.** If you are using an AirPort Base Station or compatible wireless router for Internet access, you will enter your TCP/IP settings here. If your wireless router is set up to use DHCP, a DHCP router, or BootP, you can simply choose the appropriate setting from the Configure pop-up menu, and the router will take care of the rest. If you have your router set up for static IP addresses, you will need to enter each setting manually. (Your IP address will usually be something like 192.168.1.x or 10.0.0.x, and the router address will generally be 192.168.1.1 or 10.0.0.1.) If your ISP requires you to use certain domain name servers, you will need to enter their addresses as well.

**AppleTalk.** If you will be using the AppleTalk protocol over an AirPort network, this tab is where you enable it (by checking the Make AppleTalk Active checkbox). An AirPort AppleTalk network does not require an AirPort Base Station; you can create a network between two AirPort-equipped computers directly. (See "The Internet Connect Application," later in this chapter.) You can also choose an AppleTalk zone (if applicable) and manually configure your AppleTalk node ID and network ID.

**Proxies.** If your ISP or network requires proxies, you enter proxy information in this tab.

**TAKE NOTE  ▶  Activating Multiple AirPort Port Configurations**

Many people in larger wireless network environments have access to multiple AirPort Base Stations or AirPort-compatible wireless access points, and they end up switching from one network or access point to another as they move about. One way to approach this situation is to set up multiple locations (as described in "Locations" in the main text), each containing a different AirPort configuration. This approach, however, requires you to manually switch between locations. Another way to deal with multiple Base Stations is to set up multiple active AirPort port configurations simultaneously. Mac OS X will try each until it can connect. To do this, follow these steps:

1. In the Network System Preferences pane, choose Active Network Ports from the Show pop-up menu.

2. Click the existing AirPort configuration; then click the Duplicate button.

3. Give the new configuration a recognizable name.

   I suggest "AirPort *networkname*," in which *networkname* is the name of one of the AirPort networks to which you will be connecting.

4. Click OK to create the new configuration.

5. Repeat steps 2 through 4 until you have one configuration for every AirPort network you will be accessing.

*continues on next page*

**TAKE NOTE** ▶ **Activating Multiple AirPort Port Configurations** *continued*

6. From the Show pop-up menu, choose each AirPort port configuration, and enter the appropriate settings for it, using the instructions in this chapter for configuring AirPort connections.

7. Repeat step 6 until you have entered the settings for each AirPort configuration.

8. Return to the Active Network Ports settings, and arrange the various AirPort configurations in the order in which you want Mac OS X to attempt to connect.

Mac OS X will attempt to connect to the first AirPort network listed. If it cannot connect to the first network, it will move on to the second, then the third, and so on until it is able to connect.

---

**TAKE NOTE** ▶ **Setting Up an AirPort Base Station and Network**

You can configure the Network System Preferences pane for AirPort, but if you have no wireless network with which to connect, it will not be of much use. Although it is becoming more and more common to install publicly accessible wireless networks (often referred to as 802.11b networks) in places such as—appropriately enough—airports, I'll assume that if you have an AirPort card in your Mac, you also want to set it up so you can use it in your home or office. In such a case, the first thing you need to do is configure your AirPort Base Station and create your initial AirPort network.

Note: You can use AirPort cards with third-party wireless routers instead of an AirPort Base Station. You can also use wireless PC cards in laptops, instead of AirPort cards. I am going to skip over these variations, however, and stick to Apple's AirPort technology.

The simplest (and, thus, preferred) way to set up your Base Station and network is to use the AirPort Setup Assistant software, located in the Utilities folder. This method will work only if you have an AirPort card installed, however. If you want to configure a Base Station from a Mac that does not have an AirPort card installed, or if you want to make any changes that cannot be handled by the Setup Assistant, you will need to use the less-user-friendly AirPort Admin utility.

Note: To configure a Base Station from a Mac that does not have an AirPort card installed or to communicate to a Base Station from any Mac when you cannot get the AirPort connection to work, you need to have the Base Station connected to the Mac via a wired Ethernet network. Apple's second-generation Base Stations (the white ones) make this easier to do, because they have two Ethernet ports: one for connecting to the Internet and the other for connecting to a local network. The original graphite Base Stations have only one Ethernet port.

*Using AirPort Setup Assistant*

When you launch AirPort Setup Assistant, the initial decision you need to make is whether to set up a Base Station or set up your computer to join an AirPort network.

*continues on next page*

**TAKE NOTE** ▶ **Setting Up an AirPort Base Station and Network** *continued*

**Set up an AirPort Base Station.** If you are using AirPort for the first time (and there is no existing network already set up), choose Set up an AirPort Base Station. Note that if you use the AirPort Setup Assistant, your Base Station will be able to use only DHCP to communicate with other devices on the network. If you want to do something else (such as assign IP addresses manually), you must use the AirPort Admin utility to set up the Base Station. What will happen next in Assistant depends a bit on whether you are setting up a Base Station for the first time or modifying one that has already been set up. In either case, the Assistant walks you through the steps, including setting up the initial network. When you are done, the Assistant uploads the information to the Base Station. You are now ready to set up and join a network.

**Set up Your Computer to Join an Existing AirPort Network.** In most cases, this option accomplishes the same goal that you can accomplish via other methods, such as selecting an existing network in Internet Connect or via the AirPort menu that you can add to the menu bar (as discussed in the main text and in "The Internet Connect Application" elsewhere in this chapter).

### *Using AirPort Admin Utility*

When you first launch this application, you will get a list of all Base Stations that are accessible. If the one you are looking for is not listed, click the Rescan button to try again. If that technique fails, and you know the IP address of the Base Station, click the Other button and enter the address and password. If neither of these approaches works, you need to check your basic network connections (as described in the main text) to make sure that the Base Station is connected to the network. If you are using the Base Station for the first time, and therefore have no AirPort network setup, the Base Station must be connected via a wired Ethernet connection to the computer running the Admin utility.

*continues on next page*

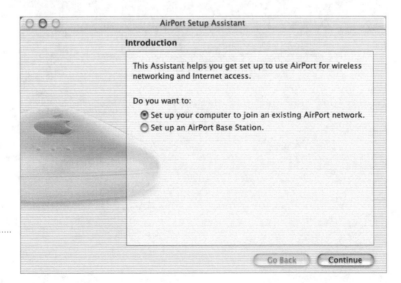

*Figure 8.4*

*The initial AirPort Setup Assistant screen.*

**TAKE NOTE ▶ Setting Up an AirPort Base Station and Network** *continued*

When the appropriate Base Station is listed, double-click it or select it and then click the Configure button to access the Base Station's settings. If the Base Station has already been configured, you will have to enter its password. If you enter the wrong password, you will get an error message that states, rather ambiguously, "An error occurred while reading the configuration."

Note: The Base Station password is separate from the password you use to join a network. Each network can have its own unique password, separate from others as well as from the Base Station password. After you enter the Admin utility, you will have a variety of choices. Following is a brief overview.

**The buttons.** Across the top of the window are four buttons:

- **Restart.** Restart (also called a soft reset) is the AirPort equivalent of restarting your Mac; it may fix some temporary problem with a connection.

- **Default.** Default loads the default version of the AirPort software to the Base Station. If you place the pointer over this button but do not click it, some pop-up text will appear, telling you the version number of the default software.

- **Upload.** If you want to upload a newer version than the default version (such as an update released by Apple), click the Upload button and then select the update file in the window that opens. (Note: In most cases, after you install an update of AirPort software on your Mac, the Admin utility will prompt you to update the Base Station immediately after you click the Configure button.)

- **Password.** The Password button shows the equivalent network password. Without going into detail, this password is used by some computers that are using a third-party card (rather than an Apple AirPort card) to connect to the Base Station.

*continues on next page*

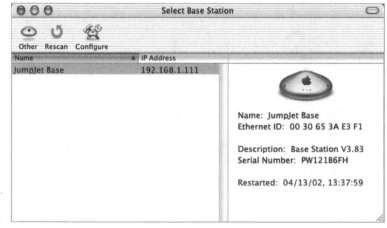

*Figure 8.5*

*The initial AirPort Admin utility screen.*

**TAKE NOTE** ▶ **Setting Up an AirPort Base Station and Network** *continued*

**AirPort tab.** This tab has two fields. In the Base Station field, you enter the name of the Base Station and its password. In the AirPort Network field, you enter the name of the network and its password. This tab has other options, such as Create a closed network. When this option is enabled, your network will not be listed in AirPort menus automatically. To access it, the user will have to enter both the name and the password of a network (such as done via the dialog box that appears after selecting the Other command in the AirPort menu bar icon's menu). This is a security feature, designed to make it harder for unauthorized users to find your network.

**Internet tab.** This tab is where you enter the settings for connecting to the Internet. Essentially, you enter the settings you would have entered in the TCP/IP tab of the Network System Preferences pane if you were not using a Base Station.

*continues on next page*

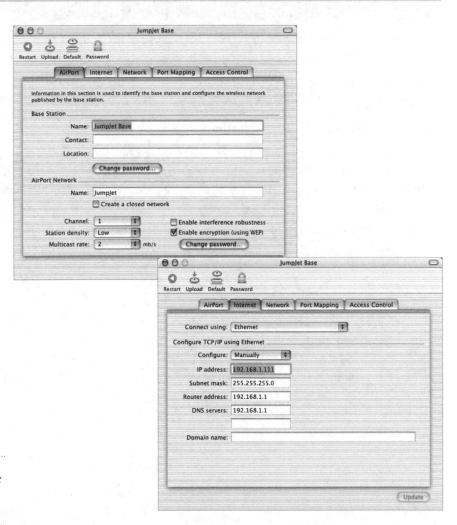

**Figure 8.6**

*The AirPort Admin utility's (top) AirPort and (bottom) Internet tabs.*

**TAKE NOTE ▶ Setting Up an AirPort Base Station and Network** *continued*

**Network tab.** This critical tab determines how the Base Station will work with the other computers on your local network. The most common choice is to enable Distribute IP addresses together with Share a single IP address (using DHCP and NAT). Alternatively, if you have a separate Internet router that is assigning IP addresses manually or via DHCP, you may choose to disable the Distribute IP addresses option and enable only the Enable AirPort to Ethernet bridging option. This lets the router handle the address sharing that would otherwise be done via the Base Station. Whatever choices you make, the text at the bottom of the window provides a summary of what you have done and how other computers must be configured as a result. This information can help you decide whether you have made the correct decision.

Admittedly, making the correct decision can be difficult if you are not familiar with how computer networks work. To help you, Apple has created a couple of PDF documents describing AirPort networking. For example, get Designing AirPort Networks for Mac OS X (v10.1) via this Web page: `http://docs.info.apple.com/article.html?artnum=120061`.

**Port Mapping and Access Control tabs.** Most users will never use these tabs. I discuss Port Mapping in "Technically Speaking: Internet Routers and Port Mapping" later in this chapter.

**Update.** When you are done making your changes, click the Update button at the bottom of the window. This action will save the changes to the Base Station and restart it.

### Do a Hard Reset of the Base Station

If you are having problems with your Base Station that none of the preceding techniques can solve (especially if the symptoms include the Base Station lights showing a color other than green), your last resort is to do a hard reset of the Base Station. To do a hard reset of a white (dual Ethernet) Base Station, follow these steps:

1. Connect the Base Station to an existing wired Ethernet network.
2. From the Network System Preferences pane, create an Ethernet port setting as follows:
   - Configure: Manually
   - IP Address: 192.42.249.15
   - Subnet Mask: 255.255.252.0
   - Router: 192.42.249.13
3. Next, unplug the cord that connects the Base Station to the wall outlet.
4. Insert the end of a straightened paper clip into the small hole on the underside of the Base Station, and hold it there.
5. Plug the power cord back in.
6. Hold the paper clip for one more second, remove it from the hole, and wait for another moment.

   When you go to the AirPort Admin utility, it will respond to the Base Station as though you had just taken it out of the box and never used it before.

*continues on next page*

**TAKE NOTE ▶ Setting Up an AirPort Base Station and Network**  *continued*

7. Choose Configure the Base Station, and do so.

   Initially, the password will be public.

8. When you're done, you can return to the Network System Preferences pane and reenter/reselect your previous AirPort settings.

**Forgot your password?** If the problem is only that you forgot your Base Station password, the procedure is simpler. Leaving the Base Station plugged in, insert the end of a straightened paper clip into the small hole on the underside of the Base Station, and hold for one second. The network and Base Stations passwords are reset to Public.

For additional details about resetting a Base Station, and especially for procedures to use with a graphite Base Station, check the Help menu for the AirPort Admin utility, the documentation that came with your Base Station, or the following Apple support documents: AirPort Base Station (Dual Ethernet): How to Reset (**http://docs.info.apple.com/article.html?artnum= 106602**), AirPort Base Station (Dual Ethernet) : How to Reload Software From Mac OS X (**http://docs.info.apple.com/article.html?artnum=106685**), and AirPort Firmware v1.0, 1.3 & 2.0: AirPort Base Station (Graphite) Forced Reload or Reset (**http://docs.info.apple.com/ article.html?artnum=58613**).

### *Create a Software Base Station?*

In Mac OS 9, Apple's AirPort software supports the capability to set up a Mac to act as a Base Station. The advantage of this capability is that you can save the expense of purchasing a separate hardware device. The main disadvantage is that the computer must always be up and running for the AirPort network to be active. In any case, this option is not included in the AirPort software for Mac OS X. Various third-party applications provide workarounds, however. The most popular alternative is IPNetShareX. A MacFixIt Web page (**www.macfixit.com/osx/ airportbase.shtml**) offers additional advice.

### *Getting Started*

After you finish setting up a Base Station and network, your next step (if you have not already done so) is to set the AirPort settings in the Network System Preferences pane, as described in the main text. Remember that what you enter here will vary depending on how you set up the Base Station's Network tab. Fortunately, after you make all these settings, you will not need to refer to them again unless problems occur.

Finally, you need to turn on AirPort and choose the desired network (usually via the AirPort menu or Internet Connect). Now you are on a wireless network. Congratulations.

# Modem

You may not think of a dial-up connection to your ISP (AOL, EarthLink, and so on) as being a network connection, but it is. The modem is linking your computer to other computers on the Internet. As a result, the settings for modem connections are located in the Network pane of System Preferences application window.

Note: The Internet Connect utility also lets you initiate dial-up connections without accessing the Network System Preferences pane as long as you have enabled Internal Modem (or another modem) as an Active Network Port.

**SEE:** • "The Internet Connect Application," later in this chapter.

**TCP/IP.** As with AirPort and Ethernet, this tab is where you enter your ISP's TCP/IP settings. The Configure pop-up menu has two options: Manually and Using PPP. If you are one of the very few people who have a dial-up connection with a static IP address, choose Manually. If you are like most users, you will choose Using PPP. The only additional data you may have to enter is the address of your ISP's domain name server.

**PPP.** This tab is where you enter the dial-up information required to connect to your ISP. To do so, follow these steps:

1. (Optional) Enter your ISP's name in the Service Provider field.

2. In the Telephone Number field, enter the phone number you dial up to connect to your ISP.

3. If you have a second number, enter it in the Alternate Number field.

   If the first number is busy or not responding, Mac OS X will try the second number.

4. Type your account name in the Account Name field.

   For some ISPs, your account name is simply your user name; other ISPs require your entire email address. Check with your ISP to be sure.

5. Type your password in the Password field.

6. If you want Mac OS X to remember your password so that you don't have to type it each time you connect, click the Save Password checkbox.

7. (Optional) If you click the PPP Options button, you can enable or disable a variety PPP settings.

   Most users will be content to leave these options at their default settings and can ignore this screen. Two choices in this screen are worth a special mention, however:

   • **Connect Automatically When Starting TCP/IP Applications**. With this option enabled, when you launch an application (such as a Web browser) and are not connected to the Internet, Mac OS X will initiate a connection automatically.

- **Disconnect If Idle for ?? Minutes**. You can set this option to log
  you off automatically if the Mac detects that you have not used the
  connection for a certain period of time. This option can be useful if
  you leave your computer with your connection still active, especially
  if you get charged by the hour, but it can be annoying if you want to
  maintain the connection despite the idle period. Note that some dial-up
  ISPs may disconnect you after a period of idle activity, regardless of
  how you set this option.

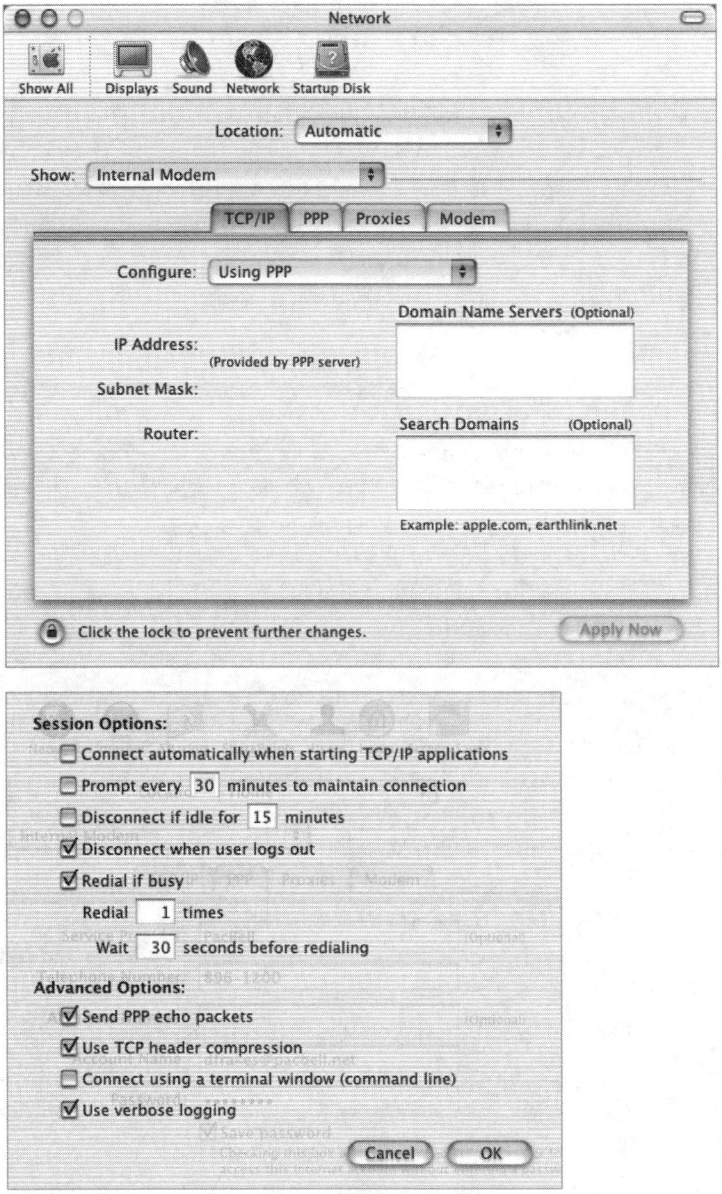

*Figure 8.7*

*The Network System
Preferences pane's
Internal Modem
settings: (top) TCP/IP
tab and (bottom)
PPP Options screen
(accessed from the
PPP tab).*

**TAKE NOTE ▶ When Connecting Automatically Is Not a Good Idea**

Although enabling Connect Automatically When Starting TCP/IP Applications can be convenient, in some cases, when you enable this option, the system will attempt to make a connection when you do not want it to. If you are not connected to an available phone line and launch your Web browser (perhaps to view a page offline), the Mac will attempt to make a connection and fail to do so.

The solution is to keep this option disabled (which is the solution I recommend). The other alternative is to create a separate location for when you are not connected to any network or phone line. Set all ports disabled in this location, and remember to switch to this location at times when you are not connected.

A slightly different variation: If you have File Sharing or Web Sharing enabled, and you have the Connect Automatically option enabled, the Mac may try to initiate a dial-up connection at startup. To prevent this situation, follow either of the suggestions I just described or turn off the sharing options via the Sharing System Preferences pane.

**SEE:** • "Blue-screen crash," in Chapter 5, for coverage of a problem with the Connect
   Automatically option that can cause a crash at startup.

**TAKE NOTE ▶ Modem Scripts**

When you select a modem model/type in the Modem tab of Network System Preferences, what you are actually doing is telling Mac OS X which modem *script* to use when initiating a dial-up connection. Because every modem is slightly different, these scripts (located in /Library/Modem Scripts) tell Mac OS X how to interact with each modem. A modem script generally describes the modem's initialization string, maximum data speed, buffer size, data-compression settings, error-correction settings, and any other special features the modem supports. You can open and view any of these modem scripts in a text editor such as BBEdit. (You can even edit them; I would advise against doing this, however, unless you know what you're doing.)

Generally, all you need to do is choose your modem's name from the Modem pop-up menu and connect. At times, however, the "right" script for your modem just doesn't work as well as it should. Your modem may try to connect at a speed your phone line can't sustain, for example, resulting in frequent disconnects. Or maybe you have a v.90 modem, but your ISP supports only the slower v.34. Choosing a different modem script from the Modem pop-up menu may help. In particular, for the Apple Internal Modem, shifting from *Apple Internal 56K Modem (v.90)* to *Apple Internal 56K Modem (v.34)* may help. In some cases, users have had better luck with the *Nifty* Apple Internal Modem selections.

In addition, modem manufacturers sometimes release updated scripts for their modems. In this case, you simply place the updated script in the Modem Scripts folder and then choose it from the Modem pop-up menu in the Modem tab.

Finally, if you really understand modem init strings and want to create your own modem scripts for Mac OS X, you can download a freeware application that creates modem scripts from **www.apple.com/downloads/macosx/networking_security/modemscriptgenerator.html**.

**Proxies.** If your ISP requires proxies, you enter proxy information in this tab.

**Modem.** This tab is where you set up your modem for PPP connections. The Modem pop-up menu is where you choose the modem model; for most recent Apple computers and PowerBooks, the model is already chosen for you: Apple Internal 56K Modem (v.90). If you have an older Mac or are using a third-party modem, choose the appropriate model. Other settings available in this tab are: error correction, sound (whether or not you can hear the modem dialing and connecting through your speakers), tone/pulse dialing, and an option to show the status of the modem in the menu bar. This final option is useful as a way to tell whether your connection is still active.

## The Internet Connect application

If you have not set your Mac to connect to the Internet automatically when you use an Internet application (Web browser, email client, and so on), you will need to connect manually to the Internet or perhaps even to an AirPort network. Even if you normally use the automatic-connect setting, at times you may want it disabled, such as when you are traveling and need to use a different dial-up number.

For such occasions, use Mac OS X's Internet Connect utility (located in the Applications folder). Internet Connect allows you to initiate a modem, AirPort, or PPPoE connection manually (the one caveat being that you can connect only via a port that is active in the Network System Preferences pane).

When you open Internet Connect, you see a small dialog box that contains only a Configuration pop-up menu. If you have only one configuration active at the moment (for example, Internal Modem or AirPort), you see only an option for that configuration. If you have multiple ports configured, the menu will include more than one option. Choose your desired port, if more than one is available, and click the Connect button to connect manually.

Click the disclosure triangle on the right, however, and you see several additional options. The options will vary, depending on your Configuration selection.

**AirPort.** For AirPort configurations, the first option is AirPort Power. You can click the Turn AirPort Off button to shut down your AirPort card. This feature is a great way to conserve battery power on a laptop. When you're ready to connect, click the button again to turn your AirPort card back on.

The second option is to choose your AirPort network. If you are in the vicinity of multiple networks, you can choose which one you want to join. If the network is protected, you will be asked to enter the appropriate password.

Also in the Network pop-up menu is an almost-hidden gem: Create Network. This option lets you create a direct, wireless Computer-to-Computer network between two AirPort-equipped computers (with no Base Station required). To do so, follow these steps:

1. Choose Create Network from the Network pop-up menu.

2. In the Name field, enter the name of your network.

   The other computer will have this name in its Network pop-up menu.

3. If you want the network to be private, enter a password and then confirm it.

4. Choose the AirPort channel you want to use.

   Usually, you can stick with the default value, but if you have problems connecting due to interference, you can set another value.

5. Click OK.

   The other computer can use its own Internet Connect utility to connect to your newly created network.

The AirPort window of Internet Connect includes the same option to Show AirPort status in the menu bar as was available in Network System Preferences.

Finally, the window provides a signal-level indicator and the ID of the Base Station to which you are connected.

**Internal Modem (or other modem).** In addition to allowing you to initiate a dial-up connection manually (by clicking the Connect button), Internet Connect's Modem configuration window provides options that extend what is listed in the Modem tab of the Network System Preferences pane.

The Telephone Number field shows, by default, the number entered in the Modem section of the Network System Preferences pane. However, you can type a different number in the field and then connect to it by clicking the Connect button. Internet Connect remembers each number you've dialed and keeps the numbers in a menu accessible by clicking the triangle to the right of the field. So if you have multiple ISP phone numbers, you can simply choose the preferred number from the menu and then connect. (Unfortunately, there is no easy way to delete numbers from this menu; for advice on how to deal with this, see "Technically Speaking: Deleting Unwanted Numbers From Internet Connect," later in this chapter.)

At the bottom of the window, you can see your connection speed (at least, the speed you had when you first connected), how long you have been connected, your IP address, and a graphical representation of data being sent and received. Note: If these graphs indicate no activity, you probably no longer have a connection, even if other settings indicate you are still connected.

You can view your connection log by choosing Connection Log from the Window menu. The log can be helpful in troubleshooting a problematic dial-up connection.

If you told Mac OS X (in the Network System Preferences pane) to save your dial-up password, it is entered here automatically. If you did not tell Mac OS X to save your password, you can type it here each time you connect.

The Internal Modem window also allows you to go to the Network System Preferences pane quickly by clicking the Edit button.

Finally, you have the same option to Show modem status in the menu bar as was available in Network System Preferences. The menu bar icon includes a menu from which you can choose a Connect option, bypassing the need to open Internet Connect at all (assuming that you intend to use default settings).

**Built-In Ethernet** (for PPPoE). If you have a DSL or cable-modem connection, and your ISP uses PPPoE, you can use this screen to connect and disconnect manually. Your service provider's name and your account name are entered automatically, using the values you supplied in the Network System Preferences pane (as is your password, if you told Mac OS X to save it). If you didn't choose to save your password, you can enter it here each time you connect. You can also choose to show your PPPoE status in the menu bar. Finally, the window allows you to go to the Network System Preferences pane quickly by clicking the Edit button.

The Status section provides your IP address, the time you have been connected, and a graphical representation of data being sent and received over your connection.

*Figure 8.8*

*The Internet Connect application window.*

**TECHNICALLY SPEAKING ▶ Deleting Unwanted Numbers from Internet Connect**

As explained in "The Internet Connect Application" in the main text, each phone number you dial from within Internet Connect is stored and is available at any time from the pop-up menu next to the phone-number field. This setup is convenient if you have multiple phone numbers for your ISP.

But what if you accidentally enter an incorrect number, or you need to use a number only for a weekend trip? You don't want those numbers to be saved for posterity, yet there is no clear way to remove phone numbers from this list.

The easiest way to delete phone numbers from this list is to use Apple's PropertyList Editor (part of the free Developer Tools CD or available from Apple's Web site). To do so, follow these steps:

1. Quit Internet Connect.
2. Launch PropertyList Editor.
3. Open the file ~/Library/Preferences/com.apple.internetconnect.plist.

   A reminder: The ~ symbol refers to is your Home directory in the Users folder.
4. Click the triangle next to Root to disclose its contents.
5. Click the triangle next to /NetworkServices/0 to disclose its contents.

   You will see a list of strings whose values are the numbers in Internet Connect's telephone-number menu.
6. Click a number you want to remove from the menu; then click the Delete button to delete it.
7. Repeat step 6 for each number you want to remove.
8. Quit PropertyList Editor.

The next time you launch Internet Connect, the numbers you deleted will no longer be included in the telephone-number menu.

## Locations

From the brief detour to visit the Internet Connect application, I now return to the Network System Preferences pane. The instructions in the preceding sections assume, for the most part, that you are using your desktop or portable Mac in an environment where your network settings are static. In many situations, however, you may have multiple groups of network settings. Perhaps you use your PowerBook at work and at home and each location requires different network settings.

Mac OS X addresses these situations through network locations. *Locations* are groups of network settings that you set up based on the environments in which you will be using your computer. You can create any number of locations sets.

Mac OS X's locations are similar to the Location Manager in Mac OS 9, in that you can create groups of settings and switch between them easily. But whereas Location Manager allows you to switch network settings, printers, time zones, startup files, QuickTime settings, sound volume, and many other things, Mac OS X's locations control *only* network settings.

On the flip side, although Location Manager was one of the more confusing utilities to confront a Mac user, locations are simple to set up in Mac OS X. In fact, if you have been using the preceding instructions to configure your network settings, you've already been working with locations, because all your initial network settings are part of a default location called Automatic.

To create a new location, follow these steps:

1. Choose New Location from the Location pop-up menu in the Network System Preferences pane.
2. Give your new location a name, and click OK.

   The new location is selected automatically.

You next need to configure the new location. To do so, use the steps outlined in "Setting up System Preferences: Network," earlier in this chapter (configure and prioritize the active ports and then configure the settings for each port).

To create a new location that is based on, or similar to, an existing location, follow these steps:

1. Choose Edit Location from the Location pop-up menu.
2. Choose the location in which you want to work.
3. Click the Duplicate button, and give the new location a name.
4. Click Done.
5. Choose the new location from the Location pop-up menu.
6. Make any necessary changes in your network settings.

When you've created multiple locations, you can switch among them easily. To do so, do either of the following:

- Choose a location from the Location pop-up menu at the top of the Network System Preferences pane. Then click the Apply Now button.

  *or*

- Choose Location from Mac OS X's Apple menu and select the desired location from the hierarchical menu.

---

**TAKE NOTE ▶ Mac OS X Server/NetInfo Manager**

You may be aware that in addition to Mac OS X, Apple offers a server-level package called Mac OS X Server. What may surprise you is that Mac OS X Server is basically the same operating system as the Mac OS X you use on your own computer, with only two major differences. The first difference is that the Server version of Mac OS X comes with server-specific and administrative tools such as NetBoot, Apple File Services, Macintosh Manager, and Web Objects—tools that provide functionality needed for a server-level product that usually are not needed in a desktop OS. Second, Mac OS X (the non-Server) can run Carbon and Classic applications, whereas Mac OS X Server runs only Mac OS X-native applications.

Thus, even the desktop version of Mac OS X can function as an adequate server in many situations. In fact, the two versions of Mac OS X use many of the same administrative databases and tools.

One of these tools is the NetInfo database. NetInfo is the central database for network and administrative data in Mac OS X, keeping track of user accounts, printers, servers, and access. Just as Mac OS X administrators need to understand NetInfo, you, as the administrator of your Mac, may benefit from understanding what NetInfo is and how to use it to your advantage. Most users of Mac OS X client will rarely, if ever, need to deal with the NetInfo database directly; but when you want or need to do so, the NetInfo Manager application (located in /Applications/Utilities) is to the tool to use.

Apple offers a document titled Understanding and Using NetInfo (`http://docs.info.apple.com/article.html?artnum=106416`) that provides a good background on this subject.

**SEE :** • "NetInfo Manager," in Chapter 3, and "Network domain," in Chapter 4, for more details.

# Setting up System Preferences: Internet

Mac OS X's Internet System Preferences pane allows you to set up default Internet settings. Similar to the Internet control panel in Mac OS 9, a Mac OS X application that supports access to Internet System Preferences settings can use these settings rather than require you to enter them separately in the Preferences dialog box of the application itself. This situation can reduce the need to enter the same data repeatedly in multiple applications.

Internet System Preferences includes four tabs: iTools, Email, Web, and News.

# iTools

Apple's iTools is a group of Apple-provided Internet tools available free to any Mac user. These tools include the following.

**iDisk** is an online storage space that allows you to store documents, music, pictures, Web sites, and movies—basically, any kind of file. In addition, Apple stocks each iDisk with software updates and a selection of third-party software (applications, music files, and even drivers for third-party peripherals).

**HomePage** helps you create your own customized Web site, including photo galleries, which is stored on your iDisk.

**iTools email** provides you a mac.com email address, accessible from any email client (including Mac OS X's Mail).

**iCards** allows you to send Apple-themed electronic greeting cards to your friends and family.

In addition, an iTools account lets you order photo prints and photo books created in iPhoto.

You can sign up for iTools and access all these features from Apple's Web site via this URL: **www.apple.com/itools**. Or you can sign up by clicking the Sign Up button in the iTools tab of the Internet System Preferences pane. If you are already a member, you can enter your iTools member name and password in the spaces provided. If you have multiple iTools accounts, you will have to reenter your settings each time you want to connect to a different iDisk—or use one of the connection methods described in "Using Connect to Server" later in this chapter.

**Figure 8.9**

*The iTools tab of the Internet System Preferences pane.*

After you enter this information, you can subsequently mount your iDisk by choosing *iDisk* from the Finder's Go menu, bypassing the need to launch Internet System Preferences.

## Email

The Email tab lets you set up your default email preferences. These preferences tell Mac OS X which email client and account should be used when you click an email link in a Web browser or when you double-click an email address file in the Finder.

From the Default Email Reader pop-up menu, choose the email client you will use to send and receive email. The options are Mac OS X's Mail and Microsoft Outlook Express. If you use another email client, choose Select and browse your hard drive for your preferred application. The default client is the one that will launch if, for example, you click an email address on a Web page.

If you are using your iTools account as your primary email account, clicking the Use iTools Email account checkbox will fill in all the account settings for you automatically. If you are using another email account (from your ISP, for example), you'll need to uncheck the checkbox and fill in the settings with information provided by your account provider. If you have multiple email accounts, you can leave this tab blank and configure the settings in Mail or your preferred email application. In any case, you can always override these default settings by using the settings options in your email application.

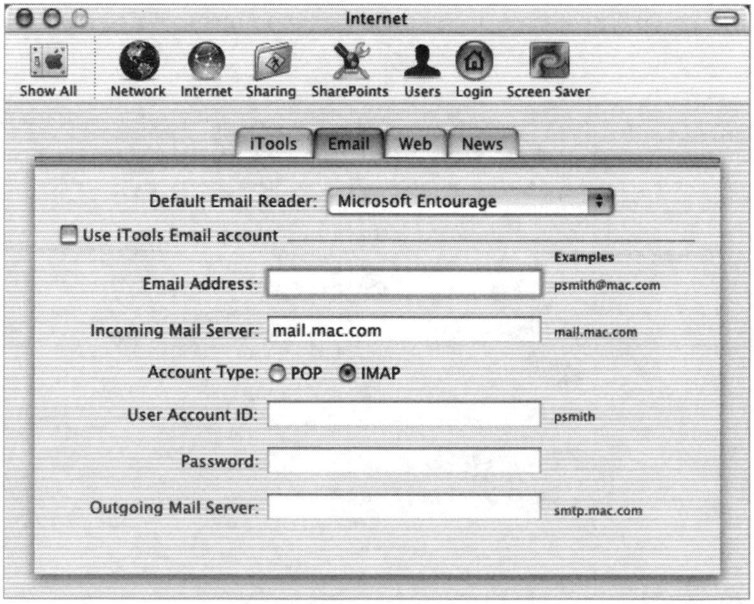

*Figure 8.10*

*The Email tab of the Internet System Preferences pane.*

# Web

Internet System Preferences' Web tab lets you specify your default Web browser and several key Web-browser settings. The choice you make from the Default Web Browser pop-up menu tells Mac OS X which browser to use if you click a URL in a document or email message or double-click a URL in the Finder.

The Home Page setting is the default address that your Web browser uses when you click the Home button. Simply enter the standard URL. You can also use a file located on your hard drive as a home page. The easiest way to do this is to open the file in your Web browser (by dragging it into an open browser window or by choosing the Open" command from the File menu). When the file loads, its local address will be displayed in your Web browser's address bar. Simply select the address, copy it, and paste it into the Home Page field.

Search Page allows you to enter the URL for your preferred search engine (Google, Yahoo!, Excite, AltaVista, and so on). This URL is used when you click the Search button in your Web browser (assuming your browser supports accessing this URL; Explorer does not).

The Download Files To field allows you to designate where on your hard drive files are saved if you click a download link on a Web page. You can type the path to your preferred folder or click the Select button to browse your hard drive and select the folder.

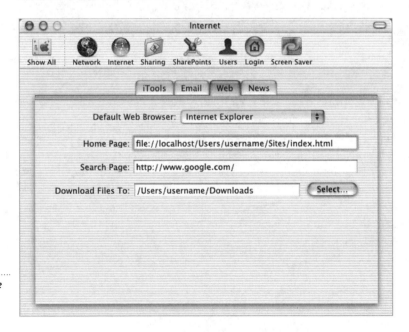

*Figure 8.11*

*The Web tab of the Internet System Preferences pane.*

# News

In the News tab, you can choose your default settings for browsing and post-ing to Usenet newsgroups. These settings will be used by most newsgroup newsreaders and will tell Mac OS X what application to open when you click a newsgroup link or URL in a Web browser, an email message, or the Finder.

The Default News Reader pop-up menu lets you choose your favorite news reader. Because some email clients are also newsgroup clients (such as Entourage, Outlook Express, and Netscape Mail & News), you may end up choosing your email client, or you can choose a dedicated newsreader program.

In the News Server section, enter the address or domain name of your news server (provided by your ISP). If your news server requires you to log in, click the Registered User radio button and enter your account ID and password.

---

**TECHNICALLY SPEAKING ▶ Internet System Preferences' Preferences**

Much of the information you enter in the Internet System Preferences pane is stored in a pref-erences file called com.apple.internetconfig.plist, located in ~/Library/Preferences. This file also holds some of the data that you access via the Preferences command in Microsoft's Internet Explorer and Entourage. The settings for Explorer's File Helpers and Protocol Helpers are stored here, for example. These Explorer settings determine what additional applications are accessed when they're needed to open certain types of files (such as StuffIt compressed files).

**Delete file to fix crash problems.** If you delete this plist file, a new version with default settings will be created the next time you launch Explorer or the Internet System Preferences pane. You will need to reenter data in the Internet System Preferences pane, as desired. Deleting this file can cure crashes in applications that access this .plist file's contents, presumably due to some corruption in the file's data.

**Prevent preferences changes from being overwritten.** When you change com.apple.internet-config.plist via an application's preferences, be cautious if you have two such applications (such as Entourage and Explorer) open at the same time. In such cases, any changes you make via *application one* may get eliminated when you quit *application two*—especially if you quit *application two* before quitting *application one*. What appears to happen is that when *applica-tion two* quits, it overwrites the changes you made via *application one*. The workaround is to quit all applications that could affect the .plist file except the one in which you intend to make changes. Then quit that application before opening any other relevant applications. After that, all should go well without further constraints.

*continues on next page*

> **TECHNICALLY SPEAKING** ▶ **Internet System Preferences' Preferences** *continued*
>
> **Helpers tab.** It appears that Apple has already created the groundwork for adding a Helpers tab to the Internet System Preferences pane. This information is essentially the same information that you access via Explorer's Preferences dialog box. This tab is not activated as of Mac OS X 10.1.3 but is likely to appear in a future update. You can get a preview of how it will work by doing the following:
>
> 1. Go to /System/Library/Preferences/Internet.prefPane.
>
>    This is the application that you access when you choose Internet in the System Preferences pane.
>
> 2. Control-click on the file to access its contextual menu and select Show Package Contents. From the window that opens, navigate to Contents/Resources/English.lproj.
>
> 3. Double-click a file called InternetPref.nib.
>
>    If you have installed the Developer Tools CD software, this file will launch Interface Builder.
>
> 4. In the window that appears, double-click the Internet Pref icon.
>
>    This icon opens a mock layout of the Internet System Preferences pane, which looks and works just like the one that you access from the System Preferences application, with one notable exception: There is a Helpers tab to the right of the News tab. No such tab appears ordinarily.
>
>    Further, if you click the Panel icon (next to the Internet Pref icon), a window called Edit Helper Application opens.

# Setting up System Preferences: Users

When you first launch Mac OS X, the Setup Assistant software requires you to set up a User account for yourself. This first account is set up, by default, for an administrative user. If you want to modify the data you entered, or if you want to add, delete, or modify additional user accounts, you do so via the Users System Preferences pane.

A user account is required for access to Mac OS X. If your computer has multiple users, you enter the name and password for your account when you log in. Each user has his or her own Users folder, with a personalized Library folder contained within. This arrangement is how each user maintains customized preferences. It is also how Mac OS X determines each user's access privileges.

In addition to providing local access to your computer (by controlling who can walk up to it and log in), user accounts control who can access your Mac remotely. If you want someone to be able to access files on your computer over the Internet or a local network (as discussed in detail in "Setting up System Preferences: Sharing" later in this chapter), that user must have an account on your computer—even if he or she will never use the computer in person.

## Adding a user

As an administrative user, you can add new users to the system. To do so, click the New User button. The resulting dialog box has two tabs: Identity and Password.

**Identity.** The Identity tab is where you provide the user's Name and Short Name. The Short Name is a nickname or shortened version (eight characters or fewer, with no spaces) of the full name. When you create a new user, a new folder is created in the /Users directory, with the user's Short Name being the folder name.

You can also choose a small icon to represent the user. (You can choose among Apple's included pictures or browse for one of your own.) If you have chosen to show the list of users at login (a choice you make in the Login System Preferences pane), this picture will appear next to the user's name.

**Password.** The Password tab is where you give the new user account a password. You can supply an optional hint to help the user if he or she forgets the password.

From here, you can also choose to give the new user administrative access by checking the Allow user to administer this computer checkbox. Be cautious— as an administrator, a user will have virtually the same access to the computer that you have, including the ability to access other users' data. The only exception is that the account of the original administrator (presumably you) cannot be modified by other administrators, although the current version of Mac OS X appears to have some bugs that may circumvent even this exception.

By choosing Edit User for their own accounts (as described in the following section), users can change their own passwords, password hints, and pictures, but not their names (short or long).

**SEE:** • "Privileges," in Chapter 3, and "Take Note: Mac OS X and Multiple Users," in Chapter 6, for more details on what it means to be an administrative user.

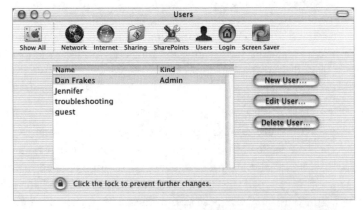

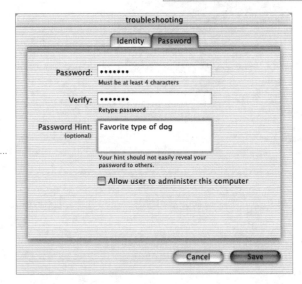

*Figure 8.12*

*The Users System Preferences pane: (from top) the main dialog box and the Identity and Password tabs that appear when you choose New User or Edit User.*

# Editing a user

As an administrator, you can edit any existing user's account by selecting the user's name and clicking the Edit User button. You can change the long name, password, icon, and administrative access. But you cannot change the short name.

The way to change the short name is via NetInfo Manager, but Mac OS X does not make this easy to do. First, you need to launch NetInfo Manager and click the padlock icon (entering your password when requested) so that you have permission to make changes. Then you will need to change virtually every instance of the short name in the database to whatever new name you want. For starters, choose *users* in the Directory Browser and then click the name you want to change. Thus, for the name *tedmac*, you would go to users:tedmac. In the fields that now appear in the bottom area of the window, change every instance of the old name to the new name. Next, you will need to change the name listed in all groups of which the user is a member (such as groups:admin and groups:wheel). Because you easily could overlook something and, thus, fail to get the change to work (or possibly mess things up so that nothing works), I recommend not doing this unless you are absolutely sure that it is necessary. Overall, it usually is easier to create a new account with the name you want to use and transfer the files to that account.

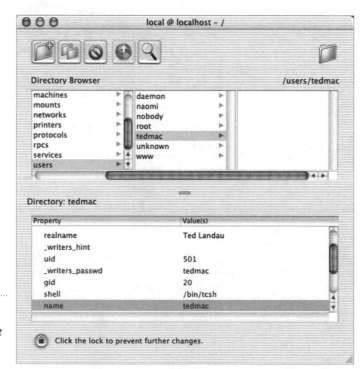

*Figure 8.13*

NetInfo Manager with the user:tedmac fields visible at the bottom of the window.

**Editing as the root user.** I once had a situation where my account mysteriously lost its administrative user status. As I was the only administrator on the system, there was no other user who could log in and restore my status. Fortunately, I had previously enabled the root user account. The solution was to log out of my account, login as a root user and access the Users System Preference. From here, I could re-enable administrative status for myself.

## Deleting a user

If you want to delete a user account, select the user's name and click the Delete User button. You will see a warning dialog box, asking whether you really want to delete the user. In addition, the dialog box will ask you for the administrator account to which you want to reassign the User folder. Because each user account has a corresponding folder in the /Users directory, and because each folder might have important files inside, when you delete a user, Mac OS X reassigns ownership of that folder and its files to the account of the administrator who deleted it. Then the folder is renamed, from *username* to *username Deleted*. At this point, the administrator can save the contents of the folder elsewhere or delete them. You cannot simply drag the folder itself to the Trash, however, as you do not have sufficient permission to do so.

SEE: • "Technically Speaking: Delete a Deleted User's Folder," in Chapter 6, for details on how to delete a deleted user's folder completely.

# Setting up System Preferences: Sharing

The Sharing System Preferences pane is where you control whether users on other computers have access to your computer and its contents. You can provide access via File Sharing, Web Sharing, FTP, and terminal (SSH) connections. You can also choose whether to allow remote Apple events.

The Sharing System Preferences pane consists of two tabs: File & Web and Application. The bottom of the pane remains the same, regardless of which tab you select, and that is where you give your computer a name. This name identifies your computer when users attempt to connect to it. Just below your computer name is your current IP address (which is needed for IP-based remote connections); you set this address in the Network System Preferences pane.

If you are using a router or an AirPort Base Station, the IP address likely will apply only to connections across a local network (such as computers connected to the router). To access your computer via the Internet, you will need to know the IP address for the router or AirPort Base Station. You can find out the address via the software for that device. For an AirPort Base Station, for example, you can access the IP address by launching the AirPort Admin utility, choosing the option to configure the Base Station, and clicking the Internet tab. Note that you may need to turn on port mapping to allow Internet access to your computer if it is behind a router.

**SEE:** • "Technically Speaking: Internet Routers and Port Mapping," later in this chapter.

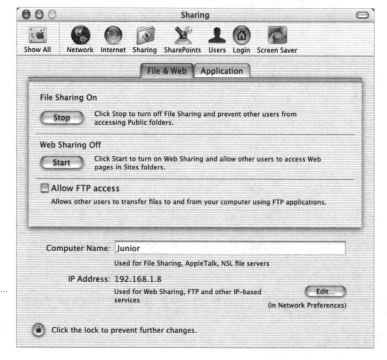

**Figure 8.14**

*The File & Web tab of the Sharing System Preferences pane.*

## File & Web tab

**File Sharing** is a way to allow users (specifically, those users who have accounts and, in a more limited capacity, guest users) to access files on your Mac from another Mac. To enable access via File Sharing, click the Start button in the File Sharing Off section. After a few seconds, the text should change from File Sharing Off to File Sharing On, and the Start button should change to Stop. Now users can log into your Mac from any other computer running Mac OS X. In addition, most Macs running Mac OS 9 or older can connect via AppleShare (which they access in the Chooser) or the Network Browser application.

You can turn File Sharing off by clicking the Stop button.

If you enabled AppleTalk in the Network System Preferences pane, and the remote computer is also on a local AppleTalk network, you should be able to connect via AppleTalk. This method is the simplest way to go, as it does not require any knowledge of the Mac's IP address. Otherwise, you will need to connect via TCP/IP, based on the IP address of the Mac.

**SEE: • "Using Connect to Server," later in this chapter, for more details.**

File Sharing in Mac OS X is similar to File Sharing in the classic Mac OS. One area in which Mac OS X differs from Mac OS 9 and earlier is with respect to *which* files remote users can access. In Mac OS 9, you could select a folder in the Finder and then choose Sharing to set up File Sharing access to that folder, including which users had access. In Mac OS X, remote access is determined largely by User accounts. Aside from Guest access, only those users who have accounts set up on it can access the Mac. Further, the limitations of their access is determined largely by the limitations they have when they're logged in locally.

A nonadministrative user who logs in *locally* using his own account, for example, will have access primarily to the files in his own Home directory, plus the files in other users' Public and Sites folders. The Public and Sites folders have privileges set to allow everyone read access. Thus, other users will be able to view the contents of the folder, as well as to open (but not edit) any documents contained therein. Those same users can also run applications in the Applications folder and can open and read many other system files, but they cannot edit or move those files.

**SEE: • Chapter 3 and 6 for more details on privileges and permissions; normal and admin users; root users; and Public, Site, and Drop Box folders.**

A nonadministrative user who logs in to his own account from another computer, via File Sharing, will have similar access to when logged in locally. There are several differences however:

- You cannot access the Shared folder in the /Users folder via File Sharing unless you are an administrator. Local nonadministrative users, however, can view the contents of the Shared folder, as well as access the files themselves, provided that the owner of each file has granted permission to other users. Thus, you should not place files in the Shared folder if you want remote users to be able to access them.

- Although users who are logged into your computer locally can view and access nonuser files on mounted volumes, users who are logged in remotely can view *only* their own User folders and the Public folders of other users. They cannot access the Sites folder of other users via File Sharing (although the contents may be accessed via Web Sharing).

- Though there is no guest account for local login, someone who doesn't have an account on your computer can log in remotely as a guest. Guest-user access is limited to Public folders.

- When logged in locally, even an administrator cannot access the contents of other users' nonpublic files unless they use root access to do so. An administrator, however, can access other users' nonpublic files when connecting to the computer remotely.

The preceding items assume that you are using Mac OS X's default sharing settings, also referred to as share points. Mac OS X provides no user-friendly way to change these settings, so you are most likely using the defaults. In Mac OS X, unlike Mac OS 9, you cannot select a particular folder in the Finder and assign File Sharing privileges to it separately. You can do this, however, via NetInfo Manager or via third-party software such as SharePoints.

**SEE:** • "Take Note: Using SharePoints," later in this chapter.

---

**TECHNICALLY SPEAKING ▶ Enabling AppleShare Logging**

In Mac OS 9 and earlier, File Sharing kept a log of all File Sharing activity that you, as the owner of your computer, could view. Mac OS X also has this capability, but it is turned off by default. To enable File Sharing logging, follow these steps:

1. Turn File Sharing on by clicking Start in the Sharing Preferences dialog box.

2. Open NetInfo Manager (in /Applications/Utilities).

3. Authenticate by clicking the lock icon and entering your password.

   This step assumes that your user account has administrative access.

4. In the middle column of the Directory Browser, click config.

5. In the right column, click AppleFile Server.

   The Directory (bottom) pane of NetInfo Manager will list all the properties in the AppleFileServer Directory.

6. Locate the property called activity_log, and double-click the Value(s) field to edit it.

   Its value should be 0.

7. Change the value of the activity_log property to 1 to turn on File Sharing logging.

8. Save your changes by choosing Save from the Domain menu.

9. Stop File Sharing (in the Sharing Preferences dialog box) and then start it again.

The next time someone logs into your Mac remotely via File Sharing, a log file named AppleFileServiceAccess.log will be created in the /Library/Logs/AppleFileService/ directory. The log's contents will be updated as it logs all future File Sharing activity. You can best view the contents by opening the log file in the Console application.

You can also enable AppleShare logging by using the third-party utility SharePoints.

**TAKE NOTE ▶ Using SharePoints**

By default, File Sharing in Mac OS X shares only the Public and Sites folders of each user's Home directory. But you can share other folders by creating other *share points*—Mac OS X's term for a shared directory. You can create and modify share points by using NetInfo Manager. An easier (and safer) way, however, is to use a third-party utility that simplifies this process. My favorite is SharePoints.

SharePoints is available as a stand-alone application or as a pane that shows up in the System Preferences application window. Although both options operate identically and provide the same functionality, the pane version is a bit more accessible (because you generally have the System Preferences window open when you are working with sharing anyway). Before making any changes, select SharePoint's Click to allow changes button and enter your administrator's password.

**Adding share points.** To add a share point, follow these steps:

1. Click the lock icon to authenticate your user name.

2. Click the "Normal" Shares tab.

3. Enter a name for your share point in the Share Name field.

4. In the Directory field, enter the path to the folder you want to share (or click the Browse button to navigate to the folder).

5. Select the Show File System Properties button to get the extended window to appear.

*continues on next page*

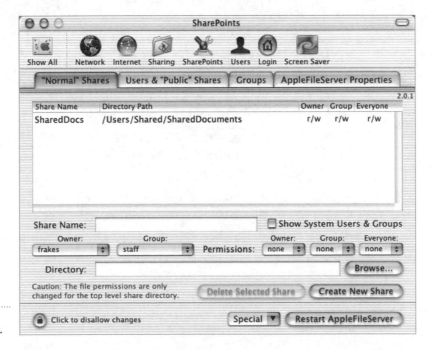

**Figure 8.15**

*The SharePoints utility main screen.*

**TAKE NOTE ▶ Using SharePoints** *continued*

6. In the extended window, set the owner and group for the folder via the Owner and Group menus.

7. Set the permissions for the folder via the three Permissions menus.

   If you set the permissions for Everyone to Read or Read/Write, any remote user can view the new share point. Note that these permissions apply only to the top-level folder; enclosed files and folders will keep their original permissions for security reasons. If you want enclosed files and folders to reflect the new permissions, you'll need to set them separately, using the Finder's Show Info window or a utility such as XRay.

8. Click the Create New Share button to create the new share point.

If you want to add another share point, repeat these steps.

To remove a share point from the list, click it and select the Delete Selected Share button. This will not undo changes you may have made to owner, group, and permissions settings, but it will prevent the folder from being accessed via File Sharing.

To edit an existing share point, make the desired changes and click the Update Share button.

**Unsharing a public share point.** SharePoints also allows you to *prevent* the sharing of a user's Public folder. If you want to disable Public-folder sharing, follow these steps:

1. Click the Users & "Public" Shares tab.

2. In the user column on the left, select the user whose Public folder you do not want to share.

3. Click the Disable Selected button below "Public" Directory Shares; or choose No from the Public Directory Shared? menu.

4. Click the Update User button.

**File Sharing Only users.** A handy feature of SharePoints allows you to create File Sharing Only users. These users can log in *only* via File Sharing . These users do not need to have local accounts, and they cannot log in via a terminal connection or FTP. To create a File Sharing Only user, follow these steps:

1. Click the Users & "Public" Shares tab, but do *not* click an existing user.

2. Fill in the information for the user in the Full Name, Short Name, Group, and UID fields.

   You can click Get Next UID if you are unsure what number to assign.

3. Click the Add New User button.

   You will be asked whether you're sure that you want to add a File Sharing Only user; then you will be asked to enter a password for the new user.

*continues on next page*

**TAKE NOTE** ▶ **Using SharePoints**  *continued*

**Create new groups.** As discussed in Chapters 3 and 6, each file and folder in Mac OS X is assigned to a group. You can view an item's group by opening the Show Info window for the item and viewing the Privileges tab. Software such as XRay allows you to change the group assignment for an item but does not allow you to create or delete groups. You *can* do this via SharePoints—something that you otherwise can accomplish only via NetInfo Manager. To do so, follow these steps:

1. Click the *Groups* tab.

2. In the Group field, type a name for the new group.

3. Click the Get Next GID button to have SharePoints find the next available group ID number.

4. Click the Add New Group button.

5. To add users to the group, select it in the Group window on the left; then add users by selecting user names in the user window on the right and clicking the addition (plus) button.

**Final step.** After making any changes in SharePoints, you need to click the Restart AppleFileServer button, which is the same as stopping and starting File Sharing manually in the Sharing Preferences dialog box.

**Web Sharing.** To enable Web Sharing, click the Start button in the Web Sharing Off section of the File & Web tab. The Start button should change to a Stop button, and the title should change to Web Sharing On.

With Web Sharing on, anyone can use a Web browser from any computer connected to the Internet to access Web pages created and stored in the Sites folder of any User directories on your computer (whether or not the person has a user account on your computer).

To access the contents of the pages in a specific Sites folder, type http:// followed by the IP address of the computer, a forward slash, a tilde, and the user's short name. For example, to access the Sites folder contents for a user named naomi on a computer with an IP address of 68.62.15.134, you would type: http://68.62.15.134/~naomi/. If you have not placed anything in the Sites folder yourself, a default index.html page supplied by Apple will appear.

When using Web Sharing, be aware of the following considerations:

- You can find the IP address for your computer (needed for the URL to access your site) in the bottom of the File & Web tab of the Sharing System Preference. However, if you use a router, this is not the address you need. Instead, you need the WAN IP address as listed by your router.

**SEE:** • **"Take Note: Internet Routers," earlier in this chapter.**

- Unless the shared computer has a static IP address (which is unlikely for users with a dial-up or a DHCP connection), the IP address will change periodically. You cannot use these dynamic IP addresses as permanent URLs. One solution is to get a static IP address, if your ISP provides this option. Otherwise, you may be able to use a *dynamic DNS service*. This assigns your machine a permanent name that remains linked to your machine despite changes in the IP address. One site that offers this service is **www.dyndns.org**. A final option, desirable if you expect frequent access to your web site, is to get a static IP address and register a domain name (such as www.*yourname*.com) via www.networksolutions.com.

- If you type just `http://` followed by the IP address for your machine (`http://68.62.15.134`, for example), you will get whatever Web pages are stored in /Library/WebServer/Documents. Mac OS X places a default index.html page in that folder, but you can replace it with your own custom pages.

- When accessing a user's Web page, be sure to put a slash after the name in the URL. That is, for example, type `/~naomi/`, not just `/~naomi`. If you leave off the last slash, you will get a localhost error (it will attempt to connect to 127.0.0.1 and fail).

- If you are using a router, accessing a user's Sites folder will likely require that you open Port 80 for the computer. This is done via the router's port mapping/forwarding feature.

**SEE:**  • **"Technically Speaking: Internet Routers and Port Mapping," later in this chapter.**

- If you want to check out how your own Web pages look in a browser via Web Sharing, you can do so most easily by substituting the word *localhost* for the IP address. Thus, Naomi could check out her site from her computer by typing `http://localhost/~naomi/`. You could also substitute 127.0.0.1 for localhost, or even omit any text at all, just by typing `http:///~naomi/` (notice the third slash).

- Via Web Sharing, unlike File Sharing, a remote user cannot access *any* files outside the Sites folder or the computer's WebServer Documents folder, which makes Web Sharing a more secure way to share files with the public than File Sharing. A user can access only files linked from a Web page accessible from the home page or via a specific URL you have given them. Thus, if Naomi placed a compressed file called *myapp.sit* in her Sites folder, a user could download it via the following URL: http://68.62.15.134/~naomi/myapp.sit.

- If a site has a document named index.html, that document will be used as the home page of the Web site. If such a document does not exist in a Sites folder, anyone trying to view the default page will receive an error message. The default setting is to *not* display directory contents.

- When you enable Web Sharing, you are actually activating a full installation of the widely used (and powerful) Apache Web server for Unix, which is included in Mac OS X. If you are familiar with Unix, you can access many more-advanced Web Sharing features (such as working with Perl scripts and CGI commands) via Apache commands entered in Terminal.

Note: An alternative, and simpler, way to create a Web site is to set it up on your iDisk via Apple's HomePage feature. This method has the advantage of providing a permanent URL that you can give other users.

**Allow FTP Access.** If you enable the Allow FTP Access checkbox, that option starts Mac OS X's built-in FTP server. Anyone with an account on your computer and an FTP client (such as Fetch, OsXigen, or RBrowser) will be able to connect to your computer and browse files by entering the IP or domain name of your computer, along with a user name and password.

Because most Web browsers support the FTP protocol, you can do this via a Web browser as well. If you type ftp://{IPaddress} in Internet Explorer, for example, a dialog box will appear, asking for a name and password. If you have an account on the specified computer, enter your name and password, and you will get a directory listing of your home directory. Each directory item will be a link; click it to view the contents of the directory. If you click a file, it is downloaded to your computer.

Note that if the Allow FTP Access checkbox is checked, FTP access will be enabled even if you have File Sharing and Web Sharing disabled.

FTP access limits users to the same access that they would have if they were physically sitting at the computer. They will have full read/write access to their own User folders, as well as read access to other users' Public folders, but they will also have read access to most other system-level files. Because read access via FTP means the ability to view and download, FTP users will be able to download system, application, and settings files located outside private User folders. They won't be able to alter or delete these files, but you should stop to consider whether you have sensitive files or information in nonprivate areas of your computer.

## Application tab

The Application tab settings of Sharing System Preferences are only needed if you intend to log in to your computer remotely (that is, from another computer not on your local network).

**Allow Remote Login (Terminal access).** Checking the Allow remote login checkbox in the Application tab allows users to access your computer via Telnet/SSH applications. You can even use Mac OS X's Terminal application for making this type of remote connection. Again, doing this assumes some familiarity with Unix.

Allowing remote login can be useful in some troubleshooting situations, as it may be possible to access an apparently frozen Mac remotely via SSH from another Mac. This method may, for example, allow you to modify or delete files that are preventing the Mac from starting up without freezing.

SEE: • "Technically Speaking: Secure Connections," later in this chapter.

• "Technically Speaking: Telnet to a Frozen Mac: Kill Processes, Run Sync," in Chapter 5.

**Allow Remote Apple Events.** Enabling Allow Remote Apple events allows AppleScripts running from remote computers to interact with your computer. Unless you have a specific reason to allow such scripts and applications from a trusted user, you should keep this option turned off, as someone could do some very malicious things to your computer by using Apple Events and AppleScripts.

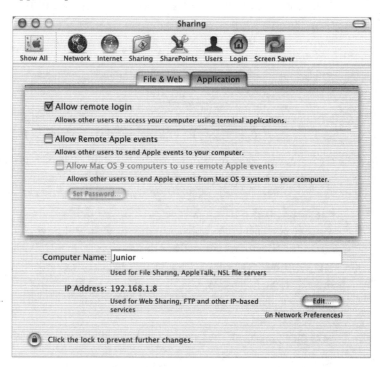

*Figure 8.16*

*The Application tab of the Sharing System Preferences pane.*

**TECHNICALLY SPEAKING ▶ Secure Connections**

Back in the days of Mac OS 9, if you wanted to connect two computers, you used common methods such as FTP or Telnet. The problem with these methods is that all text, including passwords, is sent as clear text, making it a bit too easy for hackers to grab your address and password. These methods are especially risky in a Mac OS X environment, where knowing your password could give someone administrative access to your computer.

The solution is something called SSH (secure shell). Programs that use the SSH protocol transmit text in an encrypted format, making it harder to crack. If you have enabled Allow FTP access or Allow remote login, you need to worry about this security.

Fortunately, Mac OS X built SSH into its Unix software via the OpenSSH service. To access it, launch Terminal, and use the ssh command (instead of telnet) and the sftp command (instead of ftp).

Note: When you use the ssh command, if you type ssh {*domain name* or *IP address of server*}, the command will attempt to log you on with your Mac OS X user name. To use a different name (such as the name you use on the server to which you are trying to connect), type ssh {*name of server*} -1 {*your name*}.

If you are attempting to connect to a computer running Mac OS X, you cannot use the telnet command. You must use ssh. This is determined by settings in the inetd.conf file, stored in the etc directory. Should you want to allow the less-secure alternatives, you can do so by deleting the # symbol in front of the #telnet, #shell, and #login lines of this file. You can do this from Terminal, of course, using a Terminal-based text editor such as pico. Or you can use BBEdit, which allows you to open hidden files and make changes as root (as discussed in Chapter 6).

For those who are not comfortable with Terminal, there are more user-friendly SSH alternatives. I especially like the shareware program RBrowser. TelnetLauncher is another popular choice.

## Sharing from non-Mac OS computers

If you want to share files with users on non-Mac OS computers, you can use Web Sharing, FTP, or SSH. Because each of these protocols is platform-independent, any user on a Windows, Unix, or any other computer can connect by using a Web browser, FTP client, or Telnet/SSH client, respectively. Using Web Sharing or guest access with File Sharing, users don't even need to have a user account.

**TAKE NOTE ▶ Sharing via Target Disk Mode**

If you have two or more computers connected on a local network, enabling File Sharing is a convenient way to transfer files. You can use this method to transfer files from a desktop computer to a laptop before going on a trip, for example.

For these basic file transfers, however, you can use an even easier and faster method: FireWire Target Disk mode. This method requires that both computers have a FireWire port. In Target Disk mode, one Mac acts as though it were an external FireWire hard drive that is mounted by the other computer. Then you can transfer files back and forth between the two computers at the same speed as if you had actually attached an external FireWire drive (which is significantly faster than the Ethernet connection used by File Sharing).

To use Target Disk mode, follow these steps:

1. Turn off the computer you want to use as an external drive (the target computer).
2. If you haven't already, turn on the main computer, and log in to your account.
3. Connect the two computers via a standard FireWire cable.
4. Turn on the target computer, and hold down the T key until you see the FireWire symbol on its screen.

When you see the FireWire symbol, the target computer should be mounted and accessible on the main computer.

To stop using Target Disk mode, follow these steps:

1. Drag the mounted computer/drive to the Trash (which changes to an eject symbol), or select it and press Command-E to unmount it.
2. Disconnect the FireWire cable.
3. Press the Power button on the "hard drive" Mac to turn it off.

It is important not to turn off or disconnect the target computer before you unmount it. Doing so risks damage to the data on your drive.

**TAKE NOTE ▶ Sharing via Timbuktu and Apple Remote Desktop**

The Timbuktu Pro application from Netopia (www.netopia.com) offers an alternative way to share files between two computers (even Mac OS and Windows computers). With Timbuktu Pro, you can go beyond simply sharing files; you can control a remote computer just as though you were sitting in front of it. The desktop of the remote computer opens in a window on your computer. You can observe the remote computer for collaborative work or for helping another user troubleshoot; you can even send instant messages and voice messages to the remote computer. Timbuktu Pro supports Mac OS X's Users and Privileges settings.

Apple's recently released Apple Remote Desktop provides a similar alternative. It is designed primarily for classroom environments, so that an instructor can have access to the computers of all students.

## TECHNICALLY SPEAKING ▶ Internet Routers and Port Mapping

Many users connect multiple computers to a single Internet connection, using an Internet router or AirPort Base Station and creating a small internal network (as described in "Take Note: Internet Routers," earlier in this chapter).

When it is set up, this system generally works well. If you plan to enable sharing for nonlocal users, however, an Internet router complicates things a bit. The key is that for most traffic, your Internet router knows where to send incoming Internet data because it keeps track of which computer on your network requested it. The problem with using sharing to share files with nonlocal users is that someone behind your Internet router does not initiate the connection. Rather, someone outside your home or office tries to connect to your computer via your external IP address—which basically is your router. Then your router has to decide which computer should receive the incoming data.

*continues on next page*

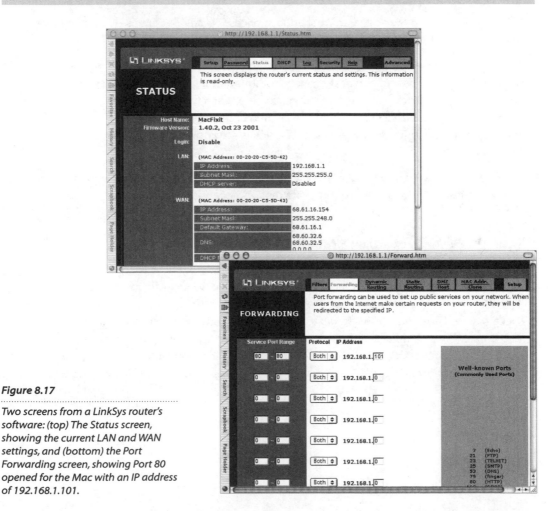

*Figure 8.17*

*Two screens from a LinkSys router's software: (top) The Status screen, showing the current LAN and WAN settings, and (bottom) the Port Forwarding screen, showing Port 80 opened for the Mac with an IP address of 192.168.1.101.*

**TECHNICALLY SPEAKING** ▶ **Internet Routers and Port Mapping** *continued*

Although this problem may sound serious, the good news is that most modern Internet routers have added support for such scenarios, using what is called port mapping (or port forwarding). In addition to its IP address, every server has *ports* that generally are reserved for different types of connections. When you point your Web browser to www.servername.com, for example, you're actually connecting to www.servername.com:80. Port 80 generally is the network port that receives requests for Web pages on a Web server.

Because each sharing service uses only certain ports, you can use port mapping to tell the router than any incoming requests that use a given port should be directed to a specific computer. For example, AFP (AppleShare, File Sharing, Apple File Service) uses port 548. If you open port 548 for one of several computers connected to your router, all File Sharing requests from the Internet will be directed to that computer. Using this feature requires that the computer have a manual IP address; thus, you could not assign addresses via DHCP. Also, a given port cannot be opened on more than one computer.

A list of ports used by various Mac OS sharing services is available via this Apple Knowledge Base document: `http://docs.info.apple.com/article.html?artnum=106439`.

The specifics of how to enable port sharing varies a bit from router to router. In general, there is a location to specify the port or ports you wish to open. In the same row, there will be a location to specify an IP address of the computer to be opened for that port. Thus, to open port 80, for Web sharing on a specific computer, you would enter 80 as the port and enter the IP address of the computer you wish to share (which is the address as listed in the computer's TCP/IP pane).

Some routers offer an additional solution: You can specify one computer to be the DMZ host. This computer will receive all incoming data requests of any type.

**TAKE NOTE** ▶ **Protection: Firewalls and Antivirus Software**

Traditionally, Mac OS computers have been among the most secure computers in terms of vulnerability to network attacks, hackers, and the like. Mac OS X continues in this trend. Mac OS X's Unix base has the potential to be more vulnerable than the classic Mac OS, if only because hackers have spent many more hours trying to break into Unix servers than Mac servers. But Mac OS X ships with most sharing services (File Sharing, FTP access, Terminal access, Web Server, and so on) disabled. So you are not vulnerable unless you choose to be. If you *do* decide to enable any short of sharing, you will likely want to enable some firewall protection.

*continues on next page*

**TAKE NOTE ▶ Protection: Firewalls and Antivirus Software** *continued*

Historically, most personal computers did not need much in the way of firewall protection. They were connected to the Internet via a dial-up connection (making the computer difficult for a hacker to nail down and preventing high-bandwidth data transfers) or on a company network that was protected behind an industrial-strength firewall managed by an IT person.

The widespread use of broadband connections, however, means that more and more computers are permanently connected to the Internet, which means more availability and greater bandwidth. In addition, computer users are more and more Internet-savvy, and the increased bandwidth has led many people to use the various sharing technologies discussed in this chapter, creating more openings for malicious people to try to exploit.

### Firewalls

The solution to many of these concerns is to set up a firewall between your computer and the outside world. A firewall can be either hardware or software. It sits between your computer (or network) and the Internet, watching the traffic coming and going, looking for anything suspicious. If the firewall detects something malicious, it tries to block it.

*   **Software.** For home users, software solutions generally are more user-friendly and more practical than hardware solutions. Actually, turning off options, such as File Sharing and Web Sharing, in Sharing System Preferences, is a form of firewall protection. But Sharing does not offer the range of options available with more full-featured firewall software. Sometimes, for example, you may want the Sharing options enabled but still retain a level of firewall protection. There are several firewall software packages you can purchase that can do this. However, Mac OS X actually has a pretty good package built right in, via Unix. Unfortunately, Apple didn't provide a way to configure it in Mac OS X 10.1, other than via Terminal.

    Once again, third-party solutions have come to the rescue. Several elegant software applications allow you to configure and manage Mac OS X's built-in firewall, including BrickHouse (my favorite), Impasse, and Sunshield.

    If you are familiar with Unix, you can access the firewall software directly, via the `<ipfw>` command in Terminal.

    A few alternatives do not rely on Mac OS X's built-in firewall; these programs include Firewalk X and NetBarrier.

*   **Hardware.** Many Internet routers have some type of firewall protection built in. If you are using an Internet router, before you go out and get a software firewall utility, check with the manufacturer of your router to see what type of firewall functionality it provides. LinkSys and Macsense are two popular brands of routers that include firewall protection.

    One other form of firewall protection is to turn off specific ports that otherwise would permit access to your computer (as described in "Technically Speaking: Internet Routers and Port Mapping" earlier in this chapter). Another method is to block access to the IP address of your computer via Network Address Translation (as described in "Take Note: Internet Routers" earlier in this chapter). See the documentation of your firewall software/hardware for specifics.

*continues on next page*

**TAKE NOTE ▶ Protection: Firewalls and Antivirus Software** *continued*

Proxy settings (as set via the Proxies tab of Network System Preferences) also serve as a form of firewall protection. However, proxies are typically only used in large network environments. To find out if you need or can use proxies, check with your Network Administrator.

*Viruses*

A firewall will not necessarily protect you from a computer virus, because many viruses arrive at your computer via email messages or downloaded files that you deliberately permitted to bypass the firewall. As a result, it is wise to have some sort of antivirus software on your computer. Norton AntiVirus, for example, now works with Mac OS X.

Note: Although no known viruses currently target Mac OS X, your Mac can still act as a carrier for passing on viruses to PC users, via email.

You should also know that many claims of potential virus attacks are actually hoaxes. There are several Web sites where you can learn more about viruses, both real and hoaxes. Symantec's SARC (**www.sarc.com**) site is a good place to start.

# Using Connect to Server

Under Mac OS X, the primary way to connect to another computer is via the Connect to Server item in the Finder's Go menu. The way to use the Connect to Server dialog box differs if the computer is local (on a local network) or remote (located outside your local network).

## Local area network (LAN) connections

To connect to another computer on a local network, simply choose Connect to Server from the Go menu. A dialog box will open.

**Connect to Server dialog box.** The terms *AppleTalk* and *Local Network* will likely appear in the list box on the left side of the window. Click the disclosure triangle to the right of the At pop-up menu if the list is not visible. If you click either term, a list of accessible computers on these networks appears in the next column, sorted by name (the name given to the computers in the Sharing System Preferences pane). There may be a brief delay before the computer names appear.

If AppleTalk has been enabled, the same computer may be listed below both headings. If so, you can connect via either option (AppleTalk or Local Network). If one method of connection seems to be faster or more reliable than the other, use that one. Otherwise, you can flip a coin. Some devices may be accessible only via AppleTalk or via the TCP/IP connection used for Local Network; in these cases, there is no choice to be made.

If the computer you want to access does not appear, you can try to connect to it by entering its address in the text box at the bottom of the Connect to Server dialog box. Addresses usually begin with afp. For local networks, simply enter `afp://{IPaddress}`. For AppleTalk, the address typically is `afp:/at/{computername}:*`. Note: You can obtain the IP address and computer name from the Sharing System Preference. If even this method does not work, sharing may not be enabled for the computer you want to access, or there may be other network-related problems. I discuss these possibilities in the "Troubleshooting File Sharing and Internet" section at the end of this chapter.

If you recently accessed a computer or server from the Connect to Server dialog box, its name should appear in the Recent Servers list in the At pop-up menu. If you want to save the name in the At menu permanently, select the server name and click the Add to Favorites button. These features allow you to make a connection more easily. Just choose the name from the menu to access that server.

After selecting the desired computer/server, click the Connect button.

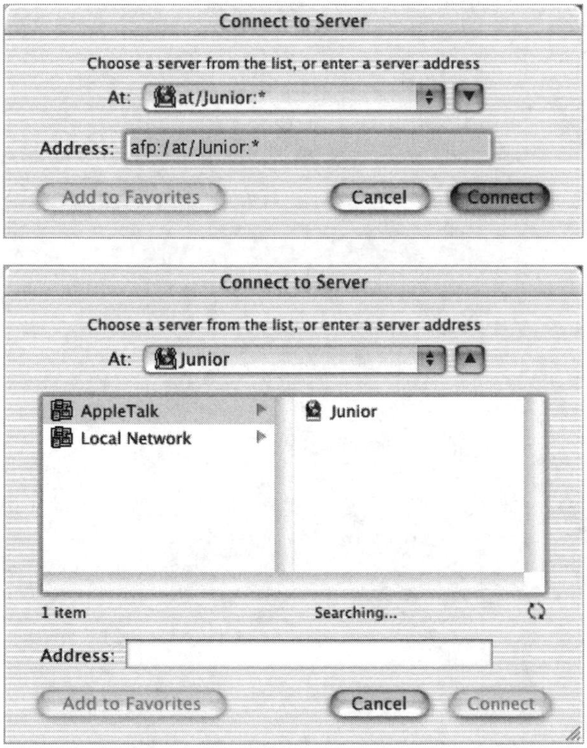

*Figure 8.18*

*The Connect to Server dialog box: (top) collapsed and (bottom) expanded.*

**Login dialog box.** If all goes well, a login window will appear after clicking Connect. From here, you can connect either as a guest (if the destination computer has this option enabled; all Mac OS X computers do) or as a registered user. In the latter case, you enter the name and password for your account on the Mac OS X computer. When done, click the Connect button.

For registered users, the Options button is enabled. Clicking this button allows you to modify several features, including Add Password to Keychain (so that you don't have to enter it the next time you connect). You also have the options to use a clear-text password and change your password.

*Figure 8.19*

*(From top) The Login dialog box, the window that appears after you log in as an administrative user (showing volumes and the admin account), and the window that appears after you log in as a guest (showing user accounts).*

**Volumes dialog box.** Next, another dialog box will appear, containing a list of volumes you may mount. Generally, the list contains all the users on the computer to which you are connecting. Select the volumes/users you want to mount, and click OK.

If you are a guest, all you will see is the names of users with accounts on the computer. You select the users whose Public folders you want to access. A guest has no other access. If you are a nonadministrator registered user, the procedure is the same, except that selecting your own folder will provide you full access to it. If a utility such as SharePoints has set up additional access, these directories will also be listed.

If you are an administrative user, you'll instead see a list containing your user Home directory name plus all currently mounted volumes and partitions. Again, select which volumes you wish to mount. Note: It is important that you do not connect to both your Home directory and the volume that contains that directory at the same time. Doing so would allow you to try to move a file from a folder in your Home directory to the same folder on the full volume, resulting in the loss of the file.

**Connection complete.** After you select which user folders or volumes you want to access, each one shows up as a separate volume in the Computer directory in a Finder window or on your Desktop (if you have chosen to show connected servers on the Desktop via the Finder Preferences dialog box). Double-clicking your own volume will open your personal Users folder. Double-clicking another user's volume opens that user's Public folder. You will be able to view any files in the user's Public folder, as well as drop files in the user's Drop Box. As discussed in Chapter 6, you can drop files into another user's Drop Box but cannot view its contents. Think of it as being a mailbox for that user; it's a safe way to deliver something to the user, but after you drop the file in, it's gone. (Before dropping a file in a user's Drop Box, make sure you've given that user privileges to read the file or to read and write it, if you prefer.) Again, if you are an administrative user, you will have complete access to the entire contents of the Mac OS X volume, including other users' folders, not just their Public folders.

You disconnect from the server by dragging its icon to the Trash. Before you do so, you can make an alias of the server icon via the Finder's Make Alias (Command-L) command. You can use this alias as a shortcut method to reconnect to the server.

**SEE:** • "Take Note: Connect to Servers via Aliases and Location Files," later in this chapter, for more details.

# Remote (wide area network; WAN) connections

If you are connecting to a remote computer, you will not see it listed in the Connect to Server dialog box below the AppleTalk or Local Network heading. You will need to enter the computer's protocol and IP address/domain name. In the Address field, type this information in the format {*protocol*}://{*IPaddress* or *name*}. Mac OS X supports several protocols:

- AppleShare, via AppleTalk or TCP/IP (example: afp://{*IPaddress* or *name*})
- WebDAV (Web Distributed Authoring and Versioning), which basically is an extension of HTML that allows for functionality much like File Sharing (example: http:// {*IPaddress* or *name*}/{*path*}/)
- SMB, the native sharing protocol for Windows (example: smb://{*IPaddress* or name}/{*sharename*}/)
- NFS exports, a common way that Unix computers share directory trees (example: nfs://{*IPaddress* or *name*}/{*path*})

You will need to obtain the relevant IP address and path information from the person with whose computer you wish to connect. After you've entered the correct address in the Address field, click the Connect button to connect. You usually will be asked for your user name and password (for the remote computer, not yours).

As is the case with local computers, after you've accessed a remote computer or server from the Connect to Server dialog box, it is saved in the At pop-up menu for easy access in the future.

# iDisks

If you have an iTools account from Apple, you have an iDisk: a storage space on Apple's iTools servers. As explained in "Setting up System Preferences: Internet," earlier in this chapter, the typical way to connect to iDisk is to choose the iDisk command from the Finder's Go menu. Doing this mounts the iDisk volume on your Desktop as though it were an external drive.

The iDisk command works only if you have entered the name and password information in the iTools section of the Internet System Preferences pane. If you did not do this, or if you have more than one iDisk that you want to access, you can use the Connect to Server command instead. Enter idisk.mac.com in the Address field. When you click the Connect button, enter the user name and password of the iTools account you want to access.

If you have multiple iDisks, an easier method is to create connection files for them.

**SEE:** • **"Take Note: Connect to Servers via Aliases and Location Files,"** later in this chapter.

Finally, many users find that accessing an iDisk via Mac OS X is quite slow. Just getting a folder to open can take many seconds. In such cases, you may have better success with the shareware program Goliath. It uses the same WebDAV technology employed by Mac OS X to access the iDisk. Rather than having the iDisk mount as a volume on your Desktop, however, Goliath opens its own directory window that lists all the files and folders on your volume. With Goliath, performance is typically much faster than with Mac OS X's native iDisk access.

**Figure 8.20**

*An iDisk icon.*

---

**TAKE NOTE** ▶ **Connect to Servers via Aliases and Location Files**

If you expect to access the same servers repeatedly, you can speed things by creating a file that mounts the server automatically when you double-click it in the Finder. You can use two approaches: aliases and (for AppleTalk servers) AFP Internet Location files.

**Aliases.** The basic idea is to make an alias of a server icon. Afterward, double-clicking the alias mounts the volume automatically. Here's how to set this up:

1. Connect to the volume via the Connect to Server dialog box.

2. When the Login dialog box appears, click the Options button and choose Add Password to Keychain.

   Note: If you skip this step, double-clicking the alias you create will take you back to this Login dialog box rather than mount the volume immediately. This method is still faster than having to go back to the Connect to Server dialog box, but I prefer the express route.

3. Enter your name and password, and click Connect.

4. Mount the volume as usual.

5. In a Finder window, click the Computer button in the toolbar to show all mounted volumes.

6. Click the server's icon, and hold down the mouse button.

7. Hold down the Option and Command keys, and drag the server's icon to the Desktop.

   This step creates an alias to the server.

   If the server icon already appears on the Desktop, you can make the alias directly from that icon by choosing Make Alias from the Finder's File menu.

Now after you disconnect from the volume, you can reconnect at any time (assuming that the volume remains on the network) simply by double-clicking the alias. If you would rather create an alias to a certain subvolume, share point, or directory, you can create an alias to it directly rather than to the main volume.

*continues on next page*

**TAKE NOTE** ▶ **Connect to Servers via Aliases and Location Files** *continued*

You can connect to multiple iDisks at the same time. If you do, however, and if you have created an alias for at least one iDisk, beware of an unusual problem. If you use an alias to connect to an iDisk, connect to a second iDisk at the same time, and then disconnect the *first* iDisk, your alias file will update automatically to point to the second iDisk. There is no workaround for this problem other than to avoid connecting to multiple iDisks at the same time.

**AFP Internet Location files.** Although aliases usually work well, they have some drawbacks. First, some servers do not allow you to add your password to the Keychain, forcing you to enter it every time you connect. Second, aliases to iDisks have a habit of reassigning themselves and no longer working.

For these cases, an alternative solution is to use AFP Internet Location files. These files allow you to include the server address, user name, password, and even a volume or share-point name. The location file then connects automatically when you double-click it.

Creating a location file is not quite as convenient as creating an alias, however. The easiest method is to use a text editor such as TextEdit, as follows:

1. Open TextEdit, and create a new blank document.

2. Type the address of the server, using one of the following formats (substituting the specifics for your server):

   - AppleShare servers:
     afp://*username:password*@{*IPaddress or name*}/

   - Specific volumes on AppleShare servers:
     afp://*username:password*@{*IPaddress or name*}/*volume*

   - Specific share Points on AppleShare servers:
     afp://*username:password*@{*IPaddress or name*}/*sharename*
     (if the share-point name has a space, change the space to %20)

   - iDisks:
     afp://*iToolsUsername:iToolsPassword*@{*IPaddress or name*}/*iToolsUsername*

3. Select the entire address in the text window; then drag it to the Desktop or any folder on your drive.

   A location file with the extension .afploc is created. This file is the same sort of file that is created if you drag a URL from your Web browser to the Desktop. You can place this file anywhere you like (in the Dock, in a folder, and so on).

When you double-click the file, it will connect you to the server automatically and mount it. You can repeat this procedure for every iDisk and server you access. You can even put all these location files in a folder and drag the folder to the Dock to have a pop-up menu of all the servers you use frequently.

**TAKE NOTE ▶ Connecting to Servers at Startup**

Mac OS 9 and earlier had an option to log in to AppleShare servers automatically at startup. Mac OS X does not include such an option directly, but you can accomplish the same functionality by using AFP Internet Location files.

After you create a location file for a server, using the instructions in "Take Note: Connect to Servers via Aliases and Location Files" earlier in this chapter, open the Login System Preferences pane. Click the Login Items tab, and drag the location file into the tab. It's probably best to drag the file to the end of the list so that it loads last.

The next time you log in, the server will be mounted automatically.

# Troubleshooting File Sharing and Internet

I have divided the troubleshooting tips in this section into separate categories, such as wireless connections and modem connections. This division is difficult to do cleanly, however, as categories can combine and interact. You can connect to the Internet via a dial-up modem, for example, which in turn is connected through an AirPort Base Station.

To help you get started, here are some general guidelines:

- If you're having trouble with AppleTalk File Sharing, you should troubleshoot your AppleTalk connection first; if that's working, then you should troubleshoot File Sharing itself.

- If you're having trouble with File Sharing or Web Sharing over the Internet, you should troubleshoot your Internet connection first and then troubleshoot File Sharing or Web Sharing.

- If you are merely attempting to use the Internet but are having trouble, you should concentrate on Internet troubleshooting, because AppleTalk and sharing are not relevant.

- If you have a working Internet connection but are having problems with your Web browser or email client, your problem is most likely with the browser or client. Focus your troubleshooting on the application's settings.

Regardless of the specific likely source of the connection problem, start with these steps:

**Check your hardware connections.** Disconnect and reconnect all cables (Ethernet cables, modem cables, power cables and so on, as appropriate). Make sure that all needed hardware is on and connected properly.

To test whether a problem is with a cable or the Mac, try swapping, if possible. Connect a suspected defective cable to another Mac, for example, and see whether the problem still occurs. Alternatively, try a new cable with the problem Mac.

**Check your Network System Preferences settings.** In the Network System Preferences pane, check and double-check that you have entered all your settings correctly. A single incorrect number or letter could prevent you from accessing the Internet. Having AppleTalk off will prevent any AppleTalk connections.

**Switch Locations and Active Network Port settings.** Changing Locations or Active Network Port settings in Network System Preferences may clear up an assortment of connection problems. I give specific examples in the sections that follow.

SEE:  • "Setting up System Preferences: Network," earlier in this chapter, for information on how to determine your correct settings and switch locations.

## Troubleshooting AppleTalk connections

If you are having trouble accessing AppleTalk devices via File Sharing (or if other users are having trouble accessing your computer via AppleTalk), the following steps will be useful in helping you isolate the cause of the problem.

**Make sure that AppleTalk is active—and active on only a single port.** Under most circumstances, AppleTalk can be active on only a single port at a time. If you have simultaneous Ethernet and AirPort connections or multiple Ethernet cards, and you are having trouble connecting via AppleTalk or printing to AppleTalk printers, make sure that you have enabled AppleTalk only for the connection method you are attempting to use.

The easiest way to do this is to check your port configurations in the Network Preferences dialog box. Check the TCP/IP tab for each configuration, and make sure that Make AppleTalk Active is checked only in a single configuration. If the option is checked for more than one configuration, uncheck the extra checkboxes and then click the Apply Now button.

> **TAKE NOTE** ▶ **AppleTalk Does Not Work When it's Active on Multiple Ports**
>
> If you have AppleTalk active on more than one port, you may find that it does not work on all of them (or on any at all). If you use AirPort for AppleTalk File Sharing but Ethernet for printing to an AppleTalk printer, you may find that Mac OS X cannot find the printer.
>
> The problem is that although Mac OS X supports AppleTalk multihoming (having AppleTalk active on more than one port at the same time), it works properly only under specific circumstances, outlined in an Apple Knowledge Base document titled Mac OS X: How to Set Up AppleTalk Multi-Homing (`http://docs.info.apple.com/article.html?artnum=106614`).
>
> If you require AppleTalk to be active on multiple ports at different times, the best solution is to create multiple locations (as described earlier in this chapter), each with AppleTalk active on a different port.

If it appears that only a single port is using AppleTalk but you are still having problems, it's possible that the Network Preferences dialog box is displaying AppleTalk information incorrectly. To check, you can use Terminal to look directly at the AppleTalk interfaces that are active. To do so, launch Terminal, and type <appletalk –s>. This command displays the active AppleTalk interface information. Each active AppleTalk interface, along with other information about the port (network number, node ID, and current zone). If you have a single listing, AppleTalk is active on a single port. (This command also provides some statistics on AppleTalk traffic; you can safely ignore this information.)

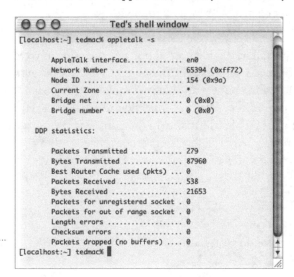

*Figure 8.21*

<appletalk –s>
*output in Terminal.*

The interface designations provided by <appletalk –s> correspond to specific ports on your Mac:

- **en0:** built-in Ethernet port
- **en1:** AirPort card, if installed (if no AirPort card is installed, second Ethernet port)
- **en2:** third Ethernet port (or second Ethernet port, if you have an AirPort card installed)

If the Network System Preferences pane claims that AppleTalk is active for a single port but Terminal tells you otherwise, try resetting the AppleTalk connection as described in the following paragraphs.

**Check whether Mac OS X can see AppleTalk devices.** If AppleTalk appears to be active (in the Network System Preferences pane), but you are unable to connect to AppleTalk devices, you should try to confirm that Mac OS can actually see AppleTalk devices on the network. You can do this by opening Terminal and typing the command <atlookup>.

If <atlookup> returns a list of all connected AppleTalk devices, including your own computer and other computers or printers, you have an active AppleTalk connection and should be able to connect to other AppleTalk devices.

If the command shows only your own computer, this result generally means that AppleTalk is active and that you are connected to an active AppleTalk network but the other devices on the network are not communicating properly. The problem is not with your computer.

If the command returns the message "The AppleTalk stack is not running," either AppleTalk is disabled on all ports or the port on which it is enabled has not experienced any network activity (so AppleTalk has not been initialized on that port). If you connect an Ethernet cable directly to an AppleTalk device or try to initiate a direct AirPort connection to another AirPort device, this action should initiate AppleTalk traffic on the port. If you run <atlookup> again and still get an error, AppleTalk is simply not active on that port. You will need to make sure that you have activated it in the Network System Preferences pane or reset AppleTalk—or both.

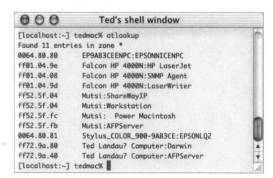

***Figure 8.22***

<atlookup> *output in Terminal.*

**Reset AppleTalk connections.** If you have checked every aspect of your AppleTalk connection and still are not getting connectivity, try the following steps to reset your AppleTalk settings. After each step, test your AppleTalk connection. After you have regained connectivity, you can ignore the subsequent steps.

1. Log out and then log back in again.

   Sometimes, the AppleTalk settings in the Network System Preferences pane don't "take" until you do so.

2. Create a new Location (using the steps outlined earlier in this chapter), switch to it, and then switch back to your original Location.

   The simplest way to set up for a Location swap is to create a new Location that has no active ports (name it *Nothing Active* for example) and then switch to it. Wait a few seconds and then switch back to the Location that is giving you problems. With luck, the problem will be gone.

3. Create a new Location, and set it up with the appropriate network settings.

   If the new location works properly, delete the original Location.

4. Zap the PRAM on your Mac by restarting and holding down Command-Option-P-R until you hear three chimes.

   Thereafter, your Mac will start up normally. Some AppleTalk settings are stored in PRAM, and if your PRAM gets corrupted, it can cause problems with AppleTalk connections.

5. Delete your Network preferences file, as described in "Take Note: Delete the Network Preferences File," later in this chapter.

## Troubleshooting wireless connections

If you have a wireless/AirPort network for local networking or Internet access and you are having connection problems, the following steps can help you isolate the problem. If you use AirPort or a wireless Internet router for Internet access and are having connection problems, try these steps before troubleshooting your Internet connection itself.

**Switch Locations.** From Network System Preferences, switching to a new Location and back again—or creating and using a new location setup—can fix a variety of AirPort-related problems:

- It may allow you to choose Turn AirPort On from the AirPort menu, which would not work before.

- It may get an AirPort network to appear in the AirPort menu or Internet Connect application, when it would not show up before.

- It may get AirPort to be listed in the Show pop-up menu in the Network System Preferences pane, where it is not present even though it is enabled in the Active Network Ports section.

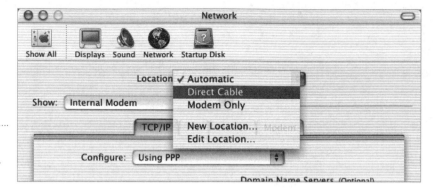

*Figure 8.23*

*Network System Preferences pane with Location pop-up menu visible.*

**Check Active Network Ports.** You might think that the most reliable way to set up a Location for AirPort is to have it be the only port configuration that is enabled in the Active Network Ports section. But I have seen a few cases in which an AirPort connection did not work unless Ethernet was also enabled.

This situation leads to another variation on this theme: The problem may be specific to how you have Active Network Ports set up in the Network System Preferences pane. I have a setup in which my iBook is set to use either Ethernet or AirPort. In such cases, if the port you want to use is second in the Active Network Ports list, the connection may not work. Thus, if Ethernet is at the top of the list, and especially if you have an Ethernet cable in the Mac's port that does not lead to an active network, the Mac may not make the AirPort connection. The solution is to switch the order of the active network ports, placing AirPort at the top.

The same solution applies if Internet Connect claims that you have a valid AirPort connection, but you cannot access the Internet.

**Remove wireless from the equation.** If you're having trouble connecting to an AirPort or wireless network, and you are also set up to connect via Ethernet, switch to Ethernet (adding the cable, if needed) to see whether you can connect.

If you are able to connect, you've verified that you have a wireless connection problem. If you are unable to connect via Ethernet either, you have a more general connection problem—one that is not specific to your AirPort connection.

Conversely, if you are able to connect to other local computers via AirPort but can not get Internet access via AirPort, this confirms that the problem is not directly with the AirPort Base Station but rather with the Internet settings or connection.

**SEE:** • "Internet: troubleshooting routers," later in this chapter.

**Check that your AirPort card is seated properly.** If the problem appears to be with AirPort but with only one Mac, check to see that the Mac's AirPort card is installed and seated properly. This procedure is an especially important first step for PowerBooks and iBooks, because the added movement and bumping that occurs with a laptop is more likely to cause an AirPort card to come loose.

**Check that your AirPort card is active.** Launch the Internet Connect application, and verify that your AirPort card is active. If it is active, the Internet Connect window should read AirPort Power: On. If not, click the Turn AirPort On button.

Alternatively, if you launch Network Utility and select Ethernet Interface (en1) from the pop-up menu in the Info tab, you can check the AirPort connection. If the Link Status line states Active, your AirPort connection is working. Note: you can tell that this setting is for a wireless connection, because the last line will read Model Wireless Adapter (802.11) or something similar.

SEE: • "Take Note: Diagnose problems with the Network Utility," later in this chapter.

**Check for AirPort signal-level strength and channel interference.** If the AirPort signal level is not strong enough, your network access will fail, even if all settings and connections are correct. You can check the signal level via either the AirPort menu bar icon or the Signal Level graph in the Internet Connect application. In the simplest cases, a weak signal level may mean that your computer is too distant from the Base Station or that the Base Station is not facing in an ideal direction. Moving your Mac closer to the Base Station, rotating the Base Station slightly, or doing both will fix this.

In other cases, the problem may be wireless channel interference. More specifically, the technology behind AirPort and wireless networking uses a narrow range of radio frequencies in the 900 GHz range. Unfortunately, that range is close to the range of frequencies used by many wireless telephones and other consumer wireless devices. Some users have reported problems with their AirPort and wireless connections in the vicinity of other consumer wireless devices. If you experience such problems, the obvious solution is to avoid other wireless devices or turn them off when you are using your AirPort card. If that solution isn't possible, the AirPort Base Station and most other wireless routers allow you to change among several channels. (Each channel has a slightly different transmission frequency.) Try changing channels until you find one that provides better connectivity. (Client computers connecting to the router or Base Station will switch to the appropriate channel automatically.)

With the AirPort Base Station, you can change the channel via the AirPort tab in the AirPort Admin Utility application; simply choose a different channel from the Channel pop-up menu. If successful, this will eliminate the interference.

Note: If you are in the vicinity of other AirPort networks, and multiple networks are using the same channel AirPort channel, your connection reliability and data-transfer rates can be diminished. Again, the solution is to change the AirPort channel to one that is less popular, which may greatly increase the reliability of your wireless network.

**Do general AirPort troubleshooting.** If all else seems well, it is time to recheck your initial AirPort setup.

**SEE:** • "Take Note: Setting up an AirPort Base Station and Network," earlier in this chapter.

## Internet: troubleshooting routers

If you are using a router, wireless or wired, checking whether it is the cause of an Internet connection problem is one of the first things you should do. If you have set up your router incorrectly, or if your ISP has taken steps to prevent the use of such routers, no amount of other troubleshooting will solve your connection problems.

The best way to determine whether the router is the problem is to disconnect the router completely and set your computer up to access your ISP directly. For most dial-up modem connections, this procedure means connecting the phone wire to the phone port on the Mac (so as to access the internal modem). For broadband connections, connect your modem directly to your Macintosh via the Ethernet port.

You will likely have to change the settings in the Network System Preferences pane to reflect this change. For example, if you had been using a manual Ethernet setting to connect your Mac to your router (probably with an IP address such as 192.168.1.101), you may need to shift to DHCP (if that is what your cable or DSL modem setup requires). To make everything go smoother, set up a separate Location with these alternative settings in advance of any problems. This allows you to preserve your initial settings and switch back to them when done.

If after connecting directly, you are able to establish a working Internet connection, the problem is not with your computer or with the connection itself but with your router or the way you have your Mac configured to access the router. In such cases, consider the following:

**Check router TCP/IP settings.** I am assuming you already checked the TCP/IP settings in Network System Preferences. However, with a router, you also need to check whether the router's TCP/IP settings are correct.

**Check for firmware updates.** The router may need a firmware update to correct some bug; check with the vendor to see whether a newer version is available. Apple's AirPort Base Station, for example, had a problem connecting to Comcast's cable Internet services. The fix required an update to the AirPort Base Station firmware.

**Check for MAC address and other ISP/router interaction problems.**
The cause of a problem may be the interaction between your ISP and your router. For example, some broadband ISPs check the MAC address of the computer before allowing a connection. If the ISP is looking for the MAC address of your Mac and instead finds the MAC address of your router, the connection will fail. One solution is to contact your ISP and request that it update the MAC address in its database. Otherwise, your router software may include a feature called MAC Address Cloning. This feature allows you to enter the MAC address of your computer in a special field in your router's software. The router sends this address to the ISP, fooling the ISP into thinking that the router has the MAC address it is seeking.

**SEE:** • "Take Note: Internet Routers" and "Take Note: What Are the TCP/IP Settings?" earlier in this chapter, for related information.

If you still cannot connect to the Internet, even after taking the router out of the equation, the router is not the direct cause. In this case, proceed with the troubleshooting advice in the following sections. You can reconnect your router after you have determined the cause and solution.

---

**TAKE NOTE ▶ 169.254.x.x and 192.42.249.x IP addresses: DHCP and AirPort**

Both the 169 and 192 IP addresses described here are symptomatic that something has gone wrong with your AirPort or DHCP connection.

- **169.254.x.x.** If you are connecting to the Internet via a DHCP server or using dynamically assigned DHCP IP addresses to route connections via a router, you may find an IP address in the 169.254.x.x range (169.254.0.0 to 169.254.254.255) in the TCP/IP settings. This address is used when the DHCP server fails to make a connection.

  You may see this address, for example, if the cable service is down when you're trying to connect to the Internet via a cable modem. Or you may see it on a computer attempting to connect to an AirPort Base Station if the computer has not connected to the Base Station or is unable to do so.

- **192.42.249.12.** This address is assigned to a new AirPort Base Station. If you update the Base Station software, it will also revert to this address. This situation is normal. Note: 192.42.249.13 is assigned after a hard reset of the Base Station.

  The 192.42.249.12 address also occurs, however, if you are trying to connect from a Base Station to an ISP via DHCP and it cannot make a connection. The likely cause may be on your ISP's end or it may be with your Internet settings. To check and make changes to the Base Station settings, use the AirPort Admin utility. An update to the AirPort software or firmware may also be the solution to this problem.

For more specific guidance on exactly what to do to fix these errors, check this two Apple Knowledge Base documents: `http://docs.info.apple.com/article.html?artnum=58618` and `http://docs.info.apple.com/article.html?artnum=58619`.

**SEE:** • "Take Note: Setting up an AirPort Base Station and Network," earlier in this chapter.

**TAKE NOTE ▶ Diagnose Problems with the Network Utility**

Apple's Network utility (located in /Applications/Utilities) allows you to diagnose various causes of Internet problems. You can use it to check whether a failure to get to a Web site is due to a specific problem with the Web site or a more general Internet connection problem. Although the scope of all that the Network utility can do is too broad to cover here, two tabs are worth a specific mention.

- **Info.** This tab provides information about your local network connection. The pop-up menu allows you to choose which network port the information refers to (en0 is the built-in Ethernet port; en1 is your AirPort card, if applicable, or a second Ethernet card). The hardware address is the unique number (the Media Access Controller, or MAC address) that identifies your computer. Your IP address is either your local IP address (if you are using an Internet router) or the IP address assigned to you by your ISP.

- **Ping.** Ping is one of the most useful tools for testing an Internet connection. If you type the IP address or domain of a remote server and click the Ping button, the Network utility will send a special kind of signal to the server and request a response. If the server answers, you know that your Internet connection is functioning properly. If it doesn't, try several others; some servers do not return ping requests, and a remote server may simply be having problems. All you need is a single successful ping result to verify your connection.

  If you cannot get the Web page of a site to load, and you cannot ping to that site—but other sites load and ping successfully, it suggests that the site is temporarily unavailable. That is, the problem is on the site end, not your end. In such cases, there is little you can do except wait for the Webmaster of the site to fix the problem.

  If you cannot ping any site successfully, it suggests a connection problem on your end.

An alternative to the Network utility is the shareware program IPNetMonitor X. I prefer it to the Network utility overall, as it does a few things that the Network utility cannot do.

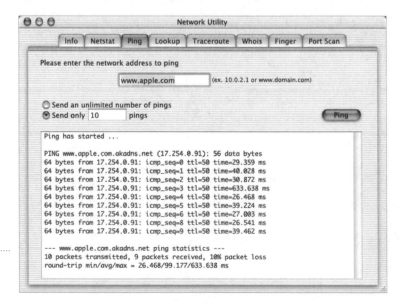

*Figure 8.24*

*Successful ping to a remote Internet server.*

# Internet: troubleshooting dial-up modems

Despite the proliferation of broadband, dial-up connections are still the most common way for home users to access the Internet. These days, most dial-up connections are made via the internal modem included with every Mac. If your modem fails to connect, or if it appears to connect but no Internet applications can access the connection, and if the advice in the preceding sections didn't solve your problem, here are some additional steps specific to standard dial-up modems.

**Check your Modem tab settings.** In addition to verifying that the Network System Preferences Modem's TCP/IP and PPP settings are correct (you did that already, right?), make sure that you have your Modem tab settings set up properly. If you don't have the correct modem model selected, for example, you may experience poor connections or may not be able to connect at all. In addition, make sure that you've selected the correct dialing method (tone or pulse). Finally, some phone systems that include voice mail send a beep when you have messages. If you use such a system, uncheck the Wait for dial tone before dialing checkbox.

SEE: • "Take Note: Modem Scripts," earlier in this chapter.

**Check Active Network Port and Location settings.** I discussed the troubleshooting value of switching Locations and Active Network Port settings in the immediately prior sections of this chapter. Here is yet one more variation on the theme.

Once, when my cable modem went down, I decided to use my internal modem via a dial-up ISP that I maintained for just such emergencies. It seemed to work OK. Internet Connect indicated that I had made a connection. But no services worked. I could not load any Web pages or get any email. It turned out that the problem was due to a glitch in how active network ports work. Even though I was dialing in through the modem, the network software was still trying to connect through the Ethernet port to the nonfunctional cable modem.

The solution is to do one of the following:

- Temporarily move Internal Modem to the top in the window that appears when you choose Active Network Ports from the Show pop-up menu. You can reverse the order when the cable modem is working again.

- Create a separate Location for the modem in which only the Internal Modem setting is active. Switch to this Location.

- Unplug the Ethernet cable (that goes to your cable modem) from your computer.

The cause of the problem is that Mac OS X considers your Ethernet connection to have priority over your modem, and because it detects a valid connection to the cable or DSL modem, it refuses to let the modem provide Internet access, despite the fact that an apparently good modem connection has been made.

**Use the Internet Connect application's Connection Log.** If you are having trouble figuring out why your modem connection is not working, checking the error messages in the Connection Log may provide a clue. To do this:

1. Open the Internet Connect application.

2. If it's not already selected, choose Internal Modem from the Configuration pop-up menu.

3. Choose Connection Log from the Window menu.

You can view information about past connection attempts, or you can use Internet Connect to attempt a dial-up connection and watch the log generate in real time. Even if you aren't able to identify the problem yourself, if you end up contacting your ISP for technical support, this log may be useful.

*Figure 8.25*

*Internet Connect's Connection Log option and an example of the log output.*

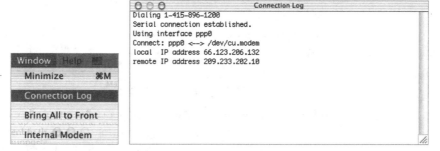

**Use verbose logging.** If the standard connection log does not provide enough helpful information, you can enable a more detail logging procedure called verbose logging. To do so, follow these steps:

1. Open the Network System Preferences pane.

2. From the Show pop-up menu, choose the modem configuration you have set up.

3. Click the PPP tab.

4. Click the PPP Options button.

5. In the Options screen, check the Use verbose logging checkbox.

6. Click the OK button.

7. Click the Apply Now button to apply your new settings.

    If you already had an Internet Connect window open, this step will generally cause it to close and then reopen.

From this point on, when you choose Connection Log in Internet Connect, the log will contain much more detail about every step of the connection process.

**Deactivate phone-line features.** Many phone lines have features such as call waiting that can cause frequent disconnects. If you have such features, check with your phone company about how to disable them when you are online.

**Check your phone line.** Unplug your modem, and hook a telephone up to it to verify that you have a dial tone and can dial out. This step will also allow you to figure out whether other phones in the house are in use or off the hook, thus preventing your Mac from connecting.

**Have your phone line checked.** If you are able to connect only intermittently and experience frequent dropped connections, it's possible that the phone lines in your home, or the area around it, are simply of poor quality. You can contact your phone company to check your phone-line quality.

**Contact your ISP.** If you've gone through every step mentioned in this section, and you still cannot access the Internet, it's probably time to contact your ISP and see whether it can figure out the problem.

## Internet: troubleshooting DSL/cable/PPPoE connections

Broadband connections are the fastest-growing type of Internet connections. They tend to be more reliable than dial-up modem connections. They are also much faster and are generally available 24/7, with no log-in procedure needed. Whenever your Mac is on, you are on the Internet. Things still go wrong, however. If the advice in the preceding sections didn't help, here are some additional steps specific to standard broadband modems.

**Reset your modem.** Turn your DSL or cable modem off (or unplug it), and leave it off for two to three minutes. (If your DSL or cable modem has a Reset button, press it first.) After turning it back on, wait a few minutes for it to resynchronize with your ISP, if necessary. Many times, this step will fix a finicky Internet connection.

Though doing so is not necessarily required, it would be a good idea to shut down your Mac and restart it after you reset your modem.

**Make sure that your computer is connected to the DSL or cable modem properly.** Most broadband modems have an indicator light (or lights) that verify that your computer is connected properly. If this light is not on, recheck the connecting cable; try a different cable if at all possible.

**Use the Internet Connect application's Connection Log for PPPoE connections.** If your ISP uses PPPoE, you can use the Connection Log that Mac OS X keeps to see detailed information about your connection attempts. The log often includes error messages that indicate the source of the problem. The procedure to set this up is the same as covered for dial-up modems in the previous section.

**Contact your ISP.** In my experience, 99 percent of the broadband problems that you will have are not your fault, and you cannot fix them. This is especially true if the problem occurs spontaneously, without your making any change or addition to the Mac that could have affected the broadband connection. In such cases, the first thing I typically do is contact my cable-modem ISP. The ISP will often tell you that there is some temporary problem with the service in your area and that the ISP is working to fix the problem. In this case, you just have to wait. Occasionally, the ISP may need to *reprovision* your modem (a technique that the cable company can do via the Internet; a repair person doesn't have to come to your house). This task is usually accomplished within a few hours of your call. As a last resort, the ISP may need to make a service call to check your connection or replace your modem.

Note: If your modem is connected via a router or any sort of wireless connection, some broadband ISPs will refuse to help you with potential router-related problems, claiming that they do not support or (in some cases) even permit their use. The fact that you use a Mac only makes matters worse, as many ISPs are less skilled in dealing with Mac setups than with Windows PC setups. In such cases, if the advice in this book is not sufficient to solve your problem, you will need to seek outside advice.

---

**TAKE NOTE ▶ Delete the Network Preferences File**

If you cannot connect to the Internet from your Mac and you are able to verify that your Internet connection is functional (perhaps because you can connect to the Internet via a second Mac), the problem could be that your Network preferences file has become damaged. In such cases, you need to delete this file (so that a new default copy is created) to fix the problem.

The Network preferences file is actually owned by root, meaning that you cannot simply drag it to the Trash. In addition, as it is located in the invisible /var folder, you can't browse to it from the Finder. You can always use Terminal to locate and delete the file (using methods discussed in Chapter 10). Or you can use a utility such as XRay. Before you start, make sure that you have a record of all your settings, as you'll have to re-enter them. Then follow these steps:

1. Launch XRay.

2. Choose Open from the File menu.

3. In the Go To field in the Open dialog box, type
   `/var/db/SystemConfiguration/preferences.xml`.

4. Click the XRay button.

   This step opens the preferences file in XRay.

5. From the File menu, choose Move to Trash.

6. Enter your account password to verify that you are a user with administrative access.

7. Quit XRay.

8. Log out and then log back in.

9. Reenter all your network settings.

Now try to connect to the Internet as you normally do.

**TAKE NOTE ▶ Network Connection Setting Causes Stall at Startup**

If you have a TCP/IP configuration set to access the Internet via a cable modem or DSL connection and that connection is not working at startup, you will get a significant delay at startup, most notably at those points where the network is accessed (when *Initializing network* and *Configuring network time* appear on- screen. If this happens, try these solutions:

- Make sure that your cable-modem connection is working. If it is not working, use the advice in this chapter to determine whether the problem is something you can fix (such as a domain name entered incorrectly in the TCP/IP settings) or something that the ISP needs to fix.

- As a temporary workaround until your Internet connection is fixed, disconnect the Ethernet cable from the Mac. Doing this should eliminate the startup delay.

I have used the slowdown as a diagnostic tool to determine quickly whether a change I made helped or hurt my attempt to fix a connection problem. If I restart and get this delay, I know that I still have problems.

SEE : • "Take Note: What Are the TCP/IP Settings?" earlier in this chapter, for related advice.

• "Startup items" and "Blue-screen crash," in Chapter 5, for related information on startup problems related to network settings.

## Internet: troubleshooting Web browsers

If you are having problems browsing the Web, consider the following.

**Fix page-loading problems.** You may find that you cannot access a certain Web site but can access others. This symptom may be accompanied by error messages such as "The specified server could not be found" or "A connection failure has occurred." If the problem is truly limited to a specific site, the cause most likely lies with the site itself, not your connection.

If these messages appear for all sites that you try to reach, however, you probably do not have a successful Internet connection. In this case, go back to the preceding sections of this chapter for advice.

The same logic holds true if a particular site loads significantly slower than most other sites do, even if you do not get any error messages.

If you get a "404" or "Page not found" error message when trying to load a Web page, this means that the particular page that you were looking for could not be found by the browser. If other pages from the same site load successfully, you may have entered the URL incorrectly. Otherwise, the Web site may have deleted the page or changed its URL.

SEE: • "Take Note: Diagnose Problems with the Network Utility," earlier in this chapter, for related advice.

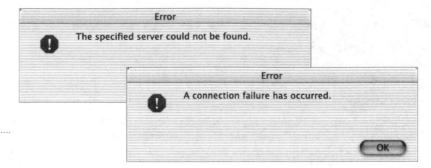

**Figure 8.26**

Two Web-browser error messages.

**Fix DNS-related problems.** If you have a valid connection to your ISP and the Internet, and you can ping IP addresses, but you are having trouble accessing Web sites by domain name (you can ping an IP address, for example, but cannot ping or browse a domain name such as www.cnn.com), the problem may be with your DNS settings. Another way to check for problems specific to domain names is to attempt to load the page via its numeric IP address instead of its domain name. If http://17.254.0.91 works, but www.apple.com does not, you have a DNS problem.

Another symptom of DNS problems is significant delays before a Web page will begin to load (but then the page loads at normal speed).

If you are experiencing these problems, open the Network System Preferences pane, and click the TCP/IP tab for the port you use to access the Internet. Verify that the values you have entered in the Domain Name Servers box match up with the settings given to you by your ISP (or that the box is blank, if your ISP instructed you to leave it blank). Because domain name servers convert domain names to their numerical IP-address equivalents, mistakes in this setting may prevent you from accessing domain names.

Note that if you switch locations in Mac OS X, and the location contains multiple network configurations (modem, Ethernet, and AirPort), it generally takes a few seconds before Mac OS X determines which of the configurations it will use. During this delay, you will not be able to resolve domain names properly. This is a good reason to disable unused network interfaces and configurations in the Active Network Ports section.

**SEE:** • "Take Note: What Are the TCP/IP Settings?" earlier in this chapter.

**Solve Java problems.** If you are having trouble using Java (either running an applet within a Web browser or as a stand-alone application), make sure that you are using the latest update of Apple's Java software. The initial implementation of Java for Mac OS X had numerous bugs, which Apple continues to fix in updates. Java 1.3.1 Update 1, for example, was an important update. You need to be running at least Mac OS X 10.1.3 to install it.

**Delete corrupt browser preferences.** This old mainstay is still valid in Mac OS X. As is the case with any application, a corrupt preferences file (and sometimes, even a corrupt bookmarks or Favorites file) can prevent a Web browser from working properly. In such cases, deleting the file is the solution. To locate the file for your browser, see "Take Note: Web-Browser Settings and Favorites Files" later in this chapter. It's a good idea to back up the file before deleting it. In case deleting it does not solve the problem, you don't want to lose all that information (such as your complete list of Favorites).

**Delete cache files.** If you enable the cache in Internet Explorer's Advanced Preferences dialog box, it stores the cache files in ~/Library/Caches/MS Internet Cache/. All the files here all end in cache.waf. Enabling this cache may or may not speed the loading of Web pages; experiment to see which method works best for you. If you ever want to delete the cache file, simply click the Empty Now button in the Preferences dialog box. Doing so may clear up problems with pages that will not update or load properly.

This cache is separate from the download cache that Explorer maintains for files that are downloaded to your drive. The download cache file is stored in ~/Library/Preferences/Explorer/Temporary Files/. There is no way to empty or delete this file from Explorer's Preferences dialog box. If you want to do so, possibly because the file has gotten very large, quit Explorer, and drag the file to the Trash.

---

**TAKE NOTE ▶ Web-Browser Settings and Favorites Files**

If you've decided that you need to delete or replace your browser's preferences files, you need to know where to find them. Here are the locations of preference, bookmark, and Favorites files for the most common Mac OS X Web browsers:

**Internet Explorer**

Preferences: ~/Library/Preferences/ com.apple.internetconfig.plist

Favorites: ~/Library/Preferences/ Explorer/Favorites.html

Toolbar Preferences: ~/Library/Preferences/ Explorer/Language.Toolbar.xml

**iCab**

Preferences: ~/Library/Preferences/iCab Preferences/iCab Preferences

Favorites: ~/Library/Preferences/iCab Preferences/Hotlist.html

**Mozilla**

Preferences: ~/Library/Preferences/org.mozilla.Mozilla.plist

Favorites: ~/Library/Mozilla/Profiles/default/bookmarks.html

*continues on next page*

**TAKE NOTE** ▶ **Web-Browser Settings and Favorites Files** *continued*

**OmniWeb**

Preferences: ~/Library/Preferences/com.omnigroup.OmniWeb.plist

Favorites: ~/ Library/Application Support/OmniWeb/Bookmarks.html

**Opera**

Preferences: ~/Library/Preferences/Opera Preferences/Opera Preferences

Favorites: ~/Library/Preferences/Opera Preferences/Bookmarks

Note that Internet Explorer uses Apple's InternetConfig preferences file; unfortunately, deleting this file also deletes the settings you've made in the Internet System Preferences pane.

---

**TAKE NOTE** ▶ **Troubleshooting Downloading Files**

Besides surfing, the thing you will most likely be doing with your Web browser is downloading software. Here is a brief collection of tips to assist you when you have trouble with a download:

- If the download attempt results in text appearing in your browser window, rather than a file on your Desktop, a workaround usually is available. In Internet Explorer, for example, hold down the Option key when clicking the download link. If that does not work, try Control-clicking the download link to bring up the contextual menu. From the menu, choose Download Link to Disk. This command will bring up the Save dialog box. Click Save, and the download should proceed.

- If the preceding technique does not work, or if you get error messages indicating that you are missing a plug-in or other software needed for the file to download, it's time to visit Helpers (in the Preferences dialog box of Internet Explorer). Helpers allow you to determine what application will post-process (for example, launch) a file after it has downloaded. You can also edit Helpers settings to specify whether a file is post-processed, saved to disk with no further processing, viewed with a plug-in, and so on.

  Note: Files that need to be decompressed with StuffIt Expander are typically post-processed automatically; this processing is actually set in Explorer's Download Options Preferences dialog box.

- Many Web downloads use the FTP protocol. You will know that this is the case for a specific download if the URL begins with ftp:// instead of http://. In such cases, using passive (PASV) mode can be the ticket to preventing download problems. Fortunately, most Web browsers use passive mode automatically. If problems occur, you can ensure this mode is used. Go to the Network System Preferences pane, click the Proxies tab, and check the Use Passive FTP Mode (PASV) checkbox.

- If all else fails, for FTP downloads, you can try shifting from using your Web browser to using an FTP client, such as Fetch or RBrowser. To do so, launch the FTP client and enter the domain name from the file's URL (the portion between ftp:// and the first slash) where the client asks for an address. No password will be needed for these public ftp sites. After you are connected, you can navigate to the directory that contains the file you want to download.

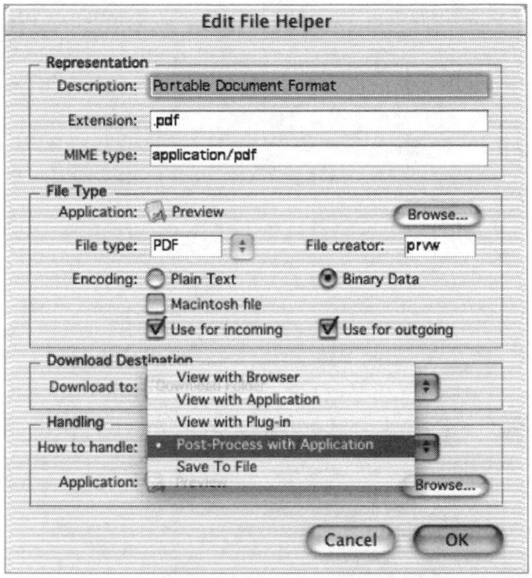

*Figure 8.27*

*Editing how to handle a file in Explorer's Edit File Helper dialog box.*

## Internet: troubleshooting email

Assuming that your network connection is working, most email problems can be traced to incorrect email settings or problems with your ISP's email server.

Also be aware that many email providers, in an attempt to block spammers from using their servers to send spam, require special procedures for sending email. For example, you may need to select to receive email before you can send email. Thus, if you get an error when trying to send email, select to receive email and then try again to send.

**Double-check your email settings.** If you are using an email client such as Mac OS X's Mail or Microsoft's Entourage, compare the settings you entered in your email client's Preferences dialog box or account information with the settings provided you by your ISP or email provider. At the very least, you will need to know your user name, password, and the mail server addresses—including whether you are using a POP or IMAP server for receiving mail (the former downloads email to your drive; the latter keeps the email stored on its server). If you entered your email account settings in the Internet System Preferences pane, verify them there. If you entered them in both your email client and the Internet System Preferences pane, make sure that the settings match.

If you are using Web-based email (such as Yahoo) instead of an email client, the situation usually is simpler. You need only enter your name and password to access the email.

**Ping the email server.** If you are having trouble sending mail, and your email client returns an error such as "Cannot contact server," use the Network utility to ping the SMTP server (this is the server that is used to send mail).

If you cannot retrieve mail (and your email client tells you that it cannot contact the server), ping the POP or IMAP server that you access to receive mail.

If you have Internet access but the server does not respond to your ping, the problem simply may be that your email server is having problems. Contact your ISP for details.

During the past year, iTools' mac.com email server has been hampered by periodic server failures. During these times, which occasionally lasted for days, users could not send or receive email. There is little you can do in such a situation except wait for the problem to be fixed.

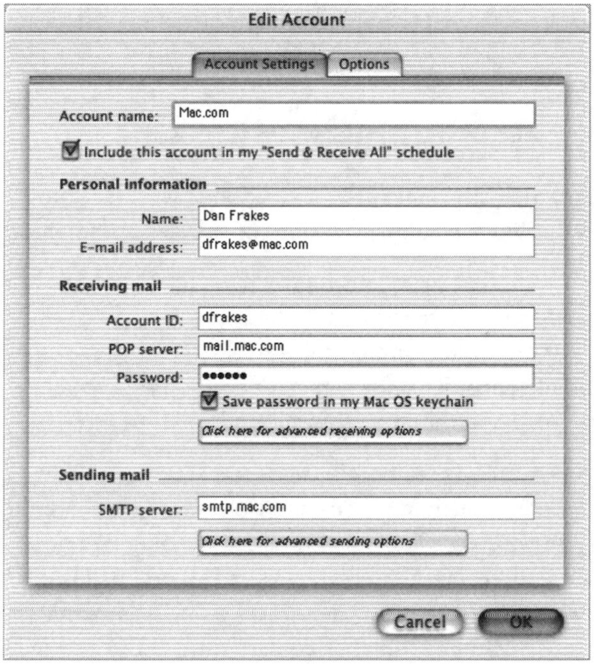

*Figure 8.28*

*Email account window in Entourage, showing email POP (for receiving) and SMTP (for sending) servers.*

# Troubleshooting Web browsing and email: Mac OS X and beyond

Yes, I know—I have not covered many Web-related and email problems. Most of these problems are not specific to Mac OS X (such as problems with browser bookmarks, getting JavaScript to work, or emailing attachments) or are specific to particular applications (such as Internet Explorer or Entourage). I have tried to restrict coverage of these issues so as to keep this already-large book from becoming unmanageable in size. For more information on these matters, I can recommend my previous troubleshooting book, *Sad Macs, Bombs, and Other Disasters*. That book has three hefty chapters that cover file sharing, networking, the Internet, Web browsing, and email. Although the focus of that book is on Mac OS 9, much of the information on these topics is general enough to apply to Mac OS X as well.

---

**TAKE NOTE ▶ iPhoto and Internet Services Conflicts**

If you cannot access the Internet from iPhoto (such as to "order prints"), it may be due to a conflict with files in the Services folders. One such folder is located at /System/Library/Services. There may be additional ones at /Library/Services and ~/Library/Services.

The iPhoto installer places three items (PrintService, Book Service, and HomePage Service) in /System/Library/Services. These are needed to use the Internet-based services offered in iPhoto.

There should also be at least two other items in /System/Library/Services that are installed by Mac OS X itself (AppleSpell.service and SummaryService.service). These items are not the cause of the problem. The conflict is due to certain third-party service files, such as one called word-services.service. The result of the conflict is that iPhoto's Order Prints, Order Book and HomePage buttons (available after clicking Share) will not work.

If you are having this Internet-related symptom, remove the wordservices file (or any other third-party services files you find in any Services folder) and see if it eliminates the problem. Note: You may need to login as the root user, or use Terminal, to do this.

If the symptom only occurs when another application (in addition to iPhoto) is open, the cause may still be related to Services. More specifically, it may be that the conflict only occurs when the application accesses a given service or it may be that the application has its own conflicting service embedded within its package. In such cases, simply quitting the offending application when using iPhoto should be a sufficient solution.

---

## Troubleshooting File and Web Sharing

If you have worked your way through all the troubleshooting advice in the preceding sections, chances are very good that you will have no problems getting File Sharing to work. Problems that may still occur tend be ones that, at least in retrospect, are considered to be obvious. Here are some examples.

**Make sure that the server you want to locate is on the network and has File Sharing enabled.** Suppose that you click an alias or location file that you created for a server or choose a server listed in the Connect to Server dialog box. Instead of connecting almost immediately, you get a long delay or an error message (such as "The alias could not be opened, because the original item could not be found" or "No file services are available at the URL"). The first thing to suspect, especially if you are trying to connect to another computer, is that the other computer is not connected to your network.

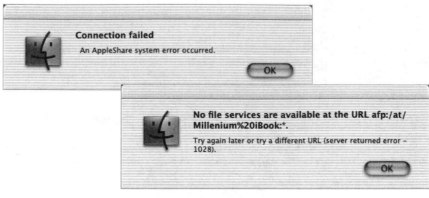

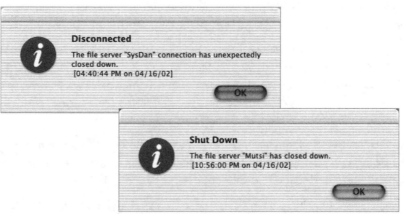

**Figure 8.29**

*Four failed-server-connection error messages: The first two (top) occur when a connection cannot be made; the second two (bottom) occur when a successful connection is broken.*

If you are attempting to connect locally from your desktop Mac to your PowerBook, for example, the connection obviously won't work if the PowerBook is shut down. If you are trying to connect to a remote computer (such as a friend's Mac), make sure that the computer is on the Internet at the time.

And always make sure that File Sharing (or Web Sharing or both, if appropriate) is turned on in the Sharing System Preferences pane on the computer with which you want to connect.

Also remember to keep the shared server active after a successful connection is established. If the computer goes to sleep or is shut down, the connection will be broken.

**Make sure that the connecting user has an account with the correct privileges.** If, when using Connect to Server, you get to the point where you are asked to enter your name and password as a registered user, but doing so leads to a "Login failed" error message, the password may have been changed, you are trying the wrong password, or the account has been deleted or modified in some way since you last accessed it.

**Make sure that the computer has an IP address.** If you are connecting two Macs via a local connection over TCP/IP (local network), both computers must have an IP address. If a computer typically connects to the Internet via PPP or DHCP and has not been used for sharing before, it may not have an IP address. In this case, when you try to connect, you will get a message that says, "The connection to this server has been unexpectedly broken."

The solution is to assign the computer an IP address. To do so, you can set up an Ethernet port to be configured manually (by creating a new port or a new location) to be used just for sharing. Then assign an IP address in the TCP/IP settings. The address should be a local private address, such as one in the 10.0.0.1 to 10.0.0.255 range. The subnet mask should be 255.255.255.0.

SEE: • "Take Note: What Are the TCP/IP Settings?" earlier in this chapter, for more information on local IP addresses and related information.

**Make sure that the connecting user is using the correct protocol and application.** As described earlier in this chapter, Mac OS X provides several methods for sharing files over a network or the Internet. Each method is accessible only when you use certain applications or protocols, however.

- **File Sharing.** The connecting user must be using a Mac OS computer that supports File Sharing. In some cases, the connection may need to be made through TCP/IP (when AppleTalk will not work, for example).

- **Web Sharing**. The connecting user can access your computer only via a Web browser.

- **FTP**. The connecting user must use a dedicated FTP client, a Web browser, or a terminal-based FTP client.

- **Remote Login/Terminal access**. The connecting user must be using a terminal application and Telnet/SSH to connect.

**Make sure that Internet router or firewall settings are not blocking access.** The settings used to prevent unwanted access to your computer sometimes prevent intended access.

SEE: • "Take Note: Internet Routers," "Technically Speaking: Internet Routers and Port Mapping," and "Take Note: Firewalls and Antivirus Software," earlier in this chapter, for more details on these issues.

**Restart sharing.** If you have made changes in your sharing preferences, user system preferences, or related settings (such as changing privileges settings for any items), you may need to stop sharing and start it again before the changes take effect.

**Log out and then log back in.** If you have made changes in sharing, sometimes they don't take effect until you log out of your account and then log back in again.

When you select Connect to Server from the Finder's Go menu, the list of servers that appears may at times include several duplicates of a particular server. At other times, a server that you know is accessible may not be listed at all. When these problems occur, here is what to do.

**Duplicate listings.** You may see duplicate listings of the same computer/server in the At pop-up menu of Connect to Server, sometimes each with a different IP address.

This situation can occur is if the computer/server has multiple IP addresses. I have seen this happen when I try to connect to my iBook, because I have my iBook set up to use a different IP address when connecting via different methods (such as AirPort vs. Ethernet). Connect to Server remembers all methods and lists them all each time. Having the multiple listings can be useful. For example, if my iBook is only connected to the Network via AirPort at the moment, I must use the AirPort IP address to connect to it. The Ethernet address would not work. With the multiple listings, I can select the address I need.

However, these duplicates can also happen for apparently inexplicable reasons and have no use whatsoever.

In any case, the duplicates appear only in the Local Network list, not the AppleTalk one. So one quick way to avoid these duplicates is to use AppleTalk, even though it often tends to be a bit slower than the TCP/IP (local network) connection.

Although unneeded duplicates will not prevent you from connecting to the server, they can be annoying. Unfortunately, there is no Clear Server Listings command available to get rid of these duplicates. The only solution is to delete the file (named slp.regfile) that stores these settings so that a new default file is created. Typically, you would do this via Terminal, because the file is stored in the invisible /var directory and requires root access to modify. Follow these steps:

1. Open the Network System Preferences pane.
2. Turn off AppleTalk for the configuration port you use to connect to AppleTalk servers.
3. Launch Terminal.
4. Type: `<sudo rm /private/var/slp.regfile>`.
5. Enter your password when you're requested to do so.
6. Quit Terminal.
7. Restart your computer.
8. Restore your network settings (for example, turn AppleTalk back on).

*continues on next page*

**TAKE NOTE ▶ Duplicate Listings in Connect to Server; No Listings in Connect to Server** *continued*

**No listings.** Occasionally, you may have the opposite problem: A server that you know has been set up correctly does not appear in the Connect to Server list. This is clearly some sort of bug. In this case, try one or more of the following:

- If you happen to know the IP address of the computer, enter it in the Address text box. This may work, even if the server is not listed. See "Using Connect to Server," earlier in this chapter, for details on how to do this.

- Often, although computer A cannot locate computer B, computer B can locate computer A. So if you have access to both computers, you can make the File Sharing connection go the other way (assuming that you have an account set up to do so). If all you want to do is copy files back and forth, the direction of the connection should not matter.

- Stopping File Sharing and then starting it again may get the MIA server to show up.

*Figure 8.30*

*An example of multiple server listings in the Connect to Server dialog box.*

**TAKE NOTE ▶ Sharing and Files in the etc Directory**

Here are two problems and solutions regarding sharing and files located in the Unix /etc directory.

**Sharing pane causes System Preferences to quit.** Selecting the Sharing pane of System Preferences may result in an unexpected quit of the System Preferences application. This problem generally is caused by a missing or corrupted inetd.conf file in the invisible /etc directory. This is a known issue with Mac OS X, and Apple has provided a utility, FixSharing, that fixes the problem. You can download FixSharing via this Knowledge Base document: `http://docs.info.apple.com/article.html?artnum=106599`.

**Web Sharing does not start up.** If Web Sharing refuses to start up, the problem may be with the settings in the httpd.conf file that contains the Apache Web-server configuration settings. The file is located in the /etc/httpd/directory. One example of this problem, and how to fix it, is provided in this Knowledge Base document at `http://docs.info.apple.com/article.html?`

**TAKE NOTE ▶ Bluetooth**

Bluetooth is the odd name given to a new technology that enables short-range wireless connections between a variety of digital devices, including computers, personal digital assistants, printers, scanners, and digital cameras.

Think of Bluetooth as the offspring of a mating between Infrared and AirPort wireless technology. With Bluetooth, similar to AirPort, you can connect to any device within a given range (it's a 30-foot range for Bluetooth). However, unlike AirPort and more similar to Infrared, you don't have to set up a TCP/IP network to use it. Any two Bluetooth-compatible devices can almost instantly talk to each other. But unlike Infrared, and more like AirPort, you don't have to point the ports of the two devices at each other for the connection to work.

To make your Mac Bluetooth compatible, you need Apple's Bluetooth USB Adapter. With this installed, launch the free Bluetooth software (available from `www.apple.com/bluetooth`) to find any compatible devices in the Mac's range. Select a listed device, and you are connected. It's that simple. One sure-to-be-popular use of this setup is to synch with Palm PDAs, eliminating the need for the Palm USB adapter.

# 9

# The Classic Environment

So you've finally decided to take the plunge and move up to Mac OS X. The only problem is that most of your software runs only in Mac OS 9. What to do? Not to worry—Apple has provided a way to run most Mac OS 9 software while you're booted from Mac OS X via a feature called the Classic environment. After launching the Classic environment (as described briefly in Chapter 3 and covered more later in this chapter), Mac OS 9 applications will run almost as though you had started up from Mac OS 9. You can shift from the Classic environment to Mac OS X and back again fairly seamlessly. You can also run Mac OS 9 Internet applications from Classic, including using the Mac OS 9 Software Update control panel to update Mac OS 9.

You didn't really start up from Mac OS 9, of course; you are still running Mac OS X. So at times, Classic will be a less-than-perfect substitute for starting up in Mac OS 9. The Classic environment—what it is, how it works, and what to do when it doesn't work—is the subject of this chapter.

# In This Chapter

# What Is the Classic Environment?

As discussed in Chapter 1, Mac OS X is such a fundamentally different operating system from Mac OS 9 that Mac OS 9 applications simply do not run in Mac OS X (and vice versa). Thus, it initially may appear that your investment in Mac OS 9 software goes down the drain when you move up to Mac OS X. Anticipating that users would not welcome such obsolescence, however, Apple provided two solutions: Carbon applications and the Classic environment.

I covered Carbon applications in Chapter 4. Briefly, Carbonizing a Mac OS 9-only application allows it to run in Mac OS X. Carbonizing an application is a developer's shortcut to having to write a Cocoa-based Mac OS X application from scratch. In many cases, a Carbonized application will run in both Mac OS 9 and Mac OS X, making these applications the lone exceptions to rule stated in the previous paragraph. Some Carbonized applications only run in Mac OS X. In either case, Carbon applications are not a perfect solution—they don't always take full advantage of Mac OS X features, and they often run more slowly than their Mac OS 9 counterparts—but they are an excellent compromise. If all Mac OS 9 software were Carbonized, there would be no need for another solution to the Mac OS 9 compatibility problem.

Unfortunately, thousands of existing applications written for Mac OS 9 will never be Carbonized or will be so only after a long delay. For these programs, the solution is to use the Classic environment (often simply called Classic), which lets you run Mac OS 9 applications *within* Mac OS X.

Some readers may have been Mac users long enough to remember the transition from the 680x0 line of processors to the PowerPC processor. The Mac OS ran PowerPC-native applications faster but emulated the older 680x0 processors so that nonnative applications could still be used just like any other application. In everyday use, PowerPC and non-PowerPC applications looked and functioned identically. Running the Classic environment under Mac OS X is not exactly the same experience, but it is still a useful metaphor for understanding what is going on. At times, you may not even be aware of the shift from Classic to Mac OS X and back.

At the simplest level, the Classic environment is a Mac OS X *application* that runs in the background and provides what is called a hardware abstraction layer. Then it boots up a slightly modified version of Mac OS 9 that runs (invisibly) on top of this layer. Classic applications then run inside Mac OS 9 just as they would on a Mac running only Mac OS 9. The main caveat is that Classic applications must be compatible with Mac OS 9.1 or later to be compatible with the Classic environment (as the Classic environment supports only Mac OS 9.1 or later).

Throughout the rest of this chapter, I use the following terms:

- **Classic Mac OS** or **Mac OS 9:** versions of the Mac OS before Mac OS X; usually Mac OS 9.1or later

- **Classic environment** or **Classic:** the Classic environment in Mac OS X

- **Mac OS 9 in Classic:** the version or copy of Mac OS 9 that is running in the Classic environment

- **Classic applications:** applications written for Mac OS 9 or earlier

## What hardware/services does the Classic environment support?

Although the Classic environment actually runs a copy of Mac OS 9, it does not necessarily support all the same hardware, services, and input/output devices and protocols that Mac OS 9 would support on the same hardware. Classic directs all in/out operations from Mac OS 9 in Classic *through* Mac OS X, rather than communicating with the hardware directly. When you print from an application in Mac OS 9, for example, your data does not go directly to the printer; the Classic environment sends the data through Mac OS X, which then sends it to the printer. Thus, if Mac OS X does not support certain hardware or protocols, Classic does not either. Likewise, some devices (such as internal modems) are not accessible to the Classic environment at all.

On the other hand, Classic can support hardware-related features that Mac OS X does not support directly, as long as the needed information is passed to the Classic environment. For example, you can still use Mac OS 9's Chooser to select a printer in Classic that is not yet supported for printing in Mac OS X. You can also use USB printer sharing in Classic, even though Mac OS X does not support this feature.

The Classic environment *does* support:

- USB
- IDE
- Built-in audio/sound
- Disk images
- Ethernet
- SCSI
- FireWire
- Built-in video

The Classic environment *does not* support:

- ADB, except for the primary keyboard/mouse, and only when used from a built-in ADB port. (Note that some crashes will require you to reboot Classic to regain the use of ADB.)

- LocalTalk

- Internal floppy drives. External USB floppy drives will work, however.

- Built-in serial ports

- Infrared ports

- PCI/PC cards (including audio, video, and SCSI cards) not supported by Mac OS X

- Modem-based applications (AOL, Z-term, and most fax software) that cannot access the modem directly from within Classic. PPP connections (in fact, all network connections) must be made under Mac OS X and then funneled to Classic applications.

## Potential problems running applications in the Classic environment

The main advantage of the Classic environment is obvious: It lets you upgrade to the latest and greatest Mac OS while letting you use most of the Mac OS 9 applications that will not run in Mac OS X. There are some down sides, however:

- There is more chance for compatibility problems, because everything you do in a Classic application is funneled through Mac OS 9, then through the Classic environment bridge, and finally through Mac OS X before it gets to your Mac's hardware.

- Applications often run significantly slower in Classic than if you had booted into Mac OS 9.

- Classic applications do not take advantage of the advanced memory and processing capabilities of Mac OS X. Applications running in Classic behave (or misbehave) just like applications under Mac OS 9. Although the Classic environment itself takes advantage of protected memory under Mac OS X (because it is simply an application), everything running *within* the Classic environment does not.

Bottom line: If there is a way to accomplish what you want to do without using Classic, you will almost always be better off doing so. Otherwise, depending on what you want to do, using Classic can be anything from a barely adequate to a perfectly fine alternative.

**SEE:** • **"Troubleshooting the Classic Environment," later in this chapter, for more specific information.**

# How to Install and Configure Classic

Guess what? You don't have to do anything to install Classic. The needed software was installed when you installed Mac OS X (or, on newer Macs, when you took your computer out of the box). As long as a version of Mac OS 9 is available somewhere on a mounted volume, you should be able to use Classic almost instantly. And all currently shipping Macs come with both Mac OS X and Mac OS 9 preinstalled. Still, before you launch Classic for the first time, you need to consider several issues.

## Do you have enough RAM?

Classic uses a lot of memory. If you intend to run Classic often, you will almost certainly need more RAM than the minimum Apple recommends for Mac OS X. I recommend having at least 256 MB of RAM and even more if you can afford it. As a bonus, you'll find that almost everything in Mac OS X is faster with more RAM.

## Do you have the right version of Mac OS 9?

As explained earlier in this chapter, Mac OS X requires Mac OS 9.1 or later to use Classic. Newer versions of Mac OS X may require even newer versions of Mac OS 9. Mac OS X 10.1 requires at least Mac OS 9.2, for example. In general, if you are using the latest version of Mac OS X (which you should be), make sure that you are also using the latest version of Mac OS 9. You can check what version of Mac OS 9 you have installed by choosing About This Computer" from the Apple menu while you're working in Mac OS 9. Or, if you are running Mac OS X, select the Startup Disk System Preference. It will list the Mac OS 9 version number for every volume that can boot from Mac OS 9.

## Should you customize the Mac OS 9 System Folder for Classic?

When you launch the Classic environment under Mac OS X, you actually start up a copy of Mac OS 9 from a System Folder on your hard drive. At other times, you may want to boot directly into Mac OS 9. To handle this, I recommend that you have two separate Mac OS 9 System Folders: one for booting into Mac OS 9 and the other one slimmed down for Classic. (I'll make more-specific recommendations about how to slim it down in "Optimizing Mac OS 9 for the Classic environment," later in the chapter.)

Because Classic does not support or need *all* the files included in a full installation of Mac OS 9, parts of Mac OS 9 are not functional under Classic. This is particularly so for many items in the Extensions and Control Panels folders. In fact, parts are *dys*functional under Classic; they can actually cause problems.

As an alternative to maintaining two separate System Folders, you could use Extensions Manager (or a commercial utility such as Conflict Catcher) to create two Mac OS 9 startup sets: one containing your full complement of startup files and another containing just those you need for Classic. Then you would choose the appropriate set depending on whether you are booting up Mac OS 9 by itself or within the Classic environment. I find this method to be less convenient than the two-System-Folder approach, however. Also, because Mac OS X modifies the System Folder used in Classic by installing extra and updated startup files and by altering preference files, having two Mac OS 9 System Folders allows your "full" version of Mac OS 9 to be free of the potential conflicts these Classic files may cause when booting from Mac OS 9.

At this point, you might be wondering why you would ever want to boot into Mac OS 9 after upgrading to Mac OS X. The answer, as detailed in several sections of this chapter, is twofold: (1) You may need to boot from Mac OS 9 occasionally to run applications that run in neither Mac OS X nor in the Classic environment, and (2) Certain troubleshooting techniques may require booting from Mac OS 9 (such as to access or delete a file that seems impossible to access/delete from Mac OS X).

## Should you partition your drive?

The problem with having two separate Mac OS 9 System Folders is where to put them. Although technically, you could maintain two Mac OS 9 System Folders as well as Mac OS X on the same volume, I do not recommend this method.

**SEE:** • "Take Note: Using Multiple Mac OS 9 System Folders on the Same Volume," later in this chapter.

A better approach is to have each System Folder in its own volume. Fortunately, you do not need to purchase an extra hard drive to do this. Instead, you can divide a single hard drive into multiple partitions, each one acting as though it were a separate volume. As this technique erases your drive, it is best to do it right away—such as the day you unpack your new Mac. If you want to partition a drive that you have been using, you'll need to back up all your data before partitioning and restore it afterward.

**SEE:** • "Take Note: Why and How to Partition," in Chapter 2, and "Take Note: Having Mac OS 9 and Mac OS X on Separate Partitions," in Chapter 5, for more details.

In the most common setup, you divide your drive into two partitions. One partition contains Mac OS X and a customized Mac OS 9 System Folder used for the Classic environment. The other partition contains a separate full Mac OS 9 System Folder that you use when you boot directly into Mac OS 9 (or any other OS version that your Mac can use, should you want). A less common alternative is to have three partitions: one for Mac OS X and one each for the two Mac OS 9 systems.

**TAKE NOTE ▶ Using Multiple Mac OS 9 System Folders on the Same Volume**

As noted in the main text, you can have a single volume/partition with multiple Mac OS 9 System Folders (one for use in Classic and one for use as a bootable Mac OS 9). Such a setup adds a few more wrinkles, however.

The first problem is that the Classic environment does not fully support multiple Mac OS 9 System Folders on the same partition. The Classic tab of the System Preferences window has only an option for which *volume* you want to use for Classic. If you have multiple Mac OS 9 System Folders on that volume, there is no way to select one or the other. After you choose a volume, Classic uses the Mac OS 9 System Folder that was used most recently as a bootable System Folder. In other words, if you recently booted your Mac into Mac OS 9, the System Folder you used will be the one that Classic uses the next time it boots up. So if you want to use a *different* Mac OS 9 System Folder on the selected volume, first you need to choose it in the Startup Disk pane of the System Preferences window (which *does* support multiple System Folders), restart, and then reboot back into Mac OS X. The next time you use the Classic environment, your preferred System Folder will be used.

The other disadvantage of having multiple Mac OS 9 System Folders on the same volume is that Mac OS X sometimes gets confused. Even if you follow the instructions for getting Classic to use a particular System Folder, it still uses the wrong one sometimes. If so, you will be asked to allow Mac OS X to modify it (which, presumably, you don't want to do, because one reason you wanted two System Folders in the first place is so that Mac OS X wouldn't modify one of them). In addition, sometimes Mac OS X modifies preferences files in the Mac OS 9 System Folder used by Classic. If Mac OS X modifies the wrong files, you may have problems later when you try to use it boot into Mac OS 9, or your Classic environment may not work correctly.

# Optimizing Mac OS 9 for the Classic environment

Before using the Classic environment for the first time, you can take several steps to make sure that it will run faster and be more stable. These steps work best if you complete them before you launch Classic for the first time. To make these changes, you should boot up your computer by using the copy of Mac OS 9 that you will be using for the Classic environment. Then follow these steps:

1. Make sure that you have version 9.2.1 or later of the Startup Disk control panel before using that copy of Mac OS 9 in the Classic environment.

   If not, you can get it by using the Software Update control panel or by downloading it from the Apple Web site. If you have updated to the latest version of Mac OS 9, as recommended earlier in this chapter, this update should already be done.

2. Make sure that Soundtrack sounds are disabled in the Appearance control panel.

   These settings are an issue mainly if you're installing Mac OS X over a copy of Mac OS 9 that you've been using for a while.

3. Delete the Navigation Services folder inside the Preferences folder in your System Folder.

   Again, this folder is an issue mainly if you're installing Mac OS X over a copy of Mac OS 9 that you've been using for a while.

4. Remove the Hosts file from the Preferences folder in your System Folder.

   Once again, this file is an issue mainly if you're installing Mac OS X over a copy of Mac OS 9 that you've been using for a while.

5. In the TCP/IP control panel, uncheck Load Only When Needed. To do so:

   Launch the TCP/IP control panel and choose User Mode from the Edit menu. Check the Advanced checkbox; then click OK. Next click the Options button in the main TCP/IP window. From the options that appear, uncheck the Load Only When Needed checkbox. Finally, close the TCP/IP control panel, saving changes when requested.

6. Disable unneeded startup files.

   Veteran Mac users may remember the days of 16 MB of RAM, when they tried to trim their startup files (extensions and control panels) to the bare minimum. Ironically, those days are back with the Classic environment. Just as the Classic Mac OS uses RAM at startup, the Classic environment takes a big chunk of RAM when you use it, and the more startup files you have enabled, the more RAM the Classic environment uses. In addition, extensions and control panels (especially third-party ones) have a much greater chance of causing problems in Classic than in Mac OS 9 itself. Therefore, you can reduce how much RAM Classic uses—and reduce the chance of conflicts—by cutting down on startup files.

   Ideally, you would want the copy of Mac OS 9 that Classic uses to be as lean and mean as possible; it will run faster, use less memory, and be more stable. This means disabling all extensions and control panels that you do not absolutely need, typically by using Extensions Manager or Conflict Catcher.

In fact, beyond the obviously essential files such as System and Finder, very few things are absolutely required by Mac OS 9 when you use the Classic environment. If you open Extensions Manager, choose the As Items view option, and click the Package column to sort by package name, you will see several items that are part of the Classic compatibility environment. These items are the only ones specifically required for Classic.

Although it's beyond the scope of this book to provide a complete list of the startup files in a Mac OS 9 System Folder, as well as to discuss whether you should keep them enabled or disabled for use in Classic, several other resources provide information on startup files, including Conflict Catcher, InformINIT, and Extension Overload.

7. Install any additional necessary startup files.

Some applications and hardware you will be using in the Classic environment may require startup files (extensions or control panels) to function properly. If so, this step is a good time to install them, because they may not install properly when you're using the Classic environment. If you use Microsoft Office 98 or 2001, for example, you should run each of the Office applications once so that Office will be able to install and configure its System Folder files. While you're using the Classic environment, if you ever get an error message that a Classic application will not run because you are missing certain files, there is a good chance that you need to boot into Mac OS 9 and reinstall the application to get the necessary startup files installed.

8. Launch Classic, and allow it to modify the System Folder.

When you boot into Mac OS X and start the Classic environment for the first time, Mac OS X will ask you whether it may add a few items to the Mac OS 9 System Folder. You must allow it to add these items. If you don't, you will not be able to use the Classic environment, and you may have to do a full reinstallation of the copy of Mac OS 9 that Classic uses. The items installed and updated by the Mac OS X installer are:

**Root level of System Folder**

- ProxyApp
- Classic
- Classic Support
- Classic Support UI

**Control Panels folder**

- General Controls

**Extensions folder**

- Apple Guide
- AppleShare
- Classic RAVE
- File Sharing
- LaserWriter
- OpenTpt Remote Access
- PrintingLib
- QuickDraw 3D RAVE

**TAKE NOTE** ▶ **Control Panels/Extensions in Classic vs. Mac OS X**

Many Mac OS 9 control panels and extensions continue to work when run from Classic. However, they will only affect the Classic environment. For example, menu modifiers such as Action Menus will work in Classic, but you will see your custom menus only when a Classic application is active.

However, many other control panels and extensions do not work at all in Classic. They may be disabled automatically when Classic is launched, ignored if you use them or even cause startup conflicts if installed. Action GoMac and RAM Doubler are two examples of such files. As suggested in the main text, the best way to avoid problems with these extensions is to disable them.

Here are some general guidelines that should help you figure out what works and what doesn't:

- Classic settings that would conflict with Mac OS X (such as appearance, virtual memory and File Sharing settings) are ignored or refused. These settings are handled entirely by Mac OS X. For example, if you try to launch the Memory control panel from Classic, it will fail to open. Instead, you will get a message that says: "That application or control panel is not supported by Classic." In other cases, the control panel may open and allow you to make changes; but the changes will be ignored.

- Similarly, the Classic environment shares whatever networking protocols and connections Mac OS X provides. What this means is that you must establish your network, AirPort, or dial-up connections under Mac OS X; your Classic applications will be able to use them just like any Mac OS X application would. For example, while you can open the TCP/IP control panel in Classic, most changes are prohibited. Instead, it lists the settings that you created in Mac OS X.

- Mac OS X applications use the Internet settings in Mac OS X's System Preferences window, whereas Classic applications use the settings in the Mac OS 9 Internet control panel (which you can also configure by using the Internet Config utility). This means that, if you click a URL or email address in a Classic application, it may open in a different browser or email client than it would if you clicked the link in a Mac OS X application, depending on whether the two settings are different.

**SEE:** • "Startup conflicts," later in this chapter, for how to disable startup files and resolve potential extension conflicts.

*Figure 9.1*

*Error message that appears when you attempt to open a control panel or application that cannot open in Classic.*

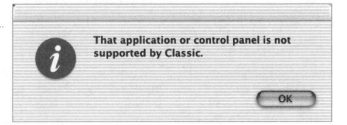

That application or control panel is not supported by Classic.

OK

# Using Classic

After you have the Classic environment and Mac OS 9 installed and optimized, you are ready to use your Classic applications from Mac OS X. The following sections explain what to do after you start up from Mac OS X.

## Select the Classic environment volume

Before you launch Classic for the first time, you need to select the Mac OS 9 volume you want to use for Classic. This step is especially important if (as I recommended earlier in this chapter) you have more than one mounted Mac OS 9 System Folder. To make this choice, follow these steps:

1.  Open Mac OS X's System Preferences window, and select the Classic pane.

2.  From the Start/Stop tab, select a volume from the list in the Select a startup volume for Classic scroll box.

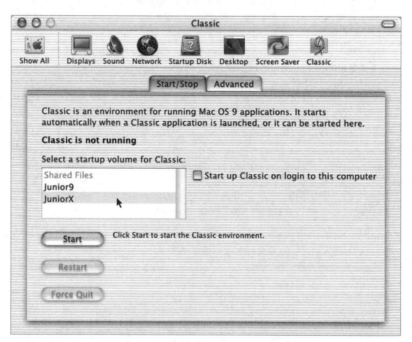

*Figure 9.2*

*Select a Classic startup volume from Classic System Preferences.*

Only volumes with a valid Mac OS 9 System Folder should appear, but a volume with Mac OS 9 on it may be dimmed in this window and unable to be selected, typically because the Mac does not see the System Folder as being blessed.

**SEE:** • "Take Note: Blessed Systems and Starting Up," in Chapter 5.

In such a case, the following procedure typically will get the volume to be accessible from the Classic System Preferences window:

1. In the Startup Disk pane of the System Preferences window, select the desired Mac OS 9 volume as the startup volume.

2. Do not select to Restart. Instead, select to return to the Classic System Preference (such as by selecting Classic from System Preferences' View menu).

3. Before the Classic pane appears, a sheet will drop down, asking whether you want to change the startup disk. Click the Change button.

4. Now the Classic System Preferences pane should appear, and you should be able to select the desired volume. Do so.

5. Return to the Startup Disk pane to undo the change you just made.

## Launch Classic

You can launch the Classic environment under Mac OS X in three ways:

- **Manually.** Click the Start button in the Start/Stop tab of the Classic System Preferences pane.

- **Launch at login.** Check the Start up Classic on login to this computer checkbox in the Start/Stop tab of the Classic System Preferences pane. Now whenever you start up your Mac in Mac OS X, Classic will launch automatically.

- **Launch a Classic application.** If Classic is not running, and you try to launch a Classic application, the Classic environment will load automatically; then the application will launch.

Overall, the preferred option is to launch Classic manually. Occasional problems have been reported with the second and third options. When Classic is set to start up at login, for example, you may get a prolonged spinning pointer when you try to copy/paste from a Classic application to a Mac OS X one.

**SEE:** • **"Can't Copy and Paste from Classic to Mac OS X," in Chapter 6, for more details.**

Whichever method you use, when Classic starts to load, a window will say, "Classic environment starting from {*name of the volume where Mac OS 9 is located*}." This window also includes a Stop button. You can stop Classic from loading by clicking this button. You may want to do this, for example, if you launched a Classic application accidentally, causing the Classic environment to launch. It is safer, however, to let Classic load completely and then shut it down from the Classic tab of the System Preferences window. In fact, if you click the Stop button, a warning dialog box appears, stating "It's best to stop the Classic environment from System Preferences (after Classic starts)."

**Figure 9.3**

The window that
appears when
Classic is loading.

In the Classic startup window, you will also see a disclosing triangle in the lower-left corner, indicating that the window can be expanded. If you click this triangle, the window expands to show what looks like a Mac OS 9 startup screen. You will see the Mac OS 9 graphic, just as though you were booting into Mac OS 9; eventually, extensions and control panels will appear across the bottom of the window, just as they do when Mac OS 9 is booting up. As mentioned earlier in this chapter, this is exactly what is happening; an entire iteration of Mac OS 9 is being loaded. But because the Classic environment is simply an application running on Mac OS X, you can do other things on your computer while it loads!

Another way to tell that Classic is launching is that the Classic icon (a gray Mac OS face with an orange 9) will appear in the Dock, bouncing to indicate that it is launching. In addition, the Classic tab of the System Preferences window will state that Classic is starting.

After Classic is fully loaded, you will notice ... well, you won't notice anything. Unfortunately (or fortunately, depending on your point of view), Apple provides no feedback that Classic has launched. The Classic icon disappears from the Dock, and Classic does not show up in any menus as a running application. You have several ways to tell whether the Classic environment is running, however:

- If a Classic application is running, its icon will appear in the Dock, just like the icon of any other application.

- If you go to the Classic System Preferences pane, it will state, "Classic is running." In addition, the Start button will change to Stop, and the Restart and Force Quit buttons will be available.

- If you choose Force Quit (such as from the Apple menu), *Classic Environment* will be listed as one of the applications you can force quit.

- In ProcessViewer, the Classic environment shows up as *TruBlueEnvironme*. From Terminal, the top command lists the Classic environment as *TruBlueEnv*.

- Some shareware/freeware utilities maintain a Classic icon in the Dock and provide visual cues about whether Classic is running. Typically, you can access a menu from these icons to start or quit Classic. Two such applications are Classic Toggler and Classic?.

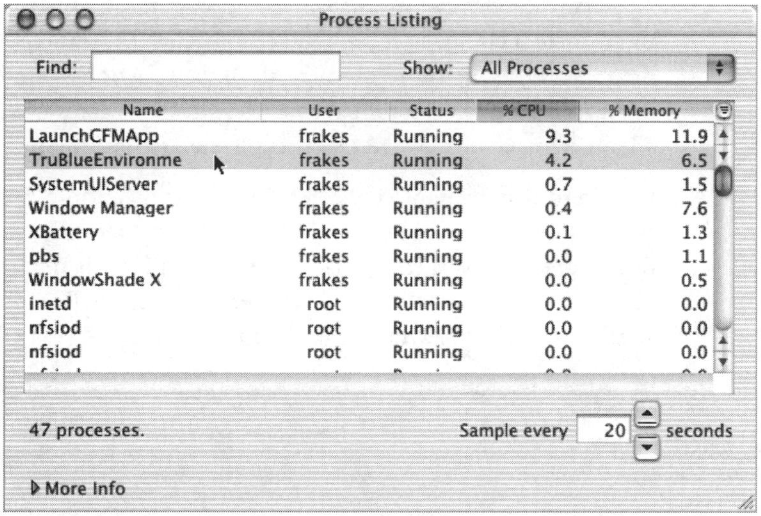

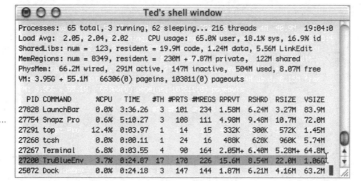

**Figure 9.4**

*ProcessViewer lists TrueBlueEnvironme; this means that Classic is running.*

**Figure 9.5**

*Terminal lists TruBlueEnv; this means that Classic is running.*

## The look and feel of Classic

When the Classic environment is running, if you launch a Classic application, it appears to launch just like any Mac OS X application. The application's icon bounces in the Dock as it is loading and remains there as long as the application is running. However, there are some differences:

**Menu bar.** When a Classic application is active, all menus and the menu bar switch to the Mac OS 9 Platinum appearance (gray with black text), and you see a menu bar arranged exactly as it would be in Mac OS 9. This situation has two major consequences: (1) All the Mac OS X additions to the menu bar, especially those at the right end (Date & Time, Volume icon, AirPort signal strength, Displays, and so on) vanish and are replaced by whatever Mac OS 9 would place there; and (2) The Apple menu shifts to the Mac OS 9 Apple menu. This second phenomenon can be an advantage, because you can choose Mac OS 9 control panels, the Chooser, and other items from the Apple menu.

Alternatively, you can use a shareware program called MR 9 Menu to bring up the Classic menu even if no Classic application is running. Or, you can simply drag the Apple Menu Items folder from the Classic System Folder to the Dock to create a Dock icon for the folder. You can then access items within the Apple Menu Items folder via the Dock icon's hierarchical menu.

One item that overlaps between the two versions of the Apple menu is Recent Items. This item provides a short list of the most recently used applications and documents. Conveniently, Mac OS X's Recent Items menu includes Classic applications you have run, and vice versa. Thus, the Recent Items lists will be similar regardless of whether you are in a Mac OS X or a Classic application.

**Figure 9.6**

Menu bar in Mac OS X when (top) a Classic application is active and (bottom) a Mac OS X application is active.

**Figure 9.7**

Apple menu in Mac OS X when (left) a Classic application is active and (right) a Mac OS X application is active.

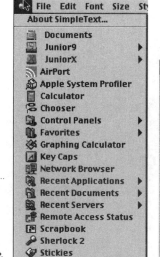

**Windows.** Windows in Mac OS X-native applications use the Aqua interface, including the trio of colored jewel buttons in the top-left corner (described in Chapter 3). Windows in Classic applications look and act as they do in Mac OS 9, using the Platinum appearance. You can even use the WindowShade effect with Mac OS 9 windows—a feature not included with Mac OS X (although a third-party utility called WindowShade X can provide it).

Similarly, Open and Save dialog boxes in Classic applications work as they do in Mac OS 9.

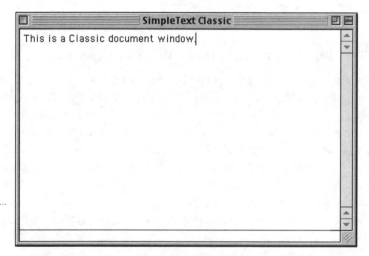

*Figure 9.8*

*A document window of a Classic application.*

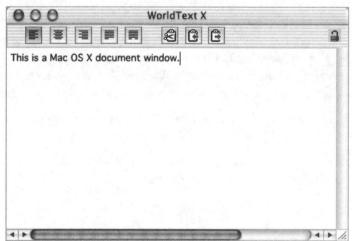

*Figure 9.9*

*A document window of a Mac OS X application.*

**Fonts.** Classic applications typically access only fonts in the Mac OS 9 Fonts folder. In particular, they will not access fonts in the various Library folders of Mac OS X. On the other hand, Mac OS X applications will recognize fonts placed in the Mac OS 9 System Folder that Classic uses.

Also, Mac OS X does not permit you to add fonts to or remove fonts from a font suitcase file, as you can in Mac OS 9, even when you're accessing these files with Classic running. Third-party utilities such as Suitcase can work around most of these limitations.

SEE: • Chapter 4 for more information on fonts.

---

**TAKE NOTE ▶ File Navigation in Open/Save Dialog Boxes**

Classic applications running in the Classic environment may use either of the two Open and Save dialog box types used in Mac OS 9. The first type is the older small white dialog boxes, called *Standard File Package* dialog boxes. They are also called *modal* dialog boxes because you cannot do anything else on your computer until you dismiss the box by opening/saving a file or canceling. You cannot even move or resize the box itself. The second type is the newer *Navigation Services* dialog boxes. These gray dialog boxes can be resized and moved, and they offer a few more menu and button options. They are modal only for the application in which they were opened. If you are using Internet Explorer, for example, and you choose its Save As command to open a dialog box, you can still switch to another application and use it while the Explorer dialog box remains open.

The Open and Save dialog boxes used by Mac OS X applications are different from either Mac OS 9 type (although they are also called *Navigation Services* boxes). They have the Aqua appearance. In addition, each document gets its own Open/Save dialog box. If you have several documents open in a native application and use the Save or Save As command, the resulting dialog box is attached to the currently active document. You can switch to other applications, or even to other documents within the same application, while the dialog box remains open.

Note: Carbon applications running native in Mac OS X may use either Mac OS 9 or Mac OS X type dialog boxes, largely depending on how the developer wrote the application.

SEE: • "Take Note: Open and Save Sheets," in Chapter 3, and "Opening and Saving: Saving files," in Chapter 6, for additional information.

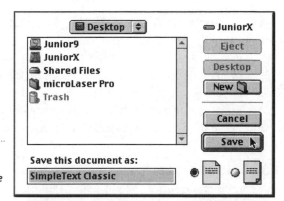

**Figure 9.10**

A Mac OS 9
Standard File
Package Open/Save
dialog box.

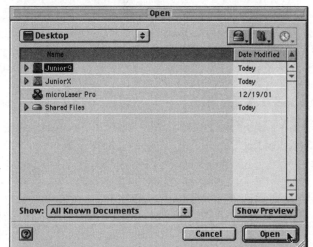

**Figure 9.11**

A Mac OS 9
Navigation Services
Open/Save dialog
box. Some Mac OS X
Carbon applications
may also use this.

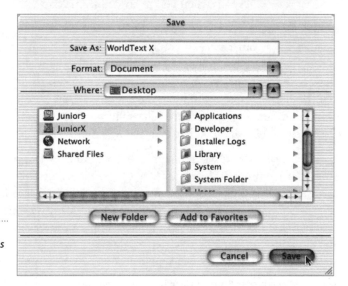

**Figure 9.12**

A Mac OS X
Navigation Services
Open/Save dialog
box.

# Desktop Folders in Mac OS 9/Classic vs. Mac OS X

If you routinely save files to the Desktop, and you boot back and forth between Mac OS X and Mac OS 9, you may notice that files saved to the Desktop in Mac OS 9 are no longer on the Desktop when you boot into Mac OS X, and vice versa, because the Desktop is handled differently by Mac OS X and Mac OS 9.

**Booting from Mac OS 9.** The Classic Mac OS was designed as a single-user environment; everyone shares the same files and folders (Mac OS 9 did introduce a Multiple Users feature, but that's another story). In Mac OS 9 and earlier, every hard drive or volume contains an invisible folder called, appropriately enough, Desktop Folder. If you have more than one volume mounted, there is thus more than one Desktop Folder available. Any items from a volume that are moved to the Desktop are stored in the Desktop Folder for that volume. However, the contents of all Desktop folders are visible together on what seems to be the sole Desktop of Mac OS 9.

**Booting from Mac OS X.** In Mac OS X, every user has his or her own Desktop Folder. This folder, called Desktop, is located at the root level of each user's Home directory (/Users/*user name*/Desktop/). When you log in to your Mac OS X account, anything you place on the Desktop is placed in your private Desktop folder. If someone else uses another account to log into your computer, he will never see—or even be able to access—the contents of your Desktop.

This also means that files saved to the Mac OS X Desktop do not appear on the Mac OS 9 Desktop when you're booted from Mac OS 9, and vice versa.

A related issue is that some Classic applications save files to the Desktop by default (or by your choice, if you click the Desktop button or pop-up menu in the Save dialog box), but they will most likely save them to the Mac OS 9 Desktop rather than the Mac OS X one. If you do not realize this situation, you may be surprised to find that the document you expected to see on your Mac OS X Desktop is not there. The solution is to locate the document on the Mac OS 9 Desktop, rather than the Mac OS X one.

A similar issue occurs when taking screen captures by using Command-Shift-3 or Command-Shift 4. In Mac OS X, the resulting files are saved to the user's Desktop. In Mac OS 9, however, the files are saved to the root level of the volume that contains the Mac OS 9 startup System Folder. When running Mac OS X, the files are also saved to the root level of the volume that contains the Mac OS 9 System Folder used for Classic, if you take a screen capture when a Classic application is the active application.

**SEE: • "Take Note: Screen Captures," in Chapter 5, for related information.**

**How to access the Mac OS 9 Desktop from Mac OS X.** You have two basic ways to access Mac OS 9 Desktop Folders when you're running Mac OS X, depending on which Desktop Folder you want to access:

- When running Mac OS X from a volume that also has Mac OS 9 installed, you will likely find an alias on your Desktop called *Desktop (Mac OS 9)*. One such alias is created for each user that has an account on your Mac. Double-click this alias to open and view the contents of the Mac OS 9 Desktop Folder for that volume. This alias is useful because the Mac OS 9 Desktop Folder icon on the startup volume is invisible and could not otherwise easily be opened.

- On all mounted volumes other than the Mac OS X startup volume, you will find a folder called Desktop Folder. This folder contains the Desktop items stored on that volume. If the volume contains the Mac OS 9 System Folder that you use for Classic, this is the Desktop Folder where items will go when you save files to the Desktop from Classic applications.

**SEE:** • "Take Note: The Location of Desktop and Trash Folders Desktop," in Chapter 3, and "Desktop (Mac OS 9) file is a symbolic link," in Chapter 6, for related information.

**How to access the Mac OS X Desktop from Mac OS 9.** If you boot from Mac OS 9 and need to access your Mac OS X Desktop, locate the Users folder (at the root level of the volume containing Mac OS X). Within it, locate the folder with your Mac OS X User name on it. Inside that folder will be the your Mac OS X Desktop Folder.

## Applications and Documents folders in Mac OS 9/Classic vs. Mac OS X

Mac OS 9 maintains certain applications in the Applications (Mac OS 9) folder. Similarly, it may store the documents you create in its Documents folder. Both of these folders are located at the root level of the Mac OS 9 volume.

There is also a Mac OS X Applications folder at the root level of the Mac OS X volume. In addition, there is a Documents folder in the Home directory of every user.

These Mac OS 9 vs. Mac OS X folders, despite their overlapping names, are separate. This situation can become a bit confusing. Open/Save dialog boxes in Mac OS 9 default to the Mac OS 9 Documents folder, for example, whereas Mac OS X dialog boxes default to your personal Documents folder. If a file appears to be missing, check both the Mac OS 9 and Mac OS X folder locations.

# Troubleshooting the Classic Environment

As the Classic environment is actually a copy of Mac OS 9, many of the same problems that can occur while you're running Mac OS 9 can occur in Classic. Unfortunately, troubleshooting Mac OS 9 is a topic too large to tackle here. Indeed, I've covered it at great length in a separate book, *Sad Macs, Bombs, and Other Disasters*. Some troubleshooting issues are specific to interactions between Mac OS 9, Classic, and Mac OS X, however. I cover a selection of those issues in this section.

One overall advantage of using the Classic environment instead of booting into Mac OS 9 is that Classic acts like just another Mac OS X application. Although a freeze or crash in a Classic application might take down the Classic environment, Mac OS X and Mac OS X applications will keep chugging along as though nothing had happened; you can relaunch Classic while you work on other things. It also means that you can troubleshoot the Classic environment while you are doing other things in Mac OS X; restarting Classic does not take over your whole computer.

## Startup conflicts

Just as Mac OS 9 loads files at startup (mainly files in the Extensions and Control Panels folders of the Mac OS 9 System Folder), so does the Classic environment. Just as you can watch the icons of these files appear across the bottom of the startup screen as they are loaded in Mac OS 9, you can see them appear in the Classic Startup window as the Classic environment loads. Because of this similarity, Classic is susceptible to the same startup-file conflicts (often called extension conflicts) that can occur when you're booting from Mac OS 9. This situation can lead to anything from a minor problem when you're accessing a command in a certain Classic application to a fatal crash of Classic as it attempts to load.

**Startup with extensions off.** The surest way to minimize such problems is to use a slimmed-down and optimized Mac OS 9 System Folder for Classic, as I recommended earlier in this chapter. If problems persist, you will want to determine whether an extension is causing the conflict.

The most direct way to do this in Classic is via the settings in the Advanced tab of Classic System Preferences. In particular, you can choose the Turn Off Extensions option from the Startup Options pop-up menu before starting or restarting Classic. This method is equivalent to starting up Mac OS 9 with the Shift key held down at startup. If you have any problems with getting this option to work, you can choose the Use Key Combination option instead and make the Shift key the key to use at startup. This method, too, should launch Classic with all extensions disabled. In either case, if the problem no longer occurs, a startup file was the cause.

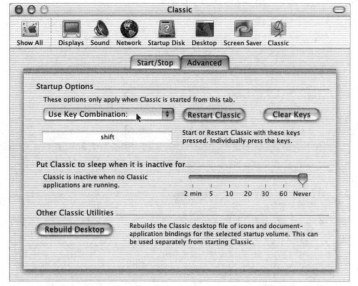

**Figure 9.13**

*The Advanced tab of Classic System Preferences, with Use Key Combination selected in the Startup Options pop-up menu.*

**Delete/ replace Classic files.** The next step is to figure out which startup file or files are responsible for the conflict. One frequent cause of such conflicts is one of the files that Mac OS X installs in your Mac OS 9 System Folder for Classic compatibility. At the root level of your System Folder are four of these files: Classic, Classic Support, Classic Support UI, and ProxyApp. Try moving these files to the Trash, emptying the Trash, and then starting up Classic normally. Mac OS X should ask you for permission to add these files back to your System Folder; allow it to do so. If your Classic startup conflict is gone, the problem was most likely that one of those files was corrupted, and replacing them with new copies solved the problem.

**Check the Startup Items folder.** If you have aliases to servers in the Startup Items folder (in your Classic System Folder) and those servers are not accessible to mount, Classic will fail to launch successfully. Instead, Classic will hang indefinitely at the point where it tries to mount the servers.

**Isolate the startup-file conflict.** If the problem is not solved by the previous suggestions, you will need to hunt down the startup file or files that are causing the problem. Those of you who have isolated startup-file conflicts in Mac OS 9 know the procedure well; although it fairly straightforward, it is also quite tedious and time-consuming.

SEE: • "Take Note: Isolating Startup-File Conflicts," later in this chapter, for specific details.

**TAKE NOTE** ▶ **Isolating Startup-File Conflicts**

When a startup file does not load properly, conflicts with another file during startup, or conflicts with other software used after startup is complete, you have a startup-file conflict. To track down the offending file or files, follow these steps:

1.  If your problems began recently, the chances are good that a newer startup file is causing the problem, so disable files that you recently installed and see whether the problem goes away.

    If it does, you can add these newer files back one at a time until you find out which one (or more) caused the problem.

    To disable a file, drag it out of the Mac OS 9 System Folder (the one used by Classic) and restart Classic. Alternatively, you can use Extensions Manager, as described in the following step.

    If testing newly added files does not solve the problem, the cause is likely third-party shareware extensions or control panels added to your System Folder. One or more of those files may not be compatible with Classic or is conflicting with other files.

2.  Launch Classic with only the startup files that came with Mac OS 9 enabled.

    To start up with just Apple's Mac OS 9 files enabled, first choose Open Extensions Manager from the Startup Options pop-up menu in the Advanced tab of the Classic System Preferences window. Then click the Start/Restart Classic button. This action will cause Extensions Manager to open as Classic launches. When Extensions Manager opens, choose Mac OS 9 All from the Selected Set pop-up menu; then click Continue.

    If the conflict no longer occurs, one of the files you disabled was the cause of the conflict.

    If the problem persists, you can restart Classic with Mac OS 9 Base selected in Extensions Manager. This method enables an even smaller set of Apple startup files—just those files that are considered to be essential. If the conflict no longer occurs, one of the Apple files that you disabled was the cause of the conflict. The chances are quite slim that Mac OS 9 Base will find the culprit if Mac OS 9 All does not, however.

Note: In versions of Mac OS 9 before Mac OS 9.2.1, selecting Mac OS 9 Base or Mac OS 9 All in Extensions Manager disabled the required Classic compatibility files (such as Classic Support UI, discussed in the main text). In this case, you would need to create a custom set that added these files to the Base or All sets. Fortunately, you can prevent this hassle simply by making sure that you are using the latest version of Mac OS 9.

When you have determined whether the offending file is an Apple file, you will likely need to determine which of the numerous possible files is the actual culprit. This process can be tedious. Here are two suggested ways to go about it:

•   **Extensions Manager.** Use Extensions Manager to enable and disable files selectively, restarting Classic each time. The recommended approach is to disable half of all files the first time. If the half that remain still produce the conflict, disable half of those files. Keep doing that until the problem no longer occurs. At this point, shift to the group you just disabled and continue the process. Eventually, you will be left with just one file: the culprit.

*continues on next page*

**TAKE NOTE ▶ Isolating Startup-File Conflicts** *continued*

- **Conflict Catcher.** If that process sounds too tedious (which it is!), you can try Casady & Greene's Conflict Catcher (www.casadyg.com). This utility automates the process for you. In fact, Conflict Catcher works even better in the Classic environment than it does in Mac OS 9. When you're using Classic, you don't have to restart your machine to do testing; you simply reload Classic. You can work on other things while testing proceeds. Conflict Catcher 9 also allows you to maintain separate extension sets for launching Classic vs. booting in Mac OS 9—helpful if you are using the same Mac OS 9 System Folder in both cases.

**Figure 9.14**

Two utilities to help isolate startup-file conflicts: (top) Extensions Manager and (bottom) Conflict Catcher.

**TAKE NOTE ▶ Shared Library Manager StartUp Conflict**

In a well-known startup conflict, the symptom is (1) a crash on the launch of Classic or (2) Classic's taking a very, very long time to launch. If you use Extensions Manager or Conflict Catcher to determine whether a startup-file conflict is the cause, you may discover that Shared Library Manager (located in your Classic Mac OS 9 Extensions folder) is identified as the culprit. Sure enough, if you disable this file, the symptom goes away.

The only problem is that your Classic Internet access, and possibly other functionality, also goes away. The Shared Library Manager is critical for the use of numerous library files, including the Open Transport files needed for Internet access in Classic. Fortunately, you usually can fix this problem without disabling Shared Library Manager.

The solution is to reboot in Mac OS 9; then delete your TCP/IP preferences file (stored in the Preferences folder inside the System Folder). This method will delete all your saved settings, so save a copy of the settings information before deleting the file. Next, create a new default setting configuration (via the TCP/IP control panel) that duplicates the preferred setting information in your Mac OS X Network System Preferences window. The next time you launch Classic, the problem should be gone. If the problem recurs, repeat the fix, this time locking the TCP/IP preferences file (by checking the Locked checkbox in its Get Info window).

**SEE:** • **"Internet connection problems," later in this chapter, for related information.**

• **Chapter 8 for more information on Network System Preferences.**

**TAKE NOTE ▶ The CarbonLib Extension**

Running Carbonized applications in Classic requires the presence of a file in your Extensions folder called CarbonLib. Apple frequently updates this file, sometimes releasing a new version between updates of the OS itself. Each new version fixes bugs in the preceding version. Thus, if you are having problems running Carbonized applications within Classic (or even from Mac OS 9 itself), the general recommendation is to make sure that you are using the latest version of CarbonLib.

You can check VersionTracker (**www.versiontracker.com**) for the latest version, including whether a beta version is available (typically accessed via a set of developers' software called CarbonLib SDK). Although I generally recommend caution in using beta software, a beta version of CarbonLib may be the only cure for a current problem.

On the other hand, a bug may appear in a new version of CarbonLib; you would suspect this problem if a symptom appears immediately after you update. The temporary solution is to downgrade to the old version. Thus, I recommend keeping a copy of the previous version whenever you update CarbonLib, just in case a downgrade appears to be worth a try.

## Font conflicts

As discussed earlier in this chapter, Mac OS X uses fonts in the Fonts folder of the Classic System Folder. So Classic fonts can cause problems for Mac OS X, including an inability to start up Mac OS X, even if you never launch Classic.

Isolating which font may be the cause of a problem can become quite time-consuming. In general, suspect older fonts, especially bitmap fonts and fonts in font suitcases. To test a suspected font, remove it from the Mac OS 9 System Folder that Classic uses, and restart Mac OS X. If the suspected font problem is preventing Mac OS X from starting up, boot from Mac OS 9 or from a bootable Mac OS 9 CD, and remove the font from the System Folder.

Alternatively, if the problem is specific to running Classic, you can use Conflict Catcher to isolate problem fonts in the same way that you use it to isolate problems with startup files. Following are a few more examples of font problems that can occur:

- Simply having too many fonts in the Classic System Folder can cause startup problems for Mac OS X. In general, keep fonts in the Classic System Folder to a minimum. Whenever possible, move the fonts to the Fonts folder in your Home directory's Library folder; Classic will still be able to access them.

- Certain fonts in the Classic Fonts folder may cause any Carbon application running in Mac OS X 10.1 to crash on launch. Classic does not need to be running for this problem to happen. Crashes logged by Console will most likely have the following text at the top line of the list: "#0 ... In FindTablesInNFNT." Mac OS X 10.1.1 or later should fix this problem.

- Some applications may run exceptionally slowly in Classic. This problem happened to me with GoLive 4.x and 5.x. I found that reducing the number of fonts (especially PostScript fonts) in the Classic Fonts folder resulted in a substantial improvement in GoLive's responsiveness.

**SEE:** • **Chapter 4 for more information on fonts.**

• **Chapter 5 for more information on startup problems.**

## Rebuilding the Classic Desktop

Just like Mac OS 9, the Classic environment occasionally loses track of which documents should be opened with which applications or which applications are actually on your hard drive. As in Mac OS 9, the most common solution is to rebuild the Desktop. When you're booting in Mac OS 9, you typically do this by holding down the Command and Option keys at startup, as just mentioned in the previous section.

One advantage of working with Classic, however, is that you do not have to restart Classic to do a rebuild. Instead, simply go to the Advanced tab of Classic System Preferences and click the Rebuild Desktop button. A progress bar will appear to show you when the rebuild is complete.

The one disadvantage of this method is that if you have more than one volume, only the volume with the copy of Mac OS 9 that Classic is using will be rebuilt. In Mac OS X 10.1 or later, if you have multiple Mac OS 9 volumes, a better approach is to hold down the Command and Option keys as Classic launches (just as you would when booting in Mac OS 9) or have the Command and Option keys selected automatically via the Use Key Combination option in the Advanced tab of Classic System Preferences. Both methods will bring up dialog boxes for each partition/volume, asking whether you really want to rebuild your Desktop. The best part about this procedure is that it will rebuild the Desktops of multiple volumes in parallel, making the rebuild much faster than the sequential rebuilding that occurs when booting in Mac OS 9.

## Classic application freezes

If a Classic application freezes, and you cannot seem to quit it by using the standard Quit command (either by choosing it from the application's File menu or by pressing Command-Q), you can still likely force-quit the application. To do this, hold down Command-Option-Escape. In the Force Quit window that appears, choose the offending application, and click the Force Quit button.

Typically, a Force Quit of a Classic application will cause the entire Classic environment to quit. In fact you will get a warning when you attempt the Force Quit that says: "This may cause all applications running in the Classic environment to quit immediately." If you Force Quit anyway, you can simply relaunch Classic.

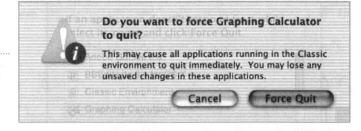

*Figure 9.15*

*The warning that appears when you attempt to Force Quit a Classic application.*

More rarely, the application will quit, but Classic will remain active. Even in this case, you should save your work in other Classic applications and restart the Classic environment (in the Classic tab of the System Preferences window) to prevent further problems.

Sometimes, a Force Quit will not work, especially if the problem occurs while the application is launching. The Dock icon continues to bounce endlessly, but the application never opens. If you Control-click the application's icon in the Dock, the pop-up menu may say that the application is not responding. In this case, follow the advice in the following section, "Classic environment freezes."

**SEE:** • "Use Force Quit," in Chapter 5, for more details on how to force-quit applications in Mac OS X.

## Classic environment freezes

As is true when you're booted from Mac OS 9, a freeze of even one open application in Classic often freezes the entire environment. Symptoms of this problem in Classic include:

- You cannot launch any Classic applications, even though the Classic tab of the System Preferences window says, "Classic is running."
- A blank menu bar appears when you attempt to bring a Classic application to the foreground.

If this happens, try to force-quit from any Classic application. If you cannot do this, try quitting Classic by clicking the Stop button in the Classic tab of the System Preferences window. If none of these methods works, you will need to Force Quit the Classic environment. To do this, try one or more of the following techniques until you are successful:

- In the Classic tab of the System Preferences window, click the Force Quit button.
- With a Mac OS X application active, choose Force Quit from the Mac OS X Apple menu, select Classic Environment in the Force Quit window, and click the Force Quit button.
- Open Mac OS X's ProcessViewer utility, select TruBlueEnvironme, and choose the Quit Process command from the Processes menu.
- Use the top command in Terminal to identify the process ID number (PID) of TruBlueEnv and then type kill {PID} to kill the Classic process.

**SEE:** • "Kill from Terminal," in Chapter 5, for more details.

If none of these methods work, you should restart your Mac. Even better, shut down the Mac; then restart.

Finally, as mentioned earlier in this chapter, having Classic launch automatically at startup (via the Classic System Preferences setting) can trigger freezes in certain situations. If problems persist, disable this option and launch Classic manually instead.

**"The Classic environment is not responding "message.** An Apple document states: "After clicking Stop in the Classic pane of System Preferences, an alert box appears with this message: 'The Classic environment is Not

Responding. You may click Cancel and attempt to save any changes to open documents...' If the Classic pane of System Preferences states that 'Classic is not running,' then your stop attempt was successful, and the message is inaccurate in this circumstance. The Classic environment has indeed been properly shut down. You may click either Force Quit or Cancel to dismiss the inaccurate alert message. To avoid the issue entirely, you may shut down the Classic environment by choosing Log Out from the Apple menu and logging back in."

**SEE:** • **Chapters 3 and 5 for more information on ProcessViewer and on restarting the Mac after a freeze.**

• **Chapter 10 for more information on Terminal.**

## Problems launching applications

In theory, Classic applications will load in the Classic environment, and Mac OS X-native applications will open in Mac OS X. In practice, what should happen and what actually happens don't always coincide.

**"Cannot be used in Classic" error.** Occasionally, if you attempt to launch a Mac OS X application (especially from the Dock while Classic is running), the application may attempt to launch in Classic. If it cannot do this, you will get an error message that says: "This version of {*application name*} cannot be used in the Classic environment." This situation can also happen if you double-click a document for which you have both a Classic and Mac OS X version of the same application (for example, if you have two copies of Internet Explorer—one for each OS—and you double-click an Internet Explorer document). Essentially, this problem is due to a bug in Mac OS X. If you click OK and attempt to relaunch the application, the application usually will work. Sometimes, you have to make sure that you are not actually in the Classic environment by switching to a Mac OS X application first.

**Wrong version accessed.** When you have both Classic and Mac OS X versions of the same application on your drive, the Mac OS 9 version may open in error.

If you have both variants of the same Web browser, for example, and you do not have the Mac OS X version running, clicking a URL from within a Classic application (such as a Classic email client) will likely launch the Classic version of the Web browser instead of the Mac OS X version. The reason is due to the way that the Classic environment looks for applications to open files. First, it looks to see whether the appropriate application is already running and, if it does not find the application open, it looks to launch the application. In such cases, Classic may see only the Mac OS 9 version (not recognizing a Mac OS X package .app file as being a legitimate application) and will launch the Mac OS 9 version. The solution is to keep the Mac OS X version of your Web browser running or to launch it before clicking a URL.

A similar problem can occur if you have both the Mac OS 9 and Mac OS X versions of StuffIt Expander. The Mac OS 9 version may launch when you expect the Mac OS X version to be used. The solution is easy. Because StuffIt Expander 6.0.1 or later is a Carbon application that will run in both Mac OS X and Mac OS 9, simply delete all earlier versions from your drive.

**SEE:**  • "Technically Speaking: Understanding Packages" in Chapter 2.
  • "Technically Speaking: Troubleshooting StuffIt Engine.cfm" in Chapter 3.
  • "Document opens in the wrong application," in Chapter 6, for related information.

**When you want to use the Classic version instead.** Finally, you may *want* to open some Carbon applications in Classic rather than in Mac OS X. (Maybe you have an application that has a spelling checker that works in Mac OS 9 but not in Mac OS X, so you prefer to use the Mac OS 9 version.) If you open the Show Info window for certain Carbon applications and check the Open in the Classic environment checkbox, the application will always load in the Classic environment.

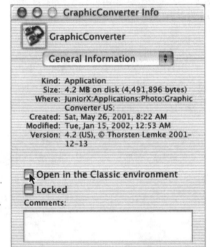

*Figure 9.16*

*The Open in the Classic environment option in the Show Info window of a Carbon application.*

**TAKE NOTE ▶ Applications Packages with Two Application Versions Inside**

Some application packages (AppleWorks 6 is a prime example) work in Classic or Mac OS X by maintaining two separate versions of the application within the application package file. The appropriate "inside the package" application for the current OS gets launched when you double-click the package icon. Unlike applications that consist of a single Carbonized version that can run in either Mac OS X or Classic, however, the Show Info window for these dual-application packages does not include the Open in Classic Environment checkbox. When you are running Mac OS X, AppleWorks 6, for example, will always launch its Mac OS X version, even if Classic is running. The Mac OS 9 version will launch only if you boot from Mac OS 9.

*continues on next page*

**TAKE NOTE ▶ Applications Packages with Two Application Versions Inside**
*continued*

What can you do, in such cases, if you want to force the Classic version to be used when you're running Mac OS X? Follow these steps:

1. Open the AppleWorks package via the Show Package Contents command in the contextual menu.

2. Navigate to the MacOS Classic folder, and open it.

   You will see the Classic AppleWorks icon.

3. Double-click the icon to launch AppleWorks.

   *or*

   Drag that icon to the Dock. With this method, whenever you click the Dock icon, the Classic version will launch.

   Similarly, dragging the Mac OS X version of AppleWorks (located in the MacOS folder) to the Dock can ensure that the Mac OS X version gets launched, just in case some error is resulting in the Classic version's getting launched.

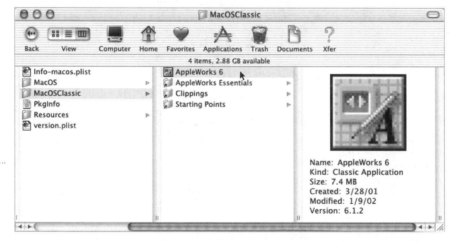

*Figure 9.17*

*The Classic version of the AppleWorks application in the AppleWorks package.*

**Mac OS X error message appears when you're launching documents in Mac OS 9.** Occasionally, when you're booted in Mac OS 9, an error message may appear when you double-click a document, saying that you need to be running Mac OS X to use the software you just tried to launch.

This message occurs, as you would expect, when you try to launch a Mac OS X application in Mac OS 9. It also occurs if you double-click a document that was created with a Mac OS X application (because this document will attempt to load the Mac OS X application as well).

The problem is that the message may also appear when you're trying to open a document that should launch a Mac OS 9 application, especially if you also have a Mac OS X version of the application installed. This situation has been known to happen after Microsoft Office X is installed. In this case, when you boot in Mac OS 9 later and double-click an Office document—even one that you created and saved in a Mac OS 9 version of Office (such as Office 2001) —the OS may attempt to launch the Mac OS X version of the Office application. You will have an advance warning, because the icon of the document will have shifted to the Mac OS X version of the document icon.

This problem has a variety of workarounds. My recommendation is to rebuild the Desktop when you're booting in Mac OS 9, as described in "Rebuilding the Classic Desktop," earlier in this chapter. If that technique alone does not work, first compress the Mac OS X version of the application (using a program such as DropStuff) and rebuild the Desktop. Then you can decompress the compressed application.

## Problems installing software

Although Classic software installers will run in the Classic environment, they will not necessarily work properly. Due to Mac OS X's use of permissions, Classic installers, if not written properly, can try to install in to or write to directories for which the user does not have enough privileges. To make things worse, the error messages that result are not always clear. If you get strange errors when you're trying to install Classic software, try rebooting in to Mac OS 9 and then running the installer again. In fact, it is probably a good idea always to boot into Mac OS 9 before updating/installing Classic software.

One exception: In current versions of Mac OS X, you can run the Software Update control panel for Mac OS 9 and update Mac OS 9 software from within the Classic environment.

## Copy/Paste problems

Classic and Mac OS X share the Clipboard, and you can cut and paste between Classic and Mac OS X applications just as you can between two applications in Mac OS 9. Mac OS X and Classic applications don't always use the same data types for Clipboard content, however, so some copy/paste operations between Classic and Mac OS X applications will fail. The Mac OS 9 Clipboard may not recognize the format of a particular clip from Mac OS X, for example; thus, you will lose the clip's formatting when you paste it into a Mac OS 9 application. Typically, you can prevent this problem by dragging the content directly from one application to the other, or from one application to the Desktop, and then from the Desktop to the second application.

**SEE:** • **"Can't copy and paste from Classic to Mac OS X," in Chapter 6, for related information.**

# Memory problems

Mac OS X eliminated the need to separately set the memory allocation for each application. But the issue remains for Mac OS 9 applications run via Classic.

**Application memory.** Although Mac OSX allocates RAM dynamically to Mac OS X applications and the Classic environment itself, Classic applications use memory just as they do when you're booted in Mac OS 9. Each application can use only as much RAM as you have allocated to it in its Get Info window. If an application is having memory-related problems, you may need to allocate more memory to it. To do so, follow these steps:

1. Quit the application; then select it in the Finder.

2. Choose Show Info from the File menu (or press Command-I).

3. In the Show Info window, choose Memory from the pop-up menu.

4. Increase the application's Preferred Size. I recommend starting with an increase of 25 to 50 percent.

5. Close the Show Info window.

6. Relaunch the application.

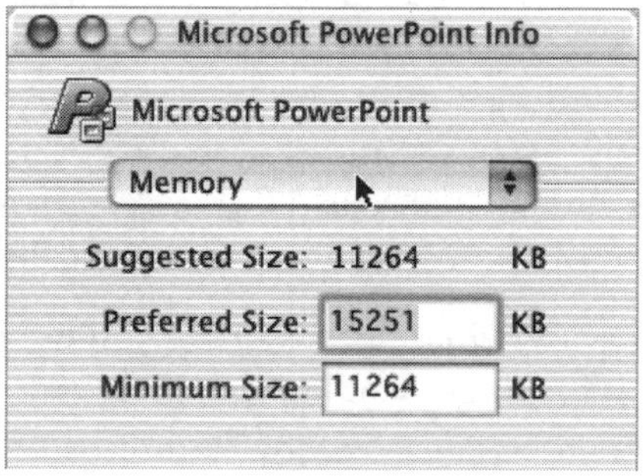

*Figure 9.18*

*The Memory options of the Show Info window for a Classic application.*

**Virtual memory.** Because memory management is handled by Mac OS X, the Classic environment always operates as though virtual memory is disabled. As a consequence, Classic applications that require virtual memory (and there are only a few that do) will not function properly in the Classic environment. Unfortunately, no workaround is available for this problem right now, other than to boot into Mac OS 9 to use these applications.

# Printing problems

Printing in Classic is similar to printing in Mac OS 9; open the Chooser (available from the Classic Apple menu) to select a printer and then print from within your applications.

There are some special considerations, however, when printing from Classic:

- Although Mac OS X supports non-AppleTalk serial-port printers, you cannot print to such printers from within Classic, because Classic cannot access serial ports through Mac OS X. Similarly, you cannot print to LocalTalk-connected printers from Classic.

- If your printer requires a PPD file or driver in Mac OS 9, and you don't have it installed, you'll need to install it before you can print. If it is just a PPD file that is needed, you can install it while running Mac OS X, by dragging the file to the Extensions/Printer Descriptions folder in the Classic System Folder. Otherwise, if you need to run an Installer utility, you may have to boot from Mac OS 9 to do so.

- Classic does not support Mac OS 9 desktop printers. Neither does it use the Mac OS X print queue. To monitor your Classic print jobs, you must use the PrintMonitor application (located in the Extensions folder of the Classic System Folder).

If you are still having general problems getting documents to print in Classic, consider the following:

**PrintMonitor memory.** Some problems printing from Classic may be solved by increasing the memory size of the Classic PrintMonitor application. The application is located in the Extensions folder of the Mac OS 9 System Folder. Increase its memory by opening the Get Info window for the application, choosing Memory from the pop-up menu, and replacing the Preferred Size setting with a larger value (perhaps double or triple its initial size).

**Background printing.** Background printing is a Mac OS 9 feature of the LaserWriter driver (selected in the Chooser). If the feature is enabled, it may prevent printing from within the Classic environment. To work around this problem, disable background printing. To do so, follow these steps:

1. Choose Print from the File menu of a Classic application to open the Print dialog box.

2. Choose Background Printing from the pop-up menu.

3. Choose Print in: Foreground (no spool file) rather than the default Print in: Background option.

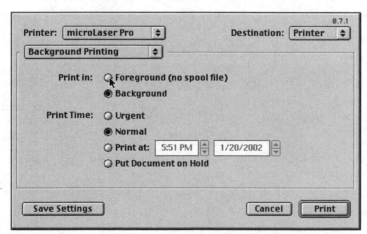

*Figure 9.19*

*The Background Printing options in the Print dialog box.*

**AirPort.** If you can print to an AppleTalk printer over an AirPort connection via Mac OS X, but not via Classic, Classic's AppleTalk control panel may be set to AirPort. Although this choice might seem to be the correct one, it is not. Instead, select Ethernet Slot 1 (or, if this option is not available, Ethernet or Ethernet Built-In). The TCP/IP control panel should have a similar Ethernet setting. For this control panel, however, the setting is established when you first launch Classic and cannot be modified. So if the setting is incorrect, you will need to boot in Mac OS 9 to fix it.

**SEE:** • "Internet connection problems," later in this chapter, for more details.

**Print in Mac OS X with Classic active.** If you are having general problems printing in Mac OS X while Classic is active, be aware that some printers will not print when Classic is running. In this case, the solution is to quit Classic before attempting to print.

**SEE:** • Chapter 7 for more general information on troubleshooting printing problems.

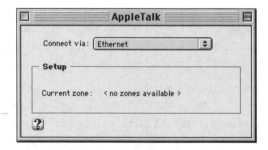

*Figure 9.20*

*AppleTalk control panel in Classic.*

---

**TAKE NOTE ▶ Save as PDF File to Print in Classic**

In several situations, a document may refuse to print in Mac OS X but will print in Mac OS 9. Some USB printers are supported in Classic but do not work under Mac OS X itself, for example. So if you are using a Mac OS X application, you will be unable to print.

The solution is as follows:

1. In the Print dialog box of the Mac OS X application, click the Preview button instead of the Print button.

   This step converts the file to a PDF (Acrobat) document and opens the file in the Preview application.

2. Save the file as a PDF file.

Another method is to choose Output Options from the pull-down menu in the Mac OS X Print dialog box, check the Save As File checkbox, choose PDF as the file type, and then save the file.

*continues on next page*

**TAKE NOTE** ▶ **Save as PDF File to Print in Classic**  *continued*

In either case, assuming that you have a version of Acrobat that opens in Classic (Acrobat 4.x or a Classic version of Acrobat 5.x, for example), you can open the resulting PDF document in Classic and print from there.

Similarly, Classic supports USB printer sharing, whereas Mac OS X does not. You can use the same procedure to print to a shared USB printer.

## Sleep problems

The ability to put the Mac to sleep is a great energy-saving feature. It works in Mac OS X, whether or not Classic is running. However, the combination of Classic and sleep presents a few special problems.

**Slow wakeup.** Waking from sleep is dramatically faster in Mac OS X than in Mac OS 9. But if Classic is running and a Classic application is active (the frontmost application), wakeup time can slow dramatically. To speed up waking from sleep, be sure to switch to a Mac OS X application before putting your computer to sleep.

**Wake-from-sleep crashes.** Numerous users have reported crashes in waking from sleep if the Classic environment is running when the computer is put to sleep (and especially if a Classic application is the active application). Some of these reported crashes are mild (the Finder quits and Classic quits); others are as serious as kernel panics. Although Apple apparently fixed many of the causes of this problem in its most recent Mac OS X updates, and although the problem may affect some Mac models more than it does others, if you experience problems on waking your computer, it may pay to make sure that Classic is stopped before letting your computer go to sleep. Or at least make sure that a Mac OS X application or the Finder is the active application.

**Putting Classic to sleep.** In the Advanced tab of the Classic System Preferences window is an option to put Classic to sleep when it is inactive for a specified time. This option is separate from the overall sleep mode of the Mac; it is designed to minimize the processor and memory use of the Classic application when you are not using Classic but do not want to quit it. I have found, however, that when Classic wakes from this inactive state, I am more likely to have a freeze or crash than if I did not let it go to sleep at all. If this appears to be happening to you, set the inactive time in the Classic System Preferences window to Never.

# Internet connection problems

When you first launch the Classic environment, Mac OS X actually alters the configuration setting for Mac OS 9's TCP/IP control panel (stored in the TCP/IP Preferences file in the Classic System Folder). More specifically, it creates a new configuration named Classic. This configuration is used to funnel all TCP/IP traffic in Classic through Mac OS X.

Normally, this situation works wonderfully, allowing you to access the Internet via Classic applications without requiring any separate configuration of Mac OS 9. You just launch Classic, and everything works! Occasionally, however, your Mac OS 9 Internet applications may fail to work even though Mac OS X applications are connecting to the Internet with no problems.

**Mac OS 9 vs. Mac OS X settings conflict.** The most common cause of Classic Internet problems is because Mac OS X can detect the correct connection type automatically and switch to the correct network settings, whereas the settings in Mac OS 9's TCP/IP control panel remain static.

To elaborate, when Mac OS X creates the Classic configuration in TCP/IP, it chooses the first type of connection specified in the Active Network Ports section of Mac OS X's Network System Preferences window. If your first setting is AirPort, and your second is Ethernet, Classic's TCP/IP setting will be AirPort. As long as Mac OS X is connected to the Internet via an AirPort connection, everything is fine. The problem occurs if you switch from an AirPort connection to an Ethernet connection. Mac OS X will detect the change and switch automatically, but Classic will continue to think that it should be using an AirPort connection. If no AirPort connection is available, the connection will fail.

Unfortunately, this problem has no permanent fix. If you get bitten by this bug, the workaround is to delete the TCP/IP preferences file in the Mac OS 9 System Folder before you launch Classic. When you launch Classic, Mac OS X will create a new configuration that corresponds to the current Mac OS X connection. If you switch connection types again, the problem will reappear.

Note: If you frequently boot into Mac OS 9 by using the System Folder used for Classic, you may have created additional TCP/IP configurations for accessing the Internet from Mac OS 9. If you delete the TCP/IP preferences file, as suggested earlier in this section, all these additional settings will be deleted. To prevent this problem, save a copy of the preferences file outside the System Folder before you delete the file. When you're booted from Mac OS 9, you can drag the copy back into the Preferences folder to restore your additional settings.

**Corrupt TCP/IP preferences.** More generally, Mac OS 9's TCP/IP preferences file seems to become corrupt much more often in Classic that it does in Mac OS 9. Problems with the TCP/IP preferences file can even prevent Classic from starting up at all. If you are having Internet connection problems in Classic, or startup crashes, throw away the TCP/IP preferences file and launch the Classic environment again.

SEE:  • **Chapter 8 for more information on troubleshooting Internet problems.**

# Classic Quick Fixes

Following are brief descriptions of an assortment of problems related to the use of Classic and their known solutions/fixes.

## Files locked in Mac OS 9

When you're booted in Mac OS 9, you can lock files via the Locked checkbox in the Get Info window for the file. This locked/unlocked setting carries over to Mac OS X. If you try to throw away a file that was locked in Mac OS 9, Mac OS X will not let you do so. In fact, it will most likely not even allow you to place the file in the Trash, claiming that you do not have "sufficient privileges."

In most cases, you can still delete the file in Mac OS X by opening the Show Info window for the file and unchecking its Locked checkbox.

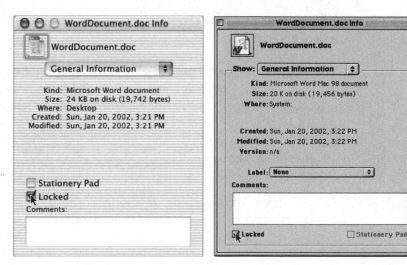

*Figure 9.21*

*The Locked check-box in (left) a Mac OS X Show Info window and (right) a Mac OS 9/Classic Get Info window.*

SEE:  • **Chapter 6 for much more information on problems with deleting files, locked and otherwise.**

## Clippings files in Mac OS 9 vs. X

A text clipping file is created (from applications that support this feature) when you drag a selection of text from a document to the Desktop. Typically, double-clicking these files opens a window displaying the text contents.

**Opening clipping files created in Mac OS X when you're booting from Mac OS 9.** If you create a clipping file in Mac OS X, the file will not open when you're booted in Mac OS 9. Double-clicking it in Mac OS 9 instead results in an error message that says, "This file is used by the System Software. It cannot be opened."

The solution is to use any utility that allows you to change the creator of a file, either in Mac OS X (by using a utility such as XRay) or in Mac OS 9 (by using a utility such as Snitch). Change the creator of the clipping file from MACS to drag. Now the file will open in Mac OS 9 as expected.

Opening a Mac OS 9-created clipping file in Mac OS X works without making any modification of the file's attributes.

Note: Depending on what you drag to the Desktop, you may create different types of clipping files, such as picture clippings and Internet address clippings.

**Clipping files with long names.** Sometimes, a text clipping created in Mac OS X has a name more than 31 characters long. Because Mac OS 9 does not support file names this long, if you try to copy one of these clippings to another Mac or a file server running Mac OS 9 or earlier, you will get an error. The solution is to rename the clipping file with a shorter name.

## "Ensure that TruBlueEnvironme is setuid" message

When you try to launch Classic, you may get an error message that says, "You are running Classic without supervisor (root) privileges. Ensure that TruBlueEnvironment is setuid and owned by root, or re-install Classic." A likely solution to this esoteric complaint is to uncheck the Ignore Privileges on This Volume checkbox (located in the volume's Show Info window) for the volume that contains the Classic Mac OS 9 System Folder. Classic should now launch.

Otherwise, it is likely that Mac OS X cannot locate a blessed Mac OS 9 System Folder or there is no Mac OS 9 System Folder to be located. In the former case, you need to bless the System Folder (as described in "Select the Classic environment volume" earlier in this chapter). In the latter case, you need to install Mac OS 9 on a mounted drive.

## "The operation could not be completed" message

Occasionally, when you're trying to eject a CD or unmount a disk image file, you may get an error message that says, "The operation could not be completed because the disk is in use," even though nothing on the CD or image appears to be in use. In such cases, quitting Classic should allow the image or CD to unmount or eject.

SEE:  • Chapter 6 for more information on ejecting disks.

## Disappearing pointer

Sometimes, the pointer disappears when you're using a Classic application. You have two quick ways to fix this problem:

• Press Command-Tab to switch to a Mac OS X application; then click somewhere in the application. When you switch back to the Classic application, the pointer should be visible.

• Move the (invisible) pointer all the way to the edge of the screen so that when you click, you are clicking the Desktop. Then switch back to the Classic application.

## Classic application and folder names

If a Classic application and its enclosing folder have the same name (such as Claris Emailer), the application may not launch in Classic. The solution is to rename the application or the folder so that they have different names.

## Volumes do not mount when booting from Mac OS 9

A volume that was formatted when installing Mac OS X will not mount when booting from Mac OS 9 if the Mac OS 9 disk drivers are not installed. If this happens, the obvious solution is to install them. To do so, boot in Mac OS 9 from some volume (use a Mac OS 9 Install CD if no hard drive is available) and launch Drive Setup. Select the name of the volume that will not mount and select Update Driver from the Functions menu.

The problem can be prevented by making sure that the Install Mac OS 9 Disk Drivers option is enabled when installing Mac OS X—either from (a) the Install Mac OS X utility on the Mac OS X Install CD or (b) the Partitions tab in Disk Utility in Mac OS X. The option is enabled by default.

# 10

# Unix for
# Mac OS X Users

I've said it before. The core of Mac OS X is an operating system whose origins predate the Mac itself: Unix.

For most users, the fact that Unix exists on the Mac will be as relevant as the fact that REALbasic exists as a programming language for Mac OS X. You don't need to bother with either just to use a word processor or a Web browser.

Still, as I have asserted before, troubleshooters do not have the same luxury. When things go wrong and the standard Mac OS X techniques do not work, you will often need to resort to Unix. Indeed, I have peppered the preceding chapters of this book with tips (primarily in sidebars) that demonstrate the use of Unix, either via third-party Aqua utilities that serve as a graphical front end to the Unix features or via the direct access provided by the Terminal application.

The Terminal application is the focus of this chapter.

# In This Chapter

# Understanding Unix

The point of this chapter is not for you to become a Unix expert. That's an admirable goal, and I certainly would encourage you to do so, if you're motivated. But the goal here is just to provide enough understanding of how Unix works to enable you to do those Mac OS X troubleshooting tasks that will benefit from using Terminal. Welcome to Unix for Mac OS X.

**SEE: • Chapters 1 and 4, for more background on Unix in Mac OS X.**

## What is Terminal?

The Terminal application is located in the Utilities folder of the Applications folder. Terminal is your window to the Unix world. If you were to use a computer running Unix and nothing else, the only way you would be able to interact with the computer would be through an environment much like Terminal.

Terminal is an incredibly powerful tool that provides key troubleshooting capabilities that you cannot access any other way. If you are familiar with Unix, it also allows you to do almost anything that you could do from a standard Unix machine, such as setting up and running Perl scripts; setting up cron jobs; and accessing FTP, Telnet, and Apache Web-server software. It is no wonder that many more advanced users have been almost drooling at the prospect of what can be done with this combination of Unix and the Mac.

Potentially, Terminal is also a very dangerous tool, especially if you are not familiar with how to use it. A small error could result in your deleting a good part of the data on your drive without even getting a warning from the Mac about the trouble that's about to happen.

Terminal uses a command-line interface, which means that (1) it accepts only text input and produces only text output, and (2) all interactions are made via the keyboard, with almost no use of the mouse.

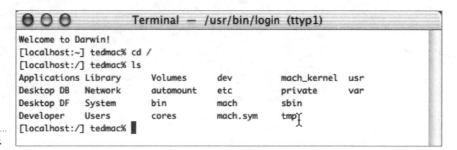

*Figure 10.1*

*A Terminal window.*

**Terminal's menus.** Although the focus of Terminal is the command-line window that opens when you launch it, Terminal also has traditional Mac menus in the menu bar at the top of the display. Most of these menus customize the display (the Font menu, for example) or assist you in navigating the Terminal window (the Control menu, for example). The Shell menu provides the option to open multiple Terminal windows, as well as to save or print Terminal output. The Inspector command in the Shell menu opens a window in which you can set various display parameters, such as the window size, the font, and the colors of the display. These options, as well as others, are also accessible when you choose Preferences from the Terminal menu. The difference is that changes in the Inspector window box affect only the currently active shell, whereas changes in the Preferences window affect all future shell windows.

In most cases, you can leave all the defaults alone. For basic troubleshooting needs, you rarely have any reason to modify these settings.

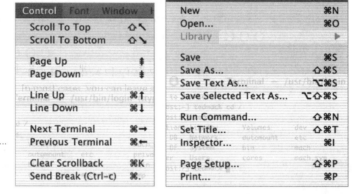

*Figure 10.2*

Terminal's (left)
Control menu and
(right) Shell menu.

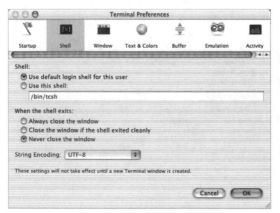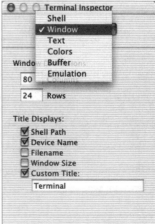

*Figure 10.3*

Terminal's (left)
Preferences window
and (right) Inspector
window.

**TECHNICALLY SPEAKING ▶ What's a Shell?**

A shell in Unix refers to a command-line interpreter. That is, when you type a command such as <ls>, the shell determines the response to the command.

On the Mac, you typically have only one "shell": the Mac OS itself. Although this metaphor is not perfect, you could think of different versions of the Mac OS as being different shells. Thus, if you have both Mac OS 9 and Mac OS X on your Mac, and you shift between them, commands will work differently. Command-N, for example, creates a new folder in Mac OS 9 but opens a new Finder window in Mac OS X. Changing shells in Unix can have the same effect.

In terms of the basic Unix commands you will be working with in this chapter, however, all shells work pretty much the same way. Mac OS X's Terminal defaults to the tcsh shell (known as the terminal-based C shell). Other popular shells are sh (called the Bourne shell) and csh (called the C shell).

You can change to a new shell simply by typing its name in the Terminal window and pressing Return. For example, to shift to the sh shell, type <sh> and press Return. To revert to the preceding shell, type <exit>.

Another way to access a different shell is to have a shell window open in an alternative shell. I explain how to do this in "Technically Speaking: Modifying the Window Title: An Example of Using Terminal Preferences," later in this chapter. Unless I explicitly state otherwise, however, I recommend that you stick with the default tcsh shell.

**The env command: What shell are you using?** The title bar of Terminal windows will likely indicate what shell you are using. If the title bar says login, you are using the default login shell (tcsh). Otherwise, you can determine your current shell by typing <env> (for environment). You also get a host of other basic information, such as the OSTYPE (darwin) and HOSTTYPE (macintosh).

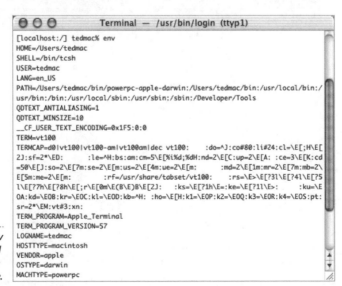

**Figure 10.4**

*Output from the env command: The shell name is listed in the SHELL=/bin/tcsh line.*

**TECHNICALLY SPEAKING** ▶ **Modifying the Window Title: An Example of Using Terminal Preferences**

When you launch the Terminal application, a window will open. The name of the window will be something like /usr/bin/login (ttyp1).

You can modify this name via Terminal's Preferences command. To do so, select the Window pane, and look at the Title Displays setting. You will see that the title lists the Shell Path (/usr/bin/login) and the Device Name (ttyp1). The shell path refers to the program used to determine what shell is opened. In this case, it is the default login shell (which happens to use tcsh).

Note: Shell programs are stored in the /bin directory.

If you want to have a different shell open in a new window, go to the Shell Preferences pane, deselect "Use default login shell for this user," and select instead "Use this shell." The tcsh shell is the default as well, but you can change this setting to something else, such as /bin/sh. If you do, when you press Command-N to open a new shell window, the title will indicate the change in the selected shell.

Returning to the Window pane, if you prefer not to see the Unix jargon in the window title, you can uncheck the Shell Path and Device Name checkboxes and choose Custom Title instead. Now you can type any title text you want.

Finally, if you make any customized changes in a particular shell window, you can save the changes as a .term file via the Save command. You can choose to have Terminal launch that .term file at startup, either by choosing the option to enable this feature in the Save dialog box or by selecting the "Open this .term file" option in the Startup pane of the Preferences window.

*Figure 10.5*

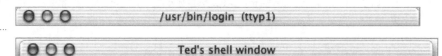

*The title bar of a Terminal window (top) before and (bottom) after changes are made in the Preferences settings.*

**TAKE NOTE ▶ Unix Problems and How to Fix Them**

If you thought that some of the error messages in Mac OS 9 or Mac OS X were too cryptic for your taste, you'll get no relief with Unix's error messages. They are usually worse.

**Unix error messages.** When Unix does not like what you typed, you will often get an error message. The most common error you will make is that you did not type the command correctly. It may be that you made a typographical error (such as misspelling a word), typed a pathway that does not exist, or attempted to use an option that requires more information than you provided.

If Unix has a good guess as to what went wrong, it may prompt you with its guess about the solution (for example, revising the input) and then ask, "OK?" If you like its guess, type <y> (for yes). Otherwise, simply press Return (for no).

Error messages may otherwise just give an indication as to what went wrong. For example, if you mistyped a name, Unix may say, "No such file or directory." This is your clue to check whether you typed the name incorrectly or are trying to access a file that does not exist.

In other cases, Unix may offer a brief line or two indicating the format of the command and some common options, such as "Usage: cd [-plvn][-|<dir>]." This feedback usually means that you used an invalid option or typed something incorrectly. If you are familiar with the use of the command, the feedback may be helpful.

**Stopping Unix.** Sometimes, after typing a command, you may wait indefinitely and still not have the command-line prompt reappear. This may be exactly what is supposed to happen. Unix has entered a mode where the command line will not return unless you specifically instruct it to do so. Typically, typing <q> or <exit> will get the prompt to return.

Other times, it may be that Unix is doing some intensive processing; the command line will return when it's done. You just need to be patient.

Otherwise, you may have the Unix equivalent of a freeze. To fix this problem, press Control-C or Command-period. This action will halt whatever process was in progress, but you will regain the ability to enter further commands.

You can use the same commands if the output from some earlier command continues to scroll and scroll, with no end in sight. At least one of these commands should bring the scrolling to a halt.

As a last resort, you can always close the window or quit Terminal.

*continues on next page*

> **TAKE NOTE** ▶ **Unix Problems and How to Fix Them** *continued*
>
> To prevent such freezes or excessive scrolling from occurring the next time, make sure that you typed the initial command correctly. If you are not sure if you did, type <man> to check the manual for the problem command, to make sure you are using the command correctly. If this action still fails to turn on any light bulbs, you'll probably need to consult a book on Unix or seek other outside help.

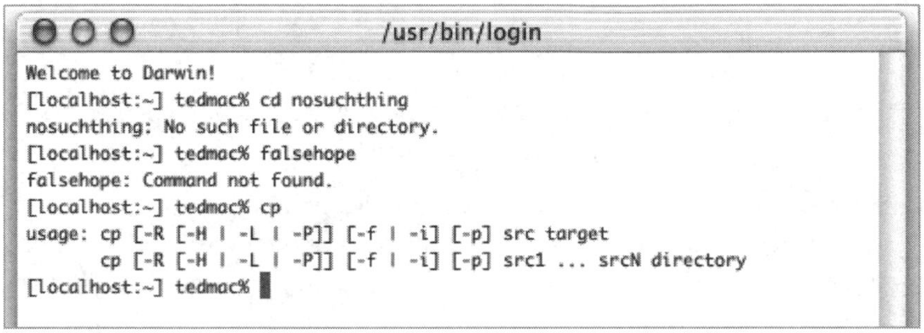

**Figure 10.6**

Three examples of Unix feedback when something goes wrong.

```
                         /usr/bin/login
Welcome to Darwin!
[localhost:~] tedmac% cd nosuchthing
nosuchthing: No such file or directory.
[localhost:~] tedmac% falsehope
falsehope: Command not found.
[localhost:~] tedmac% cp
usage: cp [-R [-H | -L | -P]] [-f | -i] [-p] src target
       cp [-R [-H | -L | -P]] [-f | -i] [-p] src1 ... srcN directory
[localhost:~] tedmac% ▮
```

# Launch Terminal

When you launch Terminal, a window opens, saying, "Welcome to Darwin." The next line is the command-line prompt. It will typically read:

[localhost:~] *username%*

*localhost* is the name Unix uses to refer to your computer, regardless of what you named it in the Finder.

The next text indicates the name of the directory at your current location, which in this case is the root level of your Home directory. The tilde (~) is a standard Unix abbreviation for this location.

*username* is the short name (set up in the Users System Preferences dialog box) of the logged-in user—presumably, you. It is also the name of the folder for your account inside the Users folder in the Finder.

The % symbol is the indication that Terminal is ready to accept your typed input. The symbol may be different, or absent, in different shells.

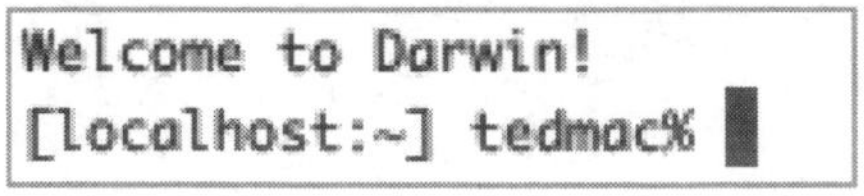

**Figure 10.7**

Terminal's command-line prompt.

```
Welcome to Darwin!
[localhost:~] tedmac% ▮
```

## The logout command

To log out of a Terminal session, type <logout> or press Control-D. You do not need to log out before quitting Terminal, however. When you quit Terminal (by pressing Command-Q), Terminal will log you out automatically after asking whether you really want to quit.

## The man command

If you want to know more about any Unix command, simply type <man> (for manual), followed by the name of the command. To learn more about the ls command, for example, type <man ls>.

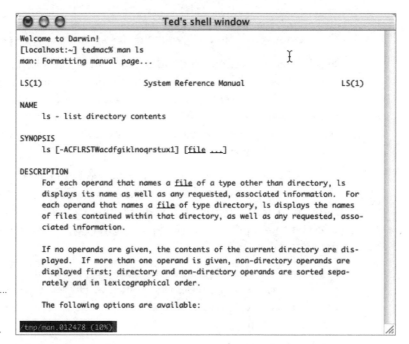

You can even type <man man> to find out about the man command itself.

The output of a man request often assumes that you already know a good deal about how Unix commands work. Don't expect it to be a tutorial. But even if you are a Unix novice, you may glean some useful information from this output, especially about the various options that work with a command. Unlike the Mac, which has menus and checkboxes, Unix gives you no easy way to guess what options are available. Without the man command to tell you what your options are, you might never know.

Most man output exceeds what can fit on a screen. To see more, just keep pressing the Return key. If you want to exit before the output is done, press the Q key.

Several Aqua-based utilities, such as ManOpen, provide access to the man output from the Finder.

## The sudo and su commands

If you type a command in Unix and get a "permission denied" or "operations not permitted" error message, you probably need root access to do what you want to do. There are two ways to do this:

**Use su.** To get root access, type <su>. When you type this command and press Return, you will be asked for your password. If you are an administrator, after you give your password, the prompt will change to something like:

```
[localhost:/Users/username] root#
```

You are now a root user and will remain so until you type <exit> or <logout>.

Note: After using su to change to the root user, your Home directory changes to that of the root user. This means that shortcuts (such as the ~ symbol) that indicate a Home directory now refer to a different Home location. To address this situation when you type commands, you may want to enter the absolute path for a file. Just typing the file name itself my no longer work, even if it worked before you shifted to root access.

**Use sudo.** Alternatively, to get root access, you can type <sudo> as the first part of further commands to appear on the same line. You will again be asked for your password. In this case, you retain root access only for the command or commands on that line; you do not need to type <exit> to get back to your previous status.

In general, you should prefer to use sudo rather than su, unless you need to retain root access over a series of commands. However, you may occasionally find that one of these commands does not work as expected. In such a case, try the other command. Almost always, at least one of them will be successful.

**SEE:** • "Take Note: Root Access," in Chapter 3, for more details.

# Unix: Listing and Navigating

OK. Now that the basics have been covered, you're ready to do something useful with Unix. I'll start with how to list the contents of a directory and how to move to different directories.

# The ls command

The ls (list) command lists the contents of your current directory location. When you first launch Terminal, you arrive by default at the root level of your Home directory. Thus, typing <ls> gives you a list of every item in your Home directory. You can compare this list by clicking the Home button in the toolbar of a Finder window. The items that you see in the window should be the same files that are listed in Terminal.

**Figure 10.9**

The items in your Home directory, as viewed in (top) the Finder and (bottom) Terminal.

**Figure 10.10**

The same Home directory, as listed after (a) <ls -a> and (b) <ls -l>.

**Options.** Most commands in Unix have optional arguments that can be appended to the command. These options usually start with a hyphen, followed by an uppercase or lowercase letter. You can see a complete list of options for any command by typing <man> for that command. The ls command has two especially important options:

- **ls -a.** This option lists adds the invisible items (the ones that start with a dot) to the list of items displayed. Typing this command for your Home directory would, for example, reveal the .Trash directory, which is where most of your files go when you drag them to the Trash.

- **ls -l.** This option outputs the long form of the directory listing. Each item is listed in its own row, followed by an assortment of additional information. Most important, the additional information includes each item's permissions settings, owner, and group name. If you have read earlier chapters of this book (especially Chapters 3 and 6), you already know what these items are used for. I also review the topic as it applies to Terminal, in "Changing permissions," later in this chapter.

You can combine options in the same line, using only one hyphen if desired. Thus, to get a list that both includes invisible items and is in the long form, you can type either <ls-a-l> or <ls-al>

**ls of any directory.** What if you want to see a list of some location other than where you are now? You can do so by typing <ls> followed by the absolute or relative pathway to the directory you want to view.

Suppose, for example, that you want to see what's in the Documents directory of your Home directory. Assuming that you are still in your Home directory, simply type: <ls Documents>. This command is a relative pathway command. Unix assumes that you are starting your path at your current directory location; thus, it looks for a directory called "Documents" in your Home directory.

Suppose that you want to see the contents of the root-level Applications folder. The simplest way is to type the absolute pathway—the pathway that starts at the root level of the volume itself. In this case, type <ls /Applications>. The initial slash instructs Unix to start the path at the root level of the volume.

By the way, Unix commands are almost always case-sensitive. Thus, typing <ls /Applications> is not the same as typing <ls /applications>.

**SEE:** • **"cd and related commands,"** later in this chapter, for more on pathways and navigational commands.

• **"Take Note: Folders vs. Directories,"** in Chapter 4, for background on absolute and relative path names.

**TAKE NOTE** ▶ **Unix Shortcuts**

Having to type a long string of pathways and command options can get to be a pain, especially when one typographical error can ruin the entire line, requiring you to start over. That's one of the reasons why a Mac-like interface is often preferred. Still, Unix offers a variety of shortcuts to help reduce the amount of typing you have to do. Here are my most-used shortcuts:

• **Tab.** Whenever you start to type a path name, press the Tab key at any point; Unix will fill in the remainder of the item name that matches what you are typing. If Unix finds more than one match in a given directory, it will list all possible matches, allowing you to continue typing until you have a unique match. Then you can try Tab again. For example, if you type <ls /Ap> and then press Tab, Unix will fill in the rest of the name (Applications) for you. This shortcut is a great time-saver, especially for long file names that contain spaces, as the Tab key also uses the correct notation for spaces in pathway names.

• **History.** Press the up-arrow key at any point, and the last command you typed will appear. You can keep pressing the up-arrow key to go back in your history for as many commands as Terminal is tracking. You can use the down-arrow key to traverse to your starting point again. When you find the command you want to use again, simply press Return, and it will execute.

• **Wildcards.** The asterisk (*) is a wildcard character; it is a match for any number and sequence of characters. For example, suppose that you are in your Documents directory and want to delete (remove) every item that ends in .html. Instead of typing each item separately, you could type <*.html> just once after the remove (rm) command. The use of the asterisk instructs Unix to match every file that ends in .html, no matter what precedes it.

  The question mark (?) is also a wildcard, except that it is a substitute for a single character. Suppose, for example, that you want to match every file that ends in .dmg or .img. You could type <*.?mg>. This command matches every file, no matter what precedes the dot, as long as it ends in any character followed by mg. Assuming that no files end in some other combination of a character plus mg, except img and dmg, this command would do the trick.

• **Drag a Finder icon.** This last trick is not a Unix trick, exactly, as it depends on the Mac OS. But it works. If you drag a Finder icon to the Terminal window, it pastes the pathway of the icon in the current location of your text input. Numerous Aqua-based utilities also allow you to select an item and copy its Unix pathway to the Clipboard; Locator is one such utility. Then you can paste its path into Terminal.

  Thus, to list the contents of a particular directory in Terminal, type <ls> followed by a space and then drag to the Terminal window the Finder icon of the directory you want to list. Its path will appear. Press return and the directory list will appear.

**TAKE NOTE ▶ Spaces in Path Names**

When you type path names, Unix interprets a space as being the start of a new name. Thus, if you type <Research Report> as a file name to be used with some command, such as cp or rm, Unix would think that you are referring to two separate file or directory names—one called "Research" and another called "Report"—rather than to a single item called "Research Report." To instruct Unix to include the space as part of a single name, you have two options:

• Place a backslash before the space. That is, type <Research\ Report>.

• Put the name in quotes (ideally, double quotes, although single quotes usually work as well). That is, type: <"Research Report">.

Preceding any character with a backslash (\) eliminates any special meaning that it may have. Thus, preceding a space with a backslash says, "Treat the space as a space, not as a name divider."

Putting a term in quotes tells Unix to treat everything within quotes exactly as typed; again, no special meanings are assigned.

You can get into big trouble if you are not careful about how you type file names, especially if you add a space where you did not intend and do not use quotes or backslashes. Suppose, for example, that you wanted to delete your entire Applications folder (not that I would recommend doing this). To do so, type: <rm -R /Applications>. There should be no space between the / and the A. This is critical. Suppose, instead, you accidentally placed a space after the / and before the A, so you actually typed: <rm -R / Applications>. Unix would now interpret the / and the Applications as being two separate items. The initial / is interpreted to mean the volume root directory. Thus, you are instructing Unix to delete the entire root directory! That is not what you wanted to happen. Surrounding the name with quotes, even if they are not needed (that is, even if there are no spaces or special characters in the name), would protect against this error.

Note: When you use the Tab key to complete a name, Unix automatically and correctly adds backslashes in front of each space in the name.

## cd and related commands

Sometimes, it is not enough to list the contents of a directory; you want to move to the directory itself. Among other things, moving to the desired directory can simplify working with items in that directory. For example, when you are at a specific directory, just typing <ls> will list its contents; you no longer need to enter the directory's path each time.

To move to any directory, you use the cd (change directory) command. To move to the Applications folder, for example, type: <cd /Applications>.

Here are some related navigational commands:

- If you want to know what directory you are in, type: <pwd> (print working directory).

- To move to the root level of the volume, type: <cd />.

- If you want to return to your Home directory quickly, type <cd> with no path specified.

- Use the ~ symbol to indicate an absolute path to your Home directory. Thus, to go to the Documents directory in your Home directory, no matter where you are located, type: <cd ~/Documents>.

- You can use relative pathways to navigate. This method saves time, because you don't have to type the longer absolute path. Thus, if you want to move to the Documents directory and you are in your Home directory, just type: <cd Documents>.

- You can use dots in pathnames to assist in navigating. For example, suppose that you are in the Documents directory and want to go back to your Home directory. In this case, you could type <cd> to do so. But there is a more-general shortcut to go up one level no matter where you are. To do so, type: <cd ..>. To go back more than one level, you can type this command multiple times. Or, to go back two levels with one command, type: <cd ../..>.

  A single dot refers to the current directory. Thus, <cd ./Documents> tells Unix to go to the Documents directory within whatever directory you are in. In most cases, the single dot is not needed; simply typing <cd Documents> would have worked just as well. But the dot is necessary for some commands other than cd. For example, as explained in "Executing Unix commands," later in this chapter, you may need the single dot when you're trying to execute a command located in the current directory.

# Unix: Changing Permissions

Permissions are the Unix equivalents of the settings that you access in the Privileges pane of the Show Info window for Finder items. Permissions settings determine your ability to open, modify, copy, and delete items on your drive. The Privileges settings of the Show Info window are a subset of the options that you access via permissions settings in Unix. Changing the Show Info settings modifies the underlying Unix settings. But you can make changes in Unix that you cannot make in the Show Info window.

I have discussed changing permissions settings in several chapters of this book, especially in Chapters 3 and 6. I will give you a brief review here as permissions apply to working in Terminal.

**SEE:** • **"Privileges" in Chapter 3, "Permissions/Privileges Problems with Opening Files" in Chapter 6, and "Problems Copying and Moving Files" in Chapter 6, for more background on these topics.**

Unix assigns a minimum of nine permissions settings to each item: a read (r), write (w), and execute (x) value for the owner of the item; the group assigned to the item; and everyone else. Each of these settings can be either *on* (you have the needed permission) or *off* (you don't). In brief, r refers to the ability to open and view a file, w refers to the ability to modify a file, and x refers to the ability to execute/run a program. These settings are also used for directories and folders but have slightly different meaning. For directories, for example, the execute permission needs to be enabled before the r and w settings have any effect at all. In fact, when it's used with directories, the x bit is more often called the search bit than the execute bit, because it needs to be on before you can search or view the list of contents.

**Figure 10.11**

*Permissions settings in Terminal. (top) A sample of items in a directory in a Home directory. (bottom) A sample of items in an /Applications directory.*

```
drwxrwxrwx   23 tedmac   staff      738 Feb 20 15:15 Recovered
-rwxr-xr-x    1 tedmac   staff     4827 Feb 20 13:54 StickiesDatabase
-rwxrwxrwx    1 tedmac   staff     5221 Jun 26  2001 console output.rtf
```

```
drwxrwxr-x   11 tedmac   admin   330 Feb 28 20:32 Roxio Toast Titanium 5.1.2
drwxrwxr-x    3 root     admin   264 Sep 15 00:02 Sherlock.app
drwxrwxr-x    3 root     admin   264 Sep 11  2001 Stickies.app
drwxr-xr-x    3 root     wheel   264 Sep 15 00:03 System Preferences.app
```

In Terminal, when you use the ls -l command to view a list of directory contents, you see the permissions settings for each file in the far-left column. A drwxrwxr-x listing would be a common setting for programs in the Mac OS X Applications directory, for example. Here's what this permissions setting means:

**d.** The initial d means that the item is a directory (or folder in Mac OS X jargon). In this example, it may seem odd that applications are considered to be folders. Remember, however, that most Mac OS X applications are really .app packages, which are simply special types of folders. If an item is a single file instead of a folder, the initial character would be a hyphen (-).

- **owner rwx.** The first trio of rwx means that the owner of the application has read, write, and execute permission. As indicated in the columns to the right in the figure, for applications installed by Mac OS X, the owner is root.

- **group rwx.** The second rwx means the same thing for members of the group. As indicated in the column to the right, for most applications installed by Mac OS X, the group is admin. As all administrative users are in the admin group, they all have complete access to the items in this directory. Note: For most files in your home directory, the owner will be you and the group will be staff.

- **everyone r-x.** The third trio, r-x for everyone else, means that all other users can access and execute the application but cannot modify it.

The precise implication of having no modify access can get a bit tricky. (Can you move the application out of the Applications directory without modify access? Can you modify a text file within the .app package? Can you delete the application?) What you can or cannot do is determined by a combination of the permissions settings for the item itself and for its enclosing directory or directories. I cover most of the specifics in Chapter 6.

In this chapter, my focus is not what all these settings mean but how to use Unix commands in Terminal to edit these settings. You may need to edit these settings when the editing ability of the Show Info window's Privileges pane is not sufficient. The Show Info window does not allow you change the owner of a file, for example.

In earlier chapters, I emphasized the use of Aqua-based utilities, such as XRay and Get Info, as a graphical front end for these Unix commands. These utilities allow you to make the desired changes without having to launch Terminal or remember any Unix jargon. In general, I find using these utilities to be more convenient and less time-consuming than going to Terminal. But it pays to have at least a rudimentary idea of how you would make these changes in Terminal.

## The chmod command

You use the chmod (change mode) command to change permissions (also called "mode bits"). At any time, you can use the ls -l command to examine the current settings and confirm that a change was made as you intended. (Note: In the following commands, I assume that you are in the parent directory of the item you want to modify, so you only need to enter the name of the item. Otherwise, you would need to include a relative or absolute path.) You can use the chmod command in two ways.

**Octal method.** The first method requires entering numbers to indicate the permissions settings you want to use. This method is called the octal method because it has eight possible values (0 to 7). A 0 implies no access, and 7 means all access for the given type of user.

Each type of access (r, w, and x) has an assigned numeric value. x is assigned 1, w is assigned 2, and r is assigned 4. If you want to give more than one type of access (such as both read and write) to a given category of user, you add the numbers for each individual access type.

Thus, the octal notation for read and write (rw-) access is 6 (4 + 2). The octal notation for complete access (rwx) is 7 (4 + 2 + 1). And so on. There is a separate numeric value for each of the three types of users: owner, group, and everyone. Thus, the octal notation for rwx access for owner and group, but r-x access for everyone else, is 775. To set this permission for a file called test.app, for example, you would type:

<chmod 775 test.app>

A slight disadvantage of the octal method is that, if you want to make a single modification (perhaps removing write access for the group), you still need to reenter all the octal values. Thus, to make the group assignment change for test.app, you would need to type:

<chmod 755 test.app>

**Symbolic method.** In the symbolic method, you use an equation format that describes what you want to do. The equation has three parts:

1. Pick which category of user the change will affect (u=user, which is the same as owner; g=group; o=other, which is the same as everyone).

2. Indicate whether you want to add (+), remove (-), or set (=) a permission for that user category.

3. Select one or more permission types (r, w, and x).

Again, suppose that you want to change the permission of the test.app file from rwxrwxr-x to rwxr-xr-x. With symbolic notation, you would type:

<chmod g-w test.app>

This command says, "For just the group setting, remove the w access."

Another example: To set rwx access for group and other, overwriting the current settings, you would type:

<chmod go=rwx test.app>

**Special mode bits.** In addition to read, write, and execute, you may encounter some less-well-known mode bits: the sticky bit, setUID, and setGUI.

**SEE:** • **"Sticky bits and the Drop Box" and "Technically Speaking: setUID and setGID," in Chapter 6, for more information on these settings.**

You can use the chmod command to change these special mode settings. To do so via the octal method, you add a fourth digit in front of the initial three: 1 enables the sticky bit, 2 enables the setGID bit, and 4 enables the setUID bit.

Suppose, for example, you wanted to enable the sticky bit for a directory called myitems that currently has rwxr-xr-x access. To do so, without changing existing rwx permissions, type:

<chmod 1755 myitems>

If you use <ls – l> to see the permissions settings after making this change, you will see that it now reads rwxrwxrwt. The t at the end, rather than an x, indicates that the sticky bit has been enabled.

As another example, to enable the SetUID bit for a file called myfile, precede the standard octal notation with a 4. That is, type:

<chmod 4755 myfile>

If you now use ls -l to see the permissions settings for the file, it will read rwsr-xr-x. The s at the end of the first trio of letters indicates that setUID has been enabled for the owner (setUID always applies just to the owner).

For those that prefer to use the symbolic method, you can make the same changes, although I will omit going into the details here.

**Aqua alternatives.** A reminder: If you don't want to bother with any these techniques, you can use an Aqua-based utility such as XRay instead. A convenient tutorial feature of XRay is that it shows the ls command info (such as rwxrwxrwx) and chmod command input (such as chmod 777) for whatever change you make. You can use this information to compare the changes you make in XRay with what you would have done in Terminal.

## The chown and chgrp commands

Although the preceding methods edited the permissions of the owner and group of a given item, they never actually changed the name of the owner and group. To do that, you use the chown (change owner) and chgrp (change group) commands.

The format is quite simple. You type the command, the new owner or group, and the path name of the item to be changed. To change the group of a file called testfile to staff, for example, type:

`<chgrp staff testfile>`

Similarly, to change the owner of an item called test.framework from root to yourself (*yourname*), type:

`<chown `*yourname*` test.framework>`

OK, it's not quite that simple. You cannot change the group assignment of an item unless you are the owner of the item. A greater obstacle is that no one but the root user can change the owner of an item. You cannot even change the ownership of a file you own. Thus, typing this chown command will lead to an "operation not permitted" error.

True, as I discussed in Chapter 6, copying a file from one directory location to another may modify the ownership of the file. But that is a separate issue from modifying the permissions of a file directly.

The solution is to use the su command to get temporary root access (assuming that you are an administrative user). To do so, type the following:

`<su>` (and enter your password when requested)
`<chown `*yourname*` test.framework>`

Theoretically, typing <sudo chown *yourname* test.framework> in one line should also work, but I have had problems getting it to do so. The two-line approach has been more reliable.

Be aware that changing the ownership or group of an item could mean that you can no longer modify or even access the item via your normal user status. If a file has rwx access for the owner and no access for any group or anyone else, and you are no longer the owner, you cannot access that file in any way. The only way around this restriction would be to get root access again and modify the file—or change its ownership back to you, or change its group permissions, so that you can modify the file later without needing root access.

### The chflags command

The chflags command is used to change flags. I gave an example of its use in Chapter 6, using it to turn off the immutable flag to allow a file to be deleted.

In brief, you if you type <chflags nouchg myfile>, you are turning off (no) the immutable flag (uchg) for the file named myfile. Again, you can do the same thing in a utility such as XRay.

This technique is similar to locking and unlocking files from the Finder's Show Info window. Sometimes, however, the Finder may indicate that a file is unlocked even though this flag is set. That's when you may need to use this command.

**SEE:** • "Deleting files," in Chapter 6, for more details.

# Unix: Copy, Move, and Delete

In most cases, when you want to copy, move, or delete files, you will do so in the Finder. Occasionally, when the Finder fails to carry out the operation successfully, you may find that using Terminal solves the problem.

Remember that any changes you make in Terminal will affect the location of these files in the Finder as well. These are two interfaces to the same files, not two parallel universes.

**SEE:** • "Technically Speaking: Copying from Terminal," in Chapter 6, for one example.

### The cp command

The cp (copy) command is the equivalent of the Mac's Copy command. It creates a copy of the file without deleting or modifying the original. A simple format for this command is:

```
<cp oldfilename newfilename>
```

This example assumes that you are in the directory of the old file. In this case, a new copy of the original file is created in the same directory.

**Copy to a different location.** If you want to have the new file reside in a different directory, you will need to specify its path. Assume you are at the root level of your Home directory, and you want to copy a file called report.doc to your Documents directory, where you want it to be listed as report42.doc. In this case, type one of the following:

```
<cp report.doc Documents/report42.doc >
```

or

```
<cp report.doc ~/Documents/report42.doc >
```

or

```
<cp report.doc /Users/yourname/Documents/report42.doc>
```

**Copy with the same name.** Now suppose that you are content to have the name of the new file be the same as the name of the original. In this case, you can leave off the file name in the second path. Thus, to move a file called song.mp3 from the root level of your Home directory to your Music directory, you could type:

```
<cp ~/song.mp3 ~/Music/>
```

**Batch copy.** You can combine the cp command with wildcard notation (such as *) to copy several files at the same time. Thus, to copy all files that end in .mp3 to the Music directory, you could type:

```
<cp ~/*.mp3 ~/Music/>
```

**Copy directories.** So far, I have been talking about copying files. If you try to use the cp command to copy a directory—one called testfolder, for example—it will fail. You will get an error that says "cp: testfolder/ is a directory (not copied)."

To solve this problem, you need to type <cp –R>, followed by the path name or names. The –R option is the recursive option. (Note: For typing "R," using uppercase or lowercase seem to work equally well, although don't count on this being so for all commands.) Thus, to copy testfolder to the Documents directory, type:

```
<cp –R testfolder /Documents/testfolder>
```

In this case, you should end the second path with the desired name of the new directory, even if it is the same name as the original. If you are using wildcards in the name of the first path, however, you can just specify the destination directory in the second path. Thus, the following command will take all items, files, or directories that begin with test and copy them to the Documents directory without changing any names:

```
<cp -R /test* /Documents/>
```

**Using ditto and CpMac instead of cp.** One problem with the cp command is that it copies only the data fork of an item. This situation is not a problem when working with files created in Unix, as every Unix item consists only of a data fork. Mac files (especially those initially written for Mac OS 9), however, are often divided into two forks: data and resource. The cp command is incapable of copying resource forks, so it will not successfully copy files that contain one. Two commands can help solve this problem.

- **ditto.** The ditto command, included with Mac OS X's basic Unix software, makes exact copies of directories and their contents, including resource forks, making sure not to change permissions, symbolic links, or anything else. It is particularly useful for backing up directories or volumes.

- **CpMac.** The CpMac command, included on Apple's Mac OS X Developer Tools CD, copies both the data and resource fork of a file but otherwise works similarly to the cp command.

SEE: • "Technically Speaking: Copying from Terminal" and "Technically Speaking: Move Your Home Directory to a Separate Partition," in Chapter 6, for more information on the ditto and CpMac commands.

## The mv command

The mv (move) command follows almost exactly the same structure as the cp (copy) command. The main difference is that mv deletes the original file, so that only the moved version remains. As its name implies, you appear to move the file to its new location, rather than copy it. Thus, if you wanted to move the report.doc file, instead of copying it, to the Documents directory, you would type:

```
<mv report.doc Documents/report42.doc>
```

You can also use the mv file to rename a file. That is, if you move a file to the same location where it currently exists, you have simply renamed the file.

The mv command works equally well with files or directories. Like the cp command, you can use it to move multiple items. Unlike the cp command, no –R option is needed.

SEE: • "Permissions/Privileges Problems with Copying/Moving Files," in Chapter 6, for a discussion of how moving vs. copying may affect permissions.

## The rm command

The rm (remove) command deletes files and directories. To use it, type <rm> plus the name of the item or items you want to delete. If you want to delete a directory, including all items in the directory, add the –R option. Thus, to delete a song.mp3 file from your Desktop, type:

<rm ~/Desktop/song.mp3>

To delete the Music directory and all its contents from your Home directory, type:

<rm -R ~/Music>

You can remove multiple items, either by typing them individually or by using a name with a wildcard. Remember that you can also add a path name by typing <rm> and a space and then dragging the Finder icon of the file or files you want to delete to the Terminal window. You could thus delete both of the preceding files with one remove command. To do so, type:

<rm -R ~/Music ~/Desktop/song.mp3>

As I discuss in "Take Note: Spaces in Pathway Names," earlier in this chapter, you need to be especially careful when using the -R option; otherwise, you may inadvertently remove more than you intended.

SEE:  • "Take Note: Using rm: Risk Management," in Chapter 6.
      • "Using Unix to Delete Files," in Chapter 6.

**The rmdir and mkdir commands.** If a directory is empty, you can use the rmdir command to delete it. If you want to create a new directory, use the mkdir command. In both cases, follow the command with the path name of the directory to want to delete or create. Thus, to create a directory called mp3files in your Home directory, type:

<mkdir> ~/mp3files>

# Executing Unix Commands

When you type <ls>, <cp>, <rm>, or almost any of the other commands I have discussed in this chapter, you are executing (or running) a built-in Unix command. But you are not limited to what is "built-in." Just as you can add software to your Mac beyond what ships with the Mac OS, you can add new software to run in Unix.

To run a "built-in" Unix program, you need no special command to precede the name of the file. To run the ls command, for example, you do not need to type <run ls>. Neither do you need to include the relative or absolute path to where the ls command file resides. You need to type only <ls>. Whatever you type as the first term in a line, Unix understands that you want it to be treated as a command to be run and executed.

For commands to run in this manner, two conditions must be met:

* The execute (x) bit must be enabled for the file.
* The file must be in a directory that Unix searches when it looks for commands that match what you typed.

When you type a command such as ls, the OS checks specified directories where it knows to look for executable files. If it finds a file that matches the name you typed, it executes and runs the file. One of the directories where Unix looks, for example, is the volume root level /bin directory. Thus, all commands in that directory will work as described, by just typing their name. Commands such as ls, cp, and kill are stored in this directory.

To see a complete list of all directories searched by a Unix shell, type <env>. In the output that appears, examine the PATH line. All the searched directories are listed, separated by colons.

**SEE:** • **"Take Note: What and Where Are the Unix Files?" in Chapter 4, for more information on bin and related directories.**

Another way to see the PATH listing is with the echo command. In its simplest form, echo simply prints to the screen whatever text follows the command. Thus, if you type <echo ls>, it causes the next line to output ls. You can also use it in combination with the $ character to print the value of a variable. Thus, if you type <echo PATH>, you simply get the word PATH as output. But if you type <echo $PATH>, you get the list of all directories searched by the shell, just as would appear in the PATH line of the env output.

*Figure 10.12*

*The PATH line in output from the env command.*

```
PATH=/Users/tedmac/bin/powerpc-apple-darwin:/Users/tedmac/bin:/usr/local/bin:
/usr/bin:/bin:/usr/local/sbin:/usr/sbin:/sbin:/Developer/Tools
```

Not included in the list of directories in PATH is /Developer/Tools. If you have installed the software from the Developer Tools CD, however, this directory is where a collection of Unix commands supplied by Apple is stored. The CpMac command, discussed earlier in this chapter, is one such command.

All the commands in the Tools directory have their execute bit set, so there is no problem with that. But if you type just <CpMac> followed by the needed path names, the command will not work. Instead, an error message appears that says "Command not found," because Unix does not check the Tools directory for commands.

**SEE:** • **"Take Note: The Developer Tools CD," in Chapter 3.**

• **"Technically Speaking: Copying from Terminal," in Chapter 6.**

So how do you get a command such as CpMac to run? There are several options. Some details get beyond the scope of this book. But the following sections provide an overview.

## Type the command path name

If you type a correct absolute or relative path for a command, Unix will execute it, even if it is not in one of the default directories that Unix searches.

Thus, to run the CpMac command from any directory location, type:

```
</Developer/Tools/CpMac>
```

If you are in the directory that contains the command file (/Developer/Tools, in this example), you can take a shortcut and just type:

```
<./CpMac>
```

---

**TAKE NOTE ▶ Open Mac OS Applications in Terminal**

You can open almost any Mac OS applications via Terminal, and they launch just as they would if you double-clicked them in the Finder. To do so, type:

```
<open pathname>
```

To put a clock on your Desktop, for example, type:

```
<open /Applications/Clock.app>
```

There is no real advantage to opening a file this way, but if you are already working in Terminal, it may be more convenient than going back to the Finder to locate the application.

I found a use for this command in one case. TinkerTool provides an option to add a Quit Finder (Command-Q) command to the Finder's Finder menu. If you use this option, the Finder quits without relaunching. It relaunches automatically if you quit all other open applications via the Dock. Otherwise, there does not appear to be a convenient way to get the Finder back. A solution: Launch Terminal from the Dock. (Ideally, you previously placed an permanent icon for Terminal in the Dock.) Then, from within Terminal, type:

```
<open /System/Library/CoreServices/Finder.app>
```

The Finder will relaunch.

Note: "Take Note: Opening .app Files from Within Terminal," in Chapter 6, provides a variation on this theme. It covers how to open certain programs located within a .app package, using the <./pathname> method.

# Use your Home bin directory

As a rule, I recommend not adding files to the Unix root-level directories, such as /bin, as any change you make might get eliminated in a Mac OS X update or could otherwise cause problems. Also, you need root access to add files here, which makes it less convenient. Thus, although moving the CpMac file to the /bin directory would allow CpMac to run without your having to type its pathway, I would not do this.

Fortunately, an alternative accomplishes almost the same goal but without the risks or hassles: Move CpMac (or whatever software you wish) to the bin directory in your Home directory. If you check the PATH line in the env command, you will notice that it lists /Users/*yourname*/bin directory as a directory that is checked for executable commands. A minor problem is that there is no bin directory in your Home directory; Mac OS X does not install one by default. But you can create one. Putting it all together, here is what you do:

**1.**   Create a bin directory in your Home directory via the Finder (press Command-Shift-N while in your Home directory and name the folder bin) or by using Terminal (type: <mkdir ~/bin>).

**2.**   Copy or move the CpMac file from its location in /Developer/Tools to the newly created bin directory.

Again, you can do this via the Finder or via Terminal. To do so in Terminal, type:

<cp /Developers/Tools/CpMac ~/bin>

**3.**   Before trying to use the command, open a new shell window in Terminal, or just quit Terminal and relaunch it.

**4.**   Type: <CpMac>

Unix will now recognize it as a Unix command.

To get all the files in the /Developer/Tools directory to work this way, copy all of them to the new bin directory.

**Limitations and alternatives.** A limitation to having the file or files in your Home directory is that the command will not work when someone other than you logs in. If access by other users is important, you could repeat the same procedure for each local user on your drive. A less tedious method, although it gets back to manipulating the root level Unix directories, is to create a bin directory in the /usr/local directory. Files placed here should be accessible to all users.

As a final alternative, you could instruct Unix to add the relevant directory (/Developer/Tools, in this case) to the list of directories that it searches for commands. See "Take Note: The .cshrc File: Saving the alias and set path Commands," later in this chapter, for details on how to do this.

# Create an alias

In Unix, the alias command creates a shortcut for another longer command. Suppose, for example, that you don't want to make any of the changes described in the preceding section for getting a command to run. Instead, each time you want to run the CpMac command, you do type </Developer/Tools/CpMac>. But as you use this command frequently, you decide that you would prefer a way to invoke the command with less typing. What can you do? Create an alias. To do so, type:

<alias CpMac /Developer/Tools/CpMac>

Now when you type <CpMac>, it will act as an alias for the longer command.

The name you choose for the alias need not have any similarity to the name of the original command; it could be anything you want. For example, you could type:

<alias cp2 /Developer/Tools/CpMac>

Now when you type <cp2>, it will invoke the CpMac command.

**Override existing commands.** You can even use an alias to override the meaning of an existing command. If you always use <ls -al> to list the contents of a directory in the long form with invisible files included, you could type:

<alias ls ls -al>

Now whenever you type just <ls>, Unix will interpret it as <ls -al>. Thus, you have altered the meaning of the existing ls command.

If you later want to invoke the original ls command while maintaining the alias, type: <\ls>. The backslash tells Unix to interpret the command "literally," without substituting any potential alias. If you ever want to delete the alias and revert to the default use of the command, type: <unalias ls>.

**Aliases vs. aliases.** In Unix, an alias (as described here) means something entirely different from what the word means in Mac OS X. The Unix equivalent of a Mac OS X alias is a symbolic link.

**SEE:** • "Aliases and Symbolic Links," in Chapter 6, for more information on this distinction.

**Aliases are not saved.** A limitation of aliases is that they are forgotten when you close the shell window. This means you will have to re-create them each time you launch Terminal.

However, there is a way to circumvent this limitation. You can save and run not only aliases of one-line commands but any sequences of commands. To do so, create a shell script. Shell scripts, described in the following section, offer the most flexibility of all the execute options described in this chapter.

> **TAKE NOTE ▶ The .cshrc File: Saving the Alias and Set Path Commands**
>
> A file called .cshrc is located at the root level of your Home directory in typical Unix systems. This file—and, thus, the commands it contains—is checked and run each time you open a new shell.
>
> A related file, also typically in Unix Home directories, is the .login file. The .login file is used for operations that run only at login, whereas the .cshrc file is used for operations that run each time a new shell is opened (which you can do without logging in again). Together, these files allow you to customize the Terminal environment from its default settings.
>
> Note: Like all files that start with a period, these files are invisible in the Finder.
>
> A problem for Mac OS X users is that Mac OS X does not place .cshrc or .login files in the user's Home directory by default. You can create your own, however. I focus here on using the .cshrc file. Note the following points:
>
> **alias.** To save aliases that you create via the alias command, add the alias commands to the .cshrc file.
>
> **set and paths.** Type <set> at any command prompt to see a list of environmental (env) settings that can be modified. You similarly use the set command to make these modifications. For example, relevant to the discussion in the main text, you could change the list of paths that Unix searches when it looks for commands. Thus, to add the /Developer/Tools directory to the search path, type:
>
> <set path = ($path /Developer/Tools)>
>
> Changes that you make with the set command, like those that you make with the alias command, are not saved when you start a new shell. Again, to make the change permanent, you need to add the relevant set command to your .cshrc file.
>
> As an experiment, I created an empty .cshrc file in my Home directory and added the set path line cited above to it. I used a Unix text editor called pico to do this in Terminal, but you could just as well use BBEdit Lite. (BBEdit's Open Hidden command allows you to open and work with invisible files.) After quitting and relaunching Terminal, all commands in the /Developer/Tools directory could now be run just by typing their name.
>
> Similarly, adding an alias command to the .cshrc file worked for making alias commands permanent.

## Use a shell script

A shell script is the Unix equivalent of what macro utilities, such as QuicKeys X, do in Mac OS X. A shell script is not limited to any particular length, so you can use it to carry out what would otherwise require a long sequence of commands.

In Chapter 6, I described the following sequence of Unix commands:

```
<sudo rm -R ~/.Trash/>
<sudo rm -R /.Trashes>
<sudo rm -R /Volumes/volumename/.Trashes/>
```

**SEE:** • **"Files in Trash window may come from multiple locations," in "Use Unix to delete files," in Chapter 6.**

You need to repeat the third line for every mounted volume. This sequence makes sure that everything in your Trash bin is deleted, no matter where the Trash items are stored. I will now describe how you can create a shell script to execute this sequence of commands.

**Create a shell script.** If you use this sequence often, you might prefer a way to invoke the entire sequence without having to keep retyping it. This procedure not only saves time but also prevents any problems that could occur from mistyping a command. To accomplish this task, you need to create a shell script. Follow these steps:

1. Launch the freeware text editor BBEdit Lite.

   Note: You could use a Unix text editor, such as pico. But Mac users will likely be more comfortable with a Mac utility.

2. In the BBEdit Preferences window, select Text Files: Saving.

3. In the window that appears, click the Unix radio button for Default Line Breaks.

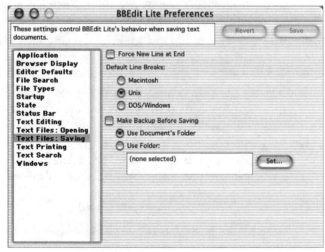

*Figure 10.13*

*BBEdit's saving preferences window.*

4. Close the Preferences window.

5. Open a new blank document.

   This step is important; don't use any document that you opened or created before making the preferences change. You need to complete steps 2, 3, and

4 only one time. The preferences change should be preserved. So the next time you launch BBEdit, you can proceed directly to step 6.

**6.** For the first line, type: <#!/bin/tcsh>.

This line is optional if you want to use the default shell, as in this case. Otherwise, you will need to enter the path of the shell you want to use. For a common shell, often preferred for shell scripts, type: <#!/bin/sh>.

**7.** Type the sequence of sudo rm commands, pressing Return at the end of each line, including the last line.

Again, you may need to type several variations of the last line, once for each partition or volume that you have mounted. Substitute the actual volume name where *volumename* is located in the command. If you are unsure what volumes are available, type <ls /Volumes> to see a list.

In some cases, you may need to end every line but the first (#!) line with a semicolon. With the semicolon, you should not need to press Return. The semicolon will be interpreted as a Return character. If one method does not work, try the other.

**8.** Save the file, ideally giving it a name that ends in .command, such as deleteall.command. The .command extension is needed to run the command from the Finder in some cases. Save the file anywhere in your home directory; the root level of the directory is fine.

**9.** Using either XRay (in the Finder) or the chmod command (in Terminal), change the permissions of the file so that the execute (x) permission is enabled for owner, group, and other (referred to as world in XRay).

**SEE:** • "Technically Speaking: **How the OS Selects a Document/Application Match: Using XRay** " and **"Permissions/privileges problems with copying/moving files,"** in Chapter 6, for more information on using XRay.

**10.** Return to the Finder. If you want the command file to launch and execute automatically when you double-click it in the Finder, do one or both of the following:

**a.** Open the Show Info window for the deleteall.command, and in the Open with Application tab, select Terminal as the application. If you do this, ending the file name with .command is not necessary.

**b.** Use a utility such as XRay to delete the file's creator. In XRay, you do this by changing the creator from R★ch (the creator code for BBEdit Lite) to No specific creator (which leaves a blank creator code).

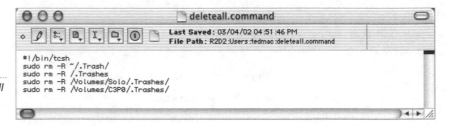

*Figure 10.14*

*The completed shell script, open in BBEdit.*

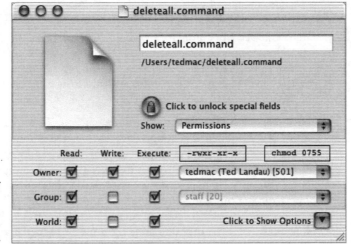

*Figure 10.15*

*How a .command file's settings appear in XRay after making the changes to make it a double-clickable shell script.*

**Run a shell script.** You can run a shell script in several ways:

- **Double-click the script file.** When you double-click a shell script file in the Finder, it will launch in Terminal, carry out the designated commands, and log out.

  In the deleteall example, Terminal should ask for your password before executing, as you are asking to run as root. Also, if you get an error message that says, "No such file or directory," one or more of the Trash directories is empty. You can ignore this message. The script will still empty the Trash.

- **Drag the file icon to the Terminal icon.** Dragging the file icon to the Terminal icon will launch the script. You need to do this, as opposed to double-clicking the file, only if you skipped step 10 in the preceding section.

- **Use Terminal's Run Command menu item.** You can run any command, shell script or otherwise, via the Run Command item in Terminal's Shell menu. In the window that appears when you select the command, type the text box the path to the command file. For the deleteall example, assuming you saved the file in the root level of your home directory, type: <~/deleteall.command>. Then click the Run button. The command will execute in its own shell.

- **Execute it from Terminal's shell window.** Launch Terminal, and type the path to the command after the prompt. If you saved the file in your Home directory, type <~/deleteall.command>.

  If you want, you can also move the script to your Home bin directory. Now you can launch the script simply by typing its name: <deleteall.command>. In this case, as you will likely no longer care if the file is double-clickable in the Finder, you can eliminate the .command extension from its name. With the extension gone, you can run the command from Terminal just by typing: <deleteall>.

One advantage of running the command from Terminal, rather than launching it from the Finder, is that after the command is completed, you are not logged out automatically. Thus, you can continue typing commands after the script is run without needing to open a new shell window. If the shell script deleted a file, for example, you can continue as though you had deleted the file with an rm command instead of having deleted it via the script.

However, even though you are not logged out, Terminal still treats the script as an independent subprocess that opened and closed after it ran. Unix users refer to the script as a *child* of the initial *parent* process. After the script is run, you are back at the parent level. An important implication is that any changes that the script makes that would get undone when you log out will still be undone after the script is run. Therefore, you cannot use a shell script in this way to run a list of alias commands. The aliases will be forgotten after the script is run, just as they would after you log out.

Fortunately, there is a way to get the results of aliases commands (or any other commands with the same problem) to be preserved after a script is run: Use the source command.

- **Use the source command.** Suppose that you created a shell script to run a list of alias commands, such as the alias ls ls –al command I mentioned earlier in this chapter. The text might look like this:

```
#! /bin/tcsh
echo "load aliases";
alias ls ls -al;
```

The script would continue with as many additional alias commands as you wanted to include.

Note: The echo line is optional. It provides feedback when you execute the shell, so that you can tell that it ran successfully. This is desirable, because an alias command produces no immediate output on its own.

You can create this shell script via the method described earlier in this chapter and run it. Suppose that you called it loadaliases and placed it in your Home bin directory. When you type <loadaliases> in Terminal, the script will run successfully. But when you next type <ls>, the alias will not execute. As I explained in the preceding section, this is because the alias change is not preserved after the script is run. To solve this problem, use the source command: <source *pathname*>. In this case, type:

```
<source ~/bin/loadaliases>
```

Note: In some shells, you use a dot (.) rather than the word source. Type <. ~/bin/loadaliases>, for example.

The source command runs the script in the current shell rather than in a separate subshell, preserving the changes. Try it!

*Figure 10.16*

*Running a shell script via the source command preserves an alias command contained in the script.*

```
[localhost:/Applications] tedmac% source ~/bin/loadaliases
enable aliases
[localhost:/Applications] tedmac% ls
total 24
drwxrwxr-x  25 root    admin    806 Mar  8 15:12 .
drwxrwxr-t  28 root    admin    908 Mar  8 15:12 ..
-rw-rw-rw-   1 tedmac  admin   8196 Mar  8 15:12 .DS_Store
drwxrwxr-x   5 root    admin    264 Jan 28 17:00 Acrobat Reader 5.0
```

Shell scripts, like Unix itself, can get much more elaborate than I have described here. But even with what you know now, shell scripts are a valuable tool. Even if you use Terminal occasionally, for a few command sequences, turning the sequences into scripts can save you time as well as eliminate the need to remember what to type.

# Other Unix Commands

From the dozens of Unix commands that exist, I've selected a few more that can help you in troubleshooting Mac OS X.

## The df command

The df command tells you the amount of space used by every volume on your drive. The first row is for your OS X startup volume. The various columns indicate the volume's capacity in terms of the amount used, the amount available, and the percentage of capacity used. The last column (Mounted on) includes the names of volumes as displayed in the Finder; the exception is the name of the startup volume which is listed simply as /.

*Figure 10.17*

*The output of the df command. Ignore the lines where the capacity is 100 percent. The remaining lines refer to actual mounted partitions or volumes.*

```
[localhost:/Applications] tedmac% df
Filesystem          512-blocks      Used     Avail Capacity  Mounted on
/dev/disk1s9          53858288  16218360  37639928    30%    /
devfs                       78        78         0   100%    /dev
fdesc                        2         2         0   100%    /dev
<volfs>                   1024      1024         0   100%    /.vol
/dev/disk0s9          20969696  11920000   9049696    56%    /Volumes/Solo
/dev/disk0s10         19113016   3477944  15635072    18%    /Volumes/Luke
/dev/disk1s10         42090840  11317408  30773432    26%    /Volumes/C3PO
/dev/disk1s11         21269816    980448  20289368     4%    /Volumes/Offsite
automount -fstab [288]        0         0         0   100%    /Network/Servers
automount -static [288]       0         0         0   100%    /automount
[localhost:/Applications] tedmac% █
```

# The touch command

To create a new blank document file or update the modification time of an existing file, type:

<touch *filename*>

If no file by your selected name exists in the current location, Unix creates one. If the file already exists, Unix updates the "last modified" time for the file to the current time. As always, you can type a relative or absolute path to the file to create or modify a file in a location other than the current location.

# The head, tail, cat, and more commands

Most of the time, if you want to view the contents of a text file related to troubleshooting, you will likely prefer to use Mac applications, such as TextEdit and PropertyList Editor. If you are at work in Terminal, however, it may be more convenient to look at a file's contents directly in Terminal. If you need to view the file's contents without editing it, you have several choices.

**head and tail.** These commands output the first 10 and last 10 lines of a file, respectively. You can request to see more or fewer than 10 lines by adding a number option to the command. To see the first 20 lines of a file called my.doc, for example, type: <head –20 my.doc>.

**cat.** Use the cat command, followed by a file name, to see an entire file, if it is not so long as to exceed the scrollback buffer of Terminal. Note: The size of the scrollback buffer is set in the Buffer pane of Terminal's Preferences window.

**more.** Use the more command for long files, especially ones that would exceed the scrollback buffer. The output appears much like the output of the man command. That is, output stops when the screen is filled; to see more of the file, you need to keep pressing the return key (advances line by line) or the space bar (advances screen by screen). Type <q> at any point to quit the output display and return to the command prompt.

*Figure 10.18*

*Output from the head command.*

```
[localhost:~/Library/Preferences] tedmac% head com.apple.finder.plist
<?xml version="1.0" encoding="UTF-8"?>
<!DOCTYPE plist SYSTEM "file://localhost/System/Library/DTDs/PropertyList.dtd">
<plist version="0.9">
<dict>
        <key>AppleNavServices:GetFile:0:Path</key>
        <string>file://localhost/Applications/Utilities/</string>
        <key>AppleNavServices:GetFile:0:Position</key>
        <data>
        AMsBHw==
        </data>
[localhost:~/Library/Preferences] tedmac% █
```

# The find and locate commands

Similar to using Find in the Finder, Unix has its own commands to help you find items from within the Terminal application.

**find.** In its basic form, the find command displays a list of every item in the directory you specify. Thus, to display a list of *all* files and directories in the Applications directory, including items contained within subdirectories within the Applications directory, type:

`<find /Applications>`

As .app packages are considered to be directories in Unix, the resulting list will include the items within every .app package. This is probably much more than you wanted to see, which limits the usefulness of the command. In fact, you will likely want to press Command-period to halt the scrolling output that results from the command.

You can get less output by limiting the scope of your search, assuming you knew that the limits still contained what you wanted to find. For example, if you knew the item you wanted was in the Utilities folder inside the Applications folder, you could type `<Applications/Utilities>` as the path name, instead of just `</Applications>`.

To further limit (or extend) your search, you can use wildcards in any part of the search term. Thus, you could type `</Applications/Utilities/Disk*>` as the path name for the find command. This command would match any items in which the segment of the path name that corresponds to the root level of the Utilities directory begins with the word Disk. In other words, it would match Disk Copy.app and Disk Utility.app. But it would also list all the items within these two packages as matches. For example, /Applications/Utilities/ Disk Copy.app/Contents/Info.plist would be a match, because Disk Copy.app is in the matching spot of the path name.

You can also use the find command to limit matches only to items where the search term is in the actual name of the file (that is, the search term must be in the very last segment of a path name). This more limited search is probably closer to what you typically want. To do this, you need to use the -name option. You combine the -name option with the file name (or part of a file name, with wildcards added) that you are seeking. Thus, to find every file name in the /Applications directory that contains the word chess, type:

`<find /Applications -name "*hess*" -print>`

Similarly, to find all file names that end in .mp3 in your Home directory, type:

`<find ~ -name "*.mp3" -print>`

You could use the Finder's Find command (Sherlock) to do a similar search, but the results would not be the same. Sherlock does not list files contained within packages; the Unix find command does. Here is some further advice about using the find command:

- If you are going to use wildcards with the -name option, the file name should be in quotes.

- Without wildcards, the find command will find only an exact match. The full name of the Chess application is Chess.app, even though you see only the word *Chess* in the Finder. Thus, the application itself will not appear as a match in a search for the exact term *Chess*. A search for *Chess.app* or *Chess★* would get a match.

- Unix is case-sensitive. Thus, in the Chess example, I left off the initial *C* so as to search simultaneously for *Chess* and *chess*.

- Unix texts recommend the *-print* option be added to the end of the find command line (as in the preceding examples) to get the results displayed on the screen. In the Darwin version included with Mac OS X, however, I have not found this option to be necessary.

- If you get messages that read "permission denied" for certain directories, and you believe that what you are searching for is in those directories, you will need to search again with root access (using the su or sudo command).

The find command has numerous options not described in this chapter. You can type <man find> to see the full range of this command. But I recommend not bothering. The rules that determine what output you get with find can be confusing—even to experts. And no matter what you do, it will often wind up that you don't get what you are seeking. If the find command is not producing the results you want, using the advice presented here, you can try using the locate command instead. It works similarly to the find command for simple searches but may be easier to use. Otherwise, search via Mac OS X, and bypass Terminal altogether.

*Figure 10.19*

*Output from the find command with the -name option selected.*

```
[localhost:~] tedmac% find /Applications -name "*hess*"
/Applications/Added/Super Get Info.app/Contents/Resources/English.lproj/Super Get Info Help/
gfx/sgi_chess_perm_tab.jpg
/Applications/Chess.app
/Applications/Chess.app/Contents/MacOS/Chess
/Applications/Chess.app/Contents/Resources/chess.icns
/Applications/Chess.app/Contents/Resources/chess.tiff
/Applications/Chess.app/Contents/Resources/ChessApp.tiff
/Applications/Chess.app/Contents/Resources/ChessDoc.tiff
/Applications/Chess.app/Contents/Resources/English.lproj/Chess.nib
/Applications/Chess.app/Contents/Resources/gnuchess.book
[localhost:~] tedmac%
```

```
[localhost:~] tedmac% locate /Applications/*hess*
/Applications/Chess.app
/Applications/Chess.app/Contents
/Applications/Chess.app/Contents/Info.plist
/Applications/Chess.app/Contents/MacOS
/Applications/Chess.app/Contents/MacOS/Chess
/Applications/Chess.app/Contents/PkgInfo
/Applications/Chess.app/Contents/Resources
/Applications/Chess.app/Contents/Resources/ApplicationNameImage.tiff
/Applications/Chess.app/Contents/Resources/chess.icns
/Applications/Chess.app/Contents/Resources/chess.tiff
/Applications/Chess.app/Contents/Resources/ChessApp.tiff
/Applications/Chess.app/Contents/Resources/ChessDoc.tiff
/Applications/Chess.app/Contents/Resources/COPYING
/Applications/Chess.app/Contents/Resources/English.lproj
/Applications/Chess.app/Contents/Resources/English.lproj/.snd.snd
/Applications/Chess.app/Contents/Resources/English.lproj/3d_black_sample.tiff
/Applications/Chess.app/Contents/Resources/English.lproj/3d_board.tiff
/Applications/Chess.app/Contents/Resources/English.lproj/3d_pieces.tiff
/Applications/Chess.app/Contents/Resources/English.lproj/3d_plastic.tiff
/Applications/Chess.app/Contents/Resources/English.lproj/3d_white_sample.tiff
/Applications/Chess.app/Contents/Resources/English.lproj/black.tiff
/Applications/Chess.app/Contents/Resources/English.lproj/black_bishop.tiff
/Applications/Chess.app/Contents/Resources/English.lproj/black_king.tiff
/Applications/Chess.app/Contents/Resources/English.lproj/black_knight.tiff
/Applications/Chess.app/Contents/Resources/English.lproj/black_pawn.tiff
/Applications/Chess.app/Contents/Resources/English.lproj/black_queen.tiff
/Applications/Chess.app/Contents/Resources/English.lproj/black_rook.tiff
/Applications/Chess.app/Contents/Resources/English.lproj/Chess.nib
/Applications/Chess.app/Contents/Resources/English.lproj/Chess.nib/objects.nib
/Applications/Chess.app/Contents/Resources/English.lproj/clock.tiff
/Applications/Chess.app/Contents/Resources/English.lproj/Credits.rtf
/Applications/Chess.app/Contents/Resources/English.lproj/Localizable.strings
/Applications/Chess.app/Contents/Resources/English.lproj/SpeechHelp.xml
/Applications/Chess.app/Contents/Resources/English.lproj/white.tiff
/Applications/Chess.app/Contents/Resources/English.lproj/white_bishop.tiff
/Applications/Chess.app/Contents/Resources/English.lproj/white_king.tiff
/Applications/Chess.app/Contents/Resources/English.lproj/white_knight.tiff
/Applications/Chess.app/Contents/Resources/English.lproj/white_pawn.tiff
/Applications/Chess.app/Contents/Resources/English.lproj/white_queen.tiff
/Applications/Chess.app/Contents/Resources/English.lproj/white_rook.tiff
/Applications/Chess.app/Contents/Resources/gnuchess.book
/Applications/Chess.app/Contents/version.plist
[localhost:~] tedmac% █
```

**Figure 10.20**

*Output from the locate command without the path in quotes.*

**Locate.** The locate command also finds (or locates) files. It has no options to select and so is simpler to use. In its basic format, you simply type:

<locate *searchterm*>

For example, if you type <locate /Applications/*hess*>, you will get a list of all items that include the term *hess* in the segment of their path name that immediately follows the Applications segment.

Note: When you use the find command with just a single argument, the procedure is called fast-find; it works almost the same as locate. Apparently, locate was created as an addition for those Unix variations that did not include the fast-find feature. In Terminal, both fast-find and locate are included, so you get your choice. Thus, typing <find /Applications/*hess*> will produce the same result as the locate command.

Recall that typing <find /Applications -name "*hess*" -print> yields a different and smaller subset of results. It lists just those items with *hess* as part of the file name. Thus, the item /Applications/Chess.app/Contents will be a match for /Applications/*hess* when you use locate but not when you use find with the -name option.

Enclosing a locate search term in quotation marks changes the results you get. With quotation marks, an item is considered a match if the search term is anywhere in the path name of the item. To make this distinction clear, consider these examples:

- If you type <locate /Applications/*Resources*>, you will not get any matches. This is because the word *Resources* does not appear at that location in the path name of any file.

- If you instead type <locate "/Applications/*Resources*">, you will get many matches. This is because it will match every item that includes the term *Resources* anywhere in its path below /Applications.

Three other points of interest about how locate works:

- If you type <locate "/Applications*hess"> (note the lone asterisk!), you will only get a single match. It will match the only file in which hess is at the very end of its path name: /Applications/Chess.app/Contents/MacOS/Chess.

  This is one place where the fast-find version of the find command works differently from locate. If you type <find "Applications*hess">, you do not get any match.

- The locate command (as well as the fast-find variation of the find command) searches a database that is updated periodically (assuming that you leave your Mac on all the time). The find command, used with options such as -name, does a real-time search of the entire contents of a volume. As a result, locate typically is much faster, especially for a large volume filled with files. But it also means that locate may not match an item, if the item was added after the last update to the database.

  You can update the database at any time by typing the command <sudo /usr/libexec/locate.updatedb>.

- If you type a search term with no path and no wildcards, locate interprets it as a search to start from the root directory. Thus, typing <locate hess> will match every item that contains *hess* anywhere in its path name on every mounted volume. This can be a fast and convenient way to use Terminal to search for matches on all your volumes at the same time.

# Beyond This Chapter

This chapter is obviously not the last word on everything that might be said about using Unix in Mac OS X. For those who want to know more, the following information should set you on the right path.

## Mac utilities that are front-ends for Unix commands

For users who would like to take advantage of the Unix features included with Mac OS X but would rather not learn how to deal with Terminal, numerous shareware developers offer Aqua-based utilities that provide a Mac-like graphical interface to the Unix commands. These utilities are often referred to as front-ends for Unix functions.

I have already cited many of these utilities throughout this book. The most frequently mentioned are XRay and FileXaminer, the ones that access Unix's permissions settings.

Other examples include: MacJanitor and CronniX (for dealing with Unix's cron jobs, as covered in Chapter 3); Perfboard, Renicer, and Xoptimize (front-ends for vmstat, renice, and update_prebinding Unix commands, respectively, as covered in Chapter 6); BrickHouse (which accesses the ipfw firewall commands, as covered in Chapter 8) and SharePoints (which access Unix's file-sharing features, also as covered in Chapter 8). Locator is a front-end for the locate command described in this chapter.

Some of Apple's own Mac OS X utilities are essentially front-end utilities. ProcessViewer, for example, is an alternative to Terminal's top and kill commands. The Web Sharing option of the Sharing System Preferences dialog box accesses Unix's Apache Web-server software.

Knowing how to use Terminal frees you from dependence on these utilities. If you can use Terminal, you can do anything that can be done with Unix on a Mac. But using these utilities frees you from having to learn how to use Unix. Take your choice.

SEE: • "Technically Speaking: Log Files and Cron Jobs," in Chapter 3.
  • "Use Force Quit," in Chapter 5, for coverage of the kill command.
  • "Technically Speaking: Monitoring and Improving Performance," in Chapter 6, for coverage of the top, vmstat, renice, and update prebinding commands.
  • Chapter 8, for more information on firewalls and file sharing.

# Examples of using Terminal elsewhere in this book

This chapter gathered together the essentials of the Unix commands and procedures you need to know as a Mac OS X troubleshooter. In earlier chapters of this book, I covered specific examples of the application of these commands, plus several commands that were not mentioned in this chapter.

The following list is a review of the most notable Unix-related references from other chapters of this book:

- "Technically Speaking: Using Terminal to Save the Installer File," in Chapter 2
- "Technically Speaking: Don't Use Mac OS 9 Software Restore on a Mac OS X Volume," in Chapter 2
- "Privileges," in Chapter 3
- "Take Note: Root Access," in Chapter 3
- "Take Note: The Developer Tools CD," in Chapter 3
- "Create a Bootable CD," in Chapter 3
- "NetInfo Manager," in Chapter 3
- "Terminal" in the "Applications and Utilities" section of Chapter 3
- "Technically Speaking: Log Files and Cron Jobs," in Chapter 3
- "Darwin," in Chapter 4
- "Take Note: Folders vs. Directories," in Chapter 4
- "Blue-screen crash," in Chapter 5
- "Technically Speaking: Understanding Kernel Extensions," in Chapter 5
- "Take Note: Screen Captures," in Chapter 5
- "Log in as Console," in Chapter 5
- "Use Force Quit," in Chapter 5
- "Run fsck," in Chapter 5
- "Technically Speaking: Telnet to a Frozen Mac: Kill Processes; Run Sync," in Chapter 5
- "Take Note: Restart Without Restarting," in Chapter 5
- "Optimize Mac OS X volumes," in Chapter 5
- "Permissions/privileges problems with opening files," in Chapter 6
- "Permissions/privileges problems with copying/moving files," in Chapter 6
- "Sticky Bits and the Drop Box," in Chapter 6
- "Technically Speaking: setUID and setGID," in Chapter 6
- "Technically Speaking: Copying from Terminal," in Chapter 6

- "Technically Speaking: Move Your Home Directory to a Separate Partition," in Chapter 6
- "Technically Speaking: Conceptualizing Directories in Unix," in Chapter 6
- "Take Note: Using rm: Risk Management," in Chapter 6
- "Use Unix to Delete Files," in Chapter 6
- "Files in Trash window may come from multiple locations," in Chapter 6
- "Technically Speaking: "How the OS Selects a Document/Application Match: Using XRay," in Chapter 6
- "Technically Speaking: Monitoring and Improving Performance," in Chapter 6, for coverage of the top, vmstat, renice, and update prebinding commands
- "Take Note: Changing the Default Paper Size in Page Setup Dialog Boxes," in Chapter 7
- "Error –108 When Attempting to Select a Printer in Print Center," in Chapter 7
- "Technically Speaking: Secure Connections," in Chapter 8
- "Troubleshooting AppleTalk connections," in Chapter 8
- "Take Note: Duplicate Listings in Connect to Server; No Listings in Connect to Server," in Chapter 8
- "Take Note: Sharing and Files in the etc Directory," in Chapter 8

## Unix information beyond this book

If you are motivated to learn still more about Unix, many resources are available.

**Books.** The two books that I return to most often are:

- *Teach Yourself Unix in 24 Hours, 2nd Edition,* by Dave Taylor and James C. Armstrong Jr. (SAMS Press, 1998). This book is a good place to start your journey.
- *Unix Power Tools, 2nd Edition*, by Jerry Peek, Tim O'Reilly, and Mile Loukides (O'Reilly Press, 1997). This book is an exhaustive resource of just about every imaginable Unix tip and trick.

**Web sites.** Numerous online tutorials and reference databases are available. I have found the following to be especially useful:

- Unix Reference Desk (www.geek-girl.com/unix.html).
- Unix Tutorial for Beginners (www.ee.surrey.ac.uk/Teaching/Unix).
- Carbonized Interactive Unix Tutorial (www.macinstruct.com/tutorials/unix/x/index.html). This tutorial is rather basic, but it uses the Terminal application in Mac OS X, as opposed to the more common platform-neutral tutorials.

# Index

# V

# W

# OS X

## Watch for these titles:

**The Little Mac OS X Book**

By Robin Williams
ISBN: 0-201-74866-5
672 pages • $29.99

**Mac OS X Advanced:
Visual QuickPro Guide**

By Maria Langer
ISBN: 0-201-74577-1
312 pages • $24.99

**Mac 911**

By Chris Breen
ISBN: 0-201-77339-2
352 pages • $29.99

**Mac OS X 10.1:
Visual QuickStart Guide**

By Maria Langer
ISBN: 0-321-11631-3
336 pages • $19.99

**The Macintosh Bible, 8th Edition**

By Clifford Colby and
Marty Cortinas
ISBN: 0-201-70899-X
984 pages • $34.99

**iMovie 2 for Macintosh:
Visual QuickStart Guide**

By Jeff Carlson
ISBN: 0-201-78788-1
216 pages • $19.99

**AppleScript for Applications:
Visual QuickStart Guide**

By Ethan Wilde
ISBN: 0-201-71613-5
480 pages • $21.99

**Real World Mac OS X
Server**

By John Welch
ISBN: 0-201-78264-2
800 pages • $44.99

## Look for updated editions of your favorite books at
# www.peachpit.com

# WWW.PEACHPIT.COM

**Quality How-to Computer Books**

About

News

Books

Features

Resources

Order

Find

Welcome!

## Visit Peachpit Press on the Web at www.peachpit.com

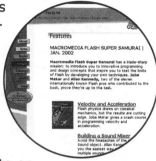

- Check out new feature articles each Monday: excerpts, interviews, tips, and plenty of how-tos

- Find any Peachpit book by title, series, author, or topic on the Books page

- See what our authors are up to on the News page: signings, chats, appearances, and more

- Meet the Peachpit staff and authors in the About section: bios, profiles, and candid shots

- Use Resources to reach our academic, sales, customer service, and tech support areas and find out how to become a Peachpit author

## Peachpit.com is also the place to:

- Chat with our authors online
- Take advantage of special Web-only offers
- Get the latest info on new books